Self Impr... Life-Writing, Autobiografiction, and the Forms of Modern Literature

MAX SAUNDERS

OXFORD
UNIVERSITY PRESS

OXFORD

UNIVERSITY PRESS

Great Clarendon Street, Oxford, OX2 6DP,
United Kingdom

Oxford University Press is a department of the University of Oxford.
It furthers the University's objective of excellence in research, scholarship,
and education by publishing worldwide. Oxford is a registered trade mark of
Oxford University Press in the UK and in certain other countries

First Edition published in 2012
First published in paperback 2013

British Library Cataloguing in Publication Data
Data available

Library of Congress Cataloging in Publication Data
Data available

ISBN 978–0–19–957976–1 (Hbk.)
ISBN 978–0–19–965769–8 (Pbk.)

Printed in Great Britain on acid-free paper by
MPG Books Group, Bodmin and King's Lynn

2 4 6 8 10 9 7 5 3 1

SELF IMPRESSION

'I am aware that, once my pen intervenes, I can make whatever I like out of what I was.' Paul Valéry, Moi.

Modernism is often characterized as a movement of impersonality; a rejection of auto/biography. But most of the major works of European modernism and postmodernism engage in very profound and central ways with questions about life-writing. Max Saunders explores the ways in which modern writers from the 1870s to the 1930s experimented with forms of life-writing—biography, autobiography, memoir, diary, journal—increasingly for the purposes of fiction. He identifies a wave of new hybrid forms from the late nineteenth century and uses the term 'autobiografiction'—discovered in a surprisingly early essay of 1906—to provide a fresh perspective on turn-of-the-century literature, and to propose a radically new literary history of Modernism.

Saunders offers a taxonomy of the extraordinary variety of experiments with life-writing, demonstrating how they arose in the nineteenth century as the pressures of secularization and psychological theory disturbed the categories of biography and autobiography, in works by authors such as Pater, Ruskin, Proust, 'Mark Rutherford', George Gissing, and A. C. Benson. He goes on to look at writers experimenting further with autobiografiction as Impressionism turns into Modernism, juxtaposing detailed and vivacious readings of key Modernist texts by Joyce, Stein, Pound, and Woolf, with explorations of the work of other authors—including H. G. Wells, Henry James, Joseph Conrad, Ford Madox Ford, and Wyndham Lewis—whose experiments with life-writing forms are no less striking. The book concludes with a consideration of the afterlife of these fascinating experiments in the postmodern literature of Nabokov, Lessing, and Byatt.

Self Impression sheds light on a number of significant but under-theorized issues; the meanings of the term 'autobiographical', the generic implications of literary autobiography, and the intriguing relation between autobiography and fiction in the period.

MAX SAUNDERS is Director of the Arts and Humanities Research Institute, Professor of English and Co-Director of the Centre for Life-Writing Research at King's College London, where he teaches modern English, European, and American literature. He studied at the universities of Cambridge and Harvard, and was a Research Fellow and then College Lecturer at Selwyn College, Cambridge. He is also the author of *Ford Madox Ford: A Dual Life*, 2 vols. (Oxford University Press, 1996), and has edited five volumes of Ford's writing, including an annotated critical edition of *Some Do Not . . .* , the first volume of *Parade's End* (Carcanet, 2010) and the new Oxford World's Classics edition of *The Good Soldier* (OUP 2012). He has published essays on Life-writing, on Impressionism, and on Ford, Conrad, James, Forster, Eliot, Joyce, Rosamond Lehmann, Richard Aldington, May Sinclair, Lawrence, Freud, Pound, Ruskin, Anthony Burgess and others.

Praise for *Self Impression*

'Saunders's account . . . is the most important recent contribution to the genealogy of modern literature . . . The paradoxy of autobiografiction never disorients him; rather, it inspires plentiful pithy wisdom in a book that seems to end every paragraph aphoristically. Theory and history, history and form get their due recognition, and the book as a whole is an apt and exciting tribute to its subject, capable of everything necessary to prove that life-writing has meant everything to literary modernity.'
Jesse Matz, *Modern Language Quarterly*

'a remarkable achievement, laying the foundation for future studies of life-writing genres and their relationship to fiction; it provides us with the critical tools and methodologies that will diversify our understanding of life-writing genres and their evolving place in literary history.'
Journal of Victorian Culture

'a hugely impressive enterprise, in which Saunders wears his formidable erudition and theoretical expertise gracefully and wittily'
Andrew Radford, *Year's Work in English Studies*

'a very important intervention into a number of arenas . . . a very welcome contribution to the fields of auto/biographical, late nineteenth-century and modernist studies . . . opens up new ways of thinking about life-writing and, in particular, the relationship between autobiography and fiction . . . a very rich and rewarding study . . . It engages very productively with autobiographical theory, arguing extremely convincingly for more flexible models of generic identity . . . subtle, informed and persuasive'
Laura Marcus, Goldsmith's Professor of English Literature, University of Oxford

'This is a captivating study . . . the range of the book is . . . breathtaking; it is a work of great scholarship and subtle erudition . . . a work of strikingly new perspectives on modernism . . . Saunders's work is ambitious in scope, depth and conceptualisation, while the sophistication of his theoretical analyses are couched in a readable style . . . It will make an extremely important and original contribution to the fields of nineteenth-and twentieth-century literary criticism and is a welcome and much needed addition to recent theorisations of life-writing.'
Dr Susan Jones, English Fellow, St Hilda's College, University of Oxford

'Qui saura me lire lira une autobiographie, dans la forme.'

(Paul Valéry)

To Alby,
For whom 'autobiografiction' is just the work of a lie-lie man.

Acknowledgements

It is the acknowledgements in a book that are often the purest examples of 'autobiografiction'. 'Many people' are customarily thanked for their collaboration in the very work over which the author has just asserted his or her sole moral right. Other names are invoked to give credibility to a work whose existence might well surprise them.

Thus several friends and scholars have contributed ideas and information to this work that proved more useful than they may have realized. In particular I'd like to thank John Attridge, David Herman, Brian Hurwitz, Vicki Mahaffey, George Myerson, Sita Schutt, and Alex Zwerdling. Among those who know how much they have done to help its evolution, I'm especially grateful to the following, who heard or read earlier drafts, and offered extremely valuable suggestions: Laurel Brake, Ron Bush, Dame Antonia Byatt, Keith Carabine, Kate Fullbrook, Sara Haslam, Richard Kirkland, Laura Marcus, Jerome Maunsell, Richard Proudfoot, Paul Skinner, Anna Snaith, John Stokes, and Neil Vickers.

Vesna Goldsworthy deserves special thanks; for generosity with her time, in volunteering to read much of the book; and for her encouragement nonetheless. She could be said not only to have assisted at its birth, but also to have stood in as fairy godmother, showing me how its title might be turned inside out.

Andrew McNeillie, the book's original commissioning editor, was also wonderfully encouraging while a book he hadn't seen was assuming its final shape; and wonderfully stoical when he saw its final scale. I am extremely grateful to him, and to his successor Jacqueline Baker, and Ariane Petit and the staff at Oxford University Press for their exemplary help and advice and support throughout the publication process; and to Elizabeth Stone for her tactful and attentive copy-editing.

It has taken several periods of leave to complete this work, and I'm grateful to the Arts and Humanities Research Board (as it then was) for awarding me a semester's research leave in 2002; and I'm especially grateful to the Department of English, and the School of Arts and Humanities at King's College London, for their generosity in granting sabbatical leaves, and for their support of such an extended project.

Earlier versions of a few parts of this book have appeared in print. The versions appearing here are so different as scarcely to constitute republication; but I am grateful—and not only for the legalistically minded—to the editors and publishers for permission to republish any material from the following essays:

' "Things Passed Over": Ruskin, Modernism, and Autobiography', *Ruskin and Modernism*, ed. Giovanni Cianci and Peter Nicholls (Basingstoke: Palgrave,

2001), reproduced with permission of Palgrave Macmillan; 'Reflections on Impressionist Autobiography: James, Conrad and Ford', *Inter-relations: Conrad, James, Ford, and Others* in the series 'Joseph Conrad: Eastern and Western Perspectives', gen. ed. Wieslaw Krajka (Lublin/Columbia University Press, 2003); 'Biography and Autobiography', *Cambridge History of Twentieth-Century English Literature*, ed. Laura Marcus and Peter Nicholls (Cambridge: Cambridge University Press, 2004); 'Life-Writing, Cultural Memory, and Literary Studies', in *Cultural Memory Studies: An International and Interdisciplinary Handbook*, Edited by Astrid Erll and Ansgar Nünning in collaboration with Sara B. Young (Berlin and New York: Walter de Gruyter, 2008); 'Autobiografiction: How the Edwardian Stephen Reynolds identified a new genre among the experiments of his time', 'Commentary' essay, *TLS* (3 October 2008); 'Autobiografiction: Experimental Life-Writing from the Turn of the Century to Modernism', *Literature Compass*, 6:2 (2009).

For permission to quote from the *Selected Poems 1908-1969* by Ezra Pound I am grateful to the estate of Ezra Pound and Faber and Faber Ltd.

For permission to reproduce visual images I am grateful to the following:

The estate of Alfred Cohen, for 'Confrontation Bergamasque' on the dust-jacket; The Cecil Higgins Art Gallery (Bedford Borough Council), Bedford, England, for Arthur Hughes' drawing of Mark Rutherford; The Galton Collection, UCL Library Services, for Galton's composite portrait; and the Society of Authors, for the illustrations from Virginia Woolf's *Orlando*.

Contents

List of Illustrations

Introduction

'every portrait that is painted with feeling is a portrait of the artist, not of the sitter.'[1]

'I am convinced of the phenomenalism of the *inner* world also: everything that reaches our consciousness is utterly and completely adjusted, simplified, schematised, interpreted—the *actual* process of inner 'perception', the *relation of causes* between thoughts, feelings, desires, between subject and object, is absolutely concealed from us, and may be purely imaginary.'[2]

'*The highest as the lowest form of criticism is a mode of autobiog*raphy.'[3] When Wilde put this paradox in the Preface to *The Picture of Dorian Gray* it was to pre-empt, or at least to mock, a low form of criticism. Beastliness is in the eye of the beholder, it implies. Anyone finding his book depraved is merely betraying a depraved mind. Part of the comedy of his remark comes from its suave version of childish name-calling: 'immoral yourself!' But his returning of his accusers' condemnations on their own heads is both more significant than that, and also (as this book hopes to show) deeply representative of its time. In posing the book as mirror of the critic's mind—or portrait, perhaps, of the reader's soul—Wilde is also placing the autobiographical at the heart of any act of reading or criticizing. '*It is the spectator, and not life, that art really mirrors.*'[4] Wilde imagines his critic reading his fiction biographically, condemning the author on the basis of a work of art. He parries by threatening to read the criticism biographically. If his novella reveals him autobiographically, then the imaginary critic's perceiving of obscenity reveals *him* or *her* just as much. This study is primarily concerned with the ways in which these categories of autobiography, biography, fiction, and criticism begin to interact, combining and disrupting each other in new ways, from the late nineteenth century to the early twentieth. It investigates experiments in literary portraiture from impressionism to modernism, arguing that new relationships emerge between autobiography, biography, and fiction which enable a new account of modern literature to be told.

---

[1] Oscar Wilde, *The Picture of Dorian Gray*, ed. Michael Patrick Gillespie (New York: W. W. Norton, 2006), p. 9.
[2] Nietzsche, Nov. 1887–March 1888, *Will to Power*, Book 3, in *Complete Works*, vol. 15, ed. Oscar Levy, trans. Anthony M. Ludovici (Edinburgh: T. N. Foulis, 1910), no. 477; p. 7.
[3] Wilde, *The Picture of Dorian Gray*, p. 3.
[4] Ibid., p. 4.

From one point of view Wilde's aestheticism is the end-point of Romanticism. This remark about autobiography can be seen as extending the core Romantic concept of expression from something the writer does to something the reader does too. From another point of view, though, his aestheticism is something other than Romanticism. The paradox about criticism as autobiography can also be read as a rejection, or the beginning of a rejection, of Romanticism, a negation of Romanticism's attempt to tie literary works to the personality of their author. According to this view, instead of saying that the work doesn't just express me, but it expresses you just as much, he would instead be saying that the work doesn't express me; it expresses you instead. Rather than late Romanticism, this would be early modernism—the beginning of the claim for the impersonality of the work of art; for the art-work seen as an autonomous object, not explicable by or reducible to or even meaningfully connectable to its author; Art for Art's Sake, not for the sake of self-expression. The paradox is thus genuinely double-edged. It extends the reach of autobiography, to cover genres not normally thought of as autobiographic. But it simultaneously calls the autobiographical into question.

Wilde had, of course, a compelling reason to play such games with the concept of autobiography. It enabled him to write about homosexuality without condemning himself in the eye of the law as a homosexual. But his gesture has wider significance, standing as a riposte to the whole massive nineteenth-century investment in biography. Carlyle had famously written that 'No great man lives in vain. The history of the world is but the biography of great men.'[5] The rapid establishing of biography as the quintessential Victorian genre seemed to say that not just history, but art, literature, thought—all human productions—were best accounted for biographically. It was time for a reaction, and the banner of Art for Art's Sake (rather than for the sake of a life) was one facet of it. That it wasn't the only facet is evident from the case of Nietzsche, who wrote in *Beyond Good and Evil* that all philosophy is 'the confession of its originator, and a species of involuntary and unconscious auto-biography.'[6] The strategy is similar to Wilde's, and perhaps even more paradoxical, since it claims that even philosophy—the very discourse that most aspires to transcend the contingency of the human, and attain to pure reason, general truth; the last discourse we tend to read *as* autobiography—nonetheless can be so read. (Nietzsche's own strategy was to make his own philosophy consciously autobiographical.) If discourses of impersonality such as criticism or philosophy can be read as autobiography, then all writing, all art, is equally susceptible. As Gertrude Stein would put it: 'Anything is an autobiography [. . .].'[7] And again this returns us to Wilde's

---

[5] Lecture, 'The Hero as Divinity', repr. in *Heroes, Hero-Worship and the Heroic in History* (New York: The Macmillan Company, 1897), p. 39.

[6] Nietzsche, *Beyond Good and Evil*, trans. Helen Zimmern (London and Edinburgh: T. N. Foulis, 1914), p. 10.

[7] Gertrude Stein, *Everybody's Autobiography* (New York: Random House, 1937), p. 5.

paradox. That no genre can escape the impress of the autobiographic means that no author can say a work isn't autobiographic. This appears to preclude Wilde from arguing that *Dorian Gray* is not autobiography. Indeed, that isn't quite what he says in the Preface. And it certainly isn't what Basil Hallward says to Lord Henry in *The Picture of Dorian Gray*, when he tells him: 'every portrait that is painted with feeling is a portrait of the artist, not of the sitter.'[8] Hallward sees art as in a double-bind, arguing that impassioned art cannot but be autobiographical; but critics should not read it as autobiography. He worries that the portrait of Dorian will give him away. 'The reason I will not exhibit the picture is that I am afraid that I have shown in it the secret of my own soul', he says. Because the age cannot be trusted to see the art instead of the autobiography: 'An artist should create beautiful things, but should put nothing of his own life into them. We live in an age when men treat art as if it were meant to be a form of autobiography. We have lost the abstract sense of beauty.'[9] Wilde's way of escaping from this double-bind in the Preface is to double it back onto persecutory critics, who thereby put themselves in the *Picture*. It is a small step (though also a great leap) from Wilde's sense of how readers read themselves into a text, to Freud's sense of how each man kills the thing he loves—unconsciously. Thus the paradox is that while every text is autobiography, no reader can know for sure in what way it is, because every reading is itself a species of involuntary and unconscious autobiography, and distorts the features of the writerly autobiographer into those of the readerly one. Wilde's and Nietzsche's strong claim for the autobiographical thus paradoxically turns the nineteenth century's investment in biography against itself. The very gesture that seemed to legitimize interpreting writing in terms of the author's biography simultaneously makes it unreliable.

Though Wilde and Nietzsche were influential in the development of modernism, they have been an even greater source of inspiration for postmodernists. And this universe of undecidable encounters between unconscious autobiographers is a decidedly postmodern one, in its relativism, playful irony, relish for the simulacrum, and its celebration of multiple perspectives instead of grand narratives. Where biography offered the Victorians the promise of a shared social judgement of an individual's life, the hope of objective knowledge and moral certainty, autobiography has become the quintessential postmodern genre (if it is a genre, which postmodernism cannot know) precisely because of its freedom from all these things. There has been a veritable surge of critical interest in autobiography since the 1980s: not only because more and more writers are exploring it, including writers who might have been expected to be suspicious of it as a form—philosophers, psychoanalysts, materialist critics and historians, and so on—but also because critics have increasingly turned to it as a legitimate field of study. This book is not a study of what I call 'formal' autobiography, or

---

[8] *The Picture of Dorian Gray*, p. 9.
[9] Ibid., pp. 9, 15.

(following Philippe Lejeune) 'contractual' autobiography—in which real author, narrator, and the name on the title-page all coincide, and seek to interpret their own life—though the second chapter and conclusion in particular do discuss it. Instead, my subject is how modern writers in the late nineteenth and early twentieth centuries found new ways to combine life-writing with fiction.

Life-writing has been an area of major development in literary studies since the 1970s, and many of its key theorists are discussed here. Yet it remains a contentious term, covering a wide range of texts and forms. Indeed, its contentiousness arises at least partly because it seems, to some, to cover too many. As one leading British biographer, Hermione Lee, writes, it is sometimes used 'when different ways of telling a life-story—memoir, autobiography, biography, diary, letters, autobiographical fiction—are being discussed together.'[10] Though, as Lee notes, another main usage is 'when the distinction between biography and autobiography is being deliberately blurred'. These are the main senses in which I shall be using it. The term 'autobiography' was coined as Romanticism took shape towards the end of the eighteenth century. Paradoxically, this is also the period in which the view began to emerge that all writing had an autobiographical dimension. According to this view, which became increasingly consolidated through the nineteenth century, and which is even shared by postmodernism, the distinction between autobiography and other forms such as biography or fiction is thus *always* blurred.

So the term 'autobiography' has a radical ambiguity. It can mean a mode of writing that is separate from other forms (drama, poetry, fiction, and so forth), and that exists purely for telling the story of your own life. Or it can be used to describe something about all those other forms too. The best illustration of this is the way we use the adjective 'autobiographical'. When we speak of an autobiographical novel, say, we are applying the term to something that is not a formal autobiography, but that has some qualities or content of autobiography in it. To talk of an autobiographical autobiography would be to sound tautological and self-contradictory at once.

In his seminal essay 'Autobiography as De-Facement' (1979), Paul De Man theorized the reading of autobiography by arguing that it is not a genre at all but, precisely, a mode of reading. Wordsworth writes a poem—*The Prelude*; we read it as autobiography. But De Man is talking of works which are explicitly autobiographical: in the first person, and where that person is evidently the author. But neither of those things need be true in an autobiographical novel. De Man doesn't register the difference between 'autobiography' and 'autobiographical', and his failure to distinguish them problematizes his argument for the rhetorical importance of the name. He famously advances the figure of prosopopeia ('the fiction of an apostrophe to an absent, deceased or voiceless entity,

---

[10] Hermione Lee, *Body Parts* (London: Chatto & Windus, 2005), p. 100.

which posits the possibility of the latter's reply and confers upon it the power of speech'), arguing that 'Prosopopeia is the trope of autobiography, by which one's name [. . .] is made as intelligible and memorable as a face.'[11] In autobiographical fiction, the protagonist's name is not (or at least isn't usually) 'one's name', but someone else's. This doesn't exactly negate De Man's position that 'It appears, then, that the distinction between fiction and autobiography is not an either/or polarity but that it is undecidable', since we cannot decide exactly how much fiction there might be in an autobiography, nor exactly how much autobiography there might be in a fiction.[12] But it does cast doubt on his doubt about autobiography's generic status, in that his scepticism is enabled by a kind of sleight of hand in glossing over the difference that our language-use recognizes, between autobiography and the autobiographical. He invokes Gérard Genette's discussion of Proust's *A la recherche du temps perdu* as readable as both fiction and as autobiographical. But the fact that a modernist author blurs generic boundaries does not invalidate the concept of genre. It may highlight the inevitable overlappings of genres, since genres are not pure entities. Saying an autobiography contains fiction is comparable to saying epics contain history, myth, or indeed fiction. So they do, but that does not mean epic isn't a genre. As Derrida argued in 'The Law of Genre', texts 'participate' in genres to which they cannot 'belong.'[13] So it is with autobiography and with the novel.

Reading something as 'autobiographical', then, is different from reading it as 'autobiography'; its autobiographical dimension can be covert, unconscious, or implicit. A sentence in a biography may purport to refer to its subject—Dr Johnson, say—but we are at liberty to read it as autobiographical: as telling us instead or as well about Boswell. The 'autobiographical' has become something of a blind spot in life-writing theory. This study reconsiders what 'autobiography' and 'autobiographical' mean in this period of the long turn of the century, from the 1870s to the 1930s, and how autobiography relates to other forms, especially biography and fiction.

The two senses of 'life-writing' distinguished by Lee are then not as distinct as they might have seemed. We need the term to hold the varieties of life-writing forms together because individual works tend to combine them anyway; and readers can move across the generic borders as writers can. Our postmodern ways of thinking about biography is much more aware of, and open to, these elements of autobiography and fiction in all life-writing. Such generic blurring is characteristic in another way, though. Life-writing is fundamentally intertextual.

---

[11] Paul De Man, 'Autobiography as De-Facement', *Modern Language Notes*, 94:5 (1979), 919–30 (p. 926).

[12] Ibid., 921.

[13] Jacques Derrida, 'The Law of Genre', *Critical Inquiry*, 7:1 (1980), 55–81 (p. 65): 'Every text participates in one or several genres, there is no genreless text; there is always a genre and genres; yet such participation never amounts to belonging. And not because of an abundant overflowing or a free, anarchic, and unclassifiable productivity, but because of the *trait* of participation itself.'

Biographies quote freely from their subjects' letters or diaries or speeches where available. Memoirists quote conversation they claim to remember verbatim. One might think autobiography would provide the greatest generic purity, relying only on acts of memory for its sources. Yet autobiographers, too, quote documents, others' biographies, their own journals or novels, though by the same principle of generic fusion such sources will themselves be already fused. Siegfried Sassoon's *Memoirs of an Infantry Officer* (1930), say, which offers a fictionalized account of Sassoon's life as 'George Sherston', quotes from his diaries written in the trenches. The effect is to ground the narrative in immediate testimony. Yet Sassoon's own diaries, which have since been published, reveal something arresting. He often describes himself in the third person, as if he needed to view himself as a character in a novel, in order to write about his experiences. The diary is thus already fictionalized. The diary extracts in the *Memoirs* have then been rewritten—re-fictionalized—in order to make them sound more autobiographical; they have been translated into, or back into, the first person, and framed within a semi-fictionalized narrative. Not all life-writing plays such complex games with intertextuality and hybridity, but many literary examples do something of the sort.

The study of life-writing has generated further neologisms to indicate the new critical emphases, and two kinds of these must be introduced here. First, *auto/biography*.[14] This compresses two key aspects, acting both as shorthand for 'autobiography and/or biography' (useful when generalizing about works of both types) and also as a term for individual works that fuse together autobiography and biography (thus corresponding to Lee's two senses of 'life-writing', though connoting extended life-narratives and excluding other auto/biographical forms such as letters, diaries, or travel writings).

Both aspects are necessary for my argument. The first, because much of what is said about one form can apply to the other at the same time (as in the example from Wilde, in which an autobiographical work is given a biographical reading, which is in turn another autobiographical act). The second, because there has been a particular surge recently in what might be called 'relational memoirs'— voyages round one or more parent, a sibling, or friend. A representative example of this development is provided by the copy of the *Guardian* 'Review' of 11 September 2004, that happens to be at hand at the time of writing this paragraph (read that as my autobiography, if you're that kind of critic) about half of which is devoted to auto/biography. The present book sees such work as developments of the experiments in auto/biography of a century earlier.

Just as the postmodern view of biography and autobiography is that they cannot be kept entirely separate from each other, and that the term 'auto/biography' can condense their interrelations, so two further terms have begun

---

[14] See for example Laura Marcus's excellent study, *Auto/biographical Discourses* (Manchester: Manchester University Press, 1994).

to gain currency recently to indicate that auto/biography itself cannot be kept entirely apart from fiction; that however truthful or candid an autobiography might be judged, it is nonetheless a narrative, and shares its narrative features with fictional narratives. These terms, 'autobiografiction' and 'autofiction', are comparably double-jointed, indicating both that auto/biography can be read as fiction, and that fiction can be read as auto/biographical. 'Autobiografiction', the term used here, if the more cumbersome, connotes more clearly the literary relationship that is central to this book: that between fiction and a self's autobiography, rather than that between fiction and a self. The term 'autofiction' has emerged more recently, in association with particular postmodern figures, especially the writer Edmund White and the autobiographer and life-writing critic Serge Doubrovsky.[15] 'Autobiografiction' seems to require the invention of *biografiction* to accompany it, and, alas, *auto/biografiction*, for the sake of exhaustiveness as well as symmetry.

Although I had wanted to avoid terms of professional jargon, the alternative of spelling out what was meant each time—such as 'fiction which draws on biography and/or autobiography'—seemed far more awkward. I tried to console myself that 'autobiography' too had once seemed as objectionable. Indeed, the first use recorded by the *OED*, from 1797, is an argument for not using it, commenting on the term 'self-biography' that 'We are doubtful whether the latter word be legitimate: it is not very usual in English to employ hybrid words partly Saxon and partly Greek'; but objecting to a new-fangled but entirely Greek compound: 'yet autobiography would have seemed pedantic.'[16] The decisive

---

[15] See the entry for 'Autofiction' in Margareta Jolly, ed., *Encyclopedia of Life Writing: Autobiographical and Biographical Forms*, 2 vols (London and Chicago: Fitzroy Dearborn, 2002), vol. 1, pp. 86–7. The term was coined by Doubrowsky in 1977 on the cover-blurb of *Fils* (Paris: Éditions Galilée, 1977), where he defines it as: 'Fiction, d'événements et de faits strictement réels; si l'on veut, *autofiction* [. . .]'. Martin Middeke uses (and perhaps coined) the term 'biofiction' to identify a strand of postmodern writing which falls within Linda Hutcheon's category of historiographic metafiction (discussed in Chapter 12), but which is specifically concerned with literary biography and with Romantic writers. I use the term 'biografiction' (for the symmetry with 'autobiografiction') to include such works, but also to refer to fiction thematizing any forms of biography from any period: Middeke, Introduction to Werner Huber and Martin Middeke, eds, *Biofictions: The Rewriting of Romantic Lives in Contemporary Fiction and Drama*, (Rochester, NY: Camden House; Woodbridge, Suffolk: Boydell and Brewer, 1999). Merle Tönnies applies it to contemporary fiction concerned with the way biographical narrative combines fact and fiction, taking her examples from Graham Swift, Ian McEwan, and A. S. Byatt: Tönnies, 'Radicalising Postmodern Biofictions: British Fictional Autobiogaphy of the Twenty-First Century', in *Fiction and Autobiography: Modes and Models of Interaction*, Salzburg Studies in English Literature and Culture, vol. 3, ed. Sabine Coelsch-Foisner and Wolfgang Görtschacher (Frankfurt: Peter Lang, 2006), pp. 305–14. Tillotama Rajan uses a different term, 'autonarration', to mean much the same as 'autobiografiction' as defined in Chapter 4—namely autobiographical experiences strung on a fictionalized narrative—though the absence of a marker of fictionality in the term makes it less useful. See Rajan, 'Autonarration and Genotext in Mary Hays' *Memoirs of Emma Courtney*', *Studies in Romanticism* 32:2 (1993), 149–76.

[16] 'Art. IV.': review of I. D'Israeli, *Miscellanies; or, Literary Recreations*, *Monthly Review*, 2nd series, 24 (1797), 374–9 (p. 375).

factor, however, was the discovery that the term 'autobiografiction' was not in fact a late twentieth-century, postmodern coinage to describe contemporary metafiction, but one which appears in the middle of the period discussed here, in 1906, and which described earlier forms of literary hybridization. This made it seem not a retrospective imposition of a specialized critical jargon, but an indication that the writers under consideration were thinking precisely in such terms of generic fusing and metamorphosing. It is an indication, too, of the tendency of 'autobiography' to co-exist with an anxiety about genre and terminology. In the end I came to feel that the formal distinctions important to this study were under-appreciated precisely because there wasn't an agreed vocabulary for them, and so have adopted and adapted terms where they seemed convincingly to clarify such distinctions. Thus while these terms are the product both of a postmodern critical sense that the boundaries between genres have been dissolving, and of the experiments of postmodern writers in dissolving them even further, my argument is that such developments enable us to see how earlier writers were already concerned with similar generic fusions.

The idea of 'autobiografiction' is used here in two related ways. First, theoretically, to explore the profusion of modern literature's experiments with life-writing. Indeed, one story of the novel in English is of a troubled relation between fiction and autobiography, from fictive autobiographies by Robinson Crusoe, Tristram Shandy, or Jane Eyre, to autobiographical novels like Dorothy Richardson's *Pilgrimage* or D. H. Lawrence's *Sons and Lovers*. This distinction is partly a matter of form. An autobiographical novel need not be cast into the form of an autobiography, though it might be, as in the fictive autobiographies *David Copperfield* and *Villette*. But it is also a matter of content. At least some of an autobiographical novel must refer to the author's life, whereas you can write a fictional autobiography by an imaginary character like Lemuel Gulliver. We are familiar with the idea that all creative writing must be autobiographical in some way. You don't have to have actually turned into an insect to be able to write 'Metamorphosis'; but you probably have to have felt alienation, or abjection. Fiction can be 'autobiographical' in many different ways.

The most autobiographical of autobiographical novels is arguably the *roman à clef*. In its purest form, one might say that only the names of the characters have been changed. If one changed them back to the real names of the original people, it would no longer be a *roman* at all, but biography, or autobiography. But of course novelists change more than just the names, and even a *roman à clef* might include invented episodes and speeches. So a novel might be auto/biographical in its characters, but not in its plot or dialogue. Or, vice-versa: it might tell a real story, but reinvent the characters involved. Or it might use some real people, events, or language, but combine any of these with invented material. It might be true to autobiographical feelings about real events, but not to the events themselves. Or it might realize autobiographical fantasies. And so on.

Those would all be examples of works in fictional form but with some kind of autobiographical content. But there's an important (but often occluded) distinction between that combination and novels that are autobiographical in *form*: that is, which are written as if they were autobiographies, but fictional ones, either because an author is fabricating passages from his or her formal autobiography, or because they are written by fictional characters. These various kinds of forged confessions get called pseudo- or mock-autobiographies, but the interchangeability of those prefixes is unhelpful. Instead I propose distinguishing between pseudo-autobiographies, which just *impersonate* the form, and mock-autobiographies that actually *parody* it.

The story of fictional works in auto/biographical form such as these is my central subject. This book is not primarily concerned with 'autobiographical novels' which reveal aspects of their authors' lives; nor with untruths in auto-biographies which conceal or distort aspects of their authors' lives; though it inevitably touches on both.

The second way in which the idea of 'autobiografiction' is used here is thus historically, to demonstrate how the relations between the component terms underwent a decisive transformation in the long turn-of-the-century, from the 1870s to the 1930s. On both counts these relations constitute a surprisingly untheorized aspect of modern literature. Or at least, of literature in English. In her excellent book *Biography and the Question of Literature in France*, Ann Jefferson explores 'the role of biography in the construction of the idea of literature', seeing 'conflicting responses to biography' as 'a key driver in the literary history of France of the past two and a half centuries.'[17] In French Studies especially, to take biography as one's subject is to risk appearing conservative; and to be denying or ignoring gods of post-structuralism such as Roland Barthes, who envisioned 'The Death of the Author', and Michel Foucault, who asked 'What is an Author?' Jefferson notes how in such work: 'authorial personality and circumstance appeared as an obstacle to what was considered to be most interesting and valuable in literature, namely, the thing that makes it literary.'[18] Part of the power of her thesis is its evident translatability into English literature. As she observes, both 'literature' and 'biography' are eighteenth-century terms in all major European languages.[19] Though there are important precursors in English biography before the eighteenth century (arguably from Asser's Life of King Alfred), it is with Dr Johnson's *Lives of the English Poets*, and Boswell's *Life*

---

[17] Ann Jefferson, *Biography and the Question of Literature in France* (Oxford: Oxford University Press, 2007), p. 25; the second and third quotations are from Edward Hughes's review, *Times Literary Supplement* (22 February 2008), p. 13. Roland Barthes, 'The Death of the Author', in *Image, Music, Text*, trans. Stephen Heath (London: Fontana, 1977), pp. 142–8. Michel Foucault, 'What is an Author' (1969), in *Language, Counter-Memory, Practice*, ed. Donald F. Bouchard (Ithaca: Cornell University Press, 1980), pp. 113–38.

[18] *Biography and the Question of Literature in France*, p. 2.

[19] Ibid., p. 1.

of Johnson, that literary biography makes its presence felt, and that the writing of literary biography becomes a primary vehicle for articulating critical values and defining the literary canon—and thus the nature of literature itself.

The present book advances a comparable claim: that modern English literary history is shaped by its conflicting responses to life-writing—especially autobiography and biography. These have helped to define the literary field, the canon, modern and modernist literature, and modes of interpretation. Most importantly, they have in turn incited experiments in new literary forms of life-writing, forms which both extend the limits of auto/biography, and which make use of it, turning it into something different—something more like fiction, though something that often perplexes attempts to categorize it. Where my approach differs from Ann Jefferson's is that I give a stronger emphasis to autobiography as well as biography; and to the relationship between life-writing and fiction. These things were crucial in eighteenth-century English literature too. Indeed, it might be objected that the examples of Swift, Defoe, Sterne, the Brontës, and Dickens suggest that autobiografiction drives the English novel continuously from much earlier on; and that my claim for a turn-of-the-century development is overstated. I accept that the inventiveness of writers like Swift and Sterne produces forms we like to think of as modern, whereas there is little in postmodern fiction not already in their anti-novels (which are also anti-autobiographies). To do justice to their work and that of their contemporaries would require another, probably longer, book. But there are four better reasons for beginning this one in the late nineteenth century.

First, because the energy of autobiografictional experiment abates for most of the nineteenth century. There are brilliant exceptions, certainly: Carlyle's *Sartor Resartus* (1833–4); Kierkegaard's *Diary of a Seducer* (1843). But these are sports, in a period in which the establishing of sincerity and earnestness were paramount, and the documentation of a real life became the prime mode of guaranteeing them. In other words, Victorian culture was in many ways inimical to the playing of fictional games with the forms of autobiography or biography. In realist fictions such as *The Mill on the Floss, Middlemarch,* or *Jude the Obscure,* the content often has a strong autobiographical element, and the form often has a strong biographical element. Maggie Tulliver, say, is virtually tracked from cradle to watery grave. But there's no formal confusion.

Second, and paradoxically, the very earnestness of autobiography begins to work against it. Autobiography experienced a crisis in the later nineteenth century, partly because its project came to seem impossible. Developments in the form that constantly push towards the limits of self-understanding keep discovering that the self has a perplexing capacity to elude such attempts at description. Deconstructive readings of founding autobiographic texts by Rousseau and Wordsworth have argued that autobiography was always a self-undoing project. In the *fin de siècle* texts considered here, it undoes itself differently. The subject's experiences are too mobile and keep changing their aspect to be susceptible of definitive understanding. It is as if the attempt to establish autobiographical sincerity culminates in an anxiety that sincerity is all the autobiographer can hope for, when knowledge of the self and its world are felt to be dissolving. At the same time, autobiography as a form comes to seem conventional, and its conventionality to preclude the rendering of individuality.

The third point is that when mid-Victorian texts resort to autobiografiction, it is not because they share this scepticism about autobiography. This is especially the case with women's writing. When Charlotte Brontë offers *Jane Eyre* as 'An Autobiography', what is at stake is less a matter of ludic formal invention and more of the creation of subjectivity—of a female subjectivity which would have been difficult to express outside fictional form. In an era when most biography and formal autobiography narrated the lives of men, fiction paradoxically becomes an arena for granting female experience an equivalent reality in the public sphere. The production of fictive autobiography in such cases can be seen as an expression of a baffled desire to write autobiography, rather than a despair about the form itself. Whereas the period under consideration is the one in which the realist novel and naturalist theatre also become transformed. In a sense, the story told in Part I of this study is one of the disintegration, around the turn-of-the-century, of what might be called (by analogy) auto/biographical realism—narratives confident they could deliver objective truths in narrating a life—as authors (re)discover the fictionality that is inextricable from auto/biographical narrative as it is from the novel or the drama.

Though nineteenth-century fiction drew deeply on auto/biographical material, such material is usually lent to characters who, though they might be writing their experience down for our benefit, are not presented creative artists, but as artless recounters and transcribers of their experience. (David Copperfield is an exception, but the scarcity of such fictional-novelist-narrators proves the rule.) This leads on to the last reason for positing new versions of autobiografiction at the turn of the century: the emergence of the modernist *Künstlerroman* (or novel about the development of the artist) which coincides with the new kind of experimentation combining the fictive and the auto/biographical constituting the subject of this book.

Thus (unlike Jefferson in her discussion of French literature) I am more concerned here with the later phase of the story, up to the point where modernism begins to turn into postmodernism. Since autobiografiction is a prime postmodernist mode, the story could be continued, to include contemporary postmodern experiments in 'faction', 'autofiction', autobiographical documentary film, blogging, and so on. But that phase is more familiar to us, and better documented; whereas part of the interest of this study is the light it can shed on the pre-history of postmodernism. The chronological range of the book is thus perforce relatively narrow. My argument is that the 1870s to the 1930s represent a cusp, in which a variety of forms evolve very rapidly, but share a fascination with the fictional possibilities of life-writing-forms. Though the arrangement is broadly chronological, with the first half devoted to late Victorian or Edwardian writing, and the second to modernism, the aim is to show that experiments in autobiografiction provide a continuity from late nineteenth-century to early twentieth-century literature; thus several chapters (especially Chapter 2 on Ruskin and Proust and Chapter 5 on the taxonomy of faked lives) range transhistorically across the period.

Just as the chronological range has been confined to manageable proportions, the geographical range is focused primarily on English literature, with some attention to American and European texts. While some postcolonial texts make brief appearances, I recognize that autobiografiction also plays a major role throughout colonial and postcolonial literature, from turn-of-the-century works like the 'foundational Australian feminist classic' *My Brilliant Career* (1901) by Miles Franklin, to postmodern novels like Salman Rushdie's *Midnight's Children* (1981).[20] Its transformations of history and fact can make it a potent form in identity politics and resistance to oppression.

This study comes out of a sense that criticism has not adequately described the relations between modernism and life-writing; and in particular, that it has offered two versions of that relation which have become truisms despite appearing to contradict each other. On the one hand, the classic New Critical view (initiated by modernists themselves) that modernist impersonality requires a rejection or abjuring of biography, a view which tended to undervalue autobiographical utterance, whether in lyric or narrative poetry, or in autobiographical prose forms. On the other hand, the account of the modernist autobiographical novel, especially the *Künstlerroman*, such as Proust's *A la recherche*, Lawrence's *Sons and Lovers*, Joyce's *A Portrait of the Artist as a Young Man*, or Woolf's *To the Lighthouse*. A certain kind of exclusionary critic might argue that some of these novels (Lawrence's, say) are not 'impersonal' enough to count as modernist. Nevertheless, the autobiographical is central to modernist narrative, and never far from the surface even in the extended poetry of Pound or Eliot. How, then, are we to construe modernism's engagement with life-writing?

The overall argument depends upon three interconnected acts of synthesis, and the interpretative consequences of each. First, it considers modern and modernist texts in relation to auto/biography, precisely in order to demonstrate how profoundly such writing is exercised by the idea of auto/biography. There has been good work on Virginia Woolf's or Gertrude Stein's crucial engagements with biography and autobiography respectively, say, which has brought out their

---

[20] Ian Henderson to Max Saunders, 15 April 2008. Henderson also notes that 'What is considered by many the "Great Australian novel" is autobiografiction, titled *Such is Life* (1903), purportedly by "Tom Collins" who decides on an experiment of narrating his life of the same day of each year for a series of years. It's really a novel by Joseph Furphy, though it is still as frequently published as by Collins. The "real" stories are submerged under Collins's fractured and unreliable narrative in what he has failed to notice about the people whom he encounters at various different moments.'

energies of parody, fictionalization and criticism of both forms. Such criticism has been important in the separate worlds of Woolf or Stein studies, and also in the studies of gender, sexualities, and feminist studies of authorship and subjectivity. But I argue that such approaches to these works need to be connected to each other, and to studies of other modern writers, including men as well as women, and set against a broader literary-historical context, so as to bring out how a surprising number of major works of European modernism and postmodernism—by Rilke, Joyce, Proust, Pound, Woolf, Mann, Svevo, Stein, Sartre, Nabokov, and others—engage in very profound and central ways with questions about life-writing. Where those modernists who inveighed against auto/biography did so in response to its prevalence and pervasiveness, so their interventions can be redescribed as contributions to the modernist discourse of auto/biography and auto/biografiction. Reading such interventions in this way makes clear the extent to which modernism is often not negating auto/biography but making it new. Thus to synthesize modernism and life-writing is to redefine modernism.

This synthesis of modernism with auto/biography enables the second synthesis: that of autobiography and fiction into 'autobiografiction'. Many modernist works (by Dorothy Richardson, May Sinclair, Richard Aldington, H. D., for example, in addition to those already cited) have been recognized as belonging to an older tradition of the autobiographical novel, specifically the *Bildungsroman* (or novel about education) or the more specialized version of it, the *Künstlerroman*. But these have tended to seem at odds with modernism's programme of impersonality and innovation. The present study seeks to resolve this tension by arguing that the whole category of the 'autobiographical novel' is inadequate to describe modernist engagements with auto/biography; and that (as suggested above) instead it represents only a part of a broader concern with the fusing of genres of auto/biography and fiction. The claims for the synthesis of autobiography and fiction are that it brings out how many modernist works exist through such generic fusion; that it reveals modernism's precursors in this regard; and that it advances our understanding of the function of the 'autobiographical' in literature, and enables a new account of the relations between autobiography and fiction.

The third synthesis brings modern auto/biography and auto/biografiction into relation with impressionism. Another notable feature of recent scholarship on modernism has been a rehabilitation of the concept of 'Literary Impressionism'; an attempt to show that it was elbowed out of the way to make room for versions of modernism that emphasized an epistemological break with its immediate precursors, but that reinstating it gives a new kind of coherence to the longer story of the development of modern literature. Here, too, there has been good work on particular authors in relation to impressionism and modernism, especially Henry James, Stephen Crane, Joseph Conrad, Ford Madox Ford, Anton Chekhov, Katherine Mansfield, Virginia Woolf, and Jean Rhys. There have also been some impressive overviews. In Paul B. Armstrong's *The Challenge of Bewilderment*, for example, the focus is on a trio of writers working at the turn of the century—James, Conrad, and Ford—whose work is seen as distinctive in its emphases on epistemology and phenomenology—key impressionist emphases too. According to this view, impressionism emerges as a useful description for the literature of a transitional phase as realism turns into modernism. In another study, Jesse Matz's *Literary Impressionism and Modernist Aesthetics*, a longer narrative of impressionism is posited, from the British empiricist and sceptical traditions in philosophy in the seventeenth and eighteenth centuries, through the aestheticism of Walter Pater, and into modernist writers such as Proust, James, Conrad, Ford, and Woolf. Here the emphasis is on the continuities from realism through impressionism and aestheticism to modernism. Thus rather than being limited to a transitional *fin de siècle* moment, impressionism is used to character-ize essential features of classic modernist texts themselves.

However, the main emphasis in this recent critical work has been on novels, whereas impressionism is a particular challenge to the concept of the self and its representation. Armstong and Matz know this, yet still disattend to their subjects' self-representations in autobiography. Just as there has not been a full account of the relations of modernism to auto/biography, nor has there been one of impressionism and auto/biography. I argue that auto/biography needs to be considered if we are properly to make sense of the interrelations between literary impressionism and modernism. There are several further interpretative conse-quences of this third synthesis. Literary impressionism can be seen as being driven by concerns about life-writing. Modernism's relation to literary impres-sionism is also revealed as focused on life-writing. And finally, just as modernism is transformed by its engagement with life-writing (and the categories of auto-biography and fiction are transformed by their engagement with 'autobiogra-fiction'), so auto/biography and autobiografiction are transformed by their engagement with impressionism.

Literary history from the late nineteenth century to the mid-twentieth century is thus re-read as a series of responses to impressionism's challenge to subjectivi-ty—to the experience of perception, the experience of time, and the intelligibility of the self. The resultant account of modern writing brackets off the received periodizations that divide impressionism from aestheticism from expressionism from modernism, and offers instead a narrative running from Walter Pater to Gertrude Stein and beyond. I argue that the general claim enables a series of particular claims; that the proposed narrative offers a background against which many key modernist works can be made to yield new kinds of sense.

This book thus explores the ways in which modern writers have engaged with forms of life-writing—biography, autobiography, memoir, diary, journal—in-creasingly for the purposes of fiction. It is concerned both with the use of fiction as a resource for autobiography, and with auto/biography as a resource for fiction. The main focus is on experiments in literary portraiture, self-portraiture, imaginary portraiture, and literary impressionism from the 1870s to the 1930s, understood as provoked by a growing unease with auto/biography through the nineteenth century. When the founding editor of the *Dictionary of National Biography*, Leslie Stephen, wrote: 'my own story of my own life is somehow altogether wrong', he was describing the 'strange sensation' of discovering an old letter, which showed how his memory had been 'ever since letting facts drop, and remoulding others, and colouring the whole with a strangely delusive mist.'[21] He turns this into an argument for the importance of letters to biography, and for preserving any correspondence from 'a possible biographee', as a means of preserving facts, and their original shapes and colours. But by the same token his language bespeaks a fundamental scepticism about the truthfulness of auto-biography, which is very much characteristic of its time. Expressions of unease with the forms of biography and autobiography rose to a crescendo towards the end of the nineteenth century. They were not unprecedented, of course. Scepti-cism about autobiography is as old as autobiography, and as the fictional satires of autobiography already cited. But for much of the nineteenth century such scepticism receded. Not only was it the age of 'the biography of great men', but it was also the age of the great autobiographies of men.

Yet in the second half of the nineteenth century, the reaction against the proliferation of life-writing begins to set in. When *The Diary of a Nobody*, the mock-diary of a late Victorian London clerk, Charles Pooter, first appeared anonymously in *Punch*, between 26 May 1888 and 11 May 1889, the first episode carried an introductory footnote which testifies precisely to the sense of autobiography having come to seem problematic:

As everybody who is anybody is publishing Reminiscences, Diaries, Notes, Autobiogra-phies, and Recollections, we are sincerely grateful to 'A Nobody' for permitting us to add to the historic collection.[22]

Two years later, J. M. Barrie took up the mockery of what had come to seem a glut of memoirs, publishing a satirical letter in the *Fortnightly Review* purporting to issue from a 'Society for Providing Material for Volumes of Reminiscences.'[23] It says the society was formed in 1881—the year of Mark Rutherford's *Autobi-ography* (a major crux in the history of autobiography, as argued in Chapter 3), 'to supply a real want':

By that time it was already popular and remunerative for persons of fifty years or over to publish their reminiscences in two vols. 8vo, and I need scarcely say that the public appetite for such provender has not abated.[24]

---

[21] Leslie Stephen, 'Biography', *National Review*, 22 (October 1893), 171–83 (at 179). I'm grateful to Jane Darcy for drawing my attention to this passage.
[22] *Punch*, 94 (26 May 1888), 241.
[23] J. M. Barrie, 'Pro Bono Publico', *Fortnightly Review*, 48, new series, 1 July–1 December 1890 (vol. 54 old series), 398–407. I'm grateful to John Attridge for telling me of this article.
[24] Ibid., 398.

Would-be autobiographers are advised to tell 'characteristic' anecdotes, by which it means gossip about personal traits rather than ideas or arguments: that is, not what Cobden said about Corn Laws, but that he spoke with his mouth full. The essay explains: 'The Society for Providing Material for Reminiscences has a large quantity of such anecdotes always on stock. In ordering please say what celebrity you want something characteristic about.'[25] Its shrewdness about the market— about, precisely, the commodification and celebrification of reminiscence— makes its satire mordant. It mentions the current sudden need for anecdotes about the explorer Henry Morton Stanley, whose *How I Found Livingstone* had appeared in 1872, and who had returned to London in April 1890 after the relief of Emin Pasha, published *In Darkest Africa*, and been married in Westminster Abbey in July.[26] Most of the rest of the article consists of sample anecdotes (including a hilarious parody of gossip about Carlyle),[27] with prices in shillings appended. It ends with a paragraph of testimonials, including this splendid evocation of the indefatigability of autobiographical fatuity:

When I sat down to write my reminiscences I found that I could remember nothing of interest. I had met many of the famous persons of their day, but if they did or said anything remarkable in my company (which I question) I have forgotten it. Had it not been for you I would have had to abandon my project. Please send me by return another two Thackerays (mild), a Carlyle (full-flavoured) and a Stanley (pathetic), for which I enclose postal orders for *30s*. Please do not go beyond that sum.[28]

Though *The Diary of a Nobody*, *Punch*'s note about it, and Barrie's satire all make comedy from autobiographical vacuity, concerns about the form took more anxious forms too (or perhaps rather one should say that the comedy ministers to the anxiety, which, as we shall see, had appeared several decades earlier). This anxiety about autobiography persists into the twentieth century. William Dean Howells was still wondering, in 1904, whether readers of autobiography had not 'been having rather too much of a good thing' of late.[29] Most of the works discussed in the rest of this book could be said to issue from just such a sense of autobiography having come to seem newly problematic; and their formal experiments can be seen as their attempts to solve the problem.

   The first part of the book argues that the pressures of secularization and psychological theory unsettled the categories of biography and autobiography, and that this disturbance stirred up a proliferation of fictional experiments with the forms of life-writing. It seeks to recover the variety of this experimentation, in order to extend our understanding of the role of life-writing in the period.

---

[25] J. M. Barrie, 'Pro Bono Publico', 399.
[26] Ibid., 400.
[27] Ibid., 402.
[28] Ibid., 407.
[29] Howells, 'The Editor's Easy Chair', *Harper's*, 108 (1904), 478–82 (p. 478).

Criticism of the individual modernists discussed in Part II, when it has touched on auto/biography, has been dogged by the question of how autobiographical particular works are. What has been studied less often is modernist fictionalization of the *forms* of life-writing. This is one of the three fertile and under-explored areas this study seeks to open up. The others are: the notion of imaginary portraiture (pioneered by Pater, but surprisingly pervasive into the twentieth century); and the related notion of literary works by imaginary authors. Imaginary portraits (whether imagined pictures within texts, like Dorian Gray's portrait, or texts presented as portraits in words) prove a richly ambiguous theme. They also prove surprisingly accommodating to the idea of fictional authorship and imaginary works of literature. The book argues that these concepts, forms, and tropes regularly co-exist in this period (and that most but not all of them occur in each instance): portraiture; imaginary portraits, particularly collections of such portraits; and (because these portraits are often of imaginary artists), imaginary art-works; and particularly, imaginary works of literature. These imaginary writings occur across a range of genres: diaries, journals, autobiographies, biographies, and even prose fiction and verse. Study of these phenomena is used to enable a fresh approach to key modernist texts in Part II, with particular emphasis on Joyce, Stein, Pound, and Woolf.

In short, it is a book about the explosion of literary activity where the borders between autobiography, biography, and fiction intersect. It draws upon the upsurge of recent theoretical work on auto/biography, as well as that on impressionism. It seeks to contribute to literary history by attempting a taxonomy of the varieties of modern transformations of life-writing; and to shed new light on two important periods through the lens of life-writing.

OUTLINE

Part I: Modern Ironizations of Auto/Biography and the Emergence of Autobiografiction: Victorian and *fin de siècle* Precursors

Chapter 1, 'Im/personality: The Imaginary Portraits of Walter Pater', begins with Walter Pater as a key figure, representing a gateway from impressionism to modernism and beyond. It discusses the implications of Pater's impressionist aesthetics for modernist writers, and explores his investment in the notion of the 'Imaginary Portrait' in literature, arguing that while Imaginary Portraits can be found in earlier writing, they become increasingly important over the following decades.

Chapter 2, 'Aesthetic Auto/biography: Ruskin and Proust', argues that the notion of 'aesthetic autobiography', attached by Suzanne Nalbantian to the modernist autobiographical *Künstlerroman*, in fact originates in the way earlier writers such as Ruskin and Gosse develop literary forms to construct their lives as aesthetically motivated. Ruskin's impressionist autobiography is investigated as a precursor of early twentieth-century literary autobiographies by James, Conrad, and Ford. Particular attention is paid to time, memory, impressions, and reading. The chapter proposes a changing view of 'mediation' through the period, arguing that realism denies the mediation of reality by art; impressionism accepts the mediation of reality, but locates it in the process of perception and consciousness; modernism combines this interest in phenomenology with an awareness of how language or form mediates between the subject and the object; whereas Postmodernism is founded on a denial, or suppression, of the objectivity of the object. The chapter concludes with a discussion of Proust (of all modernists the most indebted to Ruskin, and a sophisticated analyst of impressionism), from the rejection of biography in *Contre Sainte-Beuve* to the fictionalization of autobiography in *A la recherche*. The essay on Ruskin, 'On Reading', is used to show how, as for Ruskin, autobiography is an act of reading, for Proust reading is an act of autobiography. Ruskinian impressionism is thus seen as also anticipating the modernist fictionalized auto/biography discussed in Part II.

Chapter 3, 'Pseudonymity, Third-personality, and Anonymity as Disturbances in *fin de siècle* Auto/biography', is the first of four chapters exploring the turn-of-the-century disturbances in the relation between life-writing and fiction. It argues that 'autobiography' begins to seem a problematic category in the period, and gets displaced towards fiction. The chapter focuses on 'Mark Rutherford', not just for his autobiography, but for his later inclusion of the story 'A Mysterious Portrait'. Other authors discussed include George Gissing, H. G. Wells, Henry Adams, Samuel Butler, and Edmund Gosse. The various displacements of auto/biography are shown to complicate Lejeune's concept of the autobiographic contract guaranteeing the identity of author, narrator, and subject.

Chapter 4, 'Autobiografiction', develops this account of autobiographical writing which swerves into fiction. It explores the hybrid form identified in Stephen Reynolds's 1906 essay 'Autobiografiction'. Reynolds's arguments are examined in detail. The significance of the body of work he identifies, fusing spiritual experience, fictional narrative, and the essay, is discussed in relation to a growing resistance to conventional forms of auto/biography. One of Reynolds's chief examples is A. C. Benson. Two of his works are analysed, with particular attention to his elaborate play with the forms of life-writing, and with pseudonymity and posthumousness. Benson's approach to the spiritual through autobiografiction is contextualized in terms of secularization, psychical research, and the emergence of psycho-analysis. The chapter concludes with a discussion of the trope (deriving from the Nietzsche-Wilde/subjectivist views outlined at the start) that fiction is the best autobiography.

Chapter 5, 'Auto/biografiction: Counterfeit Lives', examines the converse displacement to that considered in Chapters 3 and Chapter 4, looking instead at cases where fiction-writers colonize the forms of life-writing, producing a variety of fake diaries, journals, biographies, and autobiographies. It takes a different approach to most of the other chapters, consisting of brief accounts of many works rather than sustained readings of a few. A taxonomy of modern engagements with life-writing is proposed. The chapter moves on to discuss Galton's notion of 'composite portraiture' as a way of thinking about the surprisingly pervasive form of the portrait collection. The main examples are from Ford, Stefan Zweig, George Eliot, Hesketh Pearson, Gertrude Stein, Max Beerbohm, and Arthur Symons; Isherwood and Joyce's *Dubliners* also figure. Where Chapters 3 and Chapter 4 focused on books with a single central subjectivity, Chapter 5 looks at texts of multiple subjectivities. It concludes with a discussion of the argument that multiple works—an entire oeuvre—should be read as autobiography.

The shorter Chapter 6, 'Literary Impressionism and Impressionist Auto/biographies', is really a coda to the first half of the book, arguing that an alternative contemporary response to the disturbance in life-writing is represented by the impressionist autobiographies of the novelists James, Conrad, and Ford. It discusses the recent rehabilitation of the concept of literary impressionism in theoretical studies of fiction. While its discussion of the impression looks back to the studies of Pater, Ruskin, and Proust, it also looks forward to the modernists discussed in Part II.

Part II: Modernist Auto/biografiction

Chapter 7, 'Heteronymity I: Imaginary Authorship and Imaginary Autobiography', develops the earlier discussions of life-writings by fictional narrators to consider sustained acts of creative impersonation: works entirely (or almost entirely) presented as written by imaginary authors. It introduces Fernando Pessoa's practice of heteronymity. In this context a surprising reading of Joyce's *Portrait* is proposed, building on the presence in the work of Stephen's writings (poem, journal, etc.), to suggest that the entire book might be read as not just a case of free indirect style, with Joyce rendering Stephen's consciousness, but as possibly Joyce's impersonation of the autobiographical book Stephen might have written. Italo Svevo's *Confessions of Zeno* is proposed as a comparable example of a fictionally-authored self-portrait.

Chapter 8, 'Heteronymity II: Taxonomies of Fictional Creativity', discusses the taxonomy of imaginary literary works (supplementing the taxonomy of fictionalized life-writings proposed in Chapter 5), and their scarcity during the nineteenth century. It concludes the discussion of Joyce, and ends with an account of Stein's *Autobiography of Alice B. Toklas* as an indisputable example of a fictionally authored auto/biography.

Chapter 9, 'Auto/biographese and Auto/biografiction in Verse: Ezra Pound and *Hugh Selwyn Mauberley*', suggests a new reading of one of Pound's most contested works in terms of the contexts provided in Part I. In particular, Pound's parody of aestheticism is compared to Beerbohm's in *Seven Men*. The critical tradition has been excessively preoccupied with trying to identify the speakers and 'originals' of each section of *Mauberley*. I argue that, seen in relation to the growing interest in portrait collections, composite portraiture, the disturbances in auto/biography, and imaginary art-works, this poem sequence can be read as a parody of the forms of literary memoir, through which Pound also explores autobiography.

Chapter 10, 'Satirical Auto/biografiction', asks whether the kind of reading offered in the previous chapter disarms the possibility of modernist satire, deflecting our attention from criticism to autobiography. This chapter discusses two less equivocally satirical modernists by way of counter-arguments to this objection. Wyndham Lewis's *Time and Western Man* contains some of the most forceful modernist attacks on the auto/biographic; yet Lewis offers the book as itself a kind of intellectual self-portrait. Conversely, Richard Aldington's *Soft Answers* is read as a portrait collection, adopting modernist parodies of auto/biography in order to satirize modernists such as Eliot and Pound. I argue that (as in the case of Pound, and according to the argument introduced in the Preface) not only can satire be auto/biography, but auto/biography can also be satire. Indeed, Pound was shown in Chapter 9 to be writing both in verse; and in the next chapter Woolf is shown to do both in prose. The chapter concludes with a discussion of how the First World War transformed the crisis in life-writing.

Chapter 11, 'Woolf, Bloomsbury, the "New Biography", and the New Auto/biografiction', focuses on the British modernist whose work represents the most sustained fictionalizing engagement with biography. It recounts changes in biographical theory in Woolf's lifetime; especially her father's *Dictionary of National Biography*; the influence of Freud on Bloomsbury; Woolf's own critical discussions of biography; and New Criticism's antagonism to biographical interpretation; though it also draws on recent biographical criticism of Woolf. It discusses *Jacob's Room* and *Flush*, but concentrates on *Orlando*, arguing that it draws on the notions of imaginary and composite portraits discussed earlier. Whereas *Orlando* is often read as a 'debunking' of an obtuse biographer-narrator, I show how Woolf's aims are much more complex. First, the book's historical range is alert to the historical development of biography; and the narrator is no more fixed than Orlando, but transforms with each epoch. Second, towards the ending the narrator begins to sound curiously like Lytton Strachey, himself the arch-debunker of Victorian biographical piety. Thus *Orlando* is read as both example and parody of what Woolf called 'The New Biography'. The chapter reads Woolf in parallel with Harold Nicolson's *Development of English Biography*, and also his book *Some People*—a text whose imaginary (self)portraiture provoked her discussion of 'The New Biography' as well as contributing to the conception of *Orlando*.

Chapter 12, 'After-Lives: Postmodern Experiments in Meta-Auto/biografiction', is a coda considering the after-life of modernism's engagements with life-writings covered in Part II. It begins by sketching how the ideas traced in this study of imaginary portraiture, imaginary self-portraiture, and aesthetic autobiography figure in experiments in life-writing by two authors coming after modernism: Jean-Paul Sartre in *Les Mots*; and Vladimir Nabokov in *Speak, Memory*.

The second section sketches ways in which postmodernism has drawn upon and extended the tradition of experimentations with life-writing. Here the emphasis is on metafictional strategies, especially those of auto/biografiction and imaginary authorship. Auto/biografiction can be understood as a strand of what Linda Hutcheon defines as 'historiographic metafiction', focusing on the representations of individual life-stories rather than on representations of historical crises or trauma. Modernist works explicitly thematizing their own processes of representation (such as *Orlando* or *The Autobiography of Alice B. Toklas*) are reconsidered as pioneers of the Postmodern development that might be termed 'auto/biographic metafiction'. Key examples discussed are A. S. Byatt's *Possession* (as biographic metafiction); Doris Lessing's *The Golden Notebook* (as autobiographic metafiction); and Nabokov's *Pale Fire* (as auto/biographic metafiction). Where historiographic metafiction represents a Postmodernizing of the historical novel, auto/biographic metafiction represents a Postmodernizing of auto/biography.

The 'Conclusion' argues that auto/biography is shadowed by the alter-ego of scepticism, whether directed at the reality or intelligibility of selves; their representability, or the adequacy of the available forms of representation. It summarizes the resulting positions of anti-subjectivity and autobiograficton, arguing that the sceptical engagements with life-writing display a markedly performative dimension, using theoretical concepts from Judith Butler and Sidonie Smith. The notion of the performative reintroduces the ideas of fictionality and creativity to the heart of the autobiographic project; and to that extent could be said to inscribe even in formal autobiography some of the key qualities discovered here in more hybrid works, of 'autobiografiction' and imaginary writing. A literary autobiography's relation to a fictional oeuvre is discussed as working according to Derrida's logic of the supplement, with a comparable effect: posing autobiography as outside fiction, but infiltrating the autobiographical into the fiction, and thus reciprocally, the fictional into the autobiography. What such arguments bring out is how autobiography and fiction, while posed as mutually exclusive, are in fact profoundly interdependent, and constitute throughout the last two centuries a system of modern self-representation which might itself be termed 'autobiografiction'.

METHODOLOGY

When I claim a text engages with life-writing, I mean this in a formalist sense, as when a work is cast in a life-writing form, as auto/biography, a fake diary or journal and so on. Much of my analysis is formalist, in that it attends to what writers say about the forms of life-writing, and how they transform those forms. But formal properties are not adduced as ends in themselves. My argument is that the formal games Modern writers play with life-writing constitute acts of criticism. (Just as criticism and philosophy can be read as modes of autobiography, so autobiographies can be read as works of philosophy or criticism.) Modern engagements with life-writing are important because they accumulate into a developing and sustained critique of the conditions of self-representation; of the writing of subjectivity. And this critique provides the groundwork for much contemporary literary theory. It is no surprise that post-structuralism arose through a series of responses to writers like Wordsworth, Nietzsche, Proust, Joyce, or Sartre. But it may come as a surprise how central to the emergence of recent theory were such writers' engagements with life-writing.

One discovery while researching this study was of how attentive the writers were to the ways in which their work was framed. My readings necessarily attend to the effects of such framing, and to how frames can produce *mises en abymes*. Here too, my account is necessarily formalist, though it gives considerable attention to what Kevin Jackson calls 'Invisible Forms', such as title-pages, pseudonyms and heteronyms, or prefatory and editorial material.[30] Taken with the attention given to composition and publication history, this may sometimes have the appearance of New Historicism or the History of the Book. But, rather, the focus is on how the material circumstances of composition and publication, like the 'invisible forms', themselves become increasingly thematized and fictionalized during the period.

The main argument of the book is that from the 1870s to the 1930s autobiography increasingly aspires to the condition of fiction and that this rewrites the literary history of modernism, to show that, far from negating life-writing, modernism constantly engages with it dialectically, rejecting it in order to assimilate and transform it.

Such an argument might provoke at least three related objections. First, that it implies an outmodedly narrow definition of modernism. Nowadays we talk of modernisms, their institutions and networks, rather than restricting ourselves to its self-appointed high priests such as T. S. Eliot or Ezra Pound. Second, that the poetics of impersonality is a particularly masculinist formulation, and that once we focus on the gendering of modernism the old monolithic definitions crumble away. Third, that historically the major modernist experiments with life-writing occur *after* the classic high modernism of *Ulysses* and 'The Waste Land' in 1922, whether because female modernists like Woolf and Stein react against the

---

[30] In this respect my analysis differs from that offered by Mary Ann Caws in her *Reading Frames in Modern Fiction* (Princeton: Princeton University Press, c.1985), which understands 'frames' in a more numinous sense of devices to focus a reader's attention. Most of the techniques I discuss would qualify as examples of what she calls 'the *insetting* of text and picture within text as narrated and pictured', p. 16. Kevin Jackson, *Invisible Forms: A Guide to Literary Curiosities* (London: Picador, 1999). See Chapter 7 for further discussion.

patriarchal tendencies of male modernists, or because writers begin to return to auto/biography as 1930s documentarism begins to take over from high modernism after the flood of First World War memoirs appearing from the late 1920s.

While there is much force in all these objections, I believe my argument leads to different conclusions. While contemporary Modernist Studies is refreshingly open to the range of modernisms, it has not addressed the range of modernist experiments in life-writing. One thing this study demonstrates is how modern fictionalizations of life-writing develop in terms of literary networks, with writers not only responding to each others' work, but thematizing the networks themselves. My discussions focus on aesthetes (Chapters 1, 2, and 9), social realists (Chapter 3), impressionists (Chapter 6), modernists (Chapters 6–11), and the Bloomsbury group (Chapter 11), and show that the diversity of auto/biografiction allows a more precise taxonomy of modernisms. They show how engagements with life-writing can be said to characterize early and high modernism too, and even the work of the very canonical male high modernists who are taken to be so opposed to auto/biography. They also establish how auto/biografiction's masquerades include gender masquerades, making it a mode attractive to writers wanting to queer their picture. Autobiografiction and homoeroticism seem to coincide (for obvious reasons, when to write candid sexual autobiography could land a person in prison). Just as life-writing has been the missing person of modernism, so autobiografiction has been missed by historians of sexuality or queer theorists.

The term 'engagements' has been used to include hostile attitudes, as well as the appropriation and critique of life-writing forms, techniques, terms, and ideas, to produce works which are not auto/biography, exactly, but often closer to fiction—which are, or are becoming, 'autobiografiction'. I take it that the transformation of biography from gigantic Victorian hagiography to the psycho-analytically inflected debunking miniaturism of Strachey's *Eminent Victorians*, say, was one of the factors that led Eliot to formulate the poetic as that which would be immune from biographical reduction. Another way of putting it, would be that rather than thinking of modernism as a discourse of impersonality, we should think of it as a discourse of personality plus impersonality, or, to introduce another neologism, *im/personality*: one in which the relation between autobiographical subjectivity and aesthetic objectivity is being reinvented.[31] And just as modernism can be understood as in dialogue with the New Biography, so the New Biography can be seen as modernist, or as assimilating the modernist challenge to Victorian biographical concepts such as 'personality'. Strachey pitches his camouflaged camp tone precisely to suggest that his Victorians are not so much living out the demands of their personalities, but are *performing* those personalities. He repeatedly catches them posing—living out fantasy selves

---

[31] See Chapter 1.

through which they personify 'conscience' or 'mercy' or 'heroism', while trying to convince others—and themselves—of what are essentially fantasy perform-ances. In short, his biographies are studies in the autobiografictions perpetrated by his subjects. Thus although there might seem to be a tension between an impersonalist high modernism, and self-conscious Bloomsbury life-writing, from another point of view, the function of the New Biography is precisely to vaporize the conventional biographical (and critical) notions of 'personality' or 'character' by showing how thoroughly permeated with fictionality they have always been. Modernism's play with masks, personae, unreliable narrators, and its engage-ment with psychoanalysis too, while they can all be seen as attacks on traditional ways of writing about the lives of people, or understanding character, can themselves be understood as not so much an abandonment of these things, but an attempt to find new ways of doing them. Classic modernist works do not so much ignore or annihilate life-writing. Rather, they parody it, play formal games with it. These practices merely become more visible from the late 1920s, in works like *Orlando* (1928) and *The Autobiography of Alice B. Toklas* (1932).

A more traditional kind of modernist scholar might voice a different objec-tion: that I am trying to re-imprison modernists in the very system they were trying to escape—the tyrannical hold of 'character', 'personality', and other concepts fetishized by Romanticism's investment in self-culture, and by biogra-phy and autobiography—and that to read an attack on life-writing as a continu-ation of it is perverse, and denies artists any possibility of changing anything. In some cases I would not disagree: an Imagist poem is not a life-story; where modernism is most corrosively anti-Romantic and anti-Humanist it has little truck with life-writing—in Wyndham Lewis's fiction, say, or the criticism of T. E. Hulme or T. S. Eliot. But even Eliot's poetry does strange and rich things with life-writing: not only in his early monologues by speakers who feel they have not had a life—J. Alfred Prufrock, or the Lady of 'Portrait of a Lady'—but even in that most austerely modernist of works, 'The Waste Land'. Since, though we might not have realized it from the poem, the notes tell us that it is united by the single 'personage' of Tiresias, who, like Orlando, has changed genders, and whose visions span many human lifetimes. To Cyril Connolly, writing close to modernism, in *Enemies of Promise* (1938), the key dichotomy was indeed between personality and impersonality.[32] He distinguished between what he called the 'Mandarin' and the 'vernacular' or 'colloquial' styles. It was the latter which he understood as a quest for impersonality—for the erasing of the artist's personality so as to appeal to the mass, like cinema. Whereas the Mandarin category, which includes high modernists such as Joyce and Eliot, seemed to him embarked on a quest for personality. Even if we feel he had ignored the Mandarins when they argued for impersonality, the fact he could formulate it

---

[32] Connolly, *Enemies of Promise* (London: George Routledge & Sons, 1938), for example pp. 16, 22, 76, 79–80.

so differently suggests that the boundaries between personality and impersonality in modernism are harder to draw than we might have thought.

Once one starts asking questions about the role of 'life-writing' in modernism, it becomes clear that rather than being a movement in which literature and life-writing are severed, it can be redescribed as one which investigates their relationship in new ways. My aim is to show how widespread the phenomenon is; and also how, as some of these examples indicate, what's happening is something different from the conventional form of the autobiographical novel, or the *roman à clef*. As with Proust's *A la recherche*, or Joyce's *Portrait*, the books are not just novels based on autobiographical experience; they also thematize the question of life-writing; they are concerned with how to *write* the autobiographical (in Marcel's novel; or Stephen's journal). Autobiografiction, then, is important not to suggest that the same old autobiographical novels were somehow still carrying on in the background, but to suggest that the question of the relation between fiction and autobiography was in contention—in crisis, even.

My argument is that these modernist experiments with the forms as well as the contents of autobiography were prepared for by turn-of-the-century autobiographical writing: in particular by writers like Mark Rutherford, Samuel Butler, George Gissing, A. C. Benson, and Edmund Gosse, in which a marked element of fictionalization enters into autobiography. The book aims to develop a coherent account of these modern engagements with life-writing, and to offer a sustained argument for an increasing experimentation with the hybrid form of 'autobiografiction'. This concept, and related concepts such as literary impressionism, imaginary portraiture, and fictional authorship, are developed throughout, though a more sustained theoretical consideration of the significance of auto/biografiction is saved for the Conclusion.

PART I

MODERN IRONIZATIONS OF AUTO/BIOGRAPHY AND THE EMERGENCE OF AUTOBIOGRAFICTION: VICTORIAN AND *FIN DE SIÈCLE* PRECURSORS

1

Im/personality: The Imaginary Portraits
of Walter Pater

·

'Through a dreamy land he could see himself moving, as if in another life, and like another person [...] it was as if he must look round for someone else to share his joy with: for someone to whom he might tell the thing, for his own relief.'[1]

IMPRESSIONISM AND THE SELF

Auto/biography. Impressionism. Modernism. Writers on all three of these terms have been well aware of the difficulty of defining them. Each is so broad as to cover a vast range of work, even within a narrow chronological span. This raises various problems of selection, not least of which is the extent to which the selection may be self-serving. A particular thesis attracts discussion of the works which best exemplify it; but if the critic selects only those works that support the thesis, its general validity is called into question. To put it another way, definitions of the terms are shaped differently by different selections of material. A study such as this, which sees Joyce's *A Portrait of the Artist* as (amongst other things, certainly) an engagement with auto/biography; which sees Flaubert as an impressionist; and which sees Ford Madox Ford as a modernist, makes the case for different understandings of these three terms than would be the case were Edmund Gosse's *Father and Son* taken as representative early twentieth-century auto/biography, Flaubert taken as exemplary realist, and Joyce's *Ulysses* as paradigmatic modernist novel.

As the example of Flaubert suggests, chronology is part of the problem of selection too. If he can be considered an impressionist, then when does impressionism begin? The question of when modernism begins is equally vexed. Literary historians of autobiography too propose different foundational fathers: does the genre properly begin with Wordsworth, with Rousseau, or even with Augustine? My attempt to demonstrate the interrelations between auto/

---

[1] Walter Pater, *Marius the Epicurean* (London: Dent, 1934), ch. 19: 'The Will as Vision', p. 178.

biography and modernism, using impressionism as the intermediary which makes those relations newly intelligible, thus needs to acknowledge, right at the start, the problem of precisely *when* to start—or even the problem of claiming that there is such a thing as a starting-point at all, rather than a gradual evolution of forms. Since I argue that to limit discussion of modernism's engagement with auto/biography to the early twentieth century is to falsify the story, isn't it equally false to limit it to the long *fin de siècle*, from 1870 to 1930? If, as I have suggested, aestheticism is both the end of the thread of Romanticism and the beginning of its unweaving, isn't it necessary to go back at least to there?

The short answer, which is yes, would make for too long a book. So, although I shall certainly refer to Romantic and pre-Romantic works occasionally, the discussion will concentrate on the long turn-of-the-century. And instead of a starting-point, or founding moment, I propose a gateway as the entry into my topic, with Walter Pater as its gatekeeper.

The celebrated 'Conclusion' to *The Renaissance*, in which he urges that 'To burn always with this hard, gem-like flame, to maintain this ecstasy, is success in life', has been taken, rightly, as a manifesto for aestheticism, as well as for impressionism.[2] It is something else besides: a manifesto for himself. Not only because it is a manifesto for how he aims to live—as an aesthete, an impressionist—but because it ponders the implications for the notion of the self of both aestheticism and impressionism; and also because it ponders their implications for the representation of that self; for the writing of auto/biography. It thus appears as a crucial account of a modern consciousness in which impressionism, modernity, and auto/biography intersect. 'To regard all things and principles of things as inconstant modes or fashions has more and more become the tendency of modern thought', his ending begins. As it continues, he embraces that modernity. He starts with what he calls 'the whole physical life', which he describes as a 'perpetual motion' of the elements and forces of which we and the natural world are composed:

That clear, perpetual outline of face and limb is but an image of ours, under which we group them—a design in a web, the actual threads of which pass out beyond it. This at least of flame-like our life has, that it is but the concurrence, renewed from moment to moment, of forces parting sooner or later on their ways.[3]

Then he moves on to 'the inward world of thought', where, he says, 'the whirlpool is still more rapid, the flame more eager and devouring'. That something can be imaged as both a flame and a whirlpool might give us pause, but pause is what Pater will not give us. His argument is as eager and devouring of

    [2] Pater, 'Conclusion', *The Renaissance: Studies in Art and Poetry: The 1893 Text*, ed. Donald L. Hill (Berkeley: University of California Press, 1980), p. 189.
    [3] Ibid., pp. 186–7.

images as he finds experience to be of impressions: 'a drift of momentary acts of sight and passion and thought.'[4] These impersonal images of personality, as paradoxically at once energy and form—hard gem-like flames, rapid whirl-pools—are clear precursors of modernist formulations; such as Ezra Pound's assertion that: 'The image is not an idea. It is a radiant node or cluster; it is what I can, and must perforce, call a VORTEX, from which, and through which, and into which, ideas are constantly rushing.'[5] (In another statement on Vorticism, for the first number of *Blast*, Pound had included Pater and his fellow Impressionist Whistler as amongst Vorticism's 'Ancestry', misquoting Pater's dictum that 'All art constantly aspires towards the condition of music', having just denounced both impressionism and Futurism as 'the CORPSES of VORTICES'.)[6] What the modernists rejected, though, was the aesthete's tone of wistful resignation and helplessness as all that is solid melts impressionistically into air.

Pater's impression of the self deserves quoting at length on several counts: for its imagining of impressionist autobiography; for its argument that, conceived in terms of impressionism, all our knowledge and perceptions of anything *are* autobiography; for its expression of an anxiety about solipsism; and for its resolution of that anxiety through the dissolution of that very self that seemed imprisoned by itself:

At first sight experience seems to bury us under a flood of external objects, pressing upon us with a sharp and importunate reality, calling us out of ourselves in a thousand forms of action. But when reflexion begins to play upon those objects they are dissipated under its influence; the cohesive force seems suspended like some trick of magic; each object is loosed into a group of impressions—colour, odour, texture—in the mind of the observer. And if we continue to dwell in thought on this world, not of objects in the solidity with which language invests them, but of impressions, unstable, flickering, inconsistent, which burn and are extinguished with our consciousness of them, it contracts still further: the whole scope of observation is dwarfed into the narrow chamber of the individual mind. Experience, already reduced to a group of impressions, is ringed round for each one of us by that thick wall of personality through which no real voice has ever pierced on its way to us, or from us to that which we can only conjecture to be without. Every one of those impressions is the impression of the individual in his isolation, each mind keeping as a solitary prisoner its own dream of a world. Analysis goes a step farther still, and assures us that those impressions of the individual mind to which, for each one of us, experience dwindles down, are in perpetual flight; that each of them is limited by time, and that as time is infinitely divisible, each of them is infinitely divisible also; all that is actual in it being a single moment, gone while we try to apprehend it, of which it may ever be more truly said that it has ceased to be than that

---

[4] Ibid., p. 187.

[5] Pound, *Gaudier-Brzeska* (New York: New Directions, 1974), p. 92.

[6] 'VORTEX. POUND', *Blast*, no. 1 (June 1914), 153–4. Pater's statement is from 'The School of Giorgione' in the *Renaissance* (London: Macmillan, 1913), p. 140. Pound's version is 'All arts approach the conditions of music'.

it is. To such a tremulous wisp constantly re-forming itself on the stream, to a single sharp impression, with a sense in it, a relic more or less fleeting, of such moments gone by, what is real in our life fines itself down. It is with this movement, with the passage and dissolution of impressions, images, sensations, that analysis leaves off—that continual vanishing away, that strange, perpetual weaving and unweaving of ourselves.[7]

This is too long to inscribe over a gateway, even to somewhere as capacious as Hell, in which Pater appeared to have become unable to believe. As paraphrase, perhaps 'Abandon the soul, all ye who enter here' would serve. Or perhaps, 'abandon the notion of a continuous self'. So it is fitting that Pater's tone is itself discontinuous, weaving and unweaving an exhilaration at what is literally an ecstasy—a standing outside the self—as well as a baffling simultaneous sense of loss of that self and of entrapment within it. There is something odd about an argument that starts with the dematerialization of the solid physical world getting to an image of the immaterial 'inward world of thought' as bounded by a thick wall. And indeed, what his argument does immediately after that, is to take the notion of the self, and dematerialize that too. The self has been redefined as the vanishing away of the self; the weaving and unweaving of the self. What Pater has done is to substitute for the traditional notion of the *soul*, as something timeless (immortal), moral, substantial enough to be judged, and fixed (in the sense that the eventual judgement is predetermined), *a self*: something which is transient; whose morality is to sustain an ecstasy of experience, rather than strive for 'the fruit of experience';[8] and which, as soon as you concentrate on it, dissolves. To this extent Pater is also part of the story of secularization in the nineteenth century, in which the spiritual 'psyche' is reconceptualized as mind, as the psychological; and his bouts of agnosticism are the direct consequence of his impressionist vaporization of the self. (It is true that his later work such as *Marius the Epicurean* allows the religious to return, to co-exist with the aesthetic, whether for the purposes of aestheticizing the sacred or sacralizing the aesthetic. But such inconsistencies merely show Pater steadfast in his conviction of impermanence.) His descriptions of impressions of the physical world anticipate the ways in which pictorial Impressionists were soon to approach the representation of objects:

when reflexion begins to play upon those objects they are dissipated under its influence; the cohesive force seems suspended like some trick of magic; each object is loosed into a group of impressions—colour, odour, texture—in the mind of the observer.

This is one of the best accounts of Monet, though published the year before Monet began exhibiting with the group later called Impressionists. A Monet haystack becomes a field of light; the stones of Rouen Cathedral dissolve into

---

[7] Pater, 'Conclusion', *The Renaissance*, pp. 187–8.
[8] Ibid., p. 188.

sunset; his Houses of Parliament blend into the London fog. Literary impressionism can go further, following in Pater's next footstep, subjecting the processes of thought and experience ('impressions, unstable, flickering, inconsistent, which burn and are extinguished with our consciousness of them') to the same analysis with which pictorial Impressionism dematerialized the world into light and beauty. And where Impressionist painting often aspires to the condition of temporality—rapid brushwork, attention to changes in light, and transitory effects of leaves, snow, cloud, smoke, fog, water, and so on—but is always ultimately confined to the atemporality of the picture surface, literary impressionism can discuss time, change, process, as Pater does here.

There are two objections to this contrast. Art historians may object that while the paint may be static, the eye (as Ernst Gombrich argued) is not, and Impressionism in paint was particularly concerned with the experience of ocular movement, the temporality of perception.[9] Others might object that Pater's words are as fixed on their page as Monet's paint on its canvases. To some extent the argument about the moving eye counters this objection, since it is at least as true for the eye moving through words as for one looking around a canvas. The words may be static, but our encounters with them are not, as reader-response criticism has shown. What is less contentious is the essential contrast between pictorial and literary impressionism. That literature can provide representations not just of the outside world, but of the inner world too; of the world of perception, knowledge and consciousness.

Pater's words were mobile in another sense, however. He kept revising the text (as well as the title) of *Studies in the History of the Renaissance* (as it was first called, in 1873), and in particular rethinking the relation of this passage to the whole. 'This brief "Conclusion" was omitted in the second edition of this book', he wrote, 'as I conceived it might possibly mislead some of those young men into whose hands it might fall.'[10] As Laurel Brake explains in her entry on Pater in the Oxford *Dictionary of National Biography*, imputations of homosexuality had endangered his college fellowship, and his advocacy of passion and experience might have been construed as evidence of a desire to corrupt the young.[11] By the third edition in 1888 (which had been retitled *The Renaissance: Studies in Art and Poetry* since the second edition of 1877) a revised version of the conclusion was

[9] E. H. Gombrich, 'Standards of Truth: The Arrested Image and the Moving Eye', *Critical Inquiry*, 7:2 (1980), 237–73.

[10] Pater, *The Renaissance* (London: Macmillan, 1893), p. 247. Indeed, the 'Conclusion' itself originated earlier, ahead of the work it follows, as the last section of Pater's anonymous review of 'Poems by William Morris', *Westminster Review*, 90 (October 1868), 300–12. See Samuel Wright, *A Bibliography of the Writings of Walter H. Pater* (New York: Garland, 1975), pp. 3–4. I am grateful to Laurel Brake for alerting me to the textual history of the 'Conclusion'.

[11] See Richard Dellamora, *Masculine Desire: The Sexual Politics of Victorian Aestheticism* (Chapel Hill: University of North Carolina Press, 1990) for an excellent discussion of homoeroticism in Pater's Oxford milieu.

restored. It now began with the footnote explaining its textual history: 'On the whole, I have thought it best to reprint it here, with some slight changes which bring it closer to my original meaning.' When, though, did that original meaning originate? The chapters of *The Renaissance* had begun as separate essays, and the Preface incorporated material from the earlier essays 'Diaphaneitè' and 'Coleridge's Writings'. Brake comments that Pater's method of production—of 'accreting work over time and reproducing, reordering, and cutting and pasting it to form a shaped sequence—was to characterize, in various permutations, all of his subsequent books except *Marius the Epicurean*.[12] This is an important point, insofar as it brings out the way the apostle of perpetual motion could not let his writings stand still. (Christopher Ricks properly reprehends Pater for not letting the words of other writers stand still either, as he revised them into misquotation.)[13] But the image of 'cutting and pasting' makes the method sound more mechanical than Pater would have wished. And the claim about *Marius* oddly ignores the way such revision can progress: oddly, because Pater himself announces in the footnote that *Marius* is a reworking of the 'Conclusion' to *The Renaissance*: 'I have dealt more fully in *Marius the Epicurean* with the thoughts suggested by it.'

That Pater's generalizations about impressions, and about the appreciation of works of art, were prone to be read as confessions of homosexuality speaks volumes about how the Nietzsche–Wilde argument that philosophy and criticism could be read as autobiography was far from being far-fetched. Pater's case has two further significant implications for the history of auto/biography. First, his method of accretion and revision is more than a personal idiosyncrasy. It is, instead, the condition of modern autobiography. The great autobiographical projects of modernity are more often than not cases of repeatedly revised texts, as were Pater's: Wordsworth's *Prelude*; De Quincey's *Confessions of an English Opium Eater*; Mill's *Autobiography*; the self-analyses in Freud's *The Interpretation of Dreams*; the autobiographical fiction of Proust and Joyce; the memoirs of Ford or Nabokov. Once one is committed to the Romantic conception of the self as a dynamic, organic process, then the representation of that self becomes problematic where it aims for definitiveness, totalization, completion. The view of the self as process produces a text that is itself in process. The 'perpetual weaving and unweaving of ourselves' is represented by a perpetual weaving and unweaving

[12] Laurel Brake, entry on Pater in the *Oxford DNB*.

[13] Ricks, 'Walter Pater, Matthew Arnold and Misquotation', in his *The Force of Poetry* (Oxford: Clarendon Press, 1984), pp. 392–416. Ian Small, *Conditions for Criticism* (Oxford: Clarendon, 1991) considers Pater's rewriting and re-attribution of quotations as indicative of one of his 'principal intellectual concerns', 'to engage with concepts of textual and historiographical authority' (p. 104). Samuel Wright calls such moveable texts as 'Aesthetic Poetry' and the 'Conclusion' 'Multi-form articles': *A Bibliography of the Writings of Walter H. Pater*, pp. 164–70.

of texts. Angela Leighton gives a suggestive reading, arguing that 'the ways in which this passage mimes "the passage and dissolution" of its own meaning are astounding. The subject is the self, "the individual", but more than any modernist destabilizing, Pater enacts a dissolving of the ego which leaves almost nothing.' What it does leave, of course, is style: 'Pater's real gift lies not so much in what he says, however, which is often second-hand paraphrase, but in the way he says it.'[14]

This leads on to the second point: Pater is significant for the way he did not write auto/biography. How could he write the *autos*, the self, if that self were a process of dissolution and vanishing? That is, he did not write formal autobiography: *My Life*, by Walter Pater. The Victorian autobiographer, if he can be called that, who wrote *My Secret Life*, and gave his first name only, 'Walter', illustrates another aspect of Pater's predicament: that Walter's secret life was his sexual adventures, and his book is pornography. Pater's sexuality was the life he needed to keep secret. He kept his life secret enough for Wilde (according to Max Beerbohm) to be able to quip, on hearing of his death: 'Was he ever alive?'[15] 'It remained for biographers, critics, historians, and novelists in the twentieth century to piece together the elusive traces of his life,' says Brake, 'much of which had been withheld or destroyed by his family and friends, and to claim him variously as an important early modernist, and writer of gay discourse.'[16]

IMAGINARY PORTRAITS

Nevertheless, much of what he did write was, if not formal autobiography, nonetheless auto/biography. As Laurel Brake explains: 'he developed the portrait/biographies of *Studies* into a hybrid genre of fiction and history which he called the "Imaginary Portrait"'. The first, an autobiographical short story called 'Imaginary Portrait: The Child in the House', appeared in *Macmillan's Magazine* in 1878. *The Renaissance* is structured as a sequence of biographical studies— 'portrait/biographies'—which give an impression of their subject rather than an exhaustive official biography: very much the kind of brief lives that Lytton Strachey was to advocate in the preface to *Eminent Victorians* a third of a century later. This form, the portrait/biography, can also be turned to autobiographical use, as in 'The Child in the House'. But, as we have seen, the ostensibly biographical portrait can be read autobiographically too, whether it is the portrait

---

[14] Leighton, *On Form: Poetry, Aestheticism, and the Legacy of a Word* (Oxford: Oxford University Press, 2007), pp. 91, 90.

[15] Richard Ellmann, *Oscar Wilde* (London: Hamish Hamilton, 1988), p. 50.

[16] Brake, *ODNB*. I am also grateful to John Stokes for initially directing me towards Pater's Imaginary Portraits.

of Leonardo da Vinci or of Dorian Gray. Whether the emphasis is on biography, or as in the 'Conclusion', on criticism, the essays were also intended as autobiography, to the extent that they are intended as expressions of Pater's point of view, taste, personality. All the essays, in short, qualify as examples of auto/biography, if in different ratios. Laurel Brake contests this view, arguing that the *Imaginary Portraits* and *Marius* represent a turn away from autobiography and into fiction; that because the 'Conclusion' to *The Renaissance* 'was read so blatantly as autobiographical once it was signed', Pater 'took refuge in historicized and imaginary characters'. Certainly the *Imaginary Portraits* make no autobiographical disclosures admissible in a court of law. But they can certainly be read as continuing autobiography by other means; rather as Lawrence Evans, for example, describes *Marius* as Pater's *apologia pro vita sua*; Carolyn Williams endorses this idea of an 'autobiographical valence' in Pater's fiction, commenting how often the character of Marius has been seen as 'a recognizable mask for Pater's own "epicurean" sensibility.'[17] Indeed, it is precisely as 'sensibility' that he has inscribed himself in literary history. Harold Bloom defines him as the kind of critic whose 'value inheres neither in his accuracy at the direct interpretation of meaning in texts nor in his judgments of relative eminence of works and authors. Rather, he gives us a vision of art through his own unique sensibility, and so his own writings obscure the supposed distinction between criticism and creation.'[18] Or between criticism and auto/biography. Bloom quotes an epiphanic passage from the crucial chapter of *Marius*, 'The Will as Vision', commenting: 'All of Pater is in this passage.'[19]

Pater himself (if that isn't a contradiction in terms) felt both that 'The Child in the House' was something new—'the modern expression of a modern outlook'—and that it was the logical summation of his previous work.[20] He also discussed it in terms suggesting that it represented to him a form of imaginative autobiography: 'Child in the House: voilà', he wrote (*prétentieux? lui?*): 'the germinating, original, source, specimen, of all my *imaginative* work.'[21] Pater's critics have perhaps been too ready to accept his own appraisal of his achievement. William Buckler, for example, describes 'The Child in the House' as:

---

[17] Lawrence Evans, *Letters of Walter Pater* (Oxford: Clarendon Press, 1970), p. xxx (cited in Carolyn D. Williams, *Transfigured World: Walter Pater's Aesthetic Historicism* [Ithaca: Cornell University Press, 1989], p. 185); Williams, *Transfigured World*, p. 184. Also see Gerald Monsman, 'Gaston de Latour and Pater's Art of Autobiography', *Nineteenth-Century Fiction*, 33:4 (1979), 411–33.

[18] Harold Bloom, ed., *Selected Writings of Walter Pater* (New York: Columbia University Press, 1974), p. vii.

[19] Ibid., p. xv.

[20] Quoted by William E. Buckler, *Walter Pater: Three Major Texts* (New York and London: New York University Press, 1986), p. 39.

[21] Ibid.

the first pure example of a new species of writing that showed not only that he had creative intuitions that were inadequately satisfied by even the most imaginative reaches of conventional criticism, but also that prose literature itself lacked a precisely appropriate form for the expression of certain kinds of awarenesses that were being pressed upon the imaginative consciousness by mutually reinforcing developments in modern thought and in modern man's need to announce his spiritual whereabouts.[22]

By failing to define any of the key terms here—the 'new species of writing'; the 'creative intuitions'; the 'appropriate form'; or the 'certain kinds of awarenesses'—as if in paler imitation of aestheticism's pallor, Buckler weakens the force of his claim. His closing flourish about modern man's need 'to announce his spiritual whereabouts' both takes Paterian spirituality uncritically, and appears oblivious to the difficulties Pater and his contemporaries had determining the whereabouts of their spirituality. That said, there is something innovative about the *Imaginary Portraits*, and Buckler puts it well when he more modestly calls them 'new literary adaptations': 'non-fictional fictions and critical non-criticisms.'[23] I take that to mean that Pater enacts critical views without writing criticism of real artists; and that he writes about fictional artists in the manner of non-fiction—that is, of life-writing. And if, as Paterian critics tend to do, we consider Pater's only finished novel, *Marius the Epicurean* (1885), as another Imaginary Portrait, then his assessment of 'The Child in the House' as the origin of all his '*imaginative* work' is accurate.[24] Laurel Brake gives a better account of the continuities, better not least for indicating how the origin of Pater's imagination of (self-)portraiture came earlier than he thought:

The links between these 'portraits', the fictional 'life' of Marius, and the earlier biographies of the historical figures in *Studies* are palpable; in *Studies* the 'real lives' were sketched imaginatively, as characters in narrative; and in the fiction, the imaginary lives are historicized and documented. In both cases these subjects, fictional and real, are comparable to Browning's array of speakers in his dramatic monologues: they stand stolidly between the writer and his audience, substituting their first person 'I' for his; they screen him *from* his audience.[25]

The volume of *Imaginary Portraits* (1887) comprises four pieces: 'A Prince of Court Painters'; 'Denys L'Auxerrois'; 'Sebastian Van Storck'; and 'Duke Carl of Rosenmold'. Pater wanted to include 'The Child in the House', but changed his mind rather than change his text, which he had characteristically decided would

[22] Ibid., pp. 38–9.
[23] Ibid., p. 39.
[24] Bloom, *Selected Writings of Walter Pater*, p. xxii. His selection, like other modern editions, classes 'The Child in the House' as an imaginary portrait, and argues that the form is one of Pater's three main modes. Laurel Brake to Max Saunders, 29 January 2007.
[25] Laurel Brake, *Walter Pater* (Plymouth: Northcote House, 1994), p. 45. However, on p. 44 she makes it clear that what such screens conceal is, precisely, autobiography, arguing that *Marius* 'cunningly finds a vehicle for autobiography in the fictional genre of *Bildungsroman*'.

be necessary.[26] 'Emerald Uthwart' was published separately, but has been appended by subsequent editors, as have also occasionally 'The Child in the House', 'An English Poet', 'Apollo in Picardy', and even the longer portrait 'Gaston de Latour.'[27] The portraits are set in different places and different historical periods. The four men all die young. They are not all aesthetes. Sebastian Van Storck is rather impatient with all those Dutch landscape paintings, though his reasons for rejecting them might sound suspiciously Paterian:

The fine organisation and acute intelligence of Sebastian would have made him an effective connoisseur of the arts, as he showed by the justice of his remarks in those assemblies of the artists which his father so much loved. But in truth the arts were a matter he could but just tolerate. Why add, by a forced and artificial production, to the monotonous tide of competing, fleeting existence? Only, finding so much fine art actually about him, he was compelled (so to speak) to adjust himself to it; to ascertain and accept that in it which should least collide with, or might even carry forward a little, his own characteristic tendencies.[28]

Otherwise, he is a beautiful object of the aesthetic attitude. (Emerald Uthwart is both a 'Young Apollo', and also someone with the physiognomy of 'those who have the imaginative temper in excess'; one of the few schoolboys 'who find out, almost for themselves, the beauty and power of good literature'.)[29] The method here is characteristic. The person, and the age, are interpreted via the 'fine art' of the time and place. Thus 'Sebastian Van Storck' begins: 'It was a winter-scene, by Adrian van de Velde, or by Isaac van Ostade.' Nature, as Wilde said it did, is imitating art, rather than vice versa.[30] Just as Pater approaches the idea of the Renaissance through portrait/biographies of artists, so he approaches Flemish Golden Age painting, French Neoclassicism, or German Romanticism through these Imaginary Portraits. In a sense, they are portraits of an age as much as of a person; portraits of art; of the imagination at its historical best. Yet their fictionality makes them more significant still.

What exactly is an 'Imaginary Portrait'? In painting the word 'portrait' inexorably gestures towards an actual subject. A painter may title a work 'Portrait of a Woman', and not identify the model, but there would normally have been a model. Or the painter may represent people he has not seen: figures from history

---

[26] Denis Donoghue, *Walter Pater: Lover of Strange Souls* (New York: Knopf, 1995), p. 196.

[27] 'Emerald Uthwart' was first published in the *New Review*, 6 (1892), 708–22, and 7 (1892), 42–54; and included (together with 'A Child in the House' and 'Diaphaneitè') in *Miscellaneous Studies*, ed. Charles Shadwell (London: Macmillan, 1895). There was a separate publication with the subtitle *An Imaginary Portrait* (Portland, ME: Thomas B. Mosher, 1899). See for example *Imaginary Portraits by Walter Pater: A New Collection*, ed. Eugene J. Brzenk (New York, Evanston and London: Harper and Row, 1964).

[28] *Imaginary Portraits* (London: Macmillan, 1922 [repr. of the 1910 Library Edition]), p. 88.

[29] 'Emerald Uthwart', *Miscellaneous Studies*, pp. 223, 221, 249.

[30] According to Vivian in Wilde's *The Decay of Lying*, 'Life imitates art far more than Art imitates life': *Complete Writings of Oscar Wilde* (New York: The Nottingham Society, 1909), vol. 7, p. 33.

or legend. But a Virgin and Child, say, would not be titled 'portrait'; though it may represent its subjects as the artist, or the viewer, would like to imagine them. According to Martine Lambert-Charbonnier, the expression 'Imaginary Portrait' refers to precisely this 'specific tradition in painting':

When the artist wished to represent a historical figure whose features had remained unknown, he could represent his idea of what the person must have looked like, especially by using a model of his own time. The practice was very controversial during the Renaissance in Italy when dealing with the portrait of a saint, because it dangerously blended profane and religious matters.[31]

History, it is true, has bequeathed us paintings of individuals that tantalize us into imagining who the subjects might have been, and what they might have been like. The *Mona Lisa* is only the most famous example; the museums are full of portraits of unknown men and women. Unknown to us, but not to the painter or the sitter. It was this form of biographical curiosity Pater said he hoped to arouse. He wrote of 'The Child in the House': 'I call the M.S. a portrait, and mean readers, as they might do on seeing a portrait, to begin speculating—what came of him?'[32] History has also left us portraits that we like to imagine as particular historical individuals: Shakespeare; Christopher Marlowe. Again, the picture may not be of the author whose book cover it illustrates; but it is bound to be *of* someone; almost certainly a real person, but if a real portrait of someone else, then an imaginary one of the author whose work it illustrates.

There are also literary antecedents. Walter Savage Landor had published *The Imaginary Conversations of Literary Men and Statesmen* between 1824 and 1829. These were dialogues, between historical figures such as 'Pericles and Sophocles', 'Washington and Franklin', 'Chesterfield and Chatham'. Though the conversations were imagined, the historical figures were not. They take their place at the head of a line of fictional life-writings such as Mark Twain's diaries of Adam and Eve, and Maurice Baring's *Lost Diaries* (discussed in Chapter 5). Pater's 'A Prince of Court Painters', which is subtitled 'Extracts from an Old French Journal', is an instance of these fictional remains of real or at least well-known people. But whereas Twain and Baring take comic liberties with scripture, history, and literature, Landor's imaginary conversations and Pater's Imaginary Portraits play their biografictional games seriously.

---

[31] Martine Lambert-Charbonnier 'Poetics of Ekphrasis in Pater's "Imaginary Portraits"', in *Walter Pater: Transparencies of Desire*, ed Laurel Brake, Lesley Higgins, and Carolyn Williams (Greensboro, NC: ELT Press, 2002), pp. 202–12 (p. 208).

[32] Pater to George Grove, 17 April 1878: *Letters of Walter Pater*, ed. Lawrence Evans (Oxford: Clarendon Press, 1970), p. 48. At this stage Pater called the piece 'The House and the Child', and said: 'It is not, as you may perhaps fancy, the first part of a work of fiction, but is meant to be complete in itself; though the first of a series, as I hope, with some real kind of sequence in them [. . .]'. Ibid.

In Pater's case, the concept of an 'Imaginary Portrait' is especially paradoxical. Imaginary portraits of real people; or portraits of imaginary people? Either way, they are roughly the auto/biographical equivalent of Magritte's painting 'La trahison des images' ('The Treachery of Images'; 1928–9), of a pipe, captioned 'Ceci n'est pas une pipe.'[33] As Wolfgang Iser explains:

> If 'portrait' denotes a picture of a person, 'imaginary' makes it clear that the picture does not aim at likeness, but is fashioned by an overmastering fantasy, which is bound to reveal a good deal about the 'artist' himself.[34]

Iser goes on to observe that this paradox is 'all the more remarkable as Watteau, Dionysus, and an eighteenth-century duke are historical figures and not purely invented characters.'[35] There are two points to be made about this paradox. First, that it is more than a *jeu d'esprit*; a Wildean riposte, say, to a criticism that a portrait was a bad likeness of its sitter: 'My dear Cecil, all my likenesses are bad: the only realistic portraits are imaginary.' Pater means his paradox solemnly. These are works which *take the form of the portrait*, but free it from the chains of referentiality; so as to allow the hard gem-like flame of personality to burn all the brighter. It is important to my argument that Pater's essays take biographical form, whether portraits of real or imaginary subjects, but turn it into something else: they are exercises *in* form, in fiction, in impression-ism. One way in which they are more than biography—and this is the second point—is that they are also auto/biography: imaginary *self*-portraits, as Iser indicates. This is more obvious with 'The Child in the House', perhaps. But it's also evident in 'A Prince of Court Painters', in which he chooses Watteau's student, the Flemish painter Jean Baptiste Pater, 'whom the author regarded as his ancestor.'[36] (Landor had indicated in a footnote to 'Oliver Cromwell and Walter Noble' that Noble was his ancestor.) The *Imaginary Portraits* are rightly described as mixing autobiography and fiction. But their way of mixing them needs to be distinguished from the autobiographical novel, in which a book is presented as fiction, but can be read as, or even proved to be, autobiographical. Pater crosses the boundary in the other direction, offering work in the form of non-fictional biography, which he encourages us to read as fiction, and autobi-ography. Put neologistically, auto/biography has become auto/biografiction. The autobiographical enters into even the Imaginary Portraits that do not seem based on Pater's own life. This is because they are acts of his imagination. Their aim is to present an impression in writing that we can admire as we might admire a portrait by Leonardo or Giorgione without knowing whom it is of. What we

---

[33] Los Angeles County Museum of Art, California.

[34] Iser, *Walter Pater: The Aesthetic Moment*, trans. David Henry Wilson (Cambridge: Cambridge University Press, 1987), p. 154.

[35] Ibid.

[36] Laurel Brake, *ODNB*.

admire in such portraits is the style of their artist, the beauty of their composition and execution. Pater's Imaginary Portraits are thus in a sense portraits of his imagination—hence imaginary self-portraits that present the self as the 'Conclusion' to *The Renaissance* imagined it, only visible as it turns into something else—as here, another self. Put alongside the biography/portraits of *The Renaissance* (which themselves compose the autobiography of an aesthetic imagination) the Imaginary Portraits show Pater is significant not only for his delineation of aestheticism; nor only for the role he assigns the impression in his aesthetics; but also for the way he combines these concerns with experiments in forms of auto/biography which perform what is effectively a deconstruction of subjectivity.

Indeed, it is his talent for fusing together different modes that the Imaginary Portraits are so distinctive. As Maurizio Ascari concisely defines it: 'the imaginary portrait lies at the intersection of autobiography, biography, the short-story, myth, the history of art, of ideas, of manners, of events.'[37] In one of the fullest recent explorations of this topic 'The Imaginary Portrait: Pater's Contribution to a Literary Genre', Elisa Bizzotto argues that Pater draws together three 'typologies.'[38] The first is 'the Victorian short story as expressed by the sub-genre of the proto-aesthetic novellas of Rossetti, Morris and [Simeon] Solomon'; and also other nineteenth-century narratives 'set in the past or exploiting and re-elaborating historical, mythological or legendary motifs', such as Mérimée's 'La Vénus d'Ille', Hawthorne's *The Marble Faun*, Flaubert's 'La Légende de saint Julien l'hospitalier', and George Eliot's *Romola*. The second is what she calls 'the critico-biographical mode', represented by Plutarch, Vasari, Aubrey's *Brief Lives*, Johnson's *Lives of the Poets*, Hazlitt's *The Spirit of the Age: Or, Contemporary Portraits*, Landor, Sainte-Beuve's *Portraits littéraires* and *Portraits contemporains*. The third typology is autobiography; specifically 'the greatest expressions of confessional literature by Augustine and Rousseau, together with some nineteenth-century English works written in the same vein', such as Wordsworth's *The Prelude*, De Quincey's *Confessions of an English Opium Eater*, and *Suspiria de Profundis*, or Newman's *Apologia*. She adds to this typology the 'basically autobiographical essay writing of such disparate authors as Marcus Aurelius, Montaigne, Sir Thomas Browne, Pascal and Lamb', which she calls 'histories of a conscience'. Though these 'typologies' are all immensely broad, they do help define Pater's emphases: the aesthetic; the historic; the auto/biographical. As in stories such as Rossetti's 'Hand and Soul', Pater focuses on 'the protagonist's inner world', and their visionary sensibility (even if his protagonists, unlike those

[37] Ascari, 'The Mask without the Face: Walter Pater's *Imaginary Portraits*', *Textus*, 12:1 (1999), 97–112 (p. 98).
[38] Elisa Bizzotto, 'The Imaginary Portrait: Pater's Contribution to a Literary Genre', in *Walter Pater: Transparencies of Desire*, ed. Laurel Brake, Lesley Higgins, and Carolyn Williams (Greensboro, NC: ELT Press, 2002), pp. 213–23 (pp. 218–19).

of Rossetti, Morris, or Solomon, tend not to achieve their epiphanies, unless in death).[39] Bizzotto is right, too, about the relevance of biography and autobiography:

> the new form appears as markedly autobiographical and biographical and conforms to another typical trend of the nineteenth century, the age of the institutionalization of biography in England and of the success of modern autobiography, modeled on Rousseau's *Confessions* and accordingly registering the author's innermost impulses and sensations.[40]

However, the force of this argument is to show Pater as of his time. The clearer the extent of his drawing on contemporary developments in aesthetic fiction, biography and autobiography, the less clear his 'contribution'. Where that contribution does seem most significant—especially for his modernist successors—is in the fusing specifically of the fictional and the auto/biographical. It is not only that the forms on which he draws are themselves already hybridized— the aesthetic fiction itself represents a weaving together of different aesthetic media, literature, and painting; the other novels and tales fuse fiction with history, legend or myth; the 'critico-biographical' tradition announces itself as a compound; the autobiographical fuses narrative with confession or the essay— it is also that to combine these forms or 'typologies' (the term already bespeaks an uncertainty about their generic status) is to produce something which is itself such a complex hybrid as to undermine its admissibility to the 'genre' to which Bizzotto claims Pater is contributing. Rather than being experienced as contributions to a stable 'genre', then, the Imaginary Portraits are experienced (like the Paterian self) as a weaving and unweaving of their different components. What makes the combinations so unstable is precisely the way Pater fuses forms traditionally valued for their truth-telling—portraiture, history, essay, biography, autobiography—with the counter-factual energies of fiction, imagination, and myth. His experiments were not unprecedented. But what has not been appreciated is how his achievements in the Imaginary Portraits are as much a matter of form as of content. It isn't just in terms of his handling of quotations and attributions from others, or even of his own texts, that he is concerned (as Ian Small argues) 'to engage with concepts of textual and historiographical authority.'[41] He also engages with the authority of the *forms* of auto/biography or history, fusing them with the forms of fiction and criticism. It is in this transformative engagement with the forms of life-writing that much of his originality lies.

[39] Iser, *Walter Pater: The Aesthetic Moment*, p. 154. 'Pater [. . .] leaves no doubt about the price to be paid if the aesthetic attitude is sustained; it finds its paradoxical fulfillment in continual failure.'

[40] Ibid., p. 215.

[41] Small, *Conditions for Criticism*, discussed in note 13 above, p. 104.

Where Arnold saw criticism as a 'disinterested' pursuit of objective valuation, to enable culture to perfect the individual, Pater is concerned with the expression of personality, and argues that the more perfect the artist or aesthete, the closer will be the inward life and its outer expressions. To that extent his position is the opposite of T. S. Eliot's advocacy of an impersonal theory of poetry in 'Tradition and the Individual Talent'; though Pater's sense of the self's trick of disappearing when you try to see it as it really is, is a necessary preliminary to modernist impersonality, as we shall see. 'The artist and he who has treated life in the spirit of art desires only to be shown to the world as he really is.'[42] This is yet another version of the argument that all expression is autobiography. In the Preface to *The Renaissance* Pater takes up the Arnoldian phrase about seeing 'the object as in itself it really is', and turns it inward: 'in aesthetic criticism the first step towards seeing one's object as it really is, is to know one's own impression as it really is, to discriminate it, to realize it distinctly.'[43] It's a first step on a journey he can only travel hopelessly, though, since as we have seen from the solipsistic argument in *The Renaissance*, his impressionism precluded confidence in being able to see objects as they really are, objectively. What Pater wants is to see the *subject* as in itself it really is; but with a clarity and wistful alienation that sees it as if it were an object—while knowing that even that cannot be done; that such a self will always be only an imaginary object. And that is what the essay does, for him, beneath the surface, or behind the veil. As both artist and someone who has treated life in the spirit of art, at some level Pater clearly is writing about himself, and nowhere more than in that sentence does he want to show to the world himself as he really is: an aesthete. His essays, then, offer a form of displaced autobiography; another version of the imaginary self-portrait.[44] His contrasting terms of the 'outer life' and the 'inward' are indicative of a sense (widespread in the period, and discussed in Chapters 3 and 4) that autobiography needs to be displaced, from the outer towards the 'inner life'; and from formal autobiography to autobiografiction.

Pater's celebrated essay 'Style', placed first in the volume of *Appreciations* (1889), argues that 'The line between fact and something quite different from

---

[42] Pater, 'Diaphaneitè', *Miscellaneous Studies*, p. 253.

[43] Arnold, 'The Function of Criticism at the Present Time' (1864; published in *Essays in Criticism*, 1865), *Selected Criticism of Matthew Arnold*, ed. Christopher Ricks (New York: New American Library, 1972), p. 92. Pater quotes Arnold's phrase directly before giving this impressionist adaptation of it: 'Preface' to *The Renaissance*, p. x. Ricks adduces how it was Wilde who took the 'next step': 'The highest criticism, then, is more creative than creation, and the primary aim of the critic is to see the object as in itself it really is not': 'The Critic as Artist', quoted in Ricks, *The Force of Poetry*, p. 392.

[44] Martine Lambert-Charbonnier, in *Walter Pater et Les Portraits Imaginaires* (Paris: L'Harmattan, 2004), comments on the essayistic as well as autobiographic qualities of the Imaginary Portraits, arguing that 'le "portrait imaginaire" se rapproche des essais' (p. 169); and (apropos 'Sebastian Van Storck') that: 'La forme littéraire que choisit Sébastien, hésitant entre l'abstraction du traité et l'intimité du journal, exprime les tensions de son âme' (p. 171).

external fact is, indeed, hard to draw.'[45] Again, this may stand as ushering in our postmodern scepticism as to whether there is a line there, or a line to be drawn there, at all. It does so by ushering in a modernist concern with technical self-consciousness. It is once one begins to study prose as *style* rather than for the truth-content of what it argues, that the line becomes hard to draw. Where Nietzsche and Wilde proposed reading philosophy and criticism as revealing of their authors, Pater takes a theologian as an example of how words presented as rhetoric can be read as autobiography:

In Pascal, for instance, in the persuasive writers generally, how difficult to define the point where, from time to time, argument which, if it is to be worth anything at all, must consist of facts or groups of facts, becomes a pleading—a theorem no longer, but essentially an appeal to the reader to catch the writer's spirit, to think with him, if one can or will—an expression no longer of fact but of his sense of it, his peculiar intuition of the world, prospective, or discerned below the faulty conditions of the present, in either case changed somewhat from the actual world.[46]

The scepticisms run deep here. Arguments may be worthless. The reader may not be able or willing to 'think with' the author. The attempt to express fact issues instead in the expression of the author's sense of fact. It is almost, though not altogether, a classic statement of nineteenth-century subjectivism. Subjectivism—the theory that 'values are reflections of the feelings, attitudes, and responses of the individual, and have no independent objective or external reality or source' is a particular problem for ethics, since any value judgement can be dismissed as merely an expression of the emotional state of its utterer.[47] Subjectivism is an aspect of the growing nineteenth-century sense of a dissociation between fact and value; an anxiety that our deepest-held beliefs and values could no longer be taken as grounded upon factual truth. It is a response to secularization and agnosticism. That is why—especially with a theologian such as Pascal—a reader may no longer be able or willing to assent to an author's thinking. The loss of faith in a transcendental being undermines the foundation of any possibility that thought can transcend the subject. We are back in the solipsistic 'narrow chamber of the individual mind' of *The Renaissance*. And again the vista of infinite regress that Wilde anticipates opens up. Pascal's argument delivers not fact but his sense of fact. Your reading of Pascal delivers not Pascal but your sense of Pascal. My reading of your reading of Pascal delivers not your reading but my sense of it. We have gone through the looking-glass into Bloomland, where all readings are misreadings.

---

[45] Pater, 'Style', *Fortnightly Review* (December 1888), repr. in *Appreciations* (1889). *Appreciations: With an Essay on Style* (London: Macmillan, 1907), p. 8.
[46] Ibid., pp. 8–9.
[47] Peter A. Angeles, *A Dictionary of Philosophy* (London: Harper and Row, 1981), p. 277. Also see Alasdair MacIntyre, *After Virtue: A Study in Moral Theory*, 2nd edn (London: Duckworth, 1993), who uses the alternative name, 'emotivism'; chs 2 and 3.

What Pater actually offers here is both less and more than subjectivism. He starts from the premise that an argument must consist of fact(s) to be worth anything. He then argues that argument inevitably, at some point, fails to apprehend fact, giving interpretation of fact instead. He also argues that it is difficult to define where this point falls—a formulation which recalls the opening statement about the difficulty of defining the difference between fact and 'something quite different from external fact'. Besides raising the question of the status of his own argument (since surely that too is liable to diffract fact) this appears so to problematize the whole notion of 'fact', or our ability to be sure about what is and isn't fact, as to make anyone philosophically minded give up. If we don't, the worse prospect looms: if fact is what makes arguments worth anything; and all arguments depart from fact; then no argument is worth anything. That is, an argument that seemed to be trying to define the minute supplement of a rhetorical effort that lets you glimpse the rhetorician's autobiography behind the performance suddenly turns inside out, suggesting that the supplement is in fact the whole story, or the only story that's worth listening for. What started off seeming to subordinate the writer's spirit to his argument, ends by putting it the other way up: if Pascal's theology is undermined by his personality, then all his arguing, in the end, delivers only his personality. The value of the writing is in what it expresses about the pleading and appealing of the person writing it, rather than any truth about the world or about religion. Pater's apparent diffidence about where to draw the line might conceal an audacity in drawing it so that *everything* is on the side of 'something quite different from external fact'. His qualifications seek to reassure us that he is only pulling the rug from under us in the gentlest way: the line is hard to draw between fact and something different from fact; it's hard to know when we're getting the something different; but don't worry, it only happens from time to time; we may not be seduced by this differentness; but even if we are, it is only 'somewhat' different from the actual world. But of course, if it's so difficult to differentiate fact from 'non-fact' (and note how careful Pater is not to call it that!), then how can we know that the non-fact is so intermittent or slight?

Pater's Imaginary Portraits make, and are intended to make, the line between fact and imagination particularly hard to draw. But where they do so most is in a surprising, paradoxical way. I have characterized them as using life-writing forms for fictional purposes. In practice this is less misleading than it might sound. One is immediately aware that the form of a journal, or a factual biography, is actually a device; that the characters are fictional characters, and that the form is itself part of the fiction: a fake journal; a portrait of an imaginary person. Take the opening of 'Duke Carl of Rosenmold':

One stormy season about the beginning of the present century, a great tree came down among certain moss-covered ridges of old masonry which break the surface of the Rosenmold heath, exposing, together with its roots, the remains of two persons. Whether the bodies (male and female, said German bone-science) had been purposely buried there was questionable. They seemed rather to have been hidden away by the accident, whatever it was, which had caused death—crushed, perhaps, under what had been the low wall of a garden—being much distorted, and lying, though neatly enough discovered by the upheaval of the soil, in great confusion. People's attention was the more attracted to the incident because popular fancy had long run upon a tradition of buried treasures, golden treasures, in or about the antiquated ruin which the garden boundary enclosed; the roofless shell of a small but solidly-built stone house, burnt or overthrown, perhaps in the time of the wars at the beginning of the eighteenth century.[48]

Few readers would mistake this for history or biography. Not only is its chronology so vague, but its story-like quality is so evident. Indeed, the stories are nested: the folk-legend of buried treasure nested within the nineteenth-century speculation about how these bodies got here, and how the house was destroyed; both these nested within the framing narrative. At all levels the stories display markedly Gothic traits: mysterious treasures; antiquated ruins; suggestions of revolutionary upheaval and overthrow; concealed corpses; enigmatic causes of death; storms; even the science is Gothic—'German bone-science'; and of course the name in the title, compacting beauty and decay. The whole narrative is a pastiche of the Gothic; as suggested already, a portrait of a mode of imagination; of style as much as of a man. But then, 'The style is the man', is the maxim of Buffon's which Pater quotes approvingly in his essay on style.

Here we arrive at another knot of paradoxes, such as to make us wonder if Pater realized how modern, or postmodern, he was being in his antiquarianism. For if he writes in a pastiche of an earlier style, how can the style be Pater? Or is it only him ironically, just as it is only Gothic ironically? Or can Pater's stylistic mastery only be glimpsed as it vanishes behind the style of someone quite different? Is it ultimately a style of impersonation—the doing an impression of a Gothic narrator? Or should we measure his achievement in the gaps between the different impersonations, so that, again, as with the kind of impressionist who mimics real voices, his skill in effacing himself behind so many different portraits is what we admire? Such questions are also raised by the master-parodist of modernism, James Joyce, who, especially in *Ulysses*, forges a style from a disappearance of his own style behind a set of parodies of each phase of the history of English prose.[49] Rather than claiming, as some critics do, that Joyce is parodying Paterian style in the *Portrait*, we need to consider the possibility that what Joyce admires in Pater is the ability to evolve a style by ironizing other styles.

To argue that readers are unlikely to mistake his Imaginary Portraits for real ones might seem to trivialize the method of imaginary portraiture as a coy pose

---

[48] *Imaginary Portraits* (London: Macmillan, 1922), p. 119.
[49] See especially Hugh Kenner, 'Joyce's Anti-Selves', *Shenandoah*, 4:1 (1953), 24–41; and his *Joyce's Voices* (London: Faber, 1978).

easily seen through. I hope I have shown how Pater was doing more than that. The Imaginary Portraits are experiments designed to exemplify the views he was formulating in his critical prose: demonstrations of how problematic it is to distinguish fact from fiction. The more decisive criticism is that he didn't always succeed, and that we don't confuse Duke Carl with a real person any more than we confuse Pater with Leonardo. Though he continually intimates how indefinite the received definitions of truth have become, he does not have the courage of his lack of convictions. Not compared to Wilde, certainly; though Wilde's criminal conviction shows what Paterian diffidence had to recommend it.

However, from another point of view, that very diffidence is the more radical position. For all the scepticism of Wilde's epigrams, at the centre of the stage is always the performance of Wilde's personality. By presenting personality *as* performance, Wilde is certainly throwing down the gauntlet to conventional notions of essential selfhood. But that the performance was always quintessential Wilde undermines the undermining. With Pater, something much stranger happens. For if his fictional portraits are not mistaken for real people, it's less clear what happens when he works the paradoxical form the other way, presenting his own experience as if it were that of someone quite different. Most commentators agree that 'The Child in the House' is transposed autobiography; that 'Emerald Uthwart' was prompted by a return to his old school and the rekindling of homoerotic memories. But in what does the imaginariness of these portraits then consist? Is it merely a matter of changing the names, places, and such specific details. Or are they quite different from biographical fact in other ways? As readers, we certainly cannot know where to draw that line. Equally, to accept the psychoanalytic concept of the unconscious is to believe that no one can tell their Real from their Imaginary. Did Pater know, or think he knew? It seems to me that his perpetual qualifications towards uncertainty indicate that he thought we couldn't know; that for him, the self *is* an imaginary portrait.

Such, then, are the challenges Pater presents to the modern writer of autobiography or fiction. The self exists only in its disappearance, or as a process of weaving and unweaving. Representations of the self are as unstable as the self they try to represent. The expression of subjectivity has come to appear impossible, endless, and dangerous. There is a clear line from Pater's self-unweaving to the modernist fragmentation of subjectivity in Joyce's imaginary self-portrait as Stephen Dedalus, Eliot's as Tiresias in 'The Waste Land', or Pound's as both 'E.P.' and 'Mauberley' in *Hugh Selwyn Mauberley*. If his formal self-consciousness and emphasis on the experience of art as epiphany anticipate the modernisms of Proust, Joyce, and Woolf, his Imaginary Portraits are postmodern simulacra improbably materializing out of Renaissance portraits. Of course Pater is not the only source of such challenges, fusings of genre, and reconsiderations of subjectivity. One of the aims of the first half of this book is to demonstrate the extent to which they can be found elsewhere in *fin de siècle* culture. Modernists may have had other aesthetes than Pater specifically in mind. But the Aesthetic movement was certainly one of the things they were reacting against (as we shall see in the discussions of Joyce, Eliot, and Pound). Some readers will feel that my claims for Pater's significance are exaggerated, and that my discussion of him in relation to modernism makes him sound more modern than he was. Not Adam Phillips, who rightly identifies modernist tendencies in *The Renaissance*, but overstates the modernity of its overall appearance:

The Renaissance now looks like what we have come to think of as a modernist text. It is densely self-referential: providing, intermittently, an implied commentary and critique of itself. It is also [...] drawing attention, sometimes obtrusively, to its own medium.[50]

My claim is not that anyone could mistake Pater's Imaginary Portraits for works of modernism, but simply that he represents cultural transformations that were to become crucial in the early twentieth century. This is not to say that his work isn't often painfully precious; monotonously poignant; at its most self-regarding when it affects to be least so. Indeed, where modernists engage most closely with Paterian aestheticism is precisely in ironizing its self-regard; in highlighting aestheticism's tendency towards self-parody when it takes itself as solemnly as Pater, rather than as farcically as Wilde. Pater is, if you like, ultimately, a convenient fiction for focusing on the reinvention of modern life-writing: a bit of an imaginary portrait himself.

It doesn't seem plausible now that Pater's writing could have corrupted the young in the way that the author and the authorities feared (though if young men discovered passion and experience through reading his auto/biography, it was probably as well that they got a life). Yet he did influence the young in other ways. As the rest of this book is designed to show, subsequent impressionist and modernist writers can be seen as responding to the challenges Pater's work presents. Their responses are indicated both by the fact that they engage with auto/biography, and that it is more central to what they write, than has generally been recognized; and by the way they engage with it, by experimenting with its forms, turning them around and inside out; by blurring the boundaries between biography, autobiography, criticism, impressionism, and fiction.

Wilde reviewed Pater's *Imaginary Portraits* admiringly, saying: 'Mr. Pater is an intellectual impressionist.'[51] What did Pater make of Wilde's imaginary portrait of Dorian Gray? Wilde's energy elicited one of his liveliest pieces, and it is liveliest where it touches on some of the ideas developed in his essays and portraits. He starts by praising the life of Wilde's dialogue, while accepting his view of 'life, as he argues, with much plausibility, as a matter of fact, when it is really awake, following art'. There is a delightful suggestion here of how reading

---

[50] Adam Phillips, Introduction to *The Renaissance*, Oxford World's Classics (Oxford: Oxford University Press, 1998), p. [vii.]; Leighton, *On Form*, p. 87, 'He might, then, be called a modernist before his time.'

[51] Oscar Wilde, 'Mr. Pater's Imaginary Portraits', *The Pall Mall Gazette* (11 June 1887), 2–3.

Wilde made him feel 'really awake', thus giving a small demonstration of just how art can lead life. Yet how really awake do we have to be to be concerned about that matter-of-fact phrase 'matter of fact'? What kind of fact is it to say that life follows art? If it does, wouldn't that mean that all facts were products of imagination before they were objectively true? Saying that Wilde makes his case with 'much plausibility' suggests that the argument is not watertight. And again there is the familiar strategy of reassurance which cannot reassure. He doubts that Wilde is right to identify the commonplace with the middle class. But the middle classes are unlikely to be soothed to hear that it is artists—especially artists like Wilde and Pater—who set the agenda, instead of facts, respectability, heterosexuality, or money.

The way Pater identifies the central interest of the novel tells us more about his own Imaginary Portraits:

> Its interest turns on that very old theme, old because based on some inherent experience or fancy of the human brain, of a double life: of Doppelgänger—not of two *persons*, in this case, but of the man and his portrait.[52]

This is well said of Wilde, but as well said of Pater too, who (perhaps sensing himself as, in some ways, Wilde's double) had not one double life but two: as necessarily covert homosexual, and as self-effacing artist. For the phrase 'the man and his portrait' is double-edged. Apropos of Wilde it refers primarily to Dorian and the imaginary painting. Apropos of Pater it evokes the relation between the author and his Imaginary Portraits, and thus reflects back on to Wilde, raising the question Wilde predicted would dominate his book's reception, of the relation of author to book, and whether the morality of Lord Henry or Dorian Gray doubled that of Mr Wilde; a question Wilde was inimitably to answer best: 'Basil Hallward is what I think I am: Lord Henry what the world thinks me: Dorian what I would like to be—in other ages, perhaps.'[53] The way Pater expresses this interest in Wilde's story is revealing in other ways. What, for example, are we to make of that equivocation over whether the Doppelgänger theme is old 'because based on some inherent experience or fancy of the human brain'? Is it because the double life means two things: inherent experience for covert homosexuals, something only imagined for everyone else? Or is it a recurrence of the familiar uncertainty over where fact ends and imagination begins? And what is the relation between these two readings? Does a sexuality that dare not speak its name generate an epistemological and ontological anxiety about whether our experience is factual or imaginary? Or does the subjectivist crisis disturb our categories of sexuality too, making us aware of what Freud was

[52] 'A Novel by Mr Oscar Wilde', *Bookman* (November 1891): reprinted in Pater, *Essays on Literature and Art*, ed. Jennifer Uglow (London: Dent, 1971), pp. 142–5.

[53] *The Letters of Oscar Wilde*, ed. R. Hart-Davis (London: Hart-Davis, 1962), p. 352.

soon to call the 'polymorphously perverse';[54] of how it can be an inherent experience that our desires might not be unitary?

One way in which art may lead life is by giving us a clear appreciation of such uncertainties. So perhaps what Pater likes in Wilde's book, or one of the things he likes, is how the use of the Doppelgänger theme expresses these very uncertainties, and expresses them for Pater's own work as much as for Wilde's. For an imaginary portrait could be described as a Doppelgänger of a 'fancy of the human brain'. That is to say that the relation between man and portrait could be taken as an expression of a possible resolution to the anxiety over the fact/imagination distinction; that the double life as factual man and man of imagination meant he could combine inherent experiences and fancies of the human brain, as a way of overcoming anxiety about how to divide them. This isn't a matter of saying merely that becoming a writer let him grant space to the play of fantasy, but also that these literary portraits symbolize how everybody's life is already double; that the engagement of imagination with fact is what constitutes our lives.

If that were all, an artist's life would perhaps be a happier lot. But there is also something disconcerting about his phrase 'inherent experience'. He probably means by it 'particular to the brain, but nonetheless factual; existing within it'; as opposed to something purely fancied by the brain, but having no real existence. The 'Conclusion' to *The Renaissance* had argued that 'experience' dwindles the object down into impressions we have of the object, and that these in turn dwindle down as we try to think them. All experience is thus already internal to our minds, inherent in them. The phrase 'inherent experience' may be intended merely to remind us of this view. But it also connotes something the phenomenologists were soon also to start studying: what might be called the experience of experience; the impression the mind has of its own processes of receiving impressions. As with all forms of the subjective turn since Romanticism, there is a reassuring side to this. Idealism, and the species of Idealism which is impressionism, in arguing that we project our categories onto the world, precludes the possibility of apprehending the world directly. This has the corollary of trapping us within our own experience—remember Pater's image of 'each mind keeping as a solitary prisoner its own dream of a world'—and rendering the objective world unknowable. Understandable, then, that a common modern response is to concentrate on what we can be certain of: our subjectivities; and to try and base rigorous knowledge upon what we can know of our own consciousness; as phenomenology was to do. Yet, as we shall see—and as we have seen, in Pater's style of uncertainties—consciousness proves as hard as anything else to be certain about—or perhaps harder. Very much for the reasons

---

[54] Sigmund Freud, 'Introductory Lectures on Psycho-Analysis', *The Standard Edition of the Complete Psychological Works of Sigmund Freud*, trans. James Strachey, 24 vols, vol. 15 (London: The Hogarth Press and the Institute of Psycho-Analysis, 1963), p. 209.

Pater gives: that the very act of analysis seems to displace the experience it wants to analyse. (Which corresponds to one of the most telling criticisms of Pater's portraits: that the ostensible subjects get displaced by Pater's reveries about them.) That perplexity of analysis follows from the original problem of being unsure how to differentiate fact from imagination. If you cannot tell how much a painting is being disfigured by your way of looking at it, how can you tell whether your way of looking at things isn't itself distorted by your way of looking at your way of looking? By simply substituting your impressions for their sources, you have merely moved the problem along. There is no reason why you should have a more objective view of your impressions of an object than of the object itself. Your thoughts about your own imaginations may themselves be equally imaginary.

If this sounds like another way of saying that Paterian impressionism deconstructs the self, it is. But it is also to say that the impression of the double life—man and portrait, fact and imagination, author and text—cannot redeem the self from its dissolution. That is perhaps why Pater sounds so elegiac in the contemplation of beauty: to be really woken to experience is to become aware of that experience's vanishing away. What Pater does, particularly in the form of his *Imaginary Portraits*, is to pose one final challenge: one that he didn't fully confront himself, but which becomes crucial, in different ways, for subsequent impressionists, modernists, and postmodernists. In brief, this is to postulate fact and imagination as ultimately indistinguishable, even when thinking about our own experience. In the essay on 'Style' he makes a distinction between 'the literature of fact' and 'the literature of the imaginative sense of fact.'[55] A fact is still a fact even if we have an imaginative sense of it; and the existence of a literature of the imaginative sense of fact seems here not to threaten the idea of a literature of fact. But the *Imaginary Portraits* do not just give an imaginative sense of fact—the kind of engagement with history represented by *The Renaissance*, say. Instead, they offer imaginary facts. In a way it is another version of the question 'what if we draw the line so that there is only imagination and no fact?' But now, instead of producing uncertainty about god, nature, or other people, it turns that uncertainty within, and calls into question the ontology of our impressions, feelings, ideas, and memories: in short, of our subjectivity.

'THE CHILD IN THE HOUSE'

To explain why this is so influential a challenge, and why the form of Imaginary Portraits pose it, we need to think again about what Pater is doing when he writes one, and to return to the argument that it is when he fictionalizes his own

---

[55] 'Style', *Appreciations*, p. 8.

experience that self-uncertainty becomes most radical. In 'The Child in the House' Florian Deleal encounters an old man walking, and as they talk, the man mentions the place where Florian had lived until the age of twelve. That night he dreams of his childhood house, and the vividness of the dream prompts an introspection. It was, the narrator tells us, 'just the thing needed for the beginning of a certain design he then had in view, the noting, namely, of some things in the story of his spirit—in that process of brain-building by which we are, each one of us, what we are.'[56] This is all in the first paragraph. The remaining twenty-three pages tell that story of 'brain-building'. That the story is autobiographical is evident not so much from occasional biographical markers—the father's early death; the house in the suburbs; the family connexion with Watteau; the closeness of Florian's and Pater's ages (though, as Denis Donoghue notes, even such markers are inextricably fictionalized)[57]—as from the outcome of the brain-building process; and also from the way Florian's design of noting his development is what Pater has written. For the child the house builds is an aesthete, like Pater: someone sensitive to 'two streams of impressions, the sentiments of beauty and pain.'[58] Readers of *The Renaissance* would have noticed many other Paterian characteristics in the way Florian's story is told. Not only the aesthetic privileging of experience, and attention to impressions, but the emphasis on how experience can be broken down into those impressions:

Our susceptibilities, the discovery of our powers, manifold experiences—our various experiences of the coming and going of bodily pain, for instance—belong to this or the other well-remembered place in the material habitation—that little white room with the window across which the heavy blossoms could beat so peevishly in the wind, with just that particular catch or throb, such a sense of teasing in it, on gusty mornings; and the early habitation thus gradually becomes a sort of material shrine or sanctuary of sentiment; a system of visible symbolism interweaves itself through all our thoughts and passions; and irresistibly, little shapes, voices, accidents—the angle at which the sun in the morning fell on the pillow—become parts of the great chain wherewith we are bound.[59]

The language of 'shrine', 'system of visible symbolism' and 'great chain' connotes a larger public world. But Pater's paradoxical technique is to redirect portraiture from the publicly visible exterior, to the subjects' interior worlds; and from conventional notions of how to build a child's character, to a sense of how, in the weaving of a self, it is the impressions that seem insignificant at the time,

---

[56] Pater, *Miscellaneous Studies*, p. 172.

[57] Donoghue, *Walter Pater: Lover of Strange Souls* (New York: Knopf, 1995), p. 181, demonstrates that 'Pater never lived in such a house; his father didn't die abroad, the actual moves from Stepney to Enfield and later to Canterbury didn't at all resemble the move in the story.'

[58] *Miscellaneous Studies*, p. 180.

[59] Ibid, pp. 177–8.

which turn out to have been formative in memory, once they have vanished away:

> So the child of whom I am writing lived on there quietly; things without thus ministering to him, as he sat daily at the window with the birdcage hanging below it, and his mother taught him to read, wondering at the ease with which he learned, and at the quickness of his memory. The perfume of the little flowers of the lime-tree fell through the air upon them like rain; while time seemed to move ever more slowly to the murmur of the bees in it, till it almost stood still on June afternoons. How insignificant, at the moment, seem the influences of the sensible things which are tossed and fall and lie about us, so, or so, in the environment of early childhood. How indelibly, as we afterwards discover, they affect us; with what capricious attractions and associations they figure themselves on the white paper, the smooth wax, of our ingenuous souls, as 'with lead in the rock for ever,' giving form and feature, and as it were assigned house-room in our memory, to early experiences of feeling and thought, which abide with us ever afterwards, thus, and not otherwise.[60]

The trajectory from here to Proust and Joyce is clear: the story of the artist's life is one of intense impressions that will become epiphanies when resurrected in memory later. That 'great chain wherewith we are bound' perhaps anticipates the 'chain of the hours, the sequence of the years' which Proust imagines encircling the sleeper at the start of *A la recherche du temps perdu*.[61] Two other features stand out, which are characteristic of Pater, though they also reverberate in later writers' works. First, the disconcerting impersonality: 'the child of whom I am writing.'[62] The circumlocutoriness of this locution for 'Florian' suggests that the child is someone other than Florian, which of course he is. But as a way of writing about oneself it is even stranger. The transposition of autobiography into fiction, via the name of 'Florian', is thus given multiple motivations. Is it the result of a proper modesty and discretion about his sensitivity and epicureanism? A concern about being interpreted as 'morbid'? Or is it that for Pater his memories seem like those of another person: that the child about whom he is writing, although it is actually him, doesn't feel like him? Third-person autobiography is always a disconcerting genre, though it can prove a peculiarly expressive one, and we shall encounter other versions of it later.

The other characteristic, which again both is and is not in modernism and postmodernism, is the way the piece moves between the physical and the metaphysical, between fact and imagination. Just as experience can be analysed down to impressions, so Florian's development is reducible to effects of light, colour, materiality, temperature, sound, and so on. What the narrator says is that this is a story of the spirit, and that material things are spiritualized as they

---

[60] Ibid., pp. 176–7.

[61] Proust, *Swann's Way*, trans. C. K. Scott Moncrieff (London: Chatto & Windus, 1971), p. 3.

[62] In *Præterita* Ruskin was to use a similar turn of phrase 'the child whose history I am writing'. *Library Edition: The Works of John Ruskin*, ed. E. T. Cook and A. Wedderburn, vol. 35, *Præterita and Dilecta* (London: George Allen, 1908), p. 51.

interact with the child's imagination. The building is a 'half-spiritualised house', and 'sensible things' 'figure themselves on the white paper, the smooth wax, of our ingenuous souls'. The word 'spirit' feels like a carefully chosen alternative to 'soul.'[63] When the soul is introduced here, it is done so figuratively, as something constructed by impressions, produced by writing on its white paper or tabula rasa. (The vocabulary suggests that of the Lockean or Humean account of impressions.) But the effect of saying that this series of impressions of the physical world built the soul is to imply that the equation can be worked in both directions. Indeed, Florian's take on Christianity is precisely of its operating in the other direction: the 'translating' of 'spiritual verity into things that may be seen';[64] and the notion of translation indeed implies an interchangeability between matter and spirit. Analysing the child in the house produces the house in the child: the building materials that have constructed this spirit. (There is perhaps a line, too, from Pater's image of 'the house of thought' to Henry James's image of the House of Fiction.)[65] Here the aesthetic spiritualization of materialism begins to turn into its opposite, a materialist de-construction of the notion of spirituality. This is implicit even in the curious vocabulary of 'brain-building', which seeks to reassure the bourgeoisie that aestheticism has the solidity of bricks and mortar, only to end by implying that ultimately religion and morality are only effects of impressions of the physical world. This is why Florian became 'unable to care for, or think of soul but as in an actual body', thus repudiating religion and explaining both Pater's agnosticism and another reason why he may have wanted to fictonalize himself.[66]

Florian's dream 'did for him the office of the finer sort of memory, bringing its object to mind with a great clearness, yet, as sometimes happens in dreams, raised a little above itself, and above ordinary retrospect.'[67] The 'house and garden of his dream' recalls the 'dream of a world' that each mind keeps a solitary prisoner.[68] In it, he sees 'a child moving'. This taps into the ancient tradition of dream visions and their defamiliarization of habitual situations and notions. But again (and as in many previous dream visions) the experience, and the status of the experience, is profoundly ambiguous. So far the emphasis in my analysis has been on the uncertainties about fact and imagination, or fact and value. But Pater's posing of the uncertainty over where to draw the 'line between fact and something quite different from external fact' in the Imaginary Portraits also renders uncertain the line between someone's subjectivity and something quite

---

[63] Christopher Ricks argues that 'Pater, like many who are more sure of the need for spirituality than of the existence of the spirit, does not know quite what to make of the word *spirit*': Ricks, *The Force of Poetry*, p. 396.

[64] *Miscellaneous Studies*, p. 187.

[65] Ibid., p. 184.

[66] Ibid., p. 187.

[67] Ibid., p. 172.

[68] Ibid., p. 173.

different from it; between the identity of self and other, or writer and reader. Paterian memories, like impressions, are alienated from the self that is remembering or receiving them. The Imaginary Portraits thus aspire to the condition Pater admired of diaphaneity, insofar as neither writer nor reader can be sure whose subjectivity they portray.[69] Whose life is it anyway?

The key moment in Pater's *Marius the Epicurean*, which provides the epigraph to this chapter, follows Marius's awakening from a dream, into a vision that itself feels like a dream: 'Through a dreamy land he could see himself moving, as if in another life, and like another person [...]'. Rather as the 'Conclusion' figures the self as a perpetual weaving and unweaving, so 'The Will as Vision' chapter of *Marius* figures it as a perpetual dreaming and waking: 'he passed from that mere fantasy of a self not himself, beside him in his coming and going, to those divinations of a living and companionable spirit at work in all things, of which he had become aware from time to time in his old philosophic readings [...].'[70] Pater's dreams, being in excess, suggest that he is aware of what they are doing to memory. So, in a sense, in 'The Child in the House', though Pater's prose is not his memory, and the more Paterian the prose becomes the further it gets from the Child's memory. Or alternatively, the nearer it gets to the child, the further it gets from Pater's memory of being that child. The elegiac, alienated tone intimates that the child has died; this effect is consolidated by the moment when the child returns for a last look at the house just after the family have left, and it is unfamiliarly empty. It is as if it is the house that has died, and taken the child that existed in the house with it. The effect is comparable to the passage in Book V of *The Prelude*, 'There was a boy, ye knew him well ye cliffs / And islands of Winander', in which Wordsworth writes about a boy whose psychology sounds like his own, as if he were another, now buried in the churchyard. Florian is the only subject of Pater's Imaginary Portraits who does not die young. But through these various displacements of loss, 'The Child in the House' reads as elegy, not only for the past, for childhood, but also for the self. This is deeply characteristic of Pater, who seems unable to think of himself other than in terms of autobiographical retrospect or elegy (understandably, if our impression of our impressions fines down to a 'continual vanishing away'). As it seems to 'Emerald Uthwart', whose present experience 'was almost retrospect even now, with an anticipation of regret [...].'[71]

The autobiographer does not just recover memory, but elaborates and narrativizes it; loses it, perhaps; certainly turns it into something quite different: 'a self not himself'. Its physical being becomes different: firing synapses turn into words

---

[69] As for example in the essay 'Diaphaneitè' (1864), which though it predates the Imaginary Portraits, is another candidate to be read as both Imaginary Portrait and Self-Portrait: *Miscellaneous Studies*, pp. 251–9.

[70] *Marius*, p. 179.

[71] 'Emerald Uthwart', *Miscellaneous Studies*, p. 228.

on a page. The experience of it becomes different: introspection becomes writing and reading. An autobiographer's life is thus a double one too: a perpetual sense that the narrativization eludes the memories that prompted it. According to this view, all autobiography is (to some extent) imaginary self-portraiture; inevitably appears to fictionalize the life, the self. Pater writes of himself in the third person not only because the child is other to the man, but because his writing about the child seems other than his memories of being that child.

These arguments are couched in general terms, and as we shall see, they apply to other work at the borders of life-writing and fiction. My contention is not only that Pater posed them, if not for the first time, in fresh and apposite ways that represented a challenge to subsequent writers of auto/biography and auto/bio-grafiction. It is also that the forms he uses heighten these questions in specific ways. It isn't just that in writing out his memories he defamiliarizes them, becomes estranged from them, and from himself. It is also that this estrangement puts into question whether they are his memories at all. Are they (to recall his remarks on Wilde's portrait of the double life) 'based on some inherent experience or fancy of the human brain'? Are they transpositions of impressions he did actually receive? Or can we read them as examples of Pater's skill in fancying experiences he hasn't had? The dichotomy is not clearly demarcated. If a memory is a fancy of the human brain, does that preclude it from being part of our experience? Psychoanalysis tells us that our fantasy life is integral to our life story. Aestheticism goes less far (it's too interested in self-consciousness to be as interested in the unconscious) but also further: for the aesthete the life of imagination is superior to the life of fact. Art leads the life we live. Life for Art's Sake. Thus the life we can imagine has a greater reality than our factual life. Art is 'the finer sort of memory', 'raised a little above itself, and above ordinary retrospect'. That is what Pater's Imaginary Portraits are: memories raised to a higher power, so that they have the unreality of dreams.

At this level there is the possibility of a very real confusion of categories, between lived and imagined experience. This takes two forms. The form of Pater's Imaginary Portraits, in which autobiographical experience is displaced on to fictional characters. 'These aren't *my* memories, they're Florian Deleal's or Emerald Uthwart's.' The other form is what psychologists now call false memory syndrome: when you are convinced you have a memory of something which didn't actually happen to you. It may never have happened at all; or it may have happened to someone else. At face value this might appear a startling claim. How can we be wrong about whether a memory is ours or not? Yet one need only think of the stories families tell to children about what they did when they were younger, to see how such memories may be constructed. This may produce a different (and harmless) scenario, in which a child acquires a memory, which is theoretically false in that it wasn't a memory the child had in the first place, but is actually true in that it is a memory of something that did actually happen to the child (but which amnesia had entirely erased). False memories are more problematic when they are of events that did not actually occur, or conceal events that did. Such questions are pertinent to the autobiographer, who must ask whether memories genuinely come from within ('inherent experience'), or whether they mightn't have been suggested by the fancy of other humans' brains.

IM/PERSONALITY

This shades off into an area with which impressionist and modernist auto/ biography and autobiografiction has particularly engaged: the way reading gives you experience of the subjectivity of others, a major part of which is the experience of the memories of others. As modern literature, in parallel with phenomenology and psychoanalysis, turned increasingly to the nature of con-sciousness and its representations, this curious phenomenon has come to the fore. As Georges Poulet has written of the experience of reading: '[B]ecause of the strange invasion of my person by the thoughts of another, I am a self who is granted the experience of thinking thoughts foreign to him. I am the subject of thoughts other than my own.'[72] Readers of auto/biography are the subjects of memories other than their own. This can be disconcerting, because, as Ford Madox Ford writes, memories are 'the most intimate and most inviolable portion of a man.'[73] It was Ford who amongst modernists took the Paterian impressionist position furthest. Not only did he assert the primacy of impressions over facts, but he also refused to draw a line between his own memories and the memories of others he had read about. One example to which he keeps returning is a memory of reading W. H. Hudson:

Twenty-five years ago—really twenty-five years ago—I lay on my back on the top of the great shoulder of the downs above Lewes—looking into the crystalline blue of the sky. There drifted above me frail, innumerable, translucent, to an immense height, one shining above the other, like an innumerable company of soap bubbles—the globelike seeds of dandelions, moving hardly perceptibly at all in the still sunlight. It was an unforgettable experience.... And yet it wasn't my experience at all. I have never been on that particular down above Lewes, though I know the downs very well. And yet I am not lying! In the 'nineties of the last century, I read that passage in *Nature in Downland*—and it has become part of my life [...] So Mr. Hudson has given me a part of my life [...] That is what you mean when you say a man is a creator...a creative artist.[74]

[72] Georges Poulet, 'Phenomenology of Reading', *New Literary History*, 1:1 (1969), 53–68 (p. 56).

[73] Ford Madox Ford, *A History of Our Own Times*, ed. Solon Beinfeld and Sondra Stang (Bloomington and Indianapolis: Indiana University Press, 1988), p. 15.

[74] Ford, *Thus to Revisit* (London: Chapman and Hall, 1921), pp. 77–8. Ford must have read the book not in the nineties but after it was published in 1900! For further discussion of this story see my *Ford Madox Ford: A Dual Life*, 2 vols (Oxford: Oxford University Press, 1996), vol. 2, pp. 14, 449–54.

This represents a further turn of the impressionist unscrewing of the self. Instead of analysing the self down to the impressions that have constituted it, Ford reads it as constituted (at least in part) by others' texts. What both analyses share is the notion of taking something apparently very personal, and translating it into, or breaking it down into, the impersonal; something quite different from the self.

Impersonality is of course one of modernism's central tenets, and it may appear counter-intuitive to claim it as prefigured in aestheticism and impression-ism, which are more often seen as heavily invested in the notion of personality. I do indeed make that claim, but in such a way as to reconfigure all three movements as centrally preoccupied with the paradoxical relationship between personality and impersonality—a preoccupation which is expressed through their successive engagements with auto/biography and autobiografiction. Person-ality is as important a notion for modernism as Impersonality is for impression-ism. What modernist impersonality is impersonal about is arguably nothing less than personality. Thus when Pound formulated the principles he, H. D., and Richard Aldington had agreed upon in 1912, he wrote that rather than produc-ing poems stating their feelings directly, for the Imagists 'the natural object is always the adequate symbol.'[75] But what is it that the natural object is the adequate symbol *of*? In Pound's celebrated haiku,

> *In a Station of the Metro*
> The apparition of these faces in the crowd;
> Petals on a wet, black bough.[76]

It doesn't make sense to say the natural objects symbolize themselves. The energy of the haiku associates the images in the two lines, suggesting an analogy or metaphor. The natural objects—petals on a bough—are the symbol of the human: the faces in the crowd. But they are also the symbol of the 'apparition' of these human faces, appearing to the poet (as, perhaps, a train suddenly pulls into a station). That the petals are stuck to the wet bough suggests that the flower is blown; dying. To the poet's mind, the faces in the underworld of the Metro suggest their own ghosts, or apparitions. Thus in an example like this, the natural objects symbolize something other than themselves: they evoke the observer's thoughts and feelings towards them: in this case, what Pound imagines about what he has seen in the Metro. Imagists and modernists theorizing about the 'concrete' thus tend to tell only part of the story. True, they wanted to move toward 'Direct treatment of the "thing" whether subjective or objective';[77] but not as an end in itself; rather, as a way of expressing attitudes towards things, as they impress themselves on the personality of the writer; or because (as Pater's

---

[75] Pound, 'A Retrospect', *Literary Essays*, ed. T. S. Eliot (London: Faber, 1954), p. 5.
[76] Pound, from *Lustra* (1916); in *Selected Poems* (London: Faber, 1973), p. 113.
[77] Pound, *Literary Essays*, p. 3.

Child grows to understand) things can suggest or produce emotions. 'The emotion of art is impersonal', wrote Eliot, catching the paradox precisely.[78]

Thus the discourse of *im/personality* (another necessary neologism, to indicate the inseparability of these apparently opposing terms: how else to understand why the most personal of modernists, D. H. Lawrence, writes of 'the great impersonal which never changes and out of which all change comes'?)[79] will thread its way through subsequent chapters. The autobiographical is the alter ego of modernist impersonality, as when Paul Valéry wrote: 'En vérité, il n'est pas de théorie qui ne soit un fragment, soigneusement préparé, de quelque autobiographie' ('In truth, there's no theory that isn't a carefully prepared fragment of some autobiography').[80] What remains of this chapter before it vanishes away, will merely suggest ways in which the *fin de siècle* posed the issue of im/personality, to indicate a new way of conceptualizing its challenge to subsequent writers, as well as Pater's legacy to modernism.

Pater uses the word 'impersonal' in two ways. It is part of his praise of Wilde, the 'Personality' par excellence. 'There is always something of an excellent talker about the writing of Mr Oscar Wilde', his review begins. This means that in his hands, as opposed to those who write didactic rather than dramatic dialogues, 'the form of dialogue is justified by its being really alive'. There's something of a paradox here already, since if all the characters are redolent of Wilde's excellent talk the life of the dialogue as being an interaction between different personalities would be compromised. Pater confesses to liking the artist Basil Hallward better than the other characters in *The Picture of Dorian Gray*, but then qualifies himself: 'It should be said, however, in fairness, that the writer is impersonal: seems not to have identified himself entirely with any one of his characters.'[81] The novel is thus a genuine dialogue between artist, cynic, and narcissist. This praise follows immediately from Pater's wondering at how Hallward's sensibilities 'idealise the world around him, the personality of Dorian Gray, above all, into something magnificent and strange'. The characters have sensibility and personality. Wilde is impersonal. Saying that Wilde doesn't identify completely with any of the characters may in part be a pre-emptive defensiveness against identification as a homosexual. But it is also a critical appreciation; and this is the other sense in which he uses the word, in his essay on 'Style', and while discussing the writer who was above all to come to exemplify the artistic ideal of

---

[78] Eliot, 'Tradition and the Individual Talent' (1919), in his *Selected Essays*, 3rd enlarged edn (London: Faber and Faber, 1951), pp. 13–22 (p. 22).

[79] See Lucia Boldrini, *Biografie Fittizie* (Pisa: ETS, 1998), p. 45, who uses the notion of '(im)personalità'. Lawrence, Letter to Henry Savage, 19 January 1914, *The Letters of D. H. Lawrence*, vol. 2, ed. George J. Zytaruk and James T. Boulton (Cambridge: Cambridge University Press, 1981), p. 138.

[80] Valéry, 'Poésie et Pensée Abstraite', in his *Oeuvres*, ed. Jean Hytier (Paris: Gallimard, 1957), vol. 1, pp. 1314–39 (p. 1320).

[81] Pater, 'A Novel by Mr Oscar Wilde', in *Essays on Literature and Art*, ed. Jennifer Uglow (London: Dent, 1971), p. 143.

impersonality for impressionist and modernist writers: Flaubert: 'the martyr of literary style.'[82] Pater is developing the idea of the style being the man:

The style, the manner, would be the man, not in his unreasoned and really uncharacteristic caprices, involuntary or affected, but in absolutely sincere apprehension of what is most real to him.[83]

Pater quotes a French critic on Flaubert, arguing that style for him was 'a certain absolute and unique manner of expressing a thing, in all its intensity and colour'; and that 'the *matter,* the basis, in a work of art, imposed, necessarily, the unique, the just expression, the measure, the rhythm—the *form* in all its characteristics'. Style is thus a discipline of giving an objective reality to this material (including, of course, the material of the subjective experience of a Frédéric Moreau or an Emma Bovary). Pater comments: 'If the style be the man, in all the colour and intensity of a veritable apprehension, it will be in a real sense "impersonal".' Again, note the paradox. The artist apprehends what is personal ('most real *to him*'). The art is impersonal. Just at the point where Pater's late Romanticism turns all art into autobiography, aestheticism's style-worship turns the autobiographic into the impersonal. Indeed, the impressionist paradox doesn't only comprehend aesthetics, but all consciousness. If all we perceive is our impressions of the world, all experience is autobiographical; but by the same token, that autobiography only consists of our impressions, rather than delivering a coherent and self-present subjectivity having the impressions. If the Paterian self is self-deconstructing, so is Paterian or impressionist autobiography. Modernism's negation of personality begins here, as does its advocacy of stylistic and technical self-consciousness.

Why was it that im/personality became a pressing concern at the *fin de siècle?* The introduction of Flaubert suggests one answer. As the prestige of science increased, realists and naturalists felt the way to overcome the disjunction between fact and value, objective and subjective, was to give their work the appearance of fact and objectivity; to efface the figure of the creative artist from the picture (rather as science was effacing a divine creator from its view of the world). But this quest for impersonality contradicted the theory, inherited from Romanticism, of art as expressive. Some of the paradoxes of aestheticism or impressionism result from trying to work through this double-bind; as Ford put it: 'the Impressionist author is sedulous to avoid letting his personality appear in the course of his book. On the other hand, his whole book, his whole poem is merely an expression of his personality.'[84] Expression, according to these principles, has become oblique. What the work of art expresses is not its overt subject,

---

[82] Pater, *Appreciations*, p. 27.

[83] Ibid., p. 36.

[84] Ford Madox Hueffer, 'On Impressionism', *Poetry and Drama*, 2 (1914), 166–75, 323–34 (p. 323).

but something hidden, effaced. The implication for autobiography is that the autobiographical in art will be found elsewhere than in formal autobiography. As Gerald Monsman argues of Pater, most of his work is autobiographical; but his 'overriding strategy is to reveal himself covertly by deploying through critical or fictionalized critical utterances "a self not himself".'[85] Pater is thus an early instance of the trope that will return in later chapters, whereby writers argue that fiction is their true autobiography. It also helps account for the experimentation combining auto/biography and fiction which provides the core of this study. Auto/ biografiction allows writers to express and efface personality at the same time.

The association of the cult of personality with transgressive sexualities suggests another answer. The celebration of personality could provide a coded, and thus legitimate, expression of a homosexuality otherwise censored. Accordingly, the rejection of aestheticism by modernists such as Pound and Wyndham Lewis is as much a homophobic as aesthetic response. Yet there is a broader social context for the aesthetic celebration of im/personality. The political dimension is crucial, as Alison Hennegan explains apropos of Wilde's *The Soul of Man Under Socialism* (1891):

The word 'personality' is central to the essay just as the fact of personality was central to Wilde's understanding of the world. For him the term conveyed full 'personhood', the manifestation of each human being's true self, undistorted by baneful influences, un-shackled by false restrictions [...][86]

This, too, is a paradoxical position, since as Hennegan comments: 'Ironically, in this period, so pre-eminently the Age of Personality, the self, on which personality depends, was under concerted attack [...]'. She argues that the attack on the self came from evolutionary theory, sexology, and the forces of materialism in science. To this should be added not only the materialist strand in socialist thought itself—the Marxist form of dialectical materialism according to which 'personality' was merely symptomatic of bourgeois ideology—but also the process we have been investigating, whereby literature was playing its part in the deconstruction of subjectivity.

Hennegan also notes the cultural context:

This was the first age of The Personality, the Celebrity, whose words were swiftly communicated via the personality interview, whose face became familiar to thousands through the photographs reproduced in papers and on the postcards sold in shops and advertised on the back of magazines.[87]

---

[85] Monsman, 'Gaston de Latour and Pater's Art of Autobiography', p. 413; and his *Walter Pater's Art of Autobiography* (New Haven and London: Yale University Press, 1980), p. 7. The quotation is from *Marius*, p. 179.
[86] Alison Hennegan, 'Personalities and Principles: Aspects of Literature and Life in *Fin-de-Siècle* England', in *Fin de Siècle and its Legacy*, ed. Mikuláš Teich and Roy Porter (Cambridge: Cambridge University Press, 1990), p. 204.
[87] Ibid., p. 185.

Where Walter Benjamin discussed 'The Work of Art in the Age of Mechanical Reproduction', this offers the notion of the mechanical reproduction of the artists themselves. There had been literary celebrities before, certainly: Dr Johnson; Byron; Shelley, Dickens. But the media were changing, and changing the process of publication from something which published a book, to something which made public a personality.

PORTRAITURE

The idea of the portrait was under attack too, as Wilde understood. The notion of the literary portrait is central to this study. Though there is a long tradition of calling literary descriptions of people 'portraits', whether in life-writing or fiction,[88] literary portraiture changes markedly through the long turn-of-the-century from the 1870s to the 1930s. The 'portraitist of today', wrote Emil Ludwig in 1925, 'is first of all a psychologist.'[89] Ludwig specialized in the '*biographie romancé*,' defined sternly by the *Oxford Companion to German Literature* as a form 'in which much carefully gathered source material was fused and presented in a manner more appropriate to fiction'. His method was a frankly de-historicized concern with 'personality':

> once again we turn our attention to the personality *per se*, the personality almost devoid of temporal co-ordinates, considering the volume, intensity, and resistance of its vital forces, the restless fluid of its emotional configurations, and the balance between its impulse towards action and its repression through precept. Whereas our fathers asked, 'How did the individual harmonize with his world?' our first question is, 'Does he harmonize with himself?'[90]

This perhaps made it all the more striking that the personalities he was to ask that question of were world-historical figures: in *Goethe* (1920); *Napoleon* (1924); the Kaiser *Wilhelm der Zweite* (1925); *Bismarck* (1926); *Lincoln* (1930); *Michelangelo* (1930); *Hindenberg* (1935); *Cleopatra* (1937); *Roosevelt* (1938); even *The Son of Man* (1928) about Jesus. Edmund Gosse (of whom more in Chapter 3) had announced in 1911 that it was biography's psychological turn that marked its modernity—'The true conception of biography, therefore, as the faithful portrait of a soul in its adventures through life, is very modern'[91]—though his choice of

---

[88] See for example Catherine J. Lewis Theobald, 'Layers of Portraiture in *Manon Lescaut*: Changing Modes of Representation in a Changing Society', *French Forum*, 28 (2003), 1–19.
[89] Emil Ludwig, from 'Introduction: On Historical Portraiture', *Genius and Character* (1925; translated 1927), quoted in in James L. Clifford, ed., *Biography as an Art: Selected Criticism, 1560–1960* (London: Oxford University Press, 1962), p. 135.
[90] Ibid.
[91] Edmund Gosse, 'Biography', *Encyclopedia Britannica*, 11th edn (Cambridge: Cambridge University Press, 1911), vol. 3, p. 954. He goes on to argue that 'Moreover, the peculiar curiosity

the ancient term 'soul' for what psychologists were beginning to call (using the ancient Greek for soul) the 'psyche' seems concerned not to let it become too modern—like psycho-analysis, say.

The inward turn such work represents in biography corresponds to a major change in the practice of portraiture in the visual arts, as realism and impressionism gives way to Post-Impressionism. For the first time since the Renaissance, the portrait moved away from realistic representation of visual appearance. With the expressionist energies of Van Gogh, the geometric reductions of Cézanne, or the stylized Tahitian pictures of Gauguin, the emphasis shifts from 'photographic' realism to an attempt to express an 'inner' world. With the abstractions of Cubism and Vorticism, representationality is often abandoned almost entirely. With the analytical-Cubist portraits of Picasso and Braque, it is sometimes hard enough to identify a human form at all; the notation of a guitar and a hat may indicate a musician, but the portrait has been separated altogether from the individual identity of the sitter.

As in Impressionist painting, such developments are both inspired by, and in opposition to, the development of photography. But photography, which is often treated in art history as if it offered an unmediated realism, offers something rather different in Victorian portrait photography, when backdrops were often fantasy ones provided by the studios; and sitters had to remain still for a long exposure time, adopting a pose that they thought best reflected themselves, or showed them as they wanted to be represented. Indeed, it was that desire to present themselves in the best light that led the conservative French writer Barbey d'Aurevilly to object to biography and photography, in his 1867 essay 'Les Photographies et les biographies', as 'the siamese twins of a single vanity.'[92] In portraits of thinkers, writers and artists, a 'visionary' pose was often adopted—as in Julia Margaret Cameron's poignant images of Herschel or Tennyson—with the eyes staring into the far distance.

That even a process as mechanically transcriptive as photography records someone posing rather than just being, poses a challenge to an essentialist conception of the self. Instead, it shows selves caught in the process of constructing themselves; the self performing itself, and grasped by the viewer as an effect of perception, interpretation, performance. The implications of this performative notion of subjectivity for autobiography and auto/biografiction will be enacted in the Conclusion.

All portraiture, photographic ones included, could thus be said to involve an 'imaginary' component: an expression of the artist in the subject; of the artist's imagination of that subject—even if it's himself. Portrait photography too

---

which legitimate biography satisfies is essentially a modern thing; and presupposes our observation of life not unduly clouded by moral passion or prejudice.'

[92] Ann Jefferson, *Biography and the Question of Literature in France* (Oxford: Oxford University Press, 2007), p. 95.

1 Sir John Herschel with Cap, 1867.

attempted to conjure up that 'inner life', which we shall see playing an increasingly important part in the writing of auto/biography and auto/biografiction. The reading of the inner life from the visual surface is symptomatic of the increasing subjectivism, interiorization, psychologization, that we have seen in Pater. Though it is also possible that technical developments in the photographic resolution and clarity of the prints intensified as well as reflected such a process.

All novels could be said to contain portraits, with an imaginary component; indeed, to constitute collections of such imaginary portraits. Some even style themselves portraits: *The Portrait of a Lady*; *A Portrait of the Artist as a Young Man*. Though there is no clear line to be drawn here either, this study is concerned primarily with works that explicitly and significantly address the notion of portraiture, whether by thematizing it, or displaying a self-consciousness about the concept and its implications. Hence several of the works discussed here feature portrait paintings or photographs. The increasing self-consciousness about portraiture, about representation, means that the writers discussed here do not simply portray, but write about the problems of portrayal. The conventions of portraiture that realism needed to remain invisible begin to get in the way; the fictionality of characterization is beginning to show up; in short, the imaginariness becomes as visible as the portrait.

Just as the mobility of Paterian impressionism is best understood as in opposition to a new form of portraiture, that of the portrait photograph (though Pater collected photographs of his friends from Elliot and Fry, where he lodged his own photograph for others to buy),[93] so the *fin de siècle* discourse of im/personality needs to be understood in the context of the publicizing and marketing of authors. Authors' lives now became double in a different way, in that their role as public figures could seem at odds with their senses of their private selves.

Pater was never as prominent a public figure as Wilde. He died in 1894, just before the trial of Wilde first made then broke the pre-eminent literary personality of the age. By 1910, the year Virginia Woolf said that 'human character changed',[94] he was in danger of being effaced by the next generation; by the Post-Impressionists exhibited in London by Roger Fry that year; and by the modernists like Conrad, Ford, Proust, Pound, Joyce, Eliot, and Woolf herself, all then producing or on the verge of producing work that was to rethink the issue of im/personality. Yet 1910 was also the year in which a collected edition of Pater's work was published. The collected edition put Pater back in the public eye just at a crucial moment when modernists were formulating or reformulating their aesthetic strategies. So perhaps it isn't merely a critical fancy to suggest that the challenges his work presents were part of the reason 'human character changed.'[95]

There is little explicit trace of Pater in the writings of those modernists—a few disparaging remarks by Woolf in reviews of others' work; a passing reference in *The Good Soldier* to 'the mental spirituality of Walter Pater';[96] echoes of a Paterian sensibility in Stephen Dedalus. Perhaps the most visible trace was when Yeats printed the famous passage from the essay on Leonardo da Vinci

---

[93] I am grateful to Laurel Brake for this information.

[94] Woolf, 'Character in Fiction' (1924; subsequently reprinted as 'Mr Bennett and Mrs Brown'), in *The Essays of Virginia Woolf*, vol. 3, ed. Andrew McNeillie (London: The Hogarth Press, 1988), pp. 420–38 (p. 421).

[95] Woolf had acquired Pater's collected works between 1902 and 1905. See Perry Meisel, *The Absent Father: Virginia Woolf and Walter Pater* (New Haven and London: Yale University Press, 1980), pp. 16–17 n. 24.

[96] Ford, *The Good Soldier* (London: John Lane, 1915), p. 20.

(1869), meditating on Mona Lisa ('She is as old as the rocks upon which she sits'), as the first exhibit in his 1939 *Oxford Book of English Verse*. Nevertheless, there is by now a body of criticism adumbrating Pater's influence; especially on Joyce and Woolf. In Joyce's case, it is in the *Portrait* that commentators have detected a likeness of Pater. Perry Meisel, for example, argues that it echoes 'Emerald Uthwart', and describes Stephen as Paterian.[97] Frank Moliterno argues for the influence of *Marius* on *Portrait*.[98] Sometimes the line of influence is traced indirectly, as by Karl Beckson, who relates Joyce's *Portrait* to the 'intensely autobiographical imaginary portrait', 'A Prelude to Life', by Arthur Symons, who acknowledged his debt to Pater.[99] John Paul Riquelme discusses the Paterian influence on both Joyce and Stephen.[100] In the case of Woolf, it is *Orlando* that most obviously draws on the Paterian Imaginary Portrait.[101] Denis Donoghue, whose biographical study of Pater reads him as a proto-modernist, makes one of the strongest claims: that Pater 'is audible in virtually every attentive modern writer—in Hopkins, Wilde, James, Yeats, Pound, Ford, Woolf, Joyce, Eliot, Aiken, Hart Crane, Fitzgerald, Forster, Borges, Stevens, Ammons, Tomlinson, and Ashbery.'[102] Perry Meisel makes another strong claim for Pater's influence, writing that 'Joyce, Eliot, Pound, Stevens, Hardy, Conrad, James, even Lawrence, each is obligated to Pater in particular ways'. He argues that it is as a critic and essayist that his impact on Woolf was most profound. Though, as he notes, before 1898 the only volume of Pater in Woolf's father Leslie Stephen's library was a first edition of *Imaginary Portraits*, so that it was in the form of this volume that 'Virginia first experienced Pater directly'. 'Woolf's fiction, like Joyce's,' he continues, 'has no clearer anticipation in English prose than Pater's own fictional portraits.'[103] Yet, as his telling title indicates—*The Absent Father: Virginia Woolf and Walter Pater*—Pater is a paradoxical influence, one who seems relevant in his absence as much as in his presence.[104] Meisel quotes Wyndham Lewis, spotting how:

[97] Meisel, *The Absent Father*, pp. 139, 61.

[98] Moliterno, *The Dialectics of Sense and Spirit in Pater and Joyce* (Greensboro, NC: ELT Press, 1998).

[99] Beckson, 'Symons' "A Prelude to Life", Joyce's *A Portrait*, and the Religion of Art', *James Joyce Quarterly*, 15 (1978), 222–8. 'A Prelude to Life', *The Collected Work of Arthur Symons* (London: Martin Secker, 1924), vol. 5, pp. 3–32, was included in the volume *Spiritual Adventures*, discussed in Chapter 7.

[100] Riquelme, in the *Cambridge Companion to James Joyce*, ed. Derek Attridge (Cambridge: Cambridge University Press, 1990), p. 103; discussed in Chapter 7.

[101] Bizzotto, 'The Imaginary Portrait', p. 222, discusses Eugene Brzenk's tracing of *Orlando* back to Pater.

[102] Donoghue, *Walter Pater: Lover of Strange Souls*, p. 7.

[103] Perry Meisel, *The Absent Father*, pp. 12–13.

[104] Meisel, ibid., p. 73 suggests Woolf's essay 'Reading' is influenced by Pater. Leighton, *On Form*, p. 96 suggests that Denys L'Auxerrois may have inspired Woolf's 'Solid Objects'.

'aestheticism', though in truth rampant and ubiquitous, is on all hands violently dis-
owned: and although the manner of Pater is today constantly imitated, on the sly, and his
teaching absorbed along with his style, he is scarcely *respectable* in the intellectual sense.[105]

Understood in this way, Pater's influence is pervasive, and well documented.
But such criticism has focused mainly on Paterian style; or on a Paterian aesthetic
and sensibility, whether in the character-types dramatized, or in the narratorial
emphases on consciousness, impressions, vision, epiphany, fluidity, self-dispersal,
or disintegration. My purpose, by contrast, is to explore the ways in which
formal experiments in works such as Pater's were developed and transformed
by Edwardian and modernist writers. Elisa Bizzotto concludes her account of the
Imaginary Portraits with a claim for the influence of their *form*, rather than
merely their style or their aestheticism: 'despite the opinions of a few critics,
recognition of aesthetic portraiture as a seminal literary mode is occasional, and
the real hold of the genre on twentieth-century prose writing remains as yet
underestimated.'[106] Much of the following book seeks to provide such an
estimate, while broadening out its terms of reference to include aesthetic self-
portraiture, and twentieth-century verse as well as prose. In doing so, I am
offering three further, inter-related, aspects of the modernist engagement with
aesthetic (self-)portraiture: gender and sexuality; ideas of im/personality; and life-
writing forms.

A cogent reason why aesthetic portraiture's legacy has not been gauged is
proposed by Lesley Higgins. She argues that Wilde's praise of Pater ensured that,
after the scandal of the Wilde trial, and in 'masculinist high modernist culture',
'beauty's most radical champion' could not but be repressed or evaded.[107]
Modernists, that is, didn't want to admit the influence, whether to themselves
or to others. But—as Lewis was hinting by italicizing the word 'respectable' into
an innuendo—what happens is worse than inattention to aestheticism, or passing
over it in silence. When T. S. Eliot, for example, looked back from the vantage
point of 1930, he wrote of Pater:

His view of art, as expressed in *The Renaissance*, impressed itself upon a number of writers
in the 'nineties, and propagated some confusion between life and art which is not wholly
irresponsible for some untidy lives.[108]

This ostensibly confines Pater's influence to 'the 'nineties', thereby effectively
precluding any influence on himself (Eliot, born in 1888, hadn't reached his
'teens when the 'nineties ended). It further seeks to limit Pater's significance by

---

[105] Lewis, *Men without Art* (London: Cassell, 1934), p. 145.
[106] Bizzotto, 'The Imaginary Portrait', pp. 222–3.
[107] Lesley Higgins, 'No Time for Pater: The Silenced Other of Masculinist Modernism', in
Walter Pater: Transparencies of Desire, ed Laurel Brake, Lesley Higgins, and Carolyn Williams
(Greensboro, NC: ELT Press, 2002). *Transparencies of Desire*, pp. 37–54 (p. 37).
[108] T. S. Eliot, 'Arnold and Pater', *Selected Essays*, p. 442.

claiming that what influence he was, was bad. Writers had 'untidy' lives long before Pater; the euphemism here conceals under its cloak of magnanimity the insinuation of a particular form of untidiness that best not have its name spoken. This is perhaps as mild as one could expect a writer, by then Catholic, to be, who was suggesting (in that claim that Pater confused art and life) that what was pernicious was the way Pater's art encouraged a homosexual lifestyle. It might be countered that such a critique of aestheticism was itself guilty of a confusion of art with life. The 'masculinist modernists' such as Pound and Eliot repeatedly focus their criticism on aestheticism's language rather than its morals. Pound admired the advocacy of 'good writing as opposed to the opalescent word, the rhetorical tradition.'[109] What he meant by that conjunction of opalescence and the rhetorical is perhaps best elaborated by Eliot, writing in 1920 on Swinburne:

> The morbidity is not of human feeling but of language. Language in a healthy state presents the object, is so close to the object that the two are identified.
> They are identified in the verse of Swinburne solely because the object has ceased to exist, because the meaning is merely the hallucination of meaning, because language, uprooted, has adapted itself to an independent life of atmospheric nourishment.[110]

Yet such criticisms are not purely linguistic. They apply to language the discourse of degeneration and decadence. Aesthetic language, as Eliot implies, is 'unhealthy'; malnourished; unnaturally detached from the world it describes. In its showy fixation on ornament, it has become opaque. Pound's word 'opalescent' puns between the jewellery beloved of *fin de siècle* writers, and the lack of clarity he sees as resulting from such a fixation. The implication is that perversity or morbidity of language derives from a perversity or morbidity in the aesthetes. Eliot's concern with 'confusion between life and art' is also the basis of his landmark essay 'Tradition and the Individual Talent', which asserted that good writing must separate the two: 'the more perfect the artist, the more completely separate in him will be the man who suffers and the mind which creates.'[111] This influential theory of poetic impersonality set its modernist face against aestheticism's cult of 'personality'. However, as we have seen, Pater's representation of subjectivity is remarkable for the extent of its self-unweaving. Furthermore, Eliot's comment about Pater reveals the extent to which Eliot's formulation of impersonality occurs very much under the shadow of Pater. Pater is an absent father for Eliot too. His anxiety that art should not be made from the artist's untidiness doesn't only express an anxiety that his own writing, in the aftermath of his nervous breakdown, might be compromised by its own inability to draw the line between the personal and the impersonal; it also

---

[109] Ezra Pound, 'Mr Hueffer and the Prose Tradition', *Poetry*, 4:3 (1914); repr. as 'The Prose Tradition in Verse', in Pound's *Literary Essays*, pp. 371–7.

[110] T. S. Eliot, 'Swinburne as Poet' (1920), in his *The Sacred Wood* (London: Methuen, 1980), pp. 148–9.

[111] Eliot, 'Tradition and the Individual Talent', p. 18.

expresses, perhaps, a specific anxiety of influence. The author of the aesthetic world of 'Portrait of a Lady' must have recognized his early poems as Imaginary Portraits. J. Alfred Prufrock, Gerontion, the Tiresias of 'The Waste Land', are all Paterian in their conception. Partly because the poems give us an interior, visionary world, rather than the dramatized utterance of the Victorian dramatic monologue. Also because, as Iser says of Pater's imaginary subjects, they 'are placed right in the heart of a crisis which destroys them, and their death indicates that the resultant dislocation of man and world cannot be set right even temporarily.'[112] (Admittedly, Eliot's transformations of the Paterian Imaginary Portrait are as significant as his attraction to it. Rather than trying to convey the impression that we might be reading auto/biography, Eliot perplexes us about who and where and what his characters can possibly be: are they alive, dead, real or imagined?) And finally because Eliot's poetry itself deals exactly with 'the hallucination of meaning'. I am not merely arguing that Eliot's poetry engages with Pater; but that even his attempts to disavow that engagement themselves bear Paterian traces. That is, Eliot's attempts to police the line between art and personality could be traced back to Pater's attempts to erase that line. The modernist aspiration towards impersonality sets its mask against Pater's face, only to find that, in Henry James's extraordinary obituary remark to Edmund Gosse, Pater was 'the mask without the face';[113] that this ostensible religion of personality had already impersonalized itself.

To accept Pater's erasure of the line between art and personality, then, is to read all writing as auto/biographical. Eliot, by contrast, argues that the more auto/biographically an art-work can be read, the more imperfect the art. But in this antithesis, we can see the synthesis which the following book reads modernism (*contra* Eliot) as attaining: a literature that makes new art forms out of auto/biography, much in the way that Pater had already done, by seeing that once you consider life-writing as *form*, rather than mere transcribed experience, it offers a new resource for art. Instead of posing as a point of leverage outside the sphere of art (with reference to which art can be read as something else), it becomes something else which art can find pleasure in. Instead of reading literature as auto/biography, Pater reads auto/biography as literature, and makes literature out of auto/biography, precisely by demonstrating the impossibility of keeping such forms separate.

In the work of the other modernists discussed here—especially Proust, Joyce, Stein, Pound, Aldington, Ford, and Woolf—we shall see how the Paterian fusion of life-writing and artistic experiment in the Imaginary Portraits may also have been responsible for subsequent works in which the boundaries between auto/biographical and fictional *forms* were programmatically confused. That is, what is most original about Pater's work is not that he uses auto/biography; not that he

---

[112] Iser, *Walter Pater: The Aesthetic Moment*, p. 154.

[113] James to Gosse (13 Dec. 1894), in *Henry James: Letters*, ed. Leon Edel, vol. 3 (London: Macmillan, 1981), p. 492.

smuggles it into works which might normally be expected to exclude it; but that he fictionalizes it. Unfortunately, his greatest gifts were not as a fiction-writer, as even his greatest champions concede. 'Pater had no gifts for narrative, or drama, or psychological portrayal, and he knew this well enough', says Harold Bloom.[114] What he did best was develop an intermediate, or hybrid, genre, in which fiction, auto/biography, history, essay, and criticism weave together and unweave each other, in an allegory of ecstatic subjectivity. The passages that have proved most resonant are those that make a critical or philosophical point, rather than advance a plot or deepen a character, but enact a mood of poetic exhilaration and poignancy. One of the things his Imaginary Portraits revealed was what might be done with forms of life-writing if they were reformulated through critical self-questioning. His portraits make us hyper conscious not so much of their subjects, but of portraiture itself; not so much of the imaginations of their artist figures, but of the imaginariness of their selves. It is not only the figures themselves who are fictionalized, then, but the act of portraiture too. Pater isn't the only writer beginning to make play with our awareness of the fictionalization of life-writing in this period, as the other chapters in Part I will demonstrate. He figures here as exemplary of a kind of aesthetic self-consciousness that will become increasingly important in modernist engagements with life-writing, as he moves from celebrating the power of the imagination in art, to imagining the imaginary work of art.[115] In short, the conjunction of Pater's poignant deconstruction of the impressionist self, and Wilde's and Nietzsche's claims that discourses such as criticism or philosophy are also modes of autobiography, open the gates to modernist and postmodern thought about self-representation.

---

[114] Bloom, *Selected Writings of Walter Pater*, p. xxiii. Compare Donoghue, *Walter Pater: Lover of Strange Souls*, p. 199: 'Pater's most serious defect as a writer of fiction, even as a writer of romance, is that he thinks a character may be sustained by the ideas he or she is given to hold. And while he can imagine what it would be like to hold an idea, he can't imagine any consequence of holding it, the difference it would make. In his sense of the world at large it makes no difference, because he gives this world such tenuous acknowledgement.'

[115] See Small, *Conditions for Criticism*, p. 101, on the complex intertextual games Pater plays in chapter 15 of *Marius*, as when, in his account of the historically factual Cornelius Fronto he quotes from a fictional discourse by Fronto which is in fact based on Marcus Aurelius' *Meditations*. I am grateful to Malcolm Cocks for drawing my attention to this example.

2

Aesthetic Auto/biography:
Ruskin and Proust

Through art alone are we able to emerge from ourselves, to know what
another person sees of a universe which is not the same as our own [. . .].[1]

One way in which Pater's work represents a gateway into modernist engagements
with the auto/biographic is that it poses the category of what might be called
'aesthetic autobiography'. Or, to be more precise, we have seen how he presents
two versions: Imaginary Portraits give the developmental processes of the aesthetic life, which draw upon his own experience, but fictionalize and displace it
(this path leads to 'aesthetic autobiografiction'); and the biography/portraits of
The Renaissance, which, combined with the credos of the 'Preface' and 'Conclusion', give what Nietzsche called the author's 'unconscious autobiography' too
(this path leads to 'aesthetic auto/biography')—though this version may be more
a case of strategically displaced, covert or disguised autobiography, rather than
any lack of awareness on Pater's part that he was expressing the spiritual
development of an aesthete.

This chapter discusses the history of 'aesthetic' autobiography and autobiografiction. It argues that the term 'aesthetic autobiography' is best reserved for
formal autobiography written by aesthetes and impressionists, rather than being
applied to the kinds of experiment this study is calling 'autobiografiction'—
especially those written in the twentieth century. It begins with a brief consideration of autobiography written by 1890s aesthetes, and proposes an alternative
genealogy for such 'aesthetic autobiography', focusing on a reading of Ruskin's
Præterita. It moves on to consider the significance of this line of aesthetic
autobiography, and the figure of Ruskin, for modernist autobiografiction, concentrating on the example of Proust, and his reading of Ruskin.

Late nineteenth-century aesthetic autobiography is certainly not unprecedented. Many artists had written autobiographies, at least part of which are concerned
with aesthetics, such as Cellini, Rousseau, Goethe, or De Quincey. But the
aesthetic is subordinated to the autobiographic. What such autobiographies tell
us about art is part of a larger story of lives, travels, friendships, loves, adventures,

---

[1] Proust, *Time Regained*, trans. Andreas Mayor (London: Chatto & Windus, 1970), p. 262.

misdemeanours, drugs. The autobiography aspires to a totality—a representation of the plenitude of a life—and art is only a part of the whole.

Aesthetic autobiography inverts these priorities, and subordinates the autobiographical to the aesthetic. It tells the story of a life *as an artist*. The pre-eminent nineteenth-century precursor is Wordsworth. *The Prelude* discusses much more than the poet's self: the natural world; books; London; the French Revolution, and so on. But these things are always introduced for what light they can shed on what the posthumous subtitle termed *The Growth of a Poet's Mind*.

Aestheticism's 'religion of beauty' was also the cult of the self.[2] As such, one might expect it to attach a particular value to the autobiographical. In its turn from Christianity to art, from the theological to the psychological, it represents the major cultural shifts registered by most of the writers under discussion. In its concern for impressions, perception, emotion, and temporality, it constitutes an intense focus on subjectivity and how to represent it. The English modernist Richard Aldington (whose own, biografictional, experiments with life-writing forms feature in Chapter 10) wrote that: 'it was through Pater and J. A. Symonds that English readers were initiated into Goethe's "ideal of self-culture" which formed so essential a part of the æsthetic ideal.'[3] The 'ideal of self-culture' had fostered autobiography by Romantic writers (including Goethe himself). The specific aesthete's version of it, the cultivation of the artist's self, was to become central to modernism's reinvention of fiction, as we shall see. But what of the Aesthetes themselves? What form did their engagement with auto/biography take?

The first and most striking point by way of answer is that formal autobiographies by people associated with the Aesthetic movement are relatively scarce. Though Leslie Stephen had thought it everyone's civic duty to publish his autobiography, the aesthetes, who were resistant to most moral injunctions except those issuing from the morality of art, tended not to.[4] The cases of two of the most significant figures are indicative. *The Memoirs of John Addington Symonds* is a substantial autobiography, written between 1889 and 1892.[5] But it wasn't published until the end of the following century. The life of another leading aesthete, Symonds's near-homonyn, Symons, is represented chiefly by *The Memoirs of Arthur Symons*.[6] However, as John Stokes explains, that title is

---

[2] Richard Aldington used the phrase for his anthology, *The Religion of Beauty: Selections from the Æsthetes* (London: Heinemann, 1950); though as he explains (p. 45), he took the phrase from F. W. H. Myers' 1883 essay 'Rossetti and the Religion of Beauty', which he includes.

[3] Aldington, *The Religion of Beauty*, p. 19.

[4] Leslie Stephen, *Studies of a Biographer*, 4 vols (London: Duckworth 1898–1902), vol. 1, 'National Biography', p. 4. See Andrew McNeillie, ed., *The Essays of Virginia Woolf*, vol. 4 (London: The Hogarth Press, 1994), p. xiii.

[5] *The Memoirs of John Addington Symonds*, ed. Phyllis Grosskurth (New York: Random House; London: Hutchinson, 1984). Grossskurth explains that though Symonds was 'associated with the aesthetes' he was no advocate of 'art for art's sake' (p. 13).

[6] Arthur Symons, *The Memoirs of Arthur Symons: Life and Art in the 1890s*, ed. Karl Beckson (University Park: Pennsylvania State University Press, 1977).

rather misleading: the volume was assembled by the editor, Karl Beckson, from various fragments of Symons's proposed memoirs. For the most part, it is a portrait gallery of more than thirty individuals, mostly named, and including Pater, George Moore, Huysmans, Ernest Dowson, John Addington Symonds, Verlaine, Wilde, Beardsley, Gide, Swinburne, and Whistler. It is framed by two more autobiographical pieces: the first chapter, 'A Prelude to Life' 'is genuinely autobiographical and follows the pattern of a developing aesthetic sensibility.'[7] This was from Symons's *Spiritual Adventures* (1905), which will be discussed in Chapter 5. The volume closes with a garbled fragment called 'Mental Collapse in Italy' (which appears to relate to the last chapter of *Spiritual Adventures* about a nervous breakdown in Venice) taken from the account Symons published in 1930 about his mental illness twenty years earlier: *Confessions: A Study in Pathology*. Karl Beckson, who has also written Symons's biography, says of the *Confessions* that 'Despite its circumstantiality—that is, a wandering from the central point but a periodic return to it', it is 'a remarkable transformation of Symons's psychosis of 1908 and 1909 into the tentative order of confessional art.'[8]

There are autobiographies by writers who have some relation to aestheticism, but who are not normally considered members of the Aesthetic movement. As Aldington says, with some it was 'a life-long passion', with others 'a phase of varying duration.'[9] Thus autobiographies by Henry James, more often now seen as an early modernist, and by Yeats and Ford, who both went through aesthetic phases to become modernists, are certainly preoccupied with the aesthetic sensibility.

The titles of Yeats's two major autobiographic volumes are explicit, both about the development of an aesthetic attitude, and the claim made for his art. *Reveries over Childhood and Youth* (1914): we might think of childhood as the phase dominated by daydream and fantasy; for Yeats, these are simply the inspiration for the mature poet's aptitude for poetic reverie. *The Trembling of the Veil* (1922): his life and times, Ireland's mythology and nationalism, are the occasions for quasi-mystical revelation to manifest itself through the realm of appearance; the poet presenting himself as the mage who can summon such visions. Art is to be treated with the awe reserved for religion.[10] The autobiographical books by James and Ford, together with those of another impressionist with aesthetic tendencies, George Moore, will be amongst those discussed in Chapter 6.

Why the relative dearth of aesthetes' autobiographies? Part of the answer is that much of their autobiography went into their lyric verse. Another explanation is that much autobiographical material does appear in prose, but displaced, into

---

[7] Stokes to Saunders, email, 17 December 2005.

[8] Beckson, *Arthur Symons: A Life* (Oxford: Clarendon Press, 1987), p. 317.

[9] Aldington, *The Religion of Beauty*, p. 45.

[10] 'I have found in an old diary a saying from Stéphane Mallarmé, that his epoch was troubled by the trembling of the veil of the Temple. As those words were still true, during the years of my life described in this book, I have chosen *The Trembling of the Veil* for its title': Yeats, *Autobiographies* (London: Macmillan, 1980), p. 109.

works like Pater's *Imaginary Portraits* or Symons's *Spiritual Adventures*. Indeed, the movement's valuing of artifice over literal truth encouraged both these strategies. The autobiographical needed to be poetized or fictionalized, turned into *art*, before it could provide an adequate representation of the artist's subjectivity.

It may be an exaggeration, but only slightly, to suggest that the typical aesthete autobiography needs to be reconstructed retrospectively, either because the subject was no longer an aesthete when writing his autobiography if he did write one; or because it wasn't written by the subject, or wasn't published by him. I offer *In Memoriam: The Imaginary Reminiscences of Sir Max Beerbohm*, by Ira Grushow, as an example of this trope—a particularly appropriate example, since written in homage to aestheticism's imaginary (self)portraiture, as well as Beerbohm's own fascination with imaginary works.

The other main reason is indicated by the case of Symonds. When his *Memoirs* were eventually published, the very grounds for not making them public in the 1890s became the grounds for publicizing them on the dust-jacket in the 1980s: 'The Secret Homosexual Life of a Leading Nineteenth-Century Man of Letters'. If he was no longer the household name he had been for his seven-volume magnum opus on the *Renaissance in Italy*, he could be marketed as not only a homosexual, but a secret one: secret not only because he had married, and attempted to suppress his homosexual desires; but because he had not thought his *Memoirs* could be published.

Symonds explains in a 'Preface' that it was his work on other people's autobiographies (especially those of Cellini and Carlo Gozzi) that led to his 'acquiring in the process certain opinions with regard to the method of self-portraiture and considerably adding to the interest which I always felt for this branch of literature.'[11] He says that Gozzi called his memoirs 'useless', and published them from motives of 'humility'. Symonds continues:

Mine are sure to be more useless than his; for I shall not publish them; and it is only too probable that they will never be published—nobody's humility or pride or pecuniary interests being likely to gain any benefit from the printing of what I have veraciously written concerning myself.[12]

He only hints at what he means by this in the 'Preface':

Other and more important reasons—more important in their bearing on my psychological condition and the anxiety problem of the coming years—will reveal themselves to those who read the ensuing chapters.[13]

In a letter to a friend he was more explicit:

My occupation with Cellini and Gozzi has infected me with their Lues Autobiographica; & I have begun scribbling my own reminiscences. This is a foolish thing to do, because

---

[11] Symonds, *Memoirs*, p. 29.   [12] Ibid.   [13] Ibid.

I do not think they will ever be fit to publish. I have nothing to relate except the evolution of a character somewhat strangely constituted in its moral and aesthetic qualities. The study of this evolution, written with the candour & the precision I feel capable of using, would I am sure be interesting to psychologists & not without its utility. There does not exist anything like it in print; & I am certain that 999 men out of a thousand do not believe in the existence of a personality like mine. Still it would be hardly fair to my posterity if I were to yield up my vile soul to the psychopathical investigators.[14]

Symonds had collaborated with the most eminent of the period's British 'psychopathical investigators', Havelock Ellis, and his name was to appear as co-author of the first volume of *Studies in the Psychology of Sex*, on *Sexual Inversion* (1897).[15] As Ellis explains in the preface, Symonds died before the collaboration was complete. His essay 'A Problem in Greek Ethics' appears as appendix, as do some fragments he provided. Ellis says his work also supplies passages in the main text, and that he provided several of the case histories. What he doesn't say is that Symonds *was* one of the case histories. He appeared, pseudonymously or all but anonymously, as 'A' in Case XVII of *Sexual Inversion*.[16] The sexual history he revealed to Ellis is much more explicit than anything in the text of the *Memoirs*. Such displacement of autobiography via pseudonymity, anonymity, and (as Symonds may also have done in working his experience into a case history) writing about oneself in the third person, is widespread in the period, and is a subject of the next chapter. It should perhaps also be noted here that unpublication might be considered another form of autobiographical displacement.

Though he could not imagine its being published, his literary executor, Horatio Brown, said 'Symonds was anxious to have [it] preserved'. When Brown died in 1926 the manuscript was left to the London Library (though Brown said he had tried to get the British Library to accept it 'with an embargo of 50 years, against publication').[17] Symonds wrote the *Memoirs* over the five years before his death in 1893. Even then they had seemed unpublishable. After the trial of Wilde in 1895, British society became even less tolerant of homosexuality, and of the aestheticism that had been associated with it. This intolerance is the most compelling reason why aesthetes tended to avoid autobiography.

Nevertheless, the influence of aestheticism on subsequent literary auto/biography is crucial. Twentieth-century autobiographies by writers and artists are generally 'aesthetic', not merely because their authors happened to be artists, but because they investigate how they became artists. As in Ruskin's *Præterita*, the emphasis falls less on the subject's engagements with society, or with god, and more on the

---

[14] Symonds to Graham Dakyns, quoted by Grosskurth (ed.), *Memoirs*, p. 16.
[15] Ellis, *Studies in the Psychology of Sex*. Vol. 1: *Sexual Inversion* (London: Wilson and Macmillan, 1897).
[16] See Symonds, *Memoirs*, Appendix One, pp. 284–8.
[17] *Memoirs*, p. 10.

consciousness and vision; on what Richard Jefferies had called, in his passionate but strangely decontextualized autobiography, *The Story of My Heart* (1883).

The relative exiguity of aesthete's autobiography may be one reason why Suzanne Nalbantian called her study of Proust, Joyce, Woolf, and Anaïs Nin *Aesthetic Autobiography*.[18] The title does an injustice to her valuable book, though, since none of her authors wrote anything called an autobiography, or that should be called autobiography; nor was any of them a member of the Aesthetic movement. Proust might be called an aesthete, but the other three would have been likely to resent the label. All four are writers we now think of as modernist. Of course they all wrote works that are deeply autobiograph*ical*, and deeply concerned with art and the figure of the artist. She uses the phrase 'aesthetic autobiography' as a kind of shorthand for the transmutation of life facts into art works: as her subtitle has it (with unrepresentative banality): 'From Life to Art [. . .]'. I don't at all contest her argument that all four based their aesthetic on autobiographical material, and that they subjected that material to aesthetic processes, turning it into something other than life or autobiography—art. Indeed, it forms a cornerstone of my argument that modernism has a more profound engagement with auto/biography than is generally acknowledged. But I am also arguing that this engagement derived from late nineteenth-century impressionist and aesthetic experiments in auto/biography. Therefore I shall use the term 'aesthetic autobiography' in a different sense, to designate those works instead—works which *are* formal contractual autobiographies, but innovative in the way they foreground the aesthetic, and subject autobiographical narrative to the aesthetic principles the authors advocate. Like the works Nalbantian discusses, they all focus on the dawning awareness of the aesthetic life, as the process by which the subject develops into an artist. But they are mostly written earlier than the modernist works she discusses, either in the late nineteenth century or in the early twentieth century by writers whose careers had begun in the late nineteenth. 'Aesthetic autobiography' in this sense is work that falls between Victorianism and modernism; that is increasingly being called impressionist, coinciding as it does with the major art movement of the late nineteenth century, pictorial impressionism, which shifts representation from concrete objects to the processes of perception; a secular movement free from both the religiosity of the Symbolists and aesthetes, and the rationalist understanding of symbolization in psychoanalysis. Such work forms part of the prelude to the modernist experiments in auto/biography described in Part II; and so it makes more sense to describe it as 'aesthetic autobiography', so as to be able to see the extent to which the modernist autobiographical *Künstlerroman* (which Nalbantian uses the term to designate) and experimental autobiografiction actually depart from it. The modernist works Nalbantian discusses as if they were inaugurating a new kind of

---

[18] Suzanne Nalbantian, *Aesthetic Autobiography: From Life to Art in Marcel Proust, James Joyce, Virginia Woolf and Anaïs Nin* (New York: St Martin's Press, 1997).

auto/biography are in fact playing games with this pre-existent form. Her Envoi doesn't note that a degree of fictionalization is one of the main qualities which the autobiographical works by all her four authors have in common; and that this is what differentiates their work from autobiographies by aesthetes of the nineteenth century, such as Wordsworth, Ruskin, or Symonds.

Nalbantian puts together four modernist writers: Proust, Joyce, Woolf, and Nin, arguing that their rendering of their own lives represents a new development in literary form. Certainly, those writers are all doing new things with autobiography and biography. My objections are: first, that what they're doing is so new that it doesn't make sense to call it 'autobiography' any more. Just putting the term 'aesthetic' in front isn't adequate. Second, that each of her four writers does it so differently that what one needs is a sense of the extraordinary variety of ways in which writers are reimagining the forms of life-writing. Third, that what's at stake here is precisely a question of the forms as much as of the content (i.e. not just whether writers invent episodes in their fictionalized lives, or change the names or the genders of some of the people; but how they reinvent ways of narrating lives). Nalbantian's quaint discourse of life being transmuted into art fails to distinguish between these modernist fictionalizers of autobiography, and earlier but equally artful autobiographers—like Wordsworth or Rousseau, say. Finally—and this is the objection that's most relevant to the work discussed in this chapter—the term 'aesthetic autobiography' is best applied not to Nalbantian's modernists, but to the impressionist writers immediately before them, who are writing something that still looks like formal autobiography but of which the main story is one of aesthetic realization. To understand the games modernist play with auto/biography you need to see how they develop out of this earlier version of aesthetic autobiography.

I mean two things by that phrase 'aesthetic realization'. First, that the key events in the lives of Ruskin, James, or Ford are when they realize something about art. Their life stories are stories of what made them decide to be artists. But also, because the lives they have chosen or discovered are aesthetic ones, they present their lives to us as perceived aesthetically. This constitutes a major shift in the meaning of autobiography. For earlier writers it had a spiritual significance (as for Augustine, say; or Bunyan); or it had a psychological significance, as for Rousseau and De Quincey; or a social significance, as for Rousseau again, or someone like H. G. Wells. What begins to happen in these 'Aesthetic autobiographies' is that a life begins to be perceived as having a form, like the form of a work of art. In his book *Forms of Autobiography: Episodes in the History of a Literary Genre*, William Spengemann traces a sequence from 'historical', through 'philosophical', to 'poetic' autobiography.[19] Though the general outline is plausible, autobiography from Augustine onwards has manifested philosophical and poetic tendencies; and this hybridity persists into Wordsworth, Nietzsche, or

---

[19] William C. Spengemann, *Forms of Autobiography: Episodes in the History of a Literary Genre* (New Haven: Yale University Press, 1980).

Sartre. A further problem is that Spengemann's category of 'poetic autobiography' would need to include both the aesthetic autobiography of the turn of the century, and subsequent but very different modernist autobiografiction. As we shall see in the rest of this chapter, *fin de siècle* aesthetic autobiography is a transitional stage on the way towards modernist autobiografiction. The forms of autobiography have come to feel artificial: rather than giving us a direct transcription of a life, autobiography has begun to feel like a species of invention.

This wasn't a new response, but precisely what had happened when the form emerged in the eighteenth century, as novelists satirized the new modes of autobiographical writing. What seemed inherently comical in the eighteenth century began to seem normative by the nineteenth. By the time 'autobiography' is named with the arrival of Romanticism, it is already more than just an additional available genre: it is on the way to becoming the paradigm for all writing; all creativity. Coleridge's celebrated definition of the imagination as 'a repetition in the finite mind of the eternal act of creation in the infinite I AM' not only poses human creativity as legitimated by divine creation; it conversely reads divine creativity as an act of autobiography.[20] That Coleridge's autobiographical philosophizing in *Biographia Literaria* proceeds with some of the machinery of Sternean playful digressions and imaginary conversations with imagined readers is indicative of the way in which, while the exploration and presentation and assertion of self had become increasingly imperative by the end of the eighteenth century, it nonetheless emerged out of and is bound up with the presentation of fictionalized subjectivities.

But by the end of the nineteenth century, that familiarity perhaps began to breed contempt, or at least a scepticism about the forms of life-writing: they began to look odd again: something to be mocked and stretched in various directions. Such play with auto/biography was not impossible earlier, as witnessed by the strange case from the 1830s of Thomas Carlyle's *Sartor Resartus*: a parody not only of German Idealism, but of biography too, from the century's greatest champion of the value of biography. In his essay 'Biography' (1832), Carlyle performs the extraordinary juggling act of asserting the need for biography (he calls it 'almost the one thing needful') while railing against its 'Fictitious' versions in 'the lowest of froth Prose in the Fashionable Novel.'[21] Ostensibly he wants to purge biography of fictitiousness, to preserve and distill it for history: '"History," it has been said, "is the essence of innumerable Biographies." Such, at least, it should be.'[22] So what does he do? He defends the reality value of biography against the fictitious by performing a bit of fictitious biography:

---

[20] S. T. Coleridge, *Biographia Literaria: Or: Biographical Sketches of My Literary Life and Opinions*, ed. James Engell and W. Jackson Bate, 2 vols (London: Routledge and Kegan Paul, 1983), vol. 1, ch. 13, p. 304.
[21] Carlyle, 'Biography', in *English and Other Critical Essays* (London: Dent, 1915), pp. 65–79 (pp. 66, 69, 68).
[22] Ibid., p. 67.

Here, however, in regard to 'Fictitious Biographies', and much other matter of like sort, which the greener mind in these days inditeth, we may as well insert some singular sentences on the importance and significance of *Reality*, as they stand written for us in Professor Gottfried Saurteig's *Æsthetische Springwurzeln*; a work, perhaps, as yet new to most English readers.[23]

Indeed. Professor Godpeace Sourdough's *Aesthetic Paper-spurge*, or thereabouts, would be just the thing for green minds. Carlyle's argument is that the 'Reality' glimpsed in episodes of biography—King Charles being sheltered and fed by a peasant; Dr Johnson being accosted by a whore—are revelatory in ways that fiction cannot match. Interestingly, his celebration of biography does not extend to autobiography, just as his objection to the novel is that it is a solipsistic expression of self rather than an objective grasp of what lies outside the self:

These Three Thousand men, women and children, that make up the army of British Authors, do not, if we will well consider it, *see* anything whatever; consequently *have* nothing that they can record and utter, only more or fewer things that they can plausibly pretend to record. The Universe, of Man and Nature, is still quite shut-up from them; the 'open secret' still utterly a secret; because no sympathy with Man or Nature, no love and free simplicity of heart has yet unfolded the same. Nothing but a pitiful Image of their own pitiful Self, with its vanities, and grudgings, and ravenous hunger of all kinds, hangs forever painted in the retina of these unfortunate persons; so that the starry ALL, with whatsoever it embraces, does but appear as some expanded magic-lantern shadow of that same Image,—and naturally looks pitiful enough.[24]

The strategy in 'Biography' is the same as the creation of *Sartor*'s fictional philosopher Diogenes Teufelsdroeckh. But as there, the energies of fictionaliza-tion take over, and turn into something more complex and ambivalent than mere parody of escapist novels. If the existence of these works makes one wary of generalizing about attitudes to auto/biography in the period, the delayed publi-cation and baffled reception of *Sartor* suggests that it was a sport, and that most readers were not yet ready to know what to make of it.

This growing nineteenth-century unease with the forms of life-writing coin-cides with the emergence of aestheticism. Ruskin wasn't an aesthete, though he was certainly an influence on the movement. He didn't advocate art for art's sake, but art for life's sake. Ruskin is a transitional figure between a Romantic view of harmony with nature, and the aesthetic or modern view of self-consciousness and artifice. He gets his visionary experiences from the natural world. But he gets them from art, too. The rest of this chapter will concentrate on Ruskin and Proust. It will argue for the significance in the way Ruskin, and others discussed in Part I, such as 'Mark Rutherford', Samuel Butler, and Edmund Gosse, develop literary forms to construct their lives as aesthetically motivated. And in the

---

[23] Ibid., p. 69.
[24] Ibid., p. 77.

emphasis Ruskin places on 'impression', his autobiography is a precursor to the early twentieth-century literary autobiographies by James, Conrad, and Ford discussed in Chapter 6 on impressionist autobiography. Particular attention will thus be paid to impressionist preoccupations—not just with the nature of the impression, but also with time, memory, and the nature of reading. Ruskin's text draws attention both to the gaps in experience, memory, and reading, and also to the attempt to make connexions across such gaps. After examining Ruskin's use of the term 'reading' (both literally and figuratively), the chapter will move on to sketch the predominant shifts in attitude towards the notion of textual 'mediation' from realism, through impressionism and modernism, to postmodernism. It will conclude with a discussion of Proust (of all modernists the most indebted to Ruskin, and a sophisticated analyst of impressionism), from the rejection of biography in *Contre Sainte-Beuve* to the fictionalization of autobiography in *A la recherche*.

RUSKIN[25]

Like the two greatest philosophical autobiographers of the nineteenth century, Mill and Nietzsche, Ruskin experienced a nervous breakdown. All three were driven intellects, ceaselessly pushing to the limits of rationality and cultural analysis. It may be that the demons which drove them eventually took their toll. But their madness should perhaps equally be seen as a product of the logic of their age, as, in their attempts to analyse human creativity in the context of an increasing scepticism about religion and social convention, each man confronted the limits of his own intelligibility. Richard Aldington put it rather more acidly:

Among the less cultured elements of the time there was a deeply-rooted belief that artists and all who were attached to the arts and believed them to be important were mad. By a strange and triumphant coincidence, the first Slade Professor of Fine Art at Oxford was mad, or became so shortly after his appointment in 1869. As early as August, 1871, Ruskin showed himself so much the victim of hallucinations as to believe in his 'plague-cloud of the nineteenth century', with its 'strange, bitter, blighting wind', its 'dry black veil' of cloud and 'fitful shaking' of leaves, which he attributed to 'dead men's souls, flitting hither and thither.'[26]

Such a poetic or vatic discourse may seem more intelligible to postmodernists as a refusal of a utilitarian industrialism by someone forging the voice of a prophetic sage. But the other example Aldington gives of a 'serious symptom' of Ruskin's,

---

[25] An earlier version of part of this section, appeared as '"Things Passed Over": Ruskin, Modernism, and Autobiography', in *Ruskin and Modernism*, ed. Giovanni Cianci and Peter Nicholls (Basingstoke: Palgrave, 2001), pp. 97–109.

[26] Aldington, *The Religion of Beauty*, p. 12.

what he calls the 'astonishing confession' of November 1874, in *Fors Clavigera*, Letter 48, offers more compelling evidence:

I am always wanting to be something else than I am. I want to be Turner; I want to be Gainsborough; I want to be Samuel Prout; I want to be the Doge of Venice; I want to be Pope; I want to be Lord of the Sun and Moon. The other day, when I read that story in the papers about the dog-fight, I wanted to be able to fight a bull-dog.[27]

Aldington thought it strange that 'Nobody seemed to have noticed' the incipient insanity, but Ruskin certainly did, saying in the same letter: 'Does it never occur to me that I may be mad myself?'[28] Whatever one makes psychologically of such manic empathy, it has powerful implications for the modernist notion of destabilized and fragmentary subjectivities; and for how they are represented in auto/biography; and for what it is to read—not just to read stories in the papers, but the story of the self or selves.

Much has been written on Ruskin's madness.[29] My aim here is to concentrate on his autobiography, *Præterita* (1885–9), *as* autobiography; and in particular, as a form of aesthetic autobiography, which opens up the question of subjectivity, perception, aesthetic experience, and rationality in new ways; and by doing so, to foreground the links between nineteenth-century innovative autobiography, aestheticism, and modernist engagements with life-writing. *Præterita*—which Aldington called 'probably his finest piece of prose'—is an aesthetic autobiography in a double sense.[30] It structures the narrative of his life in terms of a sequence of aesthetic discoveries. It is thus an autobiography of his aesthetic experience. In doing this, like most of his work, it also constitutes an argument *for* the aesthetic: for the importance of the arts, and especially the visual arts. Ruskin's reading of his life in terms of moments of perception presents the crucial paradigm that allowed impressionism to transform itself into modernism, as the Ruskinian reading of 'nature' turns into a concern with the nature of 'reading.'[31]

Ruskin was proud of his analytic mind, and excelled in giving close analytic attention to whatever he was studying: the painting of Tintoretto; a Gothic cathedral; a word, or a line of verse.[32] And his writing demands a similar analytic saturation. He wants to change the way people look, the way they attend to their

---

[27] Ibid.

[28] Ruskin, *Fors Clavigera: Letters 37–72*, Library Edition, ed. E. T. Cook and A. Wedderburn, vol. 28 (London: George Allen, 1907), p. 206.

[29] See for example Jay Fellows, *Ruskin's Maze: Mastery and Madness in His Art* (Princeton, NJ: Princeton University Press, 1981); and Mary Ann Caws, 'Ruskin's Madness and Ours', in *Victorian Literature and Culture*, ed. John Maynard and Adrienne Munich (New York: AMS Press, 1991).

[30] Aldington, *The Religion of Beauty*, p. 13.

[31] George P. Landow, *Ruskin* (Oxford: Oxford University Press, 1985), pp. 73–4.

[32] *The Works of John Ruskin*, Library Edition, ed. E. T. Cook and A. Wedderburn, vol. 35, *Præterita and Dilecta* (London: George Allen, 1908), pp. 44, 51. (References are to this edition unless stated otherwise.) See for example the analysis of the Scottish expression 'mind' for 'remember' on pp. 464–6.

objects, whether natural or cultural. He wants to effect a revolution in taste. So it is appropriate to subject the title of his autobiography, *Præterita*, to a Ruskinian meditation. Lewis and Short's *A Latin Dictionary* defines 'Praeterita' as 'things gone by, the past'; then, in a second definition, as 'things passed over (Gr. παραλειπόμενα), a name of the books of Chronicles, because they contain what had been omitted in the books of Kings.'[33]

From one point of view, Ruskin's work is centrally concerned with capturing the *present*. The moments he presents in *Præterita* as decisively visionary—the ivy seen on the road to Norwood, and the aspen at Fontainbleau, which teach him how to draw the natural world; the sight of Mont Blanc, or the rapture in front of an unexpected masterpiece—are all vivid impressions of what were vivid impressions of objects while he was gazing at them.[34] And in this sense, the aesthetics of *Præterita* are those of its contemporaries, the impressionists. Kenneth Clark, in his 1948 Introduction to *Præterita*, said: 'Ruskin was by nature an impressionist.'[35] Ruskin defined his own writing as 'impressional and emotional.'[36] The emphasis is on the immediacy and ephemerality of perception, not the durability of the things perceived.

From another point of view, though, Ruskin's work is an attending to the *past*. To the archaeology of culture. Not for nothing was he nearly a geologist. As a geologist finds in the stones of the Alps the story of the planet, so Ruskin finds in the stones of Venice the story of Christian civilization. Like all revolutionaries, he changes the present by rewriting the past, offering a revisionist history of art, of architecture, of society. Like orthodox art historians he sees the Renaissance as a turning point. But for him it is a turn for the worse: not the ushering in of humanism and progress, but the decline of the Gothic and the origins of decadence.

This antithesis between past and present corresponds to a central fissure in Ruskin's work, between the visual and the verbal. The present of visuality contrasts with the past of narrative, of history. Ruskin's work mostly exists on the cusp between the visual and the verbal; it turns on the effort to translate pictures into words, images into narrative, buildings into history.

When Ruskin turns to his own past, it is memory that re-presents this paradox of present and past; this problem of translating impressions into autobiography. In his later years, as Dinah Birch argues, Ruskin 'became a great writer of remembrance.'[37] This paradoxical nature of memory is of course central to modernism. Proust, Conrad, Ford, Joyce, Woolf all explore the power of

---

[33] Ruskin's title may have been influenced by that of Schopenhauer's popular work of 1851, *Parerga und Paralipomena* (παρεργα translating as 'secondary business', or 'appendages').
[34] *Præterita*, pp. 311, 314–15.
[35] Kenneth Clark, 'Introduction', *Præterita* (London: Rupert Hart-Davis, 1949), p. xvi.
[36] *Præterita*, p. 67.
[37] Dinah Birch, 'Fathers and Sons: Ruskin, John James Ruskin, and Turner', *Nineteenth-Century Contexts*, 18 (1994), 147–62 (p. 161).

memory, and the relation between memory and aesthetics: the way memory can transform experience from temporality to permanence, as art does. They are also aware of how memory can transform experience in a more problematic way, from fact to impression, or, in extreme cases, from fact to fiction. Ruskin, before them, could argue that 'There is a moral as well as material truth,—a truth of impression as well as of form—of thought as well as of matter; and the truth of impression and thought is a thousand times the more important of the two.'[38]

'Præterita': 'things gone by, the past'; this denotes what is over, behind us: irrecoverable and irredeemable. But the second definition, 'things passed over', is more ambiguous. Things that have been passed over long ago? Or things that are being passed over again, gone over once more as they are summoned to memory? Another paradox of memory that becomes central as impressionism turns into modernism, is that it is only *in* memory, in retrospect, that the past can be known and understood. 'I never have known anything of what was most seriously happening to me till afterwards.'[39] Thus Ruskin, but it could as well be the baffled narrators of Conrad's *Under Western Eyes* or Ford's *The Good Soldier*. The characteristic predicament of the modernist self is bewilderment in the face of the present—the experience of mysteries, enigmas, uncertainties, which can only be resolved, if at all, later.[40] Experience, that is, can only be present to the self when it is distant in time. The modernist tragedy is that we cannot experience our own experience as we live it. But modernism explores the redemptive possibility that lost experience can be regained in memory. And the characteristic way modernism expresses this temporal self-alienation is by disrupting linear chronology, and following instead sequences of mnemonic association. Ruskin is in the vanguard here too: 'I think my history will, in the end, be completest if I write as its connected subjects occur to me, and not with formal chronology of plan.'[41] Again, we could be listening to those Conradian or Fordian narrators.[42] They are known for being 'unreliable', either because 'obtuse', or because their apparent lack of narratorial rigour or coherence raises questions about whether they are telling the whole truth. Ruskin's title raises comparable doubts. Are things passed over in the sense of overlooked, missed out? In which case, again we encounter the temporal paradox. Is it that they were ignored before, but are being attended to now? Or that even in remembering, some of what has passed is inevitably being glossed over. This is the sense Ruskin suggests in the preface,

[38] Ruskin, ch. 5 of *Modern Painters*, vol. 1 'Of Ideas of Truth', Library Edition, vol. 3 (London: George Allen, 1903), p. 104. Compare Ford Madox Ford's provocative contrast (discussed in Chapter 6, pp. 283–4) in *Ancient Lights* (London: Chapman and Hall, 1911), pp. xv–xvi, between his 'inaccuracies as to facts' and his absolute 'accuracy as to impressions [. . .]'.

[39] *Præterita*, p. 442.

[40] See Paul B. Armstrong, *The Challenge of Bewilderment: Understanding and Representation in James, Conrad, and Ford* (Ithaca and London: Cornell University Press, 1987).

[41] *Præterita*, p. 128.

[42] See Landow, *Ruskin*, p. 84, arguing that Ruskin's narrative strategies, like Tennyson's, anticipate modernist developments.

saying he would compose the book 'at ease', 'speaking, of what it gives me joy to remember, at any length I like', but 'passing in total silence things which I have no pleasure in reviewing [. . .].'[43] Yet his silence about pleasureless memories doesn't guarantee he's not remembering them. The title still leaves us with an uncertainty as to whether it evokes a conscious or unconscious process? Where there are gaps, are they the product of amnesia, repression, or suppression?

Impressionist or modernist literary autobiography is particularly exercised by this problem of self-possession. Literary life-writing has a double focus: the life and the writing. Artists' autobiographies characteristically don't just chart their family backgrounds, their social and sexual lives, but tell the story of how and why someone became an artist. People read a writer's biography or autobiography in most cases because of the subject's work: to find out how they came to write *Sense and Sensibility*, or *A la recherche du temps perdu*.[44] And this corresponds to what we have in *Præterita*. For example when Ruskin defines his 'business' as 'to give account of the materials and mental resources' with which he began to write the second volume of *Modern Painters*.[45]

For the modernist autobiographer, however, this strategy of telling the story of one's stories raises a problem. The kind of modernist impersonality asserted by Eliot, Wyndham Lewis, or Pound, seeks to detach the work of art from its biographical origin. But literary autobiography is fundamentally attached to the author's oeuvre. It poses itself as the necessary supplement to the author's other work.[46] Modernist autobiography characteristically avoids this problem by locating inspiration in intertextuality. That is, the epiphanies tend to be the author's experiences of his or her art. For Conrad, or Yeats, or Ford, as for Proust, it was what they *read*, as much as what they *did* or *saw*, that made them writers. Thus Ford begins his first volume of literary autobiography, *Return to Yesterday*, with his oldest literary recollection: reading Kipling on a train. Or think of Yeats's recollections of the impact on his youth of Shakespeare; or Conrad writing about Flaubert in *A Personal Record*. And again this is what we have in *Præterita*: a history of Ruskin's formative reading, together with a representation of what that reading was like: how it affected him.[47]

I need now to demonstrate the importance of reading (in the *literal* sense of the books he read) in *Præterita*. The autobiography famously starts with a statement (repeated from *Fors Clavigera*) about himself: 'I am, and my father

---

[43] *Præterita*, p. 11.

[44] These issues are developed more fully in Max Saunders, 'A Life in Writing: Ford Madox Ford's Dispersed Autobiographies', *Antæus*, 56 (1986), 47–69; and *Ford Madox Ford: A Dual Life*, 2 vols (Oxford: Oxford University Press, 1996), vol. 1, 'Introduction', pp. 1–16; vol. 2, chapter 23, 'Ford's Autobiography', pp. 437–67.

[45] *Præterita*, p. 389.

[46] See the Conclusion for a development of this concept.

[47] As he says in a rather defensive footnote: 'How I learned the things I taught is the major, and properly, only question regarded in this history': *Præterita*, p. 368.

was before me, a violent Tory of the old school'; but the biographical details here—paternity, temperament, politics—are immediately interpreted through literature: 'Walter Scott's school, that is to say, and Homer's. I name these two out of the numberless great Tory writers, because they were my own two masters.'[48] And he then goes on to cite his Sunday reading, such as *Pilgrim's Progress* and *Robinson Crusoe*. Within a few pages we are given an account of his learning to read and write, complete with a sample of his earliest writing.

Præterita is full of his reading. Reading the Bible. Being read to. Hearing his father reading to his mother. Re-reading. To give just the most salient examples: the last narrative chapter, 'Joanna's Care', dwells fondly and fully on his reading, together with his cousin Joan, of Walter Scott. As Ruskin extracts material from *Fors* to construct the first two chapters, we see him re-reading his own published work. Similarly, he re-reads unpublished material, as when he reprints his own diary account of meeting Turner.[49] Or, more strikingly, in the final part of the autobiography, '*Dilecta*', Ruskin goes over and publishes the correspondence and diaries that he valued and re-read.

I have proposed that a definitive moment in the transition between impressionism and modernism occurs as Ruskin ponders the nature of 'reading'; which he understands not only in its literal sense of following the letters on the page, but also in its *figurative* sense of interpreting.[50] It was the intensive training he received from his mother in Bible-reading that alerted him to how texts needed interpreting. 'It had never entered into my head to doubt a word of the Bible, though I saw well enough already that its words were to be understood otherwise than I had been taught.'[51] This sense of reading as interpreting gets applied to things other than texts. He reads people: 'my mother, as I now read her.'[52] He knew that he was primarily an interpreter; that his main gift was not to be a creator himself, but his 'faculty of seeing the beauty and meaning of the work of other minds.'[53] 'I can no more write a story than compose a picture', he writes.[54] But he had a genius for translating between picture and story. Describing himself reading shades off into describing how to read himself.

This inconceivable passive—or rather impassive—contentment in doing, or reading, the same thing over and over again, I perceive to have been a great condition in my future power of getting thoroughly to the bottom of matters.[55]

As he passes over his life again, he 'perceives' new patterns in it. That is, autobiography is a reading of the self: posing the self as a text to be re-read, deciphered, construed, retold. It worries Ruskin that his readers read him differently from the way he reads himself. In volume 2, chapter 2, he mentions

---

[48] *Præterita*, p. 13.   [49] Ibid., p. 305.
[50] See Landow, *Ruskin*, p. 74, on 'his two concerns with perception and interpretation'.
[51] *Præterita*, p. 189.   [52] Ibid., p. 122.   [53] Ibid., p. 383.
[54] Ibid., p. 304.   [55] Ibid., p. 58. Cf. p. 141.

getting letters from acquaintances who say they like him more after obtaining new lights upon his character from the book. 'Which was not the least the effect I intended to produce on them', says Ruskin: 'and which moreover is the exact opposite of the effect on my own mind of meeting myself, by turning back, face to face.'[56] Turning back to his past, in writing the book? Or turning back the pages, as he reads it over; lets his eye pass over it again?

This follows an expression of concern about what his reader is making of the book. He reads his reader reading:

In my needful and fixed resolve to set the facts down continuously, leaving the reader to his reflections on them, I am slipping a little too fast over the surfaces of things; and it becomes at this point desirable that I should know, or at least try to guess, something of what the reader's reflections *are!* and whether in the main he is getting at the sense of the facts I tell him.[57]

Setting down the facts sounds like an appeal to an empiricist objectivity. Yet Ruskin knows that the facts alone will not suffice. You need 'the sense of the facts'. Facts are something you have to make sense of: to interpret; to read. If you don't pause to read them, you slip too fast over their surfaces. Thus, paradoxically, it is the very effort to represent the facts, that leads to their being 'things passed over'.

Ruskin could thus be said to have anticipated the debates a century later in reader-based theories about how far reading is determined by texts, how far by readers, and how far by institutions or traditions of interpretation. That is, he knew how 'reading' was arguably a matter of reading something into, not just reading something off, or out of, an object.[58] Indeed, this is the core of his anxiety about 'The Pathetic Fallacy': the psychology of modernity makes all acts of perception autobiographic, since the modern mind cannot help reading itself into the world.[59]

Ruskin's career as critic of the visual was not formed by books alone, of course, but other kinds of visual experience. His earliest recollections of visual impressions are crucial too, since they are also 'read'; are just as much the occasion for interpretation. *Præterita* is rich with Ruskin's vivid visual memories. Starting from the grim recollection of how he coped with the repressive and punitive regime of his parents by learning how to 'pass my days contentedly in tracing the squares and comparing the colours of my carpet', or looking for patterns in other decorative fabrics and wallpapers.[60] Or he recounts his first encounter with painting, when he was taken to have his portrait painted at three and a half, by Mr Northcote.[61] Within a few pages we are told of a gift that combines word and image: 'the illustrated edition of Rogers' *Italy*'. 'This book was the first means I had of looking carefully at Turner's work: and I might, not without some

---

[56] *Præterita*, p. 279.   [57] Ibid.

[58] See for example Andrew Bennett, ed., *Readers and Reading* (London and New York: Longman, 1995), p. 2.

[59] *Modern Painters*, vol. 3, Library Edition, vol. 5 (London: George Allen, 1904), ch. 12, pp. 201–20.

[60] *Præterita*, p. 21.   [61] Ibid., pp. 21–2.

appearance of reason, attribute to the gift the entire direction of my life's energies.'[62] Similarly he recalls 'the really most precious, and continuous in deep effect upon me, of all gifts to my childhood': a publication called 'the *Forget-me-not* of 1827, containing an engraving of Prout's 'Sepulchral monument at Verona.'[63] Furthermore, as we can see from these examples, it isn't that the moments of vision precede interpretation; are prior to art. In *Præterita* even the crucial revelations of nature are mediated by art. As George Landow argues, Ruskin was prepared for his visions of the Norwood ivy and the Fontainebleau aspen by his experience of Turner's work; and these moments then helped him return to Turner to understand, or interpret, him better.[64]

He does not just let the prose move from the literary to the natural, but brings it back again to the image of the book. 'Thus', he says, inspired by the sight:

with so much of science mixed with feeling as to make the sight of the Alps not only the revelation of the beauty of the earth, but the opening of the first page of its volume,—I went down that evening [. . .] with my destiny fixed in all of it that was to be sacred and useful.[65]

Our perceptions of the world are, after all, shaped by what we have previously learned about it. 'My Venice, like Turner's, had been chiefly created for us by Byron', says Ruskin.[66]

One way of reading these figures would be a deconstructive one, insisting on the textuality of anything—even a mountain—that might seem to stand outside the realm of the textual. But it is perhaps best seen as at least a paradoxical figure, since it also asserts the primacy of the non-textual over the textual. When science is mixed properly with feeling, then you don't need science books: the mere sight of the Alps is itself just as instructive. The Alps become the first page in the volume of the earth's beauty.

In a passage that follows close upon this, Ruskin touches on a central problem for the impressionist autobiographer. He is describing the effect of not understanding the language of the place you're visiting:

things are learnt about the country that way which can be learned in no other way, but only about that part of it which interests itself in you, or which you have pleasure in being acquainted with. Virtually, you are thinking of yourself all the time [. . .] We did not travel for adventures, nor for company, but to see with our eyes, and to measure with our hearts. If you have sympathy, the aspect of humanity is more true to the depths of it than its words; and even in my own land, the things in which I have been least deceived are those which I have learned as their Spectator.[67]

Was Philip Larkin thinking of this passage when he called his landmark 1955 volume *The Less Deceived*? The importance of detached observation for disabusal

---

[62] Ibid., p. 29.   [63] Ibid., p. 91.   [64] Landow, *Ruskin*, p. 79.
[65] *Præterita*, p. 116.   [66] Ibid., p. 295.   [67] Ibid., p. 119.

is certainly Larkinesque, as is the sense—really the inverse of the pathetic fallacy—that such disabusal is also self-disabuse: to be less deceived about the world is to become less self-deceived. Ruskin's passage is alert to the way experience of otherness is inescapably autobiographic. In encountering the other, 'Virtually, you are thinking of yourself all the time.' In describing what he has seen, therefore, he tells us—and himself—what he is. Yet the very mechanism which enables this, also disables it. For if seeing is privileged over saying, then the words in which he tells his experiences are charged with being less true, more deceptive. If the impressionist autobiographer must translate visual memories into verbal discourse, he can only be aware of the gaps between the two.

In a sense, this notion of epistemological gaps is related to the gaps between the three main subjects of *Præterita*: people (family, friends, artists); art (painting, writing, architecture); and nature (mountains, trees, light). One could say that his figures attempt to pass over the gaps between these subjects. Thus one reading of the title suggests that 'things passed over' need not simply be omitted, consigned to oblivion because finished; but that they can be 'passed over' as ravines or mountains can. Think of those accounts of the Alpine passes . . .

Præterita, then, could be read as filling in the gaps in Ruskin's other writings: 'a name of the books of Chronicles, because they contain what had been omitted in the books of Kings'. But the title *Præterita* implies that the gaps are more radically significant. They certainly were for Henry James, perhaps the greatest impressionist autobiographer, writing from a position precisely between Ruskin and modernism:

I foresee moreover how little I shall be able to resist, through these Notes, the force of persuasion expressed in the individual *vivid* image of the past wherever encountered, these images having always such terms of their own, such subtle secrets and insidious arts for keeping us in relation with them, for bribing us by the beauty, the authority, the wonder of their saved intensity. They have saved it, they seem to say to us, from such a welter of death and darkness and ruin that this alone makes a value and a light and a dignity for them, something indeed of an argument that our story, since we attempt to tell one, has lapses and gaps without them.[68]

Modernist narrative is notoriously disjunctive: fragmentary and juxtapositional rather than connective and evolutionary. Another kind of paradox emerges from James's image here of vivid images, which insist on the gaps their absence would create. The very disjunctiveness of such images means that a story told around them will inevitably have its gaps as well: the gaps James represents as the 'death and darkness and destruction' that surrounds the epiphanic moments of vividness. Ruskin's autobiography has been described as a form of conversion narrative

---

[68] James, *The Middle Years*, in *Autobiography*, ed. Frederick W. Dupee (Princeton: Princeton University Press, 1983), p. 551.

structured around moments of epiphany; though, like so much aesthetic autobiography or autobiografiction, it tells of a conversion to aesthetics at the expense
of a de-conversion from religion. In *Præterita* he wrote how, after studying
Veronese's *Solomon and the Queen of Sheba* in Turin in 1858, 'that day, my
evangelical beliefs were put away, to be debated of no more.'[69] But the corollary
is that epiphanic narrative is by definition structured around gaps, the gaps
between the epiphanies, the passages of mundanity from which the epiphanies
stand out. This is also a function of memory and its relation to narrative. The
Freudian unconscious could be described in terms of gaps that the ego structures
and restructures itself around. But cognitive science tells us that we need to forget
in order to make room for new mnemonic connexions to be established in the
brain. Thus all our adult memories depend upon selectivity, upon the loss of
other memories. And writers, or their narrators, have many motives for not
telling the whole truth. We shall pursue these questions of forgetting, evading,
and distorting in Chapter 6 on impressionist autobiography.

Meanwhile, in a post-Lacanian, Derridean universe, we know that discourse can
never fill its own gaps: that there is an absence or lack at the heart of all we say or
think. Even if a writer wants to tell the whole truth, they cannot say everything about
a story or a person or a situation. In this sense, all narrative is 'things passed over'.
Biographically this is obviously true of *Præterita*. Kenneth Clark comments on the
'remarkable' omission of his marriage to Euphemia Gray from the narrative.[70] But
the sense of omission is much more pervasive. Ruskin cultivates a manner of
dignified innuendo, hinting that he could always tell more; as with the strangely
moving inclusion of the long letter from Rose La Touche, whom he simply names as
'Rosie', at the end of volume 3, chapter 3. He had fallen in love with her when she
was only eleven, and proposed to her when she was seventeen, and he was fifty.
'Some wise, and prettily mannered, people have told me I shouldn't say anything
about Rosie at all. But I am too old now to take advice, and I won't have this
following letter—the first she ever wrote me—moulder away, when I can read it no
more, lost to all loving hearts.'[71] He then glances at the 'shadows' that gathered
round the happiness of those days.[72] Rose had died in a nursing home in 1875, aged
twenty-seven, apparently suffering from mental illness. Her death is thought to have
precipitated Ruskin's own periods of insanity from 1877.

Autobiography never can fill all the gaps in the self, or in the sense of the self. It
can only, in James's suggestive phrase, 'glory in a gap.'[73] When Ruskin found in a
bookseller's 'a little fourteenth century Hours of the Virgin', he used the reverse

[69] See Landow, *Ruskin*, p. 83. *Præterita*, p. 496.
[70] Clark, 'Introduction', *Præterita* (London: Rupert Hart-Davis, 1949), p. xiii.
[71] *Præterita*, p. 529.
[72] Ibid., p. 535.
[73] James, 'The New Novel', in *Selected Literary Criticism*, ed. Morris Shapira (Cambridge:
Cambridge University Press, 1981), p. 332.

of the figure describing the Alpine view as the page of a book, saying now that each page opened a vision of a new world:

The new worlds which every leaf of this book opened to me, and the joy I had, counting their letters and unravelling their arabesques as if they had all been of gold,—as many of them indeed were,—cannot be told, any more than—everything else, of good, that I wanted to tell.[74]

I shall end this account of Ruskin with a sketch of how we might map the relation between nineteenth- and twentieth-century literature—between Ruskin and modernism—by considering the changing view of 'mediation' from realism, to Ruskinian impressionism, through modernism, to postmodernism:

a) Realism denies the mediation of reality by art; it is based on an attempted suppression, or disattending to, this mediation.

b) Impressionism accepts the mediation of reality, but locates it in the process of perception: in the phenomenology of vision, or the stream of consciousness.[75]

c) This emphasis on perceptual subjectivism and stream of consciousness is in modernism too. But there it co-exists with an awareness of how language or form mediates between the subject and the object.

d) Postmodernism is founded on a denial, or suppression, of the thing mediated. A scepticism about the objectivity of the object. For Postmodernists, mediation and figuration is all we have. We cannot locate a stable subject or a stable object outside the field of mediation; beyond representations. Figuration is no longer grounded in the real.

Ruskin represents a turning point between impressionism and modernism, because he can just about accept the mediation that is 'reading', but only by displacing reading from its literal, literary sense (of reading a book, a verbal text) onto a figurative, and visual sense: reading a landscape, or a painting, or a person. But this strategy of trying to steady himself against the vertigo of interpretation lures him further towards the edge. To talk of reading a landscape or a person appears to ground hermeneutics in the natural. To naturalize interpretation. But it also does the converse, opening up that ground, since nature is no longer self-present and self-declaring, but is a text demanding an interpretation: a representation of an absent essence; a gap. And so it is with autobiography. Writing, and reading, the self, may start as a strategy for plenitude, for integration, making the self cohere into a story. But the story becomes that of the self in need of such strategies; the self not self-present but passed over in the process of living; present

---

[74] *Præterita*, pp. 490, 491.
[75] See Matz, *Literary Impressionism and Modernist Aesthetics* (Cambridge: Cambridge University Press, 2001), pp. 243–4.

neither to others nor even to itself, but only recuperable as interpretation, in the act of passing over its past again, in writing and in reading.

With auto/biography this notion of mediation becomes more problematic, since the self is both subject and object; both writer and reader of itself. Postmodern autobiography tends to deny the reality of both subject and object, though it accepts the reality of reading and writing, mediation and simulation. The writer to whom we turn next, Marcel Proust, is in many ways a forerunner of this shift. The subject of *A la recherche du temps perdu*, only tentatively named once as 'Marcel', is not, exactly, the book's author, 'Marcel Proust'. Nor is he its 'object'. Rather, it is the medium, art itself, which is the book's object. Proust accepts art as mediator, but locates autobiography within it.

PROUST

Proust made two translations of Ruskin: of *The Bible of Amiens* and *Sesame and Lilies.*[76] These were the only two books he published between his first, *Les Plaisir et les jours* (1896), and *Du côté de chez Swann* (1913), the first volume of *A la recherche du temps perdu*. The prefaces he wrote for the translations are crucial documents, signalling not only Ruskin's influence, and Proust's efforts to distance himself from him; but also charting the development of Proust's conceptions of the aesthetic life, of the significance of reading, and of the significance of autobiography.

In the Preface to *La Bible d'Amiens* Proust celebrates Ruskin as 'one of the greatest writers of all times and of all countries'. But he identifies an aspect of Ruskin's writing that troubles him. Proust calls it 'idolatry'; though it's clear he means this ironically, careful to explain that he is trying to capture 'an infirmity essential to the human mind' in general, rather than to 'denounce a personal fault.'[77] He subjects a passage from *The Stones of Venice* to a morally inflected close reading of the kind Ruskin excelled in. It is a passage in which Ruskin argues that the city's destruction followed once it strayed from its religion, and that it had no excuse because that religion was superlatively expressed by its art and architecture. It is for a form of idolatry that Ruskin berates the Venetians: for worshipping 'the wantonness of wealth' and 'the desire of the eyes or pride of life.'[78] Yet, according to Proust:

[76] *La Bible d'Amiens* (Paris: Mercure de France, 1904). *Sésame et les lys* (Paris: Mercure de France, 1906).
[77] Marcel Proust, *On Reading Ruskin: Prefaces to 'La Bible d'Amiens' and 'Sésame et les lys', with Selections from the Notes to the Translated Texts*, trans. and ed. Jean Autret, William Burford, and Phillip J. Wolfe; introd. Richard Macksey (New Haven: Yale University Press, 1987), p. 54.
[78] Ruskin, quoted by Proust, ibid., p. 51.

At the very moment he was preaching sincerity, he was himself lacking in it, not by what he said, but by the way in which he said it. The doctrines he professed were moral doctrines and not aesthetic doctrines, and yet he chose them for their beauty. And since he did not wish to present them as beautiful but true, he was forced to deceive himself about the nature of the reasons that made him adopt them.[79]

He argues that though Ruskin thought beauty was subordinated to 'moral feeling and truth, in reality truth and moral feeling are there subordinated to aesthetic feelings, and to an aesthetic feeling somewhat warped by that perpetual compromising.'[80] For a Judeo-Christian it would be idolatrous to prize the aesthetic above the religious (the statue of the golden calf above the monotheistic god). But for Proust, it is idolatrous for diametrically opposed reasons: not because Ruskin actually does subordinate the religious to the aesthetic, but because he tries not to. When he draws the aspen at Fontainbleau, its beauty strikes him as a theological sign:

The woods, which I had only looked on as wilderness, fulfilled I then saw, in their beauty, the same laws which guided the clouds, divided the light, and balanced the wave. 'He hath made everything beautiful, in his time,' became for me thenceforward the interpretation of the bond between the human mind and all visible things; and I returned along the wood-road feeling that it had led me far;—Farther than ever fancy had reached, or theodolite measured.[81]

Here Proust's reservation is borne out exactly. An aesthetic experience—an awareness of beauty—seems to Ruskin to call for its interpretation as a sign of god's creating the human mind in harmony with the natural world. Ruskin implies that the theological produces the aesthetic, whereas Proust sees Ruskin's reaching towards the theological as produced by his aesthetic experiences. It is a moment of epiphany, certainly. But whereas Ruskin intends it in the theological sense of epiphany (by analogy with the manifestation of Christ to the Magi), for Proust what is made manifest is not god, but simply beauty. As he says, it is beauty that leads him to this experience; and for Proust—as for any aesthete— the only true epiphany is an aesthetic one. This is indeed the function of the epiphanies in *A la recherche*. They are moments of ecstasy—of *ek-stasis*—standing outside: outside of time and outside of the present self. As epiphany and ecstasy they perform many of the functions of their religious equivalents: they bring joy; revelation; in redeeming the time that has passed they give promise of the afterlife of experience, resurrected in memory. But they do all these things without reference to a theological basis. Where Joyce's *Portrait* shows the process of displacement or substitution, in which a religious vocation is transfigured into an aesthetic calling, Proust's vocation is secular right from the start: his Eucharist a cup of tea and a madeleine.

---

[79] Proust, *On Reading Ruskin*, p. 51.   [80] Ibid.
[81] Ruskin, *Præterita and Dilecta*, pp. 314–15.

Ruskin's greatness for Proust is in his vision of an aesthetic life: his passionate insistence that the value of human life is expressed by human creativity, in art, architecture, literature. What qualifies his admiration is his sense that Ruskin didn't have the courage of this conviction. It is a shrewder view of Ruskin than the similar one held by Richard Aldington, who argues in his Introduction to *The Religion of Beauty*, that Ruskin was 'a man of remarkable sensibility' with 'an essentially religious outlook on life, and an incoherent, capricious taste for the fine arts'. But then he goes on to concede that 'although he would not have acknowledged it, Nature and Art as the human response to Nature, really formed Ruskin's religion all along.'[82] That is the paradox Proust analyses with greater profundity. Thus in the Preface to his second translation, Proust can be heard taking Ruskin not as the last word, but as the starting-point for his own magnum opus:

And there, indeed, is one of the great and marvelous features of beautiful books (and one which will make us understand the role, at once essential and limited, that reading can play in our spiritual life) which for the author could be called 'Conclusions' and for the reader 'Incitements'. We feel quite truly that our wisdom begins where that of the author ends, and we would like to have him give us answers, while all he can do is give us desires [...] by a singular and, moreover, providential law of mental optics (a law which perhaps signifies that we can receive the truth from nobody, and that we must create it for ourselves), that which is the end of their wisdom appears to us as but the beginning of ours [...][83]

This idea was to be incorporated (as was so much of his earlier material) into *A la recherche*, in which the narrator observes: 'The writer's work is merely a kind of optical instrument which he offers to the reader to enable him to discern what, without this book, he would perhaps never have perceived in himself.'[84] The distinction Proust makes between identifying a problem in Ruskin's writing, and denouncing a personal fault, is central to another work which was to become absorbed, sublated, into *A la recherche*: what Terence Kilmartin calls 'a curious hybrid, part criticism, part fiction, which came to be known as *Contre Sainte-Beuve*.'[85] Charles-Augustin Sainte-Beuve (1804–69) is best known now as a critic (though he was also a poet, novelist, and senator), and best remembered for his low estimates of the greatest French writers of the nineteenth century (especially Balzac, Stendhal, Baudelaire, and Flaubert). His *portraits littéraires* have been seen as a model for Pater's Imaginary Portraits.[86] Proust identified what he mistrusted about Sainte-Beuve's critical method thus:

[82] Aldington, *The Religion of Beauty*, pp. 10, 17.
[83] Proust, *On Reading Ruskin*, pp. 114–15.
[84] Proust, *A la recherche du temps perdu*, vol. 12: *Time Regained*, trans. Andreas Mayor (London: Chatto & Windus, 1970), p. 283.
[85] *Marcel Proust on Art and Literature: 1896–1919*, trans. Sylvia Townsend Warner; introd. Terence Kilmartin (New York: Carroll & Graf, 1997), p. 9.
[86] See Ed. Block Jr, 'Walter Pater, Arthur Symons, W. B. Yeats, and the Fortunes of the Literary Portrait', *Studies in English Literature, 1500–1900*, 26:4 (1986), 759–76, on 'the strain of portrait essay which Pater adopted from St. Beuve's *portrait littéraire* and then made over [...]' (p. 759).

To have devised the Natural History of Intellectuals, to have elicited from the biography of the man, from his family history, and from all his peculiarities, the sense of his work and the nature of his genius—this is what we all recognise as Sainte-Beuve's special achievement.[87]

He cites Hippolyte-Adolphe Taine (1828–93) too, who pursued the Naturalist method even more systematically, praising Sainte-Beuve for being innovative in carrying 'the methods of natural history into the history of moral philosophy.'[88] What Proust objects to in Sainte-Beuve's method is that it is biographical: ' "I do not look on literature", said Sainte-Beuve, "as a thing apart, or, at least, detachable, from the rest of the man and his nature".'[89] 'Sainte-Beuve's great work does not go very deep', says Proust: he 'never altered his shallow conception of the creative mind.'[90] In trying to grasp the writer through the external contingencies of a life, he falsifies the essential nature of the writer's life:

And so, by failing to see the gulf that separates the writer from the man of the world, by failing to understand that the writer's true self is manifested in his books alone, and that what he shows to men of the world (or even to those of them whom the world knows as writers but who can only resume that character when they put the world behind them) is merely a man of the world like themselves, Sainte-Beuve came to set up that celebrated Method [. . .] which consists, if you would understand a poet or a writer, in greedily catechising those who knew him, who saw quite a lot of him, who can tell us how he conducted himself in regard to women, etc.—precisely, that is, at every point where the poet's true self is not involved.[91]

'[W]omen, etc.—precisely'. A homosexual author in an age which condemned homosexuality might be particularly concerned that his work should not be defined biographically. But Proust's opposition to biographical criticism goes deeper, and is enshrined in that claim that 'the writer's true self is manifested in his books alone'. That is the basis of the 'gulf that separates the writer from the man of the world': they manifest different forms of subjectivity; the writer's cannot be found anywhere but in his or her books. While this is an argument against a biographical method—the Naturalist method of Sainte-Beuve or Taine—it is also a redefinition of the biographic: a claim that there is a 'true self' that is manifested; but that it is manifested elsewhere than where biographical critics would have us believe. This is a form of the argument that Philippe Lejeune discusses (though he associates it with Gide and Mauriac), which claims that a writer's true autobiography is to be found in his creative work.[92] Thus

---

[87] *Contre Sainte-Beuve*, in *Marcel Proust on Art and Literature: 1896–1919*, p. 95.
[88] *Contre Sainte-Beuve*, p. 95.   [89] Ibid., p. 98.
[90] Ibid., p. 107.   [91] Ibid., pp. 106–7.
[92] Phillipe Lejeune, 'The Autobiographical Contract', in *French Literary Theory Today*, ed. Tzvetan Todorov (Cambridge: Cambridge University Press, 1982), pp. 192–222 (p. 216). This notion is explored further in Chapters 4 and Chapter 5, and in the Conclusion.

whereas his work on Ruskin had been primarily concerned with aesthetics, *Contre Sainte-Beuve* is Proust's first major engagement with life-writing.

Contre Sainte-Beuve begins with a rejection of the intellect as a mode of recreating impressions:

> Every day I set less store on intellect. Every day I see more clearly that if the writer is to repossess himself of some part of his impressions, get to something personal, that is, and to the only material of art, he must put it aside. What intellect restores to us under the name of the past, is not the past. In reality, as soon as each hour of one's life has died, it embodies itself in some material object, as do the souls of the dead in certain folk-stories, and hides there. There it remains captive, captive for ever, unless we should happen on the object, recognise what lies within, call it by its name, and so set it free.[93]

This is why Proust rejects Sainte-Beuve's biographical method. It is the product of what he calls Sainte-Beuve's 'astonishing intellect.'[94] As readers of *A la recherche* will recognize, that distinction between 'What intellect restores to us under the name of the past' and repossession of impressions arising from a chance encounter, is the distinction fundamental to Proust's art:

> my work is based on the distinction between involuntary and voluntary memory, a distinction which not only does not appear in Mr Bergson's philosophy, but is even contradicted by it [. . .] To my way of thinking, voluntary memory, which belongs above all to the intelligence and the eyes, offers us only untruthful aspects of the past; but if an odour or a taste, re-encountered in totally different circumstances, unexpectedly reawakens the past in us then we can sense how different this past was from what we thought we could remember, from what voluntary memory offered us, like a painter working with false colours.[95]

Indeed, it is striking how fully the opening of *Contre Sainte-Beuve* anticipates the programme of *A la recherche*: the preoccupation with 'impressions'; the project of attempting to 'repossess himself'; the quest for the past through accident and material objects and analogy; the magic of naming. What Proust opposes to the method of Sainte-Beuve, the falsifications of the intellect, is a mode of autobiography, but one that is structured according to the flashes of involuntary memory and metaphor rather than the analytic processes of intellect and chronology. Yet at once he acknowledges a difficulty. He is convinced that the 'relative inferiority of the intellect' is 'perhaps for an artist the greatest of all' intellectual problems; but that paradoxically 'it is intellect we must call on to establish this inferiority.'[96] 'And if intellect only ranks second in the hierarchy of virtues', says Proust, 'intellect alone is able to proclaim that the

---

[93] *Contre Sainte-Beuve*, p. 19.
[94] Ibid., p. 142.
[95] Proust, interviewed by Elie-Joseph Bois, *Le Temps*, 13 November 1913; trans. Roger Shattuck, *Proust* (London: Fontana, 1974), p. 169.
[96] *Contre Sainte-Beuve*, p. 25.

first place must be given to instinct.'[97] This is true insofar as the faculty of judging or ranking is an intellectual one. Yet precisely what Proust's technique is not—both in *Contre Sainte-Beuve* and *A la recherche*—is 'intellect alone'. He finds forms which assimilate the intellect into the aesthetic. His style is notoriously discursive, complex, intelligent. But he seeks to persuade by beauty rather than by force of argument. This might sound uncomfortably close to what he criticized in Ruskin. If Ruskin chose moral doctrines on aesthetic grounds, isn't Proust choosing intellectual doctrines on aesthetic grounds? Yes, he is: but unlike Ruskin he believes the aesthetic *is* moral; is philosophically as well as psychologically *true*. And where Ruskin could only accept the aesthetic by translating it to the theological, Proust is fully self-conscious in accepting the aesthetic as his basis. To put it another way, where Romanticism sees an analogy or parallel between vocations of the spiritual and the aesthetic, for a writer like Proust (and also, as we shall see in the next sections, like James, or Joyce too) the aesthetic has taken the place of the theological.

In *Contre Sainte-Beuve* the form Proust finds is to use the intellectual challenge to the superiority of intellect as an introduction to, or frame for, the autobiographical. Even on the first page he moves immediately to autobiographical reminiscence. The first example is the celebrated epiphany near the start of *Du côté de chez Swann*, when the taste of the madeleine soaked in tea summons up and allows him to repossess involuntary memories of his past self. Or almost, since in *Contre Sainte-Beuve* the same effect is produced by 'some slices of dry toast.'[98] Other memories that prove crucial in *A la recherche* make their first appearance here too: the church seen from a train, and the uneven paving stones of St Mark's square in Venice—both figure in the 'Prologue'. The first chapter, 'In Slumbers', is where *A la recherche* begins, with Proust remembering the disorientations of falling asleep. As he explains, these intimate moments are offered as a more authentic representation of self, or a representation of a more authentic self, than anything that the method of intellect or biography could achieve: 'Compared with this past, this private essence of ourselves, the truths of intellect seem scarcely real at all.'[99]

Yet one can see why Proust felt the need to recast the material. The form of *Contre Saint-Beuve* doesn't work. The epiphanies don't amount to very much; they are presented too discursively. In *A la recherche* Proust turns the form inside out. The theorizing about the value of involuntary memory is still there, but is absorbed within the autobiographical. The memories are now the frame which can incorporate their discursive justifications. So that by the time we reach *Le*

---

[97] *Contre Sainte-Beuve*, p. 26.
[98] *Marcel Proust on Art and Literature*, p. 19. See Joshua Landy, *Philosophy As Fiction: Self, Deception, and Knowledge in Proust* (Oxford: Oxford University Press, 2004), p. 14, on 'The Madeleine Proust Never Ate'.
[99] *Contre Sainte-Beuve*, p. 24.

Temps retrouvé we have the fullest possible sense of the self that is being repossessed at such moments. At the same time he inverts not only Ruskin's priorities but his development. *Præterita* was Ruskin's last book; he began as an aesthetician and ended an autobiographer. Proust began, as an artist, with auto/biography.

Proust thus begins what was to prove in a real sense his life's work through an argument against biography, and by offering instead a new form of autobiographical writing. It is a shift which is, essentially, the story of the emergence of modernism, and central to the argument of this book. He incorporates moments of epiphany that also clearly provide the impulse to write *A la recherche*. Proust did not publish *Contre Sainte-Beuve*, and as Kilmartin says, its status in Proust's oeuvre, and its relation to *A la recherche* is problematic. He cites Philip Kolb's work on the *Carnet de 1908*, which demonstrates that 'at the time Proust was working simultaneously on a novel and on a study of Sainte-Beuve, that he kept switching from one to the other, and that the two became closely interlocked until at a certain stage the novel took over.'[100] But this is slightly misleading, since what the published text of the version he is introducing shows is that right from the beginning the critique of Sainte-Beuve was inextricable from the material that was to form the basis of the novel. And that is its relevance for this study: Proust's novel begins, as it ends, in the transformation of auto/biography.

The epiphanies that flood through the narrator in an overwhelming succession throughout the last chapter of *Le temps retrouvé* (Proust calls it a chapter, but it is as long as a Virginia Woolf novel) are 'aesthetic' in two senses. First, they allow him to grasp his life aesthetically, as something with a pattern, with a beauty that is accompanied by a feeling of joy. The aesthetic becomes an alternative to the biographic: to seeing the self externally, with the intellect, as a chronology of facts and an analysis of 'character'. This seeing life in terms of aesthetics goes hand in hand with—or is itself produced by—the increasing tendency to *treat* life aesthetically; and in particular to treat it according to the aesthetics of fiction: in short, to begin to fictionalize it. The varieties of fictionalizing displacements or disturbances of auto/biography are the subject of the next four chapters.

The second sense in which the Proustian epiphanies are 'aesthetic' is that the corollary of their revelation is the narrator's realization that he should write his book about them. In *Le temps retrouvé* he steps backwards and trips on an uneven paving stone. It is another moment of physical disorientation which heralds a temporal one, since it recalls a similar stumble in St Mark's square. Again it releases a feeling of joy. But in this case it is more specifically a moment of literary vocation:

Just as, at the moment when I tasted the madeleine, all anxiety about the future, all intellectual doubts had disappeared, so now those that a few seconds ago had assailed me

---

[100] Kilmartin, *Marcel Proust on Art and Literature*, p. 10.

on the subject of the reality of my literary gifts, the reality even of literature, were removed as if by enchantment.[101]

A few pages later this absence of self-doubt begins to be replaced by the more positive presence of a creative self-confidence. 'I had the feeling that perhaps beneath these signs there lay something of a quite different kind which I must try to discover' he says: 'some thought which they translated after the fashion of those hieroglyphic characters which at first one might suppose to represent only material objects'. Next he realizes what this decryption will actually involve: 'And this method, this apparently sole method, what was it but the creation of a work of art.'[102] This leads in turn to a further flash of insight that what this work has to be is autobiographical:

And I understood that all these materials for a work of literature were simply my past life; I understood that they had come to me, in frivolous pleasures, in idleness, in affection, in unhappiness, and that I had laid them up in store without divining the purpose for which they were destined or even their continued existence [. . .][103]

That is, he is explaining to us the process by which he arrived at the decision to write the book we have been reading. Hence the celebrated paradox whereby *A la recherche* ends with the narrator's decision to begin writing it: a book written to explain how it came to be written. There are several observations to make on this realization. First, he has left it until the very end of his immense work to explain it, rather than telling us at the start, as he did in *Contre Sainte-Beuve*, with anticlimactic results. Second, his attitude to the intellect has itself shifted. Rather than being the faculty which must be used to demonstrate its own inferiority to impressions, he now sees it as something that can 'enshrine' them in literature, so that they may be communicated:

I felt, however, that these truths which the intellect educes directly from reality were not altogether to be despised, for they might be able to enshrine within a matter less pure indeed but still imbued with mind those impressions which are conveyed to us outside time by the essences that are common to the sensations of the past and of the present, but which, just because they are more precious, are also too rare for a work of art to be constructed exclusively from them.[104]

---

[101] *Time Regained*, p. 223. Also see pp. 267–8: 'And thus my whole life up to the present day might and yet might not have been summed up under the title: A Vocation. Insofar as literature had played no part in my life the title would not have been accurate. And yet it would have been accurate because this life of mine, the memories of its sadnesses and its joys, formed a reserve[. . .].'

[102] Ibid., p. 239.

[103] Ibid., p. 267.

[104] Ibid., p. 266. Compare *A la recherche* (Paris: Gallimard, 1954), vol. 3, p. 423; trans. and discussed by Roger Shattuck, *Proust*, p. 127. This passage offers a revealing contrast with Joyce, who arguably did attempt, in the epiphanic method of *Portrait of the Artist*, to construct a work exclusively from such impressions.

If he had already realized this when writing *Contre Sainte-Beuve* (in which he juxtaposed intellect and impression), that experiment showed him that simply narrating the impressions was not enough; not even if they were intercalated with critical arguments against the method of the intellect. For, in the chapters of *Contre Sainte-Beuve* not discussing Sainte-Beuve, he switches into autobiographical mode, telling of his epiphanic moments, and asserting that they are more real than anything a critic like Sainte-Beuve could have found out about him from reading documents or interviewing his friends and family. What he doesn't make clear is *why* they are so real; why they matter to him. In *A la recherche*, the focus of the narrative shifts. While it starts by narrating epiphanies, the narrative becomes the search for a way to understand them, which turns out to be the method of recreating them as art. In order to tell this story, he has to incorporate the intellectual quest within the aesthetic (rather than, as he had tried to do in *Contre Sainte-Beuve*, to frame the epiphanic within an intellectual argument about biographical method). The intellect now is given its place, which is as the subject of the narration. That is, rather than delivering his intellectual arguments, he narrates them. He tells the story of his thinking about his impressions. That is why the novel is a story of a search, or a research, for lost time, rather than a lyrical account of its recovery. As Roger Shattuck says, '*The Search* shows a man trying to find his mind—his whole mind.'[105] That mind cannot be simply named or made transparent (as Rousseau had hoped his *Confessions* could make his soul transparent).[106] It must be quested after, much as the whole mind sought by Freud, different though it was from Proust's conception of mind, could also only be approached through the labyrinth of analytic narrative. Proust, then, is neither attacking the intellect, nor asserting it or delivering its results. He is narrating its quest; telling a story of mental process: 'I felt . . .'; 'I thought'; 'I understood . . .'.

In a sense all these aspects of the quest are already implicit from the beginning. The most celebrated of 'Proustian moments', the ecstasy of the madeleine, is an epiphany of self. But it is also an incitement not only to understand it, but to recreate it as autobiographical writing:

An exquisite pleasure had invaded my senses, but individual, detached, with no suggestion of its origin. And at once the vicissitudes of life had become indifferent to me, its disasters innocuous, its brevity illusory—this new sensation having had on me the effect which love has of filling me with a precious essence; or rather this essence was not in me, it was myself. I had ceased now to feel mediocre, accidental, mortal. Whence could it have come to me, this all-powerful joy? I was conscious that it was connected with the taste of tea and cake, but that it infinitely transcended those savours, could not, indeed, be of the same nature as theirs. Whence did it come? What did it signify? How could I seize upon and define it?

[105] Shattuck, *Proust*, p. 128.
[106] Rousseau, *The Confessions*, trans. J. M. Cohen (Harmondsworth: Penguin, 1975), p. 169.

[. . .] It is plain that the object of my quest, the truth, lies not in the cup but in myself
[. . .] I put down the cup and examine my own mind. It is for it to discover the truth. But
how? What an abyss of uncertainty whenever the mind feels that some part of it has
strayed beyond its own borders; when it, the seeker, is at once the dark region through
which it must go seeking, where all its equipment will avail it nothing. Seek? More than
that: create. It is face to face with something which does not so far exist, to which it alone
can give reality and substance, which it alone can bring into the light of day.[107]

This magnificent passage may come from a book that is not quite autobiography,
but it remains one of the best things written about autobiography—as well as
about the turning of it into autobiografiction. Its full implications only unfold
after the 3,000 or so pages that separate it from the climactic realizations of *Le
temps retrouvé*; so their echo of its challenges are not only perfectly justified (it is
the critic's juxtaposing of them here that may make them sound repetitious), but
enact across the span of the book the recapturing of sensation across the abyss of
past time.

Proust's quest to grasp the meaning of his impressions out of time leads him to
fuse impression, intellect, and narration into a single act of creation. But this is
not to say that the book is directly autobiographical. Its transformations of key
facts are well documented: as for example his inversion of his homosexuality; his
substitution for the devastating death of his mother of the deaths of other women
(the narrator's grandmother; or Bergotte). Some changes may seem less significant; but in a book preoccupied with the power of names, even a conventional
fictional disguising of a real person takes on a different colouring; or, in a book in
which the greatest mysteries are initiated by the most mundane materialities,
changing a piece of toast to a madeleine is not neglible. Suzanne Nalbantian
describes his aesthetic process in general as one of 'dislocation, adumbration,
multiplication and mystification.'[108]

Yet even if it were 'directly autobiographical', Proust argues that it wouldn't be
so in any straightforward way. That is, it wouldn't correspond to a directly
biographical account of its author, in the manner of Sainte-Beuve:

And this is one reason for the futility of those critical essays which try to guess who it is
that an author is talking about. A work, even one that is directly autobiographical, is at the
very least put together out of several intercalated episodes in the life of the author—earlier
episodes which have inspired the work and later ones which resemble it just as much, the
later loves being traced after the pattern of the earlier. For to the woman whom we have
loved most in our life we are not so faithful as we are to ourself, and sooner or later we
forget her in order—since this is one of the characteristics of that self—to be able to begin
to love again.[109]

---

[107] *Swann's Way*, 'Overture', pp. 58–9.
[108] See Nalbantian, *Aesthetic Autobiography*, pp. 67–9.   [109] *Time Regained*, p. 279.

So an account of a single love affair might refer to several women (who might have been several men). An epiphany may conflate similar experiences with madeleines *and* toast. There is even the suggestion, in the phrase about 'the later loves being traced after the pattern of the earlier' that not only does the writer write about similar episodes as if they were only one episode, but that he may live them as if they were only one. Here again Proust is close to Freud: in this case to the idea of transference, in which the subject projects unconscious feelings about one person (a parent or sibling, say) onto another person (their analyst, their boss, their partner, their friend), unconsciously letting a past relationship shape a present one.[110] Either way, Proust implies that the literary work (again like psychoanalysis) discovers or creates a truth about the self that is different from the truth of objective biography. Or (still like psychoanalysis) he says that selves are multiple; that what is wrong with biographical criticism is that:

this method ignores what a very slight degree of self-acquaintance teaches us: that a book is the product of a different *self* from the self we manifest in our habits, in our social life, in our vices. If we would try to understand that particular self, it is by searching our own bosoms, and trying to reconstruct it there, that we may arrive at it.[111]

This deeply paradoxical idea that the truest autobiography must come 'face to face with something which does not so far exist', and must create that face; the idea of the creation of a self different not only from the one known to others, but even from the self known to ourselves; both is and is not to say that the autobiographical self must be invented; found in fiction.

Proust performs a series of similar equivocations about the relation of the self to the book. In *A la recherche* this idea that 'a book is the product of a different *self*', alternates with a more mystical one: the idea that the self *is* a book; or that what the autobiographical writer does is look into his mind and read it *like* a book; and that it is this book which produces the self. He argues that this imaginary book was already pre-existent within him.[112] It is what guarantees the autobiographicality of the book he is going to write (or has written):

As for the inner book of unknown symbols [. . .] if I tried to read them no one could help me with any rules, for to read them was an act of creation in which no one can do our work for us or even collaborate with us [. . .] at every moment the artist has to listen to his instinct, and it is this that makes art the most real of all things [. . .] This book, more laborious to decipher than any other, is also the only one which has been dictated to us by reality, the only one of which the 'impression' has been printed in us by reality itself. When an idea—an idea of any kind—is left in us by life, its material pattern, the outline of the impression that it made upon us, remains behind as the token of its necessary truth.

---

[110] See J. Laplanche and J.-B. Pontalis, *The Language of Psycho-Analysis* (London: The Hogarth Press and the Institute of Psycho-Analysis, 1983), pp. 349–56 and 455–62.

[111] *Contre Sainte-Beuve*, pp. 99–100.

[112] *Time Regained*, p. 242.

The ideas formed by the pure intelligence have no more than a logical, a possible truth, they are arbitrarily chosen. The book whose hieroglyphs are patterns not traced by us is the only book that really belongs to us [. . .] What we have not had to decipher, to elucidate by our own efforts, what was clear before we looked at it, is not ours. From ourselves comes only that which we drag forth from the obscurity which lies within us, that which to others is unknown.[113]

One effect of saying that the autobiographical art work has to be read within the self, that the self is the book wherein it is encrypted, is to move from an essentialist notion of the self as fully self-present and deliverable, to the notion of the self as a narrative: as something extended over time, and which has to be read and interpreted.

In a provocative recent essay the philosopher Galen Strawson argues against the view widespread in the humanities that we experience our lives, our selves, as narrative.[114] He opposes to this 'Diachronic' orientation what he calls the 'Episodic' style of temporal being, which doesn't experience narrative linkage between the well-remembered parts of its past. Though he concedes that the distinction is not absolute: that sometimes 'Episodics' may have a clear sense of the continuity of their existence through time, and sometimes 'Diachronics' may not. But he believes the categories are both radically different and genetically determined. It is because he believes himself to be an Episodic, and to share this characteristic with several of our authors (Proust, Ford, Woolf), that he feels it imperative to give Episodics their due in an age predisposed towards narrativity. This is philosophy as autobiography (though perfectly consciously so), as well as philosophy about autobiography. What immediately strikes one about his application of the distinction to authors, however, is how arbitrary it seems. Certainly there is a high investment in the episodic in Proust, as there is in Ford and Woolf. That is what is meant when definitions of modernism generally include the notion of 'epiphany', 'moments of being', and so on. Yet from another point of view, while to talk about the abandonment of narrative connectivity in a haiku by Pound is one thing, it makes little sense to deny that novels like *A la recherche* or *The Good Soldier* are narrative. Certainly all three novelists experience episodes of extraordinary intensity. But, as we have seen from Proust's account of the experience arising from the madeleine, it isn't that he experiences episodically but writes narratively. Instead, from the moment he has had the experience he begins to think about it in narrative terms. If his notoriously complex syntax doesn't exemplify a deeply diachronic mentality it's hard to know what would. Conversely, writers such as Wordsworth, Dostoevsky, and Conrad, all of whom Strawson categorizes as Diachronics, while all masters of narrative, are surely

---

[113] *Time Regained*, pp. 240–1.

[114] Galen Strawson, 'A fallacy of our age: Not every life is a narrative', *Times Literary Supplement* (15 October 2004), 13–15. See the Conclusion for a further discussion of arguments about the narrative construction of the self.

equally haunted by the episodic: Wordsworth's 'Spots of time'; Dostoevsky's epileptic ecstasies; Conrad's bewildered impulses. Surely all these authors, like most people, are capable of both modes, and oscillate between them. But while I don't think the distinction is material in the way Strawson wants it to work, it is valuable in helping us to think about the ways in which auto/biographers combine the Episodic and the Diachronic: how they establish narrative connection between the crucial moments which seem to disrupt narrative. Proust's trope of the book within the self which the autobiographer must read suggests that the episodes of epiphany are already narrativized, and their story merely has to be . . . well, read, created, or, in the other metaphorical turn we glimpsed earlier (in the figure of hieroglyphics), translated:

So that the essential, the only true book, though in the ordinary sense of the word it does not have to be 'invented' by a great writer—for it exists already in each one of us—has to be translated by him. The function and the task of a writer are those of a translator.[115]

Fine if you're essentially a one-book writer—however great, gigantic, and multi-voluminous the book—but if not, not. Where does this idea of a writer being capable of one 'true book' leave those who have written a multitude of great but different works: Chaucer, Shakespeare, Dostoevsky, James, Conrad, Joyce, and so forth? It would either have to privilege one above the rest—to see *Hamlet* as Shakespeare's 'essential' autobiography, or *The Brothers Karamazov* as Dostoevsky's—or to read their whole oeuvre as a single book, with each work contributing a different chapter.[116] Either way, the implication is that the autobiographer must try to turn his experience, however episodic, fragmentary or multiple, into a single narrative.

Although the imaginary Proustian book within the self is read by introspection, that process can take many forms. According to Proust, one can also read oneself by reading other people's books; as in that image of a book as 'a kind of optical instrument' enabling the reader to discern what 'he would perhaps never have perceived in himself'. Reading, that is, also becomes an autobiographical act. It helps us to experience 'our true life', of which we would otherwise remain unaware:

But this discovery which art obliges us to make, is it not, I thought, really the discovery of what, though it ought to be more precious to us than anything in the world, yet remains ordinarily for ever unknown to us, the discovery of our true life, of reality as we have felt it to be, which differs so greatly from what we think it is that when a chance happening brings us an authentic memory of it we are filled with an immense happiness?[117]

Reading another's book to look into yourself might sound the converse of looking into the book of yourself and reading another self in it. But they are

---

[115] *Time Regained*, p. 255.

[116] The implications of this idea for literary autobiography are developed in Chapter 5 and in the Conclusion.

[117] *Time Regained*, p. 242.

really analogous processes for Proust. In both cases one reads an unknown book to discover an 'other' self. From one point of view Proust might appear to take one step further into the Paterian prison of impressionist solipsism. Where Ruskin is marching up mountains, sketching trees and describing buildings, Proust is contemplating his narrative, and finding all other selves to be himself. As Terence Kilmartin observes:

what he had to say about other writers—or painters or musicians—was intimately bound up with his own artistic aspirations and his own literary sensibility. Cool, objective analysis is not his forte; his criticism is subjective, intuitive, impressionistic; he enters into a symbiotic relationship with the authors and artists he writes about.[118]

However, it wasn't only a matter of recasting others in his own image. As the passage about art revealing our 'true life' indicates, there is an element of defamiliarization involved. It is because the life art shows us 'differs so greatly from what we think it is' that we are able to enjoy it. According to this view, the way in which reading can be an autobiographical act is by letting us see our self as other. Proust's critical gift was inextricable from his talent for giving impressions of other selves; recasting his own literary self into the styles of others. As Kilmartin continues:

The famous parodies, which he described as 'literary criticism in action', bear witness to this gift of empathy: 'I set my inner metronome to his rhythm,' he said of his pastiche of Renan, 'and I could have written ten volumes in the same style'.

Thus, from another point of view, in Proust one can hear modernism begin to rattle the prison bars of *fin de siècle* solipsism. For where impressionism and aestheticism are preoccupied with the self and its cultivation, part of modernism's quest for objectivity involves turning subjectivity inside out. Rather than trying to put the self into a book (the fantasy of the essentialist autobiographer), Proust locates the book within the self. The book is on the inside and the self outside it, reading it. But as it does so, it perceives that the book is the self; just as the 'exquisite pleasure' which invades his senses with the taste of the madeleine makes him feel full of an 'essence'. That term is already doubly metaphysical (an essence like a scent, or like a soul?). But Proust can even turn the metaphysical inside out: the 'essence was not in me, it was myself'.

Thus where Ruskin reads the objective world, but reads it as a monologic scriptural text, modernism reinvestigates the nature of reading. To tell the story of how it does so would require a different book. But many of our authors would also figure amongst its chief characters. Proust (whether writing on Ruskin, Sainte-Beuve, or the book of himself); James's reading of his own work for his New York edition; Joyce's parodies; the autobiography of Pound's autodidactic reading that is his *Cantos*; the attention to the reader in the criticism of Woolf or

---

[118] Kilmartin, 'Introduction', *Marcel Proust on Art and Literature*, p. 14.

Ford; all these contribute to modernism's exploration of the nature of the reading experience. Again this may seem solipsistic, in the suggestion that what is at stake is what goes on inside the head of the modernist author who happens also to be reading. But Proust introduces two important counter-arguments into *Le temps retrouvé*. First, that the notion of the immanent book of the self is not a case of aesthetic elitisim, because it is in everybody; not just the artist. Second, that just as literature makes us aware of our own lives, it makes us simultaneously aware of the lives of others.

Real life, life at last laid bare and illuminated—the only life in consequence which can be said to be really lived—is literature, and life thus defined is in a sense all the time immanent in ordinary men no less than in the artist [. . . .] art, if it means awareness of our own life, means also awareness of the lives of other people [. . . .][119]

Thus if another person's book is an optical instrument that enables us to see into ourselves, like most optical instruments it can be turned around. If it helps us to see the book that is in ourselves, that book in turn can help us to see what is in other selves.

What does Proust have to say about reading others' books, as opposed to the book of the self? Curiously, his most extended discussion, the essay 'On Reading' prefaced to his translation of *Sesame and Lilies*, ostensibly argues that 'Reading should not play the preponderant role in life assigned to it by Ruskin.' As in *Contre Sainte-Beuve*, Proust proceeds by moving from criticism to autobiography, discussing his own childhood reading, and saying that 'what it mostly leaves in us is the image of the places and the days when we did this reading.'[120] While this appears to play down the role of reading, as something which only serves to heighten the self's other experiences such as those of time and place, it soon becomes clear from his distinction between reading and conversation that he sets a very high value on reading, provided that it is active—and active in a specifically autobiographical mode:

reading, contrary to conversation, consisting for each of us in receiving the communication of another thought, but while we remain all alone, that is to say, while continuing to enjoy the intellectual power we have in solitude, which conversation dissipates immediately; while continuing to be inspired, to maintain the mind's full, fruitful work on itself.[121]

When Matthew Arnold said that the note of the modern was 'the dialogue of the mind with itself' his suggestive paradox expresses an unease both about the mind (it is fragmentary) and the idea of dialogue (a dialogue within the self cannot be a meeting of truly other minds).[122] He anticipates the modernity of Proust's idea of reading, which is the mind's fruitful work on itself. How better to express that

---

[119] *Time Regained*, p. 262.
[120] Proust, *On Reading Ruskin*, p. 110.   [121] Ibid., p. 112.
[122] Matthew Arnold, 'Preface to First Edition of *Poems*, 1853', in *Selected Criticism of Matthew Arnold*, ed. Christopher Ricks (New York: Signet, 1972), pp. 27–8.

'intellectual power', than in realizing the ambiguity inherent in the idea of doing work on the self ('à rester en plein travail fécond de l'esprit sur lui-même').[123] Is this working to understand the self—autobiography?—or working on the self in order to transform it—autobiografiction? Here reading is seen as providing an experience comparable to the Proustian epiphanies: rather than being in two times, or two places, we are in two minds, having our own 'intellectual power', combined with the 'communication of another thought.'[124] As we have already seen, this combination heightens understanding both of ourselves and of others: autobiography and biography: auto/biography.

When we understand something in someone else's book, it is implied, what happens is not cognition but recognition: we are taken back to something in ourselves that we may not have been aware of beforehand. (Here the theory is close to Plato's theory of knowledge as recognition of ideal forms.) This spark of recognition, for Proust, whether it comes from other writers' books, or from the book of the self, should ideally stir the reader into creativity, in order to write the book that is already being read in these acts of recognition: the book of the self. It might be objected (as T. S. Eliot objected about Middleton Murry or D. H. Lawrence, say)[125] that Proust is no less passive in the face of his aesthetic epiphanies than a religious person is in accepting the authority of a god; that he has merely substituted an 'inner voice' for a religion, and granted it the authority that he denies to scripture. But Proust's image of the book in the self has cunningly anticipated that objection. For even when the text he is reading is the book of himself, he doesn't let it reify into 'a material thing, deposited between the leaves of books', but sees it as 'an ideal we can realize only through the intimate progress of our thought and the effort of our heart.'[126] That is the point of his paradox whereby the book has to be read in order to be created, in order for autobiografiction to be written. The book in the self, which seemed a mystical, or metaphysical, or metaphorical idea, materializes into an actual book as we read it: a work of autobiografiction, like *A la recherche du temps perdu*.

Joshua Landy notes that '*Contre Sainte-Beuve* leaves its narrator on the threshold (perhaps) of a future work, rather than having him draft a number of potentially unrelated "sketches".'[127] In other words, Proust's decision to leave us with the idea that the book we have been reading is the *Kunst* Marcel's *Bildung*

---

[123] Proust, *On Reading Ruskin*, p. 112. For the French text, see Proust, *On Reading*, trans. and ed. Jean Autret and William Burford (London: Souvenir Press, 1972), p. 30.

[124] Compare Georges Poulet, 'The Phenomenology of Reading', *New Literary History*, 1 (October 1969), 53–68.

[125] For examples see Eliot, 'The Function of Criticism' (1923), in *Selected Essays*, pp. 23–34 (on John Middleton Murry's discussion of the 'inner voice'; and his *After Strange Gods: A Primer of Modern Heresy* (London: Faber, 1934), p. 59.

[126] Proust, *On Reading*, p. 118.

[127] Joshua Landy, *Philosophy As Fiction: Self, Deception, and Knowledge in Proust* (Oxford: Oxford University Press, 2004), p. 47.

has been preparing him to write, was made after *Contre Sainte-Beuve*. That decision leaves the whole of *A la recherche* delicately poised between two readings. Insofar as it is autobiography, there is an unproblematic identity between the subjectivity being enunciated, and the author of the book. But insofar as it is a fiction, the splitting between the book's author, Marcel Proust, and the narrator-character, 'Marcel', troubles the author-function. Marcel's 'sketches', that is, are offered as fictionally authored, and the novel contains literary works supposedly written by a fictional character. What's more, Proust's decision to give the novel a cyclic form in which the ending announces the beginning of its writing, has the curious effect of retrospectively turning the whole novel into an imaginarily authored book (one which contains *mises en abymes* of fictionally authored sketches within itself). As we shall see in Part II, such experiments in imaginary authorship and fictional creativity are a marked component of later modernist auto/biografiction.

The line traced here of 'aesthetic autobiography' from Ruskin towards Proust indicates one route by which impressionism transforms itself into modernism via a re-imagining of auto/biography—the central topic of this book. The four remaining chapters of Part I will consider various other routes by which writers made parallel journeys. They include further developments of aesthetic autobiography towards fiction. Chapter 3 discusses works in which writers disturb the act of naming in auto/biography through pseudonymity, anonymity, or the use of the third person. Chapter 4 considers 'autobiografiction'; Chapter 5 examines fictionalizations of aesthetic autobiographical writing (developing the form of imaginary portrait collections). Chapter 6 considers impressionist autobiography by writers who were primarily novelists.

There is some chronological justification for the ordering of these chapters. The main books discussed in Chapters 3 and 4 are from the late nineteenth century to 1915. Chapter 5 surveys the whole period of this study from the 1870s to the 1930s. The main works discussed in Chapter 6 are all from the twentieth century, and most from the eight years before the outbreak of the First World War, though it includes some material from the 1920s and 1930s. However, in fact all four chapters refer to works across the period from the 1870s to the 1930s, and the aim is not to suggest a chronological development through these various forms of autobiographical displacement, but rather the opposite: that this period experiences an over-layering and cross-fertilization of diverse life-writing forms; and that this simultaneity helps explain how writers were able to combine being impressionists, aesthetes, modernists, and autobiographers in different ways. The separation of the chapters has been made on conceptual, formal, and thematic grounds, to indicate how the displacements of auto/biography relate back to the work studied in the first two chapters; how increasing fictionalizations look forward to the experiments in modernist autobiografiction discussed in Part II; and how impressionism offers a key to the transition from one to the other.

3

Pseudonymity, Third-personality, and Anonymity as Disturbances in *fin de siècle* Auto/biography: 'Mark Rutherford', George Gissing, Edmund Gosse and Others

If Proteus be taken to represent that Reality which all save metaphysicians believe to be real, he represents especially that half of it which I have (elsewhere) called *Otherness*, that is to say, whatever is not *ourself*. And just as the essential, unshareable *ourself* is what we feel, to wit: moods, passions, efforts, hope and fear, liking and disliking; so the *not-ourself* (other persons as well as other things, and even our own personalities when viewed as if they were not our own)—the *Otherness* in short, is, on the contrary, *seen*, because it is outside us.[1]

'a man defines himself by his make-believe as well as by his sincere impulses'.[2]

SO-CALLED AUTOBIOGRAPHY

When Anthony Trollope published a volume called *An Autobiography* in 1883 his title implied that it is only one possible version of his life, though he ended it with a scepticism about the kind of truth any version of autobiography could tell:

It will not, I trust, be supposed by any reader that I have intended in this so-called autobiography to give a record of my inner life. No man ever did so truly,—and no man ever will. Rousseau probably attempted it, but who doubts but that Rousseau has confessed in much the thoughts and convictions rather than the facts of his life? If the rustle of a woman's petticoat has ever stirred my blood; if a cup of wine has been a joy to me; if I have thought tobacco at midnight in pleasant company to be one of the elements of an earthly Paradise; if now and again I have somewhat recklessly fluttered a £5 note over a card-table;—of what matter is that to any reader? I have betrayed no woman. Wine

---

[1] Vernon Lee, *Proteus: Or the Future of Intelligence* (New York: Dutton, 1925), pp. 12–13.
[2] Albert Camus, *The Myth of Sisyphus*, trans. Justin O'Brien (Harmondsworth: Penguin, 1975), p. 18.

has brought me no sorrow. It has been the companionship of smoking that I have loved, rather than the habit. I have never desired to win money, and I have lost none.[3]

The conception of the 'inner life' here is so different from anything envisaged by Rousseau that one would like to be able to give Trollope the benefit of the doubt, and suspect irony in the way he tantalizes readers with banal revelations he is determined not to give them. Yet the comment about Rousseau is perplexing: not the insinuation that Rousseau can't be trusted about the facts he gives about his life—that has become a truism of commentary on the *Confessions*. Rather, it is the notion that giving 'the thoughts and convictions rather than the facts' is a bar to recording the 'inner life'. What Trollope appears to mean by 'inner life' is what we would think of as 'private life'—personal habits, amusements, and appetites, rather than public works and duties. What the passage does not seem to allow is that there is any conception of the 'inner life' beyond such banalities. True, he may not have told us much more about his inner life if he had disclosed trivial affairs or addictions. But that would be because such things didn't signify much about his inner thoughts, feelings, hopes, dreams, or fantasies, rather than because they couldn't be told accurately, or because if they could be told accurately, they would disclose the inner life. The legacy of Romanticism and its aftermath was to prise apart the facts of a life from its imagination or value, and to locate that value in thoughts, passions, and convictions, rather than in mere facts. Trollope's position here is in striking contrast to the autobiographical writings that we tend to value most from the nineteenth century, by writers such as Wordsworth, Mill, Ruskin, and Newman: writers who brought a new psychological depth and moral inwardness to autobiography in the Victorian period.

'So-called autobiography' is a telling phrase. Again there is an ironic note. 'So-called' implies it is not in fact an autobiography (which is to be expected if writing the life of one's self is an impossibility). Yet his volume is indeed 'so-called': *An Autobiography*. The reference to Rousseau indicates that one meaning of 'so-called autobiography' is when a writer distorts the facts of his life. Or the irony may signal the unease with conventional forms of autobiography manifesting itself forcefully in the years just before Trollope published his. But there is another meaning, which emerges at about the time of Trollope's autobiography, and which casts its shadow over much of the most interesting auto/biographical work for the following fifty years. This refers to works which are called auto/biographies but are in fact something else: fictions; and works which are written by 'so-called' autobiographers: that is, by authors whose names are replaced by pseudonyms on the title-pages of their purported auto/biographies; works that I shall later term pseudo-autobiography. Such works, and related strategies of authorial displacement, are the subject of this chapter.

---

[3] Trollope, *An Autobiography*, ed. Michael Sadleir and Frederick Page, World's Classics (Oxford: Oxford University Press, 1980), pp. 365–6.

'MARK RUTHERFORD'

The classic and representative example is *The Autobiography of Mark Rutherford, Dissenting Minister* (1881), written by William Hale White (1831–1913). Such pseudonymity might appear to issue from a sense of delicacy or shame. 'Mark Rutherford' is beset by religious doubt, and loses his faith: a trajectory that would have been painful to confess publicly at the time, particularly for a minister. Yet White himself, though he had been born into a Dissenting family, and was educated to become a minister, had been expelled from theological college in 1851 for holding 'unsafe' views about scriptural authority, and entered the Civil Service instead when he was twenty-three; though he did sometimes preach in nonconformist chapels in the 1850s.[4] Rutherford's career (though it draws on, and elaborates Hale White's own early youth and scepticism) is thus considerably fictionalized.[5] As his biographer C. Macdonald Maclean writes, 'While the first two books cannot be regarded as a "Confessions", still less can they be regarded as factual autobiography.'[6] She quotes Hale White saying: 'I wish sometimes I could write, as a warning, a real history of my own inner life'; yet she claims that it is as a record of this 'inner', or spiritual, life, that it has truth-value: 'Fictional though many of the events be, the delineation of the growth of a human soul is as faithful as that given in *The Prelude*.'[7]

Like Mill, whose *Autobiography* had been published in 1873, Hale White had also undergone the kind of mental 'crisis' that it required courage to confess. As the *Oxford DNB* explains:

Casting about for employment Hale White took up a schoolmastering post in Stoke Newington, where he lasted only a few hours, fleeing for his sanity after a terrible night of vastation, a kind of spiritual urban angst, bouts of which recurred all his life (nervous breakdowns in effect).

The book is a novel cast in the form of an autobiography, published under the central character's name, and offered as 'Edited by his Friend, Reuben Shapcott'. It ends with an editorial note saying: 'Thus far goes the manuscript which I have in my possession. I know that there is more of it, but all my search for it has been in vain. Possibly some day I may be able to recover it.'[8] Shapcott worries that

---

[4] The words 'Dissenting Minister' were silently removed from the title-page of the second edition of 1888.

[5] Charles Swann, 'Autobiografiction: Problems with Autobiographical Fictions and Fictional Autobiographies. Mark Rutherford's Autobiography and Deliverance and Others', *Modern Language Review*, 96:1 (2001), 21–37. My debt to this important essay is discussed in the next chapter.

[6] C. Macdonald Maclean, *Mark Rutherford: A Biography of William Hale White* (London: Macdonald, 1955), p. 276.

[7] Ibid., pp. 276, 278.

[8] *The Autobiography of Mark Rutherford, Dissenting Minister* (London: Trübner & Co., 1881), p. 176.

2 William Hale White / 'Mark Rutherford' by Arthur Hughes, 1887.

Rutherford has misrepresented himself, and says 'I still cherish the hope that some day or the other I may recover the contents of the diary.'[9] The *Autobiography* was so successful that White published several other books as by 'Rutherford': *Mark Rutherford's Deliverance* appeared in 1885—the conclusion to the

[9] Ibid., p. 179. Three volumes purporting to be Rutherford's journal did indeed appear: *Pages from a Journal* (1900); *More Pages from a Journal* (1910); and *Last Pages from a Journal* (1915); though Shapcott has disappeared from these books.

Autobiography, again 'Edited by his Friend, Reuben Shapcott'. There's another note at the end of the *Deliverance*, which starts: 'Here ends the autobiography. A month after this last holiday my friend was dead and buried.' Shapcott says his papers included 'a mass of odds and ends, some apparently written for publication'.[10] As with the *Autobiography*, this note leaves the door open for more posthumous publication. And indeed a whole series of other books followed. Some were novels, or like novels: *The Revolution in Tanner's Lane* (1887); *Miriam's Schooling and Other Papers* (1893); *Catherine Furze* (1893); and *Clara Hopgood* (1896). Like the *Autobiography*, all these volumes are presented as edited by Shapcott. But 'Shapcott' was clearly a fiction too; a device enabling White to go on publishing as 'Mark Rutherford', even after Rutherford's supposed death. And what he says about the manuscript of the *Autobiography* cannot have been true: either the rest didn't exist yet, or if it did, White wouldn't have needed to search for it.

The *Autobiography* was White's first book. It's not surprising that its success encouraged him to follow it up with more books by 'Rutherford': But it is surprising that almost all his work appeared under the pseudonym. The only works he published under his own name were translations of Spinoza, biography—*An Estimation of the Charge of Apostasy Against Wordsworth* (1898), and *John Bunyan* (1907)—or bibliography (*A Description of the Wordsworth and Coleridge MSS in the Possession of Mr T Norton Longman*, 1897): all works by or about others. When the focus was on his own life or thought, he became Mark Rutherford.

The advantages of publishing in this way are clear. By making Shapcott's editing look like an act of friendship and piety—publishing the literary remains of someone recently dead—White might take the edge off criticisms from people who disapproved of Rutherford's agnosticism. They might be less inclined to speak harshly of the dead; especially someone who could inspire the friendship Shapcott speaks of. Pseudonymity can provide a protective disguise. White may not have wanted all his acquaintances and neighbours to know of his spiritual doubts. Despite the success of the books, he remained unwilling to declare publicly that 'Mark Rutherford' was his pseudonym; and this despite the fact that his identity had been revealed in the *Westminster Review* in 1883, just two years after the *Autobiography*, and two years before the *Deliverance*.[11]

---

[10] *Mark Rutherford's Deliverance* (London: Trübner & Co., 1885), pp. 162–3.

[11] Valentine Cunningham, Oxford *DNB* entry for Hale White. See Don Cupitt, 'Introduction', in William Hale White, *The Autobiography of Mark Rutherford and Mark Rutherford's Deliverance, edited by his friend Reuben Shapcott* (London; Libris, 1988), p. viii. W. Robertson Nicoll, 'Memories of Mark Rutherford', in *A Bookman's Letters* (London: Hodder and Stoughton, 1913), pp. 366–7, quotes from the *Westminster*: 'Not long ago Mr. Hale White published a remarkable little book, which attracted very much less attention than it deserved, *The Autobiography of Mark Rutherford, Dissenting Minister.*'

Indeed, it's not even clear if it is a pseudonym, exactly. We tend to think of pseudonyms as assumed names authors use to conceal their identities as the authors of books that would reveal something of themselves they would rather keep private. A pseudonymous autobiography in that sense is like a *roman à clef* in which the only fact that has been changed is the name of the author (rather than the characters). To the extent that *The Autobiography of Mark Rutherford* tells Hale White's own story, 'Mark Rutherford' is that kind of pseudonym. But to the extent that Hale White changes his own story into fiction, it's something more: 'Mark Rutherford' becomes a fictional identity, someone whose story differs from that of his author. In structural terms, a pseudonym is normally taken to refer to the author, while concealing his or her identity. Whereas the 'Mark Rutherford' who does things Hale White did not, refers to someone who doesn't exist: a fictional character, who also writes his (fictional) autobiography: namely, a heteronym (to use the term coined by Fernando Pessoa, which will be discussed further in Chapter 7). In short, when writers fictionalize their autobiography, they're doing more than writing a novel; they're writing a book by someone else: an imaginary author. Because the *Autobiography* combines Hale White's autobiography with fiction, 'Mark Rutherford' hovers between pseudonym and heteronym.

But what is also striking about his case is how representative it is; how many other writers around the turn of the century are displacing their autobiographies into various kinds of pseudonymity; and into various forms of fiction. It might seem strange that the publisher T. Fisher Unwin produced a book series in the mid-1890s called the 'Autonym Library'. 'Autonym' is now a term of identity politics: the name by which a social group designates itself; but here the older sense is meant, of using one's own name. But the series name plays on that of the publisher's earlier series, begun in 1890 and successful enough to run to fifty-four titles: the 'Pseudonym Library'. Publishing a book under a pseudonym is one thing. If the name on the title-page is unfamiliar, we are likely to assume it belongs to a new writer, or a little-known one. But publishing a book in a series called the 'Pseudonym Library' is to advertise its pseudonymity: to reveal that the name conceals another name, which may be better known. Effectively it converts pseudonymity into anonymity. And as with anonymity, the effect is to arouse curiosity in the reader as to the writer's real name. Whatever benefits anonymity or pseudonymity offer a writer—psychological, social, legal—here they have also become a commercial strategy, which could reward both author and publisher.[12]

Pseudonyms abound at the turn of the century. Those disguising gender have received much recent critical attention: 'Vernon Lee' (used by Violet Paget); 'Michael Fairless' (used by Margaret Fairless Barber); and 'Michael Field' (used interestingly to disguise not only a gender shift but an autobiografictional double

---

[12] See Troy J. Bassett, 'T. Fisher Unwin's Pseudonym Library: Literary Marketing and Authorial Identity', *English Literature in Transition 1880–1920*, 47:2 (2004), 143–60.

act, by Katherine Harris Bradley and her niece and ward, Edith Emma Cooper). Yeats's friend the Scottish poet William Sharp is a rare case of a man using a female pseudonym: 'Fiona Macleod'.

Pseudonymity of course has a long history; longer than that of autobiography. What's new about these developments at the turn of the century is the appearance of pseudonymous or anonymous autobiography (as opposed to fictional autobiography). After all, biographical curiosity is inextricably tied to a specific known individual; so there is something deeply paradoxical about the idea of an anonymous or pseudonymous autobiography. Not all pseudonymists were autobiografictionists. George Russell published his poems and essays as 'Æ'. Whereas others certainly did write autobiografiction, like Vernon Lee, whose prose such as *Laurus Nobilis* (1909) combines aesthetic essay with personal reminiscences of 'spiritual' experience.[13]

The apparatus of *The Autobiography of Mark Rutherford* is not in itself new. Nick Groom sees it as a continuation of an earlier fashion, in which 'Many early eighteenth-century novels called themselves "histories" or "lives" and were framed with prefaces disengaging the writer from the work, or claiming that a manuscript had been "found" (usually in a peculiar place), or that the work had been edited from the papers of a friend.'[14] But the 'Rutherford' phenomenon is different in several ways: not just because of the repeated use of the same device and pseudonym; but also because the kind of life narrated is different: less picaresque; unexceptional in external events, but striking only for its psychological focus; and because it has the feel of authentic autobiography rather than fiction. What happens in a case like Hale White's—and it's indicative of much turn of the century autobiography—is that the inner life seems to have split off from the outer. People no longer feel that a record of the outer life will answer to their sense of selfhood. It's common to refer to this epoch of increasing interest in psychology; and of the birth of psychoanalysis, as the 'inward turn' (though we also need to see it as the end of a longer process beginning with Romanticism). Autobiography turns inward too; but the effect of that turn is not only to produce more personal, intimate stories, but to produce more fictional ones. It's another phase of profound creative uncertainty about life-writing, comparable to that which produced the great Romantic experiments in autobiography by Rousseau, Wordsworth, Goethe, and De Quincey. And perhaps, like Romanticism, it also reflects a transformation of belief in the supernatural. As Victorian agnosticism begins to bite, writers like Hale White beginning to doubt their

---

[13] Vernon Lee, *Laurus Nobilis: Chapters on Art and Life* (London: John Lane, The Bodley Head, 1909). See for example p. 119, on the effect of 'pleasant memories': 'Such moments, such modes of being, ought to be precious to us; they and every impression, physical, moral, æsthetic, which is akin to them, and we should recognise their moral worth. Since it would seem that even mere bodily sensations [. . .] accustom us not merely to health of our body, but also, by the analogies of our inner workings, to health of our soul.'

[14] Groom, *The Forger's Shadow* (London: Picador, 2002), p. 112.

god feel that that doubt entails a doubt about themselves—about how far they can know their inner selves, and how far they can trust or believe their own motives. The instabilities of autobiografiction, then, can express these uncertainties about the self.

Mark Rutherford's Deliverance is intriguingly characteristic of this method. As with many of the works studied here, the title-page—a key site for the notion of autobiography as a contractual enterprise, as posited by Philippe Lejeune—deserves a close look: 'Mark / Rutherford's / Deliverance / Being / The Second Part of his Autobiography / edited by his friend / Reuben Shapcott'.[15] That of course is different from 'Deliverance / Mark Rutherford', and creates an ambiguity as to whether the book we are about to read is *Deliverance* by an author called Mark Rutherford, or a book called *Mark Rutherford's Deliverance*. Even if the latter, it is still presumed to be by Rutherford, since edited by his friend. But this second possibility raises a further ambiguity. Is it Deliverance *by* Mark Rutherford, or the Deliverance *of* Mark Rutherford? If the latter, then who has given it that title? Certainly it could be 'Rutherford' himself, writing about himself in the third person—which, as we shall see, is itself a significant strategy particularly at this period. Or is it a title given to the book by the editor, commenting on the significance his labours have let the work reveal? After all, in a sense it is Shapcott's supposed editorial labours that have delivered Rutherford's autobiography to the publisher, and thus to the public.

The *Deliverance* begins with an 'Editor's Note' at the start, saying that he wishes to correct a misunderstanding. 'It has been supposed that I set him up as hero'; whereas, Shapcott says:

This is the very last thing I should have thought of doing. I always knew him to be weak, the victim of impressions, especially of self-created impressions; and I always pitied him for his propensity to entangle himself in problems which he had not the power to solve [. . .] But I knew also he had great qualities.[16]

The phrase 'self-created impressions' evinces just the kind of ontological uncertainty it describes. The editor means the impressions of the world that were the projections of Rutherford's mind, and which made life seem more depressing than it is; but the author recognizes how 'self-created impressions' are impressions the self creates of itself too: the element in which autobiografiction lives. As we shall see in several of the authors discussed in later chapters, autobiografiction provokes precisely this uncertainty and anxiety. Self-creation is both a liberation, and, as Pater foresuffered, a prison. (After all, part of Rutherford's depression stems from the feeling that it isn't just the world that seems without hope, but himself as well.) Such anxiety produces a corresponding anxiety as to the impression the self created by autobiografiction might make on its readers. We shall also see more such prefatory comments in which fictional editors worry

---

[15] London: Trübner, 1885.   [16] First edition, 1885, p. [vii].

whether they have created the right impression. Such anxiety might itself be symptomatic of a further ontological uncertainty. If it expresses concern about the dangers of autobiografiction being misread, it could equally be seen as a realistic device particularly suited to fictions presented in the form of edited life-writing: creating the impression of the self of the anxious editor, wanting to create the right impression of his anxious subject. 'Shapcott' had ventured a judgement on Rutherford at the end of the first edition of the first volume, saying: 'I will just add what my opinion of Rutherford was up to this point in his life. He was emphatically the child of his time [. . .] The old order of things had gone, and a new order of things had not arisen [. . .]'.[17] But this was cut for subsequent editions. Perhaps White felt it made him sound too like the hero of a novel. Or perhaps he felt it would have jarred slightly against the more critical preface to the second installment, when they were published together in 1888.

After some 160 pages of the *Deliverance*, the narrative ends, and is followed by a note signed 'R. S.' explaining how his friend died of an 'unsuspected disease of the heart', exacerbated by his violent employer. The note ends:

> On looking over his papers, I found the sketch of his life and a mass of odds and ends, some apparently written for publication. Many of these had evidently been in envelopes, and had most likely, therefore, been offered to editors or publishers, but all, I am sure, had been refused. I add one or two by way of appendix, and hope they will be thought worth saving.[18]

It is a cunning strategy, repeated from the *Autobiography*, capitalizing on its success, and allowing White to continue producing bits of Rutherford's literary remains indefinitely. The 'one or two' odds and ends appended to the *Deliverance* are two essays, 'Notes on the Book of Job', and 'Principles'. Their topics clearly supplement the spiritual questions of the autobiography. But when the two volumes of the *Autobiography* were combined into one, for the second edition of 1888, a third short piece, 'A Mysterious Portrait', was added. This is more oblique in relation to the volume; more like a short story.

It is cast as a reminiscence about a bachelor friend. Rutherford visits him late in life, and admires the portrait on his study wall of 'a singularly lovely woman'.[19] Noticing Rutherford's interest, the friend tells the story of the picture. One night in 1817 he was riding in a coach, fell asleep, and woke up to find a lady in the opposite corner. He is too struck by her to be able to start a conversation, and when he next comes round, she has gone. No one else saw her; the guard says no-one had got on or off since the last stop, and he must have been dreaming. The friend doubts this, and says he had never 'suffered from

---

[17] The Libris edition of the *Autobiography* (London, 1988) restores this passage, on pp. 119–20.

[18] *Mark Rutherford's Deliverance*, p. 163.

[19] 'A Mysterious Portrait', in *The Autobiography of Mark Rutherford and Mark Rutherford's Deliverance* (London: Trübner & Co., 1888), p. 313.

ghost-like visitations'.[20] What's more, her blue neckerchief is in the coach. Later he makes enquiries in the neighbourhood, but can find no other trace of the woman. Though he was 'smitten' by her, the impression appears to fade. He prospers, gets engaged, is ruined, gets dis-engaged. Years later he has to make the same journey, and still suffering from 'my ancient enemy—the weakness in the chest', again travels by coach.[21] The repetition brings back the memory. And when he arrives in Newcastle, he catches sight of the woman again in the street. He follows her. She goes into a bookshop. But when he goes in two minutes later, she has disappeared, and again no one else has seen her there. He is devastated, and doubts 'whether my brain was actually sound or not'.[22] For a time he is 'completely broken'.[23] His obsession with what he calls his 'spectral friend—if spectre she was' comes to dominate his existence, and prevents him from further involvement with any other or actual woman.[24] Then he visits the Academy in London, and is amazed to find exhibited there a drawing of her face. He tracks down the artist to try to discover her identity. When he asks who sat for it, the artist replies: 'Nobody'; 'it was a mere fancy sketch'.[25]

It's an effective story, whose early nineteenth-century setting suits its Romantic emphases on passion, dreams, visions, and the possibility of the supernatural. Its engagement with the idea of the imaginary portrait, though, is very much of the *fin de siècle*. It conducts this on two levels. The bachelor is an imaginary portrait. It may draw upon White's feelings (he wouldn't have been the first man to have been haunted by a memory of a beautiful woman), but not upon the biographical facts of his life: he was certainly no bachelor, having married his first wife when he was twenty-five. The imaginary portrait of the bachelor contains the imaginary portrait of a woman, in a double sense: not only a portrait of a subject who doesn't actually exist; but a portrait conceived by its artist as a representation of an imaginary woman.

The story is powerfully suggestive, and one thing it suggests is a kind of allegory about art—that the idealization or fictionalization of art can satisfy our desires in an ideal way which any actual object cannot. The bachelor can live with the portrait, but his encounter with the possibly spectral woman has left him uninterested in any other women. (Rutherford's *Autobiography* tells us how much he valued what he calls 'purity of life', meaning abstinence from sexual indulgence.)[26]

Whatever its signification, it is a curious note on which to end the volumes containing the autobiography. Its inclusion and positioning raise the question of whether White had something else in mind other than merely to present an impersonation of someone's haphazard literary remains. What if the structure of the eventual complete *Autobiography* is careful crafted by White, behind the mask of the loyal (but no less spectral) friend and editor Shapcott? The reason for

---

[20] Ibid., p. 315. [21] Ibid., p. 318. [22] Ibid., p. 319. [23] Ibid., p. 319.
[24] Ibid., p. 321. [25] Ibid., p. 322. [26] *Autobiography*, p. 10.

asking this question is that 'A Mysterious Portrait' is a different kind of text from the *Autobiography* or the other two pieces: it is more evidently fictional. True, it goes through the motions of purporting to be an autobiographical reminiscence about 'Rutherford''s bachelor friend. But it has the feel of a mysterious romantic tale that sets it apart from the rest of the two volumes.

This leads one to ask what difference it makes to those volumes. What is the relationship between 'A Mysterious Portrait' and the *Autobiography*? Even to pose that question is to suggest one answer: that the story somehow reflects, or comments upon, or allegorizes, the *Autobiography*; that the *Autobiography* is in its own way a 'mysterious portrait', and that the story can be read as an allegory for the identity of 'Rutherford' too: someone who doesn't actually exist, but who (being a work of art) can have a greater effect on his readers than any actual reminiscers. According to this view, the *Autobiography* is a 'mysterious portrait' not only because 'Rutherford' too has dedicated himself to an ideal which perpetually eludes him; but also because he is a mysteriously imaginary portrait himself; a fiction; part of the period's fascination with portraits in literature as well as the visual arts; and the way they turn into what Pater called 'Imaginary Portraits'.

Including the story thus ironizes the autobiography, casting a doubt on its authenticity which is a literary equivalent of the theological doubt it retails. The story is careful to establish the grounds of the ambiguity about the woman's existence. The bachelor may have been dreaming; he may have been ill; he may have been suffering from bad nerves. Or (if we read backwards, from the vantage point of modernism's unreliable narrators), perhaps he was making it all up, after noticing his friend eyeing the picture. He says he has had it for a long time, though he hasn't shown it to the narrator before. But perhaps that isn't true. Perhaps he has just bought it, sees the narrator wondering about it and what it might reveal about the bachelor, and is thus prompted to spin him a good yarn, perhaps to mock his prurient curiosity. That is perhaps an implausibly extreme suggestion. But part of my argument is that modernism's unreliable narrators represent a development from turn-of-the-century unreliable autobiographers like 'Rutherford'. Scepticism about the woman's existence mirrors scepticism *in* the *Autobiography*. It also opens up the possibility of scepticism *about* the *Autobiography*; that it too may be a fiction. If the *Autobiography* is fictional, then so is the story of 'A Mysterious Portrait', which is after all told as by the same narrator. Conversely, once one entertains doubts about the existence of 'Rutherford', one is suspecting the unreliability of the narration. And once that possibility is granted, why stop at the level of doubting Rutherford's claim to be simply recounting what his bachelor friend said; why not also doubt what the bachelor says? One effect of adding this story is thus to convert the *Autobiography* and *Mark Rutherford's Deliverance* into something more like volumes of imaginary portraits: of Rutherford; of Shapcott; of the bachelor.

The story ironizes the *Autobiography* in this general way, subjecting it all to a sceptical distancing. Once it is considered as fictionalized, more specific ironies emerge, particularly where it claims to be honest. For example, while he is largely dismissive of the value of his education, 'Rutherford' says that it nonetheless conferred the advantage of 'a rigid regard for truthfulness'.[27] Yet the fictionalizing of an autobiography suggests a more flexible regard for truthfulness. If such narrative ambiguities seem like the postmodern games of metafiction, it is because they provide important antecedents for postmodernism too. But there is more to them than that, as can be seen in a crucial passage from 'A Mysterious Portrait'. After the bachelor sees and loses the woman for the second time and has a form of mental breakdown, he says he 'tried to take up with a science, and chose geology' while he was recovering.[28] Perhaps the methodological rigour of geology, and the solidity of its materials, were supposed to ground him again. But the soundness of geology as science was precisely what was undermining to other certainties, those of religious faith—as Ruskin, another enthusiastic amateur geologist had found:

You speak of the Flimsiness of your own faith. Mine, which was never strong, is being beaten into mere gold leaf, and flutters in weak rags from the letter of its old forms; but the only letters it can hold by at all are the old Evangelical formulae. If only the Geologists would let me alone, I could do very well, but those dreadful Hammers! I hear the clink of them at the end of every cadence of the Bible verses.[29]

That was in 1851. If the geologists seemed to be chipping away at the biblical tables of time eight years before the publication of *On the Origin of Species*, how much more disturbing must those hammers have been by the 1880s? By putting a story about someone turning to geology alongside the autobiography of a doubting minister, White was proffering a rather secular tract for the times, perhaps. The bachelor isolated from human sympathy is an allegory for mankind isolated from belief in divine sympathy. Subjectivism emerges as belief in god atomizes, because a god who could know what we feel would guarantee the objectivity of those feelings; would act as the universal other to whom everybody could express their feeling and reading and thinking. Without that reassuring sense of an audience; a transcendental other in which to confide, to whom to confess, the sense of self becomes insecure. This, ultimately, is why it is in the late nineteenth century that we find this re-emergence of forms of auto/biographical displacement—in fictionalized, anonymized, or otherwise impersonalized auto-biography such as White's; in imaginary portraiture; and in imaginary creativity.

---

[27] *Autobiography*, p. 10.
[28] 'A Mysterious Portrait', p. 319.
[29] Ruskin to Henry Acland, 24 May [1851], *The Letters of John Ruskin: 1827–1869*, Library Edition, ed. Cook and Wedderburn, vol. 36 (London: George Allen, 1909), pp. 114–15 (p. 115).

'Mark Rutherford', then, is significant as a representative of Victorian agnosticism and secularization. As Charles Swann indicates, 'One modern orthodoxy
has situated the *Autobiography* in that good old Victorian tradition, novels of
faith and doubt, novels that are frequently semi-autobiographical', such as J. A.
Froude's *Nemesis of Faith* (1849), or W. D. Arnold's *Oakfield; or, Fellowship in
the East* (1853).[30] Don Cupitt, for example, is representative of this 'orthodoxy',
claiming in his Introduction to a modern edition that to its first readers of 1881,
the *Autobiography* was 'obviously a *Bildungsroman*, a novel describing an individual's character development and spiritual pilgrimage'.[31] Yet how wrong this is
can be seen from the third edition of 1889, which appends quotations from
contemporary reviews: one page of comments on the *Autobiography*, which seem
to assume its truth as autobiography; followed by one page of comments on the
Deliverance, which are not so sure. William Dean Howells, assessing both
volumes for *Harper's Magazine*, for example, said the books 'may yet mark a
new era in English fiction', only to add: 'We hardly know, indeed, whether to call
them fiction, they carry so deep a sense of truthfulness [...]'.[32] He describes
them as 'by an unknown hand', indicating that the *Westminster Review*'s identification of White had not become widely known.

White is thus also significant for signalling a disturbance in the sense of the
autobiographic: a sense that autobiography has begun to seem a genre that
requires the qualifier 'so-called' before it. He has a further significance for our
purposes, in combining imaginary self-portraiture with other forms of imaginary
portrait. Auto/biography has never been entirely untroubled, assuredly. The
pseudo-autobiographies and pseudo-epistles that constitute many of the best
eighteenth-century novels testify as much, as do the pseudonymous pseudo-
autobiographies by Charlotte Brontë, *Jane Eyre* and *Villette*. In the first edition,
Jane Eyre's narrative is doubly displaced: '*Jane Eyre: An Autobiography* / Edited
by Currer Bell'.[33] Even the mid-nineteenth-century precursors in spiritual crisis
narratives are also precursors in troubling the identity between author and
autobiography. Both *Nemesis* and *Oakfield* have fictionalized Shapcott-type
editorial figures; and the first edition of Oakfield was published under the
orientally displaced pseudonym of 'Punjabee'.[34] However, it is the argument of
this chapter that disturbance of the auto/biographic returns with particular force
at the turn of the century, from about 1880 to 1930. It isn't that it withdraws

---

[30] Swann, 'Autobiografiction', p. 24.
[31] Cupitt, Introduction, in *The Autobiography of Mark Rutherford and Mark Rutherford's
Deliverance*, p. [vii].
[32] *The Autobiography of Mark Rutherford and Mark Rutherford's Deliverance* (London: Trübner &
Co., 1889), pp. [327–8]. Howells's review (not attributed in the third edition of the *Autobiography*)
is from his column 'The Editor's Study': 'Two Remarkable Examples of Sincerity in Fiction', *Harper's*,
72 (1886), 485–6.
[33] *Jane Eyre* (London: Smith, Elder, 1847).
[34] *Oakfield: Or, Fellowship in the East*. By Punjabee, 2 vols (London: Longman, 1853).

thereafter; rather, that it takes different forms as modernism turns into post-modernism. What distinguishes the *fin de siècle* disturbance can be seen when pseudonymity such as 'Rutherford''s is taken alongside other forms of authorial displacement: shift of person; anonymity; or even deferral of publication. Just as Trollope needs to distance himself from autobiography, by calling it 'so-called', so a surprising number of authors find comparable ways to displace autobiography. It is a striking fact that much of the classic auto/biographical writing of this period involves just such authorial displacement.

These disturbances and displacements relate to the development traced in the last chapter, of an 'aesthetic' sense of life and life-writing. As the forms of life-writing become uncomfortably visible—begin, that is, to feel like clichés, and to that extent, distortions of real lived experience—writers become more conscious of the constructedness of written lives; of their artistry. This can involve two related perceptions: seeing one's own life as a work of art; and becoming conscious of the act of telling it as drawing on the resources of art. Though no aesthete, White found the fictionalizing of his literary identity congenial; its ambiguities echoing his religious doubt.[35]

The plot of *The Autobiography of Mark Rutherford* is essentially that also used by other classic *fin de siècle* autobiographical books, such as Samuel Butler's *The Way of All Flesh*, and Edmund Gosse's *Father and Son*, and represents a radical transformation of the conversion narrative: the narrative of 'de-conversion'; of the turn away from the faith of the Victorian Father, as in Mill's move away from his father's narrow Benthamite Utilitarianism to embrace the cultivation of the self through literature.[36] Such Oedipal complexities persist into the post-Freudian twentieth century, though the paradigm is as often the turn from rationalism as from religion, as in Mill's or Yeats's conflict with their fathers' Utilitarianism, or Ford's with his father's Germanic academicism. What so many twentieth-century literary autobiographies have in common—whether they are turning away from religion or rationalism—is their telling the story of the turn towards an art of consciousness. It may seem perverse to describe it as also a turn towards a 'religion of consciousness', when so many of our writers are abandoning orthodox faith.[37] But as 'Rutherford' explained—in one of several 'literary remains'-type books published before Hale White's death—Victorian agnosticism involved not just doubt about Christianity but the attempt to find or construct alternative beliefs for oneself: 'A religion is but a general direction, and the real working Thirty-nine Articles or Assembly's Catechism

[35] Swann, 'Autobiografiction', p. 37, suggests doubt about the status of the text as fact or fiction makes it 'a real text of faith and doubt.'

[36] See John D. Barbour, *Versions of Deconversion: Autobiography and the Loss of Faith* (Charlottesville: University Press of Virginia, 1994).

[37] For example, the phrase is used of Henry James, by F. O. Matthiessen in *Henry James: The Major Phase*; reviewed by Robert B. Heilman, *New England Quarterly*, 18:2 (1945), 268–71 (p. 269).

each one of us has to construct on his own behalf.'[38] It isn't just that autobiography in this period is drawn towards the story of deconversion; but that in the wake of deconversion, hope is offered by the religion of auto/biography. In another passage from the same entry in *More Pages from a Journal*, headed 'Ourselves', Rutherford writes of biography as having the power to create the human, body and soul:

If we devote ourselves, for example, to the works and biography of any great man, the pleasure and moral effect come when we have read him and re-read him and have traced every thread we can find, connecting him with his contemporaries. It is then, and then only, that we understand him and he becomes a living soul. Flesh and blood are given by details.[39]

This appears to be a typical Carlylean justification of the value of biography. But when we read it in the context of 'Rutherford''s fictional authorship, what then? Since the *Autobiography* has pseudonymized not only Hale White but his actual contemporaries (such as George Eliot), and thus frustrated attempts to connect him with them; and since the 'details' it gives are often fictionalized; then such a definition appears to negate the truth of value of reading 'Rutherford'.

When Basil Willey wrote his influential chapter on 'Mark Rutherford' in *More Nineteenth-Century Studies* he placed him amongst what his subtitle called *A Group of Honest Doubters*. He values Hale White for his 'intellectual honesty', and though he notes of the account of his life after his expulsion from New College 'The *Autobiography* and the *Early Life* give differing accounts of this period', he doesn't seem to think that Hale White's fictionalizing of events undermines his book's honesty.[40] This is partly because he reads the book as centrally concerned with 'ideas and beliefs'. Honesty of intellect is what matters, rather than autobiographical verifiability. He demonstrates, perhaps, his own form of intellectual scruple in continuing to worry at the relation between ideas and autobiography, however. 'Why so much biographical detail in a book purporting to deal with ideas and beliefs rather than with people?' he asks. And his answer appears to go back on its earlier separation of intellectual and factual veracity:

It is because with Mark Rutherford the man and the beliefs are inseparable. In his lifelong toil of rebuilding a workable new faith from the ruins of the old, he had no other cement with which to bind its fragments than what his own experience, inward and outward,

---

[38] 'Mark Rutherford', *More Pages from a Journal: with Other Papers* (London: Oxford University Press, 1910), p. 178.
[39] Ibid., pp. 176–8 (p. 177).
[40] Willey, *More Nineteenth-Century Studies* (Cambridge: Cambridge University Press, 1980), pp. 200, 203.

could supply. In this he is representative of a half-century which, if it did not abandon faith entirely, had to do just this [...][41]

Though Willey makes an eloquent case for Hale White's importance, it sounds dated now, and bears the impress of its milieu. For a History of Ideas man, writing in 1956 in a Cambridge where the widespread acceptance of Practical Criticism had displaced an interest in biography, the relation between thought and experience might seem strange. The point is that the ideas are not just ideas for Hale White or his contemporaries, but ideas about how to live, and why. But this seems less surprising than the way Willey makes his case by entirely suppressing the element of fictionality in the *Autobiography*: the pseudonymity; the fiction of posthumous editing; the reshaping of outward experience, certainly, if not inward experience too. One can see why. Concede that Hale White changed the facts of his experience, and the argument that that experience offered the only 'cement' to bind together his fragments of faith collapses. The experience wasn't the only cement, since he could make up different experience. The man and the beliefs are not inseparable if the man could fictionalize the story of how he arrived at those beliefs.

Certainly Hale White was himself preoccupied with the questions of honesty and sincerity. In a posthumously-published paper on William Sewell's *Christian Morals*, he wrote:

Lastly, the book provokes an examination of that virtue which we call sincerity [...] His insincerity, so far as it proceeds from an earnest wish to prove what he holds to be true and of the utmost moment, may be a virtue compared with the indifference of his critics. Always, when a man devotes himself to an idea or a cause, does the temptation to dishonest advocacy present itself.

What is the test of insincerity? In gross cases its detection is easy, but who by an unfailing rule shall determine its presence in its most insinuating and dangerous form?[42]

Since the *Autobiography* is very much the story of a man detaching himself from 'an idea or a cause', its author passes his own test of sincerity. Yet 'What is the test of insincerity' in an autobiography in which the author alters his story and disguises his name? Autobiografiction, that is, itself 'provokes an examination of that virtue which we call sincerity', since it is itself an 'insinuating' form, 'dangerous', if not morally, certainly to our sense of the securities of auto/biography.

I accept that 'Rutherford' is important, and representative. But my argument is that he is representative as much for his move towards fictionalizing his autobiography as for his expression of honest doubt. Or, more accurately, he is important for the way his living of doubt also casts doubt on the form of autobiography; on the authority of narrative to narrate that very doubt. Willey argues that because religious doubt was so devastating, Hale White had to ground a new sense of self and belief in 'biographical detail'. But to ignore how that biographical detail is also subject to doubt, is to miss one of the main grounds of his representativeness. The question to ask, it seems to me, is not 'Why so much biographical detail' in a book purporting to be about ideas, as 'Why so much fiction' in a book purporting to be autobiography? The meditations on doubt in the *Autobiography* go so deep, I would argue, that they expose the way in which the dissolution of belief systems undermines the epistemology of the self too—its sense of coherence and integrity. Hale White's use of the persona is more than a ploy of self-protection. It is an expression of how that self is no longer protected from doubts about itself. Yes, the *Autobiography* is grounded in biographical experience because experience is all we have; but also because we're no longer sure we really have that either. The self has become problematic, and the problematic form of semi-fictionalized autobiography expresses Hale White's sense of no longer being secure in his own subjectivity. The way 'Rutherford' expresses Hale White's 'honest doubt' is by exploring the dubious faith offered by a semi-fictionalized autobiography. The form produces a comparable doubt in its readers too. The uncertainty of the book's first critics over whether to categorize it as autobiography or fiction bears out De Man's characterization of autobiography as a mode of reading, and suggest that autobiografiction, too, is in the eye of the beholder.[43]

GEORGE GISSING, MORLEY ROBERTS, AND H. G. WELLS

Yet there is another possible explanation for Willey's disattention to the significance of 'Rutherford''s fictionality, and this is very much of its time. To demonstrate this I want to adduce another example, this time a biographical rather than autobiographical work, from later in our period: *The Private Life of Henry Maitland: A Record Dictated by J. H.: Revised and Edited by Morley Roberts*. It was first published in 1912, and bore the following Preface, which is worth quoting at length:

This book was dictated by J. H. mostly in my presence, and I consider it well worth publishing. No doubt Henry Maitland is not famous, though since his death a great deal

---

[43] See Swann, 'Autobiografiction', p. 23. Where the *Athenaeum* (23 April 1881), 555, confidently reviewed it under the heading 'Novels of the Week', the New York *Nation* (2 June 1881), 392–3, hesitated between reading it as an as 'actual autobiography' or a 'work of the imagination' in the tradition of *Robinson Crusoe*. Swann observes that by contrast: 'Critics had no difficulty in deciding that Gissing's *The Private Papers of Henry Ryecroft* (however autobiographical) was a fiction'; p. 33.

has been written of him. Much of it, outside of literary criticism, has been futile, false, and uninstructed. But J. H. really knew the man, and here is what he said of him. We shall be told, no doubt, that we have used Maitland's memory for our own ends [. . .] Here is a writing man put down, crudely it may be, but with a certain power. There is no book quite like it in the English tongue, and the critic may take what advantage he will of that opening for his wit. At any rate we have a portrait emerging which is real. Henry Maitland stands on his feet, and on his living feet. He is not a British statue done in the best mortuary manner. There is far too little sincere biography in English. We are a mealy-mouthed race, hypocrites by the grave and the monument [. . .] In the whole book, which cannot be published now, there are things worth waiting for. I have cut and retrenched with pain, for I wanted to risk the whole, but no writer or editor is his own master in England. I am content to have omitted some truth if I have permitted nothing false [. . .] Here is life, not a story or a constructed diary, and the art with which it is done is a secondary matter [. . .] The full manuscript, which may possibly be published after some years, is, in the meantime, placed in safe custody.

MORLEY ROBERTS[44]

As Jacob Korg says: 'no one seems to have been in any doubt whatever as to the real identity of "Henry Maitland" or most of the other thinly disguised perso-nages in the book'.[45] For 'Henry Maitland' was understood to be a portrait of Roberts's friend George Gissing. Ford Madox Ford, for example, was writing only two years later as if this were common knowledge. He thought it 'a bitter bad book', not because it 'gave away a number of the confidences of poor dead Gissing' or 'may have inconvenienced several other people too'—'You must not have to do with authors unless you are prepared to have that sort of thing happen to you; that is all there is to it'—but because of what he sees as its lack of 'imagination' and 'invention'.[46] Ford's standard of how far auto/biography should imagine and invent tended to exceed that of his contemporaries. But his point is that it is a novel—like others, he saw the fictionality of Roberts's claim to be the editor rather than the author—and fails by this standard. Others, such as H. G. Wells, criticized the inaccuracy of Roberts's book; though he too described it as a novel.[47] Frank Swinnerton's study of Gissing had also been published in the same year as Roberts's *Private Life*, and may have helped readers

---

[44] *The Private Life of Henry Maitland* (London: Eveleigh Nash, 1912), pp. vii–xi. The book was reissued, once before Willey's discussion of 'Mark Rutherford'—Roberts revised it for a second edition, published by Nash & Grayson in 1923—and then just two years after the publication of Willey's book—a new edition, using the latter text, with notes by Morchard Bishop (itself a pseudonym, for the novelist Oliver Stonor), was published by the Richards Press in 1958, with the subtitle 'A portrait of George Gissing'. So although Willey doesn't discuss it, and I can't prove he had it in mind, the book remained visible for long enough for this to be probable. The Kessinger Publishing Co.'s 2004 reprint keeps Maitland's name in the title but substitute's Gissing's in the text.
[45] Korg, *George Gissing: A Critical Biography* (Brighton: Harvester, 1980), p. 47.
[46] 'Literary Portraits—XXVIII. Mr. Morley Roberts and *Time and Thomas Waring*', *Outlook*, 33 (1914), 390–1.
[47] H. G. Wells, *Experiment in Autobiography: Discoveries and Conclusions of a Very Ordinary Brain (since 1866)* (London: Victor Gollancz and the Cresset Press, 1934), vol. 2, p. 567.

to make the identification. More recent critics have continued to accept it as essentially a biographical portrait, and to warn about its inaccuracy.[48]

However one categorizes it generically—biography, fictionalized biography, biographical novel, *roman à clef,* novel—it bears striking formal similarities to the *Autobiography of Mark Rutherford.* The central figure's name is altered. The text is said to be edited from a manuscript. In each case the text is produced with the aid of a fictional intermediary: Shapcott the editor; 'J. H.' who dictates Maitland's story.

Why did Roberts present his material in this form? In part, the answer will depend on a decision about genre. If it's read as a novel, the name-change is an assertion of its independence from fact. If a biography, then the reasons would probably be to do with tact. Gissing had died only a few years before, in 1903. It may have seemed too soon after his death; potentially too hurtful to surviving family, friends, or fellow-litterateurs, to identify the story as Gissing's. But then of course that raises another question. If it's a biography, but can only tactfully be published in a form which conceals the identity of the subject, why publish it at all? Or doesn't publication on these terms recategorize it as a novel?

I shall return to these questions, but first want to suggest that this way of reading it—as actually about Gissing, but for some reason thinly veiling his identity—was perhaps how Willey was reading the *Autobiography of Mark Rutherford*: as written according to a convention that certain auto/biographical subjects required a tactful disguise, but one which the cognoscenti could easily decode. It might, then, have been such a logic that made it possible to read 'Rutherford' in the 1950s as unproblematically an instance of autobiography and intellectual honesty.

By contrast, the *Private Life* pushes this strategy so far it begins to look like something quite other. It doesn't shirk from telling the more sensational aspects of Gissing's biography which would still have been shocking to the Edwardian bourgeoisie. In it Roberts, or J. H.,

describes the quixotic youth stealing to help the prostitute he loves, his poverty in America, his miserable life as a hack writer and teacher with an alcoholic wife in London lodgings, his opinions on contemporary literature and literary life, his odd attitude to women, loathing of imperialism, disastrous second marriage, and last idyll with his French translator.[49]

So there's a cornucopia of reasons why Gissing's name and intimates might need or prefer to be protected from scandal. Yet the invocation of such tact seems disingenuous. To tell such a story, and to insist in the Preface that it's a true story,

---

[48] Adrian Poole, for example, simply includes it in a list of 'the basic works of biography': *Gissing in Context* (Basingstoke: Macmillan, 1975), p. xi. Swinnerton, *George Gissing: A Critical Study* (London: Martin Secker, 1912).
[49] Sandra Kemp, Charlotte Mitchell, and David Trotter, *Edwardian Fiction: An Oxford Companion* (Oxford: Oxford University Press, 1997), p. 344.

that J. H. knew the subject well, that it's based on a real manuscript, which is even more shocking and required censorship—these are all incitements to a prurient curiosity; designed to increase publicity and sales, by tantalizing its readers about who Maitland might really be, and what else he might have done. The idea of tactful disguise, in this reading, is invoked in bad faith. It is itself a fiction, since the disguise is ultimately no disguise—as the reception of the book demonstrated. To say this is to read the book as a *roman à clef,* in which the author bases characters on real people and intends readers to be able to identify them.[50] What's odd about this possibility is that the *roman à clef* generally has some satiric aim; whereas that doesn't seem to have been the purpose of the *Private Life.*

Roberts's complaint that 'We are a mealy-mouthed race, hypocrites by the grave and the monument' is another example of bad faith, since the book requires that attitude to achieve the prurient reaction it seeks. But it emerges from an argument about the state of British biography which anticipates the Bloomsbury version of 'The New Biography', discussed in Chapter 11. Or, to put it another way, Roberts's attack on British hypocrisy indicates that he has bad faith in his readers; that he doesn't trust them not to condemn Gissing the man for the facts of his life, whereas they will be more prepared to countenance them in the guise of fiction. He was probably right, but it means that whereas 'Rutherford' is (as Basil Willey says) Hale White's alter ego—an externalization of what he mistrusted in himself—the disguises of 'Maitland' and 'J. H.' are both mere mechanisms of self-exculpation. Gissing is not to be blamed for his life, because 'Maitland' is fictional. Roberts is not to be blamed for writing a tribute to such a fellow, because 'J. H.' dictated it.

What I have described as 'bad faith' might be more sympathetically viewed as a predicament in which Roberts feels the ground of biography shifting under his feet as he writes it. Take the notion of the 'Private Life' in his title. This, too, could be read as a promise of salacious revelations. Yet it could be seen, conversely, as indicative of the drive behind most of the life-writing studied here: to prioritize the inner life over the outer, public one; to give the core of the man, what he really cared about, rather than the official pieties of the obituary or Official Biography—what Roberts calls the 'mortuary manner'. 'But then comes the Official Biography [. . .] and the poor man dies', wrote Ford, 'no man being willing to read an author's books when he can read salacious, moral, or merely imbecile details about the Great Man's [. . .] say, affection for his doggie-

---

[50] Conrad, for example, appears to have associated Roberts with the *roman à clef.* In a letter to Edward Garnett, 26 March 1900, he describes his aim in collaborating with Ford on *The Inheritors* as follows: 'I set myself to look upon the thing as a sort of skit upon the political (?!) novel, fools of the Morley Roberts sort do write.' His editors cite Roberts's novel *The Colossus: A Story of To-Day* (1899) as an example: *The Collected Letters of Joseph Conrad,* ed. Frederick Karl and Laurence Davies, vol. 2 (Cambridge: Cambridge University Press, 1986), p. 257.

doggies'.[51] Whereas Morley's Preface asserts that by transgressing the proprieties of conventional biography he has enabled 'Maitland' to stand 'on his feet, and on his living feet'. By presenting his biography with an admixture of fiction, then, he hopes to heighten its reality. Yet this too is an aesthetically double-jointed strategy. 'Here is life, not a story or a constructed diary, and the art with which it is done is a secondary matter.' True, it's basically Gissing's actual story, not a made-up story about a made-up character. Yet it isn't exactly 'life' either; it violates one fundamental principle of biography: giving the subject its proper name; and it fictionalizes the process of its composition, transposing Roberts's writing of a biography into his writing down of a dictated memoir by someone else. Why, then, does he interpose the figure of 'J. H.'? If this is a part of the art he has used, why say it is 'a secondary matter' just as he is placing it at the head of the book? The obvious answer is that 'J. H.' is a device which enables him to write a more direct, un-mealy-mouthed biography than would be acceptable if appearing to come from his own person. By distancing himself from the composition, he can write in a more explicit way than readers of conventional biography would expect. To put it crudely, he can put it 'crudely'. When he says the 'art with which it is done is a secondary matter', he is defending an apparent artlessness: 'In this almost childishly simple account of a man's life there is the essence of a literary epoch. Here is a writing man put down, crudely it may be, but with a certain power.' The crucial word here, working to redeem the idea of any 'crudeness', is 'power': the compensation of lack of sophistication. Using the word 'childishly' is probably also a pre-emptive move against critics disturbed by the book's explicitness about sexuality and criminality, asserting a fundamental innocence in the telling. This power and innocence, it is claimed, constitute its originality: 'There is no book quite like it in the English tongue.' The account which offers 'the essence of a literary epoch' stakes its claim to make an epoch itself.

This of course constitutes an argument for Roberts's art behind 'J. H.''s apparent artlessness; which then subverts his statement that 'the art with which it is done is a secondary matter'. Personally I am not making high claims for Roberts as an artist. His fictionalizing of the book's utterance, as 'J. H.''s, is as subject to the criticism of bad faith as the other tropes in it already discussed. He does not sustain the fictionalization with the imagination and invention of Joyce presenting Stephen Dedalus; or of Stein pretending Alice B. Toklas has written her autobiography; or of Woolf's extended parody of biographical conventions in *Orlando*. But when the *Private Life* is read alongside the *Autobiography of Mark Rutherford*, its significance, its representativeness, becomes clear. Like 'Mark Rutherford', 'Henry Maitland' responds to a disturbance in the practices of auto/biography. Both works manifest the turn towards an increasing fictionalization of life-writing; towards the aestheticization of auto/biography; towards

---

[51] Letter to the Editor of the *American Mercury* [November 1936]: *Letters of Ford Madox Ford*, ed. Richard Ludwig (Princeton: Princeton University Press, 1965), pp. 265–7 (at p. 267).

auto/biografiction. They do not take this process as far as to their modernist successors, certainly. What Willey says of Hale White could apply to either man: 'If he could not take life as an art, neither could he take art as a life.'[52] But I am arguing for a view of Hale White as more of an aesthete in his view of the presentation of a life, and suggesting that it is only by disattending to the context he provides for 'Rutherford''s autobiography—the machinery of fictional manuscript and editor, the publication together with a fiction such as 'A Mysterious Portrait'—that he could be seen otherwise. Certainly, like Gissing, he had the cultural sensibility to recognize that his was a period of turbulence in auto/ biographical forms; and to grasp how this turbulence offered new narrative possibilities.

Perhaps the best gloss one could put on Roberts's book is that *The Private Life of Henry Maitland* is a form of homage to Gissing's own experiment in making play with life-writing: *The Private Papers of Henry Ryecroft* (1903), in which a Preface, signed by 'G. G.' purports to introduce a selection from Ryecroft's journals, written after a friend bequeathed him an annuity, and he was able to retire from his work as a struggling hack-writer. Ryecroft, who is said to have died a year earlier, is described as having been sensitive and reticent, someone who 'shrank from argument, from self-assertion'. 'G. G.' finds that after reading the three manuscript volumes, which were 'Assuredly [. . .] not intended for the public', he knows 'the man better than before'. The journals thus are presented as giving a more direct access to the inner life. The Preface offers 'a word or two of biographical complement, just so much personal detail as may point the significance of the self-revelation here made'.[53]

In some ways the structure follows that of *The Autobiography of Mark Rutherford*. Rycroft's life is clearly close to Gissing's, as Rutherford's is to Hale White's. Both are fictionalized alter egos. Though 'G. G.' is intended to be identified as Gissing, obviously a real person, his function is similar to Hale White's fictional Shapcott, selecting, editing, prefacing, and publishing posthumously a friend's self-revelatory manuscript.[54] But where Hale White's text is fictionalized autobiography, Gissing's is an autobiographical novel, and the author was identified from the first edition as 'George Gissing'. The 'arrangement' 'G. G.' gives the selections is to organize them simply into four sections, 'Spring', 'Summer', 'Autumn', and 'Winter', to do justice to Ryecroft's feeling for the natural world. (Though he also provides an index, to sustain the fiction of presenting the material editorially.) The freedom he gives himself to re-order the original journal entries thus produces a narrative that no longer mimics autobiographical

---

[52] Willey, *More Nineteenth-Century Studies*, p. 187.

[53] Gissing, *The Private Papers of Henry Ryecroft* (London: Constable, 1928), pp. ix–xi; vii.

[54] The first edition of *The Autobiography of Mark Rutherford* did not have a preface; only the unattributed epigraph poem about a man on his deathbed. White added a Preface signed 'R. S.' for the second edition, which was included in subsequent editions.

narrative. It is, presumably, the model Roberts had in mind when he wrote of 'a constructed diary'. Or at least, *Ryecroft* produces a double effect, of autobiographical material being worked over for aesthetic reasons. But it is Ryecroft's own aesthetic sensibility, expressed in his journals, that legitimates such working-over. Gissing ends the journal-selection with a passage in which Ryecroft contemplates the passing of a year (which thus legitimates 'G. G.''s organization of the material into the cycle of a single year). Ryecroft contemplates how the sense of time passing accelerates as life becomes more familiar, and especially so for him now that he has found happiness. This resigns him to the possibility of his life having an ending:

Now, my life is rounded; it began with the natural irreflective happiness of childhood, it will close in the reasoned tranquility of the mature mind. How many a time, after long labour on some piece of writing, brought at length to its conclusions, have I laid down the pen with a sigh of thankfulness; the work was full of faults, but I had wrought sincerely, had done what time and circumstance and my own nature permitted. Even so may it be with me in my last hour. May I look back on life as a long task duly completed—a piece of biography; faulty enough, but good as I could make it—and, with no thought but one of contentment, welcome the repose to follow when I have breathed the word 'Finis.'[55]

Such an expression of self-satisfaction—however mitigated by the acknowledgement of faults—is exactly the kind of thing it would be hard for a writer of the period to voice in his or her own person. There is another kind of self-satisfaction, though, in the putative editor's choice of this passage as the conclusion. Ryecroft could not have known that the book of his journals would end with that particular enunciation of the word 'Finis'. We are supposed to feel it as a deft bit of editorial shaping—and of course of novelistic shaping behind that. But the passage is more suggestive still. What Ryecroft exhibits here is really a classic instance of aesthetic sensibility: imagining life as art; his own life as a book.[56] In which case 'self-satisfaction' is perhaps too moralistic (except for critics who want to be moralistic about the whole aesthetic project). Rather, it is a case of what one might call aesthetic 'self-appreciation'. As an autobiographical writer, the fictionalized Ryecroft thus exhibits the tendency, in aesthetic autobiographers from Ruskin to Hale White, of apprehending one's life aesthetically. From the point of view of a study of 'autobiografiction', though, the significance of the *Private Papers* is that this aesthetic autobiographical position is contained within something else: a fiction. Reading it as a novel, we are conscious that Ryecroft's wish that he will be able to look back on his life as if it were a book is shadowed by our knowledge (and

[55] *The Private Papers of Henry Ryecroft*, p. 267.
[56] Charles Swann almost makes the same case. Though he stops short of seeing Ryecroft's as an aesthetic understanding of his own life, he does see it as a form of self-alienation, arguing that Ryecroft 'views his life as a structured text, something produced rather than lived, a biography rather than an autobiography (close, indeed, to an aesthetic work), something external to Ryecroft's self': 'Autobiografiction', p. 35.

Gissing's) that that is exactly what it is. It is a book trying to be a life, rather than a life trying to be a book. The fictional use of a form of life-writing sets up a pair of facing mirrors. Fiction can impersonate the auto/biographical; but this in turn reflects back on auto/biography, as subject to the rules of art (narrativization, fictionalization, description, metaphor, selection and so on, in this case). That is to say, as the aesthetic attitude seeks to turn life into art, it increasingly wants to fictionalize auto/biography; which issues in a new composite: autobiografiction.

There are fewer similarities between *Henry Ryecroft* and *Henry Maitland* (other than their both being based on Gissing). But the similarities that exist are nonetheless important. First, 'G. G.''s Preface, telling us enough of the life to be able to read Ryecroft's writings, is a pseudo-biography—that is, a piece of writing in biographical form about a character given a fictional name. The same is true of Roberts's *Private Life*. Of course Roberts is writing about an alter ego of his friend Gissing, whereas Gissing is writing about his own alter ego. But the second point is that both exploit the play between auto/biography and fiction. Both see auto/biographical forms as newly available as resources for experiment, for short-circuiting conventional expectations of life-writing.

A final example in this chapter of how modern writers rediscovered the possibilities of pseudonymity for reimagining the writing of auto/biography comes from another friend of Gissing's, H. G. Wells. In 1915 Wells published a curiosity entitled *Boon, the Mind of the Race, the Wild Asses of the Devil, and the Last Trump*. *Boon* is perhaps best known to literary historians as the book that sparked the quarrel between Wells and Henry James, issuing in an important exchange of letters in which both writers argued for their respective aesthetic positions.[57] Not only the tone, but the entire structure of the book is high-spirited, as not only the title but the rest of the title page makes clear. It purports to be 'a First Selection from the Literary Remains of George Boon, Appropriate to the Times, Prepared for Publication by Reginald Bliss . . . with An Ambiguous Introduction by H. G. Wells'. Wells's introduction is ambiguous precisely about whether he has written the entire book or not—so much so that it was felt necessary to add a parenthetic confession to the title-page of the second edition of 1920 after his name: '(Who is in Truth the Author of the entire Book)'; and to change the spine, from '*Boon*: by: Reginald: Bliss: Introduced: by: H. G. Wells' to '*Boon*: by: H. G. Wells'. The Introduction asserts that 'Bliss is Bliss and Wells is Wells. And Bliss can write all sorts of things that Wells could not do.' But this latter sentence undermines the attempt to keep the two apart, suggesting that Wells is using Bliss as a persona, as indeed he is doing, and as was immediately apparent to readers like James, to write things he would not write in his own person. When he talks of the 'pressure of a certain intimacy between Mr. Reginald Bliss and myself', we read between the lines that the word

[57] See Leon Edel and Gordon Ray, eds, *Henry James and H. G. Wells* (London: Rupert Hart-Davis, 1959).

'intimacy' is a covert admission of identity. The ambiguous play about the relationship between Bliss and Wells in the Introduction distracts us from (and thus draws attention to) another relationship: that between Boon and Wells. For of course Boon is his alter ego too; has the same literary friends, such as James; writes books with titles that evoke Wellsean hobby-horses such as 'The Mind of the Race'.[58] Indeed, Wells's son Anthony wrote that his father 'once spoke of *Boon* as the most self-revealing thing that he ever wrote'.[59]

The playful ambiguity is sustained in the text, which begins: 'It is quite probable that the reader does not know of the death of George Boon, and that "remains" before his name upon the title-page will be greeted with a certain astonishment.'[60] Indeed. The humour is even rather black considering the fact that the book appeared during the war. Boon is said to have been working on the three books listed in the title, but appears to have been unable to finish them:

> I must confess I was monstrously disappointed when at last I could get my hands into those barrels in the attic in which Boon had stored his secret writings. There was more perhaps than I had expected; I do not complain of the quantity, but of the disorder, the incompleteness, the want of discipline and forethought.[61]

Barrels? The comic note sounds at once, not only suggesting something intoxicated in Boon's material, but also swiping at the scraping of barrels that the publication of 'literary remains' often entails. Bliss's disappointment enables Wells to distance himself from Boon's work, the chaos of which is redeemed by the order of his own. It also licenses him to quote and paraphrase selectively, rather than having to present an entire manuscript (such as *The Autobiography of Mark Rutherford*). The play with personae goes even deeper within the text, when Boon himself starts distancing himself from his own work, and invents the fictional persona of Hallery to deliver the Presidential Address to a 'World Conference' on the Mind of the Race. Bliss finds other scraps of documents together with the Address, in which Boon wonders why 'he himself didn't somehow like this Hallery that he had made'; and explains: 'I invented Hallery to get rid of myself, but, after all, Hallery is really no more than the shadow of myself [. . .]'.[62] And from there, says Bliss, 'Boon suddenly went off into absurdities'; but absurdities, we might note, which bear not only on the play

---

[58] See, for example, Wells, 'World Brain: The Idea of a Permanent World Encyclopaedia', written in 1937 for the new *Encyclopédie Française*, and reprinted in his book *World Brain* (London: Methuen, 1938). I am grateful to Dr Gert Morreel for drawing my attention to this essay.

[59] Anthony West, *H. G. Wells: Aspects of a Life* (Harmondsworth: Penguin, 1985), p. 52.

[60] H. G. Wells, *Boon, The Mind of the Race, The Wild Asses of the Devil* and *The Last Trump* (London: T. Fisher Unwin, 1915), p. 9.

[61] Ibid., p. 12.

[62] Ibid., pp. 163, 169. The proliferation of alter egos goes further still. As John Batchelor notes, there's also a Wellsian character called 'Wilkins': Batchelor, *H. G. Wells* (Cambridge: Cambridge University Press, 1985), p. 120.

with pseudonyms by Wells, but in the period more generally: '"Should all literature be anonymous?" he asks at the head of a sheet of notes.'[63]

There are three main points to be made about *Boon* in the context of this discussion of fictionalized life-writings. First, the machinery of Wells's text is by now familiar. Dead fictionalized author (like Rutherford, Ryecroft, or Maitland); manuscript edited selectively by fictionalized editor (like Shapcott); book introduced by author (like 'G. G.'); generic indeterminacy. Second, though, in Wells's case the generic indeterminacy goes deeper. The works discussed so far raise different degrees of uncertainty about their ratios of biography, autobiography, and fictionalization. Wells introduces a note of comedy, pastiche, and parody in *Boon* which was not present in Hale White, Gissing, or Roberts. Rather than the pathos of Rutherford's spiritual crisis, or Ryecroft's aesthetic struggle, Wells gives a comic version of the aesthetic life. This tonal difference is part of his method of distancing himself from aesthetes such as James, and their vision of art as hieratic vocation. Whereas I have been reading these earlier writers as ironizing the forms of auto/biography, Wells is not only doing that, then, but parodying them. That is, *Boon* is both another example of fictionalized auto/biography, taking its place alongside *Rutherford*, *Ryecroft*, and *Maitland*; and it is also a parody of them. This book has argued so far for a late nineteenth-century phenomenon of subtle experimentation with life-writing, as the forms of auto/biography began to seem less secure, less reliable than before. By 1915, and the advent of modernism, it appears that that phenomenon had itself become subject to scepticism, to ionization, even to parody. Though Wells (above all in *Boon*) distanced himself from modernist formalists like James, Conrad, and Ford, *Boon* anticipates the more ludic experiments with autobiografiction by modernists such as Aldington, Stein, and Woolf, discussed in Part II. Like them, Wells also anticipates postmodern experiments. *Boon* falls between *The Autobiography of Mark Rutherford* and later twentieth-century experiments in auto/biografiction such as Nabokov's *Pale Fire* or Byatt's *Possession* (discussed in Chapter 12). If Wells is parodying the Rutherford/Ryecroft/Maitland phenomenon of fictionalized auto/biography, then, he is also extending it. To read *Boon* as an Edwardian country-house discussion novel (like Galsworthy's *The Country House*, or W. H. Mallock's *The New Republic*), as an attack of 'ill-temper', a symptom that Wells 'had plainly lost his balance', is to miss the way in which its energies derive from the emerging tradition of autobiografiction.[64]

Third, these energies derive not only from Wells's play with the *life* of his fictional alter ego, but from his play with Boon's and Bliss's *writing*. *Boon* includes another feature which, as we shall see, is increasingly bound up with experiments in autobiografiction: the presentation of imaginary literary works: texts purportedly written not by the actual author but by a fictional character.

---

[63] Ibid., p. 171.
[64] See Batchelor, *H. G. Wells*, pp. 71, 96.

Like Hale White and Gissing, Wells doesn't just describe the life of his fictional writer; he writes some of that character's writing. This will be explored in detail in later chapters, and especially Chapter 7. But it needs to be introduced here, because in a sense the production of pseudonymous texts introduces it, but also introduces a definitional problem.

Any first-person narrative in which the narrator is identified by a name other than the author's can be described as fictionally authored; either because it is a text purportedly written by a fictional character, or (as in the admittedly unusual case of Stein's *Autobiography of Alice B. Toklas*), as a text in which the authorship is fictionalized. (Toklas was not a fictional character, but the idea of her having written an autobiography was fictional.) But this definition is so broad as to include novels with first-person narrators, which abounded for two centuries before the period under consideration. It isn't tenable to claim that it is a new device discovered at the *fin de siècle*. But there do seem to be at least three crucial differences between the way nineteenth-century novelists like Dickens and Charlotte Brontë use it, and the uses writers such as Wells, Joyce, and Stein make of it.

First, there is a generic difference. *David Copperfield, Great Expectations, Jane Eyre, Villette* were recognized as novels. They drew on the form of autobiography, but the author's name on the title page, or in Brontë's case a pseudonymous editor's name ('Currer Bell') distinct from the narrator's name, gives away the fictionality of the autobiographical performance. In Dickens's case, there's also a degree of parody of that performance, as when David Copperfield begins:

Whether I shall turn out to be the hero of my own life, or whether that station will be held by anybody else, these pages must show. To begin my life with the beginning of my life, I record that I was born (as I have been informed and believe) on a Friday, at twelve o'clock at night. It was remarked that the clock began to strike, and I began to cry, simultaneously.[65]

The anticlimax of the first sentence, the tautology of the second, and the comedy of its parenthesis (that seems momentarily to be saying he was told and believes that he was born), the flatness of 'It was remarked' alongside the mechanical comedy of striking clock and crying child, all establish Copperfield's performance as a comic one. Though the plot of the novel has him becoming a novelist, the awkwardnesses of this beginning raise doubts about how seriously we are expected to take him as an artist. His words here are not the text of a conscious artist (as Stephen Dedalus's writing in the *Portrait of the Artist as a Young Man* is presented as being, say). The *Bildungsroman* has not yet become the *Künstlerroman*. David Copperfield is delivering an autobiographical narrative. He claims to be writing a formal autobiography—his 'life'; but this is somewhat undermined by the slightly plodding play on the words 'my life'. If Dickens is trying to

---

[65] Dickens, *David Copperfield* (Harmondsworth: Penguin, 1976), p. 49.

suggest Copperfield's awareness of the formal possibilities of autobiography, his beginning, conventionally, at the beginning, shows him not availing himself of them. Copperfield only alludes to his literary career in order to bracket it off: 'It is not my purpose, in this record, though in all other essentials it is my written memory, to pursue the history of my own fictions. They express themselves, and I leave them to themselves.'[66] By contrast, Dickens's awareness of the possibilities of autobiographical form as a fictional resource is what energizes the writing. (Indeed, his own, abandoned, attempt to write his autobiography appears to have been the germ of the novel.)[67] It's published in the form it is because it's by Dickens. If he had sent it to a publisher as by 'David Copperfield', doubtless they would have either rejected it or made him revise it. Anyhow, that phrase 'the hero of my own life' lets the mask slip. This is going to be adventure, romance, fiction.

Second, while all the works under consideration here are in some sense fusing different genres, there is a difference in the direction in which they are crossing the border between autobiography and fiction. *Robinson Crusoe* is a novel impersonating autobiography. *Tristram Shandy* parodies it. *David Copperfield* is a novel which strays towards it. In the twentieth-century novel of an artist's growth—*A la recherche du temps perdu*, say—an autobiography is worked into a novel. Eighteenth- and nineteenth-century narratives of the picaresque characteristically attempt to give verisimilitude to their presentations by making it look as if the protagonist is telling their own story: to make their inner life, their subjectivity, more empathetic; to bring the experiences closer to the reader. Modernist autobiographical works tend to distance the work from the author so as to gain objectivity on material that is disturbingly close to the author.

Third, and of most relevance in this chapter: there is a difference—admittedly in degree rather than of kind—between what Hale White does with 'Mark Rutherford', and what Wells does with 'Bliss' and 'Boon'. Hale White was essentially writing his own formal autobiography, altering some of the details, and then adopting the pseudonym and machinery of death and editorial resurrection. The disguise is superficial, as it is in *Henry Ryecroft* or *Henry Maitland*. Hale White and Gissing are both essentially presenting their own 'inner lives', their own imaginations, but obliquely so as to protect themselves from charges of egotism, theological depravity, or self-pity. What they are not trying to do is enter fully into the imaginative life of someone other than themselves: to create 'heteronyms'. This is what Postmodern versions of fictional authorship tend to do, as in *Pale Fire* or *Possession*. Wells is not quite doing that either. His satire prevents him from taking entirely seriously Boon's creativity. The point is rather that he is a failure as a creator, unable to order or complete his life's work. And anyway, Boon is not very distant from his creator. As suggested, he is an alter ego;

---

[66] Ibid., p. 758.
[67] *Oxford Reader's Companion to Dickens*, ed. Paul Schlicke (Oxford: Oxford University Press, 1999), p. 144.

a device for Wells to work out his anxieties about unrealizable projects, and about the uneasy combination in his work of grandiosity and bricolage. Yet insofar as he is a representation of what Wells mistrusts in himself, he is someone at least partly other than Wells in his entirety. He says Bliss can say things Wells cannot; but so can Boon, because it is the scrapings Wells gives of his writings that are closer to fully fictional authorship.

The contrast between *Ryecroft* and *Boon* is instructive, because though (as suggested above) Ryecroft's writing is closer to Gissing's than Boon's is to Wells, in formal terms the fiction of his being another person is more sustained. Not only the material in the supposed journals, but also the form in which 'G. G.' condenses them, and the biographical detail he gives, mean that a reader could mistake Ryecroft for a real person, whereas it's clear from Wells's title-page that Boon is a role. Fictional authorship is thus a complex phenomenon, which cannot be assessed on formal grounds alone, but which involves an interaction of form, tone, generic confusion, reader's expectations, and the relation of fictional author to real author.

PSEUDONYMITY, ANONYMITY, THIRD-PERSONALITY, AND THE RHETORIC OF AUTOBIOGRAFICTION

Why is it important to the study of autobiografiction? Because the disturbances in auto/biography charted so far introduce a comparable disturbance in the idea of authorship. The games writers play with fictional authorship, fictionally authored texts, are inextricable from the games they play with the forms of auto/biography. They are experimenting not only with the *forms* of life-writing, but the *writing* of those life-forms. The argument has been that the narration of subjectivity had come to seem increasingly problematic; that the advance of secularization had introduced a profound scepticism into the notion of subjectivity itself. If humanity had so misconceived its place in the world, and the nature of that world, had it not also misconceived itself? Once you entertain this view, and worry that you can no longer be sure of knowing yourself, then your attempts at expressing yourself become alienated. The act of expression, of utterance, of narration, of writing, expresses not you but something other, or at least something that may or may not be you—you can no longer be sure. This is consonant with psychoanalysis' subsequent view of the unconscious, because both are products of the nineteenth century's increasing preoccupation with what is hidden in the self, what cannot be grasped rationally even when it does manifest itself. Matthew Arnold's poem 'The Buried Life' (1852), for example, is a classic expression of the Victorian anxiety about self-unintelligibility. 'Fate', says Arnold, in order to save us from ourselves, to protect our 'genuine self' from 'capricious play':

Bade through the deep recesses of our breast
The unregarded river of our life
Pursue with indiscernible flow its way;
And that we should not see
The buried stream, and seem to be
Eddying at large in blind uncertainty,
Though driving on with it eternally.[68]

Arnold is explicit (perhaps too much so, given his subject) about how once you see the 'genuine self' as opaque, then our autobiographic acts are profoundly compromised:

And long we try in vain to speak and act
Our hidden self, and what we say and do
Is eloquent, is well—but 'tis not true![69]

The problem is how to 'let us be true', as he put it in 'Dover Beach'. The emphasis here is on how our (what we would now call) conscious attempts to express our 'hidden self' are foredoomed to failure; a failure which only exacerbates the desire to know the unknowable:

There rises an unspeakable desire
After the knowledge of our buried life;
A thirst to spend our fire and restless force
In tracking out our true, original course [. . .][70]

Yet the language here intimates a converse anxiety. If the 'unregarded river' is the 'river of our life'—its 'true, original course', 'its way' are what directs our life—then what is the true source of our words? Rather than seeing them as conscious, fully transparent attempts to express the unconscious and hidden, might it not equally be the other way around: that the words issue from the unconscious? If this is the subjectivist position, it is also the Freudian account of parapraxis as emblematic of how the unconscious speaks through our every word.[71] Its effect is to render our utterance problematic, out of conscious control, other.

I am not arguing that anxieties about subjectivity begin in the late nineteenth century, of course. The case of Arnold shows that they were pressing for a mid-Victorian writer, and in some form they have existed in much earlier literature: *Oedipus, Hamlet, Faust*. Nor am I arguing that the literary uses of pseudonymity begin with the texts discussed here. Pseudonyms abound in periods of literary controversialism, such as the Renaissance or the eighteenth century. They were

---

[68] *The Poems of Matthew Arnold*, 2nd edn, ed. Kenneth Allott and Miriam Allott (London: Longman, 1979), pp. 286–91; ll. 30–44.

[69] Ibid., ll. 64–6.

[70] Ibid., p. 256, l. 29; p. 289, ll. 47–50.

[71] See Sebastiano Timpanaro, *The Freudian Slip: Psychoanalysis and Textual Criticism* (London: Verso, 1985).

widely used by women writers throughout the nineteenth century, introducing the potential for another form of anxiety: an ontological gender uncertainty produced by disconnecting texts from gendered author-identities.[72] (When Hale White lodged with John Chapman, who fronted the radical *Westminster Review*, his fellow-lodger was 'the woman who actually ran the paper, Marian Evans, not yet the novelist known as "George Eliot".')[73]

The most mercurial exponent of literary pseudonyms is probably the mid-nineteenth-century philosopher Søren Kierkegaard. As Jonathan Lear explains, at the time 'the use of pseudonyms was a literary craze. Reviewers in *Flyveposten*, for example, were so enamoured of signing their articles with letters that they ran out of upper and lower case letters of the Greek and Latin alphabets and had to begin using numbers.'[74] But Kierkegaard's self-immersion in pseudonymity is so extensive and intricate as to take it to a new level of profound ontological questioning. His best-known works, such as *Either/Or*, *Fear and Trembling*, *Repetition*, *The Concept of Dread*, *Philosophical Fragments*, *Stages on Life's Way*, or the *Concluding Unscientific Postscript*, were published under various pseudonyms. The *Postscript* ends with 'A First and Last Declaration', signed with Kierkegaard's own name, which acknowledges that he is the author, 'as people would call it', of these works. 'My pseudonymity or polynymity has not had a casual ground in my *person*' he continues, 'but it has an essential ground in the character of the *production* [. . .]':

For I am impersonal, or am personal in the second person, a *souffleur* who has poetically produced the *authors*, whose preface in turn is their own production, as are even their own names. So in the pseudonymous works there is not a single word which is mine, I have no opinion about these works except as third person, no knowledge of their meaning except as a reader, not the remotest private relation to them, since such a thing is impossible in the case of a doubly reflected communication.[75]

Kierkegaard says that his relationship to these heteronyms 'combines in a unity the function of being secretary and (ironically enough) that of being the author of the author or authors.' And, as Johnathan Lear comments, 'he makes this request which, I find, haunts from beyond the grave': 'My wish, my prayer, is that, if it

---

[72] Alexis Easley, *First Person Anonymous: Women Writers and Victorian Print Media, 1830–70* (Aldershot: Ashgate, 2004) argues that: 'By examining discontinuities in women's authorial identities and texts, rather than assuming individualized, consistent authorial personae, we can explore the ways that anonymity allowed women to appear and disappear in their work—to be at once creators and constructions, cultural agents and culturally produced texts. Likewise, it enables us to view pseudonymous publication as a strategy designed to complicate the authorial position, rather than a defensive means of obscuring an essential "self" or "voice"'; p. 7.

[73] Oxford *DNB* entry for Hale White.

[74] Jonathan Lear, 'Author of Authors', *Times Literary Supplement* (28 January 2005), 3–4.

[75] Kierkegaard, *Concluding Unscientific Postscript*, ed. Walter Lowrie, trans. David F. Swenson (London: Humphrey Milford and Oxford University Press, 1941), p. [551].

might occur to anyone to quote a particular saying from the books, he would do me the favor to cite the name of the respective pseudonymous author.'[76]

This claim to write as the 'author of the author or authors' is a crucial manifesto of the notion of imaginary authorship, or heteronymity. And a work such as *Diary of a Seducer* (1843) is a superb example of fictional life-writing—a fictionally authored diary. Because so much of Kierkegaard's work concerns the relation between the theological and the aesthetic, in many ways he also anticipates the turn towards the aesthetic view of a life story outlined here (though in the spirit of ironic and theologically motivated resistance to it). His case illustrates how turn-of-the-century pseudonymity in life-writing is not unprecedented. But it does not enter the mainstream of English writing for several decades.

The experiments under discussion, besides being significant in themselves, are also important for the way they interact with other forms of modern writing, especially novels. *Boon* has already given us one example. Another is provided by the novel Ford was writing when he criticized *Henry Maitland* as 'a bitter bad book': *The Good Soldier*. That novel's narrator has been seen by many critics as obtuse to the point of implausibility or absurdity; like 'J. H.''s dictation, there is something 'almost childishly simple' about Dowell's innocence, his generosity towards the friend who has systematically cuckolded him, then destroyed the girl he loves. Dowell, too, insists on the truth of his story, and how the apparent artlessness of its telling guarantees that veracity; though as with Roberts's Preface ('But J. H. really knew the man, and here is what he said of him'), the insistence on artlessness only draws attention to the artfulness of the impersonation: 'I console myself with thinking that this is a real story and that, after all, real stories are probably best told in the way a person telling a story would tell them. Then they will seem most real.'[77]

'Seem'? Does that concede that they're not in fact real; that a story is by definition something unreal? (Ford claimed in the 'Dedicatory Letter' he wrote later for *The Good Soldier* that 'the story is a true story' and that he had 'had it from Edward Ashburnham himself.'[78] This is borne out by a vignette he included in an earlier book, *The Spirit of the People*, in which he described the fraught but repressed parting at a station of a married man and his ward who have fallen in love, which obviously forms the germ of the novel's plot and one of its most powerful scenes. And yet the biographical identities of these two are not known: Ford only refers to him as 'P—' and no one has been able to identify them.) *The Good Soldier* combines Dowell's autobiographical story with his attempt to write biographically about Edward Ashburnham. It is about the private lives of both men and their wives. It presents a sympathetic picture of a man in the grip of his sexuality to an extent that was judged as depraved by some

---

[76] Lear, 'Author of Authors'. *Postscript*, p. [552].
[77] Ford, *The Good Soldier* (London: John Lane; the Bodley Head, 1915), p. 213.
[78] Ibid., p. 3.

of its first readers. Though it is obviously a novel, and very different from Roberts's book, these similarities all suggest that Ford may have had the *Private Life* echoing in his mind when writing *The Good Soldier*, and especially when constructing its intricate labyrinth of autobiografiction.

Hale White later came to share Trollope's view of the impossibility of truly writing the 'inner life', as we saw; though the reason he gave was different: that: 'it would be too dangerous.'[79] What his and Roberts's books demonstrate is the increasingly widespread realization that what could be written was *fictionalized* histories of the inner life; works which would carry conviction by modelling themselves not on the fictionalized histories of inner lives found in novels, but on the life-histories found in auto/biography.

The variety of games authors are playing with pseudonymity, and the proliferation of texts playing such games, have perhaps distracted critics from attending to the paradoxical nature of the very idea of pseudonymous auto/biography. As someone possibly called John Mullan has shown in his study of *Anonymity*, until the twentieth century, many of the greatest works of English literature were published anonymously, or under that form of anonymity which is pseudonymity.[80] Though there was nothing new about the use of such literary disguises or concealments in themselves, it does appear a *fin de siècle* development to use them to present works with genuine elements of biography and autobiography—generally taken as fundamentally truth-telling discourses. Of course, since their beginnings, satirists had mocked autobiographers' self-aggrandizement and even unreliability. But such objections are based on the belief that the forms ought not to distort or mislead. And at the core of the idea of auto/biography's veracity is the naming of the subject. An autobiography told the life story of the author named on the title-page; a biography told the life story of the subject named in the title. Such truisms are the basis of the theory, most fully articulated by Philippe Lejeune, of the autobiographical 'pact' or 'contract.' Lejeune defines autobiography as 'a retrospective prose narrative produced by a real person concerning his own existence, focusing on his individual life, in particular on the development of his personality'. Lejeune's initial definition— 'brisk', as Laura Marcus says—asserts that the 'author (whose name designates a real person) and narrator are identical'; and that the 'narrator and protagonist are identical' too.[81] He sees these identifications as foundational and categorical: they 'are a matter of all or nothing, and these are, of course, the conditions which oppose autobiography [. . .] to biography and to the personal novel [. . .] Here

---

[79] Quoted by Willey, *More Nineteenth-Century Studies*, pp. 190–1.

[80] John Mullan, *Anonymity: A Secret History of English Literature* (London: Faber and Faber, 2008), p. 4.

[81] Lejeune, 'The Autobiographical Pact', in Lejeune, *On Autobiography*, ed. Paul John Eakin, trans. Katherine Leary (Minneapolis: University of Minnesota Press, 1989), p. 5. I'm indebted to Laura Marcus's discussion of Lejeune, in her *Auto/biographical Discourses*, pp. 190–4.

there is no transition or latitude. Either there is identity or there is not.'[82] In terms of naming this has some force. An author can sign their own name (like Mill) or a pseudonym (like Mark Rutherford). But in other ways, the examples we have been considering are, precisely, cases of transition and latitude. Is a text no longer an autobiography because it is published anonymously? Or because it is published with the author's initials only? And what if it is published pseudonymously? Since the name 'Mark Rutherford' did not fully designate William Hale White, his *Autobiography* may well fall foul of the contractual definition. But what of a writer like Anthony Burgess, whose two volumes of autobiography were published under the *nom de plume* he had adopted for most of his work, and yet which certainly endeavour to refer to himself, not to a fictional character? It would be open to Lejeune, or an adherent of a strict contractual theory, to rule that most of the works discussed in this book did not count as contractual formal autobiographies. But that would merely be another way of saying that during the long turn of the century, the contractual model began to give way to a much more transitional and latitudinarian form in which autobiography, biography, and fiction could fuse with each other: namely, auto/biografiction.

Lejeune's subsequent work has recognized these problems. In a fine groundbreaking essay, 'Autobiography in the Third Person', for example, he takes up the challenge presented to the contractual theory by works such as *The Education of Henry Adams*, or *The Autobiography of Alice B. Toklas*,[83] and by the related displacements of life-writing such as pseudonymity and anonymity. He still wants to recuperate such experiments back into the contractual theory, having the status of exceptions which prove the rule. But the prevalence of such works suggests instead that it isn't a rule, so much as a utopian hope that the range of auto/biodiversity can be ordered by regulation. As soon as one shifts the emphasis from the act of naming, to the act of referring, Lejeune's definitional assertions appear much less secure. 'Mark Rutherford' may not be 'William Hale White' as a name. But that's not the same as saying 'Mark Rutherford''s life wasn't Hale White's. There, surely, there is a much stronger case for latitude. The narrative, if not 'autobiography' in Lejeune's terms, is certainly autobiograph*ical*. And so it is with all our autobiografictional narratives. They both are, and are not, autobiography.

Michael Sheringham has praised Lejeune's definition because 'it ties autobiography to *reference* but not *resemblance*; to the interaction of textual "I" and extra-textual counterpart, but not to any specific kind of relationship between them.'[84] But in a sense, the problem with the theory is that reference is coming

---

[82] Ibid.

[83] Philippe Lejeune, 'Autobiography in the Third Person', *New Literary History*, 9:1 (1977), 27–50, which extends the argument of his earlier book *Le pacte autobiographique* (Paris: Éditions du Seuil, 1975). His arguments are discussed in more detail in Chapter 8.

[84] Sheringham, *French Autobiography: Devices and Desires* (Oxford: Clarendon Press, 1993), p. 20.

under attack in the period just as much as resemblance. The subjectivist position, as we have noted, also entails that if writers cannot be sure of the reality of the experience they are describing, they cannot be sure it is *their* experience. The contractual theory, that is, is little more than a clinical reduction. While it describes classic formal autobiography accurately enough, it surgically excludes texts which experiment with formal autobiography, and any issues they raise that give life-writing much of its theoretical interest.

For example, a case like that of 'Mark Rutherford' raises an issue about identity between author and narrative which goes much deeper. In opening up the possibility of dis-identification between the two—in providing an example in which an autobiography does not exactly tell the story of its author—it opens up the question of whether formal contractual autobiographies do that either. Even writers who set out in good faith to record their lives honestly will inevitably produce texts which select, distort, evade, or interpret those lives. The processes of turning experience into narrative ensure that however accurate, honest, truthful, they are, the narratives can never be identical with the experience. Which is to say that the notion of identity between author and narrator and protagonist inevitably contains an element of fictionality; that it is, as it were, a legal fiction; one which enables classic formal autobiography to proceed; but which modern autobiografiction exposes for what it is. The story we have been tracing is one of authors progressively realizing that their attempts to identify all three roles tends to transform themselves into—role-playing. Autobiografiction effectively works by the inverse of Lejeune's 'pact', since it is tied to resemblance but not to reference. The spiritual experiences in *The Autobiography of Mark Rutherford* resemble Hale White's, but are referred to a fictional name. Yet such a strategy also brings out the inextricability of reference and resemblance. If we refer the experience back to Hale White, it is because we believe it resembles his; in short, we are basing reference upon resemblance.

Part of the interest of these turn-of-the-century genre-blurring texts is how their experiments in autobiografiction suggest another way from which auto/biography can be approached. The most influential theories of autobiography have been the stylistic or rhetorical one associated with James Olney's *Metaphors of Self*; the contractual one associate with Lejeune; or the deconstructive one, exemplified by Paul De Man. My own readings draw on all three approaches. The results are generally closest to deconstructive readings. But they are reached by a different method, and by attending to different material for the most part. Texts such as *Mark Rutherford, Henry Ryecroft*, and *Boon*, that is, because they come to us as already self-divided, presenting identity and the project of self-representation as problematic, conflicted, have already done much of the work of deconstruction. They show awareness of the difficulties of writing the self, certainly; and some, as we shall see, represent the difficulties as overwhelming, and the story of autobiography as the failure to tell its story. But generally, rather than (as deconstructionists tend to do) relishing what are seen as strategies of self-defeat, writers such as Hale White, Gissing, and Wells grasp instead the freedoms offered by the emergent formal developments, and explore them as resources for new fictional experimentation, introducing energies of play and performance into auto/biography. The interest of these works owes much to the way so many of the properties of auto/biography are in flux: the styles and forms of writing (as analysed in the Olney approach); the structure of identifications between author, narrator, and character (the focus of Lejeune's contractual model, but here complicated by the interventions of fictional editors); and the modes of reading auto/biographical figurations (as analysed by De Man).

Indeed, these pseudo-autobiographies show that the notion of pseudonymity already incorporates this problematic idea of the self's non-identity with its representations. The pseudonymization of autobiography disturbs not only the category of autobiography, but that of pseudonymity too. To fictionalize the name of the autobiographer or biographee is a radically disruptive act; one which at a stroke disturbs the entire field of life-writing, and thus arguably the entire field of writing. Pseudonymity, that is, can be considered in these texts as expressing a hesitation of naming; and in particular, a hesitation in the naming of the writer (whether the writer is the author of an autobiographical text ('Rutherford', 'Ryecroft', 'Boon') or the subject of a biography ('Maitland', 'Boon' again), or the author of a biographical text (Roberts's 'J. H.'; Wells's 'Bliss'). This chapter will conclude by arguing that the hesitation over the naming of the writer manifests itself in other, related, forms in the period: namely, as it were, the use of the third person to write about oneself—what I call 'third-personality'—and the use of anonymity in auto/biography.

When *The Early Life of Thomas Hardy* (1928) and *The Later Years of Thomas Hardy* (1930) were published under the name of his second wife, Florence Emily Hardy, they must have looked like a survival of the Victorian official biography—the 'two fat volumes', with their 'air of slow, funereal barbarism', which Lytton Strachey had complained, a decade earlier, were how we commemorated the dead.[85] Yet in fact they were something quite other. They had been written in the third person by Hardy himself, to be published posthumously. It is a sly strategy, which enables him to write an autobiography without seeming to, but without introducing any confusion over the identity of the subject due to the use of a heteronym. The slyness consists in the way he splits the functions that autobiography usually binds together, of author and subject. He uses his own name as subject, but his wife's name as author. It is not a fictional pseudonym, of course, and the surname is his anyway. But it is the utterance that becomes fictionalized: the idea that the narration is given by another author. It also enables the book to claim close intimacy with its subject—if anyone knew him well, she did—and thus to claim authority, without incurring the charge of subjectivity. Florence Emily Hardy

---

[85] Strachey, *Eminent Victorians* (Harmondsworth: Penguin, 1986), p. 10. See Chapter 11, p. 452.

may not be thought an unbiased biographer of her husband, but readers would have taken her statements as pious testimony rather than as Hardy's own self-fashioning.

I do not know of any evidence that Gertrude Stein read Hardy's auto/biography, but its strategy is remarkably close to the text she published soon after it, *The Autobiography of Alice B. Toklas*. Formally Stein's work is different, and will be discussed in Chapter 8 as an example of a more playfully fictional type of imaginary autobiography. It purports to be an autobiography by Stein's partner, whereas Hardy's text purports to be Mrs Hardy's biography of its author. What they share is the device of an author writing a book about themselves, referring to themselves in the third person, but putting the narration into the person of their partner. Hardy's auto/biography is thus technically an example of both heteronymity and third-personality. This is something novels frequently combine. In a book like *Boon*, Wells is able to talk about (aspects of) himself in the third person, through using the synonyms of Boon and Bliss. What's different about Hardy and Stein is that they use the third person about their own name—if covertly.

One of the strangest and most significant autobiographies of the early twentieth century had done that overtly two decades earlier. *The Education of Henry Adams* (printed privately in 1907, and published posthumously in 1918) was written by the American historian and novelist—Henry Adams. *The Education* treats its subject's life with a strange detachment; partly through Adams's use of the third person to write about himself; but also through the tone of despondent patrician irony with which he pronounces his New England and Harvard education as equipping him only to fail in life. The sense of failure runs deep. Adams presents his life as a mind structured by outmoded values unable to comprehend the complexity of the modern world. He poses this modern complexity as a chaos, and then construes his life as an attempt to find some systematic meaning in it:

From cradle to grave this problem of running order through chaos [...], discipline through freedom, unity through multiplicity, has always been, and must always be, the task of education, as it is the moral of religion, philosophy, science, art, politics, and economy [...][86]

We might add that it is also the aim of autobiography. But Adams's quest is frustrated, because he finds that 'Chaos was the law of nature; Order was the dream of man.'[87] In the end, the only kind of intelligible pattern he can find in history is an accelerating fragmentation, in which the broadening scientific discoveries of energies and forces undermine the sense of human agency, and thus also threaten our mentality: 'The movement from unity into multiplicity, between 1200 and 1900, was unbroken in sequence, and rapid in acceleration. Prolonged one generation longer, it would require a new social mind.'[88] This is

[86] *The Education of Henry Adams* (Boston: Houghton Mifflin, 1961), p. 12.
[87] Ibid., p. 451.　　[88] Ibid., p. 498.

what Adams calls 'A Dynamic Theory of History'. Its corollary is a dynamic theory of autobiography. The postulated failure of his life as an intellectual quest for running order through chaos, for finding a unified meaning in the multiplicity of experience, entails a form of autobiographical failure. Hence his grimly punning letter to his friend Henry James, written after he had completed the *Education*, in which he both imagines autobiography as suicide, yet also enjoins it: 'I advise you to take your own life in the same way, in order to prevent biographers from taking it in theirs.'[89] Failure in the world of industrial and commercial modernity, and the concomitant sense of alienation from it, is also the source of his vision as an artist. But even the possibilities for visionariness are compromised by modernity. His celebrated contrast between the 'Virgin' of medieval Catholicism, symbolizing unity and perfection, and the dynamo he had seen at the 1900 Paris Exposition, symbolizing the energy and multiplicity of the modern age, finds its appropriate form in this splitting into multiple personalities of narrator and subject. Adams thus brings out the ambivalence of the autobiographic form, which attempts to see the self as both subjective and objective, individual and social; and tries to mould its complexity into a unified narrative.

Adams's sense of failure is bound up with his use of the third person. It gives him the distance to judge his former self *as* another. It also registers the extent to which that former self *is* another. The self that cannot understand its experience (in the sense in which it understands understanding) cannot represent it either. Being unable to find a unified meaning or system in the self's experience is tantamount to being unable to find a unity in the self. The writing of the self as an 'I' becomes an impossible project. No autobiographical narrative will be able to capture the chaos of the 'I', because the very act of articulating the self as an 'I' pre-supposes a unity in it, or imposes a unity upon it. Adams cannot do this for himself as himself; he can only do it for himself as an other. To write about yourself as 'Henry Adams' rather than as an 'I' might seem no less unified. Henry Adams is no more people than 'I' is. But the point is that the writing of autobiography in the third person introduces a split between the enunciating voice and the enunciated subject; between the narrator and Adams. This split enacts the multiplicity it describes, in the way it constantly wrong-foots the reader, who keeps forgetting that the story of 'Henry Adams' is actually being told by Henry Adams.

Pseudonymity and third-personality both represent disruptions in conventional formal autobiography. Soon we shall investigate yet further disruptions involving anonymity, initialization (the identifying of the author by semi-pseudonymous, semi-anonymous, initials only) and heteronymity. All such disruptions indicate a degree of fictionalization; are signs that autobiography was increasingly turning into autobiografiction. But how are such phenomena to be explained? My readings have given priority to the phenomenological

---

[89] Henry Adams to Henry James, 6 May, 1908; published in Appendix A of *The Education of Henry Adams*, ed. Ernest Samuels (Boston: Houghton Mifflin, 1974), pp. 512–13.

consequences of secularization. New Historicism would look to further contextual parallels—how the ideal of self-culture fed into and was in turn reconfigured by the Victorian education acts, for example; or how the notion of the 'inner life' is transformed in the period from the predominantly spiritual to the predominantly sexual. As in Adams's case, the perception of social change as generating ever more chaos (a view famously shared by that other Harvard product, T. S. Eliot) can be read as disturbing autobiographical forms and traditional coherence. One can also point to a Literary Historical model, according to which auto/biographers are influenced by autobiographical and first-person-narrated novels, to make their narratives the beneficiaries of fiction's symbolic capital.

While these are all relevant, it is also possible to argue that the seeds of auto/biography's exfoliation lie within it. That it was the performances of certain celebrated autobiographies themselves that began to make autobiography seem something other, more complex, than reliable confession. The cardinal examples, so to speak, perhaps begin with Newman's *Apologia Pro Vita Sua* of 1864. Newman's account of his spiritual history famously responded to Charles Kingsley's attack in *Macmillan's Magazine*, that Newman had said that truth need not be 'a virtue with the Roman clergy.'[90] The exchange that followed, starting with letters and pamphlets, and culminating in the *Apologia*, thus places the issue of truthfulness at its core. The *Apologia* is generally recognized as a literary masterpiece; as 'an exposition of his spiritual history, written with much sincerity and feeling.'[91] But this is to gloss over the way his 'sincerity' is precisely what is at stake. Newman's strategy is to meet Kingsley's accusations head-on. He is entirely candid from the title onwards as to the motive of his narrative as an act of self-justification: an 'apology' in the sense of a 'defence' of his life and statements (his argument, after all, is that he has nothing to apologize for). The work is thus openly an act of advocacy; a rhetorical exercise of persuasion and argument, aimed less at convincing its opponent than at convincing his audience that Kingsley had misrepresented him. When Newman published a pamphlet of the correspondence arising from the magazine attack, Kingsley responded with his own pamphlet, *What, Then, Does Dr. Newman Mean?*, bearing an epigraph from one of Newman's sermons: 'It is not more than a hyperbole to say, that, in certain cases, a lie is the nearest approach to truth.'[92] This presented Newman with, to put it mildly, a tricky rhetorical challenge. He is generally thought, especially by his admirers, to have met it magnificently. Certainly he meets it ironically, beginning the first chapter, on 'Mr. Kingsley's Method of Disputation' (that 'Method' is already ironical) by saying: 'I cannot be sorry to have

---

[90] Kingsley [as 'C. K.'], review of Froude's History of England, vols 7 and 8, in *Macmillan's Magazine* (1864), 216–17. Reprinted in Newman, *Apologia*, ed. Philip Hughes (Garden City, NY: Image Books, 1956), pp. 37–8.

[91] *Oxford Companion to English Literature*, ed. Margaret Drabble (Oxford: Oxford University Press, 2000), p. 720.

[92] Reprinted in *Apologia*, ed. Philip Hughes, p. 55.

forced Mr. Kingsley to bring out in fullness his charges against me', and going on to 'compliment him on the motto in his Title-page'. The first is an irony rather than a sarcasm in that he says it's better Kingsley elaborated his attack while Newman was still alive and could answer it; in the second case, he turns the motto back on Kingsley, suggesting that Kingsley's pamphlet is an example of the kind of thing he meant—that Kingsley had lied, but the lie enables an approach to the truth. This is an earnest of the rhetorical accomplishment to come, which has made many readers feel Newman has effortlessly outclassed his opponent.

However, the implications for autobiography are more troubling. By placing the polemical and rhetorical at the heart of the autobiographical project, he makes one wonder whether he isn't playing into Kingsley's hands. Kingsley had argued that:

If he will indulge in subtle paradoxes, in rhetorical exaggerations; if, whenever he touches on the question of truth and honesty, he will take a perverse pleasure in saying something shocking to plain English notions, he must take the consequences of his own eccentricities.[93]

One needn't accept the philistinism of the appeal to 'plain English notions' to see that the *Apologia* proceeds precisely by the 'subtle paradoxes' and 'rhetorical exaggerations' that shocked Kingsley; and which, I am suggesting, must have disturbed plain English notions of autobiography. The clash between Kingsley and Newman was a classic instance of the antithesis explored by Stanley Fish between 'serious man' and 'rhetorical man', as 'a disagreement about the basic constituents of human activity and about the nature of human nature itself.' For the foundational thinking of 'serious man', 'an original purity (of vision, purpose, procedure) is corrupted when rhetoric's siren's song proves too sweet'. For the rhetorician, 'all the human virtues, and indeed humanity itself, are wrested by the arts of eloquence from a primitive and violent state of nature.'[94]

It is also an argument about autobiography, since, in Fish's words again: 'As rhetorical man manipulates reality, establishing through his words the imperatives and urgencies to which he and his fellows must respond, he manipulates or fabricates himself [...]'.[95] For 'serious man', 'rhetorical man' has no integrity or honesty. Whereas 'rhetorical man' replies that 'serious man is himself a supremely fictional achievement; seriousness is just another style, not the state of having escaped style.'[96] As Fish shows, tracing the debate back to its Classical and Renaissance roots, the idea of a 'plain' style can be viewed in comparable

---

[93] Ibid., pp. 77–8.
[94] Stanley Fish, 'Rhetoric', from *Doing What Comes Naturally* (Durham, NC: Duke University Press, 1989), p. 482. Fish draws on Richard Lanham's distinction between *homo seriosus* and *homo rhetoricus*.
[95] Ibid., p. 483.
[96] Ibid., p. 484.

paradoxical terms, as a rhetorical position claiming an escape from rhetoric. It is no surprise that such a debate should return as writers became newly preoccupied with 'style' at the *fin de siècle*. As it does so, it contributes to an anxiety about autobiography as fabrication; as inextricable from fiction. The implication of this reading of the *Apologia* is that Victorian 'earnestness' had become problematic long before Wilde's farcical double-take on it. The effect of Newman's book is to displace autobiography from the plain English notion of honest transcription of experience, towards a model of autobiography as rhetorical performance. His candour about advocacy generated an anxiety about candour. Of course actual autobiographies have never been reducible to mere honest transcription, and the best have expressed their awareness of the problem, from Rousseau and Wordsworth onwards. But as the nineteenth century draws to a close, and the twentieth begins, more key autobiographical works contribute to the undermining of the notion of autobiography as earnest transcription. Mill's presentation of his self as a constructed polemical machine, for example; and Hale White's text, in which earnestness and candour about his spiritual history issues in disguise and relative fabrication.

BUTLER AND GOSSE

Autobiography and biography had come to be seen as quintessentially nineteenth-century modes. Carlyle, the prime advocate of biographical history, also wrote as early as 1834 of 'these Autobiographical times of ours.'[97] But the first decade of the twentieth century saw two works that signalled the reinvention of auto/biography, and provide our last two examples in this chapter.

Samuel Butler's *The Way of All Flesh* had been written by the 1880s, but was only published posthumously in 1903. At its heart is the portrayal of the conflict between tyrannical and hypocritical parents, the vicar Theo Pontifex and his wife Christina, and their long-suffering son, named, inevitably, Ernest. It is generally read as an autobiographical novel; a *roman à clef* of Butler's family, its closeness to home accounting for Butler's reluctance to publish it during his lifetime. Yet it exemplifies the generic multiplicity that we shall consider more fully in the following two chapters, being a fictionalized autobiography in the form of a pseudo-biography. That is, it is not simply 'autobiographical' in its sources, but an exercise in biographical form; or rather, in auto/biographical form, since the narrator, Overton, explicitly raises the question of how far in writing about Ernest he is also writing about himself:

Every man's work, whether it be literature or music or pictures or architecture or anything else, is always a portrait of himself, and the more he tries to conceal himself the more

---

[97] Thomas Carlyle, *Sartor Resartus*, ed. Kerry McSweeney and Peter Sabor (Oxford: Oxford University Press, 1987), p. 73.

clearly will his character appear in spite of him. I may very likely be condemning myself, all the time that I am writing this book, for I know that whether I like it or no I am portraying myself more surely than I am portraying any of the characters whom I set before the reader.[98]

Butler is clearly speaking through his narrator here: inciting readers to read the novel as autobiography. Yet there is also an irony in the fact that it is not Overton but Ernest who is the more autobiographical character. The view Overton is voicing is the Nietzsche-Wilde argument, that all utterance is autobiography. But in this context it works paradoxically against the novel being read as expressing Butler. For if Overton is expressing himself rather than Ernest, it is not the Ernest-like Butler he is expressing. Or, to work it the other way round, if Overton does express Butler, at least in some aspect, then to the extent that he is differentiated from Ernest, there is something of Ernest which is not autobiographical. It might be countered that Overton is a device Butler uses to objectify Ernest, and to conceal the autobiographical origins of the book. In which case, Overton's comment is something of a red herring. Yet it is one that slithers back to the question of autobiography. Both the autobiographical elements of Ernest's story, and Overton's comments about self-expression, are representative Victorian expressions of the importance of earnestness. But they also contradict each other. The book's autobiografictional form, that is, articulates the importance of not being earnest, or not quite earnest, just as Samuel Butler is neither quite Ernest nor, overtly, Overton.

The Way of All Flesh is very much concerned with the idea of the 'inner life'. The terrifyingly manipulative parents cannot accept that Ernest should keep any of his life private from them. Christina berates him, saying:

At times we are almost inclined to doubt whether you have a moral and spiritual nature at all. Of your inner life, my dear, we know nothing beyond such scraps as we can glean in spite of you, from little things which escape you almost before you know that you have said them.[99]

The novel tells the story of Ernest's struggle to keep his inner life to himself. But it is also the story of his increasing doubt about what that inner life is, as he realizes that his attempt to become a clergyman is false to his 'moral and spiritual nature'; not least because he comes to disbelieve that people's 'moral and spiritual nature'—including his parents'—is what he has been led to believe. Overton says it puzzled Ernest how long it took him to realize 'how much he had hated being a clergyman.'[100] But Butler has shown how, when the inner life is so intensively policed by others, its nature is called into doubt. It isn't just that Ernest comes to doubt the motives of others. In doing so, he is forced to doubt his

---

[98] Butler, *The Way of All Flesh* (Harmondsworth: Penguin, 1986), pp. 91–2.
[99] Ibid., p. 198.
[100] Ibid., p. 303.

own, and to realize the falsity of the self he has been manipulated into performing. Doubt is difficult; a gradual process of paring away of illusions, rather than a sudden epiphany; a process which doesn't oppose a secure sense of self to a hypocritical world, but which finds its realization of hypocrisy undermines its sense of self. Thus, curiously, it requires intervention from the outer world to transform the inner life. It is only while in prison that Ernest can begin to free himself. 'I suppose people almost always want something external to themselves, to reveal to them their own likes and dislikes', says Overton.[101] Autobiografiction can provide the perfect mechanism for such self-liberation. It can both express the 'inner life', but in a form fictionalized enough to maintain its privacy; and it can also present the self as external to itself—as other—so as to permit a revelation of the self's obscure desires to itself. In this sense, autobiografiction represents the dialectical concept of identity that Paul Ricoeur advances in his book *Oneself as Another*. He distinguishes between two senses of identity, associated with the Latin terms *ipse* (self) and *idem* (same), arguing that whereas the *idem*-identity implies a permanence through temporal existence, 'identity in the sense of *ipse* implies no assertion concerning some unchanging core of the personality.'[102] For Ricoeur this sense of the self-ness of the self is inextricable from the sense of otherness: 'the selfhood of oneself implies otherness to such an intimate degree that one cannot be thought of without the other, that instead one passes into the other [. . .]'. And he goes on to argue that the kind of 'otherness' he is invoking isn't merely a matter of comparing one self with another, but instead, is an 'otherness of a kind that can be constitutive of selfhood as such.'[103] While the better formal autobiographies are open to this sense of the self's otherness, autobiografiction is especially well placed to express it.

Edmund Gosse's *Father and Son* (1907) is formally a more conventional memoir, though it too is hybrid, part biography of his father, part autobiography. Philip Gosse himself expressed a central contradiction of the Victorian age: a zoologist and contemporary of Darwin's, but a Christian fundamentalist opposed to evolutionary theory. *Father and Son* charts the son's rejection of his father's faith, and discovery of an alternative vocation: the literary life (and in this respect can be seen as a precursor of the modernist *Künstlerroman*). *Father and Son* was initially published anonymously, so concerned was Gosse that his candour about his father's emotional coldness and cruelty would be castigated as impiety. In fact the book was well-received, and by the fourth impression Gosse's name had been attached.[104] Both Butler and Gosse are significant, then, for their styptic criticism of their fathers, and the Victorian fanaticism, hypocrisy,

---

[101] Butler, *The Way of All Flesh*, p. 303.
[102] Paul Ricoeur, *Oneself as Another*, trans. Kathleen Blamey (Chicago: The University of Chicago Press, 1992), p. 2.
[103] Ibid., p. 3.
[104] The textual history of *Father and Son* is explained in Michael Newton's excellent World's Classics edition (Oxford: Oxford University Press, 2004), pp. xxix–xxxv.

3 Philip and Edmund Gosse, *Father and Son* frontispiece.

and abusiveness they represent. It was a new attitude towards the family, towards religion, and towards biography. Though, as Christopher Ricks has reminded us, critique of Victorian 'cant' and 'hypocrisy' was not begun by subsequent generations, congratulating themselves on being more enlightened and less repressed: it was initiated by the Victorians themselves; as was the formal complexity within which such psychological ambivalences could be expressed.[105]

[105] Ricks, 'Introduction' to *The New Oxford Book of Victorian Verse* (Oxford: Oxford University Press, 1987), p. xxxi, quotes Humphry House writing of 'the central criticism which the great Victorians themselves applied to their own age'.

The impact of both books had much to do with their portrayal of impieties. Specifically, the struggle of both protagonists' faith in their theological father coincides with their struggles with the authority of their domestic fathers. But their shapes are also strikingly different from those of conventional life-writing. Conventionally, people read auto/biography—especially of men of letters or public figures—in order to find out more about a life of achievement. Yet, as Valerie Sanders notes of Victorian fiction and autobiography: 'By the end of the century, much of the muscularity of the earlier writing [. . .] had withered away in favour of narratives of self-doubt and indecision.'[106] We have seen how Adams frustrates any expectation of self-aggrandizement by representing himself as a failure, using the third person as a means of avoiding self pity; purporting to treat his case objectively, offering it (like John Stuart Mill) as a study of education and culture as much as a narrative of an individual life. Butler does something comparable. Even if there is something heroic about Ernest's struggle to resist his parents' influence, he is ultimately portrayed as their damaged victim; like 'Mark Rutherford', prone to mental as well as spiritual crises. The view was gaining ground in the period that such problems, considered as 'weakness' or 'morbidity' in the moral discourse of the time, were determining of personality. As the pioneering sexologist Havelock Ellis put it: 'In the degree in which I have been privileged to know the intimate secrets of hearts, I ever more realize how great a part is played in the lives of men and women by some little concealed germ of abnormality.'[107] Ellis took the idea further, suggesting that such 'weakness is the very hall-mark of genius.'[108]

Gosse's story, by comparison, is one of successful individuation: a declaration of independence from his father, and the indoctrination his father represents. But he too frustrates conventional auto/biographical expectations. Not only does he direct potentially scandalous criticism towards his father; he also prevents the book being read as a celebration of his own life. This is done in two connected ways. The book ends when the narrator stops defining himself as a son. Thus he does not describe what became of his adult life once he'd decided how to live it. Gosse had in 1904 landed what was perhaps the grandest job in the country for a man of letters, and certainly for a librarian, as librarian of the House of Lords. If he had incorporated his subsequent, and public, life, then he would have been identifiable. When public figures like Wordsworth, Pater, Mill or Ruskin write about their childhoods, readers know the sequel: that this boy became Poet Laureate, an Oxford don, philosopher and politician, or cultural sage. By not identifying himself as the author of *Father and Son* (at least to start with) Gosse thus detached his early life from its outcome, and short-circuited any potential attempt to justify the means by the end—which could be seen as an aesthetic counter to his father's evangelicalism:

[106] Sanders, 'Victorian Life Writing', *Literature Compass*, 1:1 (2004), 1–17 (p. 8).
[107] Havelock Ellis, *Selected Essays* (London: Dent, 1943), p. 301.
[108] J. S. Collis, Introduction to Ellis, *Selected Essays*, pp. viii–ix.

the youth is not judged by external patriarchal standards of damnation or salvation, but simply allowed autonomous existence.

These works by Butler and Gosse thus marked a break with the past; the beginnings of a modern subjectivity; and the emergence of what Virginia Woolf was later to call 'The New Biography'. Harold Nicolson (husband of Woolf's intimate, Vita Sackville-West), discussed Gosse in his 1927 study *The Development of English Biography*, commenting on the impact of his apparent lack of explicit filial piety:

The book is not [...] a conventional biography; still less is it an autobiography. It is something entirely original; it is a triumphant experiment in a new formula; it is a clinical examination of states of mind over a detached and limited period.[109]

As we'll see in Chapter 11, Woolf, Nicolson, and Sackville-West conducted their own experiments with the new formula of autobiografiction.

The first words we read of *Father and Son*, beginning its Preface, are an assertion of truthfulness:

At the present hour, when fiction takes forms so ingenious and so specious, it is perhaps necessary to say that the following narrative, in all its parts, and so far as the punctilious attention of the writer has been able to keep it so, is scrupulously true.[110]

The positioning of this claim gives it the feel of an oath, taken before giving evidence in court, to tell the whole truth and nothing but the truth. However, in what is to be a story of the son's turn away from the religion of the father, to the vocation of art—precisely, the story of an aesthete—in whose name could such an oath be sworn? Authorial punctilio and scruple has to stand in for external validating authority. The Preface goes on, scrupulously and punctiliously, but also rather unnervingly, to point out where the truth has not been told:

At one point only has there been any tampering with precise fact. It is believed that, with the exception of the Son, there is but one person mentioned in this book who is still alive. Nevertheless, it has been thought well, in order to avoid any appearance of offence, to alter the majority of the proper names of the private persons spoken of.[111]

The eponymous father and son are not named at all in the text; so from one point of view, the use of pseudonyms does not touch the central characters, so is arguably not central to the book. Yet from another point of view, for Gosse to call himself 'the Son' instead of 'myself' represents a nominal displacement akin to pseudonymity and into third-personality. Either way, just as the shadow of Newman hangs over the assertion of truth-telling, so the shadow of novelized Rutherfordian pseudonymity hangs over this scruple about name-shifting.

---

[109] Nicolson, *The Development of English Biography* (London: The Hogarth Press, 1927), p. 146.
[110] Gosse, *Father and Son: A Study of Two Temperaments*, ed. Michael Newton (Oxford: Oxford University Press, 2004), p. [3].
[111] Ibid., pp. 33–4.

More telling, and of course more germane to the present argument, is that statement that 'fiction takes forms so ingenious and so specious'. Gosse certainly thought his 'present hour' was witnessing an intense period of experiment, and that its ingenuity had something to do with its speciousness—that is, that the new forms were ingenious because specious: because they left readers uncertain, or even deceived them, about which kind of writing they belonged to: autobiography, pastiche, parody, or fiction? As it will be necessary to remind ourselves occasionally in this book, such risks of deception are not unprecedented, and have been present as long as novels have existed. But Gosse's remark indicates how he thought something new was manifesting itself by 1907, whereby writers seemed to have become especially ingenious in their perplexing combinations of auto/biography and fiction.

Which books did Gosse have in mind? In singling out 'fiction', he appears to be saying that unless he assures his readers of its truthfulness in advance, they might read *Father and Son* as a novel. That might suggest that he was thinking of fictions which impersonate auto/biography (like *The Private Papers of Henry Ryecroft*) rather than partially fictionalized autobiographies (like *The Autobiography of Mark Rutherford*). Yet, as all the books discussed here show, the line is hard to draw here too, and there is nothing to stop us reading Ryecroft as an aspect of Gissing's autobiography, or *Rutherford* as a novel in specious form; or *The Way of All Flesh* as both. However fictionalized such books are, they all insist on their truthfulness, and seek to substantiate it with accounts of manuscripts and dictations. Gosse does not do that; but there is a curious naivety in his apparent belief that you can eliminate readers' uncertainty about the referentiality of a literary piece of life-writing by just saying (as Balzac had, for example, in *Père Goriot*) '*All is true*'.[112]

The Preface, like the text itself, is an anxious document; and it's hard not to see Gosse's anxiety about how the book will be read as a sign that he was still struggling to escape the anxiety caused by his father's examinations of his motives. It might be better read, however, as evincing an anxiety not so much about writers speciously passing off fiction as life-writing, but about the difficulty of keeping the forms apart—even in his own work. Whether or not his disclaimer is itself a bit of specious ingenuity, he wasn't alone in thinking that a tectonic shift was occurring in the relations between auto/biography and fiction. And that it was having a transforming effect on both modes. The impersonation of auto/biography might begin as a device for verisimilitude—mimicking the modes most likely to suspend disbelief, and convince readers of truthfulness; but, conversely, it destabilizes those very modes. Once readers get used to reading novels that look like autobiographies, won't they also read autobiographies as if they are novels? A crucial essay announcing the arrival of the hybrid,

[112] Balzac, *Père Goriot*, trans. A. J. Krailsheimer (Oxford: Oxford University Press, 1999), p. 2.

'autobiografiction', appeared while Gosse was writing *Father and Son*, and is discussed in the next chapter. As that and the following chapter will demonstrate, the literary forms making play with life writing are even more ingenious and diverse than he may have realized.

Gosse ends *Father and Son* with the irreconcilable rupture between the two men. He declares his experience gives him the right to describe as an 'untruth' the idea 'that evangelical religion, or any other religion in a violent form, is a wholesome or valuable or desirable adjunct to human life.'[113] He recounts how eventually his 'self-sufficiency revolted against the police-inspection to which my "views" were incessantly subjected.'[114] After one such interrogation, in the family 'hot house', he is no longer able to suppress his doubt, and says: 'My replies on this occasion were violent and hysterical.'[115] He then quotes a long letter from his father, responding to this outburst, and trying to persuade him to return to his faith, so that the father could resume 'sweet and tender fellowship with my beloved Son, as of old'. Gosse ends by saying:

The reader who has done me the favour to follow this record of the clash of two temperaments will not fail to perceive the crowning importance of the letter from which I have just made a long quotation. It sums up, with the closer logic, the whole history of the situation, and I may leave it to form the epigraph of this little book.[116]

Philip Gosse wasn't to know that the letter urging his son to return to their former relationship was to be the end of that relationship; but Edmund's editing, selecting this letter as emblematic of 'the whole history' and its 'epigraph', recalls 'G. G.''s use of Ryecroft's passage about his life's 'Finis' to close his book of Ryecroft's diurnal writings. Gosse goes on to say that when such 'defiance is offered to the intelligence of a thoughtful and honest young man with the normal impulses of his twenty-one years', he has to choose between ceasing to think for himself, or assert his individuality and religious independence. These are the last words he gives himself:

No compromise, it is seen, was offered; no proposal of a truce would have been acceptable. It was a case of 'Everything or Nothing'; and thus desperately challenged, the young man's conscience threw off once for all the yoke of his 'dedication', and, as respectfully as he could, without parade or remonstrance, he took a human being's privilege to fashion his inner life for himself.[117]

Most of the book is written in the first person, so this shift into third-personality does indeed make one feel something decisive has taken place. And so it has. As Alex Zwerdling has argued, Gosse shapes the book as a series of episodes of solitary mental enfranchisement.[118] Its story of the emergence of an aesthetic

---

[113] *Father and Son*, p. 183.   [114] Ibid.   [115] Ibid., p. 184.
[116] Ibid., p. 186.   [117] Ibid.
[118] Zwerdling, 'Inventing the Family Memoir: Edmund Gosse's *Father And Son*', paper given to the London Modernism seminar, 6 March 2004.

'vocation' gives it a continuity with the works by Hale White, Butler, and later, Joyce. Also (again paraphrasing Zwerdling) he presents his choice as made equably, rather than in anger; and as being the last word in the 'clash of two temperaments'. Yet in fact the manuscript evidence shows that there were subsequent attempts at mediation, and that Philip Gosse was prepared to aid his son's literary life. Thus Peter Abbs's claim that 'As a documentary record we know, from other sources, that most of the facts are accurate' is inaccurate.[119] The biographer of both Edmund and Philip, Ann Thwaite has also contested this view, and added:

I have come across substantial further evidence in the father's parish notes, that shows how little Edmund cared for accuracy. (His friend Henry James once said he had 'a genius for inaccuracy'.) Edmund must have read his source materials years before, when writing his *Life of Philip Henry Gosse* (1890), then forgotten the facts and used a version of them to enrich *Father and Son*. There is a great deal of fiction in the book.[120]

So much for the Preface's truth claim. But what of Gosse's sincerity? Was his genius for inaccuracy merely a bad memory of events that had happened some forty years earlier? How conscious was he of his alterations and simplifications? Zwerdling argues that where he exaggerates the conflict and suppresses expressions of love for his father, it's because though the conclusion is set around 1870, the 'emancipatory fantasy' structuring the text expresses Gosse's state of mind when writing it. He later told André Gide of the book: 'I put the whole passion of my mind into it.'[121] In other words, it was true to his passions if not to the facts of his history. This is the same argument that has been made for other autobiographers whose reliability has been challenged, from Rousseau onwards. But if Romanticism's investment in the imagination wrenched the inner life away from the domain of facts, the early twentieth century seemed to feel that the inner life needed once more to be championed against external fact. Gosse's assumption of 'a human being's privilege to fashion his inner life for himself' is, equally, a manifesto for his right to tell the truth of his feelings about the past, rather than the factual history of that past.

What makes it such a magnificent ending to his auto/biography, though, is another kind of resonance in the phrase. For the fashioning of an inner life is not only the way the young man makes a choice about how to construct his future. It is also a description of the way in which the much older man has fashioned his inner life in book form (a 'sheaf of feelings' indeed!): self-fashioning by autobiografiction, in other words. Gosse too, then, expresses an aesthetic view of his life in this closing flourish. How the sentence works is to

[119] Peter Abbs, ed., 'Introduction', *Father and Son* (London: Penguin, 1989), p. 25.
[120] Ann Thwaite, 'Rereadings', *Guardian* Review (2 November 2002), 37.
[121] Gosse to Gide, quoted in Ann Thwaite's *Edmund Gosse* (London: Secker & Warburg, 1984), p. 431. I am grateful to Alex Zwerdling for this reference.

imply that the young man's choice of life—and his loss of the love between parent and child—is redeemed by the art that choice has produced. The book is the evidence for the rightness of his choice of aesthetic rather than religious vocation.

Yet there is also something disconcerting in this reading of the ending. Gosse wants the book to end with 'himself'. (One can see one reason why he may have felt it necessary to slide into the third person here, since to end with a triumphal assertion of 'myself' could have invited charges of egotism.) Yet insofar as he is talking about fashioning his life in a book, it is also for others, not just for himself. There is perhaps a hint of Paterian solipsism here; a feeling that the inner life can never be made entirely public, intelligible to others. Turn-of-the-century autobiography and autobiografiction tends towards this kind of political ambivalence. From one point of view it embodies an ethical imperative to make the 'inner life' available to the public sphere: to expose repressed subjectivity and repressive tyrannies—whether domestic, emotional, familial, educational. But while such turning of the inner life inside out is a contribution to public responsibility, from another point of view it can seem a retreat from it: a crisis of faith in the public sphere itself; in the objectivity of the non-individual.

There is, however, a possible explanation of this unease in the circumstances of the anonymous first-publication of Gosse's book—which was probably a contributory factor in his anxiety that his readers might take it as an ingenious fiction. As the book, and its anonymity, became a literary sensation, it offers a powerful example of a third form of auto/biographical displacement; and it is with this phenomenon of anonymity that this discussion of such displacements will conclude.

Phyllis Grosskurth has argued that: 'The typical Victorian autobiographer was acutely aware of his audience. A mutual complicity shaped the genre, and language became a screen to shelter the vulnerable egos of writers and readers alike.'[122] Add the other usual motives of wishing to protect the living mentioned in the book (even if there's only one), and to protect the memory of the dead, and we have an embarrassment of reasons why Gosse may have felt anonymous publication was appropriate. He was already an established man of letters, and didn't want to jeopardize his position by owning the book until he had gauged the reception. This may compromise his assertion of his right to fashion his inner life as he wished. But the fact that—though the book was generally judged a triumph—some dissenting voices complained of its impiety, shows that if he was cautious he had reason to be so. In *Father and Son* he was carrying out his own

---

[122] Grosskurth, in *Approaches to Victorian Autobiography*, ed. George Landow (Athens: Ohio University Press, 1979), p. 28. Quoted by Abbs, ed., *Father and Son*, p. 19.

advice of four years earlier to biographers to 'be as indiscreet as possible within the boundaries of good taste and kind feeling.'[123]

But I want to suggest three further aspects to anonymous publication that are relevant to my argument. First, loosing the book from the name liberates it as art; launches it into the space of ingenious aesthetic forms. If it had been immediately identified as by Edmund Gosse, the first reception was liable to be preoccupied by biographical questions. Was he fair to his father? Was it as accurate as he claimed? How did it compare to his 'official biography' of his father? Should he have written it, and published it? How did it affect his reputation? Did it invite reappraisal of his earlier work? Unmoored to the family name, it could only be read (other than by those who knew Gosse well enough to recognize him) as an aesthetic presentation: as (in its subtitle) 'A Study of Two Temperaments'. 'Temperament' is very much an aesthete's term, privileging sensibility and the cultivation of feeling above all. While this might seem to etiolate the book, depriving it of the energies of the actual, in effect it makes it more generally powerful. The clash between the two temperaments can then stand not just for the conflict within a particular family, but between two different epochs—Victorian and modern; two different political philosophies—authoritarian and liberal; and two different belief systems—the religious and the aesthetic.

Second, the book's anonymity may have indicated a certain resistance in Gosse to identify himself as his father's son? Anonymity signifies differently in a family memoir than in an atomistic autobiography, because the family name is, precisely, the family's name, as well as the author's. 'Edmund Gosse? Oh yes, Philip Gosse's boy.' Like Mill, worrying about what his father's doctrine of the formation of character by circumstance said about his own individuality, Gosse is likely to have wondered how far it was possible to escape from the influence of such a controlling parent. Indeed, the form he finds, which seemed to contemporaries ingeniously new, in which his autobiography is coupled with his father's biography, is to say the least a paradoxical way of expressing his emancipation from that father. This, I'd suggest, is why it mattered to him not only to have the last word, but to appear to do so without anger. For the apparent equanimity and resignation of the conclusion wants to mark its distance from the violence and hysteria of the final spiritual clash; to demonstrate that he is not still in the grip of it, but has put it behind him, with his father's influence. To call this an 'emancipatory fantasy' has some psychological truth. The psychoanalytic concept of the superego accounts for the mechanism by which early parental influence can be internalized, and continue to intervene unconsciously in adult behaviour. But there is a danger in such arguments that emancipation comes to seem something that can only exist as fantasy, and can never be realized. There are

[123] Edmund Gosse, 'The Ethics of Biography' [1903], excerpted in James L. Clifford (ed.), *Biography as an Art: Selected Criticism, 1560–1960* (London: Oxford University Press, 1962), 113–19 (p. 114).

comparable disputes over Joyce, and other writers like William Empson, committed to a project of liberation from theological control. Christian critics are inclined to argue that the passion of their struggle is testimony to the hold the religion still has on them; that it shows they are not as free as they argue. (Psychoanalysis' tendency to disarm arguments against it as signs of a 'resistance' which proves its truth is comparable; one of the reasons it is sometimes criticized as itself messianic; and equally frustrating to those trying to engage in rational public debate.)

This is where the aesthetic function is crucial. Anonymous publication—which due to the subject matter required the anonymity of the father as well as the son—enabled Gosse to demonstrate that his choice of the aesthetic rather than religious life had substance; that it was not mere youthful rebelliousness, but an alternative vocation. It was Gosse's way of proving that he had been able to achieve authentic self-transformation. Once the book had been praised on its own merits, this legitimated the idea that he had fashioned his own life. It was only then he attached his own name to it. By 1907 Gosse was already an established literary biographer, with lives of Gray (1882), Congreve (1888), Donne (1899), Jeremy Taylor (1904), Coventry Patmore (1905), and Sir Thomas Browne (1905) to his name, in addition to his life of Philip Henry Gosse (1890). But *Father and Son* showed that he could fashion his own life too. The ruse of anonymity enabled him later to assume his literary identity in his own name, rather than in the name of the father.

The third factor is that the withholding of the name, at least initially, stands for the way in which auto/biography conceals as much as it reveals. Concealing the name enables revelations that might have been thought too delicate if attached to a named father. The selectiveness of Gosse's new form implies another axis of concealment. By concentrating on his childhood—by literally ending the story when he reaches the age of majority, as it was then—he brackets off the subsequent adult life by which moralistic readers would want to judge his apostasy.

In John Galsworthy's 'A Portrait' (1910), generally taken to be a sketch of his father, it is the subject rather than the author who remains anonymous—and thus also his relation to the narrator is occluded—even though it is all but implied by the intimacy of the vignettes: the narrator accompanies him to his friend's funeral, watches him playing with his grandchildren, knows what his hand felt like to children, and so on.[124] While biographers read this nostalgic portrait (much more sympathetic towards the father than Gosse) as auto/

---

[124] Galsworthy, 'A Portrait', in *A Motley* (London: Heinemann, 1910), pp. 1–29. In *Caravan: The Assembled Tales of John Galsworthy* (New York: Charles Scribner's Sons, 1925), pp. 115–28, the date of the piece is erroneously given as 1908 in the table of contents, but it is dated as 1910 at the end. *A Motley* says the piece appeared there for the first time, and also gives the date at the end as 1910.

biographical, the effect of the anonymity is to make it read as a short story—and to make its subsequent inclusion in *Caravan: The Assembled Tales of John Galsworthy* seem natural. It is another instance of pseudonymity and anonymity working to fictionalize auto/biography.

The displacements of the name in such texts take a striking variety of forms, and by juxtaposing some of the best known the aim is not to assimilate them as a single phenomenon. As Charles Swann argues, 'anonymity and pseudonymity should not be confused. We approach a text differently if it is genuinely anonymous, if it is known to be pseudonymous, and if the identity behind the pseudonym is known.'[125] As he also explains, the approach also depends on the reader's familiarity with the names and figures. Gissing was already known as a novelist, whereas much less was known about Hale White by readers of 'Mark Rutherford' than we now know about him. The anonymity of *Father and Son* is curiously compromised, at least for readers who knew what Philip Gosse had looked like, by the placing of a photograph of the eponymous pair as a frontispiece.[126] There is also a difference between authors like Gosse (and the authors of *Nemesis* and *Oakfield* before him) who owned their pseudonymous works in subsequent editions, and someone like Hale White, who sustained his pseudonymity.[127] And between those (like Gosse) who use a pseudonym for a single work, those who use pseudonyms for some but not all their work, and those (like Hale White) who use them for most or all their work. And between those (like Hale White) who use one pseudonym serially, and those (like Kierkegaard or Pessoa) who are serial users of multiple pseudonyms.

Not only are there different degrees of both anonymity and pseudonymity, but they 'are not fully adequate descriptive terms', Swann argues, noting another aspect of much of this writing, which we could see as yet another form of auto/biographical displacement. 'Rutherford''s autobiography and novels are purportedly published after 'Rutherford' is supposed to have died. Ryecroft too has died, as has the protagonist of another book Swann discusses, *The House of Quiet*, by A. C. Benson, but published with a combination of anonymity and pseudonymity (and discussed in the next chapter).[128]

Nor are such developments confined to prose. Something comparable happens in Christina Rossetti's sequence of fourteen sonnets, 'Monna Innominata'. Rossetti performs a curious manoeuvre in which she prefaces the poems, which are all first-person love lyrics, with a note that juxtaposes the women named by Dante and Petrarch as their addressees, Beatrice and Laura, with the unnamed ladies—*donne innominate*—of earlier lyrics. This leads to imagining such ladies as themselves poets. 'Had such a lady spoken for herself, the portrait left us might have appeared more tender, if less dignified, than any drawn even by a devoted

[125] Swann, 'Autobiografiction': 21–37 (p. 30).   [126] Ibid., 30–1, 33.
[127] Ibid., p. 25.   [128] Ibid., p. 21.

friend.'[129] The note doesn't actually claim the sonnets originate from another time, another voice, or even another language (as do Elizabeth Barrett Browning's *Sonnets from the Portuguese*, which the note also cites, though as 'Portuguese Sonnets'). But it implies as much: as does the title, suggesting that the lady is not Rossetti but someone anonymous, offering her self-portrait. Thus the note poses the sequence as imaginary writing by a fictional poetess; an imaginary portrait of a self-portraitist. The ploy is comparable to Robert Browning's use of the dramatic monologue; except that few were likely to identify the author with his characters other than very loosely; whereas Rossetti's brother, William Michael Rossetti, provided a note to the sequence which seeks to turn it back into Christina Rossetti's autobiography. He claims that to anyone who knew her well, it is 'certain that this "sonnet of sonnets" was a personal utterance—an intensely personal one', and describes the introductory 'prose-note' as 'a blind interposed to draw off attention from the writer in her proper person.'[130] But what this shows is precisely the adaptability of auto/biografictional play as a way of concealing, or at least ambiguating, personality; personal utterance.

These practices of pseudonymity, third-personality, or anonymity, thus represent a range of different modes in which auto/biography becomes transformed from the end of the nineteenth century. As we have seen, there is a growing emphasis on the 'inner life', which parallels the emerging discourses of sexology and psychoanalysis. And with this goes an acceptance that in order to express that inner life, expression needs to find more oblique forms; a feeling that the received forms of auto/biography have grown a little tired; are too restrictive for the expression desired; that it is time to subject them to experimental reconfiguration. This results in a proliferation of partially fictionalized life-writings, which combine expression with concealment in different ways. The strategies described in these turn-of-the-century experiments in autobiografiction by Hale White, Gissing, Gosse, and Wells, provide the context for better-known books of the twenties and thirties, such as Siegfried Sassoon's semi-fictionalized autobiography of 'George Sherston', which appeared as *Memoirs of a Fox-Hunting Man* (1928), *Memoirs of an Infantry Officer* (1930), and *Sherston's Progress* (1936). Though Sherston has had many of Sassoon's experiences, and most of his military experiences, he doesn't share Sassoon's poetic vocation.[131] His biographer, Jean Moorcroft Wilson, connects the writing of the first volume with Sassoon's early admiration for Pater.[132] Certainly the trilogy constitutes a

---

[129] *The Poetical Works of Christina Georgina Rossetti*, with Memoir and Notes &C by William Michael Rossetti (London: Macmillan, 1904), p 58; p. 64 dates the sequence as 'Before 1882'.
[130] Ibid., p. 462.
[131] Jean Moorcroft Wilson, *Siegfried Sassoon: The Journey from the Trenches* (London: Duckworth, 2003), p. 235, notes that Sassoon's attempt to differentiate Sherston from himself caused problems when it came to Sassoon's public protest against the war in *Memoirs of an Infantry Officer*.
[132] Ibid., p. 189.

triptych of imaginary self-portraiture. *Memoirs of a Fox-Hunting Man* was initially published anonymously in 1928. It was reviewed so well, and sold so well, that it was reprinted eight times in the following six months. The *Daily Mail* revealed the author's identity on 2 October 1928, and Sassoon's name was added to the title-page for the second impression.[133] Though Sassoon had unimpeachable motives for wanting to disguise the identities of real people described in his 'Sherston' memoirs—including himself—the story of their publication reminds us how anonymity or pseudonymity are ambiguous gestures. While they can seem (and may be intended as) tentative, tactful, an anxious testing of the water with potentially controversial or disturbing material, they can have the converse effect of actually drawing attention to the question of authorship; of stirring up curiosity and publicity; of contributing to the cult of personality.

The war is said to have produced a *rappel à l'ordre*, an impulse to pull back from pre-war modernist experimentation. The proliferation of war memoirs appearing a decade afterwards might be seen as representing a comparable pulling back from pre-war experiments in autobiografiction. Yet the disturbances the war provoked in psychology, society, and history troubled the category of autobiography in new ways. It was as if war's surreal qualities demanded fictionalization to begin to capture them; and as if war re-problematized the relation between autobiography and fiction. When Samuel Hynes argues that 'Sassoon acknowledged the distorting power of memory by fictionalising his narrative', it is perhaps implicit that the distorting power of war magnified the distorting power of memory.[134] Mary Borden's *The Forbidden Zone* (1929) is a heavily stylized and aestheticized set of vignettes, testifying not only to the first-hand experience on which it is clearly based, but also to her contacts with pre-war modernist writers and artists. Set alongside the fictionalized memoirs such as those of Sassoon, it might suggest that authors found the need to fictionalize experiences that would otherwise be unbearably close, impossible to achieve any aesthetic detachment from. Yet if this was the case, so was the converse: for many writers—Graves, Ford, and Brittain, say—the first impulse was to write a novel; but it was when they found the material too intractable for that form that they recast it into memoir, however fictionalized. 'My original idea was that of a long novel', writes Brittain of *Testament of Youth* (1933), 'and I started to plan it. To my dismay it turned out a hopeless failure.'[135] Robert Graves, too, describes how 'In 1916, when on leave in England after being wounded' he began writing his account of his first few months in France in fictional form: 'Having stupidly written it as a novel', he said, he had in *Goodbye to All That* 'to re-translate it into

---

[133] Wilson, *Siegfried Sassoon*, pp. 175, p. 450 n. 1.

[134] Hynes, *A War Imagined: The First World War and English Culture* (London: The Bodley Head, 1990), p. 436.

[135] Brittain, *Testament of* Youth (London: Virago, 1983), p. [11].

history.'[136] These accounts of life-writing pose fiction and autobiography as separate categories (if Graves's version suggests a degree of slyness). As argued in the Introduction, a more dynamic shifting between fiction and autobiography can be seen in Sassoon's *Memoirs of an Infantry Officer*. When texts do this as substantially as Sassoon's *Memoirs*, the shifting back and forth between autobiography and fiction constitutes autobiografiction.[137]

Thus the First World War produced its own hybrids of autobiography and fiction, like Sassoon's; and the unprecedented experiences of the war had their own transforming effects on the conditions of subjectivity. Reviewing a study of war trauma, Adam Phillips goes so far as to contemplate the extent to which modern war shaped the concept of the inner life, issuing in 'a new way of describing the modern individual':

As the external world becomes more and more intolerable, the modern individual is seen to be living somewhere else, somewhere more real that is called the internal world. Modern warfare, Barham seems to suggest, helped to give birth to this inner world. And though this inner world was bereft of willpower, it seemed, perhaps by the same token, to be full of far more interesting things: feelings, thoughts, impressions, desires, an unconscious mind etc. It was not merely one's actions and their consequences that mattered now, but the relationship between a person's actions and this putative internal world.[138]

The First World War may well have 'helped' usher in this world. But our story of turn-of-the-century auto/biografiction shows that this concern with the 'inner world' or 'inner life' had already been well established for three decades. So Storm Jameson had understood it in 1931, writing of 'the enormous interest shown in recent years in biography and autobiography.'[139] She saw First World War memoirs as transforming autobiographical writing, arguing that 'The finest achievement of modern autobiography, and the only one that excuses and (you may say) sanctifies any others, is the war book proper.'[140] But, crucially, she also saw how such transformation had begun earlier: 'over a long period the novels written by clever young men and women have become increasingly autobiographical in content.'[141] Praising *Goodbye to All That*, she argued that 'our minds have been prepared for such books as his, for a burst of frank and undisguised self-portraiture, by a cloud of little books in which the self-portrait is thinly veiled, and by one big book—Proust's long novel.'[142] The books discussed so far

---

[136] Graves, *Goodbye to All That* (Harmondsworth: Penguin, 1960), p. 79.

[137] See the Conclusion for a theoretical consideration of this shifting process.

[138] Adam Phillips, 'Newfangled Inner Worlds', *London Review of Books* (3 March 2005), 21–2 (p. 21). Reviewing Peter Barham, *Forgotten Lunatics of the Great War* (New Haven: Yale University Press, 2004).

[139] Storm Jameson, 'Autobiography and the Novel', *Bookman* (New York) 72:6 (February 1931), 557–65 (p. 561).

[140] Ibid., p. 563.

[141] Ibid., p. 562.

[142] Ibid.

began to condense that cloud. The remainder of this study elaborates the story Jameson sketches, of how the recombining of auto/biography and fiction helped precipitate modernism.

The focus of this chapter has been on works concentrating on a single subjectivity, and reaching out from life-writing towards fiction. The next two chapters develop these arguments; first by exploring the theoretical issues; then by looking at texts of multiple personality, and focusing on the converse movement, by which fictional texts colonize forms of life-writing.

4

Autobiografiction: Stephen Reynolds and A. C. Benson[1]

'But I am a fictitious article and have long known it.'[2]

'there is for every man some one scene, some one adventure, some one picture that is the image of his secret life.'[3]

STEPHEN REYNOLDS

The foregoing chapter was drafted, much as it now reads, when your researcher was led to an essay that both seemed to confirm the argument (that the quest for the 'inner life' led to an increasing sense of generic instability and use of fictionalization) and—more surprisingly—its terminology. I first came across the term 'autobiografictions' as the title of a comparative literature conference at Goldsmiths' College.[4] Though I had felt uneasy about using it and its variants, the alternatives were unwieldier. I had become reconciled to its use, buoyed up by Laura Marcus's suggestion that auto/biographical writing appeared to necessitate or attract a high degree of neologism.[5] 'Autobiografiction' has acquired a limited currency. The web-based *Dictionnaire International des Termes Littéraires* included the term, giving merely a laconic definition, though one which promisingly brings together three of the different kinds of text under discussion here:

---

[1] Earlier versions of parts of this chapter have appeared as 'Autobiografiction: How the Edwardian Stephen Reynolds identified a new genre among the experiments of his time', 'Commentary' essay, *Times Literary Supplement* (3 October 2008), 13–15 (a publication of a revised version of my inaugural lecture given at King's College London on 15 April 2008); and as 'Autobiografiction: Experimental Life-Writing from the Turn of the Century to Modernism', *Literature Compass*, 6:2 (2009), 1–19.

[2] R. L. Stevenson to Sidney Colvin, 6 October 1894, *Vailima Letters: Being Correspondence addressed by Robert Louis Stevenson to Sidney Colvin* (London: Methuen, 1895), p. 351.

[3] W. B. Yeats, 'The Philosophy of Shelley's Poetry', in *The Major Works: Including Poems, Plays, and Critical Prose*, ed. Edward Larrissey, Oxford World's Classics (Oxford: Oxford University Press, 2001), p. 351.

[4] Held at Goldsmiths' College, 8–10 September 2003, some contributions from which were published in *Comparative Critical Studies*, 1:3 (2004): *Autobiografictions. Comparatist Essays*, ed. Lucia Boldrini and Peter Davies.

[5] Paper given at 'Autobiografictions' conference, but not published in the special issue cited above.

1. Text at the intersection between fictionnal [*sic*] and autobiographical fiction.
2. A fictionnal [*sic*] autobiography.
3. The writing of someone else's fiction.[6]

Most of the other instances apply it to postmodern fiction, which made me rashly assume that the term was itself a postmodern one, a sign of postmodernism's playful eclecticism; which is how the editors of the published papers from the 'Autobiografictions' conference treat it, saying it 'well reflects the dilemmas central to contemporary thought on auto/biography.'[7] For example, Peter J. Bailey argues that the recent proliferation of fictionalized autobiographies is indicative of 'a literary climate in which the distinction between autobiography and fiction has been sufficiently diluted so as to facilitate their melding into a form that might be called *autobiografiction.*'[8] This is typical of a tendency for critics to assume they have coined the term. 'We know that what is important is the text and not its label; however, were we to feel the necessity to find a definition less poetic than "a memoir bottled in a novel", we might invent a compound term like "autobiografiction" [. . .].'[9] Marta Dvorak uses the term (without discussing it) to denote contemporary Canadian literature characterized by what she calls 'The postmodern converging of autobiography, biography, and documentary within a single fictional space [. . .].'[10] Sometimes, late twentieth-century critics apply the term retrospectively to early twentieth-century books. Reviewing Milton Stern's book, *The Novels of F. Scott Fitzgerald*, Peter Buitenhuis commented that 'Stern uses the antique method of biographical criticism for the main part of his work, although he attempts to update the method by claiming that Fitzgerald's work is, in his barbarous neologism, "autobiografictional".'[11] André Bleikasten says that both Faulkner's *Sanctuary* and Beckett's *Murphy* should be 'considered "autobiografiction".'[12]

So I delayed reading Charles Swann's excellent essay '"Autobiografiction": Problems with Autobiographical Fictions and Fictional Autobiographies. Mark Rutherford's *Autobiography* and *Deliverance*, and Others', wrongly imagining it to

---

[6] See <http://www.ditl.info/arttest/art10086.php> (accessed 18 July 2006). I am grateful to Lucia Boldrini, for this reference. The term 'autofiction' has greater currency.

[7] *Autobiografictions. Comparatist Essays*, ed. Boldrini and Davies. In their Introduction, pp. v–viii (p. v).

[8] Peter J. Bailey, '"Why Not Tell the Truth?": The Autobiographies of Three Fiction Writers', *Critique*, 32 (1991), 1–23.

[9] Clara Bartocci, 'John Barth's *Once Upon a Time*: Fiction or Autobiography?', Associazione Italiana di Studi Nord-Americani (Italian Association for North American Studies), <http://www.aisna.net/rsajournal6/bartocci.html> (accessed 20 April 2006).

[10] Marta Dvorak, 'Autobiografiction: Strategies of (Self) Representation', *Commonwealth Essays and Studies* 24:1 (2001), 91–101 (p. 99).

[11] Peter Buitenhuis, 'The Golden Moment', *New York Times* (20 December 1970).

[12] André Bleikasten, 'Of Sailboats and Kites: The "Dying Fall" in Faulkner's *Sanctuary* and Beckett's *Murphy*', in *Intertextuality in Faulkner*, ed. Michel Gresset and Noel Polk (Jackson: University Press of Mississippi, 1985), pp. 57–72.

be a postmodern reading of Hale White's pseudonymity.[13] But meanwhile a more recent search turned up two reviews discussing Stephen Reynolds.[14] I knew of Reynolds as the author of a book about his life with Sidmouth fishermen, *A Poor Man's House*, and a younger writer befriended by Conrad and Ford Madox Ford, who published him in the *English Review*, and even supported him by giving him some editorial work on the *Review*. *A Poor Man's House* (1908) has been much admired by Labour historians (one edition has an introduction by Roy Hattersley); and I'd taken Reynolds's account as autobiographical reportage. What I hadn't known was that two years before the book was published, in 1906, he had written an extraordinary article, titled with just the one word: 'Autobiografiction.'[15] This essay, it turned out, was where Swann found his title. And what it startlingly shows is how exactly that 'converging of autobiography, biography, and documentary within a single fictional space', which to a contemporary critic seems so 'postmodern', had been identified when modernism was emerging, as characteristic of the (pre-modernist) literature of the turn of the century.[16]

It is a short but immensely suggestive piece, and in what follows I shall consider it in detail, in order to show how it sheds light not only on the literature of the end of the nineteenth century, but also on the literature to come: modernism. Reynolds's essay certainly bears on 'Rutherford', who is one of its main points of reference, along with *Ryecroft*, and A. C. Benson. Swann brings out Reynolds's acuity in connecting these works, and identifying a contemporary phenomenon, and uses his concept of 'autobiografiction' to open up the question of autobiographical personae, and to ask necessary questions about how contemporary readers could have approached the autobiographicality or fictionality of these texts. However, his discussion of Reynolds's essay is generally limited to its application to *The Autobiography of Mark Rutherford*. Whereas the essay and its title-concept are much more broadly significant—even in ways that arguably escaped their author—on several counts.

First, it shows a writer acutely aware of the interfusing of these genres of autobiography and fiction (and indeed of the discursive too, since Reynolds

---

[13] *Modern Language Review*, 96:1 (2001), 21–37.

[14] Jonathan Keates, 'Angels of resurrection', *Spectator*, 287 (15 September 2001), 41; review of Scoble's edition of Reynolds, A Poor Man's House (Tiverton: Halsgrove, 2001). *Year's Work in English Studies*, vol. 81 (2002), Julian Cowley *et al.*, 'Modern Literature', pp. 767–873 (p. 789); reviewing Scoble's biography, Fisherman's Friend: *A Life of Stephen Reynolds: 1881–1919* (Tiverton, Devon: Halsgrove, 2000).

[15] Stephen Reynolds, 'Autobiografiction', *Speaker*, n.s., 15:66 (1906), 28, 30. The essay is also discussed by Peter Keating, *The Haunted Study: A Social History of the English Novel 1875–1914* (London: Fontana, 1991), pp. 309–11. Keating notes in passing the relevance of the concept to modernists such as Joyce and Lawrence, but his main emphasis is on the presentation of society, and on a contrast between Reynolds and Wells. There is also a brief discussion in Charles Lock, 'On Biographical Proportions: A Review-Essay', *The Powys Journal*, 13 (2003), 240–7 (pp. 244–5). Margareta Jolly's otherwise excellent *Encyclopedia of Life Writing: Autobiographical and Biographical Forms*, 2 vols (London and Chicago: Fitzroy Dearborn, 2002), has no entry for 'Autobiografiction' nor for Reynolds.

[16] Dvorak, 'Autobiografiction: Strategies of (Self) Representation', p. 99.

4 Stephen Reynolds, Reynolds, *Letters*, ed. Wright (1934).

includes the essay as a component) as it was happening around him. His essay appeared the year before *Father and Son*, which it describes exactly. Second, because he found the name for it a century ago, and exactly in the middle of the long 'turn-of-the-century' period under consideration here. Though he appears uneasy with the coinage, he uses it repeatedly and resolutely, because it answers to the forms of the times. Third, his analysis of these texts led him to a theory of their genesis; and this in turn helps us to understand the relationship of his grouping of texts to other experiments with life-writing. And finally, the key themes and strategies he identifies are precisely those that are germane to our analyses: not just the question of autobiography's turn towards fiction, but the issues of egotism, of the spirit, of the 'inner life', and of the aesthetic.

The essay is brief, taking up just two dense pages of *The Speaker*. But it is extraordinarily concise and suggestive, and a key document for our purposes, both for what it says about autobiografiction, and for the fact of its discussing the form. Reynolds defines it as focused on 'spiritual experience', which he defines in turn as:

anything that reacts strongly on the mind, from a vision of heaven to a joint of beef eaten with a full perception of its meaning in life; any emotion, beautiful thing, work of art, sorrow, religion, or love, which intensifies a man's existence; anything in short that directly touches his soul.

The joint of beef is something of a hearty distraction, since (as we shall see) he privileges autobiografictions concerned with spiritual and mental crises. It's worth noting, though, that this elasticity in the definition of the 'spiritual' is one factor enabling a corresponding elasticity in the definition of 'autobiografiction' too. He is struck by the definitional problems surrounding the form. And he notes the prevalence of pseudonymity in the quest after the 'inner life'. He also suggests connections between fictionalized autobiographies and fictionalizations of other life-writing forms such as journals and letters. Indeed, in a 'Preface' he wrote for a later edition of *A Poor Man's House* in 1911, Reynolds explicitly situated his own writing in this context:

Works of fiction are frequently cast into the form of journals, diaries, letters, autobiography, and so forth. In every respect they are written down as if they were works of fact, actually as well as imaginatively true; and on the extent of the illusion their success largely depends.[17]

But the earlier essay, besides being a manifesto for the book he was about to write, is also critically more sophisticated.[18]

Reynolds begins by distinguishing 'Autobiografiction' from the two areas where the fusion of autobiography and fiction are most often noted—autobiographical fiction on the one hand, and unreliable autobiography on the other:

The phrase autobiographical fiction is mainly reserved for fiction with a good deal of the writer's own life in it, or for those lapses from fact which occur in most autobiographies. Hence the need for coining a rather dreadful portmanteau-word like *autobiografiction* in order to connote shortly a minor literary form which stands between those two extremes; which is of late growth and of a nature at once very indefinite and very definite.[19]

---

[17] 'Preface to the New Edition' (1911), *A Poor Man's House* (Oxford: Oxford University Press, 1982), [p. xv].

[18] See Scoble, *Fisherman's Friend*, p. 224: '*A Poor Man's House* was constructed according to the principles Reynolds had set out in *Autobiografiction* in October 1906; that is, a selected episode of autobiography, slightly rearranged in time and space, written to communicate a deeply-felt spiritual experience.' He also discusses the essay on pp. 135–6.

[19] Reynolds, 'Autobiografiction', p. 28.

'Autobiografiction', that is, appears to him as a recent phenomenon. He addresses its paradoxical combination of generic definiteness and indefiniteness in a surprising way, surprising not least because it anticipates the most surprising strategy of what is probably the most famous literary-critical essay of the twentieth century, T. S. Eliot's 'Tradition and the Individual Talent', with its celebrated analogy between chemical catalysis and poetic creation. Reynolds— who had read chemistry at Owens College, Manchester—finds a precise chemical image for autobiografiction's indeterminacy as to state:

Perhaps a scientific analogy may clear the ground. At one particular temperature, combined with one particular pressure, the solid, liquid, and gaseous states of sulphur are in equilibrium. Alter by ever so little the temperature or the pressure, and immediately the sulphur liquefies, vaporises, or solidifies. But so long as the very definite temperature and pressure are unchanged, the sulphur remains in that indefinite state of neither solid, nor liquid, nor gas, but something between the three. So with autobiografiction. It is so indefinite, and shades off so gradually into better marked, well-known forms, that its existence as a distinct literary *genre* appears disputable. At the same time it is the outcome of definite tendencies and has a very definite position on the literary chart. Where the three converging lines—autobiography, fiction, and the essay—meet, at that point lies autobiografiction.[20]

His delimitation of it as a 'minor literary form' is probably a show of modesty, given that it is the form in which he was to excel. Yet it also comes from the desire in his essay to identify it with narratives of spiritual crisis. That is certainly one form autobiografiction can take. If one restricts the term to cover only narratives structured like autobiography, then it refers only to the kind of work discussed in the last chapter; and not even to all the works discussed there, but only to those like *The Autobiography of Mark Rutherford*, which cover the bulk of the subject's life. According to this restrictive definition, works like *The Private Papers of Henry Ryecroft*, or A. C. Benson's *The House of Quiet* (based on a fictional journal), or *The Upton Letters* (also by A. C. Benson; structured as half of a fictional correspondence) would be excluded. But Reynolds does include *Ryecroft* and *The House of Quiet* as central examples, and raises the question of the relationship of autobiografiction to works in other forms, such as *The Upton Letters*, the *Essays of Elia*, and *Sartor Resartus*. This passage recognizes how, as 'autobiografiction' shades off into other forms, it appears much more extensive. Taken in this broader sense, it includes not only all the works covered in the last chapter, and earlier works by writers like Carlyle, or by Romantic autobiographers like Wordsworth or De Quincey, but also all those covered in the next (which fictionalize not just autobiography but all the other major forms of life-writing as well—letters, diary, journal, memoir, portrait, biography), and also all the modernist engagements with life-writing discussed in Part II. Reynolds

---

[20] Reynolds, 'Autobiografiction', p. 28.

certainly glimpses this sense in which 'autobiografiction' can be an extremely powerful concept; though his essay seems to pull back from that possibility, closing, as we shall see, with an attempt to narrow the application by another criterion. But it is in this broader sense that I use the term, and which thus provides the core concept of this study.

'Autobiografiction', says Reynolds, is 'a record of real spiritual experiences strung on a credible but more or less fictitious autobiographical narrative.' That last clause is crucial, and makes it clear how such writing is distinct from most autobiographical novels. It doesn't just use autobiographical *material*, put into the form of a novel, but uses autobiographical *form* too. His formulation is more double-jointed than it might first appear, though. Autobiografiction is 'real' autobiographical experience (the 'spiritual experiences') turned into fictional form. But it isn't just the form that is fictionalized, but the autobiographical experience itself; either because it has been altered, or because it has been attributed to someone else; reinvented as another's imaginary experience. Either way, this fictionalization is presented in what is therefore pseudo-autobiographical form. The definition requires the 'spiritual' and the 'autobiographical' to be separable, and appears to privilege the 'spiritual' as significant experience: what intensifies our lives, or touches our souls. That leaves the 'autobiographical' as the less significant circumstances, which provide the context for such experiences. The distinction appears to correspond to that between the inner life and the outer; and it implies that the spiritual experiences are not fictionalized, but the other experiences are. Yet the example of the joint of beef suggests that these lines between what is and isn't significant, and between what is and isn't fictionalized, are harder to draw. As it proves in many major modernist autobiografictions, in which spiritual significance is attributed to the most unobtrusive, everyday moments, such as dipping a madeleine in tea, or seeing a curtain fluttering in a window.

Reynolds goes on to add another, less anticipated, component: 'And it reads very like, is closely related to, an essay.' He cites Lamb's *Dream Children* as 'a beautiful short example': 'The longing for a wife and children was one of his spiritual experiences. To express it he records a fictitious fireside gathering of the wife and children he never had.' And he quotes Lamb's biographer Alfred Ainger on it: '"The emotion in this essay is absolutely genuine; the blending of fact with fiction in the details is curiously arbitrary." In other words, it is a piece of autobiografiction.' Why does Reynolds connect autobiografiction with the essay? In part, it's because he sees autobiografiction as using only *selected* autobiographical material, however fictionalized. This is likely to give it a thematic focus: spiritual crisis, aesthetic development, childhood, a friendship, and so on. That thematic focus in turn can incline the narrative toward the discursive; if, that is, the selection appears to have been made in order to make a point (this is what religious doubt is like to live through, and it's the sign of our times; this is the nature of the aesthetic life; or—in the case of the book Reynolds was soon to write—this is what working-class hardship is like in a neglected non-industrialized trade). Conversely, what the connection with the essay also does is to stretch the coverage of 'autobiografiction' to include essay-length pieces—like Lamb's.

Reynolds then names his three main exhibits, which he takes to be 'entirely typical': 'Rutherford''s *Autobiography*, *Ryecroft*, and *The House of Quiet*. (It is curious that he doesn't cite Pater or Butler, but this is perhaps because the *Imaginary Portraits* and *The Way of all Flesh* are predominantly biografictional in form.) With definitions and examples in place, he moves on to consider why autobiografiction might recommend itself to writers. What's unexpected here, especially given his emphasis on the spiritual and its crises, is that he doesn't start with the obvious answers of the advantages of disguise: concealment, protection of self and others; tact. Indeed, as a homosexual, writing only a decade after the Wilde trial, he would have been particularly sensible of the need to be guarded about his intimate life.[21] Instead, he identifies two factors. First, and with another striking chemical analogy, the idea that there is something about spiritual experience, or accounts of it, that is inherently unappealing:

Now, spiritual experience is an awkward thing to deal with in bulk. Pabulum for a few, it is spice to the many, and mightily difficult to make a dish of. Like nitro-glycerine and absolute alcohol, it positively demands absorption or dilution. It is apt to be rhapsodical, wearisome, or incredible; witness Blake's Prophetical Books, Wordsworth's *Excursion*, or the philosopher Teufelsdröckh in *Sartor Resartus*. Jefferies' *Story of My Heart*, which contains the minimum of material detail, would scarcely bear lengthening [. . .] Doubtless my friend's inner life is the most interesting thing about him, but for him to spend all day and every day in telling me of nothing except his spiritual adventures[22] would be as intolerable as for him never to stop singing 'Beer, beer, glorious beer!' Overmuch spirit becomes a thorn in the flesh.

But perhaps one needs to read that precisely as a way of negotiating queer autobiography; since a gay writer may well have been concerned as to how his psychic life would be tolerated by others. The second hint Reynolds gives as to the appeal of the genre is also curiously negative: that it might suit an author unable, or unwilling, to write fiction, or a poet inept at rhyme. At least, that is one possible motive in the sketch he gives next of how a piece of autobiografiction might come to be written. The point here is that a writer wanting to express a spiritual experience feels that none of the forms of fiction, autobiography, or the essay alone would be able to do it justice. It may even, in its miniature way, be a piece of autobiografiction itself—a sketch of how Reynolds had arrived at the aesthetic position that led him to *A Poor Man's House*:

---

[21] Christopher Scoble, entry for Reynolds in the *Oxford DNB*.
[22] Arthur Symons's *Spiritual Adventures*—parts of which would certainly qualify as essayistic autobiografiction, and which is discussed in the next chapter—had appeared the previous year.

So the genesis of autobiografiction may be imagined thus. A man, usually of an introspective nature, has accumulated a large body of spiritual experiences. He feels that he must out with it [. . .] What is he to do? Fiction is impracticable. He does not wish, or is not able, to invent such a complicated apparatus for self-expression. Besides, the story's the thing in fiction. To use that medium would be to scatter and sink precisely the spiritual experience which he wants to record. Formal autobiography would present much the same difficulty—the introduction of a large amount of (for his purpose) extraneous matter—for a man's life and the events of it, chronological sequence and completeness, are the aim in autobiography. Essays, again, would be too disconnected and would scarcely admit of an attitude frankly egotistical enough. How, then, are the pitfalls of spiritual experience in bulk to be avoided? He invents a certain amount of autobiographical detail, or (which comes to much the same) he selects from his life the requisite amount of autobiographical material, adding perhaps a quantity of pure fiction, and on that he builds the spiritual experience, with that he dilutes it, and makes it coherent and readable. The result is autobiografiction, a literary form more direct and intimate probably than any to be found outside poetry.

It is presumably because Reynolds grounds autobiografiction in spiritual experience that he feels it delivers such intimacy. And it is at this point that he entertains the idea of concealment. That is, it is because of its unusual intimacy that authors feel the need to distance themselves. The essay includes another acute passage not only discussing the qualities of pseudonymity, anonymity, and fictional posthumousness, but suggesting some of the nuances of each:

As might be expected, autobiografiction is nearly always published with some degree of anonymity. *Mark Rutherford's Autobiography and Deliverance* is indeed doubly pseudonymous, for that, and the other works of 'Mark Rutherford' are 'Edited by his [fictitious] Friend Reuben Shapcott.' *The Ryecroft Papers* [sic] purport to be the remains of a retired literary man, given to the world by George Gissing. *The House of Quiet* made its appearance as a dead man's journal, edited by his distant cousin 'J. T.'—who has since written a very similar work, *The Thread of Gold*.[23] And, after all, when a writer has revealed to the world more of his inner self than he would exhibit to his friends, it is only natural that he should wish to stay behind the scenes, at least until he finds out how the world will take his revelation—whether with inattention, ridicule, or with sympathy.

The autobiographical element of the essay comes to the fore when Reynolds concludes by discussing contemporary readers of these books. This passage too is valuable (though perhaps the more valuable the closer it is to autobiography than to autobiografiction) for giving a sense of how the genre was experienced, by actual readers most of whom were not professional critics:

Lending books discretely is often of great help in judging them. In lending these autobiografictions to all sorts of people, I have found that readers divide themselves

---

[23] As we shall see below, the questions of who edited *The House*, and whether 'J. T.' can be said to have written *The Thread*, are both more complex than Reynolds suggests. See pp. 183–7.

into two classes. One class says in effect: 'Yes, very nice indeed; fine writing, but too depressing, too introspective and too pessimistic, you know.' The other class finds them immensely inspiring and inspiriting.

The reason he offers for these polarized responses is, at first sight, not the one the essay might have appeared to lead us towards: their generic hybridity. Instead, he attributes their effect to the nature of the 'spiritual experience' they relate:

A prominent spiritual experience in most of these books is the writer's journey through the Slough of Despond. People who have gone their way, eating their bread with joy, and drinking their wine with a merry heart (see the Preface to *Mark Rutherford's Autobiography*); who are ignorant of, or determined to ignore, the Slough of Despond, find any book depressing which brings home to them the existence of it. Those, on the contrary, who are troubled in body or mind; who have been, or are, in the Slough of Despond themselves, gain courage and endurance from the knowledge that someone else has been there too, has found it just endurable and has come through. How helpful is that writer as a guide through the Slough, how calming and comforting his sympathy![24]

Those who have undergone a spiritual crisis take solace from others' tales about surviving comparable experiences. Reynolds's use of Bunyan's allegorical terminology enables him to fuse the spiritual and the psychological—those who are despondent due to loss of religious faith, and those despondent for other reasons. We would now call both 'depression', but must recognize that for writers of the period loss of faith was as genuine a grounds for depression as anything else. Part of Reynolds's strategy is to suggest that Bunyan's allegory is itself a work of autobiografiction. And that the invoking of its Slough of Despond here provides an example of why it is that narratives of spiritual crisis can be so much more affecting when they are cast into autobiografictional form. That is because the fictionalization of the autobiographical facilitates readers' empathy, not just because it cuts the material free from the name and person of the author, but because the aesthetic work that fiction performs on autobiography encourages a greater imaginative engagement with the material. The novelistic, that is, offers a range of empathetic devices which encourage one to read in a different way. For example, when we read Rousseau's *Confessions*, however novelistic they feel at times, we can rarely disattend to the question of what they tell us about a specific other historical self—that of Jean-Jacques Rousseau; or, consequently, to the question of their historical veracity. Whereas, as suggested in the previous chapter, when we read an autobiography-shaped work by someone whose name doesn't have that historical density—'Mark Rutherford', say; or that appears with no name, or just initials—then we are more likely to read it as we read a novel, and to imagine ourselves in the role of the narrator. The interiority of autobiography ministers powerfully to this tendency. Its presentation of a single consciousness, with the ability to range freely across its memories and

---

[24] Reynolds, 'Autobiografiction', pp. 28, 30.

feelings, makes it potentially one of the most intimate of forms. Of course these distinctions are not absolute. Some readers might find 'Rutherford' as 'other' as John Stuart Mill. But in general, it is the autobiografictional works that readers tend to think of as the most moving accounts of mental crises. Of course a novelist's empathetic techniques—characterization, description, focalization, free indirect style, metaphor, and so on—are open to an autobiographer too. But the more autobiographers avail themselves of them, the more their work will seem autobiografiction.

Reynolds closes the essay on this argument that the chief significance of autobiografiction lies in the psychological consolation it offers. This function helps him to tie the form to his period, which he characterizes as 'a time when the anchors of orthodox religion, robust health and tranquillity are dragging'. His own health was far from robust: his youth had been dogged by incipient tuberculosis, and he had almost died in 1903. At such a time, works of autobiografiction can 'give sailing directions for boats that have lost their rudders'. The last words seek to give the kind of spiritual uplift he sees the form as best equipped for:

> They are begetters of hope and confidence; missals of a new ceremonial that has arisen on the *other* side of doubt and trouble. In so far as literature can be dissociated from life, their importance is greater in life than in literature.[25]

The phrase 'the *other* side' intimates mortality, and thus also recapitulates the observation about posthumous publication to anticipate the argument that these autobiografictions are figuring a form of posthumous existence: a life after death, but an afterlife in literature. William Dean Howells suggested—in 1904—that autobiography was less depressing than biography, because the latter ended inevitably with death.[26] Yet Benson's autobiografiction is no less morbid. Indeed, one of the attractions of autobiografiction was that it appeared to offer an uncertain form of life after death—though arguably one more certain than biography, since we cannot be certain what others will write about us after our deaths; *pace* David Cannadine's jest that 'In our rampantly secular world, biography is the only certain form of life after death.'[27] The 'missals' might (as Swann suggests) be a swipe at Roman Catholicism and the Oxford Movement; but 'missals of a new ceremonial' also connotes the new-fangled rituals of spiritualism, seeking to summon departed spirits from 'the other side.'[28]

Swann makes the fascinating point that for its authors, purportedly posthumous autobiografiction offered the odd possibility of letting them read reviews

---

[25] Ibid., p. 30.

[26] Howells, 'The Editor's Easy Chair', *Harper's*, 108 (1904), 478–82 (p. 479).

[27] Cannadine, 'Too Golden Oldie', *Observer* (21 April 1991), Books, 61 (reviewing Martin Gilbert, *Churchill: A Life*).

[28] Charles Swann, 'Autobiografiction: Problems with Autobiographical Fictions and Fictional Autobiographies. Mark Rutherford's Autobiography and Deliverance and Others', *Modern Language Review*, 96:1 (2001), p. 36.

which were in effect their own obituaries; and thus might be seen to provide them with the impression of an afterlife that they could no longer be confident in getting from religion.[29] It makes their lives seem like Emerald Uthwart's, seen in melancholy retrospect even as he lives it.[30] Life-writing, as is often remarked, is also death-writing. Biography traditionally commemorated the dead before it began to commodify the living. Autobiography is a legacy to posterity. The rise of these forms is a response to secularization, in that they provide secular alternatives to spiritual meditations on life and death, and find new ways of performing anthropological necessities. However, to say that is to locate the mode's significance in questions of form—the shape of a life, and the point of view of the life-writer—as much as in any religious or pseudo-religious function. If Reynolds's autobiografictions are 'begetters of hope' for their readers, then, instead of offering hope of immortality on the other side of death, they offer hope of the other side of 'doubt and trouble'. In short, instead of hope of heaven, autobiografiction offers hope of beauty: 'How much beauty there is in these books the readers of *Rutherford*, *Ryecroft*, and *The House of Quiet* know very well.'[31] Autobiografiction thus allows different attitudes towards belief and scepticism, which perhaps helps explain its success and persistence. While on the one hand it can enable authors to emerge from their spiritual crises with an aesthetic vocation, on the other, as Benson's case shows, it can serve as an expression of belief, or of the desire to believe. Its fictionality can be used to foster an awareness of the fictionality in discourses claiming to be true, such as theology or autobiography. Alternatively, it can express a sense that there are truths that inhere in fictions.

I suggested earlier that there was something arbitrarily restrictive in Reynolds taking such consolatory works as his 'typical' autobiografictions. We see here that there is also a certain circularity in his argument, in that it is this restriction that then enables him to go on to claim that consolation (whether spiritual or

---

[29] Swann, 'Autobiografiction', p. 36. A curious example is provided by *The Journal of a Disappointed Man*, published as by W. N. P. Barbellion, with an Introduction by H. G. Wells (London: Chatto & Windus, 1919). 'Barbellion' was in fact pseudonym for Bruce Cummings (1889–1919). The combination of pseudonym and introduction by Wells is reminiscent of *Boon*, especially appearing so shortly after that book. Yet Cummings was a real person, who had written a real journal. His disappointment is real enough, too. He was diagnosed as suffering from disseminated sclerosis, which meant that he was forced actually to live the life Benson kept imagining, of a man of talent and imagination unable to live an active life. The *Journal* has Barbellion dying at the end of 1917. But in fact Cummings lived on until 1919, seeing the book which recorded his own death through publication, and presumably writing the synopsis and even the index which conclude it. There's no evidence Cummings fictionalized the experiences between the title page and concluding obituary note, so his book would count as pseudonymous autobiographical writing, not autobiografiction. But its fictional staging of his own death is comparable to Benson's fictions of posthumousness.

[30] Pater, 'Emerald Uthwart', *Miscellaneous Studies*, ed. Charles Shadwell (London: Macmillan, 1895), p. 228.

[31] Reynolds, 'Autobiografiction', p. 30.

aesthetic) is autobiografiction's chief function. However, just before the essay ends, Reynolds momentarily relaxes the definition:

It would be interesting to discuss in more detail all the books of this genre; to determine the relationship to it of Borrow's, Thoreau's and much of De Quincey's work, of *The Compleat Angler*, Rousseau's *Confessions*, many of the *Essays of Elia, Sartor Resartus, John Inglesant, My Trivial Life and Misfortune*,[32] *The Upton Letters*, gardening books and many others [. . .]

Ostensibly these other works are mentioned here by way of contextualization. To talk of determining their relationship with autobiografiction might suggest they are something else, and that the restricted definition stands. Yet Reynolds has already cited one of the *Essays of Elia*, 'Dream Children', as an example of something that is autobiografiction. After all, the *Essays of Elia* share many of the qualifying requirements. They are offered as a posthumous publication of writings by a fictionalized persona, edited by an anonymous 'Friend.' They adapt the form of the essay. And (as it seemed to E. V. Lucas, writing in 1914) they are 'a complete revelation of their writer's character and, with his correspondence, constitute an autobiography.'[33] So perhaps when he says it would be interesting to discuss 'all the books of this genre' the titles that follow are being given as examples of books that could or should be included. Furthermore, I also suggested that Reynolds's earlier examples were formally more fluid than his definitions. The definition requires the 'genuine spiritual experiences' to be stung on 'a more or less fictitious but very credible autobiography'. But the *Private Papers* and *The House of Quiet* string them, all or in part, on journal entries rather than autobiography. If journal entries, rearranged by the editor, are permissible, why are not letters, especially when (as in Benson's *Upton Letters*, discussed in the next chapter) they are presented in chronological sequence, and are thus arguably closer to formal autobiography. Reynolds's wondering about the relation of these texts to autobiografiction is the thin end of a wedge which would split his definition wide open—as perhaps he may have glimpsed, but then tried to fend the possibility off. He had chosen his examples, he said, 'From a number by no means great'. But admit works like these into the category, and the number multiplies immeasurably.

Which returns us to Reynolds's starting point: the 'very indefinite and very definite' nature of the form. By trying to restrict examples to narratives of the survival of spiritual crisis, he seeks to make it very definite; and very definitely the 'minor literary form' he modestly proposes. But by allowing the possibility of a more inclusive definition, he lets it appear very indefinite. What seemed a distinct *form* (spiritual experience presented through fictionalized autobiography) then

---

[32] *John Inglesant* was a romance by J. H. Shorthouse (Cornish Brothers: Birmingham, 1880); *My Trivial Life and Misfortune* was published anonymously as 'By a Plain Woman', 3 vols (Edinburgh: Blackwood, 1883).

[33] E. V. Lucas, Preface to *The Best of Lamb* (London: Methuen, 1914), p. x.

appears as a hybrid *mode* of writing (the intersection of autobiography, fiction, and essay) that can feature in any form—not just formal autobiography, but fiction, essays, biography, naturalist writing, reportage, letters, and so on. From this point of view, if it no longer appears a distinct form, it can no longer be seen as 'minor', since it cuts across many of the landmark works of literature from at least three centuries. Yet there is also something very timely about Reynolds's argument. For it indicates that the term 'autobiographical' was beginning to signify in new ways. When he says 'The phrase autobiographical fiction is mainly reserved for fiction with a good deal of the writer's own life in it, or for those lapses from fact which occur in most autobiographies', the qualification 'mainly' allows that some fiction might be called 'autobiographical' which doesn't fall into either of these two categories—precisely the kind he wants to designate autobiografiction. But how distinct a line can we draw between 'autobiographical fiction' and 'autobiografiction'? His neologism offers a way of trying to separate out the two. He would like to restrict 'autobiographical fiction' (when it's doing something more serious, or less reprehensible, than merely lapsing from fact) to work including circumstantial details from the author's life; and to restrict 'autobiografiction' to work including private, spiritual, or psychological details. It seems obvious to us that the problem with this distinction is that most substantial autobiographical writing will have to include both. But the fact Reynolds feels the need to make the distinction suggests that the meaning of the term 'autobiographical' felt problematic. His term 'formal autobiography' is indicative too. What interests him is work that cannot be called formal autobiography, but in which something autobiographical is nonetheless happening: work in which autobiography is happening by fictional means. It was no longer clear whether 'autobiographical' referred to the public, external aspects of a life, that might be recorded in an obituary or a biography; or to the 'inner life' that remained private. In other words, there had been a shift in what was understood by the 'autobiographical novel'; from event to experience; which corresponds to the general inward turn of both fiction and autobiography well attested in the period—as well as to the turn of autobiography itself towards fiction.

Reynolds died young, aged only thirty-eight, in the 1919 influenza epidemic. *A Poor Man's House* was well received. Through his association with Ford's *English Review* he encountered many leading writers of the day, including several of those discussed here. Conrad, for example, praised him to writers like Wells and Galsworthy. 'I decidedly think there is a lot in that young man', he told his agent, the year after the publication of 'Autobiografiction.'[34] I don't have any evidence of other writers having read the essay at the time, and it wasn't collected

---

[34] Conrad to Wells, 1 January 1908; Conrad to Galsworthy, 17 Feb. 1908; *The Collected Letters of Joseph Conrad*, ed. Frederick R. Karl and Laurence Davies, vol. 4 (Cambridge: Cambridge University Press, 1990), pp. 7, 43. Conrad to Pinker, 'Tuesday [8? October 1907]': *The Collected Letters of Joseph Conrad*, ed. Frederick R. Karl and Laurence Davies, vol. 3 (Cambridge: Cambridge University Press, 1988), p. 496. Also see Conrad to Pinker, 30 December 1907; ibid., p. 516.

into a book. But whether or not the essay had any direct influence, it is significant for exemplifying (together with Gosse) a contemporary formal self-awareness about modern experiments in life-writing. Reynolds had identified a new flowering of a particular hybrid variety of text, which would stimulate the development of some of the iconic works of modernism, though he wouldn't live to see most of them. He provided the earliest analysis of this phenomenon, and a remarkably shrewd one. Though he gives other explanations for its appearance than the unease with auto/biographical conventions posed by this book, that explanation is implied by his argument that autobiografiction is especially suited to express the 'spiritual' (or, to use the term of the preceding chapter), the 'inner life'.

The sheer number of works discussed in this chapter, and the chapters before and after it, and the sheer variety of their forms, demonstrate that Reynolds was right to identify a renaissance of autobiografiction as a turn-of-the-century phenomenon. But its significance is wider than he granted. By opening up the definition, to include other fictionalized life-writings (especially biography, diaries, letters), and other tones (especially the comic and ironic rather than merely the agonistic-spiritual), I hope to show that autobiografiction is not a minor form at all, but that it is a very widespread and diverse practice; and that the recovery of its turn-of-the-century energies enables a new approach to modernism, one which shows that autobiografiction is a major literary presence there too. The end of this chapter will consider some of the theoretical implications of autobiografiction, especially in relation to the arguments about autobiography raised in the Introduction. First, though, the next section will examine Reynolds's chief exhibit, A. C. Benson.

A. C. BENSON

The Introduction argued that impressionist unease with the realist novel precedes modernism. Such unease is articulated explicitly in one of Reynolds's key examples of autobiografiction, Benson's *The Thread of Gold*. Feeling that his original, anonymous Introduction had misled some readers, Benson added another for the second edition of December 1906:

One of the difficulties under which literary art seems to me to labour is that it feels bound to run in certain channels, to adopt stereotyped and conventional media of expression. What can be more conventional than the average play, or the average novel? People in real life do not behave or talk—at least, this is my experience—in the smallest degree as they behave or talk in novels or plays; life as a rule has no plot, and very few dramatic situations. In real life the adventures are scanty, and for most of us existence moves on in a commonplace and inconsequent way. Misunderstandings are not cleared up, complexities are not unravelled. I think it is time that more unconventional forms of expression should be discovered and

5 A. C. Benson, published in *The Diary of Arthur Christopher Benson*, edited by
Percy Lubbock (London: Hutchinson, [1926]).

used; and at least, we can try experiments; the experiment that I have here tried, is to present a
sort of *liber studiorum*, a portfolio of sketches and impressions.[35]

Few readers now would find anything avant-garde about Benson. Given the novels,
very unlike the average, by James, Wells, Conrad, Forster and others that had been
just appearing, his complaint against the novel's conventionality has something
about it that is, well, itself rather conventional. Yet he is so central to Reynolds's

[35] Benson, *The Thread of Gold* (London: John Murray, 1910), pp. xi–xii. Benson makes a similar
argument about the difficulties of making a novel about school life convincing in *The Upton Letters*
(London: Smith, Elder & Co., 1905), pp. 106–13. He also discusses 'impressions' in that book, p. 62.

argument,[36] was producing a remarkable variety of autobiografictional experiment, and was so widely read at the time that we need to consider him more closely.

Arthur Christopher Benson (1862–1925) was the eldest surviving son of E. W. Benson, who had been Archbishop of Canterbury. He and his two younger brothers were all prolific writers. Edward Frederic Benson is best known for his popular 'Dodo' and 'Lucia' series of novels, and also for the memoir *As We Were* (1930). Robert Hugh Benson became ordained in 1895, then became a Roman Catholic in 1903, and wrote diverse novels and religious propaganda. He also wrote a biography of Thomas à Becket, and collaborated with Frederick William Rolfe (Baron Corvo) on an uncompleted novel on the same subject: an imaginary (self-)portrait narrated by a medieval monk.[37] Robert's *Confessions of a Convert* came out in 1913. After he died the following year, Arthur, who had also written a biography of their father, published a book about him in 1915.[38] As Valerie Sanders has shown, all the brothers were serial auto/biographers, preoccupied with 'the possibilities of life writing.'[39]

In many ways Arthur Benson was a pillar of the Establishment. He had been a schoolmaster at Eton College from 1885 to 1903. During that time he published mainly hymns and song lyrics, the best known of which is 'Land of Hope and Glory' (1902). He left Eton in 1903 to edit Queen Victoria's correspondence; he became a fellow of Magdalene College, Cambridge, from 1904, and its Master from 1915 until his death.

Yet behind this public persona lies an insistent concern with what he too called the 'inner life', or 'the secret life', or with 'inner hearts.'[40] From 1897 he began keeping a diary, and continued until 1925. It is thought to be one of the longest ever written, amounting to some four million words.[41] It was while he was at Cambridge that he began publishing his autobiografiction; and a rather different private personality began to emerge, of someone afflicted by an apparently familial tendency towards depression, and an anxiety about his masculinity and

---

[36] Reynolds's images often echo Benson's, unsurprisingly given how many of Benson's works he was considering. For example, the image of rudderlessness could derive from the passage near the end of *The Upton Letters*, p. 320: 'I drift, alas, upon an unknown sea; but sometimes I see, across the blue rollers, the cliffs and shores of an unknown land, perfectly and impossibly beautiful.'

[37] R. H. Benson, *The Holy Blissful Martyr Saint Thomas of Canterbury* (London: Macdonald & Evans, 1908). Benson and Rolfe, *Saint Thomas*, ed. Donald Weeks (Edinburgh: Tragara Press, 1979).

[38] R. H. Benson, *Confessions of a Convert* (London: Longmans, 1913). A. C. Benson, *Hugh: Memoirs of a Brother* (London: Smith, Elder, 1915). *The Life of Edward White Benson by his son Arthur Christopher Benson*, 2 vols (London: Macmillan, 1899).

[39] See Valerie Sanders, '"House of Disquiet": The Benson Family Auto/biographies', in *Life Writing and Victorian Culture*, ed. David Amigoni (Aldershot: Ashgate, 2006), pp. 292–315. Sanders, 'Victorian Life Writing', *Literature Compass*, 1:1 (2004), 1–17.

[40] [A. C. Benson], *The Upton Letters*, p. 111.

[41] Only selected passages have been published, in *The Diary of Arthur Christopher Benson*, ed. Percy Lubbock (London: Hutchinson, [1926]), and in David Newsome's study, *On the Edge of Paradise: A. C. Benson, the Diarist* (London: John Murray, 1980), and his selections from the years 1898–1904 in *Edwardian Excursions* (London: Murray, 1981).

efficacy.[42] (Benson remained unmarried, as did all his siblings.) Perhaps such intimations were enabled by the masks of anonymity and pseudonymity; they seemed, at least initially to require them, since, as we have seen, when *The House of Quiet: An Autobiography* was first published in 1904, it was presented as written by an anonymous author, and edited by 'J. T..'[43] The initials are clearly another form of pseudonym in this case, since they are not Benson's own. They can also provide a form of semi-anonymity even when they are the writer's own; as when the regular Literary Causeries in the *Speaker* around 1900 were signed 'A T Q C.' Friends or readers of the *Oxford Book of English Verse* would have been able to identify Arthur Quiller-Couch, otherwise known (especially in his parodic writings) by the rather more anonymous (because it sounded pseudony-mous) initial 'Q.' A single initial tends to have an algebraic ring, especially if taken from those triads of letters beloved of algebraists: a, b, c; p, q, r; x, y, z. The algebraic effect is more likely to suggest the initial is *not* the person's own, as when the author of *The Autobiography of an Englishman* (1975) was identified only as 'Y.' For the sake of completeness, we should add 'Initialization' to Pseudonymity, Heteronymity, Anonymity, and Third-Personality in our cata-logue of varieties of auto/biographical displacement. Also 'First-Naming', as in *The Autobiography of David* ——.[44] Both these books detailed sexualities which rendered anonymity desirable. *David* —— was drawn to self-exposure of a non-autobiographical kind. 'Y' was bisexual, with sadomasochistic tendencies, and his 'autobiography' is introduced by 'S. Jacobson', who says that he has 'derived considerable value from the use of Y's text as an authentic case-history' in his own 'clinical practice as a psychiatrist.'[45] (Does he protest too much about that authenticity?) The journal author of *The House of Quiet* is only identified five pages from the end, and then only by a first name, as 'Henry.' Identifying oneself by initialization is something authors often do at the end of prefatory material. When Benson added an 'Introduction' to the second edition of *The House of Quiet* in October 1906 he signed it 'A. C. B.' But though the book had already been reprinted six times, this was the first to carry Benson's name on the title-page; so 'A. C. B.' is not an algebraic variable, but merely shorthand. There may be an effect of distancing, as I suggested with Gissing signing himself as 'G. G.';

[42] See Sanders, '"House of Disquiet": The Benson Family Auto/biographies'. In *The Thread of Gold* Benson rather disconcertingly narrates some episodes in the first person plural, but doesn't identify his companion(s).

[43] London: John Murray, 1904. Page references in the text are to the third edition of 1907.

[44] Raymond, Ernest, ed., *The Autobiography of David* —— (London: Gollancz, 1946). This intriguing text, which I'm grateful to John Thompson for drawing to my attention, appears to be a case of the real autobiographical papers of an actual person ('David' also figures as 'David P.' in Edwin Muir's *An Autobiography* (1954) (St Paul, MN: Graywolf Press, 1990), pp. 141–3), being edited by a real editor, who nonetheless presents them as verging on the fictional—presumably partly to make it sound more readable and be more saleable, though perhaps also as a way of short-circuiting any attempted prosecution for obscenity: 'After a while it became clear to me that in the midst of it all there was material for a great novel'—quoted from Ernest Raymond's introduction, on the dust-jacket.

[45] 'Y', *The Autobiography of an Englishman* (London: Paul Elek, 1975), p. 6.

but that is only a tenable argument when the prefatory material is still part of the fiction (as it is in Gissing, who is there playing the fictional role of editing another's words). This appears not to be the case with Benson's 1906 Introduction, since he begins by explaining why 'a book which has been anonymous for several years appears with an author's name on the title-page.'[46]

When Reynolds was writing his essay 'Autobiografiction', he seems not to have known this Introduction, which appeared the same month his essay was published. He still attributes the book to 'J. T..' The story of its authorship had already complicated even by then, since when *The Thread of Gold* was first published in 1905, its author was only identified as 'the author of "The House of Quiet".'[47] Reynolds had already connected *The House of Quiet* with *The Autobiography of Mark Rutherford*, as 'doubly pseudonymous'; 'Shapcott' editing 'Rutherford'; 'J. T.' editing 'Henry'. Again, though, there are different valencies to the pseudonyms. 'J. T.'s 'Prefatory Note' says 'I need hardly say that the names are throughout fictitious.' So contemporary readers knew that even 'Henry' wasn't the journal-author's real name; and that the identity of 'J. T.' was also being concealed. 'Mark Rutherford' appears to be a name that isn't concealing or fictionalizing anything. Its reappearance on other works must have confirmed the sense 'Mark Rutherford' as a real author, at least to readers who hadn't heard him identified with William Hale White. Announcing *The Thread of Gold* as 'By the author of *The House of Quiet*', removed the pseudonyms and presented the work as effectively virtually anonymous. If readers had been disconcerted by this disappearing trick, perhaps they realized that it might have been a way of tacitly acknowledging the fictionality of the earlier book; since 'Henry' says he was unable to complete a book other than his journal; he cannot have written another; so if the author of *The Thread* also wrote *The House*, 'Henry' is not a real person. Anyway, the 'Prefatory Note' to the original edition says Henry died in 1900; so *The Thread*, appearing in 1905, would have to be posthumous if his; but it doesn't have *The House*'s machinery of imaginary editor's preface. This is perhaps why Reynolds attributes *The Thread* to 'J. T.', which might seem a slip—'J. T.' is only the purported editor, not author, of the earlier book. Since Reynolds didn't yet know the true author was Benson, he may have assumed 'J. T.' were the actual author's actual initials (he was perhaps thinking by analogy with Gissing and 'G. G.')—not least because they are the only identification on the title-page. The other thing he didn't know was that another of his examples of possible autobiografiction—*The Upton Letters*—was a third pseudonymous work of Benson's, but this time not linked to any of his other books, and

---

[46] Benson, *The House of Quiet* (London: John Murray, 1906), p. v.
[47] *The Thread of Gold* (John Murray: London, 1905). The book was reprinted thrice before Benson's name appeared on the second edition in December 1906.

published under a different set of initials, 'T. B.'.[48] This had also first appeared in 1905, and was even more successful. There were another five anonymous print-ings in 1906, then a 'seventh impression' (second edition) with a new preface, in August 1906, which was the first to identify Benson as author. It might be thought to compromise Reynolds's claim to have identified a significant devel-opment that three of his examples turn out to be by the same writer (and as his article didn't appear until October 1906 he could have been aware that Benson was 'T. B.'; but Benson's name didn't appear on *The Thread* until December). The next chapter should demonstrate that the phenomenon was far more widespread, especially (as I've suggested) if autobiografiction is not confined to spiritual crisis narratives. It is perhaps the multiple presence of Benson that pushes Reynolds's argument towards the spiritual crisis form. But it also testifies to Benson's extraordinary productivity, and versatility in the invention of pseu-donymous autobiografiction. (One motive for Benson's use of pseudonyms may have been to avoid charges of over-productivity.) An anecdote of Forrest Reid's is revealing not only about the popularity of Benson's work, but also about who was and wasn't aware of his authorship of it. In 1905, he remembered:

everybody was reading, or had read, *The Upton Letters*, which had been published anonymously, though of course the authorship was known at Cambridge. I hadn't read them and was uninterested. 'Is it a book there is any necessity to read?' [someone asked,] unluckily putting the question to . . . Benson, who . . . replied with perfect urbanity, 'Not in the least.'[49]

Not known by everyone at Cambridge, clearly. If we recall Charles Swann's comment—that 'We approach a text differently if it is genuinely anonymous, if it is known to be pseudonymous, and if the identity behind the pseudonym is known'—we see that even in such a homogenous milieu different readers tend to have different degrees of knowledge about these things.[50] When Swann asks rhetorically how many readers could have known that 'Mark Rutherford' was a pseudonym, his implication—that very few of the first readers would have suspected—is surely right. But Reid's reminiscence shows how such questions are impossible to answer precisely; and why autobiografiction, and its inventive-ness in pseudonymity, provides a limit-case for attempts to determine signifi-cance by reader response, New Historicism, or textual sociology. Its generic instabilities and indefinitenesses fragment readerships, and ensure that its texts are approached differently; have multiple textual identities. That is why the study of its games with naming deserve careful attention.

---

[48] [A. C. Benson], *The Upton Letters* (London: Smith, Elder & Co., 1905). In this book Benson praises Gissing's *Ryecroft*, which contributes to a sense of a collective practice of autobiografictional writing.

[49] Quoted in Sandra Kemp, Charlotte Mitchell, and David Trotter, *Edwardian Fiction: An Oxford Companion* (Oxford: Oxford University Press, 1997), p. 28.

[50] Swann, 'Autobiografiction', p. 30.

In terms of its content, it would be hard to imagine a more dismal book than *The House of Quiet*. A young man of good family drifts through childhood, which is generally happy, though when he is six his father dies. At Cambridge an evangelical meeting precipitates religious despair, which is the onset of recurrent depression. A doctor later warns him to avoid stress, so he lives a reclusive rural invalid's life, enjoying moments of beauty, and trying to do good among his neighbours, several of whom are sketched. Just when he's reconciled to this attenuation of his ambitions, he and a new neighbour fall in love. He is on his way to propose to her when he is stricken with a fatal illness, and dies soon after. Benson's explanation of his aim is scarcely less dismal: 'I set myself to reflect how a man, with such limitations, might yet lead a life that was wholesome and contented and helpful.'[51] With its religious anxieties, the melodrama of its protagonist destroyed by even the idea of heterosexual fulfilment, its mandarin bourgeois gentility, its aestheticism of rural England, it's not hard to see why it seems less urgent now than a century ago.

But in terms of its form, it is another story. The editor introduces himself (I assume 'J. T.' is male, because most of 'Henry''s friends are, and because he describes 'Henry' coming to stay in his house, without any mention of chaperones) by saying that 'the writer of the following pages was a distant cousin of my own, and to a certain extent a friend.'[52] 'J. T.' has become his executor (another indication of his maleness), and says that 'among his papers I found this book, prepared in all essential respects for publication, though it is clear that it would not have seen the light in his lifetime.'[53] As with 'Rutherford', or John Addington Symonds, there is a sense that the material is too compromising to publish while the author is alive, though in this case it is more to do with the unwillingness to reveal mental weakness, rather than religious doubt or non-normative sexuality: what Benson calls 'an unmanly piece of morbid pathology.'[54] However, as the italicized Prefatory Note continues, it becomes much less clear what is meant by saying the book was 'prepared in all essential respects for publication.' 'J. T.' explains how he added 'a few passages from the diary for the last days, which was composed subsequently to the date at which the book was arranged.'[55] Fine. The 'following pages' are a 'book', which 'Henry' has written, and 'J. T.' has just supplemented with some late diary entries. But the first, 'Introductory' chapter from the text proper is headed with a date—'Christmas Eve, 1898'—which casts it as itself a diary entry. And it begins:

I have been a good deal indoors lately, and I have been amusing myself by looking through old papers and diaries of my own. It seems to me that, though the record is a very uneventful one, there is yet a certain unity throughout [...]

[51] Benson, *The House of Quiet*, p. vi.
[52] Ibid., p. xv.　　[53] Ibid., p. xv.
[54] Ibid., p. 206.　　[55] Ibid., p. xvi.

In a sense, it's *Krapp's Last Tape avant la lettre* (or perhaps *avant la bande*): a diary entry about reading over past diary entries. The writer goes on to explain how, though it was his 'ambition to write a book', he has not: 'I have not got the instinct for *form* on a large scale.'[56] This strikes a jarring note. What of the 'book' that 'J. T.' said was 'prepared in all essential respects for publication'? It turns out that that book is in effect an arrangement of past diary entries. Chapter 1, immediately following the 'Introductory' one is headed 'Dec. 7, 1897'; so immediately we are lifted out of the 'present' of the book's preparation or arrangement, and plunged back into the past diary entries. The writer explains in the 'Introductory' entry, rather paradoxically, that despite having the unful-filled ambition of writing a book,

now it seems to me that I have after all, without intending it, written a book,—the one book, that, it is said, every man has in his power to write [. . .] I have discarded a large amount of writing, but I have selected certain episodes, made extracts from my diaries, and added a few passages; and the result is the story of my life, told perhaps in a desultory way, but with a certain coherence.[57]

What that preparation meant, then, was less a matter of writing, and more of editing. 'Henry' may feel he lacks the 'instinct for *form*', but he has perceived a unity in his life, and an autobiography and coherence in his diary. Thus we embark on the book in the belief that its design is essentially his. But then, under halfway through the book, at the end of chapter 17, we find the only other editorial comment from 'J. T.':

[the passages that follow were either extracted by the author himself from his own diaries, or are taken from a notebook containing fragments of an autobiographical character. When the date is ascertainable it is given at the head of the piece.—J. T.][58]

There is a definite shift in the next chapter, which begins 'Now I will draw, carefully, faithfully, and lovingly, the portraits of some of my friends' (p. 106). From the next paragraph it appears that he has chosen them himself from his diaries. But otherwise, how are we to tell? 'J. T.' has already said that he has added diary passages. Whereas his note seems at odds with this, contrasting diary entries selected by 'Henry', with notebook fragments selected by 'J. T.'. The comment about dating is also perplexing. Does it only apply to the notebook, and thus imply that the notebook isn't part of the diary? Most of the preceding chapters are not dated, so the absence of a date doesn't mean a section isn't from the diaries. But then the presence of a date doesn't mean it is from the diaries, since the date may have been interpolated by the editor. There

---

[56] *The House of Quiet*, p. [1].
[57] Ibid., p. 2. Ford Madox Ford also invokes this idea that 'They say every man has it in him to write one good book' and that 'the man's one good book will be his autobiography': *It Was the Nightingale* (London: Heinemann, 1934), pp. v–vi.
[58] *The House of Quiet*, p. 105.

may be a realist explanation: that after his stroke, if that's what it is, 'Henry' stops keeping his diary, and writes fragments as he can in whatever is to hand, namely the notebook. And this would comport with the Prefatory Note's claim to have added only material from the last days—though there he says those passages are from 'the diary,' rather than a notebook. There is, in short, a formal problem. The Prefatory Note implies that any editorial additions to the book 'Henry' prepared come towards the end. Yet the insertion of the editorial note less than halfway through means that we cannot be sure who has arranged the rest of the book. This wouldn't matter if the volume were offered as 'extracts from a diary.' But given the comments about the book having been 'arranged' by the diarist, and his comments about its form and coherence, it does matter whose shape his life has been given. 'The writer of the following pages' may be supposed to be 'Henry'; but who has designed the book, or at least more than half of it?

Benson thus takes the relation between 'writer' and 'editor' further than Hale White, since 'Shapcott' comments on 'Rutherford', but doesn't intervene in the course of the *Autobiography*. The uncertain relation between 'Henry' and 'J. T.' is a kind of allegory within the text for the autobiografictional process, in which autobiographical material is used, but edited and revised into another kind of text.[59] It thus bears on the question 'How autobiographical is it?' The plot of these questions of authorship and autobiography thickened even from the time of the publication of Reynolds's essay, when Benson provided the Introduction for the second edition in 1906, then a 'Preface' to precede it in the third edition of 1907. These are both signed with Benson's initials, and need to be read in the context of his now having affixed his true name to the title-pages of both new editions. Because, as these now read: '*The House of Quiet: An Autobiography:* by Arthur Christopher Benson', a different expectation is encouraged as to how autobiographical the book might be.[60] The Introduction is a deeply ambivalent document. The book draws on his 'own slender stock' of 'impressions or

---

[59]   In the essay on 'Authorship' in *Escape and Other Essays* (London: Smith, Elder & Co., 1915), p. 224, Benson was later to write: 'My father died in 1896, and I wrote his life in two big volumes, a very solid piece of work; but it was after that, I think, that my real writing began. I believe it was in 1899 that I slowly composed *The House of Quiet*, but I could not satisfy myself about the ending, and it was laid aside.' Thus in the *House* he splits himself into two writers: presumably the bulk of 'Henry''s journal was written in 1899, but then the 'J. T.' passages were written later. Also see *House*, pp. 84 ff. on authorship.

[60]   As Charles Swann notes, Birrell, T. A., 'Notes on the new *Cambridge Bibliography of English Literature* vol. 4 (1900–1950)', *Neophilologus*, 59:2 (1975) 306–15, was categorical about how the book should be catalogued: 'Benson A. C., The house of quiet an autobiography [*sic*] 1904. This. should not be under literary memoirs; it is fiction not autobiography' (p. 312). Birrell's next correction concerns another of Benson's autobiografiction: 'Benson E. F., *As we are* 1932. Fiction, not literary memoirs. It is *not* a continuation of the same author's memoirs, *As we were.*'

experiences', but is 'in a sense a fiction.'[61] He blames critics because they 'will persist in considering any communication made through the medium of print as a solemn and deliberate manifesto of one's deepest thoughts and hopes and principles'; yet he asserts his right 'to paint pictures of the things that have seemed to me beautiful or strange or impressive.'[62] The addition of the Preface adds yet more ambivalence. Where the owning of the book in 1906, disclosing the 'secret which is no secret at all' of authorship, seemed to legitimate a more autobiographical reading of it, the Preface seeks to reintroduce an ironic or at least dramatic distancing, by presenting the protagonist as an imagined character in a fictional situation.

The effect of acknowledging his authorship was different from the case of Gosse's *Father and Son*. (Gosse was a friend of Benson's, as was Henry James, who figures at the end of chapter 5 and in chapter 6.) To see how astute Reynolds was about his period, recall the first words of Gosse's Preface to *Father and Son*, published just the following year, 1907: 'At the present hour, when fiction takes forms so ingenious and so specious [. . .].'[63] In other words, Gosse too recognized the same phenomenon, and worried that what he was trying to present as autobiography might be read as autobiografiction.[64] Gosse's echo of Turgenev appeared to situate the book in the realm of fiction, as an anglicized and singularized *Fathers and Sons*. Yet when he owned the book in its fourth impression he appeared to be affirming its auto/biographical veracity. As we saw, though, his anonymous Preface itself manifested this tension, affirming truth in terms that draw attention to the fictional. The act of owning a displaced autobiography has a different valency when the work was originally published pseudonymously rather than anonymously, however. When Benson acknowledged that he was the author of *The House of Quiet*, or *The Upton Letters*, he was acknowledging that he was the author of their personae (of both authors and editors) too; acknowledging, that is, the fictionality of the works.

Yet his 'Introduction' bears out Reynolds's speculation that autobiografiction suits those reluctant to attempt novels: 'If I had possessed any dramatic or narrative capacity', Benson writes, 'I would have made a novel out of it.' And he argues: 'I felt that if one gave the book an air of reality, there were many readers who would forgive a certain dullness and heaviness of movement and reflection, which could not be so easily pardoned in a work of fiction.'[65] So it's not a work of fiction then? As he continues, the extent to which his apparent conceptual naivety is sly *faux-naiveté* becomes apparent:

---

[61] Benson, *The House of Quiet*, 3rd edn (London: John Murray, 1907), p. xi.

[62] Ibid., pp. xii, xi.

[63] Gosse, *Father and Son: A Study of Two Temperaments*, ed. Peter Abbs (London: Penguin, 1989), p. 33.

[64] See David Amigoni, *Colonies, Cults and Evolution: Literature, Science and Culture in Nineteenth-Century Writing* (Cambridge: Cambridge University Press, 2007), p. 164.

[65] *The House of Quiet*, p. xi.

There may be people who will think it disingenuous to give to what is in a sense a fiction an air of veracity. But here again I was in a difficulty [...] My experience of the world and life has of necessity, owing to circumstances, been a limited one. If I had the inventive or creative faculty, it would be different; but I am forced by the limitations of experience and imaginativeness to draw a good deal on my own slender stock—and thus the subjective part of the book may well wear an air of veracity, for it is mostly true, while on the other hand the intimate nature of it gives every excuse for my attempting to take refuge in anonymity.[66]

Again this corresponds to Reynolds's definition. The 'subjective part'—the spiritual experiences, depressions, aestheticism—are true autobiography; he's not a skilled enough novelist to make them up; the objective part—names, facts, events, characters—are fictionalized. According to this account, the book *is* his autobiography: his *spiritual* autobiography, displaced onto an alter ego living a fictionalized version of Benson's life. After all, readers who knew anything about Benson's actual public life as schoolmaster, don, poet, editor, and man of letters would know how fictional 'Henry''s rural invalid's life was.

In a sense the difference in outward details between 'Henry''s and Benson's lives only serves to reinforce the idea that any similarities must lie at the spiritual level. Yet for the third edition Benson felt the need to add further explanation in the form of the rather anxious 'Preface'. This begins by giving an example of 'a very pathetic document' he has just read by 'a great writer' whom he doesn't name.[67] The document is a preface in which the writer tried to answer his critics, but which he was advised to suppress. Benson takes it as a 'tender lesson for all who have faithfully tried to express the deepest thoughts of their heart, frankly and sincerely, never to make the least attempt to answer, or apologise, or explain.'[68] He assures us he is not trying to answer those critics hostile to the book, but that he is only trying 'to make plain what the book itself perhaps fails to make plain, namely what my purpose in writing it was.'[69] What he says of this purpose is not very different from what he had already said: 'It was, from the first, meant as a message to the weak rather than as a challenge to the strong.'[70] Yet as he continues, he appears so keen to distance himself from 'the weak', by implying that the personality of 'Henry' was invented, that the claim that 'the subjective part' of the book was autobiographical—that in it he had 'faithfully tried to express the deepest thoughts' of his heart—seems itself weakened:

The problem, then, which I tried to present in my book, was this: I imagined a temperament of a peaceful and gentle order, a temperament without robustness and joie de vivre, but with a sense of duty, a desire to help, an anxious wish not to shirk responsibility; and then I tried to depict such a character as being suddenly thrust into the shadow, set aside, as, by their misfortune or their fault, a very large number of persons are

[66] Ibid., p. xi.   [67] Ibid., p. iii.   [68] Ibid., p. iv.
[69] Ibid.   [70] Ibid.

set aside [. . .] and I set myself to reflect how a man, with such limitations, might yet lead a life that was wholesome and contented and helpful [. . .][71]

The 'temperament' is exactly what the earlier 'Introduction' had led us to think was what 'Henry' shared with his author. Now he is claiming to have 'imagined' this temperament, and what 'might' befall it. How are we to understand this proliferation of preambles? 'Henry' provides an 'Introductory' chapter; 'J. T.' the original Prefatory Note; Benson the Introduction, then a Preface. Is it the result of a troubling anxiety that he cannot adequately explain, or even gauge for himself, the balance between autobiography and fiction? Or is it that each move seems to push the book too far in a single direction: he makes it sound too like fiction; he counters this by over-emphasizing its autobiographical sincerity? A book successful enough to have been reissued nine times within three years might indeed seem not to need apologies or explanations. Benson's language here offers another possibility. To say 'Henry' is 'suddenly thrust into the shadow' immediately connotes his being removed from the glare of society by his doctor's advice. Yet the ambiguous phrase also suggests his dark moods. And whereas Benson did not have to abjure society, he did share 'Henry''s depressions. So perhaps a sentence like this is a kind of allegory for how 'Henry''s life shadows, but is not the same as, Benson's own. Or perhaps we should read this oscillation in a different way—one closer to the spirit of Romantic autobiographers. Perhaps when Benson says 'I imagined a temperament', he not only means he imagined a temperament other than his own; perhaps he means he imagined a temperament that was his own. In other words, he may have found that in writing what he thought of as fictional, he discovered his autobiography. That would be to read the sequence of prefatory pieces less as attempts to conceal whatever the last reviews had objected to, and rather as a process of self-discovery: an imaginary self-portrait. Conversely, the prefatory excess indicates that, as autobiographers at least since Rousseau repeatedly found, the attempts 'to express the deepest thoughts of their heart' results in a deferral, a displacement, a sense of fictionalization, which seems to conceal as much as it reveals, and to make the self feel like an imaginary other. By such means, autobiografiction, like autobiography, is at its best a process of discovery rather than of mere encryption. As Paul John Eakin says, 'autobiographical truth is not a fixed but an evolving content in an intricate process of self-discovery [. . .].'[72] Benson recognizes this within his texts, not just in their prefatory material, as when he embeds a parable within *The House of Quiet*, about a traveller who, having 'ransacked the world', returns home. So the soul, he explains, 'finds after infinite trouble and weariness that it has but learnt

---

[71] *The House of Quiet*, pp. v–vi.
[72] Paul John Eakin, *Fictions in Autobiography: Studies in the Art of Self-Invention* (Princeton: Princeton University Press, 1985), p. 3.

afresh what it knew'; and finds that the 'Pearl of Price' 'is hidden after all in his own garden ground, and inscribed with his own new name.'[73]

Such works are, as Reynolds says, poised in a delicate equilibrium between autobiography, fiction, and the essay; and in a way that eighteenth-century fictional autobiography, say, is not. Benson's prefatory manoeuvres can be read as anxious adjustments to the tensions, trying to ensure that the books don't slide into awkward self-revelation on the one hand, or insincere fakery on the other. Alternatively, the anxiety of the manoeuvres can be seen as symptomatic of a problem not in the writing of the individual books, but in the categories of 'fiction' and 'autobiography' themselves, and in the relation between them. Reynolds's chemical analogy is misleading according to this view. It implies that autobiography and fiction and essay are as separate as the separate material states of solid, liquid, and gas, even if some works (like sulphur) can manifest combinations of them. But the concept of autobiografiction, and especially its resurgence, poses a different model, according to which the components cannot be kept separate. Autobiografiction, that is, shows that all autobiography has fictional tendencies, or can be read as fictionalized; and it shows that all fiction can be read autobiographically, or has an autobiographical dimension. Autobiografiction reveals the fluidity or permeability of genres and categories.

Some readers may feel that even if the intricacy of Benson's engagements with autobiografiction has been demonstrated, such interest is undercut by his insistent moralism. It is hard to see why he, or his readers, thought it wasn't obvious that *The House of Quiet* was supposed to console the weak and the socially excluded, since not only the prefaces but the book itself makes the point clearly. This problem is more apparent in the book he published the year after *The House*, *The Thread of Gold*, which Reynolds described as a 'very similar' work. This section will conclude with a brief discussion of *The Thread*, which has further light of its own to shed not only on these questions of autobiografiction and anxiety, but their relation to our themes of secularization and aestheticism.

In terms of its narrative structure, *The Thread of Gold* is even more impressionistic. There is no plot corresponding to Henry's circumscribed life and death. An unnamed narrator merely records his impressions. There is some semblance of journal-writing. The short chapters often begin by referring to the previous day, recent conversations, something just read. But there are no dates, and occasionally reminiscences take the narrative back an unspecified amount of time. The effect is to dissociate the 'spiritual experiences' even further from the contingencies of an actual life; or to suggest that it is they that make up the core of that life, rather than the conventional auto/biographical markers of names, times, and places. Benson says of his 'portfolio of sketches and impressions':

---

[73] *The House of Quiet*, p. 73.

'The only coherence they possess is that, at the time when they were written, I was much preoccupied with the wonder as to whether an optimistic view of life was justified.'[74] What he means by the title is this: 'The idea of this book, that there is a certain golden thread of hope and love interwoven with all our lives, running consistently through the coarsest and darkest fabric, was what I set out to illustrate rather than to prove.'[75] This already rings slightly false: setting out to illustrate that there *is* a golden thread is what you would do if you had already decided an optimistic view of life *was* justified, rather than being the outcome of a genuine preoccupation in wondering whether it was. Nor is it clear what the distinction signifies between illustrating the golden thread, and proving it; since surely to show it as being there is effectively to prove that it is there. Agnostic or atheist readers will thus suspect that Benson has loaded the dice before he begins. And certainly, many of the episodes seem chosen as moralistic vignettes to prove his point. A severely disabled friend finds his enjoyment of life heightened by his limitations (chapter 16). An old man who has gone blind and then deaf claims he is happier than before (chapter 20). Such examples are miniature equivalents of the plot of *The House of Quiet*, of course, and suggest that that book too comes out of the preoccupation with the question of whether life warranted optimism. In many ways, *Thread* is a manifesto to seek to account for the point of view of the earlier book. It has to be said, the episodes in *Thread* compare ill to *House*, and even less favourably to Turgenev's portrait of the paralysed peasant woman in 'A Living Relic', which is immeasurably more affecting for not being moralized.[76] Other vignettes veer from the less than sublime to the almost ridiculous, as when the narrator is happily cycling along, gets a small flying beetle in his eye, squashes the beetle and inflames his eye in trying to get it out, then wonders how the death of the creature and his own suffering could possibly be reconciled with the idea of an all-loving god (chapter 11). Yet from another point of view, the attempt to assert a benign reading of such situations can be read as expressive of a tendency to be demoralized by them. As he explains when introducing the episode of the beetle:

How strange it is that sometimes the smallest and commonest incident, that has befallen one a hundred times before, will suddenly open the door into that shapeless land of fruitless speculation; the land on to which, I think, the star Wormwood fell, burning it up and making it bitter; the land in which we most of us sometimes have to wander, and always alone.[77]

---

[74] Quotations from the fourth edition, London: John Murray, 1910; p. xii.

[75] Benson, *The Thread of Gold*, pp. xii–xiii.

[76] Turgenev's *A Sportsman's Sketches* had been translated by Constance Garnett, volumes 8 and 9 of *The Novels of Ivan Turgenev* (London: William Heinemann, 1895). 'A Living Relic' is in vol. 9, pp. 229–50.

[77] *The Thread of Gold*, p. 52.

The periphrases evoke Benson's unease in confronting depression, even as they describe its force. Or, to put it another way, if he appears to be protesting too much about suffering being redemptive, it is because he needs to cheer himself up, and not let depression have the last laugh. For at least some depressives, not being able to convince yourself that 'an optimistic view of life was justified' feels like a motive for suicide. Though Benson doesn't discuss suicide explicitly in these books, it might be seen as implicit in his autobiografictional imagining of his own death. The title of the *House* exerts an undertow in this direction, via its allusion to James Clarence Mangan's poem 'Rest only in the Grave':

> The House of Quiet, for strong and weak
> And poor and rich, I have still to seek—
> That House is narrow, and dark, and small—
> But the only Peaceful House of all.

Henry's acquiescence in the face of death makes one wonder whether Benson was keeping open the possibility that he commits suicide, since he says nothing about the actual cause of death.

Real though Benson's depression evidently was, it is intriguing how his doubts and anxieties do not really seem to touch his faith. There is a thread of mystery running through the book—a tendency to rest on a note of wonder and baffled awe: 'to wonder what it all means.'[78] He is perplexed as to why 'the Creator' appears 'to put into the hearts of our inquisitive race the desire to discover what it is all about; and to leave the desire unsatisfied. What a labyrinthine mystery! Depth beyond depth, and circle beyond circle!'[79] Such expressions of not knowing sound like symptoms of agnosticism. But Benson's predicament is that though he doesn't know why things are as they are, doesn't feel he can grasp their meaning, he is nonetheless convinced they have been made the way they are by a benign god. He doubts the meaning of life, but not the existence of god. So while the books chart a genuine spiritual crisis, his perplexity about religion is not quite the familiar story of Victorian agnosticism. The books insist on his belief with a frequency that makes them sometimes read like Christian apologetics. And yet he does feel he has undergone a spiritual crisis. It's more a question (as when 'Henry' hears the evangelical sermon in Cambridge) of feeling excluded from a direct relation to that faith, rather than doubting its truth. (So the text might be metaphorical at this level too: 'Henry''s exclusion from work and urban society might represent Benson's feeling of being kept at a distance from what he'd most like to be a part of.)

The other main element in the *Thread* is of encounters with the purely beautiful. These take many forms: moving works of art; a loving young couple; the classical buildings of Oxford. More often they involve perceptions of nature; landscapes, cloud-formations, rivers and pools; and especially a harmonious

---

[78] Ibid., p. 32.   [79] Ibid., pp. 34–5.

symbiosis between the natural world and the human, of which his view of a manor house in chapter 2 is representative. He sits down 'to drink in the beauty of the scene':

Though the name of the house, though the tale of its dwellers was unknown to me, I felt the appeal of the old associations that must have centred about it. The whole air, that quiet afternoon, seemed full of the calling of forgotten voices, and dead faces looked out from the closed lattices. So near to my heart came the spirit of the ancient house, that, as I mused, I felt as though even I myself had made a part of its past, and as though I were returning from battling with the far-off world to the home of childhood. The house seemed to regard me with a mournful and tender gaze, as though it knew that I loved it, and would fain utter its secrets to a friendly ear. Is it strange that a thing of man's construction should have so wistful yet so direct a message for the spirit? Well, I hardly know what it was that it spoke of; but I felt the care and love that had gone to the making of it [. . .] the old house had spoken with me, had left its mark upon my spirit.[80]

It is a peculiarly English form of mysticism that takes as its shrines the ancient houses of the social elite—almost as if the National Trust were the true Church of England (it had recently been founded—in 1895—to preserve the countryside from the ravages of industrialism; the beauty of stately homes and parks offering something the English could believe in). There is a line of such moments running through key works of modernism too: the voices heard in the shrubbery in Eliot's 'Burnt Norton'; Lily Briscoe's imagining of the dead Mrs Ramsay as a curtain flutters in the window in *To the Lighthouse*; and most obviously (and perhaps under Benson's influence?) the mystical association of the house and Mrs Wilcox in Forster's *Howards End*.[81]

The spiritualizing of the country house seems typically Edwardian now. But for all its fustiness, what Benson is doing has significance for the concept of autobiografiction. As in much of Forster's work, the spiritual experience is an encounter with the *genius loci*, the spirit of place. But the way Benson makes the episode affecting is through summoning the spirits of the dead: the dead faces, the 'mournful' gaze. The personification of the house stands in for the missing persons of its history. This too is very much of its Edwardian moment—the period of the Society for Psychical Research, and its scientific and pseudo-scientific attempts to investigate ghosts, fairies, and psychic phenomena.[82] Benson responds to the inanimate house with a form of imaginary life-writing—virtually a saccharined version of the plot of James's *The Turn of the Screw*. His elegiac fantasy is an essential component of the episode's beauty. What also lends it poignancy, and

---

[80] *The Thread of Gold*, pp. 13–14.

[81] Benson wrote to Forster that *Howards End* had stirred him; though curiously he said he thought 'the appeal of the *house* was a little strained': *Selected Letters of E. M. Forster*, ed. Mary Lago and P. N. Furbank, vol. 1 (London: Collins, 1983), p. 119, n.2.

[82] See Samuel Hynes, *The Edwardian Turn of Mind* (Princeton: Princeton University Press, 1975).

some of its mystical tinge, is that the house is read as his autobiography: as near to his heart, the home of his childhood, leaving its mark on his spirit. It isn't his actual childhood home, but it returns him to being the child of the house; and thus the child of Pater.

That encounter with beauty is itself essential to his notion of the spiritual. Benson's agnosticism about meaning leads him towards the aesthetic. 'I have learnt to believe in beauty', he says.[83] The aesthetic stands in for the theological; he takes beauty as a sign of beneficent providence, rather as the book of Genesis interprets the rainbow as a sign of god's covenant with man. Such moments of aesthetic exaltation accumulate into a form of aesthetic autobiography, or auto-biografiction. But there are two problems with this strategy of consolation. First, beauty moves in as mysterious ways as gods, and its intimations are as disturbing to the sense of self. When the persona writing *The Upton Letters* revisits his childhood haunts, his conviction about their beauty has the effect of dissolving him into the landscape:

Dear Woodcote, dear remembered days, beloved faces and voices of the past, old trees and fields! I cannot tell what you mean and what you are; but I can hardly believe that, if I have a life beyond, it will not somehow comprise you all; for indeed you are my own for ever; you are myself, whatever that self may be.[84]

Second, Benson's aestheticism is bound up with an intimation of mortality (as the Tennysonian echoes of this passage suggest). A later chapter of the *Thread* is headed 'After Death' (40); and many of the book's aesthetic moments depend on a sense of the afterlife, just as here the manor house appears to personify the afterlife of its dead inhabitants.[85] 'After Death' is the penultimate chapter (excluding the brief, prayer-like conclusion), and needs to be discussed briefly here. It offers a curious fantasy, introduced as 'so strange a dream or vision' the narrator says he had 'the other night.'[86] He finds himself on a cliff, looking over the sea, and becomes aware 'with a shock of pleasant surprise that my perception of the whole scene was of a different quality to any perception I had before experienced.'[87] This is because he is disembodied, and finds he can move at will through space and matter. He realizes that what feels like 'a blissful dream' is in fact life after death.[88] This is not an orthodox Christian eschatology, however, but a fantasy of Buddhist-like reincarnation, in which he imagines being repeatedly reborn, and is told by a companionable spirit: 'One suffers . . . but one gains experience.'[89] The episode is so elaborate and has such narrative coherence as to make one doubt it could have been an actual, autobiographical dream. Rather, the dream/vision frame may be designed to

[83] *The Upton Letters*, p. 212.   [84] Ibid., p. 182.
[85] For further examples of Benson family supernaturalia, see *The Temple of Death & Other Stories* by A. C. & R. H. Benson, ed. David Stuart Davies (Ware, Hertfordshire: Wordsworth, 2007).
[86] *The Thread of Gold*, p. 198.
[87] Ibid., p. 199.   [88] Ibid., p. 200.   [89] Ibid., p. 203.

allow unorthodox theology to enter the book. From another point of view, it can be read allegorically. It works as a counsel of resignation, suggesting that any actual suffering we endure will seem unimportant from this other perspective (and in those terms is reconcilable with Christianity's message of the infinitely greater importance of the afterlife to the life). Yet there are two further aspects that follow from an allegorical reading. First, it seeks to suggest that the narrator has effectively already attained such a state of enlightenment as to be able to look back on life with bemused detachment. Structurally it is comparable to the device of having 'Henry' survive his stroke to pen a few more journal entries. In both cases the narrators are positioned as if already writing from 'the other side' (as Reynolds said). They are thus able to write about their own lives elegiacally.

Second, this positioning as if from beyond death, which grants them a different, more exalted perception, can be read as allegory for the point of view of the writer—or at least, the point of view to be aimed at. In other words, the kind of out-of-the-body experience described, while it taps into a contemporary fascination with the paranormal, is also a figure for the imaginary perceptions of art; especially, perhaps, for the escape from the writer's own body that is autobiografiction. The dream of reincarnation, according to this allegorical reading, figures the writer's continual self-reinvention in the form of others' lives.

This combination of the spiritual, the after-deathly, and the aesthetic, is the structural principle of *The Thread*, and is often implicit in Benson's other writing.[90] The aesthetic grants a foretaste of existence as pure spirit; death enables a vision of life as aesthetic; the aesthetic anaesthetizes anxiety about death, translating it into a spiritual necessity. It's a combination that is inherent in the book's title, too. The idea of a thread of gold combines human artifice (mining, metalworking, weaving) with natural beauty (especially of sunsets: the prolific Benson had also published *The Isles of Sunset* in the same year, 1905), and with a metaphor for transcendence (the idea of spiritual radiance). Indeed, these elements are themselves also metaphorically interwoven: ancient traditions connect gold cloth with majesty, the sun with spiritual illumination, sunsets with death. Such metaphorical richness comes at a cost, however: the cost of metaphorical vagueness and sentimentality. Here Benson's language too is very much of its time. As Geoffrey Hill has shown, the

---

[90] For example, the following year he published *The Gate of Death: A Diary* (London: Smith, Elder, 1906). This appeared anonymously, with no authorial identification at all—no name, pseudonym, or initials. An unsigned 'Introduction' (written by the same person or persona as the diary), (pp. v–vii) is dated 'Sept. 3, 1906', and the British Museum's accession stamp (in the British Library copy) bears the date '7 Dec 06', indicating it was published after Reynolds's essay. The elements of its plot will by now be familiar. The protagonist has had a bad fall from a ladder, was in a coma, but has regained consciousness. The entries run from June to November, recalling the accident of January. Thus the accident and its aftermath and narration all fall within a single year, but that year is made to reflect the whole life—as with Gissing's *Ryecroft* and Benson's *Upton Letters*.

poetry of the years immediately preceding the First World War is repeatedly drawn towards an 'aureate' diction.[91]

The vagueness is integral to Benson's theological uncertainties. He cannot understand the rationale for suffering. But this doesn't negate his belief that there is one. The thread of gold is thus his hope that one can be perceived, and that beauty is the sign of its presence. It is tempting to say that instead of god, he finds gold; that the theological is displaced into the aesthetic. But of course his hope is that the beautiful is evidence of god's benevolence. Where other aesthetes offered beauty as an alternative to traditional religion, Benson, like Ruskin before him, sought to find beauty in religion (as in his description of the ruined 'small ancient chapel' in chapter 2, 'The Deserted Shrine') and religion in beauty. But where Ruskin (according to Proust's reading) was responding aesthetically, and trying to convince himself he was responding religiously, Benson knows his responses are grounded in the aesthetic, but hopes the aesthetic can be taken as a guarantee of religion. (Indeed, he criticized Pater on just these grounds, saying that Marius the Epicurean is attracted to Christianity for aesthetic reasons—'its sensuous appeal, its liturgical solemnities', which it shares with other religions, 'instead of emphasizing the power of sympathy, the Christian conception of Love, which differentiates Christianity from all other religious systems.'[92]) Thus part of the interest of his work is how it shows that autobiografiction need not imply agnosticism or atheism. Where other Victorians and Edwardians—such as Hale White, Butler, and Gosse—experiencing spiritual crises turned away from the theological towards the aesthetic, the author of 'Land of Hope and Glory' found hope in the glory. He was not an 'art for art's sake' aesthete. Ultimately, for Benson, the aesthetic is a sign of god's care for the human, and human art operates under licence from the divine artist. When he speaks of god as 'the great Artificer', he invokes the Romantic notion of the community between human and divine creativity. There is thus a world of difference between that and Stephen Dedalus's last sentence in *Portrait of the Artist*: 'Old father, old artificer, stand me now and ever in good stead.' Jeri Johnson annotates this as referring to Daedalus,[93] which would make it a Nietzschean assertion of imaginary parentage, of Stephen's allegiance to art, and to European classicism, over and above any allegiance to family, church, or state. (And thus the echo of the Lord's Prayer—'Our father, which art . . .'—turns it into a liturgy of the aesthetic.) In formal and generic terms, though, works of autobiografiction like Benson's were laying the groundwork for such modernist engagements with life-writing.

These two books of Benson's do all the things which Reynolds argued characterized autobiografiction. Indeed, they fit his definition so exactly as to suggest that

[91] Geoffrey Hill, 'Gurney's Hobby', *Essays in Criticism*, 34:2 (April 1984), 97–128.

[92] Benson, quoted by T. S. Eliot, 'Arnold and Pater', *Selected Essays* (London: Faber, 1972), p. 441.

[93] Joyce, *A Portrait of the Artist as a Young Man*, ed. Jeri Johnson (Oxford: Oxford University Press, 2000), pp. 213, 289.

they were the examples which most informed his thinking, and which perhaps influenced his attempt to restrict autobiografiction to consolatory narratives of spiritual crisis. The books recount spiritual experiences, displaced onto fictional narratives; use pseudonyms and fictional posthumousness; they engage with beauty. As I hope this discussion has shown, they do these things with a greater intricacy than in Reynolds's account of them. His definition of 'spiritual experience' is certainly broad enough to include aesthetic experience. But arguably the main quality he missed in them is the way they are not just works of beauty, but works *about* beauty. (Though perhaps that was what he had in mind in commenting on the essayistic component of autobiografiction, since—especially in *The Thread*—the discursive parts constitute an essay in aesthetics and theology.) We should not be surprised to find that Benson also wrote a study of the aesthete central to our study of imaginary portraiture and self-portraiture—Walter Pater.[94]

THE TRUEST POETRY IS THE MOST FEIGNING: FICTION AS TRUER AUTOBIOGRAPHY

Our readings of aesthetic and displaced autobiographies have emphasized the increasing fictionalization of autobiography. Clearly, autobiografiction is the next stage of that development. But it also represents an antithetical development: the increasing autobiographicalization of fiction. There are two aspects to this process. The *writing* of fiction in the modernist period turns increasingly to autobiographical novels of artistic development, such as we have seen with Proust, and will see in later discussions of Gide, Joyce, Pound, Sinclair, Woolf, Stein, and others. The *reading* of fiction is crucial too, and is the subject of the remainder of this chapter, which will consider a specific trope in which fiction is read as autobiography.

Reynolds's explanation of autobiografiction—as autobiographical spiritual experiences adopting fictional forms—accounts for the fictional elements in the hybrid in largely negative ways: embarrassment with the spiritual; literary incompetence; the desire for concealment. However, there are indications (as, again, we have already glimpsed) that the negative defence of autobiografiction sells it short. Instead, an argument emerges during this period that justifies fictionalized autobiography in more positive terms. This is the trope Philippe Lejeune identifies, especially in authors of the late nineteenth and early twentieth centuries, according to which works of fiction are said to be truer autobiographies than a factual, formal autobiography could be.[95]

---

[94] A. C. Benson, *Walter Pater* (London: Macmillan, 1906).

[95] Lejeune, 'The Autobiographical Contract', in *French Literary Theory Today*, ed. Tzvetan Todorov (Cambridge: Cambridge University Press, 1982), pp. 192–222 (p. 217). Lejeune's argument here was touched on in Chapter 2, and will be developed in the next chapter and the Conclusion.

What are writers saying when they claim their fiction is their true autobiography? Besides the motives already discussed, they might be taken to be expressing a despair about formal autobiography: a feeling, common to anyone who has tried to express anything, that the self slips through the mesh of language; a sense that language is too imprecise, narrative forms too restrictive; that the desire for self-expression, as Lacan has argued of all desire, is insatiable. However, these are arguments for the impossibility of autobiography altogether, not for fiction's ability to perform autobiography better. Similarly, the psychoanalytic perspective might also appear to negate the possibility of full autobiographical veracity. According to the Freudian model, the psyche will not let the truth about itself be told; not consciously, anyhow. It will repress, negate, distort, disavow, displace material, leaving the attempt at formal autobiography unreliable, full of gaps and contradictions. Something like this is implicit in Ford's account of Conrad's personality. Ford (like James, as we shall see) sees art as deriving from the artist's personal qualities. In other words, he reads fiction autobiographically. However, something strange happens to the idea of the self being expressed:

to know the really extraordinarily Promethean quality of Conrad's mind you had to realize that he was always acting a part [. . .] He had to make his desperate sorties into the wearisome and disreputable pursuit of weaving innumerable lies.[96]

Ford picks up the language of Conrad's letters which lament having to peddle lies for a living. But what in Conrad's writing sounds like a moral scruple about the disreputableness or perils of fiction, signifies rather differently when Ford implies a connection between 'weaving innumerable lies' when writing, and 'always acting a part' when living. The untruthfulness of writing has, it is implied, seeped into Conrad's mode of being in the world. This would be a different criticism from those often levelled at Conrad's formal reminiscences, of evasion or distortion, since Ford appears to have Conrad's fiction rather than his memoirs in mind; and since the comment about acting implies a fictionalization not in his memoirs but in his mind. Yet Ford is not accusing Conrad of being a liar. On the contrary, what might read as an attack is in fact meant as a defence, an explanation of why Conrad might have appeared histrionic, especially to English non-artists. Calling Conrad's mind 'Promethean' says as much, casting him as the creator of men, the ingenious fire-bringer, who stands up for the human against the severity of Olympian law. It's also a self-defence, a fragment of displaced autobiography, since Ford himself was regularly accused of untruthful reminiscence. What he is suggesting is that this is an occupational hazard for novelists: that a life spent dealing in fiction transforms the self:

The Poet—and particularly the poor devil so harried as was Conrad—must have escape from the world, anodynes, and drugs of which the lay public has neither need or

---

[96] Ford, 'Men and Books', *Time and Tide*, 17:21 (1936), 761.

knowledge. One of these is to *Poetiser un peu*—to romance a little when he talks of himself. Then that romance becomes part of himself and is the true truth.[97]

Here is Lejeune's trope again: the work of art expresses the 'true truth', is truer than conventional, factual or biographical, truth. That trope seeks to limit the claim to artists. Yet at the same time it claims that rather than autobiography being impossible, art expands its possibilities. For the aesthete, the artistic temperament allows a greater depth of self-expression in art than is achievable by non-artists. Similarly, for the psychoanalytically minded, the oblique approach of fiction permits a greater depth of self-expression, by evading the censor (as Freud argued in 'Creative Writers and Day-Dreaming').[98] Yet psychoanalysis also recognizes how the argument cannot be limited to artists. Insofar as creative writing is analogous to daydreaming, a kind of professionalized fantasy, then everybody's self is in part composed of the 'true truth' of fantasy. It isn't only professional fictionalizers who fictionalize their lives and their selves—which is to acknowledge that the self is inseparable from narrative and fictionality.

This trope that fiction is the true autobiography is thus consonant with the claims emerging in philosophical and aesthetic autobiographies that subjectivity was beginning to be felt as already aesthetic and fictionalized. While this perception can be posed as applying to everybody, there may nonetheless be good reasons why writers are more conscious of it than others, and why they might thus see it as expressing something about the writer's nature, or the nature of the writer's life. This is certainly the force Ford gives it. His point is that Conrad needed always to be acting a part because that was how he learned to elaborate fictional personae in his writing. As Hugh Kenner argued in a characteristically trenchant essay, Joyce provides another example of a writer whose histrionic personality can be seen as a continuous rehearsal of his fictional performances: Joyce 'spent his life playing parts, and his works swarm with shadow-selves'. 'Parody was the medium of his art', continues Kenner, 'and he played these parts that he might better write them. To make Bloom an authentic parody of himself, Joyce turned himself for long periods into a parody of Bloom.'[99] This seems the most satisfying explanation of what fiction-writers might mean by claiming fiction as their true autobiography: if so much of a life is spent engrossed in constructing fictionalized selves, what better to represent that life than the construction of a fictionalized self?

The claim that fiction is the true autobiography is effectively also a defence of autobiografiction. Only authors whose fiction is autobiographical, or who thread their spiritual experiences onto a fictionalized narrative, are likely to invoke it. On the other hand, as we have seen, the claim is complicated when the works in

---

[97] Ford, 'The Other House', *New York Herald Tribune Books* (2 October 1927), 2.
[98] *The Standard Edition of the Complete Psychological Works of Sigmund Freud*, vol. 9 (London: The Hogarth Press and the Institute of Psycho-Analysis, 1959), pp. 141–53.
[99] Kenner, 'Joyce's Anti-Selves', *Shenandoah*, 4:1 (1953), 24–41 (pp. 24–5).

question are works of autobiografiction rather than fiction. Whereas Lejeune argues that the trope involves conceptual sleight of hand, appearing to grant an equivalence to fiction and autobiography, while privileging autobiography as the ground of the comparison, I argue that autobiografiction shows autobiography and fiction as so deeply interfused that it's impossible to privilege either term. Certainly critics had long been aware that autobiographers distort, and novelists fictionalize their own experience. But in *fin de siècle* autobiografiction the interdependence of autobiography and fiction presents or represents itself with a new urgency and complexity.

In order to conclude this chapter with some observations on this urgency and complexity, we need to recall the arguments of Wilde and Nietzsche with which this book opened, that apparently impersonal discourses are nonetheless modes of autobiography; and the corresponding position, embodied (if that's the word) by Pater, of subjectivism, according to which, the only story I can tell is *The Story of My Heart*. This might make us feel that it is only our interior worlds that we have any authority to describe, or any likelihood of being able to describe accurately. But psychoanalysis, and the psychology of perception and memory, have shown how our instinctive knowledge of our inner world is no more reliable or total than our common-sense experience of the outer world. Freud was particularly exercised by the problem that it was precisely those memories of childhood that were likely to be the most formative which proved the least reliable, arguing: 'one is faced by various considerations to suspect that in the so-called earliest childhood memories we possess not the genuine memory trace but a later revision of it.'[100] His theorization of such 'screen memories' offers a picture of the mind according to which our memories begin in autobiografiction.

Similarly, the lack of faith in external absolutes introduces an uncertainty about the possibility of a shared language being able to frame unshared individual experience, or being able to translate one person's account of their inner world into another mind's understanding of it. Once the private world loses the sanction of the objective, theologically grounded public sphere, then it acquires a status comparable to, or even indistinguishable from, that of fiction. If your statements about yourself have no objective reality; if they express your inner life, spiritual experience, fantasy life whether conscious or unconscious, such statements will read to me as metaphorical or fictional—as denotations of a world that can have no real existence for me, in my private world.

The argument is thus from one perspective circular or self-consuming. If everything is autobiography, I read Nietzsche's philosophy as an expression of his private world, rather than a general statement of universal truth. But how can I understand his private world if there is no common ground on which we can

---

[100] Freud, 'Childhood Memories and Screen Memories', in *The Psychopathology of Everyday Life*, 1901, *Standard Edition*, vol. 6 (London: The Hogarth Press and the Institute of Psycho-Analysis, 1960), pp. 43–52 (pp. 47–8).

base our communication. Nietzsche's writing may express him, but my reading of it will express me, which means I can read his philosophy as my autobiography, but not as his.

Our discussion, which so far has tracked writers working from, or at least starting within, the conventions of autobiography, suggests a twin development. Works become increasingly fictionalized; the self comes to seem increasingly fictional. However, the Wilde–Nietzsche argument pulls in the other direction. The fictional comes to seem increasingly autobiographical. And this tendency becomes more pronounced as we move into modernism. The modernist insistence on objectivity and concreteness paradoxically results in a concentration of autobiographical fictions. The novels of Conrad, Ford, Proust, Lawrence, Richardson, Joyce, and Woolf are more profoundly autobiographical than most of the work by their Edwardian precursors and contemporaries.

Autobiography leads off into fiction; fiction leads back towards autobiography. How are we best to understand this polarity? Perhaps rather than seeing it as a contradiction, we should see it as a productive tension, as a dialectical opposition which enables a synthesis—autobiografiction—to negotiate between these extremes, in parallel with psychoanalysis, which countenances both the fictionalizing in our attempts to construct our narratives about ourselves, and the unconscious autobiography in even those utterances we do not intend to be autobiographical, such as works of fiction.

The phenomenon explored here is really an effect of a crisis in realism, or of the end of realism in painting and the novel. Impressionism signals the end of the attempt to present the real in art as if unmediated.[101] What is at stake when we talk of a new consciousness of the picture surface in painting, or the effects of linguistic technique in writing, is precisely that: a consciousness of the medium being admitted into the experience of art. This entails an awareness of how the representation is effected; how what we are perceiving *is* representation: subjective impression, not objective reality. We are encountering something constructed by the artist. That of course carries with it the possibility that what is 'made' by the artist might be 'made up', at least to some extent. Impressionism, that is, whether in painting or writing, ushers in a heightened awareness of the possibilities of fictionalizing, exaggerating, transforming, the real. That is why Impressionist portraiture shifts so naturally into imaginary portraiture.

Our discussion of imaginary portraits, from Pater to Benson, has perhaps overemphasized the anxious, even agonistic response to the implicit solipsism of autobiografiction, as consciousness of mediation and fictionalization seemed to bar any possibility of the full realization of self or others. There is, it is true, a countercurrent in both Pater and Benson: a hope, central to their different versions of aestheticism, that the subterfuges of art can liberate a truth of self not otherwise

---

[101] See Jesse Matz, *Literary Impressionism and Modernist Aesthetics* (Cambridge: Cambridge University Press, 2001), pp. 243–4.

expressible. And this current is the dominant one in Nietzsche and Wilde, who both welcome the opportunity offered by scepticism about auto/biography to demolish conventional notions of subjectivity, spirituality, and sexuality.

In the work discussed in the remaining chapters, this note of celebration of the possibilities heightened by autobiografiction begins to take over from the note of despair. The impressionist and modernist writers of the twentieth century play more exuberant formal games with auto/biography, and these are the subject of Part II. However, before moving on to consider more celebratory autobiografiction, I shall conclude this chapter by looking further at resistances to its claims.

Postmodernism finds the idea that all writing is autobiography so unobjectionable that we are in danger of forgetting what objections there might be to it. When Browning advertised his *Dramatic Lyrics* in 1842 he declared that the poems were 'always dramatic in principle, and so many utterances of so many imaginary persons, not mine.'[102] He offers characters—often artists—offering their own stories—autobiographical statements, confessions, unconscious revelations—but denies that the poems are his autobiography. In part he wanted to distance himself from his speakers' moral deficiencies—depravity, murderousness, dementia, morbidity, and so on. With the autobiographical forms of Mark Rutherford or A. C. Benson, such guarantees of distance do not apply. They could be the author's autobiography, or they could be fiction, or they could be autobiografiction—in two senses: as work in which, precisely, it is impossible to decide whether they are autobiography or fiction (though they are presumed to be either one or the other); and as work which combines autobiography and fiction. Such uncertainties carry with them a limitation. Browning's declaration of the otherness of his dramatized characters is also a declaration of imaginative independence; of the artist's ability to imagine other selves.

H. G. Wells, whose play with authorial and editorial personae we have already encountered in the previous chapter, was to produce a surprisingly strong statement against reading fiction biographically, in his novel of 1926, *The World of William Clissold*:

It would be a great kindness [...if...] William Clissold could be treated as William Clissold, and if Mr. Wells could be spared the standard charge of having changed his views afresh [...] because William Clissold sees many things from a different angle than did Mr. Polly, George Ponderevo, Susan Ponderevo, Mr. Preemby, Dr. Devizes, Dr. Martineau, Remington, Kipps, the artilleryman in *The War of the Worlds*, Uncle Nobby, Benham, Billy Prothero, and the many other characters who have been identified as mouthpieces and exponents of Mr. Wells' scandalously varied views and attitudes. And it is a point worth considering in this period of successful personal memoirs that if the author had wanted to write a mental autobiography instead of a novel, there is no conceivable reason why he should not have done so.[103]

---

[102] Quoted Robert Langbaum, *The Poetry of Experience* (Harmondsworth: Penguin, 1974), p. 74.
[103] H. G. Wells, *The World of William Clissold*, vol. 1 (Ernest Benn, London, 1926), pp. ii–iii.

The novel is presented as Clissold's eccentric attempt at something like autobiography; though, as he explains, 'It is not exactly an autobiography I want to write, and not exactly a book of confessions':

It is nothing, indeed, so systematic as a general philosophy of life I contemplate, but it is something rather more in that way than an autobiography would be. I should say that a description of my world best expresses what I have in view; my world and my will.[104]

It is a narrative concerned with framing; the first book is titled 'The Frame of the Picture'. This title is presumably to be attributed to Clissold. But the way Wells frames his novel is curiously divided. The conclusion follows the pattern of Hale White and Gissing, with Clissold's brother reporting Clissold's sudden death, delivering an obituary, and discussing his own role as the editor of the book we have been reading. Yet whereas our earlier examples had editorial prefaces too, Wells plays a different formal game, providing 'A Note Before the Title Page' in which he delivers (in his own person) what is tantamount to a manifesto against the idea of autobiografiction. He teasingly concedes that writers draw on their own experiences; but implies that it is the more trivial details rather than what Reynolds called 'spiritual' experiences that get used thus. The positioning of this note before the title page seems to indicate that anything after that point might be taken for part of the fiction, as with *Boon*'s 'Ambiguous Introduction.' Yet even as he aspires to stand outside the text, and assert that Clissold's world is not his, his concessions that writers draw on the experiences they know serve to make the line between fiction and autobiography impossible to draw. One might read this 'Note' biographically in its turn, and suggest that his reasons for wanting to screen himself from the novel were personal rather than intellectual, lest the book's dedicatee and his latest lover, Odette Keun, be identified with Clissold's Clementina; and lest Clissold's disquisition on 'Adult Love' ('I have known many women', etc.) be used to attack Wells for scandalous indiscretion.[105] But Wells's insistence that the novel not be taken for a *roman à clef* can also be read as indicating just how normative the habit of reading fiction as autobiographical had become by 1926.

Even a postmodern artist such as Jeanette Winterson sometimes wants to escape from the grip of the argument that utterance is only ever autobiographical:

Through the development of style imagination is allowed full play. The writer is not restricted to what she has experienced or to what she knows, she is let loose outside of her dimensions. This is why art can speak to so many different people regardless of time and place. It is why it is so foolish to try to reconstruct the writer from the work.[106]

[104] H. G. Wells, *The World of William Clissold*, vol. 1, pp. 26–7.
[105] Ibid., pp. 756–7. David C. Smith, *H. G. Wells: Desperately Mortal* (New Haven: Yale University Press, 1986), p. 285, equates Clementina with Odette, and says the novel treats their life together.
[106] Winterson, *Art Objects* (London: Jonathan Cape, 1995), p. 187.

Winterson, whose own work is embattled against (and in) totalitarian ways of thinking, is doubtless aware of the potential danger of biographical interpretations: namely, that they can be used to condemn or convict artists on the basis of their art. For example, also in 1926, the Nazi writer Paul Schulze-Naumberg adopted Hans Günther's contention (in *Race and Style*, 1926) that 'artists always paint their own self-portraits and that therefore their physical or racial type can be read from their paintings'. He illustrates this with examples from cubist and expressionist distortion, but uses these to conclude that the artists 'were physically and mentally degenerate.'[107] As this case shows so alarmingly, autobiography is in the eye of the beholder.

While the strong defence of autobiografiction—that it provides the truest autobiography—is a form of the Wilde–Nietzsche argument, then, it is nonetheless a special form. Whereas Wilde and Nietzsche see attempts to escape personality as nonetheless revealing that personality, and though they were presumably happy to have their own criticism or philosophy read autobiographically, they do not claim that criticism or philosophy give the *truest* or *best* autobiography. Indeed, the Wilde–Nietzsche argument is prone to conduce to negative criticism, not only of the author, for revealing himself as less noble than he purports to be, but also of the work of art, as an expression of such ignobility; as self-betrayal. As in Richard Aldington's characteristically acerbic verdict on Ezra Pound, which reads *The Cantos* as his true autobiography: 'no man can write without betraying himself, and those Cantos are a faithful picture of Ezra's strangely chaotic mind and nature.'[108] But when autobiografictionists argue that fiction is the truer autobiography, they don't mean it in this negative way. Autobiografiction can include material that writers may prefer not to own in their own person; but rather than suggesting that their fiction gives them away, either consciously or unconsciously, they are claiming that the fictional permits a *fuller* autobiography. This is partly a matter of its being able to include the shameful as well as the honourable, and thus assemble a more complete, more human, picture. But this strong defence is based on more than these claims of candour and totalization.

The claim that a fictional work best expresses the author's subjectivity is at once essentialist and transcendental, in ways that need to be historicized. We saw how, according to Reynolds, this essential, transcendental subjectivity is the locus of 'spiritual experience'. It is significant that he does not call it 'the soul', which was coming to seem an embarrassment in a secularizing, agnostic age. Spiritualism and psychical research flourished at the turn of the century for the same reason: as an attempt to recuperate the spirit in an increasingly sceptical age: to invoke, and prove scientifically the existence of, ghosts or fairies (*The Thread of Gold* includes

[107] Barbara M. Lane, *Architecture and Politics in Germany 1918–1945* (Cambridge, MA: Harvard University Press, 1968), pp. 137–8.
[108] Quoted in Charles Doyle, *Richard Aldington: A Biography* (Basingstoke: Macmillan, 1989), p. 211.

a discussion of these too).[109] Yet such efforts attracted notorious frauds and forgeries: fraudulent mediums offering consoling messages from dead relatives; or the fake fairy photographs that deceived Conan Doyle. The spiritual, in other words, came to seem a locus of fiction. One reason why writers may have felt that their spiritual experiences required fictionalization is that the spiritual had itself come to seem fictional, or at least to have affinities with fiction. Autobiografiction, that is, is the perfect form to express at once experience the author feels to be 'spiritual', coupled with an uncertainty as to the nature of the spiritual.

If one pressure on the 'spirit' is towards fictionality, another is towards 'psyche'. The period in which Reynolds identifies autobiografiction is exactly the period in which discourses of subjectivity shift from the spiritual to the psychological, psychosexual, or psychoanalytic. To argue that autobiografiction expresses a sense that one's spiritual experiences have a fictional dimension, is tantamount to adopting a psychoanalytic view of the self as self-divided, partly unconscious, a site of repression, fantasy, and the disturbing and elusive affects of transference. Autobiografiction, that is to say, also expresses a sense of the self as 'other'; that its narratives are not simply reducible to the facts of one's formal biography or autobiography.

It was possible for Reynolds to identify and name 'autobiografiction' by 1906. While his essay is very much concerned with its present moment, and shares Gosse's sense of dynamic and inventive experiment on the boundaries between fiction and life-writing, it looks backwards and forwards. His examples had been appearing since the 1880s. But he was also thinking of the work he was about to write. And he points forwards, too, to modernism. For though discussion of autobiografiction intensifies at the *fin de siècle*, autobiografiction isn't just a *fin de siècle* phenomenon. It is also the model for modernist engagements with life-writing, as discussed in the rest of this book. What modernist hostility towards, or wariness about, life-writing there was, might be understood as a reaction to precisely this explosion of autobiografiction. It seemed to have become so widespread that some modernists (like Eliot and Lewis) may have felt it necessary to avoid it as far as possible in order to clear space for their own experiments. We don't have formal autobiographies by most of the key modernists. But, as I suggested at the start, it isn't the case that modernism turns its back definitively on life-writing, even if some modernists wanted to, or thought that was what they were doing. What we do have are intense personal experiences—which Reynolds calls 'spiritual', but modernists give other (often comparably metaphysical) names such as 'epiphany', 'moments of vision', 'impression', 'image', or 'symbol'—strung on fictionalized narratives.

Two years before 1906, Joyce had begun work on 'Stephen Hero', the book he would later revise into *A Portrait of the Artist as a Young Man*. Two years later,

---

[109] Benson, *The Thread of Gold*, pp. 69–70.

Proust would begin working on the material that he would turn into his great work of autobiografiction, *A la recherche du temps perdu*. What we have in both these—as in much twentieth-century autobiografiction—is a combination of things we have seen in the turn of the century versions. The content is very similar—that sense of the inner life—interiority, subjectivity, fantasy—is also central to modernism, though it gets discussed differently there, in terms of interior monologue or stream of consciousness; or sometimes is understood as more fragmentary and episodic. But they also draw upon, and complicate, auto/biographical *forms*: not least, through the deployment of heteronymic or fictionalized *writers* within the texts: Joyce's 'Stephen Dedalus'; Proust's 'Marcel'. Whatever else they are, then, works like *A Portrait of the Artist as a Young Man*, *A la recherche*—like *To the Lighthouse*, or even 'The Waste Land' too—are works of autobiografiction.

5

Auto/biografiction: Counterfeit Lives: A Taxonomy of Displacements of Fiction towards Life-Writing

'The secret of success is sincerity. Once you can fake that you've got it made.'[1]

'"The fools don't see that when they call the portrait imaginary, they're praising it", said Harris... "Any damned son of a bitch can put down what he's heard. I'm an artist, not a reporter." He paused and then added: "There'll be ten Thomas Carlyles before there's another Frank Harris." The repetition of either is unlikely.'[2]

THE TAXONOMY OF FAKE LIVES AND LIFE-WRITINGS[3]

Stephen Reynolds explicitly excludes 'autobiographical fiction' from his account of 'autobiografiction'; but he only tells half the remaining story, omitting the other main way in which auto/biography and fiction might interfuse: that is, when, instead of autobiographical spiritual experiences threaded onto a fictional narrative, a writer presents fictional experience in auto/biographical form; when, instead of writers presenting their own experience as those of others, they present others' experiences as if those others were writing about them autobiographically, or were being written about biographically. This other version of auto/biografiction is the central subject of the present chapter. In Reynoldsian autobiografiction any element of 'faking' inheres in the fictionalizing of the narrative to accommodate the author's true experience. In this other version, both the experience itself, and the narrative containing it, is fictionalized; so an element of faking comes to the fore, even (or perhaps especially) when the lives in question are those of real people.

---

[1] Attributed variously to Jean Giraudoux or George Burns.
[2] Hesketh Pearson, *Extraordinary People* (London: Heinemann, 1965), p. 224.
[3] An earlier version of part of this section appeared as 'Biography and Autobiography', *Cambridge History of Twentieth-Century English Literature*, ed. Laura Marcus and Peter Nicholls (Cambridge: Cambridge University Press, 2004), pp. 286–303.

In Chapter 3 the *Autobiography* of 'Mark Rutherford' was constellated with auto/ biographical works by Butler, Gissing, Adams, Gosse, and Wells to demonstrate that 'autobiography' had come to seem a problematic category by the *fin de siècle*. The disturbances and displacements of the autobiographic towards the fictional discussed there coincide (both conceptually and temporally) with the challenge of Paterian impressionism explored in the first chapter. This impressionist sense of uncertainty about the self and how to write the self is crucial to all the remaining chapters, which consider different ways in which early twentieth-century writers— aesthetes, impressionists, modernists—responded to these uncertainties.

Some readers may have felt a different kind of anxiety in the yoking together of Hale White, Butler, Adams, and Gosse. Seen from another angle, all four writers are doing very different things in their negotiation of the autobiographic. This chapter will seek to disentangle such differences and suggest a taxonomy of the kinds of formal combinations of auto/biography and fiction found in the period, before going on to consider some examples in greater detail that are especially relevant to our study of imaginary portraiture—in particular one of the more perennial forms of fake life-writing in the period: the portrait-collection. It will conclude with a discussion of such forms considered as 'composite portraiture', and of how they develop the argument (discussed in the previous chapter) that the truest autobiography can be found in fiction. It will indicate that one of the most significant developments in early twentieth-century writing is this range of ways in which (at the same time that auto/biography is edging towards fiction), fiction begins to colonize forms of life-writing; to use the forms of auto/biography, journal, diary and so on as resources for experiment. Autobiografiction according to Reynolds's definition fictionalizes autobiography. Here, by contrast, we have the auto/biographicalization of fiction.

The Education of Henry Adams and Gosse's *Father and Son* are both authentically autobiographical (even if, like all autobiography, they shape, select, and partially distort). What is unusual about them is the mode of presentation. Adams's device of third-personalization, Gosse's anonymity at first, in their different ways both detach the autobiography from the person of the author: Adams from his grammatical person, Gosse from his nominal person. Butler has done something very different. While he too draws very closely on the facts of his life, he changes the names, introducing an element of fictionality that allows him to present the work as a novel. One could only call it an autobiography by a critical sleight of hand of saying the book was essentially an autobiography, and only the moral expectations of the day (piety, privacy, respect for the dead, stoicism) prevented Butler from writing it as autobiography. There may be something in this argument, since the fact that Butler didn't publish it in his lifetime may indicate that he knew, or feared, that it would be read as autobiography. Either way, it is clearly autobiograph*ical*. Or rather, auto/biograph*ical*, since, like many autobiographies, but like Gosse's in particular, the story of the self is inextricable from the biography of others.

This strategy of taking deeply autobiographical material and fictionalizing it was not in itself new. The nineteenth-century novel is unimaginable without it. Flaubert's teasing claim—'Madame Bovary, c'est moi!'—is at one level perplexing, since the life of the great ironist differed so extremely from the trapped fantasist wife (so that one has to imagine a level on which they might be compared: romanticism; boredom; sexual adventure; transgression?).[4] Yet in the classic nineteenth-century *Bildungsroman*, or novel of education, authors such as Dickens, Charlotte Brontë, George Eliot, Dostoyevsky, or Tolstoy do not incorporate just their spiritual experiences, but much of their own life-stories as well. When nineteenth-century authors include writers and artists in their fictions, they are not generally the most autobiographical characters—the painters in Balzac's 'The Unknown Masterpiece' or the sculptor and singer in 'Sarrasine', the bohemians in Flaubert's *Sentimental Education*, Eliot's Casaubon or Ladislaw in *Middlemarch*—whereas in the early twentieth century, it's the form of the *Künstlerroman* that provides many key works of the period, and represents its most significant development of the form of autobiographical novel. Not only the works by Butler and Gosse, but also Proust's *A la recherche du temps perdu*, Joyce's *A Portrait of the Artist as a Young Man*, Dorothy Richardson's *Pilgrimage*, Lawrence's *Sons and Lovers*, Sinclair's *Mary Olivier*, Woolf's *To the Lighthouse*, Rosamund Lehmann's *Dusty Answer*, and H. D.'s *Bid Me to Live*. Fictionalized autobiography evidently offered a space for women as well to enter the mainstream in a way that straight autobiography did not. Though we might also note that these examples are all also *romans à clef*: essentially pseudonymous autobiographical novels. It's a form which allows writers to appear not to be writing about themselves; which self-protection may have been especially appealing to women writing at a time when to write overt autobiography would risk still being read as appearing threateningly independent, and transgressing from the private and domestic to the public sphere.

Such fiction doesn't only encode the lives of authors and contacts; it becomes the most productive site for the representation of consciousness, gender identity, education, and the inner life. Though the boundary between fiction and auto/biography has always been blurred, and this in turn has affected the development of autobiography,[5] the twentieth century could be said to have renegotiated it in exactly these ways. However, while the modernist *Künstlerroman* might be described as 'autobiografiction' in its cross-boundary experimentation—in its emphasis on the relation between the autobiographical and the fictional as a chief

---

[4] Flaubert was said to have made the remark to the writer Amélie Bosquet. Though, as A. S. Byatt notes, he also told Louise Colet the opposite: that nothing in the book was taken from him; it was all imaginary. Byatt, 'Scenes from a Provincial Life: Part two', *Guardian* (Saturday 27 July 2002), <http://www.guardian.co.uk/books/2002/jul/27/classics.highereducation> (accessed 18 April 2008).

[5] Laura Marcus, *Auto/biographical Discourses* (Manchester: Manchester University Press, 1994), p. 258.

interest—it doesn't fit Reynolds's definition, because it is still a branch of 'autobiographical fiction'.

The work discussed in this chapter represents a departure from the tradition of the autobiographical novel (authors using fictional form and third person narrative to write about their own experiences), and in some ways represents a return to, or redaction of, the eighteenth century's interest in using the form of autobiography to present a first person narrative of someone else's (fictional) experience; producing fictional memoirs and confessions. That is, instead of auto/biography impersonating fiction (as in the autobiographical novel), in the cases discussed here we have fiction impersonating life-writing.

If we think back to 'Mark Rutherford' in these terms, we can see more clearly why his *Autobiography* is such an ambiguous production, and seems to demand a new generic classification. Insofar as its experiences are autobiographical, it is autobiographical fiction. Insofar as they are fictionalized, it's a fictional autobiography. Since both Hale White and 'Rutherford' are writers, it also qualifies as anticipating the modernist *Künstlerroman*. Not only does the *Autobiography* incorporate discussion of its own composition (from its first page); but 'Shapcott' describes Rutherford's literary remains, and includes other examples. Although in Chapter 3 I implied that the *Autobiography* was representative of a crisis in autobiography, which tended to displace the form towards the fictional, it could then just as well (or perhaps better) be seen as moving in the other direction: as a work of fiction colonizing the form of autobiography. Rather than being presented as a novel (even an autobiographical one) it adopts the disguise of formal autobiography. Furthermore, the life-facts it represents increasingly diverge from White's own, so it both is and is not autobiographical. Part of its fascination is that it does seem to be a genuinely ambiguous case, in which it is impossible to decide whether it is autobiography turning into fiction, or fiction impersonating autobiography. The form in which the volumes come to us contributes to this undecidability, as we saw, by appending a fictional work to the autobiography. Sequentially this leads us through autobiography towards fiction; but, as suggested, the juxtaposition in turn takes us back to the autobiography, to wonder whether it, too, hasn't been fictionalized, and represents a move by the author from fiction towards the form of autobiography.

This ambiguity is an immensely significant one, not just for 'Mark Rutherford', but for the period. The present chapter takes this second way of reading his *Autobiography* (as fiction impersonating life-writing) as indicative of another major category of modern writing which is inspired by the osmosis between life-writing and fiction. My argument is that these fake or pseudo- or mock-life-writings are crucial to an understanding of twentieth-century literature. How true is it to claim that fiction begins to colonize the auto/biographic in *new* ways in the twentieth century? One difference is that whereas in the eighteenth century mock-autobiographies parody a form that was still emerging, by the twentieth century, after the exfoliation of auto/biography through the nineteenth, life-writing had lost its novelty, and had come at first to seem second nature and so barely perceptible in formal terms, then conventional and outmoded. Literary fakes appear to have gone out of fashion during the eighteenth century, as a result of the American then French Revolutions.[6] After decades of Victorian earnestness they probably seemed a relief.

These changing attitudes to form are inseparable from changing attitudes to the subject of auto/biography, and to subjectivity itself. 'Invented stories contain a kernel of mystery', writes John Bayley, 'because no one—probably not even the author—knows in what relation they stand to a possible fact.'[7] Autobiografiction acknowledges that kernel of mystery in our self-knowledge, since the stories we tell about ourselves also retain their kernel of mystery. Probably not even the authors of autobiography know how their narratives relate to fact. Once we acknowledge the Freudian unconscious and the role of fantasy, then arguably all our utterance is a species of partly unconscious autobiografiction. All life-writing is susceptible to this scepticism. Much of the work discussed in this chapter has a higher degree of fictionalization than that discussed in the last two; either because it is parodic of life-writing, or aestheticized, or both. One function of these more parodic or aesthetic versions of auto/biography is to remind us of the construct-edness of auto/biography, personality, and subjectivity.

Taxonomy

In the grammar of auto/biografiction there are four fundamental formal modes:

> Autobiographical writing
> Biographical writing
> Creative/Fictional writing
> Commentary (usually of an Editorial kind)

Note how these correspond approximately to Reynolds's tripartite analysis of autobiografiction, though autobiographical writing has been supplemented by biographical (to accommodate biografictions too); and Reynolds's category of the 'essay' has been adapted to 'commentary', since this expository prose tends to discuss the auto/biographical or fictional elements. By 'formal modes' I mean grammatical or narrative modes. Thus although it is a refrain of this book that the biographical can also be the autobiographical, that is a matter of giving a biographical mode (as used in Pater's Imaginary Portraits, say) an

---

[6] See Dror Wahrman, *The Making of the Modern Self* (New Haven: Yale University Press, 2004); and Terry Castle, *Masquerade and Civilisation* (Stanford: Stanford University Press, 1986), which argues that after the French Revolution it became too dangerous to impersonate others. I am indebted to Clare Brant for drawing my attention to these arguments.

[7] Bayley, 'Other Selves', *London Review of Books* (27 October 1987), 19–20.

autobiographical reading. Thus writing in the first person is in autobiographical mode even if about someone other than the author, who may be a fictional character (such as Tristram Shandy). Alternatively, *The Education of Henry Adams* is written in biographical mode (because in the third person, as if about another) even though its content is autobiographical. Each of these four modes can be fictionalized to different degrees. They are not always clearly separable. Some autobiographical or biographical writing takes the form of commentary rather than narrative. And, as we shall see, the question of 'creative writing' is especially problematical within these hybrid forms. That is, auto/biografiction often poses the question of the art-status of its components; as when Joyce gives his young artist's poem (art, yes, but it is good art?); and then goes on to give his journal (is an artist's journal art? and if so, what about his conversation?, etc.). The four modes can also be combined in various ways, and with different ratios of each mode. For example, Rilke's *The Notebook of Malte Laurids Brigge* (1910; discussed in Chapter 8) pretends to be just what its title says: someone's notebook. The only editorial interventions are a handful of footnotes saying that a paragraph appearing in parenthesis was written on the margin of the manuscript; and the last words, a note flatly stating 'End of Journal'. The strategy is to keep us feeling that we are getting the notebook as Brigge wrote it. The fact that his marginal afterthoughts are included serves to reassure us that the inconclusiveness with which he stops is authentic. Alternatively, a single auto-biographical text can be 'framed' with an introduction and conclusion, perhaps presented as a headnote and endnote (as in Rutherford's eventual *Autobiography*). Or several autobiographical fragments can be 'edited' together, as with the diary passages 'arranged' under seasonal headings in Gissing's *The Private Papers of Henry Ryecroft*. In this case the editor feels that Ryecroft, a novelist who has abandoned novel-writing, has in his diary effectively written a novel to please only himself. Thus the diary is offered as potentially more than a diary. In the case of H. G. Wells's *Boon*, also discussed in Chapter 3, the reverse is true. Boon's creative work seems less than he claimed, whereas Bliss's commentary becomes the novel.

A representative blend of all four modes is *The Memoirs of a Failure: With an Account of the Man and His Manuscript*, published in 1908.[8] The author was Daniel Wright Kittredge, who purports to be introducing a manuscript by the 'Failure', whose name is given as 'William Wirt Dunlevy'. As Kittredge explains at the start:

Lest the name of a hitherto unknown author be totally obliterated, I am going to give a description of his curious personality, together with an account of a manuscript in his

---

[8] Daniel Wright Kittredge, *The Memoirs of a Failure* (Toronto: Albert Britnell; and James: Cincinatti: University Press, 1908). The book was reviewed in the *New York Times* on 27 March 1909.

handwriting, as bewildering as it is extraordinary, from which some extracts are now for the first time brought from obscurity into the daylight of print.

He is explicit that his interest in the manuscript is biographical; in what it reveals about Dunlevy's 'personality':

it is best to admit at the outset that the character of this man and the outcome of his life are subjects which seem destined to remain quite as inscrutable as the meaning of his manuscript. All that lies within my aim or power is simply to try to make known his personality as I have conceived it from the few facts of his life known to me, from his writings and from a slight intimacy with the man himself. What is finest to me is the man behind the manuscript; and so my part is strictly to essay at interpretative biography. I am about to tell the brief story of a life singularly strange, a life whose overmastering interest is not in public events, not in famous friendships, not in outward adventures, in nothing but the man himself.[9]

As with 'Mark Rutherford', Kittredge dwells on the machinery of the written remains; though where with Rutherford the mystery was whether more manuscript existed, with Dunlevy the mystery is whether the author exists any more. He sends the narrator an ominously funereal-sounding wooden box containing his 'private papers', asking him to keep it locked for a period of six years.[10] He intimates he may die. But the narrator hears no word for six years, opens the box, and is baffled:

Here was a mass of disconnected dreams, allegorical visions, a curious blending of fact, fiction and fancy—or—Heaven forbid—did the man actually feel what he says and do as he writes he did?

Was he simply a literary experimenter? I think not.[11]

Three-quarters of the book consist of the passages the narrator has extracted from Dunlevy's manuscript book, which is a morass of disconnected entries, with, he says, no discernible order.[12] The narrator hovers between two judgements: the literary experiment theory, which pulls the manuscript away from any autobiographical basis ('As I read, I felt that in spite of the commonness of the first personal pronoun, it was the letter and not the self'); and the pathology theory: 'To the critical eye these writings simply reveal a man of such abnormal imagination that his visions became real to him.'[13] This second judgement returns the writing to the autobiographical, but disturbingly, as 'the portrayal of a man bordering upon insanity.'[14] Kittredge published a later book called *A Mind Adrift*, which not only indicates that he was clearly drawn towards such studies of borderline mentalities, but perhaps suggests that the biografiction in the earlier book is also autobiografiction.[15] *The Memoirs of a Failure* concludes

[9] Kittredge, *The Memoirs of a Failure*, pp. 5–6.   [10] Ibid., p. 31.   [11] Ibid., pp. 33–4.
[12] Ibid., pp 41–186.   [13] Ibid., pp. 34, 36.   [14] Ibid., p. 37.
[15] Kittredge, *A Mind Adrift* (Seattle, WA: S. F. Shorey, 1920).

with a final section, 'Dunlevy Abroad?', which completes the framing, in which the narrator might seem to protest his scruples a little too much: 'it has seemed to me that it would be a breach of friendship for me to attempt to throw light upon either his family history or his private life, aside from what he gives in his own papers. It would savor too much of professional biography.'[16] But that also suggests knowledge of a possibly shameful secret. Whether madness, homosexuality, or just bohemianism, the silences and fictionalizations are further evidence of how writers were increasingly turning to autobiografiction to explore marginalized or repressed subjectivities.

One extraordinary visionary fragment—it reads like a gothic tale—describes 'The strange professor' who has invented a way of reading the minds of the dead by tapping 'the vibratory properties of matter.'[17] He says that listening to someone on the telephone—'like a voice from the other world'—gave him the idea. He gets out an Egyptian mummy and gets it to speak. Then to show he doesn't just have power over this one corpse, he takes Dunlevy to a cemetery, and inserts his tubes into the heads of various graves to let him listen to the dying thoughts of the corpses. It's a vividly ghoulish allegorization of why one might find 'professional biography' unsavoury, and gets its effect in part from making us feel that our access to Dunlevy's thoughts is comparably macabre. Eventually the narrator lets us off the hook, by recounting a meeting with an old college friend who tells him he saw Dunlevy in England, alive, but an invalid.[18]

The Memoirs of a Failure bears out (and extends beyond the turn of the century) Valerie Sanders's claim that late Victorian autobiography 'follows the pattern of the nineteenth-century novel, which in the second half of the century increasingly traces the decline and disappointment of its protagonist.'[19] But it also confirms the drift, or adrift, we have seen in such narratives (and which Sanders's own work on the Bensons has illustrated) to turn autobiography into fiction and disguise fiction as autobiography. The liminal works that resulted proved hard for critics to place. For example, though the *English Review* called the *Memoirs* 'the work of a writer of considerable imaginative and literary gifts', the review was included in its 'Essays and General Literature' section, rather than under the 'Fiction' section which follows it.[20]

As is clear from the examples given already, the best writers do not always confine themselves to one of the fundamental components of auto/biografiction, but tend to get energized by the possibilities for experimental combinations. *The Memoirs of a Failure*, like Mark Rutherford's eventual *Autobiography* or *Boon*, uses all four. In view of this, the taxonomy that follows is inevitably reductive and

---

[16] Kittredge, *The Memoirs of a Failure*, p. 191.
[17] Ibid., pp. 121–44; quotations from pp. 142, 132.
[18] Ibid., p. 197.
[19] Sanders, 'Victorian Life Writing', *Literature Compass*, 1:1 (2004), 1–17 (p. 8).
[20] *English Review*, 10 (December 1911), 183.

somewhat arbitrary. It is intended to convey the richness of the possibilities; to provide a basis for subsequent discussion of how writers complicate these categories; and also to suggest how the experimental energies of the period under discussion (the 1870s to 1930s) reverberate through later modernist and postmodernist work. For the sake of clarity I look first at works whose emphasis is more biographical, then those of a more autobiographical kind, though here too the distinction is heuristic, as one can see from the way some works appear in both categories.

Types of Biografiction

Just as 'autobiografiction', in its broadest signification, represents a variety of interactions between autobiography and fiction, we need a term that covers the variety of interactions between biography and fiction. I propose *biografiction* here,[21] which at least provides symmetry if not elegance; and which has anyway been implied by the umbrella term 'auto/biografiction'. Biografiction, then, could include biographical fiction (by analogy with the autobiographical fiction Reynolds tries to exclude), such as a novel based on another life than the author's. It could include work that corresponds to Reynoldsian autobiografiction, in which the author strings someone else's actual spiritual experience (told by a friend, read about in a book?) onto an invented narrative. It could include fake biography: fiction which assumes biographical form. Finally, it could also include fiction in some way *about* biography and biographers—indeed, work of the last two types might well tend to address the biographical process explicitly. Metabiographical fiction (the term metabiografiction were perhaps best left uncoined) has particularly flourished in the postmodern period, partly in response to the culture industry's insatiability for the biographical. However, as this book demonstrates, the perception that biography, like autobiography, can become a subject rather than merely a source for a creative writer manifested itself at the end of the nineteenth century. Three strands can be distinguished, though they are sometimes intertwined.

First, the *pseudo-biography*, that borrows biographical form to lend verisimilitude. Butler's *The Way of All Flesh*, or Thomas Mann's *Doktor Faustus* (1947), are sustained examples. Many novels borrow elements from biographical form. May Sinclair's *Mary Olivier: A Life* (1919) takes not only a biographical-sounding title, but a structure, following the phases of a life in the headings for its five books: Infancy, Childhood, Adolescence, Maturity, Middle Age—each with dates attached. It, too, is highly autobiographical, as well as being an exemplary modernist *Künstlerroman*. Much of Sinclair's own family life provided

---

[21] Of the few instances appearing on the Web, most are in French, and few in critical discourse. The equivalent term 'biofiction' also appears to be gaining some virtual currency, by analogy with the more familiar 'autofiction'.

the basis. The heroine's love for her brother Mark (based on Sinclair's brother Frank); her struggle against the tyranny and religious orthodoxy of the mother, who rejects her daughter's love in favour of her sons; her fear of hereditary madness, alcoholism, and physical weakness; her intense, unconsummated, renounced, love for several different men; and the drive to individuation and creativity seeking to escape the trammels of heredity, family, environment, society, and religion, can all be read as spiritual autobiography cast into biografictional form.[22]

Pseudo-biography can also be written with an ironic purpose (as in Mann's novel, where the plodding biographical specificity is ironized by the intimations of the demonic). Or it can be satirical, as in Richard Aldington's *Soft Answers* (1932), with scathing parodic biographies attacking modernist authors. Max Beerbohm's *Seven Men* (1919) combines the two, though the satire is gentler and is directed at types rather than individuals. It might seem surprising to cite Ezra Pound's poem-sequence *Hugh Selwyn Mauberley* (1920) here. But its subtitle— 'Life and Contacts'—intimates that Pound intends some relation to the form of a literary memoir of a minor figure. The poems themselves don't read like biography, of course; but they keep mimicking its mannerisms of style, tone, and structure. All these works are discussed in more detail in Part II. The fact that all three are examples of the portrait-collection is significant, indicating that form's particular suitability for irony and satire. Perhaps sympathy is harder to keep at bay in more extended biografictions; and perhaps the juxtaposition of contrasting individualities makes each seem more eccentric. Though, as in the cases of Pater and of Symons, as we shall see, portrait-collections need not inevitably satirize their subjects. Either way, what such collections can do—as Ann Jefferson argues, is to suggest qualities transcending the individual people or times—whether for analytic or satiric purposes.[23]

Hugh Selwyn Mauberley is also an example of the second strand, the *mock-biography*, which adopts a pseudo-biographical strategy to parody or satirize it. The prefixes 'pseudo-' and 'mock-' tend to get used interchangeably in discussions of auto/biografictional forms, which can lead to confusion (a confusion due to the ambiguity of 'mock-', which can mean substitute or ridiculing). For example Valerie Sanders calls A. C. Benson's *Memoirs of Arthur Hamilton* (1886) 'a pseudo-biography which is partly told in the first person and sounds suspiciously like Benson's own life with some adjustments'. She goes on to describe *The House of Quiet* as 'another attempt at mock-autobiography', implying the equivalence of the two terms.[24] She also calls *Memoirs of Arthur Hamilton* 'a fictitious biography, largely about himself': in other words, biografiction

---

[22] Saunders, entry for May Sinclair, *Oxford DNB*.

[23] Jefferson, *Biography and the Question of Literature in France* (Oxford: Oxford University Press, 2007), pp. 101–4.

[24] Sanders, 'Victorian Life Writing', *Literature Compass*, 1:1 (2004), 1–17 (p. 10).

is likely to be intertwined with autobiografiction too.[25] According to the taxonomy outlined here, both pseudo- and mock-biographies or autobiographies are fictitious. Pseudo-auto/biography fictionalizes with serious intent, to provide convincing impressions of authentic life-writing. Mock-auto/biography fakes life-writing for satiric or parodic purposes, which can include satire or parody of the auto/biographic subject, the biographer, or the form. In the case of *Mauberley*, the parodic energies of the mock-biography encompass both Mauberley himself, and his putative memoirist. These implications are developed in Chapter 9. Woolf's cunningly sustained *Orlando* (1928) is the best, and best-known, example, and is considered in Chapter 11 (alongside the work she was reviewing in her landmark essay 'The New Biography', Harold Nicolson's deft auto/biografictional sketches *Some People*). Orlando's 400-year life-span and change from man to woman baffle the intrusive figure of the pompous biographer. In *Boon*, Wells playfully implies the biographical memorial to the great author even if he doesn't write it. Vladimir Nabokov's *Pale Fire* (1962) satirizes the biographical process, but via the ingenious form of scholarly annotations to a poem which impose upon it the meaning of being the biography of the annotator. Kathryn Hughes recently complained wittily about being asked to review biographies of things without a pulse: London, the equation $E=mc^2$, Water.[26] Such texts trade on the current marketability of biography, rather than satirizing biographical form. But the application of anthropocentric narrative to the non-human can have an estranging effect on the form as well as the content. And sometimes this can be turned to satirical or ironic effect, as in the case of animal auto/biography, the most famous and ironic example of which is Woolf's *Flush* (discussed in Chapter 11).

In the cases of Woolf and Nabokov, mock-biography shades off into the third strand of meta-biographic fiction. Fictional works with biographers as central characters have emerged as an increasingly significant category of postmodernism. It includes works as diverse as Nabokov's *The Real Life of Sebastian Knight* (1941); Bernard Malamud's *Dubin's Lives* (1979); Julian Barnes's *Flaubert's Parrot* (1984); William Golding's *The Paper Men* (1984); A. S. Byatt's *Possession* (1990) and *The Biographer's Tale* (2000); and Tom Stoppard's plays *Arcadia* (1993) and *Indian Ink* (1995). Like most postmodern tendencies, however, it has roots in modernism, which (as the examples from Wells and Woolf suggest) was already exploring the fictionalities of biography. When Ford Madox Ford published his memoir *Joseph Conrad: A Personal Remembrance* (1924), he provocatively described it as a novel, arguing: 'a novel should be the biography of a man or of an affair, and a biography whether of a man or of an affair should be a novel . . . .'[27]

---

[25] Sanders, '"House of Disquiet": The Benson Family Auto/biographies', in *Life writing and Victorian Culture*, ed. David Amigoni (Aldershot: Ashgate, 2006), pp. 292–315 (p. 317).
[26] Hughes, Lecture 'Whose Life Is It Anyway?', in the series 'Life Writing at King's', King's College London, Thursday, 16 November 2006.
[27] Ford, *Joseph Conrad* (London: Duckworth, 1924), pp. 5–6.

Types of Autobiografiction

Just as fiction about biography has proliferated through the twentieth century, so have not only autobiographical novels, and Reynoldsian autobiografiction, but also a variety of other forms of fictional play with autobiography. These do not just represent their author's experience, but are meta-autobiographical: explicitly concerned with the auto/biographic process, and the *representation* of auto/ biography. Here at least seven broad types are distinguishable (though some are subdivisible, as indicated).

i) One is *framed pseudo-autobiographical* works, which incorporate fictional first-person material (diary entries, journals, letters, travelogues, etc.) within another narrative. We have seen examples already, such as *The Journal of a Disappointed Man* and *The Memoirs of a Failure*. Major modernist and postmodern examples occur at the end of Joyce's *Portrait of the Artist as a Young Man*; throughout Doris Lessing's *The Golden Notebook* and *The Diaries of Jane Somers*; or in A. S. Byatt's *Possession*, and Alan Hollinghurst's *The Swimming Pool Library* (1988). André Gide, positively a serial autobiografictionist as well as journal-writer, provides a range of examples right through our period, starting with his first novel, *Les Cahiers d'André Walter* (1891; *The Notebooks of André Walter*).[28] In *La Porte étroite* (1909; *Strait is the Gate*) the narrator Jérôme not only quotes the letters from his dead love Alissa, but finds her journal, excerpts of which are duly included. *La Symphonie pastorale* (1919; *The Pastoral Symphony*) is again written entirely in the form of a journal. *Les Faux-Monnayeurs* (1926; *The Counterfeiters*), which Gide called his only novel, displays a dazzling formal ingenuity, especially concerning the fictionalizing of autobiography. As the *Encyclopedia Britannica* summarizes it:

Édouard, an author writing a novel entitled *The Counterfeiters*, observes that if a counterfeit coin is thought to be authentic, it is accepted as valuable; if it is found to be counterfeit, it is perceived as worthless. Therefore, he concludes, value is wholly a matter of perception and has nothing to do with reality. The counterfeiters are thus representative of those who disguise themselves with false personalities, either in unconscious self-deception or through conscious, hypocritical conformity to convention.[29]

Or novelists who disguise themselves with the false personalities of diarists... *Britannica* calls it Gide's 'most complex and intricately plotted work', which is true, but describes it as 'a novel within a novel'. This is true too in the sense that Edouard's novel is discussed within Gide's of the same title. But what is more immediately apparent is that it is a journal within a novel. One-third of the

[28] See Justin O'Brien, 'Gide's Fictional Technique', *Yale French Studies*, 7 (1951), 81–90 (p. 88).
[29] <http://www.britannica.com/nobel/micro/733_19.html> (accessed 2 January 2007).

chapters are devoted to excerpts from Edouard's journal. In the chapter midway through the novel, 'Edouard explains his theory of the novel', he is asked how far he has got with the book. 'It depends what you mean by far' he replies:

> To tell the truth, of the actual book not a line has been written. But I have worked at it a great deal. I think of it every day and incessantly. I work at it in a very odd manner, as I'll tell you. Day by day in a notebook, I note the state of the novel in my mind; yes, it's a kind of diary that I keep as one might do of a child [. . .] My notebook contains, as it were, a running criticism of my novel—or rather of the novel in general. Just think how interesting such a notebook kept by Dickens or Balzac would be; if we had the diary of the *Education Sentimentale* or of *The Brothers Karamazof!*—the story of the work—of its gestation! How thrilling it would be . . . more interesting than the work itself. . . .[30]

As Justin O'Brien suggests, the appearance of journals in so many of André Gide's works 'suggests that the journal is Gide's form par excellence and that his imaginative works might almost be considered to be extracted from his own *Journals*.'[31] This would be more persuasive if the journal Edouard describes were Gide's own. But, as the quotation suggests, Gide is performing a much more complex counterfeiting operation. Edouard's journal, for all it may owe to Gide's own autobiographical inclinations, is a work of autobiografiction. This passage is a *mise en abyme* (a speciality of Gide's, referring to an image of the whole work within the work);[32] since what Gide has given us is precisely the 'running criticism' of Edouard's novel; the 'story of the work' rather than 'the work itself'. Edouard's point is that journals tend to write the life of the person, whereas he wants the biography of the book. Some authors have written the stories of their work's gestation: Henry James in his Prefaces to the New York edition of his novels; Thomas Mann in *The Story of a Novel: The Genesis of Doctor Faustus*.[33] Gide's fictional innovation, as in *André Walter*, is to give the 'story of the work' for a work that doesn't exist. (Earlier works frequently cite fictional fictions, as we shall see in Chapter 8; but to chart their creative processes is something new.) But by giving the novel we are reading the same title as Edouard's project, Gide gives the idea a further twist, making us wonder whether we are reading a novel about someone writing *The Counterfeiters*, or whether the book we are reading isn't in fact Edouard's novel—in which case the status of the journal entries would alter, from being Gide's counterfeit of his

[30] Gide, *The Counterfeiters*, trans. Dorothy Bussy (Harmondsworth: Penguin, 1985), Pt 2, ch. 3, pp. 169–70.

[31] O'Brien, 'Gide's Fictional Technique', 92.

[32] O'Brien, 'Gide's Fictional Technique', 88. Lucien Dällenbach, 'Reflexivity and Reading', *New Literary History*, 11 (1980), 435–49, argues that the self-reflexive figures he designates as *mises en abyme* 'supersede "authorial intervention"' (p. 441). Also see his *Le Récit spéculaire* (Paris: Seuil, 1977); trans. Jeremy Whiteley and Emma Hughes as *The Mirror in the Text* (Cambridge and Oxford: Polity Press, 1989).

[33] Trans. R. and C. Winston (New York: Knopf, 1961). A. S. Byatt, lecture on Thomas Mann at the German Embassy, London, 3 December 2008.

character's journals to Gide's counterfeit of that character's fictional counterfeit of his own journals (which would make it also a case of fictional creativity, discussed in Chapter 8).

ii) Works entirely in the form of *unframed pseudo-autobiographical works.* Technically the older form of the epistolary novel could be described in this way. But, arguably, the presentation of an entire web of correspondence, between several letter-writers, constitutes a kind of framing of each letter. It is possible for a long narrative to be presented as a single unframed letter—the collaborative novella *The Nature of a Crime* by Ford and Conrad must be one of the longest suicide notes in literary history.[34] But it is unframed pseudo-diaries or journals that constitute an extraordinarily important strand of modern fiction. Outstanding examples include Rilke's hauntingly neurasthenic *Notebook of Malte Laurids Brigge* (the minimal annotations to which concern the transcription of manuscript into printed book); and Sartre's *La Nausée* (1938), which the narrator Roquentin turns significantly from trying to write a biography, to realizing he has to write about himself: to produce the book we have in fact been reading (thus making it an explicitly hybrid example in which biografiction turns into autobiografiction). Frequently, though the bulk of the work consists of pseudo-diary, it may be introduced or annotated by an editor, as in the case of Kierkegaard's *Diary of a Seducer* (1843)—though that text offers a more equivocal case. The diary is written by someone called 'Johannes', and is introduced by a person signing themselves simply 'A', who claims to have hurriedly and secretly copied out the diary he has found by accident, in fear of being discovered. However, the editor of *Either/Or* (which includes the Diary as the last section of the first volume), who is another of Kierkegaard's fictional men of letters, 'Victor Eremita', suspects 'A' of being Johannes, and therefore the seducer.[35] Kierkegaard thus opens the door to a hall of mirrors. If one editor-persona might be lying, then so might the other, and we might as well suspect Victor Eremita of being either 'A' or Johannes or both. And since all three are fictional personae invented by Kierkegaard, he is likely to come under suspicion himself, as he well knows, for knowing too much about seduction to have a merely fictional interest in it.

There's no reason why serious auto/biografiction cannot be written in letter form too. Indeed, A. C. Benson's *The Upton Letters* (1905) is precisely that. The letters are presented by their purported author, 'T. B.', as his half of a correspondence with his friend, 'Herbert', who had to leave Britain to live abroad. After

---

[34] *The Nature of a Crime* (London: Duckworth, 1924); written 1906; first published serially 1909 in *The English Review* (under the pseudonym 'Baron Ignatz von Aschendrof') and in *transatlantic review*, 1924.

[35] See Gerd Gillhof, 'Introduction', *Diary of a Seducer* (London: Elek, 1969), p. vi.

Herbert's death his widow returns them to 'T. B.', saying Herbert had said they ought to be published. Though the letters are solicitous about Herbert's life and health, they say little about him. They are autobiografictional, recording events in 'T. B.'s life, and using them as occasions for essays on subjects such as education, religion, friendship, and of course aesthetics. Thus though epistolary in form, some of the letters are themselves written in diary form ('This letter is going to be a diary. Expect more of it.—T. B.'),[36] and accumulate into what is essentially a spiritual autobiography; hence the book gives us an example of type (iv).

The form of the pseudo-diary is important in poetry too. Many of John Berryman's *Dream Songs* are written in the form of diurnal confessions, but of an at least partly fictionalized persona, 'Henry'. Such 'confessions' all have an autobiographical dimension, drawing upon the author's personal experiences and ideas. But they are offered as fictional; as the journals of other egos than the authors'. It is at least in part Rilke's and Sartre's ability to impersonate these others that distinguishes them from Brigge or Roquentin.

Another form of pseudo-diary is exemplified by *The Whispering Gallery: Being Leaves from the Diary of an Ex-Diplomat*, which appeared anonymously in 1926. Its author was in fact not a diplomat, but the actor-turned-biographer Hesketh Pearson. His publisher, John Lane, had agreed to publish it anonymously provided that Pearson confided the diplomat's name to the firm. Pearson told Lane it had been written by a real diplomat, Sir James Rennell Rodd.[37] In fact, the book takes the form of a portrait gallery, consisting of brief biographical sketches of public figures. Three chapters treat single individuals: Lords North-cliffe ('The Napoleon of Fleet Street') and Leverhulme ('The Soap King'), and Edward VII ('The Peacemaker'). The other chapters mostly group several subjects by profession: the 'Warriors' include Kitchener, Roberts, John French, and Marshal Joffre; the chapter on 'Empire-Builders' juxtaposes Cecil Rhodes with Joseph Chamberlain; the 'Three Caesars' are the Kaiser, the Tsar, and Franz Josef'; the 'Two Despots' are Mussolini and Lenin; the 'Scribblers' include H. G. Wells, Bernard Shaw, Hardy, Henry James, Kipling, and Twain. Thus the portraits were not of imaginary people, but of the celebrities of the day. It is the portrait of the author that is imaginary, since Pearson disguises himself as a gratingly self-regarding diplomat ('Among the diplomats of Europe my name is a household word. I say this in no boastful spirit. It just happens to be so').[38] The claim that the portraits are based on the diplomat's diary is intended to guarantee their verisimilitude. The diplomat's profession has supposedly given him access to 'most of the prominent men in Europe'; and he says he has been 'amazed at the strange lack of first-hand, authentic portraiture of these national figures in the

---

[36] Benson, *The Upton Letters* (London: Smith, Elder & Co., 1905), p. 49.

[37] 'Introduction' in [Hesketh Pearson], *The Whispering Gallery*, ed. Michael Holroyd (London: Phoenix Press, 2000), pp. xviii–xxv.

[38] Ibid., p. xvii.

volumes that have glutted the book-market of late years under the heading of "Memoirs", of "Pen-Portraits", and of "Autobiography".'[39] The imaginary diary on which his portraiture is based enables him to claim that the conversations are recorded exactly—because written down immediately after the event—and are thus more accurate than they could be if recalled years later for an auto/biographical book.

The book caused something of a scandal when it first appeared. It was attacked, predictably, as a 'SCANDALOUS FAKE', making 'MONSTROUS ATTACKS ON PUBLIC MEN' (as the *Daily Mail* headlines put it), and was repudiated 'BY FIVE CABINET MINISTERS.'[40] At first the publisher was delighted by the publicity. But then the *Dail Mail* began to accuse John Lane of being party to fraud, at which point the directors started claiming they had been the victims of 'a most ingenious hoax', and charging Pearson with attempting to obtain money under false pretences. There was a trial, at which Pearson refused to plead guilty to fraud, but then admitted in the witness box to lying, saying that he had used Rodd's name to draw attention to the lie, since he obviously wouldn't have written the book. The jury was apparently moved by his candour, and acquitted him. Michael Holroyd argues that Pearson was influenced in this book, and in his other biographical writings, by both Lytton Strachey and Frank Harris, who had, he believed, 'liberated non-fiction from the obsequious routine of hagiography and transformed biography itself into an art that could be as imaginative and free as the novel'; and he claims that Pearson's experiment blazed a trail for later fictionalizing biographies such as Peter Ackroyd's *Dickens* or Andrew Motion's *Wainwright the Poisoner*.[41] Holroyd calls *The Whispering Gallery* 'an audacious, satirical work of make-believe.'[42] Many of its episodes are invented, such as the interview in which Northcliffe hopes to do a deal with the author to get hold of officially secret government information. It could thus be described as a doubly articulated fictionalization: fictionalizations of real figures, portrayed by a narrator who is himself a fictionalization of a real figure. Given the subsequent grotesque developments of media celebrity culture, we may feel now that the danger of this approach, with its focus on a particular social world of the powerful and the famous, is its proximity to celebrity gossip. If Pearson's use of the fictional narrator was intended as a parody of press sensationalism, as well as of civil service superciliousness, or of the public official's delusion of self-importance, his use of potentially scandalous subject matter is complicit with the media's love affair with celebrity trivia.

A pseudo-diary, then, is a kind of fake: the diary X might have written had X been a real person. But there is a difference between faking a diary of a fictional person, and faking the diary of a real person. Does this make *The Whispering*

---

[39] Ibid., p. xxvii.   [40] Ibid., p. xx.   [41] Ibid., pp. xiii, xxvi.   [42] Ibid., p. vii.

Gallery a fake rather than a pseudo-diary? Not quite, because there is also a difference between what Pearson was doing and what, say, the forger was doing who wrote the sixty-two volumes sold to *Stern* magazine in 1983 as Hitler's Diaries, which were later proved to have dated from after the Second World War. Both were hoping to profit from their impersonations, certainly. And both claimed authentic access to the private thoughts of historical figures. (Pearson's are offered at one remove, and of many figures; but the claim to new personal information is common to both.) Though the information offered by both texts might be equally fraudulent, the difference lies in the mode of presentation. Though Pearson may have defrauded his publisher (who may have been conscious of the deception, but acquiescent in it because of the legal protection it enabled—and so to that degree morally if not legally complicit), the authorship remained anonymous to the book's original readers. So Pearson was not passing it off publicly as the product of a particular, named, ex-diplomat. It wasn't that kind of fraud; though the 'ex-diplomat' claim fraudulently implies the book's impressions are based on first-hand knowledge of public figures.

Both these examples were offered seriously, though Pearson may have had some ironic or satirical intent. But fictional life-writing can also have great comic potential, whether as pseudo-diaries or pseudo-letters of fictional characters, or fake diaries or letters by real figures. This provides our next category.

iii) *Mock-diaries or journals or letters* mimic the forms for humorous purposes. George and Weedon Grossmith's *Diary of a Nobody* (1892) and Mark Twain's *Extracts from Adam's Diary* (1904) and *Eve's Diary* (1906) are hilarious examples. It's certainly possible for such mock-life-writing to be framed. It's a speciality of a parodist like Max Beerbohm, as in his essay 'How Shall I Word It?' which parodies a letter-writing manual of the same title by supplementing it with withering mock-epistles.[43] But the better examples tend to be unframed works. They tend to be funnier, not just because the performance has to be sustained, but because the game of fictional authorship has to be sustained along with it. They share this with pseudo-life-writing forms too, so it's unsurprising that they sometimes also share the anonymity we noted there. For example, the brothers George and Weedon Grossmith only identified themselves as the authors of the *Diary of a Nobody* three years after its first publication.[44] More often, though, the author takes the credit on the title-page for an otherwise flawless act of ventriloquism. Arguably these mock-forms are mocking not just classic autobiographical works, but, since they only establish themselves from the late 1880s, also the early classic autobiografictional works such as those by 'Mark Rutherford'.

---

[43] In Beerbohm, *And Even Now* [1920] (London: Heinemann, 1950), pp. 15–26.
[44] George and Weedon Grossmith, *The Diary of a Nobody* (London: J. W. Arrowsmith, 1892).

Another form they're inclined to mock is the portrait-collection. The master of the mock-life-writing collection was Maurice Baring. His *Lost Diaries* (1913) are miniature comic gems. The book consists of twenty fictional extracts from diaries by mythical, historical, and fictional figures including Oedipus, William the Conqueror, Hamlet, The Man in the Iron Mask, Harriet Shelley, and Sherlock Holmes. Here the juxtaposition of real with fictional figures points up the playfulness of the exercise. Baring was well known in his day, not only as a creative writer but as a diplomat, Russian expert, and war correspondent. 'He had a small but genuine literary talent', wrote Philip Ziegler, 'a genius for languages, vast exuberance and a wild imagination veering erratically between fantasy and whimsy.'[45] Much of this comes across in the high spirits of his volumes of fictional diaries and letters. 'He was one of those people of whom it is difficult to see the point unless one actually knows them', Ziegler continued. Ouch! Biographers who actually know their subjects like to claim that privileged vision. But Baring's engaging writings give a good sense of what good company he must have been. They share Beerbohm's delight in metafictional games. Indeed, one of his 'Diminutive Dramas' imagines Beerbohm as one of four prominent writers addressing the House of Commons before a vote to elect 'The Member for Literature.'[46] In the tenacity with which he plays with the forms of life-writing, Baring might be thought of in our survey as the Benson of comedy.

He begins his autobiography, *The Puppet Show of Memory* (1932):

When people sit down to write their recollections they exclaim with regret, 'If only I had kept a diary, what a rich store of material I should now have at my disposal!' I remember one of the masters at Eton telling me, when I was a boy, that if I wished to make a fortune when I was grown up, I had only to keep a detailed diary of every day of my life at Eton.[47]

Lost Diaries duly begins with 'From the Diary of Smith Minor', a pupil at 'St James's School' in September 1884 (the same date Baring started school),[48] a posher and jejune precursor of Nigel Molesworth, which makes one thankful that schoolboys aren't generally budding Pepyses. Baring's comic forays into fictional auto/biography are all bagatelles on a fantasy version of the same idea: if only legendary or mythical or even fictional figures had kept their diaries, what might those diaries be like? The *Lost Diaries* were published as journalistic pieces, and they are meant to entertain rather than seriously to reconstruct the psyches of their diarists. Most of the fun comes from the liberties they take with the received histories or legends. George Washington and Marcus Aurelius appear as insufferable prigs. The tyrants emerge as mild and misunderstood (Ivan the

---

[45] Quoted by Richard Davenport-Hines, 'Tinned Nellie', *Times Literary Supplement* (14 December 2007), 26.

[46] In Baring, *Unreliable History* (London: Heinemann, 1934). The others are based on Hall Caine, Rudyard Kipling, and Jerome K. Jerome.

[47] Maurice Baring, *The Puppet Show of Memory* (London: Cassell, 1987), p. 1.

[48] Ibid., p. 68.

Terrible hopes to be remembered as Ivan the people's friend). Sherlock Holmes makes some spectacular mis-deductions. Oedipus takes his fate in his stride: it's Jocasta who goes for his eyes with pins; otherwise he's not too bothered, and ends up cheerful at Colonus. It was a winning formula, and Baring kept mixing it. As Richard Holmes explains:

Maurice Baring invented 'lost' letters and diaries in his *Unreliable Histories* [*sic*], and suggested intriguing versions of 'alternative lives', including Shelley retiring as Tory MP for Horsham, and Coleridge completing his 'epic Kubla Khan' in fifteen volumes at the age of eighty.[49]

The Puppet Show of Memory has a diaristic energy, especially in recounting his childhood. Though Baring shrewdly observes:

On the other hand, for the writer who wishes to recall past memories, the absence of diaries and notebooks has its compensation. Memory, as someone has said, is the greatest of artists. It eliminates the unessential, and chooses with careless skill the sights and the sounds and the episodes that are best worth remembering and recording.[50]

Which is a politer, more ironic way of saying 'One never can quite trust literary men when facts are in question', as Baring has the Emperor Titus having it.[51] If a writer is reimagining his or her autobiography without benefit of diary, that's one thing. Baring does quite another thing in his mock life-writing, humorously compensating for the lack of a famous person's or character's diary or letter, in order to give them a different life from the received one. He plays on our assumption that diaries and letters, because closer to the event, are closer to the fact. While he doesn't aim for credibility—his historical figures often sound entertainingly and anachronistically modern—he infiltrates a scepticism about biographical tradition; about whether that isn't fictionalized too. The interlacing of historical, fictional, and mythological figures makes much the same point.

The mock-diary has proved a strikingly enduring form, probably for the comic possibilities it offers to express the failures, anxieties, neuroses, desires, desperations, and self-mockery that we try to keep out of our social personae. Witness Sue Townsend's *The Secret Diary of Adrian Mole aged 13 ¾* (1982), and now—with presumably a nod to Baring—*The Lost Diaries of Adrian Mole, 1999–2001* (2008); or Helen Fielding's *Bridget Jones's Diary* (1996).

iv) *Pseudo-autobiography*, in which a formal autobiography is attributed to a fictional persona, appears in two main versions; again, *framed* or *unframed*. *Framed*, or *partial*, *pseudo-autobiography* is presented by a second narrator, as

---

[49] Richard Holmes, 'Boswell's Bicentenary', at <http://web.wits.ac.za/Academic/Humanities/SLLS/Holistic/Boswell.htm> (accessed 24 April 2009). Baring's *Unreliable History* collects together his 'Diminutive Dramas', 'Dead Letters' and 'Lost Diaries'.

[50] Baring, *The Puppet Show of Memory*, p. 1.

[51] Baring, *Lost Diaries* (London: Duckworth, 1929), p. 85.

with Hermann Hesse's *Steppenwolf* (1927), which consist mostly of the 'records' left by 'Harry Haller', introduced by a friend. Or it can be presented as fragmentary, as the unconnected reminiscences making up Gissing's *The Private Papers of Henry Ryecroft*. In Nabokov's *Pale Fire*, John Shade's poem is readable as autobiographical—by anyone but its scholarly framer Charles Kinbote, who thinks it's biographical and about him, and insinuates this reading of it into his obsessive annotations. This is perhaps the most complexly hybrid example of auto/biografiction, in which Kinbote reads Shade's autobiographical poem as encrypted biography (of Kinbote); whereas Kinbote's ostensibly biographical memoir of and annotations to Shade keep turning Shade's poem into biografiction about Kinbote, and thus into Kinbote's displaced autobiography (if he's sane) or autobiografiction (if he's mad). The attention Nabokov pays to Kinbote's minute reading of Shade's poem, extreme case though it is, alerts us to the function of the introducers, editors, and annotators that recur in auto/ biografiction, which is to pose the auto/biographical as a function of reading; something that is constructed in the intersubjective relation between writer and reader. Frames come in different widths, and the distinction between framed and unframed life-writing is often problematized by these works. Whereas some of our examples—*The Autobiography of Mark Rutherford, The Memoirs of a Failure*—are unequivocally framed with an editorial and biographical preface or introduction and conclusion, in other cases the fiction of an editor is virtually effaced, as in Rilke's *Malte Laurids Brigge*.

v) Unframed, or *full, pseudo-autobiography* is a trickier form to instance. Proust's *A la recherche* is a possible candidate insofar as it is fictionalized, though the tentative identification of the narrator as 'Marcel' might seem to blur the distinction between true and pseudo-autobiography. It is at least possible to read Joyce's *Portrait* as not merely Joyce's presentation of Stephen's consciousness, but as Joyce's impersonation of the book Stephen might have written about his experience; in which case it would provide an example of a full pseudo-autobiography. This will be discussed more fully in Chapters 7 and 8, together with Italo Svevo's *Confessions of Zeno* (1923) and Gertrude Stein's *The Autobiography of Alice B. Toklas* (1933)—arguably the clearest examples of this type, though neither of these dispense altogether with a frame: Stein's closing paragraph reveals that she is in fact the author of Toklas's 'autobiography'; Svevo gives Zeno's Confessions a Preface by the psychoanalyst 'Dr S' who has instructed him to write down his memories. And it ends differently: after he gives his manuscript to Dr S, he stops writing while undergoing analysis. Then he stops the analysis, and returns to writing, this time in the form of a journal.

These examples show that, as within all auto/biografiction, many permutations of the four basic modes are possible. Creative works like poems can be included within prose narratives; journals, diaries and letters can appear within autobiographies, as can editorial interventions. The extent of the auto/ biography may vary too, covering a full life or just a part. Or, as in *Ryecroft* the editor can claim to be editing down a long span of journal-writing into a single year; or, as in *Boon*, to be editing a whole life's work into a single volume.

vi) Since pseudo-autobiography ironizes the autobiographer, it's hard to draw a line between it and *mock-autobiography*, which ironizes the form. The best modern examples have come from Twain again; not only his *Extract from Captain Stormfield's Visit to Heaven* (1909), but also the *Chapters from My Autobiography* (1906–7), which begins with parodic self-justification:

I intend that this autobiography shall become a model for all future autobiographies when it is published, after my death, and I also intend that it shall be read and admired a good many centuries because of its form and method—a form and method whereby the past and present are constantly brought face to face [...][52]

He claims he will not 'select from my life its showy episodes', and that whereas 'The usual, conventional autobiographer seems to particularly hunt out those occasions in his career when he came into contact with celebrated persons', his own 'contacts with the uncelebrated were just as interesting'. Then, with characteristic vertiginous self-mockery, the next paragraph begins: 'Howells was here yesterday afternoon, and I told him the whole scheme of this autobiography and its apparently systemless system—only apparently systemless, for it is not really that [...]'. He claims Howells 'applauded, and was full of praises and endorsement, which was wise in him and judicious. If he had manifested a different spirit, I would have thrown him out of the window. I like criticism, but it must be my way.'

Similar high spirits are manifest in *The Memoirs of Satan*, by William Gerhardi and Brian Lunn (1932). Their mockery of the form is partly a matter of teasing out the temptations that particularly beset it—to vanity (there is a chapter on 'The Birth of Vanity'), egotism ('I become the Scourge of God'), name-dropping ('I Meet Mary Queen of Scots'), salaciousness ('Love and Marie-Antoinette') and so on. But it's also a matter of time. Satan's memoirs cover more than the whole of time since the creation. God, whom he refers to as 'the All-Highest' or just 'A.H.' treated him like a son ('But whether He was really my father or not, I could never quite understand').[53] A.H. considers starting a new world as an experiment, and when he creates the Earth he sends Satan to it to observe, serve his apprenticeship—'and eventually—who knows?—take entire control of it.

---

[52] Twain, *Chapters from My Autobiography*, originally published in twenty-six instalments in the *North American Review* from 7 September 1906 (New York: Oxford University Press, 1996). This and the following quotations are from pp. 321–2.

[53] *The Memoirs of Satan*, 'Collated by William Gerhardi and Brian Lunn' (London: Cassell, 1932), p. 14.

There was something to be said for starting at the bottom.'[54] He is effectively in the role of trainee in the family business. Book One covers 'My First 1,000,000,000,000,000,000,000,000,000 Years', up to the Roman Empire. In it the authors parody the Bible, before turning to parody the rest of recorded history. The idea is that Satan isn't evil, and indeed hasn't fallen. He just cannot help interfering, out of curiosity and desire. He is actually the father of the human race, since he mates with our monkey-like ancestors, then again with Eve, which is what causes her to offer Adam the apple out of pity. As Gerhardi explained, the book is 'a history of mankind presented through the imaginary experience of Satan who, at crucial moments in the lives of famous figures, real and legendary, enters them in turn to enable him to give the inside story in every case.'[55] As that phrase 'the inside story' intimates, the device of inhabiting the lives of historical figures enables the authors to switch between biographical and autobiographical modes. *The Memoirs of Satan* thus include both biografiction and autobiografiction: imaginary portraits and self-portraits.

The book ends with an ingenious parable, in which Satan shows A.H. a film he has made of the history of the world. God hasn't been paying attention to the Earth; it was only a sideline, and he lacks omniscience and is curious how his free-will experiment has worked out. But he finds the film boring and incomprehensible, not least because, when it is speeded up, the rapid oscillations of religions and empires and fashions seem to cancel each other out. He asks if the projection can be reversed, and he prefers watching history play backwards. But he is obviously displeased, and it is immediately after this screening that Satan finds he has suddenly aged, and realizes he is no longer under A.H.'s patronage. That is the moment he falls from grace, and is sacked, leaving only one option: 'I settle down to write my memoirs.'[56] The book ends with an epilogue by 'the literary executors', which describes Satan's death, and cremation in Golders Green. The book is very much of its time, and was probably influenced by D. W. Griffith's 1916 transhistorical epic film *Intolerance*. But its play with history and time anticipates postmodern fiction such as Julian Barnes's *A History of the World in 10½ Chapters* (1989) and Martin Amis's *Time's Arrow* (1991).

Mock autobiography too can be either framed or unframed. And it can be either partial or full. The Twain examples are both unframed and yet partial—chapters and extracts, rather than the whole stories; but part of their humour is in not being prepared to deliver the whole truth (or in the case of *Chapters from My Autobiography*, perhaps from threatening that he might).

---

[54] *The Memoirs of Satan*, 'Collated by William Gerhardi and Brian Lunn' (London: Cassell, 1932), p. 15.
[55] Gerhardi's synopsis for the 1940 edition, quoted by Dido Davies, *William Gerhardie: A Biography* (Oxford: Oxford University Press, 1990), pp. 258–9.
[56] *The Memoirs of Satan*, p. 9.

An equally diverting but very different bagatelle on life-writing is *What a Life!: An Autobiography*, first published in 1911. It, too, is a collaboration, and was published under just the authors' initials: 'E. V. L. and G. M.', who were E. V. Lucas and George Morrow. The idea of a collaborative autobiography is a foretaste of the absurdity of the book. It purports to be Illustrated by Whiteley's, but what this means is that the authors made a montage of illustrations from the Department Store Whiteley's General Catalogue, linking them together with a narrative made from brief caption-like comments. (Both men worked on *Punch*, Lucas also wrote biographies.) As the dust jacket to the 1987 reprint explains, catching the book's faux-naif tone: 'One day in 1911 two Edwardian gentlemen sat down with scissors and paste and created a masterpiece.'[57] They approached Harrods first, who refused, but were 'made welcome' by Whiteley's. The result looks like Surrealism *avant la lettre*, and indeed was taken up by Raymond Queneau.[58]

Was Virginia Woolf thinking of it when she began *To the Lighthouse* with James Ramsay cutting out pictures from the Army and Navy Stores catalogue,

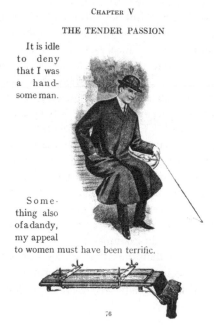

CHAPTER V

THE TENDER PASSION

It is idle to deny that I was a hand- some man.

Some- thing also of a dandy, my appeal to women must have been terrific.

76

---

[57] *What a Life!* (London: Collins, 1987).

[58] See Raymond Queneau, 'What a Life!', *Bâtons, chiffres et lettres* (Paris: Gallimard, 1950), pp. 197–207.

6 Two pages from *What a Life!* by E. V. Lucas and George Morrow (1911).

and contemplated the expressive possibilities of such montages? Or was Terry
Gilliam thinking of it, when he took similarly stilted Victorian and Edwardian
illustrations out of their contexts and put them to such surreal and slapstick ends
in his *Monty Python* animations? The humour here is complex. It comes from
trying to imagine lives for the lifeless-looking figures; from the pomposity of
their poses, and the disparity between those and some of the captions; or,
conversely (as with the image of the trouser-press) from the bathetic gap between
the inflated captions and the everydayness of the objects. (Though, as with
Surrealism, it manages to invest those objects with uncanny qualities—as with
the image of the trouser-press, which becomes charged with a wonderful erotic
innuendo.) Yet there is also a surreal pathos underlying it all. The title takes the
cliché, hovering between resignation and celebration, and turns it to suggest that
our lives are more permeated and determined by everyday objects and possessions
than we (or most autobiographers) might care to think. It mocks the form by
estrangement: because its absurdities of image and narrative and their counter-
point are so unlike conventional autobiography. But this in turn mocks that
very conventionality of autobiographical form. *What a Life!* is another indication
that auto/biography seemed ripe for mockery in the period; had come to seem

inherently absurd because of its formulaic nature that militates against the individuality it purports to express. Perhaps the Edwardian gentlemen were worried that in a society of mass consumption lives would become less distinct.

Or perhaps what troubled them was the idea of the middle classes, especially the lower-middle classes, expressing themselves through consumption. If Mr Pooter's inconsequential, non-event-ful life has its charms, a very different kind of comedy is produced by the mock-autobiography of the obnoxious prig, Augustus Carp. *Augustus Carp, Esq. By Himself: Being the Autobiography of a Really Good Man* (1924) was actually by Dr Henry Bashford, later Honorary Physician to George VI, but was published anonymously.[59] Right from the start, Augustus Carp, writing only a few years after the horrors of the First World War, reveals his full insensitivity and unapologetic self-importance. But note, also, behind that, Bashford's parody of autobiographical formulae—of what is 'customary' in the form:

It is customary, I have noticed, in publishing an autobiography to preface it with some sort of apology. But there are times, and surely the present is one of them, when to do so is manifestly unnecessary. In an age when every standard of decent conduct has either been torn down or is threatened with destruction; when every newspaper is daily reporting scenes of violence, divorce, and arson; when quite young girls smoke cigarettes and even, I am assured, sometimes cigars; when mature women, the mothers of unhappy children, enter the sea in one-piece bathing-costumes; and when married men, the heads of households, prefer the flicker of the cinematograph to the Athanasian Creed—then it is obviously a task, not to be justifiably avoided, to place some higher example before the world.[60]

vii) There is less *fiction with writing autobiography as its subject*, or *meta-autobiographical fiction*, than fiction about writing biography in the period. The works by Proust, Joyce, and Svevo already cited could be seen as instances. While this type appears an ideal postmodern form, it is relatively unexplored. However, inaugurative writers (such as Lessing, Spark, Kundera, or Coetzee) have continued to work at those frontiers of fiction and auto/biography that have proved such fertile territory in twentieth-century literature.

PORTRAIT-COLLECTIONS AND COMPOSITE PORTRAITURE

As writers began to experiment with these possibilities of auto/biografiction, one form that proved especially fruitful was that pioneered by Pater's *Imaginary Portraits*, which brings together a series of fictional life-writings about different

[59] See Thomas Jones, 'Short Cuts', *LRB* (16 November 2000), 18.
[60] *Augustus Carp, Esq. By Himself* (Harmondsworth: Penguin, 1987), p. 1.

people into a single volume. The form of the portrait-collection has its own long history, most of which is excluded here: the composite lives of Plutarch; biblical beget-ography; fairytales, folk tales, fables; Renaissance collections such as Vasari's *Lives of the Most Excellent Painters, Sculptors, and Architects*, or Aubrey's *Brief Lives*. There are collections specifically devoted to writers, such as those by George Gilfillan.[61] There are also many books entitled *Pen Portraits*— often, though not always, combining words and drawings.[62] Benson's 1906 Preface to *The Upton Letters* alludes to the Paterian legacy when (while seeking to reassure readers he hadn't meant to travesty actual Etonians) he wrote: 'All my gallery, therefore, of portraits, was purely imaginary.'[63] This is thus a potent form which combines biografiction with autobiografiction. Where it does so it differs from comic collections like Baring's, or fake collections like *The Whispering Gallery*, whose subjects were real. Such collections, though, even when not autobiographical, still enmesh life-writing with fictionality in ways relevant to our study. Works like *Lost Diaries* because they enmesh historical with fictional characters, and supply fictional sub-texts to both. Works like *The Whispering Gallery* because they claim fictional acquaintance with, and attribute fictional conversations to, real people. And collections of 'Literary Portraits' (soon to be viewed) by writers such as Ford, James, or Frank Harris, which, even when they don't fictionalize biography, give biography of writers who lived their life amongst fictions, and are thus especially inward with the relations between auto/biography and fiction. To this extent the forms of portrait-collections discussed here are different in kind from precursors such as Gilfillan's *A Gallery of Literary Portraits* (1845); or a specific form of verbal/visual composite such as *The Maclise Portrait Gallery of Illustrious Literary Characters. With Memoirs Biographical, Critical, Bibliographical, and Anecdotal Illustrative of the Literature of the Former Half of the Present Century*, which has memoirs by William Bates to accompany Daniel Maclise's lithographs.[64]

The portrait-collections focused on in this chapter are ones in which the constellation of individual portraits is understood as expressing something of the author's autobiography in addition to the multiple biographies; works in which the whole volume serves as an image of the self: a 'composite portrait'. The phrase 'composite portrait' can cover a variety of forms. In the nineteenth century there were popular series of engravings grouping together a set of

---

[61] George Gilfillan, *A Gallery of Literary Portraits* (Edinburgh, 1845); and *A Second Gallery of Literary Portraits* (Edinburgh and London, 1850); a selection was published in the Everyman's Library: *Gilfillan's Literary Portraits*, ed. and introd. W. Robertson Nicoll (London: Dent, 1909).

[62] See, for example, Helen Gray Cone and Jeannette L. Gilder, *Pen-Portraits of Literary Women*, 2 vols (New York: Cassell & Co., 1887); George Bernard Shaw, *Pen Portraits and Reviews* (London: Constable, 1932); or *Portraits and Self-Portraits*, collected and illustrated by Georges Schreiber (Boston: Houghton Mifflin Company, 1936).

[63] Benson, *The Upton Letters*, p. viii.

[64] (London: Chatto & Windus, 1883.)

portraits—of members of the royal family; famous scientists, writers, generals and so on. This tradition was continued in photography. Earlier composite daguerreotype portraits had taken the form of large plates which included numerous smaller individual portraits—of graduating university students, for example, or their teachers. As a literary designation, it can also mean several things: a grouping of several studies of individuals (such as Sebastian Faulks's *The Fatal Englishman: Three Short Lives*; 1996); a portrait of an individual, composed by assembling testimony from various witnesses: *D. H. Lawrence: A Composite Biography; Gertrude Stein: A Composite Portrait*; or *Concerning Thomas Hardy. A Composite Portrait from Memory.*[65] Or it can be used to compose a portrait of something more elusive: a nation, or a place: *A Composite Portrait of Israel*; or, bizarrely, *The Island from Within: A Composite Portrait of the Isle of Wight.*[66] Or it can refer to an attempt to represent a type, generalized from individuals: *The American Jew: A Composite Portrait.*[67]

This last example is closer to the spirit of a specific usage, for which the term was coined, that is particularly relevant to this study, which coincides with Paterian impressionism, and has been a suggestive metaphor for the possibilities of literary portraiture. This is the notion of an experimental type of 'composite portraiture' in photography, which was among the many legacies of the extraordinary personality of Francis Galton (1822–1911). Galton was first an African explorer, then a scientist. He was a pioneer in meteorology (his *Meterographica* of 1863 provided the basis of modern weather-mapping until the use of satellites); the founder of the dubious science of eugenics, and author of *Hereditary Genius* (1869) a concept in which, as Charles Darwin's cousin, he may have had a personal investment; the deviser of the system of fingerprint identification; and an investigator into colour-blindness and mental imagery.[68] Composite portraiture was an attempt to find a scientific method with which to approach cultural and moral questions. Galton used the emerging techniques of photography as a way of providing what seemed to him an inductive method for establishing the nature of cultural categories such as the 'genius' or the 'criminal'. That is, he took images of numerous particular examples, and superimposed them photographically to produce a single image of a composite 'genius', or 'criminal', or even a

---

[65] E. Nehls, ed., *D. H. Lawrence: A Composite Biography*, 3 vols (Madison: University of Wisconsin Press, 1957–9). Linda Simon, ed., *Gertrude Stein: A Composite Portrait* (New York: Avon and Discus Books, 1974). D. F. Barber, ed., *Concerning Thomas Hardy: A Composite Portrait from Memory* (London: Charles Skilton, 1968). Also see *William Whewell: A Composite Portrait*, ed. Menachem Fisch and Simon Schaffer (Oxford: Clarendon, 1991). Whewell was master of Trinity College Cambridge when Francis Galton was a student there.

[66] *A Composite Portrait of Israel*, ed. Emanuel Marx (London: Academic Press, 1980). *The Island from Within: A Composite Portrait of the Isle of Wight*, ed. Roger Sawyer (Isle of Wight: Robook, 1990).

[67] Oscar Janowsky, ed., *The American Jew: A Composite Portrait* (New York: Harper & Bros, 1942).

[68] See *Chambers Biographical Dictionary* (London: Chambers, 1990).

7 Composite Photograph by Francis Galton. Lantern slide of family composite photo-graph. Comprises photos of a father, mother, 2 sons & 2 daughters.

generalized member of a specific family.[69] The results are intriguing—not because they do what Galton wanted them to do, which now seems culturally naïve (the brooding brows and intent concentrated stare say more about nine-teenth-century stereotypes of 'genius' than about biology), but because the

[69] Francis Galton, *Memories of My Life* (London: Methuen, 1908). See ch. 18: 'Composite Portraits and Stereoscopic Maps', pp. 259–65. Also see Galton, 'Composite Portraits', *Nature*, 18 (23 May 1878), 97–100. See Philip Davis, *The Victorians*, Oxford English Literary History, vol. 8 (Oxford: Oxford University Press, 2002), pp. 7–8, for photographs of the family members contributing to this composite portrait.

images have a haunting, enigmatic quality. This is because they have a blurry indistinctness, through which something emerges that can be perceived as an individual. Whatever its shortcomings as science, and its susceptibility to eugenicist or racist exploitation, composite portraiture or photography was a suggestive idea for artistic and literary notions of representation, and particularly for thinking about the relation between particularities and generalities, between individuals and types. Thus for example, when Ford Madox Ford published his impressionist portrait of *The Soul of London* in 1905, the first volume of a trilogy about *England and the English*, one reviewer called it: 'the latest and truest image of London, built up out of a series of negations, that together are more hauntingly near to a composite picture of the city than anything we have seen before.'[70] Ford himself was to take up the idea in the third volume of the trilogy, *The Spirit of the People*, saying:

> The reader is probably familiar with what is called a composite photograph. A great number of photographs of individuals is taken, and one image being set upon another, a sort of common denominator results, one face blending into another, lending salient points, toning down exaggerations.[71]

Here he is using it as a figure for the way he has tried to represent something as abstract as 'Englishness'. But he was to return to the idea later as a way of thinking about specifically literary portraiture. In a discussion of Turgenev he says that Tsar Alexander II 'ordered the emancipation of the serfs three days after he had finished reading the *Sportsman's Sketches*':

> It is of course as impossible to know anything real about a sovereign as to know anything real about a novelist, both being so surrounded. But the figure—the sort of composite photograph—that passes for that Tsar would seem to have been intelligent, mild, well-meaning, and better acquainted—if mostly in a disciplinary manner—than are most sovereigns with the intelligentsia of his realm.[72]

This is well aware that a sovereign is so surrounded by flatterers that even a composite of their accounts is unlikely to be 'anything real'. For all his intelligence and mild, well-meaning-ness, the Tsar got to know members of the intelligentsia like Turgenev 'by their getting themselves imprisoned at the dictates

---

[70] Edmund Candler, *Daily Mail* (2 May 1905), 2.

[71] Ford Madox Hueffer, *The Spirit of the People* (London: Alston Rivers, 1907), pp. xii–xiii. See also Ford's *Between St. Dennis and St. George* (London: Hodder and Stoughton, 1915), p. 80: 'In arriving at such impressions as these the writer or the observer makes use of a method that, in photography, used to be popular in the nineties of the last century. This was called making a composite photograph. Supposing that the photographer desired to get at a rendering of A Poet rather than of any one poet, he took upon the same plate photographs of profile portraits of Dante, Shakespeare, Milton, Burns, Goethe, Wordsworth, and Tennyson. The result was a queer, blurred image, but the result was none the less striking, and the individual arrived at by this composite process had an odd but quite strong individuality.'

[72] Ford Madox Ford, *Portraits from Life* (Boston: Houghton Mifflin, 1937), pp. 154–5.

of the censor'. But what of the novelist? Why is he introduced here? True, a novelist as successful as Turgenev might be 'so surrounded' by admirers as to make it hard for a biographer to see behind the screen of fawning and ingratiation. They are also surrounded by a cloud of publicity, much of which took the form of the 'Literary Portrait'—a form in which Ford himself had specialized for three decades, and of which the essays on eleven writers that make up this volume, *Portraits from Life*, are amongst his best examples.[73] But there is a more important reason why Ford is drawn to the figure of the composite portrait as expressing something about the novelist, and it is one more germane to our purposes. It is that it expresses the relationship of the author to his work: for an author is also surrounded by the impressions of him that his work may produce. For Ford, that is to say, the nature of the writer's mind and activity render the notion of auto/biography problematic:

> Turgenev carried the rendering of the human soul one stage further than any writer who preceded or has followed him simply because he had supremely the gift of identifying himself with—of absolutely feeling—the passions of the characters with whom he found himself. . . . And then he had the gift of retiring and looking at his passion—the passion that he had made his . . . the gift of looking at it with calmed eyes [. . .] No, he was not insincere. It was perhaps his extreme misfortune . . . but it was certainly his supreme and beautiful gift—that he had the seeing eye to such an extent that he could see that two opposing truths were equally true.
>
>   It was a misfortune for his biographers and for those who believe that biographies can ever illuminate anything. For the biographer and the consumer of biographies, looking only for what they seek, find what they want and play all the gamut of their sympathies or hatreds. But Turgenev was by turns and all at once, Slavophil and Westerner, Tsarist and Nihilist, Germanophile and Francophobe, Francophile and Hun-hater, insupportably homesick for Spasskoye and the Nevsky Prospekt and wracked with nostalgia for the Seine bank at Bougival and the rue de Rivoli. All proper men are that to some degree—certainly all proper novelists.[74]

The novelist, according to this view, eludes conventional biography because in his writing he eludes the conventional biographical subject. He has to be more than a single self, and be able to interfuse himself with other, imaginary selves, and then withdraw from them and render them. And these other selves, though

---

[73] Ford had written series of 'Literary Portraits' for the *Daily Mail* and the *Tribune* in 1907, and then longer, better ones for the *Outlook* from 1913–14. See Ford, *Critical Essays*, ed. Max Saunders and Richard Stang (Manchester: Carcanet, 2002) for a selection. *Portraits from Life* was published in Britain as *Mightier Than the Sword* (London: Allen and Unwin, 1938). For an excellent discussion of this book, relating it to *fin de siècle* aestheticism and fictional portraits of imaginary authors and artists, such as James's 'The Death of the Lion' and 'The Coxon Fund' (both 1894) and 'The Next Time' (1895), Pater's *Imaginary Portraits*, and Wilde's *The Portrait of Mr. W. H.* (1889), see Maurizio Ascari, 'Mapping the Private Life and the Literary Canon: Ford Madox Ford's *Mightier Than the Sword*', in *Ford Madox Ford and 'The Republic of Letters'*, ed. Vita Fortunati and Elena Lamberti (Bologna, CLUEB, 2002), pp. 73–9.

[74] Ford, *Portraits from Life*, pp. 157–8.

they may express something about the author's self (as suggested in Chapter 4), may equally obscure or displace that self. We no longer believe that subjectivity is unitary, and perhaps no longer believe that we ever believed it was. But in Ford's formulation the novelist's subjectivity displays more than a Freudian multiplicity; instead of a dis-integrated co-existence of ego, id, and superego, Ford posits a set of contradictory performances, all conscious, but all fictionalized, such as to frustrate biography. Ford's argument here goes a stage further than the claim that a single fictionalized work can be read as the author's autobiography, to claim that to get 'anything real' by way of auto/biography you have to superimpose all the author's works—to make out of them precisely a composite portrait:

> The novel was, in fact, his religion, his country, his unchanging home and his only real means of communication with his fellow beings. So that really to know Conrad you had to read all his books and then to fuse the innumerable Conrads that are in all of them into what used to be called a composite photograph.[75]

Modern literary biography has become more sophisticated since Ford's day, and a critical biography of a writer will attempt to do something like what he suggests, though the results are more likely to trace a story of development than to produce a static image of that writer's personality. That notion of personality is unfashionably belletristic for an age more preoccupied with our own fashions of materialism and media culture, but was important at the *fin de siècle* (where, as suggested, our own fashions begin to emerge). Ford writes frequently of what he calls 'literary personality'—the auto/biography as expressed a writer's imaginative works, rather than in the records of a life.[76] He often figures 'literary personality' as a disembodied smile. As he says of Turgenev: 'I was conscious simply of a singular, compassionate smile that still seems to me to look up out of the pages of his books when—as I constantly do, and always with a sense of amazement—I re-read them.'[77] And the account of Turgenev's multiply empathetic gift is Ford's attempt to define his literary personality. Yet the effect is deeply paradoxical. The impression of Turgenev as a gentle, sympathetic observer comes across poignantly; yet his gentleness is an effect of his self-effacement through the very act of observing and identifying. So the result is a sense of a personality which is at the same time an enigma: 'One knows nothing about him. One knows less about him even than about Shakespeare. He moves surrounded by the cloud of his characters as a monarch by his courtiers.'[78] What

---

[75] Ford, 'Men and Books', *Time and Tide*, 17:21 (1936), 761–2.

[76] For a representative example of the contemporary use of 'literary personality' as a critical term, see M. P. Willcocks, *Between the Old World and the New: Being Studies in Literary Personality from Goethe and Balzac to Anatole France and Thomas Hardy* (London: George Allen & Unwin Ltd, 1925). On Ford's use of the term, see Saunders, *Ford Madox Ford: A Dual Life*, vol. 2 (Oxford: Oxford University Press, 1996), passim, but especially pp. 449–60.

[77] Ford, *Portraits from Life*, p. 144.

[78] Ibid., p. 205.

is significant about the idea of the literary portrait here is that the notion of personality appears to be on a cusp. On the one hand, Ford is asserting the importance of personality, as do writers like Pater or Benson. On the other, he's turning it inside out—showing how it is constructed, assimilated from elsewhere, performative—as in, er, Pater and Benson.

This notion of using a 'composite portrait' of an author's works to get at their 'personality' takes a different turn when, instead of fusing novels and tales, it turns to supposedly non-fictional works about other people. A further reason for discussing this example in detail before returning to earlier auto/biografiction is that *Portraits from Life*, although also a work of criticism, is itself an example of auto/biografiction, in ways which have far-reaching implications for other writers' work too. It is an autobiographical book on three levels. First, all of the writers he treats are ones he had known (in Turgenev's case, only just, by offering him a chair when probably then not quite eight). His portraits are thus, like those of a book by Henry James (who is the subject of one of Ford's chapters) *Partial Portraits*: not just highly selective sketches, but portraits of writers to whom Ford is partial. Ford himself thus figures in many of the portraits, being spoken to by James, arguing with H. G. Wells, collaborating with Joseph Conrad, and so on. It is a classic case of biography conducted explicitly as auto/biography. Some readers, preferring criticism and biography to preserve the decorum of objectivity, have objected that there is too much of the author in the book. Another objection Ford's auto/biography met with frequently was that it exaggerated or distorted the facts: that it was, in another word, auto/biografiction. Some critics, knowing that he had later become estranged from James and Conrad, doubted (unjustly) that the friendships had ever been as close as Ford claimed. Which is not to say that he didn't invent conversations, as all proper novelists do, or make provocative suggestions (such as that it was a novel that predisposed the Tsar to liberate the serfs)—though he was always perfectly frank about such romancing.

It is a trope of literary portraiture to claim this biografictional hybridity. Frank Harris, perhaps the most celebrated example of the improper auto/biographer of the period, was a serial offender, publishing four collections of *Contemporary Portraits* between 1915 and 1923. He then followed them with *Latest Contemporary Portraits* (1927), and *Confessional: A Volume of Intimate Portraits, Sketches and Studies* (1930). Further portraits are interspersed through his notorious (and notoriously imaginary) self-portrait *My Life and Loves* (1922–9; fourth, posthumous, volume, 1963). In the 'Introduction' to the first 'series' he says 'man is something more than a reporter; and that something more is the source and secret of his ineffable superiority: he is artist as well'; and he goes on to note that 'the artist-reporter is a prey to conflicting duties.'[79] '[D]uties' is a nicely Wildean touch, taking what would outrage the conventional as irresponsibility and

---

[79] Frank Harris, *Contemporary Portraits* (New York: Mitchell Kennerley, 1915), Introduction, pp. v–vii (p. vi).

recasting it as the responsibility of art. It is an impressionist's manifesto, which insists at once on his right to fictionalize the truth, and on the higher truth of his fictionalizing. Secondly, then, if a writer's fictions are his truer autobiography, then autobiografictions such as these are where a book like *Portraits from Life* is more truly autobiographical. What comes across from them is his belief in the novel as offering the fullest and least partisan account of human life; in the seriousness of the novelist's calling; and in the effects literature at its best can have on a reader. The third sense in which such a book can be thought of as autobiographical is one which returns us to the idea of composite portraiture. For, just as his method in the individual chapters is to suggest a composite portrait of each writer through a collage of details from his life and work, so the whole book assembles a composite self-portrait too, by superimposing portraits of the authors who had mattered most to him. The idea that a writer's collection of biographical portraits of others will have an autobiographical dimension too is a familiar nineteenth-century trope. Take Robert Louis Stevenson, for example, in his prefatory 'Note' to *Memories and Portraits*:

This volume of papers, unconnected as they are, it will be better to read through from the beginning, rather than dip into at random. A certain thread of meaning binds them. Memories of childhood and youth, portraits of those who have gone before us in the battle,—taken together, they build up a face that 'I have loved long since and lost awhile,' the face of what was once myself. This has come by accident; I had no design at first to be autobiographical; I was but led away by the charm of beloved memories and by regret for the irrevocable dead; and when my own young face (which is a face of the dead also) began to appear in the well as by a kind of magic, I was the first to be surprised at the occurrence.[80]

At first this sounds like a pre-emptive excuse for making a book out of what might be attacked as a random collection of ephemeral articles: an argument that the whole *is* greater than the sum of the parts, and that what connects the parts is autobiography. But Stevenson is also aware of the dangers that accompany such an argument: an implicit self-indulgence ('whatever I write is valuable because it expresses me') and post-Romantic solipsism ('whatever I write about the other is valuable for what it says about myself'). So he navigates between the Scylla of incoherence and the Charybdis of egotism. It is autobiography, but unconsciously so. As might be expected from the author of *Jekyll and Hyde*, portraits of several persons turn out to be, or turn into, a single person. The portrait-collection becomes doubled by a collection of self-portraits: a composite self-portrait. The description of being surprised by the apparition of his own face posits the autobiographical as an effect of reading. He wants his reader to read through sequentially so as to be able to share this uncanny experience of transfiguration. (There is perhaps a sense here that author and reader come together in the act of reading; that perhaps the experience of reading will be autobiographical for the

---

[80] Stevenson, *Memories and Portraits* (London: Chatto & Windus, 1887), p. vii.

reader too; though it's hard to see how readers, who do not share Stevenson's memories, can have a comparable experience, unless the text summons up their own memories through Stevenson's.) Exactly contemporary with the Nietzsche–Wilde argument about all utterance being a species of involuntary autobiography, Stevenson gives an elegant account of catching himself doing exactly that. He becomes conscious of his unconscious autobiography. Doubtless his imagination has reworked some of his memories, and fictionalization may have crept in through the mediation of narrative. But there is no suggestion that these literary pieces are offered as anything other than true memories of real people. What is different in Ford's twentieth-century practice would be closer to a postmodern scepticism about such truth-claims if it were not also in Pater; a feeling not only that the boundaries between autobiography and fiction are impossible to establish, but also that it is precisely in the moments that he crosses or confuses them that the biographical becomes most autobiographical. Because it is in such moments that the remembering self becomes most fully the writing self, and its collections of remembered portraits become most truly the self-portrait of someone whose chief characteristic is his ability to fictionalize. Charles Caramello's words on Henry James and Gertrude Stein could equally describe most of the forms of portraiture discussed in this book; that they 'used biographical portraits of other artists to construct autobiographical portraits of themselves as exemplary modern artists; and, as part of the process, they used those portraits to create artistic genealogies for themselves.'[81]

To read biography as autobiography might seem a postmodern thing to do, and at first sight it might seem surprising to find it advocated at the turn of the century. But it follows from the earlier discussion of autobiografiction, in the sense that if an element of fictionalization is recognized in biographical writing, that fictionalization must be attributable to the author rather than the subject, and thus be expressive of him or her. The pervasiveness of such reading strategies later in the twentieth century—post-postmodernism—is suggested by the stand taken against them by Kingsley Amis, who published a volume called *Memoirs* in 1991. Though the 'memoirs' are his, they are not *of* himself. Each of the brief chapters is on a specific acquaintance. Amis calls 'The kind of thing I have written here (allo- rather than autobiography).'[82] He is the centre of his circle of friends. But in an era when biography is increasingly read as autobiography, you need a term like 'allobiography' to assert that you really are trying to write about the otherness of other people.

A more systematic approach to the composite portraiture of writers was constructed by Stefan Zweig during the 1920s. He produced three trilogies of psychological literary biography, which together comprised what he titled collectively as

---

[81] Charles Caramello, *Henry James, Gertrude Stein, and the Biographical Act* (Chapel Hill and London: University of North Carolina Press, 1996), p. ix.
[82] Kingsley Amis, *Memoirs* (London: Hutchinson, 1991), p. xvi.

Master Builders, and described as 'An Attempt at the Typology of the Spirit'. *Three Masters* combined Dickens, Balzac, and Dostoevsky as examples of 'epic world-shapers who in the cosmos of their novels create a second reality side by side with the world known to us all'; *The Struggle with the Demon* took Hölderlin, Kleist, and Nietzsche as examples of 'the tragic personality driven onward by elemental urges'. The third volume, however, is the most germane here: *Adepts in Self-Portraiture*, focusing on Casanova, Stendhal, and Tolstoy as supreme autobiographers, for each of whom, whether he is conscious of it or not, 'no reality is so important to him as the reality of his own life.'[83] The series thus represents the genus of creative authorial genius, and each of the volumes a particular species of creative writer. Within each volume an evolutionary development is evident. In *Adepts in Self-Portraiture*, the three authors represent 'ascending gradations of the same creative function, self-portraiture'. Casanova is 'the lowest, the primitive gradation', only recording 'deeds and happenings', with no attempt to study 'the deeper working of the self.'[84] With Stendhal, 'The ego has grown inquisitive as to itself.' 'A new perspective emerges, arising out of the binocular vision of the ego as subject and object, out of the twofold biography of the internal and the external.'[85] 'With Tolstoy, this spiritual self-contemplation attains its highest level, inasmuch as it has now become an ethico-religious self-portraiture.'[86] So far, so Hegelian as much as Darwinian. Zweig was a prolific biographer, as well as (in his last book, *The World of Yesterday*, 1942) an autobiographer. His premise in *Adepts in Self-Portraiture* is that autobiography is fraught with possibilities for deception and self-deception, which is why so few great autobiographies have been written. He warns us that:

The art of self-deception is refined and sublimated by the wider experience, by the growth in psychological knowledge, designed to avert self-deception [. . .] Not until a man has a subtle mind are his falsehoods subtilized, refined, so that they can be detected only by one as subtle as himself.[87]

He goes on to warn us against the appearance of honesty or sincerity in autobiography. We should suspect it, as concealing 'some secret which is even more dreadful.'[88] Ostensibly the volume is cast as biography; not an autobiography that should be read according to its own strictures. And yet the argument that the strategies of a subtle mind can only be detected by one equally subtle implicitly asserts Zweig's own

---

[83] Stefan Zweig, *Drei Meister* (1920); trans. as *Three Masters* (New York: Viking Press, 1930). *Der Kampf mit dem Dämon* (1925), was to have been trans. as *The Struggle with the Demon*, and also published by Viking, but this translation didn't materialize, presumably due to the Depression. *Drei Dichter ihres Lebens* (1928), trans. as *Adepts in Self-Portraiture* (New York: Viking, 1928). Zweig followed this *Master Builders* series with a more psychological but less literary trilogy, *Die Heilung durch den Geist* (1931), trans. as *Mental Healers* (New York: Viking, 1932), on Anton Mesmer, Mary Baker Eddy, and Freud. The quotations are from the series title page facing the title page; and from p. ix. of *Adepts in Self-Portraiture*.

[84] Zweig, *Adepts in Self-Portraiture*, p. x.   [85] Ibid., p. xi.
[86] Ibid.   [87] Ibid., p. xvii.
[88] Ibid., p. x., p. xvii.

mental adequacy. When a creative writer—he was best known as a highly respected novelist at the time—presents himself as objective critic and biographer and psychologist, isn't a version of self-transformation or self-concealment in operation? Doesn't the authority with which he pronounces on the types of creativity, and creates its typology, implicitly constitute his claim to be included amongst the eminent writers he describes? Isn't he indulging in a bit of covert masterbuilding himself? Isn't his composite portrait of self-portraitists something of a self-portrait?

The fact that Ford's reference to composite photography comes up in relation to Turgenev's *Sportsman's Sketches* is significant, since that volume too is structured as a series of brief portraits: in some ways it is Ford's model, and it seems probable that he hoped his own literary personality would smile from his pages. The reference reminds us that this literary form of a portrait group has a literary history, running from Theophrastian 'Characters' through the *Canterbury Tales*, biography collections from Aubrey's *Brief Lives* to Johnson's *Lives of the English Poets*, Browning's collections of dramatic monologues, Landor's *Imaginary Conversations*, or George Eliot's last book, *The Impressions of Theophrastus Such* (1879). These works are scarcely commensurable in any other way, and draw on other traditions such as Plutarch's *Lives*, or collections of hagiography. But what they all have in common— whether dealing historically or freely with historical figures, or inventing individuals, or characterizing types—is a tension between the variety of individuals portrayed, and the presence throughout of a marked individual style of portrayal.

The Impressions of Theophrastus Such is probably the least known of Eliot's books, and one of the most curious. While it seems dry and rebarbative to some readers, its positioning between traditional moral satire and imaginary portrait-collection gives it a key place in my account of the reinvention of the latter towards the end of the nineteenth century. The narrator is dramatized to a more marked degree than is usual in Eliot's novels (though she did occasionally use a dramatized first-person narrator, as in the story 'The Lifted Veil'): the son of a country parson, a bachelor, the author of one unsuccessful book, suffering from an unrequited love for someone who doesn't even know he loves her; slightly ridiculous to others, and prone to an anxiety about health and sanity that perhaps suggests a hypochondriacal tendency: something of a pre-modernist J. Alfred Prufrock or John Dowell: a limited or obtuse narrator.[89] Theophrastus is clearly not Eliot's self-portrait, but another imaginary portrait to set alongside the figures he portrays. Most of these are only discussed fleetingly for a matter of a few paragraphs or pages. They too are poised between genres. Their names— Merman, Lentulus, Touchwood, Mordax, Mixtus, Ganymede, Vorticella, and so on—are mostly unrealistic, and point back to the classical moral satirical tradition. Yet they are nineteenth-century British provincial figures who might almost have stepped out of the corners of a George Eliot novel, if they had been

---

[89] Eliot, *The Impressions of Theophrastus Such* (London: J. M. Dent, 1995), pp. 7, 3, 6, 7.

developed into something more than personifications of single psychological quirks: the superficial pontificator in journals; the man deluded into believing himself an original thinker; the woman obsessed by her one trivial book. If one describes them as imaginary portraits not fully imagined, it is with a knowledge of what Eliot's imagination might have done with them had she not entrusted them to Theophrastus Such, but developed them herself into the centres of longer works. Some are as fully realized as anything in Pater, and the analyses are characteristically probing. Take for example Pepin, 'The Too Ready Writer':

Pepin made for himself a necessity of writing (and getting published) before he had considered whether he had the knowledge or belief that would furnish eligible matter. At first perhaps the necessity galled him a little, but it is now as easily borne, nay is as irrepressible a habit as the outpouring of inconsiderate talk.[90]

His is one of several portraits of writers in the volume, and as elsewhere Eliot satirizes habits in writing by pointing out how less tolerant of them we would be if they were inflicted on us in conversation. Pepin's predicament is presented in terms strikingly close to Pater's of solipsism and the insubstantiality of the 'object'. But whereas Pater writes elegiacally of such a predicament as the inevitable consequence of aesthetic refinement, Eliot sees it as the result of vanity, plus a habit of converting all his perceptions to 'copy' before he has savoured them:

He is gradually being condemned to have no genuine impressions, no direct consciousness of enjoyment or the reverse from the quality of what is before him: his perceptions are continually arranging themselves in forms suitable to a printed judgement, and hence they will often turn out to be as much to the purpose if they are written without any direct contemplation of the object, and are guided by a few external conditions which serve to classify it for him. In this way he is irrevocably losing the faculty of accurate mental vision [. . .][91]

None of these criticisms is likely to be levelled at George Eliot. Yet in one sense such chapters exploring the psychological dangers that attend the literary life do shade off into autobiography, if only in the sense of bodying forth anxieties about the kind of writer she wanted to avoid becoming. And this is where the book's satire turns into something different: where Eliot's advocacy of sympathetic imagination will not allow her to satirize merely to ridicule, but turns satire into moral enlightenment:

Thus if I laugh at you, O fellow-men! If I trace with curious interest your labyrinthine self-delusions, note the inconsistencies in your zealous adhesions, and smile at your helpless endeavours in a rashly chosen part, it is not that I feel myself aloof from you; the more intimately I seem to discern your weaknesses, the stronger to me is the proof that I share them. How otherwise could I get the discernment?—for even what we are averse to, what we vow not to entertain, must have shaped or shadowed itself within us as a possibility before we can think of exorcising it. No man can know his brother simply as

---

[90] Eliot, *The Impressions of Theophrastus Such*, p. 109.   [91] Ibid.

a spectator. Dear blunderers, I am one of you [. . .] And thus while I carry in myself the key to other men's experience, it is only by observing others that I can so far correct my self-ignorance as to arrive at the certainty that I am liable to commit myself unawares and to manifest some incompetency which I know no more of than the blind man knows of his image in the glass.[92]

Remember Proust's image of a book as 'a kind of optical instrument' enabling the reader to discern what 'he would perhaps never have perceived in himself'. The vocabulary of fellowship and brotherhood insist that the rights of man don't include the right to hold others in contempt. Some important consequences for the study of auto/biography follow from these ideas. Especially, that we need to know others in order to know ourselves:

Hence with all possible study of myself, with all possible effort to escape from the pitiable illusion which makes men laugh, shriek, or curl the lip at Folly's likeness, in total unconsciousness that it resembles themselves, I am obliged to recognize that while there are secrets in me unguessed by others, these others have certain items of knowledge about the extent of my powers and the figure I make with them, which in turn are secrets unguessed by me.[93]

Theophrastus' first chapter, 'Looking Inward', begins by juxtaposing biography and autobiography: 'It is my habit to give an account to myself of the characters I meet with: can I give any true account of my own?'[94] But if he carries within himself the key to others' experience, conversely they carry within themselves the key to his. That is, he cannot but give an account of his own character as he gives the characters of others. Eliot is thus well aware of the paradox, later expressed by Wilde and Nietzsche, that even the least personal utterance constitutes autobiography. Arguably, she pursues it even further, suggesting that even in the least impersonal or reticent autobiographies, such as Rousseau's, 'half our impressions of his character come not from what he means to convey, but from what he unconsciously enables us to discern'; in other words, that it isn't only non-autobiographical works, but even autobiography itself, that becomes what Nietzsche called 'unconscious autobiography.'[95]

Yet Eliot is less celebratory of this subjectivist argument, seeing it as a potential trap: 'May there not be at least a partial release from the imprisoning verdict that a man's philosophy is the formula of his personality?'[96] We saw in the first chapter how Pater, too, saw subjectivism as a prison, though it is a prison in which he was resigned to serve an imaginary life sentence. For Eliot, characteristically, it is also a matter of morals and politics. This is because she isn't content to remain inside the

---

[92] Ibid., p. 4.
[93] Ibid.
[94] Ibid., p. 3.
[95] See Nancy Henry's discussion of *Theophrastus Such* in John Rignall, ed. *Oxford Reader's Companion to George Eliot* (Oxford: Oxford University Press, 2001), p. 174.
[96] *The Impressions of Theophrastus Such*, p. 8.

world of her own imagination, but worries about the imaginative worlds of other subjectivities, and their views of her subjectivity. Reading others' arguments as their autobiographies can become morally or politically problematic when it is used to ignore their arguments: to dismiss them as *merely* expressions of prejudice or emotion. That is, while it may make a solipsist feel insured against anyone refuting his views, it can equally license anyone to ignore them. Redescribing others can all too easily be a prelude to contempt and oppression. The portrait-collection is important for Eliot because it enacts a reciprocity, a social mutuality, that offers the release from the prison house of solipsism. Portraying others may be legible as autobiography. But, conversely, autobiography is legible as biography. The habit of self/portraiture represents a mode of intersubjectivity, avoiding the traps of a delusory objectivity and a delusory subjectivity. If this is a requirement of moral health for Eliot, it is also a requirement of mental health, certainly for Theophrastus, who remarks on the complementary spectres of the 'self-flattering lunatic', or the 'lunacy of fancying oneself everybody else and being unable to play one's own part decently.'[97]

Eliot's narrator here echoes those other nineteenth-century autobiographical narrations by characters suffering from, or anxious about madness. But it also looks forward to modernist and postmodernist experiments with possibly mad narrators—in Svevo, Beckett, or Nabokov, say. It is a startlingly modern text, despite its Victorian scruples and cadences, in other ways that also bear upon auto/biography. What is at stake here is a notion of self-transformation, from autobiography to fiction, from self to art, from anxiety to pleasure. As in Eliot's novels, the central question in *Theophrastus Such* is of what we make of our lives. Eliot's real subject is the set of self-delusions that turn us into people we don't want to be, yet have nonetheless chosen, if unconsciously, to be. This is what Theophrastus investigates in himself, by seeking it out in others.

Through him, Eliot is also asking about the psychology and morality of those who choose to live (as Theophrastus does, and as did Eliot herself) by writing: by making themselves people who make something out of other people's lives, or make other people's lives up. At this—arguably existential—level, the book is indeed profoundly autobiographical. As in many of the works of imaginary portraiture under discussion here, Eliot's text is double-articulated, using a writer-character to investigate other characters, several of whom are themselves writers. Why does the dramatized narrator matter to Eliot here? Why not write the satires in her own person? A traditional moral answer is that the dramatized narrator avoids the charge of priggishness: she is not claiming to judge in her own person, but to present a judge who is himself problematic, and thus subject to her and her readers' judgement. That is, the narrator ironizes the process of moral judgement. But there is also a different kind of answer, and one more germane to

---

[97] *The Impressions of Theophrastus Such*, pp. 10, 11.

this study. By presenting the 'Impressions' of other characters as written not by herself but by the fictional author Theophrastus Such, Eliot produces a text double-articulated in another sense. It is not just a narrator-character's account of other characters (after all, many novels with first-person narrators provide as much). It is also—and the difference is crucial to my argument throughout this book—an example of the production of imaginary works of literature. When a narrator such as Esther Summerson in *Bleak House* tells her story, her status is different from that of Dickens. Even if she is writing her narrative down, she is not a professional author, writing for publication. (This is particularly evident in *Bleak House*, in which Esther is only given half of the narration, which must be supplemented by an omniscient third-person narration to make up a publishable novel. But it is also the case with novels told entirely by a first-person narrator described as writing rather than telling the story: Jane Eyre, Lucy Snowe in *Villette*, Pip in *Great Expectations*, and so on.) When realism employs dramatized narrators, it is a technique aimed at enhancing the reality of the world created inside the story; not at exploring the processes of writing the story. With the other writer-characters in *Theophrastus Such*, we are told about their works, but are not given them. In 'Diseases of Small Authorship', for example, we are told of Vorticella's one book, *The Channel Islands, with Notes and an Appendix*. From the reviews, mostly from local papers, and mostly good, because her husband is 'an important townsman' in 'Pumpiter', which she makes all her visitors read and discuss, we get a vivid sense of its unnecessariness. Which makes it unnecessary for Eliot to write it for us. But she does write Theophrastus's 'Impressions' for him; and they are, as we have seen, minutely and probingly concerned with the psychology of authorship. It is one thing to analyse this from the outside (as Theophrastus does, writing about figures such as Vorticella); it is another to write about them from the inside, *as* Theophrastus writing about others. That is, the challenge Eliot has set herself is not just to write about types, some of whom are authors; but to create an author-figure as he creates these other types: to imagine another performing acts of imagination; to write not the works that she wanted to write, but that her fictional character wanted to write.[98] Her text is thus more than just a collection of imaginary portraits; it is also a portrait of the imagination in the process of producing imaginary portraits; and, as suggested, to that extent it is also a self-portrait, painted in the distorting mirror of another's subjectivity: hence an act of double-articulated imaginary (self)portraiture. Such an exploration of the creative imagination in the process of creativity can itself be seen as a further aspect of the existential reach of Eliot's text, which may sound *sui generis* from my account of it. Yet, as we shall see, it is striking how frequently works of imaginary portraiture in the period do include versions of imaginary creativity. It represents a logical extension of the *Künstlerroman*: the desire to present not just

---

[98] See Nancy Henry's discussion of *Theophrastus Such* in John Rignall, ed., *Oxford Reader's Companion to George Eliot*, p. 174.

the artists' life, development, consciousness, but also their experience of creating, and the resulting works.

As with Landor and Browning, the form of composite portraiture fosters an interest in the border between history and imagination, and in crossing the border in both directions: in taking real historical figures (Pericles, Oliver Cromwell, Andrea del Sarto) and giving them imagined words; or in inventing figures who may draw upon historical originals, and are then inserted or re-inserted into a gallery of figures many of whom are historical, so that they too stand as if they had once been alive (Browning's Duke in 'My Last Duchess', say; or 'Porphyria's Lover'). When these portraits are cast in the form of dialogue or verse monologue, the form clearly signals the artifice. By the end of the century, the ground has shifted. The collection of imaginary portraits continues to attract authors. But they tend to be written in prose, impersonating the form of biography and memoir. This use of pseudo-auto/biography became the new border at which history and imagination meet. As the form of imaginary portrait-collections has scarcely been discussed, it may seem surprising how many significant works of the period are animated by its expressive possibilities.[99]

One distinct category of the imaginary portrait-collection is the topographical one, consisting of characters associated with a particular locale. Crabbe's *The Village*, or the *Lyrical Ballads* of Wordsworth and Coleridge, offer influential antecedents and show that the form can be equally effective in verse. The part of Robert Lowell's volume *Life Studies* bearing the subtitle 'Life Studies' collects together poems about his New England family; though the volume as a whole combines these with portraits of others, such as literary figures he had known, or unnamed possibly auto/biographical characters. Turgenev's *Sportsman's Sketches* come into this topographical category, as do twentieth-century works such as Gertrude Stein's *Three Lives* (1909) or Sherwood Anderson's *Winesburg, Ohio*, or Dylan Thomas's *Under Milk Wood*.

Such works might equally be described as story-collections, each story focusing on a different character in a community. As with Pater, the line between portrait and story is hard to draw; but (as in the visual arts) a literary portrait is concerned with personality rather than plot. So modernist stories freeing themselves from plot are likely to resemble portraits. A lot of critical work on Joyce's *Dubliners* has sought schemata that might unify the collection of disparate character studies, without seeing how such a collection has its own formal lineage. Of course, like all Joyce's fiction, *Dubliners* comprises a composite portrait of Dublin, as well as a composite portrait of the artist. But to say that is to suggest that the notion of composite portraiture is central to Joyce's aesthetic. It isn't only that 'HCE' in

---

[99] Again Ann Jefferson is an honourable exception. In her *Biography and the Question of Literature in France*, pp. 101–4, she argues for the importance of the literary portrait as a form, especially in making the transition from journalism to books, as individual journalistic sketches were collected into books.

Finnegans Wake can be read as a kind of Everyman ('Here Comes Everybody'), into whom, as with Eliot's Tiresias, other male figures in the work dissolve. *Ulysses* too can be read as drawing on the structure of the portrait-collection. That is, as well as concentrating on which Homeric book or bodily organ each chapter represents, each can be seen to be focused on a particular individual or group: Stephen, Bloom, Molly, Gerty MacDowell, 'The Citizen', and so on.

Some fictional or auto/biografictional character-galleries are connected within a single story. Christopher Isherwood's *Goodbye to Berlin* (1939) could be seen as participating in this category. The famous second paragraph of 'A Berlin Diary: (Autumn 1930)', which opens the book, may sound modern, adopting the journalistic ethos of photo-reportage: 'I am a camera with its shutter open, quite passive, recording, not thinking.'[100] Yet the 'six pieces' which Isherwood's preface claims form a 'roughly continuous narrative' can equally be seen as forming a composite photograph of Berlin, and of Isherwood. Or rather, 'Isherwood', since, like most of Christopher Isherwood's work, *Goodbye to Berlin* has complex relations to the autobiographic. He takes the *fin de siècle* play with pseudonymity and fictionalization a stage further, presenting not only his previous narrated selves but also their author as already fictionalized. He argues:

Because I have given my own name to the 'I' of this narrative, readers are certainly not entitled to assume that its pages are purely autobiographical, or that its characters are libellously exact portraits of living persons. 'Christopher Isherwood' is a convenient ventriloquist's dummy, nothing more.[101]

As we have seen with Pater's *Imaginary Portraits*, the unifying principle of the composite portrait form needn't be topographical: it can be characterological, in the spirit advocated by Galton, producing multifaceted impressions of a single type: the aesthete, the painter, the writer, and so on. This was the version practised by Edmund Gosse, who, as Hermione Lee observes, enjoyed writing 'the anecdotal portrait: profiles of famous writers in collections like *Critical Kit-Kats, Portraits and Sketches, Aspects and Impressions*, or *Silhouettes*.'[102] Or it can be characterological in the more traditional sense of assembling a set of contrasting characters, as in *The Impressions of Theophrastus Such*. It can even do both, as does *The Whispering Gallery*. A later book of Pearson's, *Extraordinary People* (1965), steers a course between the two. As he explains in the prefatory chapter, he had always 'taken delight in studying the characters of extraordinary people', which had led him to write several biographies. What most attracted him were 'strongly marked individualities' whose wit and personality went against the grain of the establishment.[103]

[100] Isherwood, *Goodbye to Berlin* (London: Chatto & Windus, 1952), p. 13.
[101] Ibid., p. 7.
[102] Hermione Lee, *Body Parts* (London: Chatto & Windus, 2005), pp. 104–5.
[103] Hesketh Pearson, *Extraordinary People* (London: Heinemann, 1965), p. 1. The chapter on Frank Harris, 'Rebel Artist', pp. 175–236 (from which the second epigraph to this chapter is taken), is entertainingly pertinent to our discussion of auto/biografiction.

The book is a portrait-collection of men (and only one woman) of science, the arts, and political thought—Henry Fielding, the Rev. Samuel Ogden, Erasmus Darwin, Anna Seward, Thomas Day, Thomas Paine, Wilkie Collins, Sir Johnston Forbes-Robertson, Frank Harris, and Bernard Shaw—who for the most part have little in common except their eccentricity. To that extent it could be seen as a Galtonian composite portrait of extraordinariness—a suggestion that is endorsed by the inclusion of a chapter on Pearson's uncle, Francis Galton himself.

In Max Beerbohm's *Seven Men* (1919) the portraits are all imaginary, and mostly of the literary world, or the sort of upper- and upper-middle-class contacts a literary man like Beerbohm might make. Beerbohm's characters inhabit the pre-war world. Richard Aldington's more satirical studies of real figures in *Soft Answers* (1932) are post-war. Again the emphasis is on the arts. Aldington satirizes both bohemian excess and the bourgeois philistinism it opposes. The fictional portraits making up Stein's *Three Lives* couldn't be further removed. Though Stein herself presided over the 1920s Parisian equivalent of modernist London, she chooses two American working-class women and a mixed-race girl as her subjects. Fiction has a long tradition of choosing characters who in real life would have been considered too humble to be biographical subjects—Pamela Andrews, Jane Eyre, Oliver Twist, Tess of the D'Urbervilles, Esther Waters—Stein's radical move is both to offer them as precisely the subjects of life-writing, while simultaneously transforming how lives might be written—rather as Virginia Woolf was to do with her 'Lives of the Obscure'.

Some of these works will be discussed more fully later. The aim of this diagrammatic introduction of them here (to each other as well as to the reader) is to make four preliminary points. First, they indicate how widespread was the *fin de siècle* interest in portraiture. The literary interest in it coincides with the visual: as photographic experimentation moves from the art-portraits by photographers such as Julia Margaret Cameron, through the composite portraiture developed by Galton, into the modernist experiments such as Alvin Langdon Coburn's 'vortograph' portraits;[104] and as painted portraits develop from realism, through Manet and the Impressionists, into Post-Impressionist and Cubist reinventions of portraiture. Second, though the category of auto/biografictional portrait-collections is arguably a loose one, the similarities between all these examples are perhaps (as with any genre) of the kind Wittgenstein called family resemblances, rather than full and strict adherence to a detailed template. As with family resemblances, most members share some of a set of traits, even if few or none display all of them. That said, it is remarkable how almost all of the texts discussed here incorporate virtually all of the following traits:

[104] Coburn took these abstract photographs by using a triangular arrangement of mirrors to produce a kaleidoscopic composite effect. Most were of inanimate objects, but some were of artists, such as Vorticism's advocate, Ezra Pound. See p. 373.

- The gathering together of a set of character sketches.

- The inclusion of artists in the group.

- An exploration of the idea of portraiture and its expressive possibilities. (Pater, Ford, and Stein had much to say about the painting of portraits, as Isherwood does about photography. Beerbohm was a brilliant caricature draughtsman as well as supreme literary parodist.)

- An exploration of the border between life-writing and fictionality.

- A marked element of autobiography, whether factual or fictionalized.

- The inclusion of writings purported to be written by the subject.

Third, as we shall see, this last characteristic proves increasingly important in auto/biografiction as impressionism develops into modernism and postmodernism, and Chapters 7 and 8 will explore it further. The fourth point, which follows from this proliferation of imaginary creativity, is that the forms of imaginary portrait, composite portrait, and fictional creation, are all especially suited to the exploration of the aesthetic; they can all be read as figures for the creative process; for how authors build up fictional characters and situations by re-combinations and transformations of auto/biography—and conversely how they might compose their own lives by re-combinations and transformations of fictionalized narratives.

The French Decadent writer Marcel Schwob is a representative example. His *Vies imaginaires* (1896) are derivative in style and tone from Pater's *Imaginary Portraits*, though they reverse Pater's combination of biographical form and fictional subjects. Though Schwob's 'lives' may be 'imaginary', the subjects whose lives they tell are not. They are real historical figures, such as the philosopher Empedocles, the writers Lucretius and Petronius, the Renaissance painter Paolo Ucello, the Native American Pocahontas, the playwright Cyril Tourneur, the pirate Captain Kidd, the murderers Burke and Hare.

Where Carlyle wanted to reduce history to biography, Schwob opposes biography to history. In the 'Préface' to the *Vies imaginaires*, subtitled 'l'art de la biographie', he argues that history as a science leaves us in uncertainty with respect to individuals, because it is only interested in their connexion to general actions and events. Art, he says, on the other hand, 'is opposed to general ideas, describes only the individual, desires only the unique. It does not classify; it *de*classifies.'[105] Biography is an art of choice, he says: 'It shouldn't preoccupy itself with being true; it should create, amidst chaos, human traits.' Like Virginia Woolf, he thought the lives of the obscure as interesting as those of the great and

---

[105] Marcel Schwob, *Vies imaginaires* (Paris: Bibliothèque Charpentier, 1896). Parts of the book were translated by Iain White as 'Selections: Marcel Schwob', *Comparative Criticism*, vol. 2, ed. Elinor Shaffer (Cambridge: Cambridge University Press, 1980), pp. 265–87. This includes a translation of the Preface, as 'The Art of Biography' from *Vies imaginaires*, pp. 285–7 (p. 285).

the good: 'to the painter's eyes the portrait of an unknown man by Cranach has as much value as the portrait of Erasmus.'[106] He defends John Aubrey for being more interested in Harvey walking off his insomnia in his nightshirt than in his discovery of the circulation of the blood; because it is such idiosyncrasies that establish individuality.

Schwob appropriates biography's authoritative narrative voice, but infiltrates into it a poetic prose which approximates to fairytale; as in the passage on the painter Paolo Uccello's lover, Selvaggia:

In the morning she would waken before Uccello, and she would be happy because she was surrounded with painted birds and beasts in colour. Uccello drew her lips, and her eyes, and her hair and her hands, and he fixed all the attitudes of her body; but he never painted her portrait as other artists do who love a woman. For the bird man did not know the delight of limiting himself to the individual; he did not remain at one place; he wished to soar, in his flight, above all places.[107]

As here, Schwob's novelistic biographical portraits have been recognized as intensely personal: as a form of aesthetic or impressionist autobiography by other means. As Robert Ziegler writes, 'these historical fictions are the vehicle for continuing self-transformation, as the act of experiencing them and writing about them serves to effect a change in the author, with each character becoming an obsolete self which is discarded in favour of new ones.'[108]

Symons

One example of the composite portrait form which follows closely in the footsteps of Pater's *Imaginary Portraits*, and which is exemplary in incorporating all of the component traits, is Arthur Symons's *Spiritual Adventures* (1905).[109] It consists of eight chapters, each focusing on an individual. Most are living some form of aesthetic life, or dying some form of premature death, or both. In the case of one, 'Seaward Lackland', the 'spiritual' adventure is concerned with religion. Otherwise, by 'spiritual' Symons generally means psychological.

---

[106] Ann Jefferson, *Biography and the Question of Literature in France*, p. 205, poses Schwob as an exception to her argument about how biography has redefined the category of literature, 'in that he does not use the literary portrait as the basis for his redefinition of the literary'.

[107] 'Selections: Marcel Schwob', *Comparative Criticism*, vol. 2, p. 284.

[108] Robert Ziegler, 'Fictions of the Forgotten in Marcel Schwob', *Forum for Modern Language Studies*, 28:3 (1991), 227–37 (pp. 227–8).

[109] Symons, *Spiritual Adventures* (London: Archibald Constable, 1905). Elisa Bizzotto, 'The Imaginary Portrait: Pater's Contribution to a Literary Genre', in *Walter Pater: Transparencies of Desire*, ed. Laurel Brake, Lesley Higgins, and Carolyn Williams (Greensboro, NC: ELT Press, 2002), p. 221, says Symons acknowledged they were modelled on Pater's short fiction. Also see Jan B. Gordon, 'The Dialogue of Life and Art in Arthur Symons' Spiritual Adventures', *English Literature in Transition*, 12:3 (1969), 105–17, for a comparison of Pater and Symons.

The book opens with 'A Prelude to Life', a first-person, and genuinely autobiographical, sketch of the narrator's childhood, somewhat in the manner of Pater's 'The Child in the House', though more direct and less wistful. The other chapters concern other people, several of whom are the narrator's friends. 'Esther Kahn' is a Jewish girl, born near the London Docks, who grows up into an actress. Her suffering in love sharpens her art. 'Christian Trevalga' is another kind of artist, a concert pianist, portrayed on his deathbed aged thirty-six. He has lost 'his sense of material things', and has visual hallucinations of music, goes mad, and dies in an asylum.[110] The fourth chapter recounts 'The Childhood of Lucy Newcome', though what this turns out to mean is the death of her childhood, brought about by the deaths of both her parents. Lucy is portrayed as a child with a vivid imagination, suffocated by poverty and grief. With 'The Death of Peter Waydelin', Symons returns to artists: this time a painter, whose life and dramatic death at the age of 24 (while trying to sketch his wife in her grief over his dying) is told by his friend. In the sixth chapter, 'An Autumn City', Daniel Roserra is a connoisseur of cities. When he marries Livia Dawlish, the question is, what will happen when he introduces his wife to 'his best friend', his best friend being Arles. The meeting is disastrous. Everything he finds soothing and atmospheric there she finds excruciatingly dull, and he begins to fear her power over him. When he relents, and takes her to Marseilles, what she finds exhilarating he finds oppressively hot and vulgar. Their incompatibility as to cities is clearly ominous for their marriage generally. The hints of the morbid and perverse in these chapters modulate into an extreme spiritual perversity in 'Seaward Lackland'. He has been dedicated to god by his mother at birth, because at the time his father, a fisherman, was the only survivor from a severe storm. Seaward becomes a fisherman too, but becomes obsessed by the idea of his religious calling, and also becomes a lay preacher. He has a curious dream in which he has been damned, and following this he is drawn to commit an unpardonable sin against the Holy Ghost, by preaching a mad sermon denying god. He is cast out by the outraged community. While he is dying, after an accident, he explains (though no-one understands him) that he committed his sin 'for the love of God': that somehow the fulfilment of his damnation is supposed to be the proof of the strength of his faith.

After the introductory autobiographical chapter (possibly fictionalized), and the six fictionalized biographical portrait sketches, with the final chapter we move into formally different territory with the fictional 'Extracts from the Journal of Henry Luxulyan'. These are framed by the narrator, who explains that when his friend Luxulyan died he had asked that his papers be sent to the narrator. These papers were mostly incoherent, but included the journal which he says he is publishing in its entirety. The narrator says he finds the journal 'disconcerting';

---

[110] Symons, *Spiritual Adventures*, p. 107.

but his assurance that 'It seems to me a genuine document' only makes it more so, arousing our scepticism about its authenticity.[111] As with several of the other spiritual adventurers, Luxulyan is a study in insanity. He begins (in a way strikingly similar to Rilke's fictional journal-writer, Malte Laurids Brigge) with an anxiety that his 'nerves are seriously out of order', and an obsession with the inevitability of his own death (though his doctor assures him there is no physical reason why he should not have a long life).[112] He has had a relationship with a woman called 'Clare', and her leaving him appears to be at least one cause of his distress.

He is introduced to the Baroness von Eckenstein, a cultured and charming lady, whose extreme disfigurement on one side of her face begins to obsess him. He is both drawn to her and repelled, and describes her as a death's head. They become friends. When he is ruined financially, she offers him the post of librarian in her superb library. He becomes aware that the Baroness's marriage is a sham: that she and the Baron are deeply alienated from each other. As Luxulyan and the Baroness become more intimate, he tells her about Clare. In return, she confides her story: how she married very young; found the Baron cold; fell in love with a young Frenchman; but was discovered in his arms by her husband. In revenge, the Baron threw vitriol in her face; then, once her bandages had been removed, invited the Frenchman to dinner to see her. The lover is appalled, and leaves the neighbourhood. Luxulyan is moved to pity by the story, and soon realizes that the Baroness has now fallen in love with him. When he had met her he had wondered at the tragic force of such a passion in her middle age. When he had heard the story of the Baron's cruelty he had wanted to see him punished. But he says he hadn't realized how the two ideas would be united in his person. He tries to suppress his repugnance, and becomes her lover, but out of sympathy and pity, or a kind of perverse desire, rather than love. This causes his nerve disorder to return. He goes to Venice to recuperate, but grows increasingly insane.[113] When the Baroness comes to look after him, he regresses to childhood, saying that 'her love is maternal'. Now he only sees her as beautiful: ' When I look at her I can see her face as it was, as it is, without a scar'—which is exactly what he had earlier predicted would happen if someone were to fall in love with her.[114]

The note of misogyny here is disturbing, and is not entirely countered by the narrator's comment about being disconcerted, not least because it sounds in several of the other stories too. But it relates to a sense of disturbance in the forms of auto/biography—for the range of the book's forms of auto/biography is striking. It includes not only autobiography (or autobiografiction), and pseudo-journal, but varieties of pseudo-biography as well, some more autobiographical

[111] Symons, *Spiritual Adventures*, p. 244.   [112] Ibid.

[113] See Chapter 2 for a discussion of the autobiographical basis of this episode as described in Symons's *Confessions: A Study in Pathology*.

[114] Symons, *Spiritual Adventures*, pp. 311, 287.

than others. Symons's own disturbance at the time was real. He suffered a major nervous breakdown in 1908, was declared insane and briefly confined to Brooke House in East London.[115] And, as we have seen, disturbances in auto/biographical forms, displacing them towards fiction, are not only characteristic of the period, but characteristically drawn towards the representation of psychological disturbance. We have already seen how this type of pseudo-journal has been an increasingly important resource for twentieth-century writers like Benson, Rilke, Gide, Joyce, Hesse, and Sartre; and how most of them use formal experimentation with life-writing to explore psychological and aesthetic crises. These arguments will be developed in relation to Svevo and Joyce (Yeats had introduced Joyce to Symons in 1902) in Chapter 7.[116]

THE MANY AND THE ONE

My discussion of portrait-collections by Ford, Stevenson, Zweig, Eliot, and Symons, has considered the ways in which such works complicate the idea, implicit in Reynolds's account of autobiografiction, and explicit in the trope discussed by Philippe Lejeune, that fiction is the truer autobiography. Rather than reading just one portrait or narrative as also a self-portrait, we are reading a group of portraits or narratives as a composite self-portrait. In one sense this is no more than what readers have always done, when feeling that all the characters in a particular novel represent aspects of their author. But a portrait-collection has a specific formal ambiguity: like a volume of poems, or of short stories, it both is and is not a single work, as the post-Freudian self both is and is not a single entity.

The trope of fiction as true autobiography is thus further complicated when we consider the relation between autobiography and fiction across such groups of works; or across the group of works constituting a writer's entire oeuvre, when true autobiography is located multiple works rather than in a single book. One may (occasionally) feel that a single work, even though only part of a writer's *oeuvre*, expresses that writer fully: Milton in *Paradise Lost*, say; Swift in *Gulliver's Travels*, or Wordsworth in *The Prelude*. But some of the cases we have been considering are very different. With a writer such as William Hale White *The Autobiography of Mark Rutherford* is only a part of the process of producing the autobiography via fiction—as demonstrated by its various sequels. In A. C. Benson's case, in addition to his own gargantuan diary, we have a group of autobiografictional works attributed to different pseudonyms. In such cases, a

---

[115] Karl Beckson, *Arthur Symons: A Life*, Oxford: Oxford University Press, 1987, pp. 261–3. I am grateful to Paul Skinner for this reference.
[116] *Selected Letters of James Joyce*, ed. Richard Ellmann (London: Faber, 1975), p. 9.

reader's sense of the autobiographical dimension emerges from the oeuvre as a whole, or at least while moving from one work to another.

The argument I have associated with Wilde and Nietzsche that all utterance is autobiography offers a challenge to the received notion of autobiography as a genre, in which it is a single work, set apart from a writer's other productions, that is supposed to totalize a life-story. Writers know this ideal of totalizing autobiography can only be an ideal, and they approach its unapproachability in different ways: through parody (Sterne); through massive elaboration (Proust); through reduction to metaphysical essentials (modernist epiphany). Yet the writing of an explicitly autobiographical book nonetheless implies the attempt to tell the essential story. If, as according to the Nietzsche–Wilde argument, any work is autobiography, then every work in a writer's oeuvre will be autobiography. Thus an entire oeuvre is itself also an accumulative autobiography; and arguably the fullest possible autobiography of that writer. The distinction between individual work and oeuvre is not always clear. In Proust's case, again, much of his early writing is read as preparation for *A la recherche*. And that work itself is both one and many. It is now thought of as a single work, but was published in distinct volumes, some of which include sections (such as 'Un Amour de Swann') which seem to tell stories separate from Marcel's, which nonetheless are expressive of aspects of Marcel's personality too. Proust is fascinated by the relation between artist and work throughout the sequence, and can be seen using the form of the *roman-fleuve* to investigate that relationship.

One example of this argument that a writer's autobiography resides in the entire oeuvre is given by Aldington again, who argued that all D. H. Lawrence's work 'forms one immense autobiography.'[117] An 'immense autobiography' might seem to justify many volumes. But this argument could equally convict someone for writing many volumes that added up to a small autobiography. Though no one could accuse Katherine Mansfield of verbosity, her statement of how an oeuvre might be generated by a core of memories is suggestive of how the argument might be used to condemn repetition and failure of imagination: 'I think the only way to live as a writer is to draw upon one's real *familiar* life [. . .] Our secret life, the life we return to over and over again, the "do you remember" life is always the past.'[118] Alternatively, this sense of a 'secret life' which a writer keeps drawing upon is consonant with the shift we have noted in the concept of 'autobiography', away from outer events and towards the 'inner life'. The psychological turn leads auto/biographers to value interiority and 'personality' over fact and morality. And this is the impressionist priority too. Impressionism is thus particularly drawn towards the trope of fiction as true

---

[117] Doyle, p. 165. Lawrence himself was not averse to such auto/biographical readings. In his preface to *Collected Poems*, he wrote that many of his early poems 'make up a biography of an emotional and inner life': Lawrence, D. H., *The Complete Poems*, ed. and introd. Vivian De Sola Pinto and Warren Roberts (New York: Penguin, 1982), p. 27.

[118] Mansfield, letter to Sarah Gertrude Millin, March [1922], *Selected Letters*, ed. Vincent O'Sullivan (Oxford: Clarendon Press, 1989), p. 258.

autobiography, because it has already discounted facts as inessential, in favour of the expression of the artist's quality of mind, or personality.

To the extent that auto/biografiction attracts writers as a means of escaping biographical capture, they might be expected to be wary of an argument that seeks to return its hybrids to autobiography. One crucial sceptical response to this position too needs mentioning here: that of Henry James's story 'The Figure in the Carpet' (1896), one of James's several enigmatic tales about writers and their biography ('The Aspern Papers' (1888) is the best known, but 'The Private Life' (1891), 'The Middle Years' (1893), 'The Death of the Lion' (1894), and 'The Real Right Thing' (1899) are comparable examples of 'biografiction'; or indeed autobiografiction, since they equally reflect James's concerns for his own privacy and posterity).[119] Its nameless narrator becomes obsessed with the idea that the works of a famous novelist, Hugh Vereker, have a secret 'finest fullest intention', and is determined to discover what it is.[120] Admittedly the story doesn't say this secret is Vereker's autobiography. But the narrator's quest to understand the meaning of Vereker's life's work is tantamount to saying the novelist's works compose his essential autobiography. Vereker himself at first appears to offer encouragement, defining his secret as 'the particular thing I've written my books most *for*.'[121] So that when he later advises the narrator to 'Give it up—give it up!', the narrator only becomes convinced he is getting closer to the secret.[122] Yet he never discovers what he seeks, and the tale ends so as to question whether he hasn't been in the grip of a delusion (in which case his life demonstrates a pattern of its own, hidden from himself, but visible to someone reading it thus). Crucially, James neither reveals Vereker's secret, nor reveals whether there is one or not; and thus places his reader in the same position *vis-à-vis* his story (and oeuvre) as the narrator is in *vis-à-vis* Vereker's work. James keeps us guessing as to how far he believes in the figure of the figure in the carpet. As he states explicitly in 'The Art of Fiction' (1884), he doesn't dispute the expressive theory of art:

There is one point at which the moral sense and the artistic sense lie very near together; that is in the light of the very obvious truth that the deepest quality of a work of art will always be the quality of the mind of the producer.[123]

But, as 'The Figure in the Carpet' shows, the problem arises when a reader tries to interpret that 'quality of the mind'. The tale thus aligns itself with Wilde's Preface to *Dorian Gray*. If neither James's story nor Wilde's Preface are exactly arguing

[119] 'The Birthplace' (1903), based on (but not mentioning) Shakespeare.
[120] James, 'The Figure in the Carpet', in *The Lesson of the Master; and Other Stories* (London: John Lehmann, 1948), pp. 149–84 (p. 149).
[121] Ibid., p. 155.
[122] Ibid., p. 159.
[123] James, *Selected Literary Criticism*, ed. Morris Shapira (Cambridge: Cambridge University Press, 1981), pp. 49–67 (p. 66).

against the expressive theory that the work expresses the quality of the artist's mind, they are sceptical about whether readers will be able to read at the requisite depth. Where readers fail, they express the superficialities of their own minds.

James famously leaves us to figure out the figure; or rather, presents his story as a trap for all but the most critically self-aware. One might observe that the pun in his title leaves us with the apparition of a person: the 'figure' might be a human figure, rather than a structural design or a rhetorical trope. Nonetheless, it is significant that, by playing such games with the figure of the 'figure in the carpet', the totalizing autobiographical interpretation of an oeuvre, James was identifying it as an existing strategy of reading. In part, what is at stake in his resistance to the reading of oeuvre-as-autobiography is aestheticism's assertion of the autonomy of art, which should not be reduced to an 'intention' which might be a moral purpose or social programme. Also, for an author jealous of his privacy, like James (or Vereker), biographical readings are not only intrusive, but also appear to negate genuine creativity—the creation of the authentically other.

Such resistance is a forerunner of Foucault's critique, in 'What is an Author?', of the biographical as a cultural institution or discourse.[124] However, such arguments are reversible. Where Foucault sees the assigning of literary texts to the name of the author as an attempt to organize the literary according to the biographical, and thus to impose a biographical limitation on interpretation (as Barthes also argues in 'From Work to Text'),[125] one can see the idea of looking for a biographical figure in the literary carpet as, conversely, a reconfiguring of the idea of biography itself: instead of finding the salient elements of an author's life in the visible traces of his lived existence, they can be sought elsewhere, in works of art. What seemed like an attempt to 'fix' texts biographically, may, instead, 'unfix' biography by dispersing it across fictional texts. As suggested above, the aesthete's assertion that it is the (single) work of art that best expresses the life can be read as expressing an uncertainty about the sense of truth, the soul, or self-presence. The assertion that it is the oeuvre that best expresses the self, instead of being seen as a conservative reduction of text to biography, can be seen as offering an even more radical challenge to all of the terms in play: biography, self, and art. This is because what it proposes is a radically *relational* model for all three. Instead of transcendental essences, they are viewed as structures or systems, and the meanings of each are produced by their relation to the whole structure or system. Here of course we are in a universe of Derridean or Kristevan textuality and intertextuality, in which not only is there nothing outside textuality, but even texts themselves do not have any autonomous existence, but only signify by virtue of their relation to other texts. In short, the emergence of autobiografiction,

---

[124] Foucault, 'What is an Author' [1969], in *Language, Counter-Memory, Practice*, ed. Donald F. Bouchard (Ithaca: Cornell University Press, 1980), pp. 113–38.

[125] Barthes, 'From Work to Text', in R. Rylance, ed., *Debating Texts* (Toronto: University of Toronto Press, 1987), 117–22 (p. 120).

and of these related tropes of art as autobiography, and oeuvre as composite self-portrait, are not just indicative of autobiography assuming new forms, but of a profound shift in the understanding of what 'autobiography' might be, and what its relation to fiction might be. These arguments about oeuvre and the relation between autobiography and fiction within it will be developed in the Conclusion.

This chapter has sought to sketch the diversity of experiments in auto/biografiction from the late nineteenth century: works of fiction which give impressions of life-writing, by or about subjectivities other than the author's. The next chapter considers impressionist auto/biography by novelists: works of auto/biography in which writers best known for fiction give impressions of themselves.

6

Literary Impressionism and Impressionist Autobiographies: Henry James, Joseph Conrad, and Ford Madox Ford

'Impressionistic writing requires the union of several qualities [...] The first thing is to see, and with an eye which sees all, and as if one's only business were to see; and then to write, from a selecting memory, and as if one's only business were to write. It is the interesting heresy of a particular kind of art to seek truth before beauty; but in an impressionistic art concerned, as the art of painting is, with the revelation, the re-creation, of a colored and harmonious world, which (they tell us) owes its very existence to the eyes which see it, truth is a quality which can be attained only by him who seeks beauty before truth.'[1]

'To feel a unity [...] in one's impressions [...] was positively to face the aesthetic, the creative, even [...] the critical life and almost on the spot to commence author.'[2]

Most of the writers discussed so far were contemporaries of the Impressionist painters, and some (as we saw in the chapters discussing Pater, Ruskin, and Benson) made the notion of the 'impression' central to their work. Others, such as Stein and Isherwood, are clearly more modern, but can nevertheless be seen as continuing and developing impressionist experiments with life-writing. The writers discussed in this chapter form a group who knew each other well and discussed each other's work, falling chronologically between these categories of aesthetes and modernists, though their practice overlaps with both: Henry James, Joseph Conrad, and Ford Madox Ford.[3] They are best known, rightly, as novelists. But they were also significant autobiographers, James completing two volumes and leaving a third unfinished; Conrad publishing two; and Ford at least five volumes that are essentially (and many other works which are largely)

---

[1] Arthur Symons, 'Impressionistic Writing', from 1923 collection *Dramatis Personae*. In R. V. Holdsworth, *Arthur Symons: Poetry and Prose* (Cheadle Hulme: Carcanet, 1974), p. 93.
[2] Henry James, *Autobiography*, ed. Frederick W. Dupee (Princeton: Princeton University Press, 1983), p. 253.
[3] See Max Saunders, 'Literary Impressionists', *Oxford DNB* Reference Group article (2008).

auto/biographical. As we shall see, these writers increasingly defined themselves in terms of impressionism, and have increasingly been so defined by recent criticism. But though there is now a substantial tradition of good criticism discussing their fiction, there has been very little comparing their autobiographical writing. And though there is now a respectable body of work comparing their fiction in terms of impressionism, there has again been very little either on the significance of impressionism in this autobiographical writing, or on impressionist autobiography as a specific mode. Yet in each of these writers there is a striking continuity between the methods of the fiction and of the autobiography; and their autobiographical books constitute a key phase in the history of modern engagements with, and transformations of, life-writing. Indeed, impressionist autobiography renders the distinction between autobiography and fiction peculiarly hard, if not impossible, to draw.[4] The autobiographies of James, Conrad, and Ford don't read like novels. They are in a different category from even the highly autobiographical modernist novels like *A la recherche du temps perdu*, *A Portrait of the Artist as a Young Man* or *To the Lighthouse*. But they are highly novelistic, and in their impressionist representations of subjectivity are approaching the positions of Proust, Joyce, or Woolf.[5] But where autobiographical novels put autobiographical material within a novelistic frame, these impressionist memoirs use novelistic tropes and techniques within the frame of formal autobiography. They represent an alternative contemporary response to the disturbances in life-writing outlined in the previous three chapters—yet another way of combining autobiography and fiction.

LITERARY IMPRESSIONISM

Impressionism has always been a problematic term, contested within both Art History and Literature. As one of its leading scholars, Richard Bretell, argues: 'There is no doubt that Impressionism is the best-known and, paradoxically, the least understood movement in the history of art.'[6] When the 'Société anonyme des peintres, sculpteurs et graveurs' put on the first of their eight exhibitions in Paris between 1874 and 1886, they didn't call themselves impressionists. It was the art critic Louis Leroy, deriding Claude Monet's sketch-like, shimmering, Japanese-influenced *Impression: sun rising*, who inadvertently gave the movement

---

[4] See Max Saunders, 'Ford, Eliot, Joyce, and the Problems of Literary Biography', in *Writing the Lives of Writers*, ed. Warwick Gould and Thomas F. Staley (London and New York: Macmillan and St Martin's Press, 1998), pp. 150–72.
[5] See Millicent Bell, 'Henry James and the Fiction of Autobiography', *Southern Review*, 18:3 (1982), 463–79.
[6] Bretell, *Modern Art: 1851–1929: Capitalism and Representation* (Oxford: Oxford University Press, 1999), p. 15.

its name.[7] Writers were soon applying the term to literature (and later to the music of Debussy and Ravel); and continued to do so through our period. Ferdinand Brunetière's essay 'L'Impressionisme dans le roman' appeared in 1879.[8] But from another point of view, what the Impressionists were painting could be said to come from literature; to take its inspiration from an influential essay by Charles Baudelaire *The Painter of Modern Life* (1863).[9] Baudelaire was writing about the pre-Impressionist painter Constantin Guys. Yet the essay can be read as anticipating Impressionism in its advocacy of the beauty of everyday life—and especially of the life of leisure in the modern city; of speed of execution; and in its preference for the ceremonies of modernity rather than adherence to the classical tradition. Similarly, we have seen how in British writing the crucial figure is Walter Pater, who had already begun to explore the notion of the 'impression' by 1873—before the first 'Société anonyme' exhibition.

The Irish writer George Moore, a champion of Impressionist painting, was one of the first fiction-writers in English to style himself impressionist. In *Confessions of a Young Man* (1886) he uses impressionist aesthetics to satirize his aesthetic pretensions, representing himself on his first page as beginning 'apparently with a nature like a smooth sheet of wax, bearing no impress, but capable of receiving any'. His *Confessions* has been described as a 'pseudo-autobiographical novel.'[10] He followed this with *Memoirs of My Dead Life* (1906), and then the three volumes on the Irish Revival: *Ave* (1911), *Salve* (1912), and *Vale* (1914), collected together as *Hail and Farewell* (1925), and described both as Moore's masterpiece, and as unreliable. While this might suggest that Moore, too, has a place in the story of autobiografiction, his memoirs are, rather, works of autobiografiction's alter ego, impressionism.

Literary critics are rightly wary about what impressionism might mean applied to verbal rather than visual art.[11] Leroy was posing what seemed to him an impossibility: making a school out of the sketchy and the numinous. Is literary impressionism like Impressionist painting; writing of intense visuality; writing which moves on rapidly (by analogy with the speed of Impressionist brushstrokes) without full elaboration; a preoccupation with the processes of perception rather than the thing perceived; particularly concerned with aesthetics and the perception of beauty? As Jesse Matz has argued, the vagueness that 'Impressionism' can connote seems integral to its signification as a critical term.[12]

---

[7] Leroy's review is printed in Linda Nochlin, ed., *Impressionism and Post-Impressionism 1874–1904: Sources and Documents* (Englewood Cliffs, NJ: Prentice-Hall, 1966), pp. 10–13.

[8] Ferdinand Brunetière, 'L'impressionisme dans le roman', *Revue des deux mondes*, 49, no. 3 (1879), p. 450.

[9] Baudelaire, *The Painter of Modern Life and Other Essays*, ed. Jonathan Mayne (London: Phaidon, 1995).

[10] Edwin Gilcher, entry on George Augustus Moore, *Oxford DNB*.

[11] See Saunders, 'Literary Impressionism', in *A Companion to Modernist Literature and Culture*, ed. David Bradshaw and Kevin Dettmar (Oxford: Blackwell, 2005), pp. 204–11.

[12] Matz, *Literary Impressionism and Modernist Aesthetics* (Cambridge: Cambridge University Press, 2001), pp. 17–18.

It is not only the nature of literary impressionism that is contested, but also its duration. In art history the chronology is much clearer. Pictorial Impressionism is decidedly an affair of the late nineteenth century and the *fin de siècle*. 'Post-Impressionism' had been identified by at least 1910, the year of Roger Fry's exhibition 'Manet and the Post-Impressionists' at the Grafton Gallery.[13] In literature one can distinguish two ways of understanding impressionism chronologically. One chronology is very specific, and sees it as exactly contemporary with Impressionism in paint: something occupying the space between realism and modernism, and coinciding with the origin of phenomenology. The other is more concerned to trace the notion of the 'impression' further back: philosophically, to its origins in British empiricism and scepticism in the work of Locke, Hume, and Berkeley; in literature, to the psychological realism of the mid-nineteenth-century; and also further forward, into and alongside modernism.

When Thomas Moser wrote in 1980 that: 'The history of literary impressionism remains to be written', after giving a sketch of the immense ground that would have to be covered—from British empiricism to phenomenology, from Dickens to Ford—he suggested that 'It will probably never be written.'[14] Since then, if its history has not been detailed on quite that grand scale, there has nonetheless been significant study of it. Besides monographs focusing on individual writers such as James, Stephen Crane, Conrad Willa Cather, and Katherine Mansfield in relation to impressionism,[15] there have also been important discussions of literary impressionism by Ian Watt and Michael Levenson, as well as some larger-scale comparative studies by Peter Stowell and Todd Bender.[16]

[13] See Samuel Hynes, *The Edwardian Turn of Mind* (Princeton: Princeton University Press, 1975), pp. 410–17.

[14] Moser, *The Life in the Fiction of Ford Madox Ford* (Princeton: Princeton University Press, 1980), pp. 123–4.

[15] James J. Kirschke, *Henry James and Impressionism* (Troy, NY: Whitson, 1981); Robin Hoople, *In Darkest James: Reviewing Impressionism, 1900–1905* (Lewisburg, PA: Bucknell University Press, 2000); James Nagel, *Stephen Crane and Literary Impressionism* (University Park: Pennsylvania University Press, 1980); John G. Peters, *Conrad and Impressionism* (Cambridge: Cambridge University Press, 2001); David Stouck, 'Willa Cather and the Impressionist Novel', *Critical Essays on Willa Cather*, ed. John J. Murphy (Boston: G. K. Hall, 1984); and Julia van Gunsteren, *Katherine Mansfield and Literary Impressionism* (Amsterdam and Atlanta: Rodopi, 1990). There are also discussions of Ford's Impressionism in my *Ford Madox Ford: A Dual Life*, 2 vols (Oxford: Oxford University Press, 1996).

[16] Watt, *Conrad in the Nineteenth Century* (Berkeley: University of California Press, 1981); Levenson, *A Genealogy of Modernism: A Study of English Literary Doctrine 1908–1922* (Cambridge: Cambridge University Press, 1984). H. Peter Stowell, *Literary Impressionism: James and Chekhov* (Athens: University of Georgia Press, *c.*1980). Todd K. Bender, *Literary Impressionism in Jean Rhys, Ford Madox Ford, Joseph Conrad, and Charlotte Brontë* (New York and London: Garland, 1997). See also James J. Kirschke, 'Impressionist Painting and the Reflexive Novel of the Early Twentieth Century', *Proceedings of the 8th Congress of the International Comparative Literature Association: Three Epoch-Making Literary Changes: Renaissance, Enlightenment, Early Twentieth Century*, ed. Bela Kopeczi and Gyorgy M. Vajda (Stuttgart: Bieber, 1980), pp. 567–73. There is also a useful selection of writing on 'Literary Impressionism' in Martin Stannard's excellent edition of Ford's *The Good Soldier* (New York and London: W. W. Norton, 1995), pp. 239–300.

But more recently the work of two critics in particular has transformed the history of literary impressionism and its relation to modernism. Paul B. Armstrong's *The Challenge of Bewilderment: Understanding and Representation in James, Conrad, and Ford* concentrates on the three writers in English most often now called impressionist, and offers a powerful philosophically inflected reading of their fiction which certainly contributes to the understanding of their impressionism. Though Armstrong doesn't discuss impressionism in detail in this book, it is his premise that 'The critical heritage has long regarded James, Conrad, and Ford as impressionists [. . .]'; and he has published essays discussing literary impressionism.[17] Where Armstrong gives the chronologically narrower account of impressionist literature (as falling between realism and modernism), the critic who has best recovered the longer history of literary impressionism is Jesse Matz, in *Literary Impressionism and Modernist Aesthetics*. This excellent study follows critics such as Frederic Jameson and Michael Levenson in arguing that impressionism is a fundamental antecedent to literary modernism. Its achievement is to establish literary impressionism as something that can be seen to have a coherent history. Matz's negotiation of the philosophical tradition investigating the mental 'impression' is a tour de force. His central literary figures include the James/Conrad/Ford trio, but these are framed with extensive discussions of both earlier and later authors: Walter Pater and Thomas Hardy; Marcel Proust and Virginia Woolf. Tamar Katz's *Impressionist Subjects* covers several of the same figures, but takes a different route, seeing impressionism as a field across which constructions of feminine subjectivity play.[18]

Jesse Matz combines several complex arguments, shrewdly relating literary impressionism not just to its philosophical influences from empiricism to phenomenology, but also to issues of sexuality, gender, and class politics. This produces readings of different nuances of literary impressionism, encompassing homoeroticism in Pater; the figure of the 'woman of genius' in James; and the argument that impressionism in Conrad and Ford involves a notion of collaboration across classes. However, it is the overall rationale of his study that is most relevant to our purposes: the argument that impressionism is the narrative that can make intelligible the transition from realism to modernism. He traces the ambiguities in the 'impression' from its empiricist origins, when it is both the passive receiving of the stamp of the world, but also the mental activity of perceiving and thinking about what is received. He begins with Proust, showing how he poses moments of intensely visual sensation and pictorial prose, only to

---

[17] Armstrong, *The Challenge of Bewilderment: Understanding and Representation in James, Conrad, and Ford* (Ithaca: Cornell University Press, 1987), p. 4; Armstrong 'The Hermeneutics of Literary Impressionism', *Centennial Review* 27:4 (1983), 244–69; and 'The Epistemology of Ford's Impressionism', in Richard A. Cassell, ed., *Critical Essays on Ford Madox Ford* (Boston: G. K. Hall, 1987), pp. 135–42.

[18] Tamar Katz, *Impressionist Subjects: Gender, Interiority, and Modernist Fiction in England* (Urbana and Chicago: University of Illinois Press, 2000).

reject them in favour of another kind of impression: the classic moments of involuntary memory in which a present impression recalls a past one.[19] It is this structure connecting impressions across time, and thereby 'regaining' or appearing to transcend time, that constitutes Proustian impressionism. By redefining the impression in this way, Matz is then able to trace striking continuities from the middle of the nineteenth century to the middle of the twentieth. The gemlike flame with which Pater wants to burn; the wondering or haunted consciousnesses of James's novels; Conrad's rigour in trying 'to make you *see*'; the modernist epiphanies of Proust, Joyce, and Woolf: all these (and one could add others: Lawrence's visionary vitalism; Eliot's Tiresias foresuffering all; Pound's desire to reconnect with the divine energies of Homer or Dante) represent a specific paradigm, which corresponds to a new way of thinking about how the mind works (where phenomenology, pragmatism, and Bergsonian vitalism co-exist); about the experience of knowing, and the relationship between perceiving and understanding.

Told in this cogent way, the history of impressionism does indeed overlap with both realism and modernism. Or, to put it a different way, it complicates both realism and modernism, showing that impressionism was not just the fundamental antecedent to modernism, but the ground on which modernism is constructed. The *style indirect libre* of Joyce as well as Flaubert is, after all, a technique for rendering impressions. Though Matz doesn't argue that Proust and Woolf are not modernists, he shows how they are also impressionists. Their work is still profoundly engaged with the idea of the impression, and how to represent it. Thus Joyce may ironize the Aesthetic movement in *A Portrait of the Artist*, but even as he does so, his method is Stephen's impressionism. What such studies bring out is the complex, suggestive energies of impressionism throughout the period from the 1890s to the 1930s; and how part of the modernism of writers like James, Proust, Conrad, Dorothy Richardson, and Woolf is precisely their concern for the impression.

Several of the authors who have since been discussed as impressionist were (at least initially) hostile or ambivalent to the term, as was Flaubert writing to Turgenev in 1877: 'After the Realists, we have the Naturalists and the Impressionists. What progress! Bunch of clowns.'[20] Henry James's judgement of Impressionist painting in 1876 may seem startlingly negative now:

The young contributors to the exhibition of which I speak are partisans of unadorned reality and absolute foes to arrangement, embellishment, selection, to the artist's allowing himself, as he has hitherto, since art began, found his best account in doing, to be preoccupied with the idea of the beautiful [. . .] None of its members show signs of

[19] Matz, *Literary Impressionism*, pp. 5–6.
[20] Quoted in Stephen Heath, *Gustave Flaubert: Madame Bovary* (Cambridge: Cambridge University Press, 1992), p. 29.

possessing first-rate talent, and indeed the 'Impressionist' doctrines strike me as incompatible, in an artist's mind, with the existence of first-rate talent.[21]

But James was later gradually to soften his views. If his remarks on Sargent a decade later are still critical—'the latent dangers of the impressionist practice' are 'the tendency to simplification and the neglect of a certain faculty for lingering reflection'—there is now more ambivalence; less absoluteness.[22] The dangers are only 'latent'; a 'tendency', rather than the inevitability of failure. He was also thinking of Sargent when he wrote in his notes for 'The Coxon Fund' that he wanted to do in words what Sargent did in paint: 'impressionize.'[23] Later still, he too can be seen moving towards a more appreciative attitude towards impressionism, particularly in literature, as Peter Brooks has argued.[24] And, as Matz shows, the concept of the 'impression' became central both in his critical work, such as 'The Art of Fiction', and his later novels—particularly *What Maisie Knew* and *The Ambassadors*. At the same time he consistently advanced the analogy between literature and painting. And the pictorial genre he often has in mind is portrait-painting, as when he titles a novel *The Portrait of a Lady* (not the unmediated lady, but the artistic 'treatment' of her). James's prefaces to his novels discuss the importance of what he called the 'central intelligence' or central consciousness. The impressionism of much of his fiction consists in its being the portrait of an imaginary consciousness: Isabel Archer; Maisie Farange; Lambert Strether. The impression, as we shall see, was also to prove central to James's major late work of non-fiction: his autobiography.

Joseph Conrad, too, was ambivalent, shifting from his early rejection of Impressionist painting, via his 'qualified praise' of Stephen Crane's writing, to a position where he himself began consciously to aim at impressionist effects.[25] Cedric Watts notes Conrad's equivocal dealings with impressionism, and quotes him on one occasion calling himself an 'impressionist from instinct.'[26] Conrad certainly understood his art as founded on impressions. He thought other writers tended to 'lean' on props such as an anecdote, a newspaper story, tradition, or history; 'while I don't', he said: 'I have had some impressions, some sensations—in my time.'[27] This was written in 1896, after he had begun *The Nigger of the*

[21] James, 'The Impressionists' (1876), in *The Painter's Eye*, ed. John L. Sweeney (London: Rupert Hart-Davis, 1956), pp. 114–15.
[22] James, 'John S. Sargent', *Harper's Magazine*, 75 (October 1887), 683–91 (p. 688).
[23] *The Notebooks of Henry James*, ed. F. O. Mathiessen and Kenneth B. Murdock (New York: Oxford University Press, 1947), p. 160: entry for 25 April 1894.
[24] Peter Brooks, *Henry James Goes to Paris* (Princeton: Princeton University Press, 2007). Also see Eloise Knapp Hay, 'Impressionism Limited', *Joseph Conrad: A Commemoration* (London: Macmillan, 1976), p. 55.
[25] Hay, 'Impressionism Limited', p. 55.
[26] Cedric Watts, *Joseph Conrad: A Literary Life* (Basingstoke: Macmillan, 1989), p. 67; *Collected Letters of Joseph Conrad*, ed. Frederick Karl and Laurence Davies, vol. 1 (Cambridge: Cambridge University Press, 1983), p. 398.
[27] Conrad to Edward Garnett, 19 June 1896: *Collected Letters of Joseph Conrad*, vol. 1, p. 288.

'*Narcissus*' as a short story, but put it to one side.[28] The afterword he wrote when it was eventually published as a novella in 1897 (and which was subsequently used as its preface) is often discussed as a manifesto of impressionism:

art itself may be defined as a single-minded attempt to render the highest kind of justice to the visible universe, by bringing to light the truth, manifold and one, underlying its every aspect.

[. . .] Such an appeal, to be effective, must be an impression conveyed through the senses [. . .] My task which I am trying to achieve is, by the power of the written word, to make you hear, to make you feel—it is, before all, to make you *see*.

Two paradoxes emerge here. First, impressionism is supposed to concentrate on the visible world. But it does this in order to get at something that cannot be perceived visually: the 'truth' 'underlying' the 'visible universe'. Conrad's celebrated credo—'it is, before all, to make you *see*' is doubly ambiguous. Does 'before all' mean before in time? (first you see the visual perceptions, then you work out what they are; what Ian Watt called 'delayed decoding'). Or does it mean 'above all': in other words, that it is less important to struggle to understand: you should just have the impressions, the sensations, the experience; be an artist rather than a philosopher? Either way, the important point is Conrad's emphasis of the word 'see', which brings out the ambiguity of that word too: to see with the eye, or with the understanding. The second paradox is that while Conrad's art renders the visible universe as a way of revealing the secrets that lie beneath it, what it finds is precisely that they *are* secrets—enigmas, mysteries. They elude rational 'seeing', and remain recalcitrantly bewildering phenomena.

Ford's case is different. He proclaimed himself an impressionist from an early stage, and became literary impressionism's most prolific exponent.[29] For him, literary impressionism precedes pictorial impressionism, and means the 'conscious art' with which an author produces impressions in words of lived impressions. He sees literature as reaching technical maturity as impressionism appears in the mid-nineteenth century in works by Stendhal and particularly Flaubert, Maupassant, and Turgenev; and he sees this line as developed by Henry James,

---

[28] Owen Knowles, *A Conrad Chronology* (Basingstoke: Macmillan, 1989), p. 24.

[29] Ford's key discussions of impressionism in literature include: *The Critical Attitude* (1911); the essay 'On Impressionism' (1914); the essay 'Impressionism—Some Speculations' (which was revised into the Preface for Ford's 1914 *Collected Poems*); the two monographs *Henry James* and *Joseph Conrad*; the critical serial 'Stocktaking' Ford contributed (under the pseudonym 'Daniel Chaucer') to the *transatlantic review* (1924); his study *The English Novel: From the earliest days to the death of Joseph Conrad*; the essay 'Techniques'; the book of critical reminiscences, *Portraits from Life* (published in the UK as *Mightier Than the Sword*); and the many passages of criticism in his other memoirs, such as *Ancient Lights* (published in the United States as *Memories and Impressions*), *Return to Yesterday*, and *It Was the Nightingale*. Finally, *The March of Literature* (1938). This is not to mention his literary journalism, most of which remains uncollected. Saunders, 'From Pre-Raphaelism to Impressionism', *Ford Madox Ford and Visual Culture*, ed. Laura Colombino (Amsterdam and New York: Rodopi, 2009), pp. 51–70, discusses Ford's gradual approach towards impressionism in literature.

and, in the twentieth century, by the formal experiments practised by modernists such as Conrad, Ford himself, and then Hemingway and Pound. Two examples give the best sense of Fordian impressionism. The first (written while he was working on *The Good Soldier*), gives an intensely visual sensation:

I suppose that Impressionism exists to render those queer effects of real life that are like so many views seen through bright glass—through glass so bright that whilst you perceive through it a landscape or a backyard, you are aware that, on its surface, it reflects a face of a person behind you. For the whole of life is really like that; we are almost always in one place with our minds somewhere quite other.[30]

The second example, from *Joseph Conrad*, is also about the building up of a superimposed multiple perspective. In this case it is an impression of a man: one who has much in common with Edward Ashburnham, the impeccable philanderer of *The Good Soldier*. And the passage describes perfectly the method of his fiction (especially *The Good Soldier*) and his autobiography:

it became very early evident to us that what was the matter with the Novel, and the British novel in particular, was that it went straight forward, whereas in your gradual making acquaintance with your fellows you never do go straight forward. You meet an English gentleman at your golf club. He is beefy, full of health, the moral of the boy from an English Public School of the finest type. You discover, gradually, that he is hopelessly neurasthenic, dishonest in matters of small change, but unexpectedly self-sacrificing, a dreadful liar but a most painfully careful student of lepidoptera and, finally, from the public prints, a bigamist who was once, under another name, hammered on the Stock Exchange. . . . Still, there he is, the beefy, full-fed fellow, moral of an English Public School product. To get such a man in fiction you could not begin at his beginning and work his life chronologically to the end. You must first get him in with a strong impression, and then work backwards and forwards over his past. . . . That theory at least we gradually evolved.[31]

Here the emphasis is on process: on the instability of impressions; how they constantly transform and astonish; how they necessitate time-shifts—the working 'backwards and forwards'. Where the first example concentrates on the phenomenology of impressionism—what the experience of perceiving things is like—the second is also attentive to its epistemology—its processes of knowing and understanding. Like most of Ford's accounts of impressionism, these both make an appeal to a form of psychological realism. They claim impressionism can represent the experience of perception or memory more accurately. That is also the claim of impressionist painting made against the then new technology of photography. To an impressionist, the camera always lies, in its hard-edged static clarity that seeks to fix the fluidity and mobility of the eye, and sharpen its vaguenesses, uncertainties, and blurs; its claim to deliver the object instead of its

[30] Ford, 'On Impressionism', *Poetry and Drama*, 2 (1914), 167–75 and 323–34 (p. 174).
[31] Ford, *Joseph Conrad* (London: Duckworth, 1924), pp. 129–30.

representations or mediations; this despite its stylized monochrome, which denies the infinite possibilities and pleasure of colour.

Just as Impressionism in painting prepared the way for pointillisme, post-Impressionism, and Cubism, so literary impressionism metamorphoses into modernism. It is particularly drawn to moments of defamiliarization, when a character's identity is threatened, when their set ways of being and doing and perceiving are disrupted, and their experience acquires a rawness and directness that makes it more real for us. In this it approaches to the stream of consciousness, which modernism was to develop out of impressionism. It also makes us more aware of the medium, construction, composition, form, techniques, just as visual Impressionism intensifies awareness of the picture surface.

Ford's criticism shows him repeatedly able to grasp immediately the significant innovations of his modernist friends such as Lawrence, Pound, Hemingway, or Rhys. His acuity is evident in his landmark reviews of Conrad and Joyce, and particularly in his pioneering insistence on what Pound called 'The Prose Tradition' in verse—the advocacy of concreteness, understatement, modern urban subjects, and freer, conversational verse forms.[32] No one who has read his scintillating—and exemplarily impressionist—account of Wyndham Lewis (encrypted as 'D. Z') blasting Ford with his denunciation of impressionism can doubt that Ford understood perfectly well how different some modernist aesthetics were from his own. Ford has Lewis grabbing his arm, force-marching him down Holland Street, telling him he was 'Finished! Exploded! Done for! Blasted in fact! Your generation has gone. What is the sense of you and Conrad and Impressionism?' 'This is the day of Cubism, Futurism, Vorticism. What people want is me, not you. They want to see me. A Vortex. To liven them up. You and Conrad had the idea of concealing yourself when you wrote. I display myself all over the page. In every word. I...I...I....'[33]

Six years later Ford reimagined the scene, this time naming Lewis. The diatribe is expanded, and the actual words are different, though the burden and force are much the same:

Mr. Wyndham Lewis (Percy) caught me mysteriously by the elbow, willed me out into Holland Street and, in his almost inaudible voice... said it....

'You and Mr. Conrad and Mr. James and all those old fellows are done.... Exploded! ... *Fichus!*.... *Vieux jeu!*... No good!... Finished!... Look here!... You old fellows are merely nonsensical. You go to infinite pains to get in your conventions.... *Progression d'effets*.... *Charpentes*.... Time-shift.... God knows what.... And what for? What in Heaven's name for? You want to kid people into believing that, when they read your ingenious projections they're actually going through the experiences of your characters. Verisimilitude—that's what you want to get with all your wheezy efforts.... But that isn't what people want. They don't want vicarious experience; they don't want to be educated.

[32] See *Pound/Ford*, ed. Brita Lindberg-Seyersted (London: Faber, 1983), pp. 16–21.
[33] Ford, *Return to Yesterday* (London: Gollancz, 1931), p. 418.

They want to be amused. . . . By brilliant fellows like me. Letting off brilliant fireworks. Performing like dogs on tight ropes. Something to give them the idea they're at a performance. You fellows try to efface yourselves; to make people think that there isn't any author and that they're living in the affairs you . . . adumbrate, isn't that your word? . . . What balls! What rot! . . . What's the good of being an author if you don't get any fun out of it? . . . Efface yourself! . . . Bilge!'[34]

The distinction between 'Cubism, Futurism, Vorticism' on the one hand, and Impressionism on the other, could hardly be clearer. But whereas one might expect Lewis as modernist to champion impersonality against the *fin de siècle* cult of personality, Ford shows it cuts both ways. Lewis's anti-humanist aesthetics issue in an argument for autobiography. Ford turns the humorous screw by doing himself exactly what Lewis requires of art: letting off brilliant fireworks; giving people the idea they're at a performance. Like much of the late auto/ biographical book from which this comes, the portrait-collection *Portraits from Life*, Ford is giving virtuoso impersonations of his writer-friends, which have an edge of caricature, satire even, that make them more than an attempt at verisimilitude. Impressionism, for Ford, then, is not reducible to the production of vicarious impressions: it can have other aims as well. Once one grasps this, then the logic of Ford's inclusive use of the term appears much stronger. What he implies is that there is a marked continuity from writers generally labelled as realists—Stendhal and Flaubert—to those who developed realism into naturalism—Zola and Maupassant—to the turn-of-the-century writers increasingly preoccupied with consciousness and form—such as James and Conrad—to those now seen as modernist, who begin to experiment with disjunctive forms (collage, time-shift, epiphany)—such as Conrad, Ford himself, or Pound, Eliot, Lewis, and Joyce. Fordian impressionism is thus not a granite monolith, but a spectrum. We should talk of impressionisms, as we now do of modernisms.[35] When we do that, the extent of the overlappings becomes even more apparent. There is no question that authors like James and Conrad were developing the methods of nineteenth-century writers like Flaubert and Turgenev. The attempt to separate off their work as modernist is inevitably arbitrary, as it would be to say that Hemingway is modernist and Ford is not, or that Woolf is modernist but May Sinclair or Rosamond Lehmann are not. Individual authors move through the spectrum themselves, some travelling distances as remarkable as those covered by James, Conrad, and Ford: Yeats, for example, who started as an Aesthete and Celtic Revivalist and ended as a modernist; or Joyce, who appears able to embody just about every phase from naturalism to postmodernism.

A modernist novel such as Virginia Woolf's *To the Lighthouse* (1927) is in many ways a Post-Impressionist work, concerned with being modern; modernist;

---

[34] Ford, *Portraits from Life* (Boston: Houghton Mifflin, 1937), p. 219.
[35] See Peter Nicholls, *Modernisms: A Literary Guide* (Basingstoke: Macmillan, 1995).

doing things differently from the preceding generation. Yet its content is very much that of the Impressionist painters: the bourgeoisie at leisure; by the seaside. Woolf shares with impressionist and modernist writers the desire to free the novel from the tyranny of story. In her key essay 'Modern Fiction' she rejects the patriarchal-institutional complex that binds us into its structures of linearity, time, and authority: 'some powerful and unscrupulous tyrant' has the writer in thrall, she argues, 'to provide a plot, to provide comedy, tragedy, love interest, and an air of probability embalming the whole [. . .]'. She goes on to ask whether novels must be like this:

Look within and life, it seems, is very far from being 'like this'. Examine for a moment an ordinary mind on an ordinary day. The mind receives a myriad impressions—trivial, fantastic, evanescent, or engraved with the sharpness of steel. From all sides they come, an incessant shower of innumerable atoms; and as they fall, as they shape themselves into the life of Monday or Tuesday, the accent falls differently from of old [. . .] Life is not a series of gig lamps symmetrically arranged; life is a luminous halo, a semi-transparent envelope surrounding us from the beginning of consciousness to the end.[36]

The trouble is that readers of prose, and especially longer, more novel-length prose, are generally less happy to get rid of stories than viewers of pictures. William Empson, for example, is both characteristically perceptive about Woolf's attention to 'myriad impressions', and aware of its limitations:

Mrs Woolf's early stories—'Kew Gardens', for instance—use what may be called the Vase of Flowers method; things seen in the same mood are described together, and there they are; two lovers and a slug; so you stop. This seems inadequate, whether derived from Chekhov or not; the range of interest (identifying oneself with all the characters and so forth) in the crudest melodramatic story is much greater than the range of interest (mainly contrast and correspondence) in a vase of flowers. Indeed, the impressionist method, the attempt to convey directly your own attitude to things, how you connect one thing with another, is in a sense fallacious; it tries to substitute for telling a story, as the main centre of interest, what is in fact one of the by-products of telling a story; it tries to correlate sensations rather than the impulses that make the sensations interesting [. . .] I think myself, at any rate, that Mrs Woolf's most memorable successes come when she is sticking most closely to her plot.[37]

Hard to disagree, as often with Empson. Or at least, it is so far as fiction is concerned. But his claim that the impressionist method is 'in a sense fallacious' because it attempts 'to convey directly your own attitude to things, how you connect one thing with another', and 'to correlate sensations' instead of 'telling a story', collapses when the story you are telling is your autobiography: the story of

---

[36] Woolf, 'Modern Fiction', *The Common Reader: First Series* (London: Hogarth Press, 1968), pp. 188–9.
[37] Empson, 'Virginia Woolf' (1931), in *Argufying* (London: Chatto & Windus, 1987), 443–9 (p. 448).

your subjectivity. Impressionist autobiography, like autobiografiction, is, precisely, a story of attitudes, connections, correlated sensations. As Ford recognized, impressionism exerts a gravitational pull towards autobiography, even
when it is ostensibly writing about another subject: 'Try how he will, an
Impressionist's book about an actual place or an actual man is bound to assume
a rather reminiscential air.'[38]

IMPRESSIONIST AUTOBIOGRAPHIES:
JAMES, CONRAD, AND FORD

Take for example the account in *Return to Yesterday* (1931) of Ford's first
meeting with Henry James, who invited him to lunch in 1896. He found
James 'the most masterful man I have ever met': 'composed and magisterial',
'in the manner of a police magistrate, civil but determined to receive true answers
to his questions'. 'The whole meal was one long questionnaire':

He demanded particulars as to my age, means of support, establishment, occupations,
tastes in books, food, music, painting, scenery, politics. He sat sideways to me across the
corner of the dining table, letting drop question after question. The answers he received
with no show at all of either satisfaction or reproof.[39]

Ford's account of this inauspicious first meeting ends with James telling a story
about Ford's uncle William Rossetti, whom 'Mr. James considered to be an
unbelievable bore', who was even able to make the story of how 'he had seen
George Eliot proposed to by Herbert Spencer on the leads of the terrace at
Somerset House' sound dull, in his 'querulous official' voice and 'Secretary to the
Inland Revenue' manner, which James mimicked. '"Is that," Mr. James con-
cluded, "the way to tell *that* story?"' Worrying later that he had portrayed James
as too waspish, Ford mused:

I will not say that loveableness was the predominating feature of the Old Man: he was too
intent on his own particular aims to be lavishly sentimental over surrounding humanity
[. . .] For some protective reason or other, just as Shelley used to call himself the Atheist,
he loved to appear in the character of a sort of Mr. Pickwick—with the rather superficial
benevolences, and the mannerisms of which he was perfectly aware. But below that
protective mask was undoubtedly a plane of nervous cruelty. I have heard him be—to
simple and quite unpretentious people—more diabolically blighting than it was quite
decent for a man to be—for he was always an artist in expression.[40]

---

[38] Ford, *A Mirror to France* (New York: Boni, 1926), p. 19.
[39] *Return to Yesterday*, pp. 11–14.
[40] Ibid., pp. 14–16, 217–18.

What he is doing here is building up a sense of the complexity of James's character—the layering of his planes of sensitivity and also cruelty: superimposing ambivalent feelings which have become overlayered in his mind through his long acquaintanceship with him. It is thus auto/biography: as much about his own experience of James, and of trying to understand him, as it is about James himself. And it is impressionist auto/biography; and as such owes much to the methods James had elaborated in the prefaces written for his New York edition. In the Preface to *The Princess Casamassima*, he wrote:

But the affair of the painter is not the immediate, it is the reflected field of life, the realm not of application, but of *appreciation*—a truth that makes our measure of effect altogether different. My report of people's experience—my report as a 'storyteller'—is essentially my appreciation of it, and there is no 'interest' for me in what my hero, my heroine or anyone else does save through that admirable process.[41]

This brings out James's continuities with aestheticism: 'appreciation' was a favourite term in the Paterian critical lexicon. He is not quite saying that he doesn't care what his characters do, only for what he thinks about their doing it; but he does say that it is only through his act of mediation that he can care about what they do. The same principle applies when his subject isn't a fictional hero or heroine, but himself. The 'interest' for him in autobiography is not in what his young self did, or said. It is in what his mature consciousness finds in those memories, or extrapolates out of them.

Ford's reminiscence of James works according to this principle. The 'interest' for him is only in James's character insofar as it makes an impression on Ford. This episode is very characteristic of Ford's autobiographical method, not only for the exquisite sense it gives of young Ford's excruciating embarrassment before this wickedly brilliant intelligence; but also for the way it intimates the feelings it represses, suggesting that such flashes of cruelty mattered to him because of the strong feeling of affection James had inspired in him. That loveableness may not have been James's predominating feature didn't stop Ford having an almost filial love for him (as is intimated by the oddity of calling someone not his father 'the Old Man'; and by raising the question of James's loveability while disavowing it).

It is also characteristic of impressionist aesthetic autobiography because both the episode, and the feelings it mobilizes, are not only about persons, but also about art. He is conscious that in recounting James's story about William Rossetti's inability to tell a story, he is telling a story himself. Conscious, too, that all the characteristics he describes in James, that might be taken for mere waspishness, are inextricable from James's genius as an artist, a 'storyteller'. His inquisitorial determination; impartiality as to the answers; his anger at Rossetti's spoiling of a story that could have been made to tell; and his being, even in his vindictiveness, 'an artist in expression': all these point to James's being a writer through and through, in every situation and mood. Like the vignette of

---

[41] James, *The Princess Casamassima* (Harmondsworth: Penguin, 1977), p. 12.

Wyndham Lewis denouncing Fordian impressionism, this is another portrait of an artist who becomes himself in his art, and in discussing his aesthetics.

In impressionism the bonds began to loosen between fact and impression; between experience and narration. I have written elsewhere about three different kinds of disjunction between fact and impression in autobiography—forgetting, evading, and distorting—tracing the different ways in which all three of these three impressionist autobiographers negotiate all three of them.[42] So I shall just recapitulate them briefly here.

(i) Forgetting

James, especially when writing about himself in his first volume of memoirs as *A Small Boy and Others*, starts from the disparity between the plenitude of consciousness and the insubstantiality of memory. He takes the fact of amnesia—that our impressions are too many and too nuanced for them all to be preserved—as a licence to elaborate. He glories in the gap: 'Wonderful altogether in fact, I find as I write, the quantity, the intensity of picture recoverable from even the blankest and tenderest state of the little canvas.'[43] He even finds a wonderfully childlike image to evoke his sense of playing on the edge. He writes of 'sitting rather queerly safe and alone, though with a dangle of legs over the edge of a precipice, on the hither side of a great gulf of history.'[44] That gulf between the mature elaborate reminiscer and the childishness of the memories being elaborated is the core of his autobiographical structures. It is also a structure he had used to great effect in his fiction, since it is also the guiding method of *What Maisie Knew*, in which the child's dawning awareness of adult motivations is elaborated in a sophisticated adult language she could not possibly command. James finds a redemptive comedy in this disparity. The loss of the past is converted into imaginative opportunity.[45] Absence makes the memory freer: the gothic voids (gulfs and precipices) become the scene of invention.

---

[42] Saunders, 'Reflections on Impressionist Autobiography: James, Conrad and Ford', *Inter-relations: Conrad, James, Ford, and Others* in the series 'Joseph Conrad: Eastern and Western Perspectives', gen. ed. Wieslaw Krajka (Lublin: Columbia University Press, 2003), 7–41.

[43] James, *Autobiography*, p. 18.

[44] Quoted by Millicent Bell, 'Henry James and the Fiction of Autobiography', p. 469.

[45] James talks of the 'inward perversity' according to which 'things vain and unintended' get converted into experience which is nonetheless valuable: 'it is quite for me as if the authors of our being and guardians of our youth had virtually said to us but one thing, directed our course but by one word, though constantly repeated: Convert, convert, convert! [...] We were to convert and convert, success—in the sense that was in the general air—or no success; and simply everything that should happen to us, every contact, every impression and every experience we should know, were to form our soluble stuff; with only ourselves to thank should we remain unaware, by the time our perceptions were decently developed, of the substance finally projected and most desirable' (*Autobiography*, p. 123).

Ford, however, is more anxious about amnesia: He starts publishing his earlier memoirs when he's worried about forgetting:

I discovered quite suddenly that I was forgetting my own childhood [...] I find that my impressions of the early and rather noteworthy persons amongst whom my childhood was passed—that these impressions are beginning to grow a little dim. So I have tried to rescue them now before they go out of my mind altogether.[46]

All three writers are spurred to creativity by that sense of a great gulf, which threatens the destruction or loss of the self. The main image for this in Conrad is the sea itself. Looking into *The Mirror of the Sea*, he contemplates his own oblivion in its obliviousness of him. He braces himself, clings to the wreckage, in the hope of 'presenting faithfully.'[47] James pirouettes comically on the brink. Writing of the Clarendon Hotel, he says: 'I recover the place itself as a featureless void.'[48] This is comic about the lack of character of some hotels—it may be true that there was nothing one would want to remember, or that was worth remembering. Yet from another point of view, obviously, a memory of a real place as a 'featureless void' can scarcely be said to *be* a memory of it at all, and is, rather, a confession of failing to remember it; and a magnificent—and humorous—recovery through turning the lack of remembered features into the achieved imagination of its featurelessness. Ford works by paradox: he asserts the accuracy of his impressions, the truth of fictions, even while acknowledging their incommensurability with fact.

(ii) Evading

Albert J. Guerard comments on how the 'evasiveness' of Conrad's *A Personal Record* is 'irritating to the biographer'. But he argues that 'The autobiography exploits [...] the now perfected technique of impressionistic fiction':

It is one of Conrad's most subtly and most deliberately constructed books. And it suggests that the technique chosen for a most evasive personal record was temperamentally suited to the writer of very personal novels. The experiments in a new novelistic form also respected a deep psychic need to control and modify one's distance from experience [...] As factual autobiography *A Personal Record* is exceptionally evasive—which makes it all the truer to the temperament it proposes to express.[49]

This is particularly true (though the phrase 'modify one's distance from experience' is itself an evasion of the main issue of evasion, of how a writer might modify the experience itself), since one of the chief characteristics associated with

---

[46] Ford, *Ancient Lights* (London: Chapman and Hall, 1911), pp. vii–viii; x.
[47] Conrad, 'A Familiar Preface', *A Personal Record*, p. xxi.
[48] James, *Autobiography*, p. 53.
[49] Guerard, *Conrad the Novelist* (Cambridge, MA: Harvard University Press, 1979), pp. 3–4.

impressionism in literature is the effacement of the artist. One could wish, though, for more explicitness about what precisely the book was evading: Conrad's emotional life? His relations with his family members? His suicide attempt?

By the time Ford was writing his later reminiscences, the war, the roaring Twenties, and then the Depression had intervened, and the codes had altered. Nonetheless, he still adheres to the code of honour that branded 'kissing and telling' as taboo (the taboo that Frank Harris, say, took pleasure in violating). Yet one can nonetheless admire his candour in writing about things that people remained reluctant to confront until much more recently: in particular, the period of nervous breakdown and continental 'nerve cures' that he recounts in *Return to Yesterday*.

One could say that evasion became the central principle of James's method, too. He is notorious for his obliqueness in relation to plot, and its direct statement. James's method, which could be extrapolated from his fiction, though it didn't manifest itself in autobiography till 1913, is to liberate mind and imagination from fact. Blink and you miss the plot of a James novel. What? Gilbert Osmond and Serena Merle are involved with each other? Merton Densher and Kate Croy have plotted to marry him to Milly Theale? If these are the salient 'facts' of *The Portrait of A Lady* or *The Wings of a Dove*, we never get anything so vulgar as the direct statement of them. Instead, we get the central consciousnesses imagining their way around them, receiving nuances and hints.

James's celebrated dream of the Galerie d'Apollon in the Louvre perhaps gives a hint as to his autobiographical method. In a striking turn, James is being pursued, then turns on his pursuer. He calls it 'the most appalling yet most admirable nightmare of my life.'[50] And part of its admirableness is perhaps due to the way it expresses what he does with consciousness, memory, perception, the world, in his writing. He can turn his anxieties about the 'other', or the lost, into his relentless intellectual pursuit of them. The autobiographer—like Spencer Brydon in 'The Jolly Corner'—is both the pursuer and the pursued.

(iii) Distorting

Adam Philips, writing about autobiography in the essay called 'The Telling of Selves', says that 'memories often make us wonder about distortion', continuing about Freud:

'Constructions in analysis,' he wrote in the paper of that title, making a significant concession to the fictive nature of the project, 'can be inaccurate but sufficient.' Constructions in autobiography can be inaccurate but sufficient. The difference, of course, is

---

[50] James, *Autobiography*, pp. 196–7.

that the inaccuracy and the sufficiency are subject only to one person's criteria, however unconscious.[51]

This is a good defence of the distortions of Impressionist autobiography, or indeed of Impressionism *tout court*. But it raises the question: what are inaccurate constructions sufficient for? Psycho-analyses have at least two criteria of sufficiency: understanding a problem (interpretation) and treating it (therapy). (Contribution to psycho-analytic theory is a further criterion from the analyst's point of view.) It's less easy to say what inaccurate *autobiographical* constructions might be sufficient for. The formula seems to point to the *effect* of autobiography, whether on the autobiographer or the audience. Constructions might be sufficient to the writer's sense of self, or for the impression of the self they want to present. Or they might satisfy the kind of impressionist writer (as described by Arthur Symons, in the passage quoted as the epigraph to this chapter) who seeks beauty before truth. The problem remains that one man's beauty is another's untruth. What is sufficient for the author might seem merely inaccurate to the reader, to whose criteria a published autobiography also becomes subject.

Distortion has been identified as an issue for all three autobiographers. As Leon Edel noted:

James wrote now in the voice of his father and his brother. When he quoted from their letters he freely revised their texts, as if they needed the same retouching given his own work in the New York Edition. When his nephew Harry protested, after *Notes of a Son and Brother* was published, at this violation of William's words, Henry explained that he was showing a marked respect. His goal was to make the documents (and his own text) 'engagingly readable'; but, he admitted, 'I did instinctively regard it at last as all my truth, to do what I would with.' He subtly altered content as well. Part of the family history had to be written as art: this was why James blended two trips to Europe into one, and made his father write a letter to Emerson in stronger language than was in the original. The novelist's visual memory for detail was extraordinary [. . .][52]

That swerve from James's distortion of documents to his 'extraordinary' visual memory for detail is itself extraordinary. There is a mild desperation in praising a writer's visual rather than verbal memory, as the biographer tries to protect James from the logic of his argument, which reveals the extent to which James's 'vision' is in fact 'revision.'[53] After all, if the verifiable documents have been rewritten, what guarantee can there be that visual memories are any less transformed? (Or is that word 'extraordinary' acknowledging as much?) Edel seems genuinely ambivalent here, honestly recording the distortions while seeking to limit any damage such recording might do to the subject. Fine to alter the content of family papers if you do it 'subtly'; if you make 'art' out of 'family history'.

---

[51] Adam Phillips, *On Flirtation* (London: Faber, 1994), p. 73.

[52] Leon Edel, *Henry James: A Life* (New York: Harper & Row, 1985), pp. 672–3.

[53] See Philip Horne, *Henry James and Revision* (Oxford: Clarendon, 1990).

Zdzisław Najder is similarly exercised by distortion in Conrad's autobiographic work; though he somewhat evasively characterizes it as 'evasion':

This evasion is superbly characteristic of the author's personal presence in *The Mirror*. The book is not an autobiography in the sense of a factual report. When we try to pin down biographical data and connect the events described as Conrad's reminiscences with documented facts, an identification often turns out to be impossible. Many 'remembered' events simply do not have plausible counterparts in Conrad's life. Neither the risky berthing of a ship at the Circular Quay in Sydney, nor the putting another one off ground after an accidental stranding (69–70), nor many other events, including the rescue of the crew of a Danish brig in 'Initiation', can be traced to facts in Conrad's biography. He was, in spite of his protestations to the contrary (64), several times a passenger on a ship; and was master of only one seagoing vessel, although he uses the plural when mentioning his 'commands' (69). Even 'The "Tremolino"', the most insistently autobiographical piece, verily bristles with details which appear to have no basis in his own experience, or which at best are lifted from some other time and place.[54]

The suggestion that the rescue of the crew of a Danish brig described in 'Initiation' may not correspond to facts in Conrad's biography is particularly alarming. The initiation is into the 'unfathomable cruelty' of the sea, in recognizing which, Conrad can say: 'I had become a seaman at last.' The chapter ends with Conrad's captain asking him sarcastically, as was his way, 'So you have brought the boat back after all, have you?' He answers, also sarcastically: 'Yes. I brought the boat back all right, sir.' Sarcasm because, though 'the good man believed me', the statement is not true.[55] The self that brought the boat back is not the same as the one that went off to the rescue. His initiation has transformed him. But how strange if this crucial, formative experience, the one Conrad identifies as the turning point of his maritime career, the moment that made him a seaman, didn't actually happen to him!

The defence might be that his other initiation—into the life of a novelist—which he describes in *A Personal Record*—has turned him into a self that produces fictions, and this is merely an example: a beautiful and meaningful, but fictional, account of initiation and transformation. That, of course, is the Fordian, impressionist defence. But the kind of evasion being suggested here is a much more problematic one than Ford's generally more overt and playful fabulation. Najder's discussion of *The Mirror* continues by distancing itself from these questions of veracity:

All that is, however, of interest mainly to Conrad's biographers. For the common reader *The Mirror of the Sea* emanates a vision of its author and his life: not reconstructed, but re-imagined, re-created; a life emotionally and intellectually coherent and meaningful.[56]

---

[54] Najder, *Conrad in Perspective: Essays on Art and Fidelity* (Cambridge: Cambridge University Press, 1997), pp. 98–9.
[55] Conrad, *The Mirror of the Sea* [and] *A Personal Record* (London: Dent, 1975), pp. 137, 142, 147–8.
[56] Najder makes similar claims for *A Personal Record*: 'All departures from factual truth are explainable by reference to this basic idea, to that underlying need: to impress coherence on his life

While I agree with this, I am struck by the claim that autobiography's fidelity to fact is irrelevant to 'the common reader'; not least because the book it appears in here is subtitled 'Essays on Art and Fidelity'. What is that 'Fidelity' that Conrad so insists upon in his autobiography if it doesn't involve fidelity to fact? What stops that 'vision' of Conrad's life—re-imagined and re-created out of experiences Conrad either didn't have, or didn't have when and where he said he did— from being a hallucination, or delusion? Likewise the vision's coherence and meaningfulness. Paranoid belief-systems, after all, are characterized by excessive, or abnormal, coherence and meaningfulness, not by their absence.

But then coherence is all that an impressionist autobiographer can claim, or wants to claim. Philosophers distinguish between the coherence theory of truth (in which the truth of a statement is a function of its coherence with the totality of other statements making up our knowledge of the world), and the correspondence theory of truth (in which the truth of a statement is a function of its correspondence to the world, or to a fact in the world). From the point of view of the reader, any autobiography can only aspire to the coherence theory, since so much of its correspondence with facts (the facts of feeling) cannot be verified by anyone but the writer. Rousseau was the first autobiographer to articulate this explicitly, arguing that what his *Confessions* needed to be true to was his feelings, his subjectivity.[57] Rousseau's defence against his modern scholars who challenge his fidelity to chronology would be that the significant truth of his *Confessions* lies elsewhere. Yet this argument concedes that any factual content is liable to fictionalization.

Ford too has been accused of distortion, notably by Arthur Mizener, who wrote in his biography:

The pain of living with his own divided nature was unendurable to Ford, and he spent much of his life and his imaginative energy inventing an alternative and more flattering image of himself that he could endure; the major source of the romancing Ford did all his life lies here.[58]

James is more knowing and ironic about his desire to impose meanings, to select, and to transform. He says of his childhood friend Napier: 'He vanishes, and I dare say I but make him over, as I make everything.'[59] David Kirby claims that this 'is neither more nor less than what any writer of autobiography does; what makes James unique in this respect is his candid willingness to discuss how he

[. . .]': *Conrad in Perspective*, pp. 107–8. And, as Keith Carabine observes (in conversation, 23 April 2002), Conrad himself says as much at the end of 'A Familiar Preface', p. xxi: quoted in the Conclusion, p. 518.

[57] See for example Rousseau, *The Confessions*, trans. J. M. Cohen (Harmondsworth: Penguin, 1975), p. 262.

[58] Mizener, *The Saddest Story: A Biography of Ford Madox Ford* (London: The Bodley Head, 1972), p. xv.

[59] James, *Autobiography*, p. 227.

"makes over" reality.'[60] Well, not quite unique, as we shall see. These three categories of separation between fact and impression assume that facts can be established, as public or documented facts can sometimes be established by biographers. But with the 'inner life' the facts of consciousness do not have a comparable self-presence, stability, or public verifiability. The paradoxical quest of impressionist autobiography is not to see how much it can pull the wool over our eyes, but to make us see this radical subjectivity of our experience, while also trying to make us see some of that experience.

INSIDE OUT

Impressionist autobiography is the story of the mind's impressions. In autobiography, if the self is represented, as Hume puts it, as 'a bundle or collection of different perceptions, which succeed each other with an inconceivable rapidity, and are in a perpetual flux and movement', then there appears to be nothing to the self *other* than the impressions that compose it.[61] This is the fear that impressionist autobiography both courts and needs to fend off. It must remain true to the psychological fact of the consciousness being subject to the stream of impressions; but it worries that the traditional notion of the self as coherent, intelligible, distinct, willing, disappears: is unwoven among its perceptions.

When, in his classic essay of 1884, 'The Art of Fiction', Henry James described the kind of experience and consciousness he wanted writing to represent, this tension is apparent:

Experience is never limited, and it is never complete; it is an immense sensibility, a kind of huge spider-web of the finest silken threads suspended in the chamber of consciousness, and catching every air-borne particle in its tissue.[62]

The fineness and exhaustiveness of such a sensibility compel him. Yet if experience is never limited or complete, then the consciousness that has the experience will be equally resistant to delimitation or definition. It is an undefined void, a 'chamber'—a term we may recall from Walter Pater, who wrote anxiously of the 'narrow chamber of the individual mind'; and who foresaw this problem (or rather, perhaps he derived it from Hume's definition of the self) of how the preoccupation with impressions tended to deconstruct the self. James was perfectly aware of this paradox whereby impressionism leads to a kind of depersonalization; that concentration on the intimate generates obscurity. In a fine essay,

---

[60] David K. Kirby, 'Henry James: Art and Autobiography', *Dalhousie Review*, 52:4 (1972–73), 637–44 (p. 638).

[61] Hume, *A Treatise of Human Nature*, ed. L. A. Selby-Bigge, 2nd edn (Oxford: Oxford University Press, 1983), p. 252.

[62] Henry James, 'The Art of Fiction' (1884), in *Literary Criticism: Essays on Literature: American Writers: English Writers* (New York: Library of America 1984), p. 52.

'Henry James and the Fiction of Autobiography', Millicent Bell points to the crucial passage that comes two-thirds of the way through the second of his volumes of autobiography, *Notes of a Son and Brother*. In it, James talks of how:

The personal history, as it were, of an imagination, a lively one, of course, in a given and favorable case, had always struck me as a task that a teller of tales might rejoice in, his advance through it conceivably causing at every step some rich precipitation—unless it be rather that the play of strong imaginative passion, passion strong enough to be, for its subject or victim, the very interest of life, constitutes in itself an endless crisis.[63]

James realizes that he is himself this subject that he seeks:

It happened for me that he *was* belatedly to come, but that he was to turn up then in a shape almost too familiar at first for recognition, the shape of one of those residual substitutes that engage doubting eyes the day after the fair. He had been with me all the while, and only too obscurely and intimately—I had not found him in the market as an exhibited or *offered* value. I had in a word to draw him forth from within rather than meet him in the world before me, the more convenient sphere of the objective, and to make him objective, in short, had to turn nothing less than myself inside out. What was *I* thus, within and essentially, what had I ever been and could I ever be but a man of imagination at the active pitch?[64]

'What was *I* thus, within and essentially'? One effect of this extraordinary image, of turning the self inside out, is to make the self look strange and unrecognizable: 'other' indeed. Turning one's self inside out captures the sense of making private interiority publicly visible—an increasingly important aspect of autobiography, as we have seen, when it aspires to express the 'inner life'. And, as Laura Marcus shows, this trope of 'inside out' has persisted both in autobiography and autobiography criticism.[65] Positing the self as something that can be turned inside out gives us the image of it as a kind of receptacle. But the turning of it inside out, while it may reveal the contents—the memories and impressions, the substance—for our inspection, has other odd effects. It releases those contents from the self, detaching them, and leaving us with a 'self' that seems oddly self-less or dematerialized. The impressions dwindle to virtually nothing by contrast with the creative mind that quests after them, and is often baffled: so what we get is how the mind makes something out of nothing or very little. That is, instead of dwelling in the grace of memory's epiphanies, James gives us the process of autobiographical self-construction. His reminiscences render an imaginary self-portrait in the sense that they show the imagination playing over, and making over, the past; beginning to fictionalize it.

---

[63] James, *Autobiography*, p. 454. See Millicent Bell, 'Henry James and the Fiction of Autobiography', pp. 466–7.

[64] James, *Autobiography*, p. 455. Proust's enabling revelation offers a similar moment of inversion: 'And I understood that all these materials for a work of literature were simply my past life [. . .]'. *Time Regained*, p. 267.

[65] Laura Marcus, *Auto/biographical Discourses* (Manchester: Manchester University Press, 1994), pp. 246–51.

The image of turning oneself inside out perhaps also suggests reading the self as like a book, that can be opened out: an aesthetic paradox George Moore invokes (whereby life imitates art): 'One reads one's past life like a book out of which some pages have been torn and many mutilated . . . .'[66]

Either way, the image of the inside-out self stands as a figure for the paradoxical effect of impressionist autobiography: the promised revelation of self in the end feels more like an effacement or dispersal of self. Impressionist formal autobiography is thus potentially a contradiction in terms. As we saw, the Paterian self produces instead manifestos for subjectivity, or its imaginary portraits. Impressionism in literature tends towards plotlessness. But impressionist novelists or autobiographers need to try to tell a story; to turn the flux of impressions into a coherent narrative. James's phrase 'teller of tales' recognizes that this project lends itself to fictionalization. Indeed the whole plot projected here, whereby the artist wants to tell the story of an artist who is someone other than him, then realizes he can tell his own story, is itself a turning inside out of the more expected trope, according to which we find the writer's autobiography within their fiction (by reading it as 'autobiograph*ical*'); whereas James finds the fiction he's seeking inside his autobiography. It is, approximately, the plot of 'The Jolly Corner'. To turn it around, one could say that while James talks of turning the inside out, what his account of that realization also does is the opposite—turning the outside into the inside, a story that was to have been an imaginary portrait, into a portrait of his own imagination.

Pater's impressionist vision of 'that continual vanishing away, that strange, perpetual weaving and unweaving of ourselves' cannot but generate an anxiety that won't go away that the self will go away.[67] Much of the work discussed in this book can be seen as a confronting of this anxiety: a contemplation of the processes by which the self is woven, and of the corollary, that the perpetual process of weaving proceeds by a simultaneous unweaving. Once impressions are located at the centre of the self, the self seems no longer to have a centre; to have become suddenly and disturbingly volatile and numinous. One way James, like the other two authors, negotiates this problem is through the effect of 'voice'. The self that is dispersed in terms of content of impressions, is recuperated through the felt personality of a distinctive style. As Leon Edel wrote: 'One hears the personal voice in every line of *A Small Boy and Others*; by degrees what is built up for us is the development of an artistic sensibility and the growth of an imagination.'[68] This, indeed, is exactly the kind of story impressionist autobiographies tell. What they can't do is tell it with the same confidence in organic process, and of the self-presence of the self that develops, as could authors like Wordsworth, or even Ruskin.

[66] *Hail and Farewell*, ed. Richard Cave (Gerrrards Cross, Bucks: Colin Smythe, 1985), p. 224.
[67] Pater, 'Conclusion', *The Renaissance* (London: Macmillan, 1913), pp. 248–9.
[68] Edel, *Henry James: A Life*, pp. 672–3.

Instead, they tell it in terms of intertextuality. Ford's autobiographical volume *Return to Yesterday* (1931) begins 'Thinking of Henry James', and soon moves on to his 'oldest literary recollection'—reading Kipling while on a train running into Rye station. It is an exploration—as is characteristic of many literary autobiographies—of how the subject became a writer, and how this process is catalysed by the experience of reading; how, in short, it is writing that makes up the writer.[69] More specifically, impressionist autobiography is at least in part the story of how the author becomes an impressionist. This story is central to James's volumes of autobiography. The project began as what James called a 'Family Book', but he said he had 'overflowed so much more than I intended about my babyhood and the few years after in the Small Boy that all that latter and more important part got crowded out.'[70] Instead, the centre is very much James's own consciousness, and what made impressions upon him.

The story of how the author becomes an impressionist is also the burden of Conrad's second volume of reminiscences, *A Personal Record*. It tells the story of his first novel, *Almayer's Folly*, and where and how it got carried about with him while he was trying to finish it. Because it is the account of how he gave up the life of the sea for the life of the mind, the story of that manuscript is the story of his initiation into the writer's life, as much as *The Mirror of the Sea* was the story of his initiation as a seaman.[71]

A Personal Record begins with 'A Familiar Preface' in which Conrad expresses a scepticism about the dangers of self-delusion that beset anyone who approaches autobiography impressionistically:

the danger lies in the writer becoming the victim of his own exaggeration, losing the exact notion of sincerity, and in the end coming to despise truth itself as something too cold, too blunt for his purpose—as, in fact, not good enough for his insistent emotion.[72]

This may be a veiled rebuke to Ford (the two men had fallen out two years previously), since it was written soon after the publication of Ford's first volume of memoirs, also in 1911, *Ancient Lights*, which Conrad had ordered in March, and in which Ford announced the radical version of impressionism that came to characterize his work:

This book, in short, is full of inaccuracies as to facts, but its accuracy as to impressions is absolute [. . .] I don't really deal in facts, I have for facts a most profound contempt. I try to give you what I see to be the spirit of an age, of a town, of a movement. This can not be done with facts.[73]

---

[69] See Saunders, 'A Life in Writing: Ford Madox Ford's Dispersed Autobiographies', *Antæus*, 56 (1986), 47–69.

[70] James to Louise Walsh, 23 June 1913: *Henry James: A Life in Letters*, ed. Philip Horne (London: Allen Lane, 1999), p. 526.

[71] See Karl, *Joseph Conrad: The Three Lives* (London: Faber and Faber, 1979).

[72] *A Personal Record*, p. xviii.

[73] The breach was in 1909 over Ford's affair with Violet Hunt, and was irreparable; though they met occasionally up to the war, and again just before Conrad's death, the meetings were of Ford's

Yet Conrad had been making similar criticisms to and about Ford since 1909. So Ford's declaration of independence from facts—also from the prefatory section of his reminiscences—could well be his response to Conrad's view of the need for restraint. Either way, Ford presents a fundamentally opposed view, which looks back to the period he is writing about, of the Wildean paradoxical aesthetes, avowing an extreme form of Paterian impressionism. And it was published two years before James, in *A Small Boy and Others*, wrote of how his memory made everything over.

'A Familiar Preface' suggests that to write autobiographically was, for Conrad, to engage in a struggle to maintain his grip on himself; to keep himself from submerging in what he called 'the chaos of my sensations': 'I have a positive horror of losing even for one moving moment that full possession of myself which is the first condition of good service'; and of good memoirs, we might add.[74] For Conrad the danger of autobiography is that imagination prevails over fact; yet one cannot do without imagination to realize, to render, to make one see the facts of the past. This is where the logic of impressionism and aestheticism points. Yet against what he saw as a nightmare of self-fictionalizing, Conrad asserts his ideal of 'Fidelity'.

Does Ford also then do 'what any writer of autobiography does': or is he doing something different? He certainly seems to have been an unusually fertile fictionalizer of his own and others' lives. Many of his friends, and his readers, have found this exhilarating and entertaining. One difference is that he writes different versions, as we saw with Wyndham Lewis's diatribe. In fact he gives at least six different accounts of that episode in different contexts.[75] In one sense this is what any anecdotalist does, telling favourite stories over and over, adapting them to their audience, experimenting with how to improve them. But such retelling is also how the fiction-writer experiments with techniques. When Ford says that because he was so involved in Conrad's work:

he could not disentangle to his own satisfaction which version of a semi-autobiographic story, like *Heart of Darkness*, was the printed story, which the preparation for the printed story, as Conrad told it to the writer, which the version that Conrad told for the pleasure of chance hearers and which was, as it were, the official autobiographic account.[76]

it was not to impugn the veracity of any of the versions, but to bear witness to Conrad's myriad-mindedness and devotion to his craft. In such remarks, Ford

seeking, and Conrad appears to have preserved his distance. Conrad to Ford, 29 March 1911: *Collected Letters of Joseph Conrad*, ed. Karl and Davies, vol. 4 (Cambridge: Cambridge University Press, 1990), p. 434. Knowles, *A Conrad Chronology*, p. xxi. Ford, *Ancient Lights*, pp. xv–xvi.

[74] Conrad, Letter to Edward Garnett, 19 June 1896: *Collected Letters of Joseph Conrad*, vol. 1, p. 288. 'A Familiar Preface', *A Personal Record*, p. xvii.

[75] The other versions are in 'On Impressionism', *Poetry and Drama*, 2 (Dec. 1914), 324; 'Thus to Revisit: IV. New Forms for the Old', *Piccadilly Review* (13 Nov. 1919), 6; *Thus to Revisit* (London: Chapman & Hall, 1921), pp. 139–40; *The March of Literature* (London: Allen & Unwin, 1939), p. 583.

[76] Ford, *Joseph Conrad* (London: Duckworth, 1924), pp. 94–5.

crucially also acknowledges that that is what he is doing. To tell multiple versions fosters something other than realism: it produces relativity, provisionality, in a word—impressionism. 'One shouldn't write *one* autobiography', as the French psychoanalyst J.-B. Pontalis put it, 'but ten of them or a hundred because, while we have only one life, we have innumerable ways of recounting that life (to ourselves).'[77] Or to others. Certainly Ford's sense of Conrad as both a man and a writer was (as we saw in Chapter 4) of someone who—very like himself—would 'romance a little when he talks of himself. Then that romance becomes part of himself and is the true truth.'[78] One might juxtapose this with James describing his father's respect for 'the true truth' as opposed to facts or details, which he treated with a contempt comparable to Ford's:

Delighting ever in the truth while generously contemptuous of the facts, so far as we might make the difference—the facts having a way of being many and the truth remaining but one—he held that there would always be enough; since the truth, the true truth, was never ugly and dreadful, and we didn't and wouldn't depart from it by any cruelty or stupidity [. . . .][79]

For all three writers, then, the 'true truth' of poetized autobiography transforms contemptible fact. Perhaps this is what it means to include in your reminiscences experiences that didn't happen, or didn't happen to you. Of course, all family narrative traditions do something like this. It is in part, perhaps, a form of wishful thinking; or a way of wishfully affecting other people's thinking. As Adam Phillips asks in his meditation on autobiography and psychoanalysis: 'What is the version of yourself that you present organized to stop people thinking about you? What are the catastrophes associated with your repressed repertoire of life-stories?'[80] But it is also a testimony to the effect of narrative, whether told by families or read in the books that make the strongest impression: impressions change; they contribute to the self; become the self; and thus change the self. The romance, as Ford said, becomes 'the true truth'.

Like James, Ford acknowledges the fictionality of his procedures; as when he says: 'Well, the lay reader should understand that *our* tongues really do follow our pens when we are engaged in writing the specious lies on which our existence depends.'[81] There is perhaps an integrity in such recognition of the disintegrity of impressionist autobiography. Ford's is a paradoxical strategy which manages to express both Conradian panic and Jamesian comic exuberance. He denies the force of facts, but couples this with intimations of the counter-factuality of the impressions that replace them. He is disturbed by the discrepancy between fact

---

[77] Pontalis, *Love of Beginnings*, trans. James Greene with Marie-Christine Réguis (London: Free Association Books, 1993), p. xv. Also see Adam Phillips, *On Flirtation* (London: Faber, 1994), p. 73.
[78] Ford, 'The Other House', *New York Herald Tribune Books* (2 October 1927), 2.
[79] *Autobiography*, p. 126.
[80] Phillips, 'The Telling of Selves', *On Flirtation* (London: Faber, 1994), p. 72.
[81] Ford, *Joseph Conrad*, pp. 157–8.

and impression, but converts his unease into agile play: into *multiple* versions (like Monet painting Rouen cathedral under different lights). He tries to recapture the uncertainty, catching the mind's doubleness when it cannot quite square its impressions with what it knows (which is also one of the best things in his fiction).

Our three degrees of separation between fact and impression—forgetting, evading, and distorting—are all ways in which autobiography could be said to begin to fictionalize. It is the third degree—distortion—which became increasingly important in twentieth-century literary autobiography. Another way of putting this is to say that in twentieth-century autobiography the distinction between autobiography and fiction gets blurred more overtly and playfully than in turn-of-the-century autobiografiction. Yet although all three writers (like most autobiographers!) perform all three, and although James's and Ford's attitudes to these degrees of separation between fact and impression are especially conducive to fictionalization, the autobiographies of all three remain ultimately within the conventions of formal autobiography. If they all display autobiografictional tendencies, they are not, ultimately, autobiografiction, either in the forms we have been encountering it around the turn of the century, or in which we shall encounter it in modernism. Rather, just as impressionism in painting or in fiction can be seen as developing out of an unease with realism, so impressionist autobiography, like autobiografiction, develops out of an unease with an autobiographical realism. They are simply parallel responses to this unease, both running right through the period. From 'Mark Rutherford' to Gertrude Stein, autobiografiction reconfigures autobiography towards fiction. From Ruskin to Ford, impressionist autobiography atomizes it into impressions.

The distinction is not and cannot be absolute, certainly. Formal autobiographies can be novelistic, and often include flights of fiction. A novel may be autobiographical. Autobiografiction often incorporates lived fact. In terms of content, that is, fact and fiction can coexist in all three. In terms of form, though, the distinction is clearer. These impressionist autobiographies do not perform the displacement of person found in the pseudonymous, anonymous, or third-person forms of Chapter 3.[82] Even if they approach the idea of the imaginary portrait or imaginary self-portrait, as I have suggested, they are not what Pater meant by the term: portraits of purely imaginary people. Nor do they thread real spiritual experiences on a fictional autobiographical narrative, as in Reynoldsian autobiografiction. The distinction is effectively a reprise of that between 'aesthetic autobiography' and autobiografiction made in Chapter 2; indeed, just as Ruskin can be described as an impressionist in his own practice (if not in his pictorial tastes), our impressionist autobiographers could equally be described as producing 'aesthetic autobiography' in their focus on aesthetic development, were it not for the desire of their authors to distance themselves from aestheticism as a movement.

---

[82] Though some of Ford's reminescential books do. *Joseph Conrad* uses the third person; *No Enemy* (New York; Macaulay, 1929) the third person and two pseudonyms.

The attempt to distinguish impressionist autobiography from autobiografiction in these ways may appear to characterize the former as formally conservative; less advanced in its experiments with generic hybridity. That would be misleading. The view of literary impressionism as a transitional mode, going beyond realism but not quite achieving modernism, may make sense in terms of fictional techniques—*What Maisie Knew* is less fragmented and obscure than *Heart of Darkness*, for example, which is in turn less experimental and technically dazzling than *Ulysses*. Yet from another point of view, impressionism's experiments in literature are not less advanced—merely different.

The final way in which Ford's autobiographical practice eventually differed from those of James and Conrad, and arguably became something other than impressionist autobiography, is when he effects a different kind of displacement: one of genre, when he publishes reminiscential books but claims they are novels. His memoir *Joseph Conrad: A Personal Remembrance*—in which he outlines their impressionist theory of the novel—proved the most controversial example; his pre-emptive categorizing it as itself a novel, written according to their theory, did little to avert criticisms from Conrad's widow and friends of the unreliability of conversations they cannot have witnessed.[83] Yet it is now seen not only as a valuable treatise on the techniques of fiction, but as a pioneering work of metafiction.[84] Ford repeated the strategy of calling his autobiography fiction in his two late and best volumes of memoirs: *Return to Yesterday*, dealing with his life before the war, and *It Was the Nightingale*, dealing with his recovery after it, and life among the expatriate modernists in Paris and Provence. Other impressionist autobiographies have been described as novels; such as George Moore's, or Frank Harris's; but that is usually a pejorative ascription made by others, and intended to denigrate their value as autobiography. Adeline R. Tintner argues that James's memoirs 'represent a new form of fiction, creative autobiography'; and that 'He himself wrote that his autobiography was a new kind of "experimental" novel.'[85] But while I agree with her conclusion—that James's *Autobiography* should be read alongside Proust and Joyce—the remarks she quotes from James certainly emphasize the aesthetic qualities of what he calls his 'book'; his 'artistic ideal', he says, is 'so literary, so compositional'—she does not produce evidence of his actually claiming it as fiction.[86] Whereas the trope Ford was using in the 1920s and 1930s is what many literary autobiographers have done since. Witness P. D. James:

---

[83] Ford, *Joseph Conrad*, p. 6.

[84] See Joseph Wiesenfarth, 'Ford's *Joseph Conrad: A Personal Remembrance* as Metafiction: Or, How Conrad Became an Elizabethan Poet', *Renascence*, 53:1 (2000), 43–60.

[85] Adeline R. Tintner, 'Autobiography as Fiction: "The Usurping Consciousness" as Hero of James's Memoirs', *Twentieth Century Literature*, 23:2 (1977), 239–60 (p. 239).

[86] Ibid., pp. 242–3.

And the past is not static. It can be relived only in memory, and memory is a device for forgetting as well as remembering. It, too, is not immutable It rediscovers, reinvents, reorganizes. Like a passage of prose it can be revised and repunctuated. To that extent, every autobiography is a work of fiction and every work of fiction an autobiography.[87]

It is a trope that turns impressionist autobiography further towards, or into, auto/biografiction.

---

[87] James, P. D., *Time to be in Earnest: A Fragment of Autobiography* (New York and Toronto: Knopf, 2000), p. xi.

PART II

MODERNIST AUTO/BIOGRAFICTION

7

Heteronymity I: Imaginary Authorship and Imaginary Autobiography: Pessoa, Joyce, Svevo

'It was this art of making one's self invisible that I considered most important and coveted most deeply . . . thus it happened later on, long after I had grown up and was practising the calling of a writer, that I frequently tried to disappear behind my creations, to rechristen myself and hide behind playfully contrived names . . .'[1]

MODERNISM AND AUTO/BIOGRAPHY?

Several of the writers discussed so far are considered modernist, especially Proust, James, Conrad, and Ford. They are sometimes seen as early modernist, or as transitional figures, working on the cusp between modernism and what preceded it, whether realism, naturalism, aestheticism, or impressionism. It has been central to my argument (following Jesse Matz) that we need to recognize the persistence of impressionism through modernism; and (where I depart from Matz) that this is nowhere more pronounced than in modernism's engagements with life-writing. With the main writers discussed in Part II of this book—Joyce, Stein, Pound, Lewis, Aldington, and Woolf—we encounter a later generation of modernists, and figures seen as central to any account of modernist literature in English. Yet the standard accounts of modernism, from the manifesto-writing of modernists themselves, have tended to articulate modernism as a negation of previous forms, techniques, and theories, not least with the two areas central to this study: impressionism and life-writing.

My discussion of Woolf's impressionism in the last chapter aimed to show that, in her case at least, impressionism and modernism co-exist—that her modernism is bound up with her rethinking of how to narrate impressions. Woolf is central to Matz's study *Literary Impressionism and Modernist Aesthetics*

---

[1] Hermann Hesse, 'Childhood of the Magician', in *Autobiographical Writings*, ed. T. Ziolkowski (London: Jonathan Cape Ltd, 1973), p. 5.

too. But otherwise it may still seem controversial to argue for an impressionist modernism. Matz, for example, says that Joyce and Lawrence are not impressionists, because impressionism involves the idea of some kind of mediation (as between body and mind), whereas they both 'seem fairly happy to believe that the body thinks.'[2] As will be clear from my discussion of Joyce in this chapter, I believe *Portrait* might incorporate a level of mediation rarely suspected. And given Joyce's hyper-consciousness of his medium in the parodic repertoires of *Ulysses* and the semantic games of *Finnegans Wake* he makes an implausible apostle of immediacy. Lawrence, it is true, may have dreamed of unmediated feeling. But what comes across in the baffled texture of his experiments of writing the passional is precisely his frustration that the medium never can escape mediation. To convey how he thinks the body thinks, he has consciously to use language. And in any case, he voiced a different objection to Impressionism in painting—that it was a doomed attempt to escape from the physical body into a realm of light.[3] If the relation between modernism and impressionism is still controversial, that between modernism and life-writing is more so. Modernists repeatedly announce the quest for objectivity, concreteness, impersonality, self-effacement. The best known such announcement is Eliot's seminal essay (already touched on in Chapter 1) 'Tradition and the Individual Talent' (1919), which likens the poet to a platinum catalyst; it says of poetry that it 'is not a turning loose of emotion, but an escape from emotion; it is not the expression of personality, but an escape from personality'; and argues that it gains its significance from its relation not to the artist's self, but to the 'tradition' of earlier works by others.[4] The implications of this argument will be explored in this and later chapters. What needs emphasizing here is the immense influence of these formalist views, which shaped the development of Practical Criticism in England and the New Criticism in America. According to their canons, critics should not try to relate literary works to their writers, whether to understand the work in terms of the life, or the life in terms of the work. To do so was to be guilty of the 'Biographical Fallacy.'[5] It followed from Eliot's argument that 'the more perfect the artist, the more completely separate in him will be the man who suffers and the mind which creates', that works which could be read as revealing 'the man who suffers' would be less than perfect art. 'Modernism and Auto/biography' thus seemed a non-subject for anyone but the historian of mediocrity.

Certainly the modernists who were generally taken during the third quarter of the twentieth century to be the canonical figures—Joyce, Eliot, Pound, and

---

[2] Matz, *Literary Impressionism and Modernist Aesthetics* (Cambridge: Cambridge University Press, 2001), pp. 243–4.

[3] Lawrence, *Phoenix*, ed. Edward D. McDonald (London: Heineman, 1936), p. 563.

[4] Eliot, 'Tradition and the Individual Talent', *Selected Essays* (London: Faber and Faber, 1951), p. 21.

[5] See Donald J. Winslow, *Life-writing: A Glossary of Terms in Biography, Autobiography, and Related Forms* (Hawaii: University of Hawaii Press, 1995), p. 7.

Lawrence—did not write their memoirs. Nor did they write biographies of others (with the possible exception of Pound's *Gaudier-Brzeska: A Memoir* (1916), which is more manifesto for Vorticism than conventional life-narrative).

Nowadays, however, this seems a reductive view, only tenable according to a very narrow conception of whom or what modernism involved. Its impact on literary studies might seem surprising, but is perhaps best explained by the influence exerted by Leavis's disciples in English teaching in schools, in an uneasy alliance with subsequent critiques of individualism: Marxism; later developments of formalism into structuralism; post-structuralism's deconstruction of the whole idea of subjectivity.

The tide turned in the 1970s, which ushered in the rebirth of studies in life-writing, though for somewhat contradictory reasons. Post-structuralist theorists such as De Man and Hartman turned their attention to autobiographical texts, while feminist and postcolonial scholars saw it as a political imperative to recover the written experience of the marginalized. New Historicism and the New Bibliography have also had parts to play in the rehabilitation of auto/biography. Though their emphases are on social energies and cultural institutions rather than individuals, their methods, studying the structures of everyday life, and day-by-day developments in the production of texts as authors negotiate with publishers and editors, are often meticulously biographical. Finally, postmodernism, too, has contributed to auto/biography's return, but again for different reasons. Its relativism has ushered in a new subjectivism; but a less anxious, more celebratory and playful version of it than the anxious Victorian one. Postmodern theories of subjectivity as constituted through narrative, combined with its scepticism about both subjectivities and about grand narratives, have renewed the sense of the indistinguishability of autobiography and fiction; and thus also the energies of autobiografiction.

What this recent work lets us see clearly now is how the New Critical view that modernism and auto/biography were inimical is wrong in two respects. First, modernists did write auto/biography—which isn't just to say that they wrote *autobiographically*. Many modernists did produce full-length autobiographies and biographies. We have seen Ford's memoir of Conrad, and his, Conrad's and James's autobiographies (James also wrote a biography, of William Wetmore Story, and a biographical study of Hawthorne). Wyndham Lewis wrote two volumes of autobiography—*Blasting and Bombardiering* (1937) and *Rude Assignment* (1950); Richard Aldington wrote one, *Life for Life's Sake* (1941); Jean Rhys died leaving *Smile Please* (1979) unfinished. Aldington also wrote several biographical books, as did E. M. Forster; Woolf wrote a life of Roger Fry (1940). Second, even when they weren't writing auto/biography, modernists were engaging with it: reinventing it, playing formal games with it, criticizing it. That engagement is the subject of Part II.

To illustrate both points, let us consider the situation a decade after the *annus mirabilis* of high modernism in 1922. Subscribers to the *Atlantic Monthly* in

1933 might have noticed something striking as they looked through the issues for that year. The centrepiece, perhaps, was Gertrude Stein's *Autobiography of Alice B. Toklas*, published in four instalments between May and August. That over-lapped with Virginia Woolf's *Flush*—her extraordinary biography of Elizabeth Barrett Browning's spaniel—which ran in the *Atlantic* from July to October. These two works, now established as classics of feminist modernism, are also amongst the most radical experiments in modernist life-writing too: a fictional autobiography purported to be written by a real person, and mainly about another real person, who in fact wrote it. And a biography of a real subject, who just happened not to be human, and which at every moment makes us aware of the games it is playing with the conventions of biography.

It is something of a coincidence that placed in the same bound volume on the library shelves these two works, applying modernist experiment to those forms that modernists often seem most to set their teeth against: autobiography and biography. Yet the *Atlantic* for 1933 contains a remarkable density of significant pieces that can be grouped together under the heading of life-writing:

'Three Days to See'. By Helen Keller.
'Confessions of a Novelist'. By Edith Wharton.
'A Civil War Boyhood'. Serial By John W. Burgess. Parts 1 and 2.
'Contrasts'. By Ford Madox Ford. [Reminiscences of Galsworthy and Moore.]
'Autobiography of an Ex-Feminist'. By Worth Tuttle.
'Christs in the Tirol'. By D. H. Lawrence.

In other words, a striking proportion of this literary magazine consists of life-writing; and much of it is by major modernist authors experimenting with the forms and boundaries of biography and autobiography. The point is not to claim any particular significance for 1933 in this respect—though other important autobiographies published that year include Vera Brittain's *Testament of Youth*, and Orwell's *Down and Out in Paris and London*. Other years could just as well be proposed as producing constellations of experimental life-writing just as significant. 1919, for example, which saw May Sinclair's *Mary Olivier: A Life*, and Max Beerbohm's *Seven Men*. Or 1922, when the last volume of Proust's *A la recherche* was published, as was Woolf's first really modernist novel, *Jacob's Room*. Or 1928, when Jean Rhys's *Postures* (later *Quartet*) first appeared, as did Radclyffe Hall's *The Well of Loneliness*, and Yeats's *The Tower*, and last but far from least, Woolf's *Orlando* (discussed in Chapter 11), another biography of a fictional character, though based on a real person (Vita Sackville-West).

It might be objected that some of these works are examples of the pre-modernist form of the autobiographical novel. Alternatively, such evidence might be taken by adherents of New Criticism to prove their point, since their canonical modernists are scarcely there. But now that we tend no longer to think of modernism as so monolithic, the idea that some modernists were more engaged with life-writing than others is scarcely objectionable. If writers like

Stein, Woolf, Lewis, and Lawrence wrote life-writings, doesn't that just mean that they weren't modernists in the same way that Joyce, Eliot, and Pound were? It needn't mean that Eliot, Joyce, and Pound were *better* modernists, merely different, more 'impersonal', ones. However, the argument of this chapter and the next, on Joyce and Pound, is that even when they seem most aloof from auto/biographical practice, even these modernists are profoundly concerned with it. Canonical modernism is often seen, with reason, as a reaction against the aesthete's cult of subjectivity. But the danger of this view is that it tends to obscure the ways in which the *question* of subjectivity is at the heart of works like *Portrait of the Artist*, or 'The Waste Land'. In the notes to 'The Fire Sermon', Eliot distinguishes, not entirely transparently, between 'spectator', 'character', and 'personage': 'Tiresias, although a mere spectator and not indeed a "character", is yet the most important personage in the poem, uniting all the rest [. . .] What Tiresias *sees*, in fact, is the substance of the poem.'[6] Insofar as Tiresias unites other subjectivities he might seem representative of the kind of impersonality Eliot advocated in 'Tradition and the Individual Talent'. Insofar as those other subjectivities traverse myth and history, he might seem representative of the tradition itself, just as his spectating is akin to a kind of envisioning. The idea of a prophet seeing things that haven't happened *yet* is analogous to the idea of the poet seeing things that haven't happened. Tiresias isn't the characters in the poem. He isn't the poet. But his presence in the poem raises the question of what a self is, and how the self of the seer relates to the selves of the seen; how the self of a personage relates to the personality which (according to Eliot) a poem should not seek to express. What subjectivity he might be said to have (in the myth he experiences female as well as male subjectivity) is markedly not of the conventional kind. Yet Eliot's characterization of him as a 'personage' realigns him with the discourses of subjectivity and im/personality. Furthermore, Tiresias's visions are themselves eerily expressive of a personality, or more precisely, a personality disorder. They share a tone of enervation, sexual disgust, anxiety, degradation.[7] Eliot knows that in the age of *The Interpretation of Dreams*, visions are taken for symptoms.

Thus although I agree with Robert Elbaz, who sees autobiography as 'a central practice in the discourse of modernism',[8] this is not to say that 'The Waste Land' is autobiography—whether Tiresias's or Eliot's. Tiresias is more like an allegory for the poet as described in 'Tradition and the Individual Talent': the catalyst who allows the fragmentary visions to combine into the new poem without being

---

[6] Note to line 218: *Collected Poems* (London: Faber, 1974), p. 82.

[7] See William Empson, 'My God, Man, There's Bears On It', in *Using Biography* (London: Chatto & Windus and The Hogarth Press, 1984), pp. 189–200, for a determinedly biographical reading of 'The Waste Land'.

[8] Elbaz, 'Preface' to *The Changing Nature of the Self: A Critical Study of the Autobiographic Discourse* (London: Croom Helm, 1988), p. vii.

'expressed' by them. But of course to say this is to acknowledge that the poem can be read autobiographically, to the extent that it allegorizes the poetic process.[9]

One line of criticism sees autobiography as a central practice in the discourse of feminist modernism. Suzanne Raitt, for example, argues apropos of May Sinclair, that 'autobiographical fiction (especially the female *Bildungsroman*, or novel of development) became increasingly common and popular after the First World War [...].'[10] She cites fiction by Dorothy Richardson, Katherine Mansfield, and Virginia Woolf as evidence of an increasingly confident exploration of femininity, of gender identities, and of sexuality. The achievements of the Suffragette movement, and the opportunities the war presented for women to work in what had been considered the masculine sphere, undoubtedly contributed both to the experiences women wanted to write about, and to their confidence in writing about them. The testimonial quality of the autobiographical was also important, as it would prove to be for other oppressed groups finding a voice in subsequent generations; especially with the Civil Rights and Gay Rights movements. However, though Raitt points 'especially' to female fiction, she recognizes that autobiographical fiction was written by men and women in the period. Some key works by male writers—D. H. Lawrence, Proust, Joyce— are no less autobiographical. It would be more accurate to say that autobiographical fiction had become increasingly inventive two or three decades earlier, as the previous chapters have sought to demonstrate. But where this was predominantly written by men before the war, it became increasingly written by women after it. One reason may have been that some modernists—those Lesley Higgins calls 'masculinist high modernist' writers such as Eliot and Pound—rejected the autobiographical precisely because it had come to seem increasingly associated first with male homosexual then with female writers.[11]

There were, however, other, more philosophically based objections. Modernist aesthetics reject the nineteenth-century paradigms of organicism and historicism. Neither Tiresias nor the other figures glimpsed in the poem are described in terms of progression, continuity, or evolution. Instead of a sense of the unfolding history of a whole life, we have the montage of fragments from different people, different texts, different times. Indeed, it is one of Eliot's chief poetic resources to present the individual subject not as intelligible through its developmental process (as in biography or the *Bildungsroman*), but as attaining what intelligibility it has only by being set against something larger than itself; something outside itself, outside the human, outside time. As the individual poem finds its

---

[9] Indeed, it was as allegory that Eliot was prepared to countenance auto/biographical readings. For example, in his 1926 Clark Lectures he wrote that: 'The *Vita Nuova* is to my thinking a record of actual experiences reshaped into a particular form.' Though he goes on to say: 'This is indemonstrable.' Eliot, *The Varieties of Metaphysical Poetry*, ed. Ronald Schuchard (London: Faber, 1993), p. 97.

[10] Raitt, *May Sinclair: A Modern Victorian* (Oxford: Clarendon Press, 2000), p. 17.

[11] Lesley Higgins, 'No Time for Pater: The Silenced Other of Masculinist Modernism', *Transparencies of Desire*, pp. 37–54 (p. 37). Discussed in Chapter 1.

meaning juxtaposed against the tradition, so the individual subject is juxtaposed against myth, history, and comparative religion in 'The Waste Land'; or, in 'The Love Song of J. Alfred Prufrock', against eschatology, eternity, and the relation between life and afterlife.

However, even in Eliot's case, then, what from one point of view looks like the rejection of auto/biography, from another looks like the transformation of it. This supports the claim made in Olav Severijnen's essay, 'The Renaissance of a Genre: Autobiography and Modernism', which argues that modernism represents the first major shift in the definition of autobiography since the Romantic period, as the techniques of modernist fiction and poetry get used in autobiography too:

In Modernist autobiography the narrating is no longer chronological or continuous, but we find experiments with possible forms of organizing the narration according to the subjective sense of time or timelessness.[12]

He makes a strong case for the appearance of radically new autobiographical writing in the period, based on the examples of Boris Pasternak's *Safe Conduct*, Stein's *Autobiography of Alice B. Toklas*, Walter Benjamin's *Berlin Childhood around 1900*, and Michel Leiris's *Manhood*. However, there are two problems with his analysis. First, most of the strategies he discusses—depersonalization, detachment, books describing their own genesis, violating the autobiographical pact—are also found from the 1870s, as we have seen in Part I. Similarly, while his account of the shift in the notion of 'autobiographical truth' from being ethical in Goethe's autobiography, to becoming aesthetic in Benjamin's, because it can only be found in images, not in 'sincerity', is persuasive, we have seen how this shift too occurs much earlier, at the *fin de siècle*.[13] Second, his generalizations, for all their elegance and superficial plausibility, are too reductive to accommodate the varieties either of modernism or of modern auto/biography which this study has sought to demonstrate. Thus the claim that 'Remembering and narrating are disconnected during Modernism' may ring true of Joyce or Eliot, but not of Proust.[14] It is based on the hypothesis that in modernism narrating is no longer dramatized; but that too would exclude early modernist works like Conrad's *Heart of Darkness* or Ford's *The Good Soldier*. Such texts like these, which are not autobiographies, and also ones like Proust's and Stein's which are more like autobiographies, also resist Severijnen's claim that, in modernism, 'The "self" of the protagonist becomes less important and everywhere the extra-diegetic narrator is superior to his intra-diegetic counterpart.'[15] It might, though, appear to describe Joyce's *Portrait*, in which, at least according to the normative reading, the (Joycean) extra-diegetic narrator is superior to his intra-diegetic counterpart, Stephen. But there is another way of reading *A Portrait*, as a

---

[12] Olav Severijnen, 'The Renaissance of a Genre: Autobiography and Modernism', *New Comparison*, 9 (1990), 41–59 (p. 54).
[13] Ibid., pp. 46–7.   [14] Ibid., p. 54.   [15] Ibid., p. 52.

modernist version of the 'imaginary portrait', which produces a very different sense of Joyce's engagement with auto/biography.

JOYCE'S *PORTRAIT*

Joyce's *A Portrait of the Artist as a Young Man* displays many of the characteristics of works discussed in earlier chapters. It is intensely autobiographical, though with its autobiography displaced onto the imaginary self-portrait of 'Stephen Dedalus'. *A Portrait* stays so close to Joyce's life, that from one point of view it scarcely counts as autobiografiction, as there's so little departure from verifiable fact (though there is a sense in which the aesthetic presentation of autobiography might be described as a form of fictionalization: an assimilation of autobiographical material into a novelistic shape). On the other hand, the circumstantial biographical evidence, as meticulously documented as is Dublin's geography in *Ulysses*, is nonetheless background: background first to the all-important 'epiphanies'; and then to the emergence of the artist whose vocation the epiphanies constitute. Joyce started writing pieces he called epiphanies from 1901–02 to 1904.[16] As the religious term implies, they are moments of intense visual realization—which might be redescribed as 'impressions', though they are also strong contenders for examples of the spiritual experiences Stephen Reynolds argued were the core of autobiografiction. Out of context they look like *fin-de-siècle* prose-poems. The first, and one of the more dramatic, was to be put into the context of *A Portrait*, in which it appears with the speeches almost identical, though with the whole passage recast as narrative rather than drama text:

[Bray: in the parlour of the house in Martello Terrace]
Mr Vance—(*comes in with a stick*) . . . O, you know, he'll have to apologise, Mrs Joyce.
Mrs Joyce—O yes . . . Do you hear that, Jim?
Mr Vance—Or else—if he doesn't—the eagles'll come and pull out his eyes.
Mrs Joyce—O, but I'm sure he will apologise.
Joyce—(*under the table, to himself*)
       —Pull out his eyes,
       Apologise,
       Apologise,
       Pull out his eyes.
       Apologise,
       Pull out his eyes,
       Pull out his eyes,
       Apologise.[17]

[16] Richard Ellmann, A. Walton Litz, and John Whittier–Ferguson, eds, *James Joyce: Poems and Shorter Writings* (London: Faber, 1991), p. 157.
[17] Ibid., p. 161.

In the version in *A Portrait* we learn that it was the idea of Stephen marrying the Vance's daughter Eileen that leads to his hiding under a table, whereupon it is Stephen's aunt, 'Dante' Riordan, who introduces the image of the eagles, rather than Mr Vance. *A Portrait* doesn't say, but Richard Ellmann does, that though Joyce's father and Mr Vance 'spoke half-seriously of uniting their first-born', the Vances were Protestant, and the aunt on whom Dante is based warned Joyce that he would go to hell if he played with Eileen.[18] In that context we can see that, however terrifying to the child, the gruesomeness of the threatened blinding was perhaps intended rather as mock-sadistic teasing. What comes across clearly in both versions is not only the way the haunting image impresses itself on the sensitive child, but how he withdraws into a world of language, images, and sounds to master it.

The 'spiritual' dimension of such an experience, that is to say, is not just a matter for Joyce of the force with which such episodes impinge on his mind. It is also a matter of how they presage, as they shape, his art. To say the narrative exists for the sake of the epiphanies is to pose *A Portrait* as autobiografiction. But here we have the beginnings of a different mode: not just an attempt to represent spiritual experiences, but an attempt to dramatize someone attempting to represent them. To the extent *A Portrait* does that, it seems to be doing the opposite of Reynoldsian autobiografiction. Rather than attributing the real experiences of the actual author to a fictional character, it would be presenting a fictional author writing their actual experiences autobiographically; and would thus be more like an example of the work described in Chapter 5: a fake autobiography. (Though there is a form of indeterminacy here, introduced via the paradox of basing your alter ego so closely on yourself, but giving him the name of a fictional character.) Yet Joyce—never one to rest on other's laurels—perhaps took these conventions a stage further. This chapter explores the reading of *Portrait* as an entirely fictionally authored book: as a book not only including Stephen's writing, but possibly entirely written by him.

THE ADVANTAGES AND OUTCOME OF THE FICTIONAL-AUTHOR READING

Such a reading could radically transform the received views of the novel, offering a way of negotiating a notorious critical impasse between two autobiographical interpretations, in which Joyce either (roughly) shares Stephen's views; or presents him ironically.[19] Harry Levin, for example, discusses *Portrait* as an unironically

---

[18] Ellmann, *James Joyce*, revised edition (Oxford: Oxford University Press, 1983), p. 26.

[19] See for example John Gross, *James Joyce* (New York: The Viking Press, 1972), 39–41; and Wayne Booth, *The Rhetoric of Fiction* (Chicago: University of Chicago Press, 1961), 324–36, excerpted in *James Joyce: 'Dubliners' and 'A Portrait of the Artist as a Young Man': A Casebook*, ed. Morris Beja (London and Basingstoke: Macmillan, 1979), pp. 188–200.

autobiographical *Künstlerroman*, arguing that 'Except for the thin incognito of its characters, the *Portrait of the Artist* is based on a literal transcript of the first twenty years of Joyce's life. If anything, it is more candid than other autobiographies.'[20] By contrast, Hugh Kenner was one of the most forceful proponents of the ironic reading, arguing that 'Stephen becomes, not an artist, but an esthete': 'Joyce was detached from what he was doing and understood fully that only an Icarian fall could end Stephen's flight to the Paterian never-never land.'[21] The parodic redaction of the title as 'A Poor Trait of the Art Less' in *Finnegans Wake* could be taken to support this view.[22] Yet Joyce's playing with his self-styling is equivocal here too: is he parodying the artlessness of the fictional Stephen, or his own younger authorial self? Robert Scholes also takes up this opposition between artist and aesthete, arguing against Wayne Booth's objection in *The Rhetoric of Fiction* that there is not enough ironic distance between Joyce and Stephen.[23]

This distinction misses what might be Joyce's most ingenious strategy, which is to construct a text that can be read as if it were the novel written by its protagonist, thus encapsulating the autobiographical reading (though in a fictionalized mode) within the ironic. It could thus be another example of the games we know Joyce enjoyed playing with his interpreters.[24] Debating the opposition between the autobiographical and ironic readings, John Gross argues that the book ends with an open question as to whether Stephen will fulfil his promise or not.[25] According to the fictional-author reading, the book which raises the question becomes its own answer—evidence that Stephen does fulfil his promise,

---

[20] Levin, *James Joyce: A Critical Introduction* (London: Faber, 1971), pp. 47, 50.

[21] Hugh Kenner, '*The Portrait* in Perspective', in Thomas Connolly, *Joyce's Portrait: Criticism and Critiques* (London: Peter Owen, 1964), pp. 25–60 (p. 41).

[22] See Michael Seidel, *James Joyce: A Short Introduction* (Oxford: Blackwell, 2002), p. 63 and *Finnegans Wake* (London: Faber, 1971), p. 114.

[23] Robert Scholes, 'Stephen Dedalus, Poet or Esthete?', *PMLA*, 89 (1964), 484–9. Reprinted in Robert Scholes, *In Search of James Joyce* (Urbana and Chicago: University of Illinois Press, 1992), pp. 70–81. Charles Rossman, 'Stephen Dedalus' Villanelle', *James Joyce Quarterly*, 12 (1975), 281–93, cites Wayne Booth's *The Rhetoric of Fiction* on the difficulty of interpreting the villanelle. Rossman criticizes Scholes's reading of the poem as validated by Joyce: 'The villanelle is not a serious sign of Stephen's artistry [...]', but portrays his 'self–deceptions', especially as he spiritualizes the physical basis of his passion for 'E. C.' (p. 292). This is perhaps a criticalized way of making Hugh Kenner's point, in *Dublin's Joyce* (Boston: Beacon Press, 1962), p. 123, that the composition starts after a wet dream. Robert Adams Day, 'The Villanelle Perplex: Reading Joyce', *James Joyce Quarterly*, 25 (1986), 69–85, surveys the voluminous debate about this small section of the novel, arguing that in terms of Joyce's or even Stephen's aesthetic principles, the poem is 'a hodgepodge of cliché and a farrago of nonsense' (p. 82).

[24] Hugh Kenner, for example, in *James Joyce: 'Dubliners' and 'A Portrait of the Artist as a Young Man': A Casebook*, p. 133, argues that Stephen does not become an artist, but is instead Joyce's 'meticulous pastiche of immaturity' (pp. 134–5). But the notion of 'pastiche' implies, or at least includes the possibility, that Joyce is impersonating Stephen's writing. It is immature, yes, and may even indicate that Stephen will never be the superior kind of artist Joyce is; but that doesn't mean he isn't the book's fictional author. On Joyce's games with his critics, see Kenner, 'Joyce's Anti–Selves', *Shenandoah*, 4:1 (1953), 24–41, and William Empson, 'The Ultimate Novel' (on *Ulysses*), in *Using Biography*, pp. 217–59.

[25] Gross, *James Joyce* (New York: Viking, 1970), pp. 39–41.

and becomes an artist in a different way from becoming a bad artist or becoming Joyce. *Ulysses* was to complicate this question, or at least the question of *when* Stephen might have written *Portrait*, by starting with him back in Dublin and still trying to find his way. Indeed, the later novel playfully alludes to the earlier, in the wonderful image in the 'Eumaeus' chapter of the sailor's tattoo portraying the tattooist as a young man.[26] The sailor's knack of pulling the skin to make the frowning face appear to smile suggests Stephen's seriousness can be read as comedy; or even that it was meant comically, though Joyce still leaves it open whether he is tipping us the wink that he was laughing at Stephen, or whether he is confirming that Stephen was parodying himself.

IMAGINARY PORTRAIT

One effect of the fictional-author reading is to redirect attention from the question of how autobiographical the book is, to the question of what kind of portrait it is. Joyce's novel is definitely an imaginary portrait (and also an imaginary self-portrait) in the Paterian sense: a portrait of someone given a fictional name, someone who does not exist in reality (even if they draw on characteristics of the author). According the reading proposed here, the novel would be an imaginary portrait in another sense: not just a work of art about a fictional person, but a fictional work of art about a fictional person. That is, it makes it an Imaginary Portrait of the Artist in a different sense from Pater's: not only a portrait of an imaginary artist, but an imaginary self-portrait by that imaginary artist. As Joyce's brother Stanislaus put it: Stephen is 'an imaginary, not a real, self-portrait and freely treated'; Joyce 'followed his own development closely, has been his own model and has chosen to use many incidents from his own experience' but he has also 'transformed and invented many others.'[27]

Insofar as Stephen Dedalus is not Joyce this seems at least logically possible. But to what extent can the work of portraiture be imaginary if its subject is actually based on a real author, James Joyce? Does the autobiographical dimension of *A Portrait of the Artist as a Young Man* militate against the reading of it as an imaginary work—Stephen's novel rather than Joyce's? The answer to this seems to me to be both yes and no, but with more no than yes. If Stephen is merely a cipher for Joyce, then the distinction between Stephen's novel and Joyce's is null. But if (as many readers do) you hear a note of parody in the presentation of Stephen, what happens to that autobiographical dimension? Is Joyce portraying the kind of artist he feared he might have become, but was confident he hadn't? Or is there an element of self-parody, at least of his earlier

---

[26] *Ulysses*, ed. Jeri Johnson (Oxford: Oxford University Press, 1993), pp. 586–7. I am grateful to Richard Kirkland for both these suggestions.
[27] Stanislaus Joyce, *My Brother's Keeper* (London: Faber, 1982), pp. 67, 39–40.

incarnation? This is the reading I prefer, not least because it allows us to adapt Hugh Kenner's wonderful comments on *Ulysses*, about Joyce turning himself into a parody of Bloom so as to be able to write him,[28] to argue that Stephen is another of Joyce's 'shadow-selves': an alter ego rather than mere ego: a parody of himself—as suggested by Joyce's comment (apropos of *Ulysses*) that he hadn't 'let this young man off very lightly, have I? Many writers have written about themselves. I wonder if any one of them has been as candid as I have?'[29] Here too Joyce binds apparently opposing arguments together: *Portrait* is critical of Stephen, but Stephen is a candid self-portrait. But of course the other implication of Kenner's subtle observation is that the self being portrayed is itself an imaginary work: a conscious performance of an already parodic nature. What the fictional-author reading does is extend this perception to that part of an author's self that is concerned with being an author.

ALMOST AUTOBIOGRAPHICAL

This is perhaps what Joyce meant when he told Stanislaus his 'idea for the novel': 'It is to be almost autobiographical, and naturally as it comes from Jim, satirical.'[30] 'Almost autobiographical' appears an unobtrusive, casual phrase, almost a truism about how fiction necessarily draws on the writer's life. But from another point of view it is profoundly significant. The 'almost autobiographical' is the realm of autobiografiction. The indeterminacy of the 'almost' recognizes the difficulty of demarcating what is autobiography from what is invention. To this extent it also sounds essentially modern. It's not impossible that earlier writers could have used the phrase of their own writing: but it's hard to imagine George Eliot saying it of *Middlemarch*, or Henry James of *The Ambassadors*. It even sounds a little too casual for the authors of Reynoldsian autobiografiction, who would presumably claim that the 'spiritual' dimension of their books was quintessentially autobiographical. What Joyce's comment indicates, then, as he was revising *Stephen Hero* into *A Portrait*, is that the entire notion of the 'autobiographical' had come into question in new ways. As with Reynolds, it could refer to entirely 'inner' experiences, which are true for the subject but are invisible to the public sphere. Or it could mean that the work selects some details from public life, and excludes others (as in Sassoon's *Memoirs of an Infantry Officer*). Or it could mean that the selected details were the starting point, but were transformed in the telling. Joyce might have meant any of these things had

---

[28] Kenner, 'Joyce's Anti–Selves', pp. 24–5. Discussed in Chapter 4.

[29] Frank Budgen, *James Joyce and the Making of 'Ulysses' and Other Writings* (London: Grayson and Grayson, 1934), p. 52.

[30] Stanislaus Joyce, *Complete Dublin Diary*, ed. George H. Healey (Ithaca: Cornell University Press, 1971), p. 12 (2 Feb 1904).

he said *Portrait* was 'almost autobiography'. But if the 'autobiograph*ical*' is already not quite autobiography, the 'almost autobiographical' is doubly removed. It might be objected that what Joyce was getting at was the opposite: that his book was almost entirely autobiographical; that rather than legitimating a reading of it as closer to fiction, the comment pulls against the pseudnoymity of 'Stephen Dedalus', and drags the narrative back towards autobiography. Yet the slight wrinkle in the terminology might reveal a multiplicity of perspectives: almost autobiographical insofar as it's Joyce's book; almost autobiography insofar as it's Stephen's.

It was precisely the sense of a work like *Portrait* being not quite autobiography that led me (in Chapter 2) to contest Suzanne Nalbantian's labelling of such modernist works as 'aesthetic autobiography'. Nor does it seem quite a novel, though it is almost a novel. It is a fusion of the two: a version of autobiografiction, certainly. Though it isn't quite Reynoldsian autobiografiction either, which required autobiographical 'spiritual' experiences to be threaded on a fictional narrative. Joyce's narrative is almost non-fictional. The fictionalization centres instead on the identity of the central figure.

HETERONYMS: FERNANDO PESSOA

Though I shall be looking at *A Portrait* with postmodernist eyes, it is also important to my argument to consider Joyce alongside other key modernists exploring the possibilities of imaginary writing, especially Rilke, Pessoa, Svevo, and Stein, all of whom were (in markedly different ways) extending the modernist novel through the writing of imaginary autobiography.

To read Stephen Dedalus as the book's fictional author is to read him as an example of what the great Portuguese modernist Fernando Pessoa called a 'heteronym'. In an excellent discussion of heteronymity, Kevin Jackson quotes Pessoa distinguishing 'his heteronyms from their far more vulgar cousins the pseudonyms':

A pseudonymic work is, except for the name with which it is signed, the work of an author writing as himself; a heteronymic work is by an author writing outside his own personality: it is the work of a complete individuality made up by him, just as the utterances of some character in a drama would be.[31]

Well, yes. Though there are two points at which we might demur. First, we have seen how pseudonyms such as 'Mark Rutherford' or those used by A. C. Benson verge on heteronyms. Their authors are doing something slightly different from writing as themselves. Or is the difference that a heteronym in Pessoa's sense

---

[31] Pessoa, writing in 1928, quoted in Kevin Jackson, *Invisible Forms: A Guide to Literary Curiosities* (London: Picador, 1999). 'Heteronyms', pp. 38–51 (pp. 41–2).

needs to be known to be a fictional performance?—an effect achieved in his case by the sheer proliferation of fictive identities. According to Jackson, 'In the space of his forty-seven years on earth, he had already experienced at least brief bursts of seventy-two lives.' There was the 'primary trio' of Alberto Caeiro, Ricardo Reis, and Alvaro de Campos, whom Jackson describes as 'three of the century's greatest poets'. Pessoa invented their physical attributes, biographies, and their entire oeuvres. But he also:

> existed, as *inter alia*, Jean Seul, the satirical French journalist and occasional poet; Mr Cross, addict of newspaper puzzles; Antonio Mora, the metaphysician; Pacecho the poet, pale imitator of de Campos; Alexander Search, the Scottish engineer (Pessoa cast his horoscope, wrote works in his name, and had visiting cards printed up for him); the Baron of Tieve, who had fallen on hard times; Vincente Guedes; Robert Anon; M. H. F. Lecher...[32]

Pessoa's oeuvre is thus quite unlike anybody else's, except in that it is everybody else's. It is *sui generis* in disintegrating both principles invoked in that expression: possession, and kind. To elaborate and inhabit such multiple identities incites a prurient speculation (which Pessoa himself anticipated, and did his best both to incite and to pre-empt) that he suffered from a multiple personality disorder. Technically one would only need one additional, fictional, personality to qualify as a multiple personality. And even had Pessoa written the work of a single heteronym, there would be a question about the ontological status of that work. But what's striking is their sheer multiplicity—not just of personalities, but of corresponding styles. Poems by Caeiro are different from those by Reis or de Campos; as Pessoa ingeniously proves by exception when he plays the game of inhabiting the style of another trying to imitate the style of another heteronym.

Such games indicate how the fascination of heteronyms also arises because trying to impersonate someone writing a work of art is different from impersonating someone speaking. This is where the second qualification to Pessoa's definition comes in, when he claims that a poem by a heteronym is an utterance by a fictional character, 'just as' a speech in a play is. Yes, both are dramatized utterances. But is it so clear that fictionalized writing is the same as fictionalized speaking? Or if it isn't, how does it differ? One way of thinking about this is to consider Pessoa's comment about 'an author writing outside his own personality', and to ask whether this is ever possible. In a trivial sense, anyone can try to forge a signature, imitate a voice, or type a letter that purports to be from someone else. Those would be examples of writing or speaking outside your person. But as soon as the notion of 'personality' is introduced, more complex issues are involved. If 'personality' is equivalent to the whole self, or the most characteristic aspects of the self, can a writer ever write from outside it? According to the Romantic view, no. If a poet, as Coleridge wrote, 'described in *ideal*

---

[32] Jackson, *Invisible Forms*, p. 48.

perfection, brings the whole soul of man into activity' (presumably the poet brings his own soul into activity so as to bring the reader's whole soul into a like activity), then writing that tried to escape from the writer's whole soul would not be poetry, or not good poetry.[33] If you adhere to such an expressive theory of art, art that tries to express another personality than the author's is a kind of fake.

But if a dramatist or a novelist can fake a convincing unconscious life as well as a convincing 'inner life' for a character, why could he or she not also fake a character producing a creative work? What is at stake here is whether art requires more than merely perfect expression. Is there a different kind, or even different degree, of faking involved, if a writer invents a character's speech for them, or invents their poem for them? The other counter-argument agrees that there is no essential difference, but pursues it to the opposite conclusion. Rather than seeing heteronymic speech as being as much a creative mystery as heteronymic writing, it sees both as comparable forgeries. This is the post-structuralist view, according to which all discourse is essentially heteronymic, in that it doesn't express us, but itself. According to this view, heteronymity is just deconstruction by other means. What is paradoxical about Pessoa's example is that on the one hand, his myriad of heteronyms seems evidence for the impersonal theory of art as advocated by Eliot. With the heteronyms he seeks to produce complete works of art that do not express his personality; indeed the sheer variety of personae seems a profound negation of the expressive theory. Yet on the other hand, at the level of the heteronyms themselves, the expressive theory still applies. Why else furnish the personae with biographies, with influences, with professions and the rest, if not to suggest a relevance of these things to their writings?

One answer to this last question could be that Pessoa uses auto/biography in an ironic way. He gives his heteronyms fictional biographies to incite biographical readings of their works from naive readers; or to mock such a tendency; or as smokescreens, faking others' biographies to obscure his own. While this account allies him with the Eliot-type high modernist advocate of impersonality, it also places him in the tradition I am trying to delineate of modernist writers engaging with life-writing. Indeed, he does exactly that in ways that align him more closely with the autobiografiction I have been discussing, in a prose work by another important heteronym (though Pessoa described him as only a 'semiheteronym . . . because his personality, although not my own, doesn't differ from my own but is a mere mutilation of it'): 'Bernardo Soares', imaginary author of *The Book of Disquietude*, an unfinished, fragmentary, 'factless autobiography.'[34]

---

[33] S. T. Coleridge, *Biographia Literaria: Or: Biographical Sketches of My Literary Life and Opinions*, ed. James Engell and W. Jackson Bate, 2 vols (London: Routledge and Kegan Paul, 1983), vol. 2, ch. 14, pp. 15–16.

[34] Fernando Pessoa, *The Book of Disquietude: by Bernardo Soares, Assistant Bookkeeper in the City of Lisbon*, trans. Richard Zenith (Manchester: Carcanet, 1996), pp. viii, ix.

'Engagement' might appear too loose a term; one which, in bringing together different kind of engagement, lumps them together, obliterating crucial distinctions between positive and negative ways of 'engaging'. Why use the one term to cover rejection as well as playful exploration? Because people, and especially as complicated people as most writers, are themselves congeries of ambivalent and contradictory responses. Playful exploration can mask, or be, a form of rejection. Rejection can be, or mask, a form of playful exploration. Even as classic a formulation as Eliot's of modernist impersonality ends with a flourish that reintroduces the personal it appeared to banish:

Poetry is not a turning loose of emotion, but an escape from emotion; it is not the expression of personality, but an escape from personality. But, of course, only those who have personality and emotions know what it means to want to escape from these things.[35]

Eliot may have included this in his penultimate paragraph to check any carping that he only advocated impersonality because he didn't have any personality to speak of. He flips the objection inside out. His chillingly elegant paradox implies that there is a class of people who do not have personality and emotions. And if only those who do have them know what it means to want to escape from them, isn't the implication that those who do not want to escape from them don't have them? In other words, writers who think they are expressing their personality and emotions are not, because they don't have them. What they are expressing is what they think is their 'personality' or their 'emotions', but in fact their art is too bad to express such things if they had them, and doesn't let them see that what they are expressing aren't those things. Eliot does not say what they are. We might speculate that what he thinks they are is false or fake personalities and emotions, derivative from a whole tradition of bad (i.e., for Eliot, Romantic) writing. This is the kind of insinuation that gives high modernism the bad names of elitism and fascism. It's a short step from denying people their personalities and emotions to denying them their civil liberties or human rights. And yet. Another effect of Eliot's flip is to put the whole theory of impersonality he has been elaborating into a new context. That context is, precisely, the auto/biographical. It suggests that the impersonal theory can itself be understood personally: as an expression of a personal desire to escape from personality. Like so much of Eliot's cunning style, this passage is self-questioning in other disturbing ways.

The other moment in which Eliot's essay seems to set its face most severely against auto/biography is (as we have seen) when he argues that while 'The mind of the poet' 'may partly or exclusively operate upon the experience of the man himself', nevertheless: 'the more perfect the artist, the more completely separate in him will be the man who suffers and the mind which creates'. Again Eliot's anti-Romantic distaste for poets who make their art from their personal suffering

---

[35] Eliot, 'Tradition and the Individual Talent' (1919), in his *Selected Essays*, 3rd enlarged edn (London: Faber and Faber Limited, 1951), pp. 13–22 (p. 21).

is evident. Yet here too there is an escape route that leads back to a form of life-writing. For, though the essay poses that 'mind' as like a 'shred of platinum' catalysing a chemical reaction, an inert and ahistorical entity, yet the creative mind has a life, even if it's different from the life of the suffering poet. And that life can be given a narrative—the story of an intellectual auto/biography, recounting formative reading, ideas, conversations, friendships, and writings.

If even as extreme an anti-personal position as Eliot's can be seen to engage with personality and life-writing at some level, where does this leave Pessoa, whose fascination with impersonal Shakespeare was matched by his fascination with the lord of personality, Oscar Wilde?[36] From one point of view he might appear to take the impersonal project a stage further: so completely to escape from his own personality as to be able to write not just impersonally, but from the position of other personalities; to write, as he puts it (while ostensibly not talking about himself), 'outside his own personality'. From another point of view, though, he takes impersonality to the point where it re-encounters personality somewhere else. He may be writing *outside* his personality, but he is writing *inside* the personalities of others. Personality, in this view, is not abandoned or escaped, but fictionalized; made imaginary. From this perspective Pessoa's heteronyms have much in common with Pater's Imaginary Portraits; especially 'The Child in the House', in which Pater depicts the aesthetic sensibility, even if he does not write Florian's work for him. It is in that act of imaginary writing, and specifically of fictional 'authorship', that the heteronym differs not only from the pseudonymous writings discussed in Chapter 3, but the Imaginary Portraits and Autobiografictions discussed in Chapters 1 and 4. That is, the salient difference of modernist heteronymity from *fin-de-siècle* displacements of identity may reside not so much in attempts to escape personality, but in moving from characters who write merely to express themselves, and get edited and published posthumously, to those who write with the aim of becoming 'authors'; who write as minds which create rather than as men who suffer.

As with Pater's Imaginary Portraits, or as with Browning's dramatic monologues, Pessoa's heteronyms can be seen as comprising a gallery of personalities; a portrait collection of the kind discussed in Chapter 5. And, as with other examples of that form, there is a sense in which, though individual imaginary personalities cannot be directly equated with the author, the *multiplicity* of them may be a better expression of the author's personality. That is, the whole collection may comprise an imaginary self-portrait in a way that no individual figure within it quite does. Pessoa wrote: 'the psychic origin of my heteronyms lies in my organic and constant tendency towards depersonalization and

---

[36] I'm grateful to Mariana de Castro for her insights into Pessoa's attitudes to Wilde and Shakespeare.

simulation.'[37] The fact that the word 'pessoa' in Portuguese means 'person' does not seem entirely irrelevant to this discussion.

The next chapter will attempt a more systematic approach to the question of imaginary writing and imaginary authorship raised by Pessoan heteronyms. For the moment let us note that the date of emergence of Pessoa's first major heteronym—March 1914—coincides with the serialization of Joyce's *Portrait* in the *Egoist*, where it made its first appearance from 2 February 1914 to 1 September 1915, before appearing in book form at the end of 1916 in the United States and early 1917 in Britain. There is no evidence of influence either way. Though (as we shall see) Joyce presents a poem written by Stephen Dedalus, this does not occur till the last 15 per cent of the novel. By March 1914, even had he been reading the *Egoist* as it appeared, Pessoa would not have seen enough of *Portrait* for Stephen to begin to be a candidate for heteronymity. Conversely, Joyce could not have known of Pessoa's heteronymic compositions.[38] The significance of the coincidence for our reading of Joyce is that it demonstrates that it was, at least, possible then for a writer to contemplate writing as another personality.

UNKNOWN ARTS

When Joyce gave the hero of *A Portrait of the Artist as a Young Man* approximately 'the name of the fabulous artificer', the legendary genius Daedalus, he must have known that its un-Irish ring would have a symbolic resonance.[39] The classical and mythological reference announces his (Joyce's/Stephen's) aesthetic allegiance. As architect, the Minoan's mastery of labyrinthine structure offers a model for the writer. As the first mortal aviator, whose ingenuity enabled him to escape an imprisoning island, he inspires Stephen's aspiration 'to fly by those nets' of 'nationality, language, religion' and escape from Ireland, as Joyce made it clear he had done himself, when he closed the *Portrait* with the courageously candid admission that the short book had been a decade in the artificing: 'Dublin, 1904 / Trieste, 191.4'[40] The book's epigraph, from Ovid, suggests another clue: '*Et ignotas animum dimittit in artes*': '[H]e sets his mind at work upon unknown arts.' The context in the *Metamorphoses* is, again, Daedalus' crafting of wings to escape the tyranny of the state: 'Though Minos rules over

---

[37] Letter to Adolf Casais Monteiro, 13 January 1935: *A Centenary Pessoa*, ed. Eugénio Lisboa with L. C. Taylor (Manchester: Carcanet, 1995), pp. 214–18 (p. 214). In the same important letter Pessoa dates the emergence of Alberto Caeiro as 8 March 1914.

[38] Joyce had sent the revised manuscript of *A Portrait* to Pound by mid-January 1914: see Ellmann, *James Joyce*, p. 350.

[39] Joyce, *A Portrait of the Artist as a Young Man*, ed. Jeri Johnson (Oxford: Oxford University Press, 2000), p. 142.

[40] *Portrait*, pp. 171, 213.

all, he does not rule the air.'[41] But the notion of 'unknown arts' here indicates that Daedalus was more than the master of known crafts. He is the 'fabulous artificer' because he is the supreme classical innovator; the master of metamorphosis. As the Ovidian source continues, his work 'changes the laws of nature'. Joyce was prepared to risk the realism of the whole book by giving Stephen such an outlandish surname. Why did it matter so much to him? One answer might be that Ovid's Daedalus is a classical, and also a secular hero; a non-Christian one. He was able to overcome the laws of nature and to fly, not by miracle, or by becoming an angel, but by himself, by the exercise of his ingenuity. If Joyce thought of Daedalus' invention as analogous to the *artist*'s invention, he is making a strong claim for the book's innovativeness.[42] Certainly *Portrait* was greeted as an inaugural book from the start, and still feels modern in many ways: for its impression of the child's self; its use of free indirect style and stream of consciousness; its fragmentation into epiphanies; and its formal and stylistic evolution—the curious fact that the style evolves with Stephen. But none of these features, impressive though they are in the *Portrait*, is entirely unprecedented in the *Bildungsroman*, in Imagism, or the *roman fleuve*. They put Joyce in the avant-garde, certainly. But do they change the laws of nature; reinvent the laws of literature? The reading of the novel explored in this chapter is one that describes a more fabulous artifice: a book so innovative that it has gone virtually unrecognized for almost a century. If Stephen chose the epigraph, then it not only illustrates his unjustified egoism, it also justifies Joyce's claim to have written a new kind of novel. One way of glossing the phrase 'fabulous artifice' would be to read it as a clue to the ventriloquial novel, which is not only 'fabulous' in the sense of notoriously difficult to bring off; but because it is 'fabulous' in the other sense: an artifice that is itself a fable: fictional fiction, or artificial artifice.

According to this reading, Stephen does eventually fulfil the Daedalean ambitions he voices at the close, and to a much greater extent than is envisaged by readers who merely find Stephen's aesthetic theorizing or first stabs at writing promising, because the entire book (rather than just the poem or journal within the book) becomes evidence for a judgement of Stephen's artistry. It can thus also accommodate criticism unconvinced by the achievements of Stephen's poem or journal. Michael Levenson, for example, reads the journal as pulling against what he calls the 'sentimental' reading of Stephen as developing into a mature artist. He sees the journal as showing Stephen poised to escape, but failing to; condemned to repeat himself, also to recapitulate in reverse the opening sequence of

---

[41] *Metamorphoses*, VIII, 188; trans. Frank J. Miller, 2 vols, vol. 1, Loeb Classical Library (Cambridge, MA: Harvard University Press, and London: Heinemann, 1971), p. 419.
[42] Fritz Senn, 'The Challenge', in *James Joyce's 'A Portrait of the Artist as a Young Man': A Casebook*, ed. Mark Wollaeger (New York: Oxford University Press, 2003), pp. 129–42, reads the epigraph as an emblem of Joyce's art; but he is especially concerned with the cryptic nature of the fragmentary quotation, and with Daedalus' art as one of ingenious combination.

the book.[43] Clearly, if Stephen has written the whole book, the loop is his design, and shows that as autobiographer he has achieved what the journal only promised. The fictional-author reading thus makes the book circular (in a different way from *Finnegans Wake*'s circularity, but more like that of Proust's *A la recherche*). At the end he has got to the point where he can forge the 'uncreated conscience' of his race by forging his own conscience; both in the diary—the base metal he needs to transmute—and in the novel's opening, when he forges his own consciousness at the early stages of its creation. The fictional-author reading also alters the status of the poem and the journal. By putting them in a new frame, they are no longer just examples of Stephen's writing at particular stages; they are examples selected retrospectively by older Stephen to illustrate his development.

Yet even if it seems far-fetched, or unoriginal, as a reading of Joyce, what I've called the 'fictional-author' reading has heuristic value in illuminating the trope I call 'fictional creativity', namely, when a writer presents us with a piece of creative writing ostensibly written by a fictional character. The next chapter will offer a taxonomy and sketch the literary history of this trope, arguing that it can thus help us place Joyce's novel. While this might seem a digression from our study of auto/biografiction, in fact it lays the groundwork for the remaining chapters in Part II, since my argument is not only that the notion of heteronymic creativity is newly important in modern writing, but that it is essential to an understanding of modernist engagements with life-writing, and is taken up in different ways by Pound, Aldington, Woolf, and Stein.

TITLE

The fictional-author theory problematizes the idea of portraiture, making us wonder who is portraying whom, and making us think again about how to read the book's title: 'A Portrait of the Artist as a Young Man'. How does it differ from James's use of *The Portrait of a Lady* as a title, for example? We could note that the idea of painted portraits in both is metaphoric; or, to put it another way, that the paintings are both fictions: imaginary portraits. And both could be seen as examples of realism's attempt to ground its reality in the reality of the visual—painting, photography, vision—anything rather than those elusive, phantasmal, unreal things, words.

In one sense, the title is a private allusion to the novel's origin in an essay Joyce had completed by January 1904, and for which Stanislaus said he had suggested the title: 'A Portrait of the Artist.'[44] It was when the essay was rejected by the

---

[43] Michael Levenson, 'Stephen's Diary in *Portrait*: The Shape of Life', *ELH*, 52 (1985), 1017–35.
[44] *James Joyce: Poems and Shorter Writings*, pp. 203, 276. The essay is printed on pp. 211–18.

Dublin review *Dana* that Joyce decided to expand it into a novel.[45] As John Whittier-Ferguson notes, 'The riddles of portraiture grow more profoundly mystifying in Joyce's succeeding works, but they are posed in his first sketch.'[46] Indeed, it begins precisely by problematizing the notion of portraiture, constrasting the way the world recognizes people, in terms of 'the characters of beard and inches', with the artist's attempt 'by some process of the mind as yet untabulated, to liberate from the personalised lumps of matter that which is their individuating rhythm [. . .]'. 'But for such as these a portrait is not an identificative paper but rather the curve of an emotion.'[47]

'A Portrait of the Artist' evolved into 'Stephen Hero', elaborating 'that ineradicable egoism which he was afterwards to call redeemer',[48] and 'Stephen Hero' was itself reconfigured as *A Portrait of the Artist as a Young Man*. The title Joyce finally settled upon gives a twist to 'A Portrait of the Artist', making it more than just a return to his earlier work.[49] The most literally minded reading of it in relation to the novel would be 'The story of Stephen Dedalus' Youth'. But the title teases us with two other possible senses.

The less obvious one takes 'the artist' as a romantic generality: the point of this portrait is what it tells you not about Stephen as an individual, nor about specifics of turn of the century Irish social life, and its effect on a sensitive boy; the point is what it tells you about the sort of person who is an *artist*. 'A portrait of artisticness.' The more obvious is the sense in which you would understand it if you found it on a painting. This is probably the sense most readers assume is important, without realizing how problematic it is when translated from the visual arts into a more metaphorical literary application.[50] If you found it on a Rembrandt, it would mean a portrait of young Rembrandt, painted by Rembrandt. It *could* be a piece of geriatric nostalgia. You'd have to look at the date it was painted to find out if it were by an ageing painter trying to recapture, at least on canvas, his youth. But it would be more likely to be a self-portrait painted when he was young.

That is to say, several kinds of elusiveness come from the word 'as' in this context. First, elusiveness of time. Does it mean 'as the young man he was when he painted it'; or 'as he was when a *younger* man than that'. Then there's the elusiveness of person. Joyce seems to be insinuating that it could also mean 'A portrait of the artist as if he were another person'; a different young man; as in a self-portrait in which the artist paints himself in costume: as Raphael

---

[45] Ibid., p. 276.   [46] Ibid., p. 209.
[47] Ibid., p. 211.   [48] Ibid., p. 212.
[49] See Hugh Kenner, 'The Cubist Portrait', in *Approaches to Joyce's Portrait*, ed. Thomas F. Staley and Bernard Benstock (Pittsburgh: University of Pittsburgh Press, 1976), pp. 171–84 (pp. 171–2).
[50] See for example James Carens, '*A Portrait of the Artist as a Young Man*', in *A Companion to Joyce Studies*, ed. Zack Bowen and James F. Carens (Westport, CT: Greenwood, 1984), p. 268.

interpolated himself into *The School of Athens* as the Greek painter Apelles; or as in the extraordinary detail from *The Last Judgement* in the Sistine Chapel, of St Bartholomew's flayed skin, bearing what is thought to be Michaelangelo's face.

For in a literal sense that is just what Joyce does give us. Not Joyce by Joyce, but Stephen Dedalus by Joyce. *Not* a portrait of the author, but a portrait of a character with close resemblances to his author when younger (Joyce was thirty-four when it was published; Stephen is about twenty when it ends). Realizing this causes a slight uneasiness as you try to work it out (precisely because it is a device that destabilizes identities). A portrait of the author, Joyce, *as* the character, Stephen. This uneasiness has perhaps led its readers to interpret the title as a rather coy way of saying that the novel is autobiographical.

This is not to deny that the character of Dedalus is based on autobiographical material, or contest the pioneering biographical work of Herbert Gorman and then Richard Ellmann, showing that Joyce had the same sort of family back-ground, same sort of education, same sort of friends, even the same sort of egotism, as Stephen Dedalus. I am not saying that all those acquaintances of Joyce who were so proud to say they had been used as characters in such celebrated books were wrong. But it is a question of how far critical readings must be constrained by biographical sources; of how far Joyce was, precisely, *using* his contacts for purposes quite other than their memorialization. Yet, as Seamus Deane suggests, if the title is taken to be ironic then the irony may be directed as much at the notion of portraiture, of representation, as at the young man.[51]

However, let us explore a quite different reading of the book, starting from a quite different reading of the title. From a literal point of view, the auto-pictorial title would only be appropriate for a novel about Stephen if he (and not Joyce) had actually written it—that is, if *he* were its *fictional* author, and it were only ghost-written by Joyce. Could we be dealing with something quite unlike the novel *A Portrait of the Artist as a Young Man* is usually praised for being: an experiment in stream of consciousness; a distillation of autobiographical material to bring out the 'epiphanies' that Joyce felt marked him out as an artist? Could we have here a novel that, instead of being Joyce's masterly rendering of Stephen's stream of consciousness, is Joyce's masterly rendering of Stephen's own rendering of his consciousness—a masterpiece of sustained aesthetic pas-tiche or ventriloquism; Joyce writing the novel his character would have written; Stephen as heteronym?

Probably not, you are thinking. Otherwise surely it would have been noticed earlier and entered the mainstream of Joyce criticism. Joyce lived for twenty-three years after its publication. You might think more than two decades of

---

[51] Seamus Deane, 'Introduction', *Portrait* (London: Penguin, 1992), p. xliii.

seeing people miss the point would have incited him to drop some hints. Nevertheless, I want to pursue the idea because it is at least possible, and possible for both formal and historical reasons (as the case of Pessoa indicates).

FICTIONAL AUTHORSHIP IN JOYCE STUDIES

When this possibility first occurred to me about a decade ago, I was rash enough to hope that it hadn't been proposed before. It certainly doesn't appear in the standard guides, introductions, casebooks, and companions discussing *A Portrait*. Yet when I gave a couple of papers exploring the idea, I was surprised by the readiness of professional Joyceans to entertain it, some saying it was effectively how they implicitly read the book. There are at least two kinds of formal justification. First, parts of the book are presented as examples of Stephen's writing. It includes works by its fictional artist—more mature and consciously composed works than the quasi-poem about the eagles pulling out Stephen's eyes: notably the poem, the villanelle that emerges as the heat of its composition is described; and the passages from Stephen's journal with which the novel ends. Many of our earlier examples of autobiografiction have been preoccupied with aesthetics. *A Portrait* goes further, not just representing the artist but representing his art. But these examples of Stephen's writing are derivative or unformed in ways the novel in which we find them is not. To read *Portrait* as presenting Stephen ironically is to see them either as youthful exercises, which need to be outgrown, or as indications that his precocity is marred by a pretentiousness, which will make him incapable of an art like Joyce's. As suggested, the fictional-author reading extends the idea of Joyce's experiments in forging Stephen's writing to its limit, taking not just isolated parts of the book but the whole to be evidence of his artistry; and taking that artistry of the whole as greater than that of the sum of its parts.

The second kind of formal justification is that this reading also merely pushes a little further the arguments often met with in Joyce criticism that the point of view, or even the narration of the book, is Stephen's. Once you grant that the novel can be read as Stephen's *thinking out* of the words of his life story, then you've granted the major part of the case; namely that *he* is, or could be, the implied narrator. The only thing remaining would be for him to write it down. Which of course he has begun to do by the end, so he could be its implied (fictional) *author*, too. The point is that Stephen is someone who lives so intensely through words and phrases, through turning his experience into epiphanic verbal sequences, that his conscience is already literary. It might be the novel that he goes about writing in his head, but never manages to get down on paper. This would create another kind of uncertainty, about whether, from his point of view, the text actually exists in written or printed form. There is no doubt that Stephen will become an artist—a writer—nor that he will write about himself, his epiphanies. So it doesn't seem impossible that the novel we have is the kind of book he is on his way toward writing...

That is to say, it's a small step from seeing the book, as many critics do, as being the product of Stephen's imagination (Joyce's free indirect style capturing an artist's work in progress) to seeing it as the product of Stephen's pen, writing down what he imagines. And yet if that is the step Joyce takes, it is also a great leap for the aesthetics of the novel to introduce not a fictional or intradiegetic narrator (ten a penny), but a fictional *artist-author*.

If it seems far fetched, it seems less so if we approach Joyce's career backwards. We know the idea attracted him later. *Finnegans Wake* is presented as written by one of its fictional characters, 'Shem the Penman.'[52] In which case, the question is then: when did the idea first occur to him? Joyce read Italo Svevo's *La coscienza di Zeno*—a fictional autobiography—with interest in early 1924.[53] Would his praise for Svevo have been as marked if he thought Svevo was borrowing a device he had pioneered himself a decade before? Or was it his way of directing a different kind of attention at his own work, as if to say: 'if you read *Portrait* alongside *Zeno* then you'll see what I was doing'? If *Zeno* were the source of the idea for Joyce, it can have influenced *Finnegans Wake* alone, his only book after 1924. Yet most of Joyce's other, earlier, sustained prose works have also been read as experiments with fictional authors. It has certainly been argued that Stephen writes some or all of *Ulysses*, published as a book in 1922, but serialized in the *Little Review* from 1918.[54] Edward Said, for example, describes the Stephen of *Ulysses* as a writer whose work, like that of Proust's Marcel, is 'a project of a never-to-be-attained future, incorporated as a beginning into another work', but says that 'Joyce and Proust encourage the reader to assume that were Dedalus and Marcel actually to produce texts, these would resemble *Ulysses* and *A la recherche*.'[55] Derek Attridge, on the other hand, considers the next logical

---

[52] *Finnegans Wake* (London: Faber, 1971), p. 125. Robert Welch and Bruce Stewart, *The Oxford Companion to Irish Literature* (Oxford: Oxford University Press, 1996), p. 190, call 'Shem the Penman' 'the autobiographical section of the work'. William York Tindall, *A Reader's Guide to James Joyce* (New York: The Noonday Press, Inc., 1959), p. 64, comments that Chapter VII of *Finnegans Wake*, 'reviews the material of *A Portrait* with Shem as another Stephen'. And on p. 274 he demonstrates a comparable use of *mise en abyme*, involving a framed letter written down by Shem (in *Finnegans Wake*, pp. 104–25): 'Dictated by A. L. P. and addressed to H. C. E., the letter was written by Shem the Penman and carried by Shaun the Post. The letter, we gather, is an epitome of *Finnegans Wake* and, like it, is at once simple and baffling.'

[53] Ellmann, *James Joyce*, p. 560.

[54] Edmund Wilson probably initiated this reading, asserting in *Axel's Castle* (New York: Charles Scribner's Sons, 1931), p. 202, that 'it is certain that Stephen, as a result of this meeting [with Bloom and Molly] will go away and write "Ulysses"'. I am grateful to Ron Bush for drawing my attention to this passage. See also Margaret McBride, *'Ulysses' and the Metamorphosis of Stephen Dedalus* (London: Associated University Presses, 2001), who speculates that Stephen may have created some of the other characters of the novel, such as Leopold and Molly Bloom. To accept that reading is not only to read the sections about the Blooms as authored by Stephen, but also the passages in which Stephen encounters the Blooms.

[55] Edward Said, *Beginnings* (New York: Basic, 1975), p. 244.

stage of speculation, that 'Stephen goes on to become the author of *Ulysses*'; though he calls the idea 'discredited.'[56]

It has even been credited that *Stephen* is the 'author' of *Exiles*, a play in which he doesn't even appear as a character:

As in *Portrait* and *Ulysses*, the artist whose image is presented can be shown to be Stephen Dedalus. Stephen does not appear in the play, however. Instead he remains 'within or behind or beyond or above his handiwork, invisible, refined out of existence. . . .' The 'framed crayon drawing of a young man' (*Exiles*, The Viking Press, 1965, p. 15) that hangs on the wall above the sideboard in *Exiles* may well be a portrait of Stephen. In the course of the play it is implied that the portrait is of Richard Rowan's father. Because Richard is a character in the play and Stephen is the theoretical author of the play, Stephen is indeed Richard's father. Stephen can be seen as the father and the ghost of *Exiles* as in *Ulysses* Shakespeare is portrayed as the father and the ghost of *Hamlet*.[57]

When the 'author' of this possibly self-parodic essay, who wisely remains anonymous, continues: 'Additional evidence can be cited to establish Stephen as the "author" of *Exiles*', readers may not be surprised to find that what is offered as additional evidence is no less tenuous. Such a case perhaps suggests why fictional-author-readings of Joyce have been confined to the more lunatic fringes such a large community of scholars is bound to have. Yet a stronger case has been made for Joyce having thought of the idea earlier than 1918, and which sees it as integral not only to the *Portrait*, but to its avatar. Kimberly J. Devlin, tracing the concepts of fraudulence and inauthenticity through Joyce's fiction, argues that *Stephen Hero* is the kind of book Stephen would have written, but then abandoned.[58] Derek Attridge makes a similar suggestion:

the reader who reads *A Portrait* together with *Stephen Hero*, the surviving fragment of its predecessor which Joyce abandoned, has a complex experience that cannot simply be described in terms of 'preliminary' and 'final' versions of the same text. One way of approaching *Stephen Hero*, in fact, is as an addendum to *A Portrait* exemplifying the type of novel that the Stephen of the end of *A Portrait* would have written—and then, by the time of *Ulysses*, abandoned.[59]

Stephen Hero was begun in 1904. Joyce began rewriting and shortening it in 1907. These intriguing suggestions imply that Joyce may already have been thinking in terms of fictional authorship before the *Portrait*. Yet Attridge leaps over that text. If Stephen is thought of as abandoning the earlier version by the time of *Ulysses*, where does this leave the *Portrait*? If Joyce might have thought of

---

[56] Derek Attridge, reviewing Robert Spoo's *James Joyce and the Language of History: Dedalus' Nightmare* (Oxford: Oxford University Press, 1994), in *Modern Fiction Studies*, 42:4 (1996), 888–90.

[57] <http://www.grammarandmore.com/edu/archive/issue11.htm> (accessed 19 October 2007).

[58] Kimberly J. Devlin, *James Joyce's "Fraudstuff"* (Gainesville: University Press of Florida, 2002).

[59] Derek Attridge, 'How to Read Joyce': <http://www.fathom.com/course/10701034/session3.html> (accessed 19 April 2009).

Stephen Hero as a book Stephen might have written, might he not later equally have thought of *Portrait* as if Stephen had written it?

Indeed, given that almost all Joyce's other major fictional works have at some time been considered as fictionally authored, it may come as no surprise that it has also been suggested that Stephen is the author of the *Portrait* itself. Joyce criticism is so industrious that there are few suggestions about his small number of books that haven't been made somewhere, however implausible. Several critics have entertained this reading; but have not elaborated it; so it remains scarcely known. This may be because it stretches credulity. There are cases of extended literary forgeries, but the more celebrated are forgeries of a series of short works (Macpherson's *Ossian*, or Ern Malley's *Poems*, say) rather than of a whole novel. Also, it might seem preposterously futile: one can understand a lesser artist forging a work by a greater: Van Meegeren's Vermeers, say. But why would Joyce invest time and energy forging a work by a jejune artist?

Indeed, the only fiction-book of Joyce's that appears not to have been attributed to a fictional character by its critics is *Dubliners*—except that Joyce himself published earlier newspaper appearances of three of its stories as by 'Stephen Daedalus.'[60] Ellmann explains this by citing Stanislaus Joyce saying that he wouldn't use his own name because he considered the *Irish Homestead* 'the pigs' paper' and was ashamed to appear in it. Yet the Joycean cunning may have already been working towards other ends. *Dubliners* is often read as a work of naturalism; as a stage through which Joyce had to pass to reach the epiphanic stream of consciousness of *Portrait* and the parodic streams of consciousness in *Ulysses*. But what if *Dubliners'* naturalism is already parodic? By interposing the heteronym between himself and his first prose book, might Joyce not be seen as ironizing not merely Dublin's paralysis, but also its crusading denouncer? That is, might not the deployment of naturalism be just as strategic a rhetorical move as the uses of free indirect discourse or parody or the invention of the language of the unconscious in the later books? That Joyce used the pseudonym for three of the stories suggests that we should at least take seriously the idea that it mattered to him to conceive of them as issuing from another person; that he may have been thinking of the pseudonym as a heteronym, or potential heteronym, in Pessoa's sense.

DISCRIMINATIONS BETWEEN YOUNG/OLDER STEPHEN AS FOCALIZED, FOCALIZER, NARRATOR, AND AUTHOR

One reaction to such claims may be to think that Joyce critics have more generous criteria of plausibility than many. What is uncontroversial is that *A*

---

[60] *A Companion to Joyce Studies*, p. 266.

Portrait is told from Stephen Dedalus's 'point of view'. It is his experience, from his earliest memories; his views of the world; his thoughts and ideas and conversations, that the book presents. In the terms introduced by narratology to avoid the vagueness of the notion of 'point of view', Stephen is the narrative's *focalizer*. The relevant narratological distinctions are between the following:

> The focalizer is the person (or agent) who sees
> The focalized is the person or thing seen
> The narrator is the person (or agent) who speaks.[61]

Stephen is the *focalized*, too, for much of the book, which is more focused on his interior world than on the external world or other people. He is also sometimes discussed, as by John Paul Riquelme, for example, as the *narrator* of *Portrait*.[62] Now the category of the narrator is less clear-cut in the modern novel than Rimmon-Kenan's distinctions make it sound. The introduction of *style indirect libre* or 'free indirect style' by novelists such as Jane Austen and Flaubert worked to fuse the voice of an impersonal narrator with the idioms of a character; so that the narrative voice of *Madame Bovary*, say, which tells Emma's story in the third person, as if he is different from the focalizer (usually Emma) and the focalized (usually Emma), sometimes tells it in her words. The question of 'who speaks' is thus problematized.

But even when—as in *Portrait*—focalizer, focalized, and narrator could all be the same person, the notion of 'speaking' is still problematic. Even if Stephen is the narrator, in what sense does he 'speak' the narrative? One problem here is the way our critical language so often erases the difference between speaking and writing, so that we say (as I am saying here, in writing) that writers 'say' things that they write. Clearly what's needed is an additional, fourth, term, 'the writer', the person (or agent) who writes. In most cases this would be the author whose name appears on the title page: in this case, James Joyce, who writes Stephen's words or thoughts for him. But in the case of fictional authors, the person who writes can be a fictional character within the book. If we think Stephen is in this position too, then it makes his role as 'narrator' something different: something consciously constructed by the character, rather than by the author.

Setting such complications to one side for a moment, let us return to the already complicated possibility of reading Stephen as 'narrator' but not 'author'. For here, too, the question of what it means to say it is Stephen who 'speaks' is already problematic. In what sense does he 'speak'? If one compares his possible role as narrator to that of a classic nineteenth-century intradiegetic narrator such

---

[61] See Shlomith Rimmon-Kenan, *Narrative Fiction: Contemporary Poetics* (London: Methuen, 1983), ch. 6.

[62] John Paul Riquelme, *Teller and Tale in Joyce's Fiction* (Baltimore: Johns Hopkins University Press, 1983), 48–85.

as Pip in *Great Expectations*, what we don't have is that sense of a storytelling voice speaking to us. The narration is no longer presented as if it were an oral performance; instead, it is an exercise in style, the performance of writing. When we are given Stephen's direct speech, that too reads like aesthetic theory, expository prose, rather than undergraduate banter. If he is not narrating to an audience, then, to whom is he narrating? One possibility—it is implicit in the notion of 'stream of consciousness'—is that rather than 'speaking' the words, Stephen is 'thinking' them; that is, that he is narrating in his head, to himself or to an imaginary listener—as he does in the Scylla and Charybdis chapter of *Ulysses*[63]—rather than narrating in conversation. To put it like that is to show up the fictionality of the Dickensian performance, though, since the audience of a written text like *Great Expectations* is equally imaginary.

Such questions are posed in a challenging way by John King, who sees them as inextricable from questions of auto/biography. His essay is primarily concerned with 'The Autobiographical Crisis of Stephen Dedalus in *Ulysses*', but—as any account of Stephen in that book tends to—it has a bearing on the Stephen of the *Portrait* too. King argues that Joyce scholarship 'has from the start, envisioned autobiographical implications in *Ulysses*.'[64] He argues that if we take Stephen as autobiographical, then 'what he argues regarding the biographical bearing of Shakespeare's plays should be crucial.'[65] As he elegantly puts it, when an autobiographical character theorizes about how to read literature auto/biographically, 'Stephen is having a *metafictional* identity crisis.'[66] The essay continues: 'if we construe Stephen Dedalus as the narrator of *A Portrait*, as Riquelme astutely does', then 'the journal entries at the novel's end and the poems in the middle section are artifacts written earlier than the body of the book, which the matured Stephen composed at a later time.'[67] King goes on to say that 'In *A Portrait*, Stephen had the gratification of writing poems and a journal, and possibly the entirety of the text itself.' While this is one of the clearer statements of the possible reading of Stephen as fictional author, it glosses over a crucial difference. Stephen 'composing' the book isn't necessarily the same as Stephen 'writing' it; nor is it the same as Stephen 'narrating' it. It might be the same; or it might be the case that Stephen 'composes' it in his head, and/or 'narrates' it to himself in his own mind, but doesn't actually write it down; that it takes Joyce, the genuine artist, actually to write the book Stephen can only imagine.

You might think that collapsing focalized, focalizer, character, and possibly narrator and even author together, would make analysis simpler, since the answer to every question would be 'Stephen'. But instead such a strategy

---

[63] I am indebted to Richard Kirkland for this comparison.

[64] John King, 'Trapping the Fox You Are with a Riddle: The Autobiographical Crisis of Stephen Dedalus in *Ulysses*', *Twentieth-Century Literature*, 45 (1999), 299–316 (p. 299).

[65] Ibid., p. 310.   [66] Ibid., p. 305.   [67] Ibid.

introduces uncertainties at every level which, if as conscious on Joyce's part as the fictional-author reading would imply, constitute the most radical critique of fictional narration of its age. All these concepts of narrating, speaking, composing, writing, become dramatized, ironized, and thus called into question. Take for example the notion of 'stream of consciousness'. The device is often thought of as a mode of, or a style justified in terms of, psychological realism. And as such, the implication is that it aims to represent the character's consciousness as it flows. The time of the narration is the time of thinking. But in the case of *A Portrait*, when is Stephen conscious of his consciousness? Do its descriptions of childhood epiphanies, say, transcribe the experiences as Stephen had them when a child? Or do they record his later memories of them as an adult? Or do they record his attempt to record them, after he has remembered them? If the last, they would be examples of Stephen being a 'stream of consciousness' author. The vividness of the experience makes them feel present; the tenses push them back into the past. Such writing might be free indirect style, in which case the past tenses would be Joyce's, but the thoughts and experiences would be Stephen's as he had them in the past. Or Stephen as narrator/composer/author might be remembering his past experiences, staging them in his memory, in his present consciousness, so as to be able to write them.

In other words, the question of the roles Stephen performs (as focalized, focalizer, narrator, or author) are complicated by the question of when he might be performing them. The autobiographical *Künstlerroman*—in which the artist character is identified with the artist who wrote the book—tends towards this complexity. Partly because the roles that would otherwise be separate are fused together. Partly because this fusion generates confusion about the source of the narrative's words. The Proustian scholar Marcel Muller detected seven different 'I's in *A la recherche*.[68] Joyce's *Portrait* is not written in the first person (except Stephen's journal at the end). Yet in this case it is the narrative which is susceptible of at least seven constructions. This is clearest when considering the scenes from childhood, in which (as in contractual or fictional autobiographies) the adult self looks back at the child self. Take for example the version in *A Portrait* of the 'epiphany' in which young Stephen is threatened with being blinded by eagles:

The Vances lived in number seven. They had a different father and mother. They were Eileen's father and mother. When they were grown up he was going to marry Eileen. He hid under the table. His mother said:

—O, Stephen will apologise.

Dante said:

[68] Muller, *Les Voix narratives dans la recherche du temps perdu* (Geneva: Droz, 1965). Muller defines the seven levels as: the hero (whose future is unknown); the retrospective narrator; the intermediary subject enabling the narrator to remember the hero; the novelist; the writer; the author, and the man (p. [8]). Roger Shattuck, *Proust* (London: Fontana and Collins, 1975), p. 43, settles for two.

—O, if not, the eagles will come and pull out his eyes.—

Pull out his eyes,
Apologise,
Apologise,
Pull out his eyes.
Apologise,
Pull out his eyes,
Pull out his eyes,
Apologise.[69]

Much in the style can be read as realist: as an attempt to transcribe directly not just the behaviour but the thought-patterns or speech-patterns of a young child. The lack of grammatical cohesion between the sentences in the first paragraph constructs this sense of childishness, as does the attempt to piece together how other people fit into his world. The repeated phrases 'Pull out his eyes / Apologize' are not assigned to a particular speaker. They might be a chant with which the adults taunt Stephen until he says he's sorry for being rude to the Vances, or for hiding under the table. Or they could be Stephen's echoing the words to himself; finding in them a rhythm that makes them even more memorable than they would otherwise have been—like a nursery rhyme or playground game. If this *first* level is of childhood experience, it is inextricable from a sense of the adult consciousness reconstructing that experience. This comes across especially, to start with, in a comic delight at the bizarrerie of childish constructions, whereby each parataxis, or each jump between paratactic sentences, introduces a kind of metaphysical vertigo. The Vances live in a number. Their parents have *difference* (from Stephen's parents? From each other?). The anaphoric reference in the pronouns starts and stops. The first two 'They's refer back to Mr and Mrs Vance. The third refers to Stephen and Eileen. The statement 'When they were grown up he was going to marry Eileen' isn't attributed to a speaker, so we can't be sure whether Stephen says (or thinks) it—in which case the transition to 'He hid under the table' might indicate that the grown-ups are shocked, or pretending to be; or perhaps that Eileen is not overjoyed at the prospect, and he has upset her; or whether one of the parents says it—causing Stephen to be upset and hide under the table. The sense of pleasure in the adult mind looking back at its childish past gives a *second* level: the adult re-living childhood memories. I haven't specified whether the childhood experiences or adult memories of them are Joyce's or Stephen's. As with most of the novel, the two are hard to separate. But given the earlier version it seems highly probable that something like it took place, so let us attribute both to Joyce in the first instances. And let us also attribute the *third* level to Joyce: that of trying to fix in language his adult memories of childhood experiences. In the

---

[69] *Portrait*, pp. 5–6.

narratological terms used earlier, the first level would be a (rather implausible?) case of the child performing all three roles: focalized, focalizer, and narrator. The second level would be a case of young Stephen being the focalized, with adult Joyce as both focalizer and narrator. The third would be young Stephen as focalized and focalizer, with adult Joyce as narrator.

We know from Joyce's biography, and his brother Stanislaus's memoir, that Dante Riordan was based on Joyce's aunt Mrs Conway.[70] For the biographer or biographical critic such details might appear to map Stephen's experiences exactly onto Joyce's. An author may have many motives for changing such a character's name that signify no more than tact or familial piety. It may even be true that when young Joyce couldn't pronounce 'Auntie' properly he said 'Dante' instead. At this point in the book we don't yet know that Stephen's family name is 'Dedalus'—that comes in the next half-page. But like 'Dedalus', 'Dante' as a name pulls away from realism, towards literature, transcendence, and myth. (There is an adult irony here too, since this Dante has more time for the Inferno than the more benign sites of Catholic eschatology.) Both name-changes introduce a *fourth* level, that of (older) Joyce objectifying his experiences as Stephen's (younger) experiences. (The brackets are unwieldy, but necessary, as we shall see.) Other changes point in this direction too. Notably the changed attribution of the eagle threat from Mr Vance to Mrs Riordan. It may be wrong to assume that the version Joyce wrote first was closer to actuality: that Mr Vance made the remark, but Joyce reattributed it to Dante to strengthen the sense of her ferocity as a character. Perhaps Mrs Conway said it, but Joyce had a reason for not attributing it to her in the earlier 'epiphany' version. Either way, Joyce was reworking the episode. And there are other elements than the names that get transformed. When he wrote it first as an 'epiphany', Joyce cast it in the form of a play scene, identifying himself as one of the parts, 'Joyce'. When he recast it into narrative, he chose to use the third person rather than the first. He could have used the first person even while using the pseudonym Stephen Dedalus. But by writing first-hand experience as third-person narration he can be seen to be trying to distance himself from his experience; to present it as objectively as possible, as if it were happening to someone else. We hear this, not just in the name-changes, but in the way the utterances also undergo a shift of tense, and possibly also of person. No one said or thought at the time 'When they were grown up he was going to marry Eileen.' What they 'actually' could have said depends on who is thought of as saying it, and to whom. If the parents, then if the sentence is indirect speech, the form they may have used would be likely to be: 'When they *are* grown up he *is* going to marry Eileen.' If they said something about a marriage it's likely to have been because the two children were playing together, in which case singling Stephen out would sound odd. So they could have said something (to each other)

---

[70] Ibid., p. 225.

like 'When they are grown up they will get married'; in which case the sentence in the book isn't indirect speech, exactly, but rather a paraphrase. Either way, the tenses have shifted, from the future projected for the children, to the past of retrospective narrative. If the parents were talking to the children, then the person has definitely shifted too. That is, they could have said to Stephen something like: 'When *you are* grown up *you are* going to marry Eileen.'

The main point here is that there is something strange about the temporality of the sentence 'When they were grown up he was going to marry Eileen.' The casting of the child's mind as it contemplates the future into the form of retrospective narrative jars just enough to make us aware of the transformation that has been worked on it. While such transformation is explicable in terms of the fourth level (adult Joyce objectifying childhood Stephen), this degree of self-consciousness is also explicable in terms of the consciousness of an older Stephen being involved as well. This introduces at least two further possible levels, in which it is now the adult Stephen who takes the place of adult Joyce in levels two and three. Thus the *fifth* level would be one in which Joyce imagines *Stephen* looking back at his own experiences. Young Stephen is the focalized; adult Stephen the focalizer; but Joyce still the narrator. One advantage of this reading is that it allows a more sophisticated account of the book's structure. Part of the function of such an episode is to mark a formative stage in the artist's development. It is, after all, the first image of flying creatures in a series which (as suggested) connects flights of imagination, desire, ingenuity, and escape and self-transformation. But it is also—if one reads the indented passage repeating and rearranging 'Pull out his eyes /Apologize' as a chant or rhyme, and if one reads it as being uttered by Stephen—one of the first examples of his playing with words; turning images into poems. Thus one question such a passage raises is: if we read it as a stage in Stephen's development into an artist, who is seeing it as this? Is it that Stephen is merely remembering it, and that it is Joyce who frames it as aesthetically significant? Or is it a case of Stephen looking back on his past, and selecting those memories which confirm his sense of an artistic vocation? The terminology of 'focalizing' isn't quite exact enough. It blurs this distinction between adult Stephen focalizing the memory as just a memory; and adult artist Stephen focalizing it as an example of Stephen's artistic tendency.

For some critics, the distinction between a Stephen who not only focalizes his memories but also selects and orders them, and a Stephen who is also the book's narrator, may seem too numinous to be useful. Certainly, if Stephen is thought of as focalizing his experience as an artist, he is already well on the way to the *sixth* level, in which he would be the narrator as well as focalized and focalizer: young Stephen as the focalized; adult Stephen as the focalizer; adult artist Stephen as the narrator. However, as suggested above, the status of the narration is itself complex. If we do feel Stephen is 'narrating' his story, he isn't doing it in a dramatized way like Conrad's Marlow, say, or Ford's John Dowell. His act of narration is not commented on, either by others or by himself—which introduces the uncertainty about the sense in which he might be imagined as 'saying' it.

It seems to me that most critics who are prepared to entertain the possibility of Stephen as narrator—and that includes many of the best Joycean critics—see the book as showing Stephen thinking about his past in ways that make clear that he has not just gone through different stages of vocation—religious, adolescent decadent, classicizing intellectual, and so on—but has recognized these as stages he has been through, and achieved an aesthetic distance from them. According to this reading, it is the vindication of his claim to be an artist that he has already begun to turn his own life into art as he remembers it; and the narrative's third person would be free indirect style. The thoughts are Stephen's, about himself; but they are told in the third person because he is thinking about himself objectively. And the book is a form of 'stream of consciousness', but the consciousness in question is a double one, in which adult Stephen is conscious of younger Stephen's consciousness. What proves Stephen an artist is not only this hyper-self-consciousness, but the way he can be seen at every stage not only responding to narrative, song, poetry, or drama, but also trying to fix his experiences in language. Such a reading usually stops short of the *seventh*, and final, level, in which Stephen doesn't only think the book, but writes it; in which he is not only its intradiegetic narrator, but its imaginary author.

AESTHETIC LOOP

If this is what Joyce had in mind, it must be acknowledged that he did it in such a way as to leave no signs that make it possible to distinguish Stephen thinking the narrative from Stephen writing it down. Or rather, since he ends the book with the journal entries that Stephen has written down, it could be objected that Joyce made it clear when he wanted Stephen's writing to be considered, so we have no reason to think of the rest of the book as Stephen's writing. Such a notion might seem like an unnecessary critical complication, best shaved off with Occam's razor. This step might seem legitimated by the novel's autobiographical proximity to Joyce. If Stephen is developing into the kind of artist Joyce was, since Joyce could write the book, so could Stephen. The journal-ending, that is, might present an aesthetic loop, whereby Stephen has reached the point where he might be able to write the book; leaving open the question of whether he is about to write it, or actually has written it. The case for the logical necessity of the Stephen-as-author theory can be made if we work the argument the other way round, from the point of view of Joyce trying to objectify his own aesthetic and critical processes. Insofar as he is presenting his own aesthetic development, or the development of an aesthetic sensibility remarkably like his own, why would he stop short with examples of Stephen's writing that don't offer much promise—a jejune decadent poem; some pretentious, aspirational journal entries? Wouldn't he also have wanted to incorporate the writing that he had been working towards, as he transformed *Stephen Hero* into the *Portrait*?

The way Joyce takes him through his religious vocation, aesthetic study, poetizing, and then journal writing, leaves him at the point of his discovery of the kind of epiphanic naturalist prose that Joyce had achieved around 1904. The point where the book leaves Stephen is thus a necessary one if he is to be plausible as its fictional author. If it doesn't show him writing *Portrait* itself, it does show him drawing ever closer to its modes. The fact that the book ends with a vision of his future work makes us wonder what that work will be. In other words, the shape Joyce has given the book poses a question about the relation between Stephen's vocation and Joyce's book, which, after all, is about the creation of the artist's consciousness from the materials of Stephen's experience.

The aesthetic-loop reading sees the autobiographical novel or fictionalized autobiography that is the *Portrait* as the next stage in Stephen's development; one which corresponds to the final stage in the book's constant evolution of styles and forms. It isn't just that the narrative voice keeps pace with focalized Stephen's age, moving from his first awkward steps in language, through his school idioms, seductions by religion and the Aesthetic movement, and the intellectualism of his university discussions. It also moves formally from the realism of the third-person childhood memories, through the aestheticism of the religious phase and the religiosity of the aesthetic phase, to stream of consciousness, dramatized dialogue, verse, and journal entries. Such a reading would thus make *A Portrait* a particular kind of recursive text, which we should read once as a narrative of Stephen's development to the point where he becomes an artist; and again, as the book he has become able to write about that development. It makes it a particularly economical form, offering two books in one. The critical history of *A Portrait*, beset by disagreements over the degree of irony Joyce intended at each point—is he criticizing Stephen's Luciferian refusal to serve god? Is he criticizing Stephen's verse?—shows the attraction for him of forms of undecidability as a mark of literary objectivity. The aesthetic-loop reading introduces a further, final level of undecidability, subjecting Joyce's own entire text to the same kind of self-consciousness and self-questioning that parts of the book invite. Indeed, one corollary of such a reading is that if we think of Stephen as the 'author' of the book, then the convenient distinction between jejune Stephen and mature ironic Joyce collapses. This in turn problematizes any assumption about narratorial irony, since we can no longer be sure that wise Joyce is safely distanced from Stephen. At this point the quest for impersonality begins to turn into its opposite, trapping the novel in Stephen's personality, in the same way that (according to the Wilde–Nietzsche argument) Joyce's book can only be an expression of his autobiography. Joyce might be using the device of imaginary authorship, that is, both to achieve a new kind of objectivity, and at the same time to bring the whole concept of objectivity into a new kind of question: in short, as a strategy of im/personality.

Critics of *A Portrait* have been shrewd in approaching this question of the narrative's status. Seamus Deane, for example, offers a formalist approach to the question of Stephen's relation to the book. He argues that Stephen begins by receiving the language of his world, but 'ends by supplanting these forms of language with his own, so that the subject of the book becomes, in a formal sense, its author.'[71] I take it that 'in a formal sense' means that Stephen is author of the book's form, if not, quite, its words; that is, that he is responsible for its structure, for the transitions, for the sequences of images and memories; that the narrative is what Stephen is *thinking*, rather than what he is *writing*. This seems borne out by what Deane says next: 'In that light the novel is a series of carefully orchestrated quotations, through which we see a young mind coming to grips with his world through an increasing mastery of language.'[72] In a later essay Deane returns to this reading of the novel as composed of 'quotations'; though now he sees them working to create uncertainties which prevent such a confident ascription of authority to Stephen or anyone else:

The story is constantly being ascribed to Stephen, and by Stephen to someone else, so that the reader is compelled to ask, but never able to answer, the question of the 'identity' of the narrator. Is the narrator the same as the author? Or is the narrator's voice as borrowed, as ventriloquial, as the voices of those in the text that are indisputably quoted?[73]

Yes. But these terms occlude a possible missing middle. Perhaps, between the possibility that the narrator might be Joyce, and the possibility that it might not be anyone, is the possibility (perhaps implicit in Deane's argument, though not stated explicitly) that Joyce might be presenting a book in which the narrator is one of the characters within the book: Stephen.

The argument that the reader can never answer the question of the narrator's identity is a compelling one. Such formal uncertainties as Joyce creates are more than literary games. They reflect epistemological and ontological uncertainties of their age: not only those nineteenth-century uncertainties, and the anxieties associated with them, about agnosticism and subjectivism discussed in previous chapters; but also the twentieth century's own uncertainties and anxieties about the knowability of the self, relating to psychoanalysis. It's hard enough to know who or what is speaking in ourselves, let alone in a book. A writer of a book cannot be sure if s/he is the one speaking, or unconsciously echoing other voices, other texts. Psychoanalysis thus problematizes the nature of autobiography, of confession. Insofar as confessional discourse is shaped by the unconscious, the author cannot know what s/he is confessing to. Confession is a text written, or

---

[71] Deane, *A Short History of Irish Literature* (Indiana: University of Notre Dame Press, 1986), p. 182.
[72] Ibid.
[73] Seamus Deane, 'Introduction' to *Portrait* (London: Penguin, 1992), p. xvii.

overwritten, or underwritten, by the other. All confession thus becomes suspect, dubious, susceptible to repression, evasion, fictionalization.

SVEVO

Yet such uncertainties also offer the writer new opportunities. Italo Svevo's novel of 1923, *La coscienza di Zeno*, is presented in the form of a fictional autobiography by Zeno Cosini, written at the insistence of his psychoanalyst to help with his analysis, and then published by the analyst in revenge for Zeno terminating his visits. Formally it looks like Rutherfordian pseudonymous fictionalized autobiography, with some entries dated journal-style, and complete with a brief heteronymous preface by the analyst, semi-anonymously using only an initial, 'Dr. S', which may or may not stand for 'Svevo' (which was in any case a pseudonym for Aron Ettore Schmitz), and coincidentally or not shares the initial of Freud's first name. Where it differs from its pre-Freudian predecessors is in invoking psychoanalysis' methods of refusing to take words at their word, but to read them against the grain, to try to understand what they are repressing, concealing, denying, fabricating, fictionalizing:

A written confession is always mendacious. We lie with every word we speak in the Tuscan tongue! If only he knew how we tend to talk about things for which we have the words all ready, and how we avoid subjects that would oblige us to look up words in the dictionary! That is the principle that guided me when it came to putting down certain episodes in my life. Naturally it would take on quite a different aspect if I told it in our own dialect.[74]

This is from the concluding chapter, 'Psychoanalysis', which ends with a note dated a year after the rest of the chapter, saying that Dr. S. has asked him to send the remainder of his memoir. This is a necessary device to explain how Dr. S. comes to have the concluding part, written after Zeno's visits to him have ceased. But it is also a very slippery passage, as a psychoanalyst would be the first to recognize, not only because it is a confession of the mendacity of confession; a confession of his mendacity in Italian rather than dialect, itself written in Italian, and by someone styling himself 'Italo', but also because it may be a double bluff, intended to undermine the analyst, and whatever he plans to do with the memoir, by undermining the truth-value of the memoir itself. So is it true that we cannot trust his statements? Or does his attempt to deny their truth merely confirm their candour, which he now regrets? Coming in a work of fictional autobiography, this is more than a translation of the Cretan Liar paradox. It not only says that all autobiography is fiction, but, in negating the truth of what he

[74] Italo Svevo, *La Coscienza di Zeno*, trans. Beryl de Zoete (1930) (Harmondsworth: Penguin, 1964), p. 351.

has already sent to the doctor, he is claiming that his confession is fiction—which might guarantee its essential truth as autobiography. He is a fictional character already; to the extent that he has fictionalized his memoir, it is an example of imaginary writing; an (almost) entirely fictionally authored book—though the frame distinguishes Svevo's novel from Zeno's memoir, which though autobiografiction, is not posed as a work of art.

The undecidability theory apropos of *A Portrait of the Artist* is pursued by Vicki Mahaffey, who provides a post-structuralist, Derridean-inflected, attempt to bring into question precisely the distinction between 'Joyce' and 'Stephen' on which so much New Critical work on the novel had got caught up:

> However, this distinction between 'author' and 'character' is itself, like all oppositions, an heuristic one, since it is impossible to be permanently inside or outside a system so long as that system and our awareness of it are subject to change. Every author is necessarily a character, or subject, and every character an author—and authority—in a dialogical process that produces no final synthesis.[75]

This is a sophisticated argument, which forms part of a compelling case about how Joyce's work transforms the notion of authorship and authority. But the deconstruction of the author/character distinction has the disadvantage of rendering impossible the kind of impersonation of authorship that may have been Joyce's aim. The danger of my argument in this chapter is that it might appear to be trying to impose a single reading (and a perverse one at that) on the text; to foreclose any uncertainties about its narration or authorship. On the contrary, my contention is merely that the reading should be kept in play, and that to do so enriches the text, suggesting an extra degree of interest in it which is compatible with the kinds of interest Joyce is acknowledged as arousing, but which has not normally been recognized in this key modernist text.

PERSON-ALITY

The difficulty of distinguishing Stephen's consciousness from that of Joyce or an implied author or narrator has much to do with the book's autobiographical dimension; but in particular, with the fact that Stephen, like Joyce, is an artist. That congruence deprives us of any confidence that we can attribute the book's artistry to Joyce rather than Stephen. With a dramatic monologue in verse or an unreliable narration in prose, readers have the sense, or at least the hope, that the character's words are interpreted for us by the framing, the shaping, produced by the author. Porphyria's Lover may be responsible for his speech as well as his crime, but Browning is responsible for the way his speech is written down, and

[75] Vicki Mahaffey, *Reauthorizing Joyce* (Cambridge: Cambridge University Press, 1988), pp. 102–3.

the way it forms a poem.[76] Jane Eyre may be writing down her story, but its patterns and rhythms of confinements and outbursts are framed by Charlotte Brontë. With *A Portrait*, it isn't only that the book's aesthetic strategies *could* be attributed to Stephen; but that many of the aesthetic interests he voices in the novel are reflected in its form. For example, we have seen how crucial to a reading of the novel is its use of person. So when Stephen discusses 'that old English ballad *Turpin Hero* which begins in the first person and ends in the third person', we cannot but wonder what bearing this has on *A Portrait*, which began, of course, as 'Stephen Hero', and which begins in the third person and ends in the first.[77] Stephen is offering the ballad as an example or emblem of the quest for impersonality. So one might take the fact that *Portrait* travels in the reverse direction as an implied criticism: all that *Bildung* and he has only reached the stage of first-personality. But even if it is a criticism of Stephen, that would not preclude the fictional-author reading. Rather than showing Stephen as still too self-indulgent to be an author, it might suggest that (by analogy with the idea of an unreliable narrator) what we have is a portrait of an unreliable artist. Alternatively, one could see the discussion of *Turpin Hero* as in accord with the autobiographical reading: Joyce starts with a fictionalized persona, Stephen, in order to get closer to himself. But it works the other way too: showing Stephen developing a stronger and stronger sense of his own identity, to the point where he can write his own portrait, and give it the novel's title.

The first-person prose narration is in practice often a more ambiguous form than the preceding paragraph might imply. While it might be convenient to assume that authors make narrators reveal themselves in ways they do not intend to, in practice we cannot always be sure that the cunning isn't the narrator's rather than the author's. It is a subtly dual form, in which the same words are at once the character's and the author's; at once narrative and novel.[78] The first-person narration offers itself as both frame and picture. Frame, because the narrator frames his or her story, comments on and interprets it for us. Picture, because the narrator is *in* the picture, is dramatized for us to interpret. It is a wonderfully elusive form. But its elusiveness is always somewhere in the foreground; in the way it keeps drawing our attention to the idiosyncrasies of the narrator.

A Portrait of the Artist as a Young Man is not a first-person narration, although it looks as if it might be about to turn into one when it ends with Stephen's first-person journal entries. But, in the reading I am considering, it is something comparable: not a story told by a dramatized narrator, but one *written* by a

---

[76] See Eric Griffiths, *The Printed Voice of Victorian Poetry* (Oxford: Clarendon Press, 1989) p. 214: 'In the dramatic monologue, the source of the pattern is distinct from the origin of the speech.'

[77] *Portrait*, p. 180.

[78] See Susanne Kappeler, *Writing and Reading in Henry James* (London and Basingstoke: Macmillan, 1980), p. 24.

dramatized *author*. For a reading of the whole novel as Stephen's composition to be convincing, however, each sentence would have to be readable as not just what Stephen *sees* (this would be realism or naturalism); nor as limited to what he *thinks* about what he sees (this would be stream of consciousness); nor as only *how he might articulate*—to himself perhaps—what he sees (this would be free indirect style); but also how Stephen would *write* about what he sees and thinks (this would be literary ventriloquism, or 'imaginary writing').

One objection to reading this novel as written by its protagonist is that any essentially realist novel written in the third person might be so read; *Sons and Lovers*? Paul Morel's letter to his psychoanalyst. *Madame Bovary*? The heroine's suicide note. For such a reading to be less trivial, we would need internal evidence of two kinds. First, that Joyce intends us to consider Stephen as a writer, and to consider his writings (evidence which the book certainly provides, by including some of Stephen's work). Second, evidence of why Joyce would want to pretend his entire novel was written by someone else.

ELOCUTIONARY DISAPPEARANCE

One passage in the *Portait*, often quoted as a key to Joycean aesthetics, could offer such evidence. It is another moment in which Stephen's aesthetic pronouncements bear heavily on the novel in which he finds himself; but also one which could support the claim that Joyce intended more than just the occasional passages to be written by Stephen. It presents a vision of the ultimate novelistic version of modernist impersonality; of what Mallarmé advocated when he wrote: 'The pure work implies the elocutionary disappearance of the poet, who hands over to the words, set in motion by the shock of their unevenness.'[79] That is, for Joyce to write Stephen's novel could be the ultimate example of the artist's aloofness from his creation; since the artist's work is concealed behind the character's. Stephen famously advocates artistic aloofness like this:

The personality of the artist, at first a cry or a cadence or a mood and then a fluid and lambent narrative, finally refines itself out of existence, impersonalizes itself, so to speak. The esthetic image in the dramatic form is life purified in and re-projected from the human imagination. The mystery of esthetic, like that of material creation, is accomplished. The artist, like the God of creation, remains within or behind or beyond or above his handiwork, invisible, refined out of existence, indifferent, paring his fingernails.[80]

If Stephen is thought of as the author, we cannot hear Joyce's voice at all. Stephen is himself conscious of a sense of alienation from his own language:

---

[79] 'Variations sur un sujet', trans. Keith Bosley, *Mallarmé: The Poems* (Harmondsworth: Penguin Books, 1977), p. 45.
[80] *Portrait*, pp. 180–1.

—The language in which we are speaking is his before it is mine. How different are the words *home, Christ, ale, master,* on his lips and on mine! I cannot speak or write these words without unrest of spirit. His language, so familiar and so foreign, will always be for me an acquired speech. I have not made or accepted its words. My voice holds them at bay.[81]

In context this is to do with speaking the English language as an Irishman (in contrast to the dean of studies, who is English). But one could read it as a veiled acknowledgement that Joyce is writing as Stephen: the language in which Stephen is presented is his before it is Joyce's. Joyce is holding his character at bay. The elocutionary disappearance of the author destabilizes language, opening up the possibilities of irony, parody, satire, and pastiche—terms that will loom larger in our discussion of subsequent modernist developments.

IRONY, PARODY, PASTICHE

In the book's penultimate sentence, Stephen's journal announces his mission: 'I go to encounter for the millionth time the reality of experience and to forge in the smithy of my soul the uncreated conscience of my race.'[82] That word 'forge' clangs somewhat. The Homeric weapon-making image seems slightly too *mock-*Homeric. The idea of 'forgery' is a little uncomfortable in relation to Stephen's lofty ambitions. But might it not be Joyce's hint that the whole book is a kind of forgery? A pastiche of Stephen's exposition of his lofty mission? How else do we account for the fact that so much of the novel reads as a parody of florid adolescent prose?—much more so than in *Stephen Hero.*

Similarly, if the mimicking of the child's thought-style in the opening is too affectionate to read as parody, the language towards the end of the novel seems decidedly parodic:

A glow of desire kindled again his soul and fired and fulfilled all his body. Conscious of his desire she was waking from odorous sleep, the temptress of his villanelle. Her eyes, dark and with a look of languor, were opening to his eyes. Her nakedness yielded to him, radiant, warm, odorous and lavish-limbed, enfolded him like a shining cloud, enfolded him like water with a liquid life; and like a cloud of vapour or like waters circumfluent in space the liquid letters of speech, symbols of the element of mystery, flowed forth over his brain.[83]

This seems clearly intended to parody aestheticism. But is it possible to specify which writer(s) is Joyce parodying? John Paul Riquelme argues for the influence of Pater, especially in the conclusion of *The Renaissance.*[84] Pater was an

---

[81] *Portrait,* p. 159.   [82] Ibid., p. 213.   [83] Ibid., pp. 187–8.
[84] Riquelme, '*Stephen Hero, Dubliners,* and *A Portrait of the Artist as a Young Man*: styles of realism and fantasy', in *Cambridge Companion to James Joyce,* ed. Derek Attridge (Cambridge: Cambridge University Press, 1990), pp. 103–30 (pp. 103–4).

important precursor for Joyce, as were other Aesthetes, such as Symons. But the parodic energies of the part of *Portrait* in which Stephen begins to write do not seem to me to be directed towards Pater; as we can see by juxtaposing a passage from 'The Child in the House' that also seeks spiritual transcendence in everyday sensuousness:

His way of conceiving religion came then to be in effect what it ever afterwards remained—a sacred history indeed, but still more a sacred ideal, a transcendent version or representation, under intenser and more expressive light and shade, of human life and its familiar or exceptional incidents, birth, death, marriage, youth, age, tears, joy, rest, sleep, waking—a mirror, towards which men might turn away their eyes from vanity and dullness, and see themselves therein as angels, with their daily meat and drink, even, become a kind of sacred transaction—a complementary strain or burden, applied to our every-day existence, whereby the stray snatches of music in it re-set themselves, and fall into the scheme of some higher and more consistent harmony.[85]

Huysmans's *A Rebours* provides a more likely source, in its provocative juxtapositions of the spiritual and the sexual:

While implanting an extra-human ideal in this soul of his [. . .] the Christian religion had also instilled an unlawful ideal of voluptuous pleasure; licentious and mystical obsessions merged together to haunt his brain, which was affected with a stubborn longing to escape the vulgarities of life and, ignoring the dictates of consecrated custom, to plunge into new and original ecstasies, into paroxysms celestial or accursed, but equally exhausting in the waste of phosphorus they involved.[86]

That Joyce modelled his parody of Stephen's youthful aesthetic raptures on Huysmans fits with Richard Ellmann's account of how Joyce moved from an 'initial liking for Huysmans' to criticism of Huysmans's formlessness.[87] And it also supports the idea that Huysmans is invoked in *A Portrait* for ironic or parodic purposes.

VILLANELLE

What is being parodied at this point is not only aesthetic prose such as Huysmans's, but Stephen's thought processes as he works himself up into an ecstasy of composition. Which leaves us with a different kind of critical problem regarding Stephen's villanelle, as it emerges over the course of several pages:

> *Are you not weary of ardent ways,*
> *Lure of the fallen seraphim?*

[85] Pater, 'The Child in the House', *Miscellaneous Studies* (London: Macmillan, 1895), p. 194.
[86] J.-K. Huysmans, *Against Nature*, trans. Robert Baldick (Harmondsworth: Penguin, 1959), p. 117. As suggested in Chapter 5, Symons's *Spiritual Adventures* offers another possible precursor.
[87] Ellmann, *James Joyce*, p. 75.

Tell no more of enchanted days.
Your eyes have set man's heart ablaze
And you have had your will of him.
Are you not weary of ardent days?[88]

The ironizing of its composition might seem to ironize the poem itself, which is in any case derivative of Nineties poets such as Ernest Dowson or Lionel Johnson. In a seminal discussion of the villanelle, Robert Scholes argues that: 'In order to fulfil the term of Stephen's aesthetic gestation, it was necessary for Joyce to present us with a created thing, with a literary work which was the product of his inspiration.'[89] Hugh Kenner read it (in keeping with his view that Joyce portrayed Stephen ironically) as parodic: as what he calls a 'meticulous pastiche of immaturity.'[90] Yet, as Scholes goes on to observe, Joyce did not write the poem in 1914, or even 1904, as a heteronymic product of his fictionalized character Stephen. He had in fact already written it around 1900–1, and showed it to Stanislaus, who says it was called 'The Villanelle of the Temptress.'[91] Stanislaus comments that it was written when Joyce was younger than Stephen's age at the corresponding point of *A Portrait*. To that extent Joyce has made Stephen's writing less mature than his own. But as he appears to have written the poem in his own person in the first place, what sense does it make to call it a 'pastiche'? Is pastiche in the eye of the beholder, as when we talk of a writer producing unconscious self-parody? Can a writer write a poem in earnest and then decide later to re-present it as pastiche? Does the fact that Joyce wrote the poem long before the novel confirm the unironic reading of *Portrait*? Or does the parodic context he gives it imply that he came to see it later as pastiche decadence? The issue here is that even if it's true that Joyce wanted to present an authentic example of the creative process, that is no guarantee of his views about the result. It may be an authentic example of an inauthentic poem. So the problem about distance cannot be easily dissolved.

The poem's provenance might seem to undermine the argument about fictional authorship. If it was already written by Joyce, in what sense can we think of it as authored by his heteronym Stephen? In his second massive reconceptualization of the work, could he not have rewritten the poem too? Does Joyce's use of his own youthful versifying testify to a failure of nerve at the prospect of full heteronymous creativity; an acknowledgement that were he to try to fake another's creative process, the result would be 'inauthentic'? Worse still,

---

[88] *Portrait*, pp. 183–8 (p. 188).
[89] Robert Scholes, *In Search of James Joyce*, pp. 70–81 (pp. 73–4).
[90] Kenner, *Dublin's Joyce* (1955); excerpted in *James Joyce: 'Dubliners' and 'A Portrait of the Artist as a Young Man': A Casebook*, ed. Morris Beja, p. 133.
[91] Stanislaus Joyce, *My Brother's Keeper*, pp. 100, 158. The poem is reprinted in *James Joyce: Poems and Shorter Writings*, p. 72.

does it undermine the creation of Stephen as a character? Is it, that is, Joyce's ultimate failure to write from outside his own personality, despite the attempt at distance represented by the pseudonym?

Joyce preserved the manuscript of the essay 'A Portrait of the Artist', and by inscribing it for Sylvia Beach implicitly sanctioned its preservation. We know only of the early version of the villanelle because Stanislaus copied his brother's early poems into his commonplace book. Early readers of *Portrait* could not have known the poem's provenance, so it may be that Joyce wanted them to think he had written it heteronymously even though he hadn't. That strategy would make it fake heteronymity: not the faking of another's writing, but the faking of that faking.

But there is a less contrived reading that can preserve the concept of fictional authorship even if this is not the purest example of it. This is to see Joyce as presenting the villanelle 'as' Stephen's poem, in the same way he presents the portrait of himself 'as' an other young man. That is, we are to read it not as early autobiographical material confirming the irrelevance of the disguise, but as if he had written it later, for his heteronym. Superficially there may seem no material difference between these two positions. But the difference is best expressed thus: rather than implying: 'this poem I wrote is the kind of poem Stephen would write, because he would become the artist I became', he is suggesting 'this poem I wrote but didn't publish is the kind of poem Stephen would write and try to publish because he is the kind of artist who wouldn't transform himself in the way I have'. (This would fit with the view that in *Ulysses* Joyce imagines the kind of life he might have had in Dublin had he not left it.) Joyce wrote in 'A Portrait of the Artist' that 'About this period the enigma of a manner was put up at all comers to protect the crisis.'[92] That 'crisis' could bespeak many turning points. But one transformation it might signify is that from imitative aesthete to ironic naturalist and parodist. The problem with both 'A Portrait of the Artist' and *Stephen Hero* is that they remain too confined within the aestheticism they attempt to diagnose. The main innovation in *A Portrait of the Artist as a Young Man* is the way Joyce introduces a variety of styles and modes that mark his escape from the limitations of a single, decadent, mode. The effect of Joyce's mastery of such variety is to turn each into a parody—a discovery that was to prove the core of *Ulysses*. I am suggesting, then, that the villanelle that was an unconscious pastiche when Joyce originally wrote it became a parody when he inserted it into a new frame: a parody of a pastiche.

Here we approach the postmodern perspective, which sees all styles as always already pastiche. To the extent that Joyce anticipated that view, *Portrait* represents a deconstruction of the notion of the 'artist' altogether. It isn't that Stephen is a second-rate artist, and Joyce a first-rate one; it is the whole project of

---

[92] Ibid., p. 212.

aestheticism, and its sacralization of the figure of the artist, that is ironized. From this point of view, the distinction between 'authentic' creativity and the faking of it is irrelevant, since all writing is faked, pastiche.

Whether Joyce imagined or believed such things may not be relevant if we return to the idea of Stephen as the book's fictional author. If he is that, or even the implied narrator, something happens to the status of his poem and his journal. They can no longer be read as Joyce's authoritative transcriptions, but become Stephen's self-quotations, thus liable to be edited, or unreliable. It would be too implausible to suggest that Stephen had plagiarized them from Joyce; but the point is that the time and person of their authorship acquire new degrees of undecidability.

The critical questions posed by Joyce's inclusion of pieces of creative writing attributed to a fictional(ized) character remain real questions, regardless of whether the reading of the entire book as fictionally authored is accepted; or whether one of the pieces of writing turn out to have been written by Joyce in his own person years earlier. Most readers are likely to find the fictional-author reading of *Portrait* in its entirety too far-fetched. Applied to a less ingenious author I'd agree that it represented a waste of ingenuity. If I am not sure, it's because it's in the nature of the idea not to conduce to certainty.

COUNTER-EVIDENCE?

It remains to ask what counter-evidence might be adduced, whether external or internal to the book. What would count as external counter-evidence? Joyce might have said that he didn't mean Stephen to be taken as the book's fictional author. But he would have only been likely to deny it had someone proposed it during his lifetime, which they appear not to have done. Otherwise, to deny it in advance would only have been to alert readers to the possibility, which he would not have wanted to do had he thought of the idea but wished to exclude or pre-empt it. What would count as internal counter-evidence? Evidence that Stephen was incapable of writing, perhaps. Or evidence that one of the *other* characters was writing a book about him, called *A Portrait of the Artist as a Young Man*. But arguably there is no such counter-evidence because there is no decisive evidence to counter. That is, there is no reason for the book to state that Stephen is not the author, when it doesn't state that he is. If *Portrait* can be read as a case of fictional authorship, the fictional author can only be *implied* rather than *declared*.

There are the pieces of Stephen's writing within the novel; but no passages of the surrounding narrative stand out as obviously *written* by Stephen, rather than as rendering things *experienced* by him. There is no way of separating out Stephen as focalizer from Stephen as fictional *author*, so there is no firm ground on which to build a distinction between Joyce's book and Stephen's. But that virtually concedes the case: if the distinction is untenable, then the narration could as well be Stephen's as Joyce's. The absence of conclusive evidence can be enabling. And that very invisibility of signs might have been the attraction of the game for Joyce: heteronymity, that is, might correspond for Joyce to the cunning and silence that Stephen advocates. To have done it too crudely would have been to give it away. A clear signal from Joyce that we're hearing Stephen's writing would itself be a kind of frame, in which to put the rest of the story. And that would be to reappear as author in the novel from which (according to the fictional-author theory) he was trying to disappear.

The only explicit sign that James Joyce is the author is on the title pages and book-covers.[93] He might, arguably, have put Stephen Dedalus's name there instead of his own (as he had for the first publication of the three *Dubliners* stories) if he had wanted to endorse the fictional-author reading. According to Stanislaus, he almost did: 'in order further to identify himself with his hero, he announced his intention of appending to the end of the novel the signature, *Stephen Daedalus Pinxit*: as on a painting ('Stephen Daedalus painted this'), indicating Joyce was thinking of the title as suggesting Stephen as the book's imaginary author.[94] Yet to put Stephen's name on the title-page would have been no less ambiguous, since it would merely function as a pseudonym (as with the *Dubliners'* stories); and as such could actually have undermined the fictional author reading (had Joyce intended it) by suggesting that the actual author were directly identifiable with the character (as his earlier announcement to Stanislaus indicated). In other words, to sign it with a fictional author's name might have made it look more like pseudonymous autobiography. By putting his name to Stephen's book, on the other hand, Joyce would be reversing that practice of putting a fictional name to his own life. We need to know the book is actually written by Joyce to be able to see the achievement of writing it as if it were written by Stephen. And the fictional author reading does not deny Joyce wrote the book; rather, it argues that the book he wrote may be of a particularly cunning kind.

The fictional-author reading makes *A Portrait* appear more postmodern than modernist. Indeed, the kinds of uncertainty discussed here (as to Joyce's attitude to Stephen; the degree of equivalence between Joyce and Stephen; and the authorship of the text) are exactly those which post-structuralist critics of Joyce most value him for. *Portrait* has been seen to anticipate Julia Kristeva's concept of the subject in language as always in process: 'The radical heterogeneity and play-of-difference of all signifying practice insures that no subject position is fixed.'[95]

---

[93] Joyce was identified as the author in the *Egoist* serial (which ran from vol. 1:3 (2 February 1914), 50–3), as well as on the Egoist and Huebsch book first editions.

[94] Stanislaus Joyce, *My Brother's Keeper*, p. 239. Joyce regretted signing his essays pseudonymously, and wrote a scathing review of a novel from the Pseudonym Library, arguing that the advantages of pseudonymity included concealing shame over bad writing. Ibid.

[95] Thomas Calvin, 'Stephen in Process/Stephen on Trial: The Anxiety of Production in Joyce's *Portrait*', *Novel*, 23:3 (1990), 282–302 (p. 284).

That, or something like it, would be the point of such ingenious autobiografictional games. What would enable Stephen (and thus, vicariously, Joyce) to escape the nets trying to prevent his artist's flight would be his turning inside out of the entire notion of the autobiographical: to make his would-be captors uncertain where exactly their victim is to be found. To prevent his work being dismissed as either merely autobiographical (and hence not truly creative) on the one hand, or as merely invention (in which case its criticisms of Irish society, politics, and religion could be discounted). In short, Joyce wanted *A Portrait* to be something very different from the classic autobiographical novel. Its profound interrogation of the notions of the autobiographical, the fictional, and the aesthetic, represent his reinvention of the notion of both the 'portrait' and the 'artist'.

The possibility of such a reading extends the reach of the Imaginary Portrait. Instead of Pater's pseudo-biographical studies, Joyce's would be pseudo-autobiographical in a curiously double sense. First because it translates its autobiographical material onto a fictionalized character; second because it impersonates that character's third-person autobiography. In this last aspect, it extends the reach not only of the Imaginary Portrait, but of fiction as well. This is by introducing the concept of the ventriloquial novel. Such a concept implies a distinction—far from problematic, as we shall see, but also far from dispensable—between, on the one hand, a narrative offered as issuing from a fictional narrator—something inextricable from the history of drama or of the novel—but which is received as the narrator's story; and on the other hand, the narrative offered as an example of that fictional narrator's *art*. The following chapter examines the taxonomy and history of this strategy of heteronymic or fictional creativity: the production of imaginary literature by a fictional author.

8

Heteronymity II: Taxonomies of Fictional Creativity: Joyce (continued) and Stein

'En art, voyez-vous, il n'y a pas de *première* personne'[1]

TAXONOMY AND HISTORY OF FICTIONAL CREATIVITY

It may seem reprehensibly postmodern to read *Portrait* in terms of fictional authorship: an anachronism, reading Joyce's novel as if it were by Nabokov or Rushdie. However, some of the best recent work on Joyce does exactly that, to bring out the ways in which modernism does anticipate postmodern or post-colonial concerns.[2] Besides, fictional authorship as such was nothing new. We have seen how the idea of a fictional work written down by its central character is as old as the rise of the English novel itself. If it seems inimical to modernism it shouldn't. It was used for major modernist works by Proust from 1913 (admittedly the conclusion to *A la recherche*, in which the entire design becomes apparent, wasn't published until after Joyce's novel; but *Le Temps retrouvé* was drafted alongside *Du côté de chez Swann*; and there's no doubt from the early volumes that what we are reading is going to be a *Künstlerroman*); and it was used by other modernists: by Pound in 1920; Svevo in 1923; Gide in *Les Faux-monnayeurs* in 1925; Woolf in 1928; and Stein in 1933. And it was to be used by Joyce himself in *Finnegans Wake*. There seems no reason why the concept should have been unthinkable by him by 1914. It was even possible for Huxley in 1928 to parody the idea of the parody-novel and the fictional *mise en abyme* (with what sounds like *Ulysses* in mind):

But why draw the line at one novelist? Why not place a further novelist within the second (imaginary) novel, and so on *ad infinitum* (as on packets of Quaker Oats there is a Quaker holding in his hand a packet of oats, on which there is another Quaker holding another

---

[1] Wilde to Gide, recalled in Gide, *Oscar Wilde: In Memoriam (Souvenirs), le De Profundis* (Paris: Mercure de France, 1910), p. 46.

[2] See for example Ronald Bush, 'Rereading the Exodus: *Frankenstein, Ulysses, The Satanic Verses*, and Other Postcolonial Texts', in *Transcultural Joyce*, ed. Karen R. Lawrence (Cambridge: Cambridge University Press, 1998), pp. 129–50.

packet, on which there is a further Quaker etc). At the tenth remove one could have a novelist who would tell the story in terms of algebraic symbols, or of internal organs, or of reaction times.[3]

Novels with fictional authorship were being written by modernists, and even parodied by other modernists. And, as stated, even if Stephen is not thought of as author of the entire *Portrait*, he is certainly author of parts of it. However far he had developed the idea by 1914, Joyce was a pioneer.

How does 'imaginary writing' differ from 'metafiction'? Metafiction is usually defined as fiction about fiction; fiction that draws attention to its own devices, its own fictionality.[4] Imaginary writing is a species of metafiction, in that to discuss or present writing by a fictional character is indeed to draw attention to both levels of fictionality—the fiction within the fiction, and the fiction that frames it. But imaginary writing is a specific form of metafiction, since not all metafiction is the product of a fictional character. Why concentrate on imaginary *writing*, rather than any other imaginary *utterance*? If what we are looking at is the dramatized production of text—someone other than the author being presented as responsible for their words—does the distinction matter between someone writing those words as opposed to speaking them? This is the kind of Derridean territory in which distinctions dissolve under your feet as you try to step over them. It seems to matter more when the author means it to matter—attaches importance to the act of writing. But it is also a question of what importance the character attaches to it: what they intend the writing to be or to do.

Autobiografiction inevitably involves imaginary writing. When a fiction impersonates autobiography, either the writer, or the story, is imaginary (or both are). As with 'Mark Rutherford''s *Autobiography*, this imaginary writing can take different forms: autobiography; journal; essay; fiction. In a sense, the only difference between Hale White's example and Joyce's is that Joyce puts all these into one work, whereas Hale White . . . well, puts them into two volumes, but several 'works', yoking the different forms together but leaving open the question of whether they are all part of the same overall work or not; and whether they have the same aesthetic status or not.

THE AESTHETIC ASPECT OF IMAGINARY WRITING

In principle, any genre or form can be presented as fictionally authored, and we have already encountered many, and will encounter more. Yet when the work the fictional author writes is a work of art, we enter a different world. Texts

---

[3] Aldous Huxley, *Point Counter Point* [1928] (Harmondsworth: Penguin, 1961), pp. 298–9.
[4] See the discussion of Linda Hutcheon's concept of 'historiographic metafiction' in Chapter 12.

containing works of fictional creativity are not unprecedented in the twentieth century, but with modernism they suddenly start proliferating.

When Chapter 5 posited 'creative writing' as one of the four modes available to auto/biografiction, the category was left unexplored. Yet, as has become clear from the discussion of Joyce, the question of what constitutes creative writing within auto/biografiction weaves and unweaves itself as much as Pater could have wished. Though it may not help us decide the undecidable, a taxonomy of different degrees of creativity within imaginary writing (as distinct from the forms of the works in which they appear) may help (in Ruskin's phrase for what he thought was all the thoughts of the 'wisest' could do for us) to 'put the difficulty into a clear shape, and exhibit to you the grounds for *in*decision.'[5] The difficult question is: what happens when what's forged or faked by creative writers is creative writing? Doesn't it turn inside out the model offered in the taxonomy in Chapter 5, which considered forms in which a real author's creative work (i.e. a novel) framed a fictional author's writing of something with a different status (i.e. a journal)? If the writing that is being faked is itself creative work, what happens to its frame? This aspect of the framing of imaginary writing will be explored here, together with the related question of how such framing affects the aesthetic aspect of what it contains.

If it isn't impossible to impersonate creativity, it is immensely difficult— perhaps to the point of hubris. Sustained examples tend to occur relatively rarely before postmodernism (some key postmodern examples will be discussed in Chapter 12). Aesthetic and modernist writers seem drawn instead to liminal modes of writing: forms that it is difficult to categorize aesthetically. Rilke, best known as a poet, would have had as good a chance as anyone (except Pessoa!) at being able to write poems that could convince as examples of works by a fictional poet like Malte Laurids Brigge. Yet he chooses to write Brigge's notebooks instead. His art is invested in producing something in a form that is not quite art; to make a novel out of something not quite a novel. Notebooks (such as Henry James's) or Journals (such as those of Delacroix or Gide) or Letters (such as Keats's) have long been read as aesthetically valuable. But their value has to do at least partly with the way they supplement other art-works, supplying insights into what the painter was painting, the poet writing, or the novelist elaborating. Take away that context (Brigge's poems, say) and we feel unable to distinguish between symptoms of genuine artistic genius and charlatanism, insanity, or self-delusion.

The aesthetic dimension has been increasingly relevant to our discussion of auto/biography and auto/biografiction. We shall see how, as modernism evolves into postmodernism, these tropes of imaginary authorship and imaginary writing will also become more relevant to the analyses of auto/biografiction about artists

---

[5] Ruskin, *Sesame and Lilies*, Library Edition, ed. E. T. Cook and Alexander Wedderburn, vol. 18 (London: George Allen, 1905), p. 76.

in the rest of the book. Yet, on the other hand, when writers introduce fictional creativity into their work, it both foregrounds the question of the aesthetic—of whether we are to read utterances as examples of the aesthetic, and if so, whose art do they exemplify?; and simultaneously destabilizes distinctions between artist and non-artist; or between author and character.

Joyce poses these questions by taking an artist as his subject, and giving us so much of his talk and writing. They are also posed implicitly by fictional works narrated by non-artist characters like Marlow in *Heart of Darkness*, George Ponderevo in Wells's *Tono-Bungay*, or John Dowell in Ford's *The Good Soldier*, due to the double-articulation whereby the words are the narrator's, yet also the writer's. They are conversation, a yarn, a fumbling attempt to write down a story in what seems like no particular order. But they are also technically sophisticated and highly self-conscious artifices, works of art. We might naively think that insofar as the words are uttered by Marlow or Dowell, they are not intended aesthetically; insofar as they are written by Conrad or Ford, they are. Yet what Ford, Wells, and Conrad all do is to introduce an uncertainty about how aesthetically competent their narrators are; all three are conscious of their listeners, about the extent to which their narratives can make the audience 'see' their characters; about the mode of telling a story. When writers like Rilke, Pessoa, and Joyce take artists as their characters or heteronyms, the aesthetics become even more complex, more fluid. If we consider a further taxonomy, this time of the aesthetic dimension of fictional utterances, it might look like this:

1) Words of non-artist offered as non-art (the Russian's cryptic notice in *Heart of Darkness*, reading only: 'Wood for you. Hurry up. Approach cautiously')[6]
2) Words of non-artist with aesthetic aims (Kurtz's pamphlet, perhaps)
3) Words of quasi-artist offered as non-art (Marlow's conversations with the Russian and others)
4) Words of quasi-artist offered as non-art by them, but considerable as art by the reader (Marlow's ability to spin yarns?)
5) Words of artist offered as non-art (Brigge's journal?)
6) Words of artist offered as quasi-art (Stephen's journal?)
7) Words of artist intended as art by them, but offered by the author as an example of failure
8) Words of artist intended as art, and endorsed by the author.

Trying to disentangle this aspect of the taxonomy raises other questions, long familiar to aestheticians. Does the status of something as an example of 'art' depend on intention? (i.e. does the artist decide what is art and what isn't?) Or does it depend on reception? (i.e. can the viewer decide that an unmade bed is not art?) Does it depend on a value judgement? (i.e. if we say an unmade bed isn't

---

[6] Conrad, *Heart of Darkness*, ed. Robert Hampson (London: Penguin, 1995), p. 64.

art, are we just saying we don't value it?) And if so, who decides on value? (In our fictional cases, the characters, the narrators, the authors, or the readers?)

For some critics, such questions seem the wrong ones to ask, because reprehensibly essentialist; because they appear to accept a view of 'art' and 'the artist' as transcendental categories, in such a way as to suppress their ideology and history.[7] Certainly the category of 'the aesthetic' should be historicized. That is precisely the point. It is very much a Romantic, post-Romantic, and especially *fin de siècle* category; which is the period of the writing being discussed. And our texts consist largely of autobiographies by writers making aesthetic discoveries; discovering themselves to be, or to have become, artists; and of fiction about artists, whether imaginary or auto/biographical. So the questions of what an artist is; what it means to be or become one; what constitutes art, are all posed by most of these works. In short, the line from aesthetic autobiography leads through autobiografiction to fictional creativity.

THE FRAMING OF FICTIONAL CREATIVITY

Imaginary writing can be considered as a form of *ekphrasis* insofar as it is held up as an aesthetic object. *Ekphrasis* normally refers to extended visual description, especially description of a work of art or artefact—Achilles' shield in Homer; Keats's Grecian Urn. In such cases, the object described exists in a different medium from the medium of the description: painting, sculpture, landscape, and so on, rather than writing. With imaginary writing the medium is the same, and to this extent it can be considered a form of *mise en abyme*. Thus Stephen's villanelle and journal, as pieces of writing embedded within Joyce's writing, are *mises en abyme*. If Stephen has written the entire book, his poem and journal would be *mises en abyme* of a second-order kind: not just art-works within art-works, but writings by a character within a narrative also written by that character. But though their medium is the same—writing—their forms (poem, journal) are different from that of *Portrait* (autobiografiction); and to that extent they are *ekphrases*.

Literary works from realism to postmodernism abound with imaginary works of art in another medium, which by definition cannot be *delivered* in words, but only *described*—though the figure of *ekphrasis*. Examples from the visual arts include: Frenhoffer's unintelligible painting in Balzac's 'The Unknown Masterpiece' ('*Le Chef d'oeuvre inconnu*'; 1831); Hawthorne's *The Marble Faun* (1860); Mikhailov's portrait of Anna Karenina; Rutherford's 'A Mysterious Portrait'; Basil Hallward's painting of Dorian Gray; Lord Mark's Bronzino that so moves Milly Theale in James's *The Wings of the Dove* (1902); the painting Lily Briscoe

---

[7] See for example Terry Eagleton, *Literary Theory: An Introduction* (Oxford: Blackwell, 1994), pp. 20–1.

struggles with then completes in *To the Lighthouse* (1927). Or novelists can describe performances; whether musical performances (Trilby's mesmerized singing in du Maurier's novel of 1894; Forster's accounts of Lucy Honeychurch playing Beethoven's last piano sonata in *A Room with a View* (1908), and of Leonard Bast listening to Beethoven's Fifth Symphony in *Howard's End* (1910)); or the *tableaux vivants* in Edith Wharton's *The House of Mirth* (1905), or in Miss La Trobe's pageant of English history in Woolf's *Between the Acts* (1941).

The presence of such works perhaps prompted writers to take the device to its next stage: to produce the work, rather than merely cite it. Thus fictional creativity could be seen as prompted by the proliferation of imaginary artists and art-works emerging from the time of Pater, Wilde, and the Aesthetic movement. The trope of fictional creativity becomes widespread through the twentieth century, and its taxonomy and its history need to be sketched.

By 'fictional creativity' I mean the subset of imaginary writing that is presented as a creative or literary work. This is the kind especially relevant to our study of aesthetic autobiography and autobiografiction. In historical terms, the phenomenon is relatively rare before the period we have been studying; not least because 'creativity' is itself a post-Romantic category. When Ann Radcliffe gives us poems purportedly written by Emily, the heroine of *The Mysteries of Udolpho* (1794), they're not intended as evidence of literary genius. Rather, they are examples of sensibility, utterly conventional expressions of the right sort of feelings for a decorous young lady. 'Creativity' isn't an issue.

All first-person narratives by fictional characters are fictionally uttered writings. In some cases the narrator claims to be writing them down. But, again, the convention until the late nineteenth century was that they are artless. The life-writings of earlier narrators are supposed to be their tales, stories. Robinson Crusoe, Moll Flanders, Lemuel Gulliver, and Tristram Shandy are trying to tell their stories, not be artists. Their views on life, morality, society, are markedly not the same as the author's own. It's the characters' naivety that is often being presented, rather than their artfulness. Gulliver may just be gullible; Tristram Shandy's project is completely mad, since as he explains he writes more slowly than he lives, so the more he writes the more life he has to cover. (His style is not seen as achieved art, but as the helpless result of his conception. His mother interrupted his father's love-making, so Tristram's conceptions keep interrupting themselves.) Their artlessness draws a line between them and their authors. It's a line some books keep trying to delude their gullible readers into forgetting, especially when the device is being used for empathetic purposes (as in Defoe) in such a way as to make us disattend to the narrators' literary skill. Such artlessness in the narrators can heighten the verisimilitude of their stories. Readers are more likely to believe them if they don't feel they are being manipulated by a skilful writer of fiction. Or it can be grounds for mockery. Where Defoe works through pastiche of travellers' tales or Newgate autobiography, Swift and Sterne work through parody and satire. Either way, the emergent authors of the novel distinguish themselves from less premeditated authors—of letters, memoirs, travel writings, treatises, pamphlets, and so forth—paradoxically by fictionalizing their life-writings. Nineteenth-century novels often feature dramatized narrators, such as the multiple narrators in Wilkie Collins's *The Moonstone*. But they tend to be used for empathy rather than satire (even when handled comically, as in Dickens); and to be telling their experiences, writing statements as for the police, rather than writing novels. We talk of their qualities as narrators, not as artists.

Yet, as we have begun to see, our key exhibits are particularly exercised over this distinction as they repeatedly destabilize it. With the advent of the *Künstlerroman*, and artist characters, this distance collapses altogether; which leaves the novelists themselves with a harder task: not to fake an artless telling, but a work of art. This means we cannot then tell whom to attribute the art to in the books. Is Marlow's eloquence the sign of an artistry that reveals him as a nascent Conrad (and thus an autobiographical persona)? Or do Conrad's framings of him by unnamed narrators and other characters indicate that he may be able to spin a yarn but he couldn't style a novel? We have seen how Joyce's *Portrait* produces hesitation over who is responsible for the art—Joyce, the real author, or perhaps Stephen, the fictional one. Because this isn't a first-person narrative, the reader has to make a greater leap to attribute it to third-person Stephen. But if the reading is accepted, it is Stephen who has made the greater leap, achieving a greater objectivity. To the extent that Stephen *is* Joyce, it appears a trivial distinction. Yet it produces a curious contradiction in the text. Joyce shows Stephen writing, implying he's a different author. But he gives him roughly his own life story, which appears to negate the differentiation. From another point of view this identification, rather than infusing Stephen's character with Joyce's subjectivity, can be seen as turning Joyce's subjective experience into something objective. This would be the classic reading of it as a modernist text, using technique to escape subjectivity and produce something 'concrete'. Arguably, the differentiation between Joyce and Stephen matters less as Stephen gets closer to being the artist who can narrate himself; that Stephen needs Joyce the narrator less and less as he gets older. Yet this claim introduces a reverse circularity, since it acknowledges Stephen as the implied narrator, and thus potentially the author. The point is that imaginary writing, or fictional creativity, is more than an aesthetic refinement. It is also a deeply destabilizing narrative strategy, which escapes any classic account of modernist 'objectivity'.

Such issues come to the fore in postmodern engagements with life-writing; which, in turn, helps us see their emergence in classic modernism. In Nabokov's *Pale Fire*, for example (discussed more fully in Chapter 12), there are two fictional authors. The poet John Shade, whose poem is presented as a work of art. Its editor, Charles Kinbote, whose extensive annotations take up most of the text. Kinbote doesn't think of himself as an artist, or of his notes as creative work.

Nabokov may be presenting them as expressions of a paranoid schizophrenic delusion. They may well, that is to say, be fiction. But insofar as they constitute art, the art is Nabokov's, not Kinbote's. If this is 'fictional non-creativity', then there is also a category of 'non-fictional creativity', whereby an artist creates art out of something that appears non-fictional. Eliot's notorious notes to 'The Waste Land', for example, are not fiction in the sense of being untrue. The allusions are correctly identified, and debts properly acknowledged. The fiction is that they elucidate the poem. To that extent they are imaginary notes. They are not attached by an editor to someone else's poem to guide readers; they are attached by the poet, as part of the poem. Thus they are (arguably) art, but not presented as such. In this respect they come close to another mode in which authorship is fictionally displaced: parody. A parody can be of a named or nameable author, and is thus akin to heteronymous creation, though the point is usually to negate or at least mock the creativity of the target; as we shall see in Chapter 10 on Richard Aldington. Or it can be more generalized, as we shall see in Chapters 9 and 11, mocking creative types: the Aesthete, the Biographer. But where writing is not presented as itself an aesthetic object, it falls outside the scope of the definition of fictional creativity.

TAXONOMY

We can distinguish at least four broad 'types' of 'fictional creativity' (each of which could be further divided). This taxonomy supplements that of relations between fiction and life-writing in Chapter 5 on fake lives. The point here is that the imaginary works do not have to be life-writings, but can just as well be works of fiction or poetry. And though autobiografiction is drawn towards using the device, it doesn't appear only within autobiografiction, but (as in some of the examples below) is also common in modern fiction. In order of increasing presence within a narrative they are:

1) Fictional citation. This is when a fictional work is mentioned, even described, but not quoted; referred to, but not delivered.

This figure is very widespread. It can be found in James, Gide, and Martin Amis, as in Amis's *The Information*, in which Richard Tull never gets round to writing his *History of Increasing Humiliation*, but ends up living out the history of his own humiliation. Amis jokes about fictional novels which are only their titles. Richard Tull's latest novel is 'deliberately but provisionally entitled *Untitled*.'[8] He has begun other novels 'all of them firmly entitled *Unpublished*. And stacked against him in the future, he knew, were yet further novels, successively entitled

---

[8] Amis, *The Information* (London: Flamingo, 1995), p. 11.

Unfinished, Unwritten, Unattempted and, eventually, *Unconceived*.'[9] There's a fine essay by Max Beerbohm on this trope, about books he wishes he could read but which don't exist, because they are only mentioned only in fictional works.[10] Borges has virtually made this type his trademark. Kevin Jackson gives a good account of the fun that can be had with such imaginary works in his *Invisible Forms: A Guide to Literary Curiosities*; but he confuses those actually shown and those merely cited.[11] A subset of this type is that in which a real work is fictionally produced, as in Borges's story 'Pierre Menard, Author of the *Quixote*'; or Eco's imagining in *The Name of the Rose* of the survival of Aristotle's lost treatise on Comedy; or Joyce's villanelle.

2) Part of a fictionally authored work is embedded or framed within a narrative. (As we have seen in Chapter 5, and in the recurrent figure of the *mise en abyme*, imaginary writing and the notion of framing are mutually implicatory.) This type perhaps covers the widest range, from brief quotation, such as the lines of unfinished poems composed and recalled by May Sinclair's *Mary Olivier*, to the inclusion of long extracts; as in A. S. Byatt's novel *Possession*, with its virtuoso range of fragments of writing by her characters (elements of novel, poem, biography, criticism, diary, letter, draft, etc.). In the *Portrait*, the last six pages, comprising Stephen's journal-entries, furnish another example.

Catherine Carswell, the Scottish novelist and friend of D. H. Lawrence, drew attention to an example in Proust that invites comparison with the case of Joyce's *Portrait*. This is the passage towards the end of the *Combray* section in volume 1:

a passage in which he not merely gives the circumstances of his hero's first literary composition, but puts before us the composed fragment itself. A few pages back and the boy has been bemoaning that, his choice of a literary career notwithstanding, his mind is blank of subjects, his intellect, at the mere idea of writing, a void.[12]

He becomes enchanted by three steeples he has seen from different angles when out driving, and suddenly 'words leap to frame themselves in his head'. She explains that the narrator says the 'actual piece of prose' is reproduced 'with only a slight revision here and there', and she says we 'may allow ourselves, I think, the presumption that it is substantially a true record'; also that the passage 'furnishes us with the key to the whole work', because 'They declare that for him there was never an actual but always a psychological perspective, and that peculiar to

---

[9] Ibid., p. 12.
[10] Max Beerbohm, 'Books within Books' (1914), in *And Even Now* (1920) (London, 1950), pp. 101–13.
[11] Kevin Jackson, *Invisible Forms: A Guide to Literary Curiosities* (London: Picador, 1999), p. 225.
[12] Catherine Carswell, 'Proust's Women', in *Marcel Proust: An English Tribute*, ed. C. K. Scott Moncrieff (New York: Thomas Seltzer, 1923), pp. 66–77 (p. 68).

himself. That is why there is no intellectual or logical means of checking Proust's observations.'[13] It might, then, seem to correspond closely to Joyce's inclusion of his own villanelle as an example of his protagonist's first literary inspiration. Yet, as Scott Moncrieff points out in a pair of footnotes, the spire and towers of Martinville which Marcel sees while driving home in Dr Percepied's carriage were based on the spires of Caen, seen from a motor car, in a much later year; and an earlier version was published in *Pastiches et mélanges*.[14] Thus, rather as we saw in Chapter 2 with the evolution of *A la recherche* out of *Contre Sainte-Beuve*, in which the aesthetic passages that were originally deployed as examples within a critical frame then become the frame itself, so here the passage that is deployed as the original germ of the whole work and as Marcel's induction into aesthetic prose, turns out to be re-fictionalized, itself a result of the aesthetic journey it purports to initiate.

This is a local example of fictional creativity. But it could also offer a key to a reading of the whole book as such, since if Marcel is a fictionalization of the author, and the whole book is the novel he eventually writes, then the whole book is fictionally authored. This possibility thus turns the novel inside out, since rather than the whole book containing a specimen of Marcel's composition, the specimen contains the possibility of reading the whole book as his—as the fully achieved work, containing within it an example of a false start.

3) The whole of a fictional work is embedded or framed within a narrative, as with Stephen's villanelle. Pasternak's *Dr Zhivago* (1957) appends forty-five pages of 'Zhivago's Poems' purportedly compiled posthumously by Yuri Zhivago's brother Yevgraf and read by his friends. There are some complete poems in *Possession*. *Pale Fire* frames Shade's poem within Kinbote's introduction and commentary.

4) The entire narrative is posed as, or readable as, fictively authored. As suggested, such works can be seen as continuations of the metafictional games initiated by eighteenth-century authors such as Diderot, Defoe, Swift, and Sterne, in which the whole work (bar the ironic warning-shot prefaces, notes by the printer, etc.) is fictionally authored. An equivocal modernist case is Ford's *The Good Soldier*, in which the narrator, Dowell, begins by saying he is imagining speaking the story to a 'sympathetic soul'; but later explicitly says that he has been writing it down.[15] Other modernist examples of fictionally-authored texts such as Svevo's *La coscienza di Zeno* or Beckett's trilogy *Molloy*, *Malone Dies*, and *The Unnameable* share the uncertain aesthetic status of Ford's narrator, who is sometimes artful but doesn't present himself as an artist. The version of this

[13] Catherine Carswell, 'Proust's Women', in *Marcel Proust: An English Tribute*, ed. C. K. Scott Moncrieff (New York: Thomas Seltzer, 1923), pp. 69–70.

[14] Ibid., pp. 69 and 106. Scott Moncrieff refers to *Pastiches et mélanges*, pp. 91–9.

[15] Ford, *The Good Soldier* (London: John Lane: The Bodley Head, 1915), pp. 17, 268–9.

fourth type in which the whole work is offered as a work of art is the rarest. Indeed, such cases are likely to be equivocal precisely because of the absence of a frame identifying the rest as fictionally authored. Among modernist fictions, Joyce's *Portrait* is an example if fictionally authored by Stephen. Proust's *A la recherche* is, to the extent that the narrator Marcel is distinguishable from Marcel Proust. Gide's *Les Faux-Monnayeurs* might be, as suggested in Chapter 5.

When Justin O'Brien describes Gide's first work, *The Notebooks of André Walter* (1891), as showing 'a young romantic hero writing the novel we are reading', it might sound like a candidate for this type of fully fictionally authored novel; and indeed one which, in its portrayal of the struggle between puritan religion and sexual love, may well have appealed to Joyce, if he read it.[16] But in fact, for all its cunning levels of fictionality, it remains an example of type 1. Though André Walter is indeed writing a novel, entitled *Allain*, Gide doesn't show it. His text is presented in the form of two notebooks, 'The White Notebook' and 'The Black Notebook.'[17] There are light editorial annotations to both by another persona. In 'The White Notebook' they're unsigned, and make comments on the text such as 'Name crossed out' or 'Word missing.'[18] Those to the Black Notebook start with one signed 'P. C.' to distinguish him from Walter or Gide.[19] The only biographical 'frame' the text provides is in the note to the last page of the Black Notebook:

This page must have been written on the 28th or 29th October. Brain fever, which caused our friend's death, broke out soon afterwards. An interval of three weeks separates these lines from the following, the last written by André Walter.

So far, Gide's experiment is comparable to Rilke's *The Notebook of Malte Laurids Brigge* or the passages Joyce gives from Stephen's journal. (Interestingly, Gide had also used 'André Walter' as a pseudonym for his first published writings, rather as Joyce had published as 'Stephen Daedalus' before the *Portrait*.)[20] But what Gide adds is Walter's plan for his novel. Walter explains on the first page of the Black Notebook: 'I have begun a new notebook which I want to reserve for the book. Yesterday I set down its general design and outlined its contents.' Gide's note here, signed 'P. C.', comments:

---

[16] Justin O'Brien, 'Gide's Fictional Technique', *Yale French Studies*, 7 (1951), 81–90 (p. 88). *Selected Letters of James Joyce*, ed. Ellmann (London: Faber, 1975), p. 230, shows Joyce had read Gide's *La Porte Etroite* by 1918.

[17] Gide, *The Notebooks of André Walter*, trans. Wade Baskin (London: Peter Owen, 1968); pp. 1–73, and 76–136 respectively.

[18] Ibid., p. 24.

[19] Baskin notes: 'Gide uses the initials P. C. to identify the friend to whom André Walter entrusted his notebooks and his novel'; ibid., p. 76n.

[20] Ibid., p. 83n: 'Under the signature of André Walter, Gide had published his first writings, "Reflections from Elsewhere—Minor Studies in Rhythm", in the literary review *Wallonie*.'

Here begin the first notes recorded by André Walter for the composition of his novel *Allain*. We thought it necessary to publish them in order to avoid destroying the integrity of the manuscript, but we have separated them from the text since they are only distantly related to the rest of the diary.[21]

Thus although it is true that the text is presented as written by Walter, and he is writing a novel, the novel we read is Gide's, not Walter's. Gide gives us Walter's preliminary work for his novel, but still not the novel itself.

THE HISTORY OF THE TROPE

When one considers it historically, the striking fact emerges that *in nineteenth century and turn-of-the-century literature, you generally only get the first type of fictional creativity, that is, fictional citation.*

Stories about artists abound which cite their works but don't deliver them. And this is true not just of works in other media, which by definition cannot be delivered in words. Though it's the great era of the *Bildungsroman*, and though the literary works of the time are peppered with writer-figures, the presentation of fictional works largely disappears, leaving only their titles and sometimes their descriptions. Examples of literary works described but not delivered include: Hugh Vereker's whole oeuvre in James's 'The Figure in the Carpet' (1896); Trigorin's stories in Chekhov's *The Seagull* (1896); Kurtz's pamphlet in 'Heart of Darkness' (1902); Stephen's essay on aesthetics described in chapter 19 of *Stephen Hero* (some of which corresponds to his impromptu lecture to Lynch in *A Portrait*). It is a trope which continues to be used—often for increasingly playful effects—all through the twentieth century, from say Clifford Chatterley's stories in *Lady Chatterley's Lover* (1928), to the screenplay mentioned in *Money* (1984)—introduced with a suitable metafictional joke as by the book's actual author, Martin Amis, rather than his equally metafictionally named character, John Self.

The nineteenth century, then, appears to have got a frisson of excitement from contemplating the idea of fictional works of literature, but was coy about actually showing them. *The Seagull* does also produce an example of fictional creativity, in the fragment (thus an example of our second type) that gets acted of Konstantin's play. But it comes across in its ponderous Symbolism as of dubious value—certainly very unlike Chekhov's own dramas. Whereas Trigorin's stories, which are only described, sound very like Chekhov's own.

There are at least three significant exceptions to this claim. First, Edgar Allan Poe, who, in 'Ligeia' (1838), prints Ligeia's poem; and in 'Fall of the House of

---

[21] Baskin notes: 'Gide uses the initials P. C. to identify the friend to whom André Walter entrusted his notebooks and his novel'; p. 76.

Usher' (1839), gives us ('if not accurately') a transcription of Roderick Usher's lyric.[22] Second, those Victorian dramatic monologues in which the narrator is a poet, and the monologue is, or could be taken to be, her or his poem; those in which, in Eric Griffiths's description, 'the fictional speaker is also fictionally writing the poem.'[23] Examples of such poets include Elizabeth Barrett Browning's Aurora Leigh; or the narrators of Robert Browning's 'Pauline' or *Sordello*. The great Victorian critic R. H. Hutton described Browning as 'a great intellectual and spiritual ventriloquist' in his ability:

> to migrate rapidly in this way from your own actual centre in the world of intellect and feeling to a totally different centre, where you not only try to speak an alien language, but to think unaccustomed thought and feel unaccustomed passions; and yet to do this, as Mr. Browning does, without really losing for a moment his own centre of critical life.[24]

If there is a perceptible unease about the notion of ventriloquism here (for all the admiration for Browning's imaginative energies), how much more disturbing must have been the idea of ventriloquizing an imaginary ventriloquist. The third, and most significant exception is Dostoevsky's passage about 'The Grand Inquisitor' in *The Brothers Karamazov* (1880), a poem supposedly written by Ivan and printed in full. As with the Poe, Dostoevksy's is another fiction of macabre transgression (think of Dostoevsky transfixed by the possibility that 'Everything is permitted'); as if both authors were conscious of violating a literary taboo.

Otherwise, the curious suppression of fictional creativity is bound up with Romantic aesthetics of 'the artist', and its sacralization of artistic creation as analogous to divine creation (Coleridge's 'repetition in the finite mind of the eternal act of creation in the infinite I AM').[25] If creation is treated as sacred, it acquires a cult of mysteries, which should not be revealed to the gaze of uninitiated mortals. It is its very invisibility that protects the artist, guarantees his authority and his work's authenticity. In a period when it was argued (as by Arnold) that Art could act as a substitute for a declining religion, human creativity becomes the new sacred mystery. This is true of Romantic pantheism, as it is of the Aesthetes' religion of beauty and art in the 1890s. And it's also what we find in Stephen's analogy between the artist and god; or as in D. H. Lawrence's vitalism. If this explanation is correct—that for post-Romantic authors, to impersonate creativity was to devalue it—it suggests a paradox about the trope of fictional citation. If there is a resistance to producing a fictionally authored text, why is it all right to produce its title, if that too is

---

[22] Poe, *Selected Tales*, ed. Julian Symons (Oxford: Oxford University Press, 1980), pp. 43–4, 69–71.

[23] Eric Griffiths, *The Printed Voice of Victorian Poetry* (Oxford: The Clarendon Press, 1989) p. 214.

[24] Hutton, 'Mr. Browning', *Literary Essays* (London: Macmillan, 1896), pp. 188–243 (p. 242).

[25] Coleridge, *Biographia Literaria*, ed. James Engell and W. Jackson Bate, 2 vols (London: Routledge and Kegan Paul, 1983), vol. 1, ch. 13, p. 304.

fictionally authored? The narrator of Muriel Spark's novel *Loitering with Intent* (1981), Fleur Talbot, repeatedly mentions her novel *Warrender Chase*, but she doesn't quote from it. Yet the title is evidently as composed as the rest of the novel. But rather than seeing the citation of fictional titles as negating the idea of a resistance to impersonating a creative text, we should perhaps see it as confirming it. The trope of fictional citation implies a difference in status between the title and the text. This too is Derridean territory, where a title appears to be outside the text it names, even though it is no less written; no less part of the work. Its ambiguous positioning, both inside and outside the text, might be what enables it to overcome the resistance to impersonation.

FAKES

The notion of the artist as a special sort of person is bound up with the notion of their inalienable individuality and originality. Romantic aesthetics, that is, urges a creativity that cannot be copied, cannot be faked. Which is one explanation of why Romanticism was so exercised over the problem of literary forgery.[26] Margaret Russett, in her book *Fictions and Fakes: Forging Romantic Authenticity*, discusses a range of counterfeit or 'fictional identities' (such as John Hatfield, the bigamist who married the 'Maid of Buttermere' posing as 'Hon. Augustus Hope'; or 'Caraboo', who was found near Bristol and taken to be a person of consequence from an island near Sumatra, but who was actually Mary Baker, an unemployed servant, who later wrote her autobiography) that coincided with 'the period that enshrined the ideal of original genius associated with Romanticism.'[27] The eighteenth and early nineteenth centuries had their forged and faked literary works too, certainly. But what's being faked is generally *texts* (letters in epistolary novels; purportedly ancient ballads and poems) rather than *artists*. Celebrated literary forgeries tend not to try to individuate the faked poets; only to produce fake poems. They don't provide the fictional context of the character producing the poetry to count as heteronyms in Pessoa's sense (though Chatterton's sustained composition of works by an imaginary fifteenth-century monk, Thomas Rowley, is perhaps an exception, curiously poised between forgery and heteronym).

Nineteenth-century literature thus finds itself in a double-bind. Whether in the psychological novel or the dramatic monologue, it claims to represent the spiritual and moral essence of its characters. It seeks to make everything visible;

---

[26] See for example recent studies by K. K. Ruthven, *Faking Literature* (Cambridge: Cambridge University Press, 2001); Nick Groom, *The Forger's Shadow* (London: Picador, 2002); and Margaret Russett, *Fictions and Fakes: Forging Romantic Authenticity, 1760–1845* (Cambridge University Press, 2006).

[27] Russett, *Fictions and Fakes*, pp. 5, 2.

yet it avoids representing artists producing their art. It is as if its legitimacy, its claim for total representation, requires a suppression of the representation of its own operations—which corresponds to realism's other marked representational paradox. Realist fiction claims to render the world sensuously. Characters are described in minute visual detail, to create the illusion of seeing them. Novels sometimes describe them as being seen like characters in a drama (as in the opening of *Le Père Goriot*) or as like figures in a painting (as in *The Portrait of a Lady*). But even when our apprehension of them is shown to be mediated by such cultural forms, it is usually forms other than writing that are invoked. The writing that seeks to convey the illusion of reality needs to suppress its own linguistic essence for the illusion to work; the more we're aware of the language, the less we're concentrating on the episode it is narrating or the scene it is describing. As soon as you're aware of the experience of reading, you're no longer doing it.

Anna Karenina or Emma Bovary are representative women; their 'being' can be faked, their talk, their letters, because these activities are general. Most of us talk, most used to write letters, and many try writing diaries. When art shows people doing these things, it shows them being the same sort of person as everyone else. Creative originality thus needed a distinction between fictional speaking and fictional writing, between creative and other kinds of writing, to validate its own authority to present other people. Realism is founded on the notion that art can capture life, but it cannot capture art.

Imaginary authorship can thus be understood as a form of questioning of the Romantic view of authorship and creativity. That explains both why the production of heteronymous writing is rare throughout the nineteenth century, and why it proliferates in modernism and post-modernism, whose novels appear to be straining at the convention that suppresses fictional creativity. The relevance of these arguments to Joyce is clear. *A Portrait* was written at a time when it had become newly possible to fake creativity. In effect, Joyce has inverted conventional fictional poetics. Instead of the author's (Tolstoy's) portrait of Anna Karenina, you have Stephen Dedalus's portrait of the author.

Joyce's *themes* might suggest *why* it had become possible to write a fictional novel; since Stephen's (and his own) break with Catholicism leaves him with an aesthetic philosophy shaped by a system that now appears fictional to a secularizing age. *A Portrait* is rightly read as a novel of intellectual and moral liberation: a *Bildungs*-epic, as Stephen frees himself from the tangled nets of church, state, and family. This is usually presented with what might be called aesthetic piety; that is, his 'vocation' is simply transferred. He *will not* serve the Pope, Ireland, or his parents; but he *will* serve art.

The relation between priest and artist is clearly central in Joyce. This, together with the way Stephen bases his aesthetic theories on Aquinas, has made it easy for Catholic critics to reconcile Joyce's radicalism with theology, since they assume the structures of authority are the same, but with the author at the top instead of god—as in Stephen's image of the author as like a god. That is to ignore the joke about him paring his fingernails (does god do that? Lynch makes a joke about Stephen's joke too, asking if god is trying to refine his fingernails out of existence, too). The nervous humour perhaps gives us a glimpse of how, even while advancing the theory, Joyce (or Stephen) is uneasy about it.

If Joyce's aesthetics had the courage of Stephen's convictions, would they not challenge the authority of the *artist* as squarely as he challenges the other authorities of church, nation, and family? And how better to do that than to make your whole book one whose 'authorship', origin, is uncertain (as Vicki Mahaffey suggests)? Stephen's art is framed if the rest of the novel is Joyce's, but not framed if it's his. The fictional author reading raises the question: is Stephen in the frame; or does he provide the frame—is he the frame itself?

In post-Romantic narratives, then, works by fictional characters pose a paradox. The novelists mean us to take the processes of their creation seriously; the attempt to fake the authenticity of the creative process is a double jeopardy. You have to create the character as well as their plausible creation, and to differentiate their creativity from your own. But it can also be seen as a challenge to the whole notion of creativity, since if secondary creativity can be faked, so can primary. This gets to the heart of postmodernist aesthetics, which revel in pastiche. It has tended to be pejorative to call a writer a ventriloquist. But it follows from my argument that the whole opposition between authentic and ventriloquial creativity is one that nineteenth-century aesthetics needed; but one that from a postmodern point of view is spurious. Fictional creations will not stay in their frames (or, according to the reading of the *Portrait*, can be written *without* a frame altogether). Finally: if Romantic aesthetics say you can't fake it, postmodern aesthetics say that creativity is, precisely, a matter of faking it.

This is not to say it's not the real thing. Postmodernist novelists tend not to use their hyper-fictionality to argue that creativity is only faking, or that life is only fictional. Instead, they believe that the experience of reading literature is a real thing, with a real relation to the lives it frames.

It is possible for a writer to make, or remake at least, for a reader, the primary pleasures of eating, or drinking, or looking on, or sex. [Novels . . .] do not habitually elaborate on the equally intense pleasures of reading. There are obvious reasons for this, the most obvious being the regressive nature of the pleasure, a *mise-en-abîme* even, where words draw attention to the power and delight of words, and so *ad infinitum*, thus making the imagination experience something papery and dry, narcissistic and yet disagreeably distanced, without the immediacy of sexual moisture or the scented garnet glow of good burgundy.[28]

Now and then there are readings which make the hairs on the neck, the non-existent pelt, stand on end and tremble, when every word burns and shines hard and clear and infinite

---

[28] A. S. Byatt, *Possession* (London: Vintage, 1991), p. 470.

and exact, like stones of fire, like points of stars in the dark—readings when the knowledge that we *shall know* the writing differently or better or satisfactorily, runs ahead of any capacity to say what we know, or how. In these readings, a sense that the text has appeared to be wholly new, never before seen, is followed, almost immediately, by the sense that it was *always there*, that we the readers, knew it was always there, and have *always known* it was as it was, though we have now for the first time recognised, become fully cognisant of, our knowledge.[29]

This is from a fictional work, about a fictional character reading a work of fiction. But it describes the kind of pleasure that makes all of us read. This experience of reading is not jeopardized by our awareness of fictionality. On the contrary, it is enabled by it. This is the answer to the realist reluctance to thematize its own writing processes. Postmodern autobiographies and novels which have drawn on modernist and earlier experiments in autobiografiction and imaginary writing will be discussed further in Chapter 12. They, like our earlier autobiografiction-ists, show an awareness that so much of our experience comes to us already mediated—by language, by writing, by visual images—that we often experience our experience not only through representation, but *as* representation.

GERTRUDE STEIN'S *THE AUTOBIOGRAPHY OF ALICE B. TOKLAS*

If the concepts of the entirely ventriloquial text and sustained fictional authorship seem unconvincing in relation to Joyce's *Portrait*, they are indisputable in the case of Gertrude Stein's masterpiece of 1933, *The Autobiography of Alice B. Toklas*. The experiments with heteronyms, with the circular *Künstlerroman*, with imaginary portraiture and fictional auto/biography that we have seen emerging tentatively from the turn of the century, become exuberantly and playfully explicit.

It's important to note that though such experiments share the trope of appearing to displace authorship, they do so in very different ways. Where Mark Rutherford writes in an autobiographical form with semi-autobiographical content but uses a pseudonym as author, Joyce writes in novel form with semi-autobiographical content and uses a pseudonym as character (or possibly a heteronym as fictional author). Pessoa writes as a number of heteronyms, giving them fictional biographies and oeuvres of often lyrical poems that express these fictional lives pseudo-autobiographically. Proust writes a book that fuses novel and autobiography, using semi-autobiographical material and tentatively identi-fying the narrator with the author's first name only.

---

[29] *Possession*, pp. 471–2.

Stein's contribution to this ferment of auto/biografictional experiment is different again. The form of the *Autobiography* is, well, autobiographical. The content, too, is autobiographical enough. There's more of Gertrude Stein in it than of Toklas herself, which perhaps makes it read more like Toklas's memoir of her companion than of herself. But Stein was a large part of her life, and the story she tells is as factual as most memoirs.[30] The fictionality of it is due not to its form or information-content, nor to its naming, since both Toklas and Stein appear as themselves. The fictional element is that Toklas did not write her autobiography. She is a real person. The story is her story, but it was written by Gertrude Stein, who playfully switches the author-attribution from herself to Toklas. Thus Toklas is not a 'fictional author' in the sense that Malte Laurids Brigge is, or Pessoa's heteronyms are, fictional. She is not a fictional *character*. But she is a fictional author in the sense that it is her *authorship* that is the fiction; not her.[31]

Yet the publication history leaves us with a puzzle as to how Stein expected readers to respond to the *Autobiography*. The first book editions, published by Harcourt in the United States and John Lane in the UK in the second half of 1933, didn't put Stein's name on the covers or the title-pages. Anna Linzie explains, 'At the time of publication, Stein requested that her name, her authorial signature, not be printed on the binding, the dust jacket, or the title page of *The Autobiography*.'[32] As Margot Norris comments, this was 'a strategy bound to confound the reader with respect to the text's authorship.'[33] However, when she continues (following Linzie) that 'When the work was published in serial form in *The Atlantic Monthly* in May 1933, readers of the installments might likewise have been genuinely surprised by the authorial reversal at the ending', they are quite wrong. The serialization in the *Atlantic* had run from May to August 1933. Each of the four instalments clearly identified 'The Autobiography of Alice B. Toklas' as 'By Gertrude Stein'. So readers of the magazine version would have

---

[30] Though one must note that Eugene and Marie Jolas published an entire pamphlet supplement of *transition* called *Testimony against Gertrude Stein*, with contributions from Matisse, Braque, and Tzara, enumerating errors in the *Autobiography of Alice B. Toklas*. See Richard Bridgman, *Gertrude Stein in Pieces* (New York: Oxford University Press, 1970), pp. 217–18.

[31] Richard Bridgman, *Gertrude Stein in Pieces*, pp. 209–17, discusses the various suggestions that Toklas may have had a hand in the writing. He concludes that (according to the evidence of the surviving manuscripts) the hand she had was entirely editorial. Also see James Breslin 'Gertrude Stein and the Problems of Autobiography', in Jelinek, Estelle C.; *Women's Autobiography: Essays in Criticism* (Bloomington, IN: Indiana University Press, 1980), p. 151. Linda Wagner Martin, 'Stein, Woolf, and Parody', in *Telling Women's Lives: The New Biography* (New Jersey: Rutgers University Press, 1994), pp. 72–7 (pp. 73–4), argues that the manuscript of *Toklas* had a different start, which was replaced by several sheets in Toklas's hand. Martin interprets this to mean that Toklas had to help Stein capture her voice before she could continue, though of course it doesn't prove that the new opening was written before the rest of the manuscript; nor that Toklas composed it, rather than taking it from Stein's dictation.

[32] Anna Linzie, *The True Story of Alice B. Toklas: A Study of Three Autobiographies* (Iowa City: University of Iowa Press, 2006), p. 57. Stein's name was indeed omitted from the front of the Harcourt Brace first edition dust-jacket (though she was mentioned on the back); but the jacket of John Lane's 1933 edition identified the book as 'by GERTRUDE STEIN'

[33] Margot Norris, review of Linzie, *Biography*, 30.1 (2007), 108–111 (pp. 109–10).

been in no doubt from the start, when they opened the May issue in which the opening of the 'Autobiography' had pride of place as the first item, that Toklas was only fictionally its author. (Incidentally, this was standard *Atlantic* style: to put the word 'By' in front of the author's name, under the title. So although 'The Autobiography of Alice B. Toklas by Gertrude Stein' conveys exactly the desired paradoxical effect—that it *is* Toklas's autobiography, but isn't *by* Toklas—we cannot be sure how far what the *Atlantic*'s house style delivered was what Stein wanted.) Readers might have been puzzled as to why someone's autobiography appeared to be written by somebody else. Or they may have realized that something surprising was being done with the form. But they couldn't have been surprised by the ending of the book unless they had forgotten the repeated authorial attributions.

The question, instead, is why the book version, published hot on the heels of the serialization, removed all attributions of Stein's authorship except the closing flourish, when the surprise had already been let out of the bag over the preceding four months.[34] Perhaps Stein felt that more fun could be had by drawing out the tease for as long as possible. She, and the publishers, would have hoped to reach a different, and broader, audience, and may have felt that creating an air of mystery about the book would be the best way to draw on the *succès d'estime* of the serialization. Turning the narrative from serial to book wasn't all a matter of taking away, however. What they added was a series of signs that foregrounded the question of authorship. First, the Harcourt dust-jacket used a striking photograph by Man Ray, also used in cropped form as the frontispiece for both the American and British first editions, of both women. Toklas is standing, brightly lit, in a doorway. But she is small, in the background of the composition, because she is just about to come in through the door. In the foreground, in the centre of the room, is the much larger figure of Stein, sitting at a table. She is not only in possession of the physical space; she is writing. As James Breslin suggests, this can be read as a kind of in-joke; a covert signal that Stein is not just an author in general, but the author of this book in particular.[35]

The text on the Harcourt dust-jacket is even more tantalizing. The front flap declares in what starts like dead-pan tones that the subject of Toklas's *Autobiography* is actually Stein:

Written with monolithic simplicity, THE AUTOBIOGRAPHY OF ALICE B. TOKLAS reveals the essential honesty of Gertrude Stein's life—a life that has been devoted to the great revolution in the arts that came with the twentieth century [. . .] Alice B. Toklas, the 'I' of the book, has been friend, secretary, editor, gardener, and a 'good vet for dogs' in Gertrude Stein's home ever since they met in 1907.

[34] John Malcolm Brinnin, *The Third Rose* (London: Weidenfeld and Nicolson, 1960), p. 311, says the *Autobiography* was published in August 1933.
[35] Breslin, 'Gertrude Stein and the Problems of Autobiography', p. 152.

But not her biographer, exactly. As it goes on, we start wondering whether that 'essential honesty' was not also a tease. To call Toklas the 'I' of the book is disconcertingly different from calling her its author. The note closes on a similar double take: 'The autobiography covers Gertrude Stein's whole life from her Radcliffe and Johns Hopkins days to the present.' An autobiography is supposed to cover someone's whole life: but that someone is normally both its 'I' and its writer. The games get even more high-spirited on the back of the jacket:

Since the first announcement of the forthcoming publication of this book, innumerable questions have been asked about Alice B. Toklas. Who is this author? What is this extraordinary book that she has written? Does she really exist? One newspaper critic, Harry Hansen to be exact, even went so far as to suggest that Alice B. Toklas did not exist. He was promptly rebuked by three correspondents [....]

The questions presumably couldn't be numbered because they didn't exist either. The three correspondents were quoted at length, reassuring readers that Toklas did indeed exist. The joke being that she doesn't exist in the way she was being claimed to exist, as 'this author'. The fact that the back flap carried a notice about Woolf's *Flush* didn't do anything to subdue the sense that life-writing was being played with here.

Some of this is surely shrewd publicity work, and it doubtless helped the book become a bestseller. But the issue to which it draws attention is central to the book's achievement.[36] Part of that achievement is to mount a critique of autobiography as a gendered form. Jill Ker Conway asks:

Given that Western language and narrative forms have been developed to record and explicate the male life, how can a woman write an autobiography when to do so requires using a language which denigrates the feminine and using a genre which celebrates the experience of the atomistic Western male hero?[37]

One answer would be: write a book like *The Autobiography of Alice B. Toklas*, which takes over the jargon of male hero-worship biography, and guys it; which also mimics the form of biographical subservience, as Stein has Toklas reiterating her awe for Stein's 'genius', as we shall see. Stein smuggles in another model of public figure life, the lesbian couple, to counter that notion of male self-sufficiency. Thus part of the smokescreen about authorship continues the Joycean project of questioning authority; with an added twist of questioning it as the preserve of male authors. It offers not just the idea of the female author, but (as implied, perhaps, by the Man Ray frontispiece) a non-atomistic collaborative production of life-writing—which is arguably an essentially more honest

---

[36] They may also have felt that to create a smokescreen around the authorship would keep the question open; whereas if they had tried to present it as by both women, critics would probably assume Stein was the prime mover.

[37] Jill Ker Conway, *When Memory Speaks* (New York: Knopf, 1998), p. 3.

form, recognizing the intersubjective nature of all life-writing. Such play with traditional notions of gender and authority bespeak a major shift, and one which Stein recognized as bearing upon the relation between fiction and autobiography:

Anything is an autobiography but this was a conversation.

I said to Hammett there is something that is puzzling. In the nineteenth century the men when they were writing did invent all kinds and a great number of men. The women on the other hand never could invent women they always made the women be themselves seen splendidly or sadly or heroically or beautifully or desparingly [*sic*] or gently, and they never could make any other kind of woman. From Charlotte Brontë to George Eliot and many years later this was true. Now in the twentieth century it is the men who do it. The men all write about themselves, they are always themselves as strong or weak or mysterious or passionate or drunk or controlled but always themselves as the women used to do in the nineteenth century. Now you yourself always do it now why is it. He said it's simple. In the nineteenth century men were confident, the women were not but in the twentieth century the men have no confidence and so they have to make themselves as you say more beautiful more intriguing more everything and they cannot make any other man because they have to hold on to themselves not having any confidence.[38]

It's a marvellous irony that it is Dashiell Hammett, the creator of the iconic hard-boiled detective Sam Spade, who voices modern man's lack of confidence. The implication is that it is now the women who have the confidence—not just social confidence, but professional confidence, including the professional confidence as writers to experiment in creating an other person, as Stein had done in the *Autobiography*, paradoxically producing something in the process that is her honest autobiography, in that it does convey what matters to her as an artist. The point is that Stein wasn't trying to produce a fake, and fool anyone that Toklas really was the author. For all its sleight of hand, the book is not only Stein's autobiography, but her impression of the kind of self Toklas might present in hers.

Stein was to continue her experiments in displaced autobiography four years later, with a volume calling itself *Everybody's Autobiography* (from which that last quotation comes), and which begins (by still performing the fiction of Toklas's authorship): 'Alice B. Toklas did hers and now anybody will do theirs.' This time the 'I' is Stein herself. But where in the earlier book Stein wrote as Toklas, now she positions herself as writing universally: 'Anyway autobiography is easy like it or not autobiography is easy for any one and so this is to be everybody's autobiography.'[39] In *Everybody's Autobiography* she says of time that 'you have to be a genius to live in it and know it to exist in it and and [*sic*] express it to accept it and deny it by creating it [...].'[40] That is what she does with

---

[38] Gertrude Stein, *Everybody's Autobiography* (New York: Random House, 1937), p. 5.
[39] Ibid., p. 6.   [40] Ibid., p. 281.

autobiography: she both accepts it—by writing it, repeatedly—and denies it—by writing the autobiographies of others—by creating it—that is, by re-creating it as a new form of autobiografiction.

In *The Autobiography of Alice B. Toklas*, Stein shares a joke with Sherwood Anderson at Hemingway's expense:

But what a book, they both agreed, would be the real story of Hemingway, not those he writes but the confessions of the real Ernest Hemingway. It would be for another audience than the audience Hemingway now has but it would be very wonderful.[41]

The joke is that Hemingway should try abandoning the style of impersonal reportage that had become his trademark, in favour of self-expression. But this critique is made in a book which itself purports to be a confessional book, but isn't; or at least, is not its purported author's confession, but an oblique confession by Stein, writing herself for a different audience than the Paris expatriates who admired her less representational experiments. It isn't just that, like much in the *Autobiography*, this tips us the wink that both its own impersonality and its own confessionality are fictionalized. It is also that her approach to the modernism of Hemingway, Anderson, and herself, is through such minuets on the theme of auto/biography.

THIRD-PERSON AUTOBIOGRAPHY

The last chapter explored the limits of the fictional-author or heteronymic reading of *Portrait of the Artist*, a reading that posits the separateness of Joyce and Stephen Dedalus, and pulls the discussion away from the autobiographical. However, whether we think of Joyce or Stephen as the 'author', it remains a deeply autobiographical work. But as such it has a very striking quality: that of being written for the most part in the third person. This is true of both the actual and the fictional author. If Joyce is presenting Stephen writing the book of his life, he could have had him using the first-person throughout, as he does at the end. If it is read as Joyce's pseudonymous autobiography, he still could have used the first person: 'I, Dedalus . . .' could have been a possible utterance in both cases. The third person can be seen as merely the sign that this is a *novel*, however autobiographical, rather than an autobiography. To that extent, Joyce is using free indirect style, which combines impersonal narration with the thought-style or speech-style of a character, in order to arouse empathy with that character; though he's using it in a new way: to project his own interiority outwards, into a fictional alter ego, rather than to take an external, omniscient third-person narrator inside the head of a fictional subjectivity. Yet Joyce's intensive use of

---

[41] *The Autobiography of Alice B. Toklas* (London: John Lane, 1933), p. 232.

autobiographical material, the emphasis on the artist's development (including the genesis of a work of art) together with his experiments with imaginary writing, and his play with the title, all pull the book back towards life-writing and autobiografiction. The kind of objectification of the self entailed by translating one's own person into a fictional alter ego corresponds to the shift of person from first to third in autobiography. *A Portrait of the Artist*, that is, also has a strong claim to be considered a third-person autobiography or autobiografiction; and can thus be seen as extending the earlier line of third-personality in autobiografiction whether or not one accepts the fictional author reading. To that extent it can also be seen as a precursor to Stein's tour de force.

Philippe Lejeune, in his intriguing essay 'Autobiography in the Third Person', begins by positing that third person autobiography is comparable to first person biography. He notes that *The Autobiography of Alice B. Toklas* is a third-person autobiography from Stein's point of view, but also a first person biography of Toklas.[42] He distinguishes between a figure of enunciation and a fictive narrator, saying of Michel Leiris:

> The author speaks about himself *as if* another were speaking about him, or as if he himself were speaking of another. This *as if* concerns only the enunciation; the statement is still subject to the strict and distinct rules of the autobiographical contract. However, if I used the same grammatical presentation in an autobiographical fiction, the statement would have to be taken from the point of view of a phantasmal pact [*pacte fantasmatique*] ('this conveys something about me, but is not me').[43]

This appears valuable for the theory of autobiografiction, as does his argument that, because of the gap between narrator and subject 'The first person, then, always conceals a hidden third person [. . .].'[44] However, the attempt clinically to separate out fictive enunciations from fictive narrators breaks down when applied to autobiografictional forms which work by obscuring whether the subject is or isn't the author (Mark Rutherford's *Autobiography*, say, is fictive enunciation where Rutherford is Hale White; fictional narration where he isn't). Similarly, when Lejeune tries to apply these concepts to *The Autobiography of Alice B. Toklas* his terminology goes awry; as the comparison with Joyce makes clear. His definition of Toklas as 'fictive narrator' misses the distinction, crucial to Stein's text, between a narrator who is a fictional character, and one who is a real person whose narration is what is fictional. Lejeune proposes the book as an example of his category of 'fictive fictions' of which he says:

> They are not pure fictions, i.e., autobiographical novels based on a novelistic pact. The general system remains that of autobiography. However, a game is grafted onto one aspect of the narrative (the character of the narrator): the autobiographer tries

---

[42] Philippe Lejeune, 'Autobiography in the Third Person', *New Literary History*, 9:1 (1977), 27–50 (p. 49 n. 32).

[43] Ibid., pp. 28, 29.   [44] Ibid., p. 32.

to imagine what would happen if someone else were telling his story or drawing his portrait.[45]

This describes the book well. *Alice B. Toklas* is certainly a fictively authored *autobiography*. But the terminology here is misleading, since it connotes a fictively authored work of *fiction*, such as Ivan Karamazov's 'Grand Inquisitor' poem, say: a fictional work by a fictional character, fictional creativity. Again, when Lejeune says: 'Now for the fictional attempt to bring another point of view into one's autobiography by creating a character in a novel': Toklas isn't an entirely created character, and doesn't even have that first courtesy accorded to fictional characters of a fictional name.[46] Nor is the book exactly a novel (as he has conceded in saying 'The general system remains that of autobiography'). Finally, Lejeune's description of how 'a game is grafted onto one aspect of the narrative (the character of the narrator)' again rings slightly untrue in this case: Toklas isn't a 'character', exactly, in the sense that fictional characters are; nor is it her 'character' that is being played with, but her role as narrator.

One of his closing questions points to research still needing to be done: 'How do we distinguish between an autobiography employing fictive fictions and an autobiographical novel?'[47] This is one of the central questions I have attempted to address here, especially in relation to Joyce. Stein's case shows how a more sophisticated vocabulary is required, which can differentiate a heteronymic poem by Pessoa (a fictionally authored creative work not necessarily autobiographical in form) from a novel like *The Notebook of Malte Laurids Brigge* (a novel using the form of fictionally authored life-writing) or from a work like *The Autobiography of Alice B. Toklas* (a fictive autobiography—fictive because not written by its narrator, and thus not *auto*biography of Toklas; autobiography of Stein, but only fictively, through the ventriloquism of Toklas).

If *The Autobiography of Alice B. Toklas* doesn't quite read like a novel—'autobiografiction' seems to catch its multiply-hybrid form much better—it has much in common with the *Künstlerroman*. But Stein eschews the pseudonymity of the modernist *Künstlerroman-à-clef* (like Richardson's *Pilgrimage*, say), opting instead for a much more complex manoeuvre, which both accepts and denies her own and Toklas's identities as themselves, by creating them as seen by each other: Stein's portrait of Toklas portraying Stein.

EGOTISM

The complexity is striking in many ways in *The Autobiography of Alice B. Toklas*, but especially in the innovative way it engages with autobiography's perpetual

[45] Lejeune, 'Autobiography in the Third Person', p. 42.
[46] Ibid.   [47] Ibid., p. 47.

nemesis, egotism.[48] Stein knew that for her to write her own autobiography, making in it anything like the claims for or assumptions of her 'genius' and innovativeness would have been exceptionable enough had she been a man. Authors like James or Conrad wrote their memoirs after the body of work that had already secured their literary reputations. Though Stein had already written important books by 1933, she was not considered the major figure she is now, or cuts in the *Autobiography*. For her to write about herself directly in that way as a woman would have been doubly exceptional. What the mock-authorship by Toklas enables her to do is not only to make such claims vicariously, but in so doing to ironize them. It's not quite that we cannot be sure how seriously she means them—there's not really any doubt she thought of herself as a great writer—but such thoughts expressed in mock Toklas-ese are both serious and comical at the same time. As Stein later put it, 'It is funny this knowing being a genius, everything is funny.'[49]

The enunciatory strategy of the *Autobiography* thus enables Stein to write her autobiography as a woman in ways which pre-empt sexist ridicule by inviting and mocking it. Here too she creates women's autobiography for the twentieth century by accepting and denying it. Such things could perhaps have been done by writing a fictionally authored biography of Gertrude Stein; rather as Hardy had done, ghosting his own life (the two volumes of which had appeared in 1928 and 1930); or perhaps as Woolf had done in her fantasy-biography *Orlando* (also of 1928). Calling it Toklas's *auto*biography, rather than her biography of Stein, did more than create smoke around the question of its authorship. Most male autobiographers have been generally expected to display more qualifications for their task than merely being someone's 'friend, secretary, editor, gardener' or even vet. The diaries and memoirs of nobodies, superfluous, disappointed or failed men are the exceptions, usually comic ones, that prove the general rule. The idea that a person like Alice Toklas should write her autobiography is part of the book's challenge. The idea that a *woman* like Toklas should is part of its provocation.

These ideas are of course complicated by the fact that Toklas was much more than 'friend, secretary, editor, gardener' or vet. She was Stein's companion and lover. Coming so soon after the trial of Radcliffe Hall's *The Well of Loneliness* (1928) in both the UK and the USA, lesbian writers like Stein had to be wary of being either explicit or earnest about their sexuality. Just as at the *fin de siècle* autobiografiction had offered a mode which could figure yet conceal the desires of heterosexual females and queer males, by the 1920s queer female versions give autobiografiction its cutting edge.[50] While the *Autobiography* is utterly reticent

---

[48] See Lynn Z. Bloom, 'Gertrude Is Alice Is Everybody: Innovation and Point of View in Gertrude Stein's Autobiographies', *Twentieth Century Literature*, 24:1 (1978), 81–93.

[49] *Everybody's Autobiography*, p. 68.

[50] Though see the discussion of 'Michael Field' on pp. 113–14.

about this aspect of their lives, it manages to imply it through the way Toklas describes herself making conversation with the wives of the male artists Stein talks to. Any scandalous potential here is offset by the way the device appears to justify Toklas's act of authorship, since it aligns her with the wives or family-members, who humbly seek to perpetuate the memories of the great—again rather along the lines of Florence Emily Hardy, had she actually written *The Life of Thomas Hardy*. Thus Stein manages to create a new form for lesbian life-writing while both accepting and denying it.

Stein's nimble ironies about genius and lesbian intimacy appear right from the start: not just in the way Toklas's 'autobiography' is entirely dominated by her life with Stein; but also in the way what she says about her life before they met, and she went with Stein to live in Paris, is dispensed with in a short section called 'Before I came to Paris', devoting a mere three pages to Toklas's first twenty-six or so years. What's more, Stein begins to dominate from the second of even those: 'In the story Ada in Geography and Plays Gertrude Stein has given a very good description of me as I was at that time.'[51] Stein is the most important element in her life, and even that part of her life Stein wasn't in, is best understood through Stein's writing. Perhaps behind this matter-of-fact statement of extraordinary intimacy (it is as if Toklas is dedicating her entire life to Stein, as in effect she did and Stein acknowledges) is a wink to the reader that it is Stein who is giving the descriptions of Toklas in this book too.

The fiction of Toklas's authorship enables her to accept and deny egotism by creating it anew:

The young often when they have learnt all they can learn accuse her of an inordinate pride. She says yes of course. She realizes that in english literature in her time she is the only one. She has always known it and now she says it.[52]

Coming from Toklas, this would mean that nowadays Stein comments on her own primacy or pride. But through her, Stein is saying it 'now', through the impersonation of Toklas, in a different way. The punctuation and typography works in similarly multiple ways. 'She says yes of course.' Who says 'of course' there? Is Toklas saying 'Gertrude Stein says "yes, of course"'? Or is she saying ? 'Of course Gertrude Stein says "yes"'? If the first, Stein is being knowing about the young. If the second, Toklas is being knowing about Stein—'Of course that's the sort of thing she'd say'—and Stein is thus being knowing about herself. The lack of punctuation ambiguates the utterances; it also creates the illusion of naivety, as if (like Molly Bloom in the 'Penelope' section of *Ulysses*) Toklas is too untrained to know writerly ways with inverted commas. And yet, again, the lack of inverted commas around Stein's speech signals covertly that such a comment doesn't need to be set off as if said by another person, because Stein is saying it now.

---

[51] *The Autobiography of Alice B. Toklas*, p. 2.
[52] Ibid., pp. 84–5.

Coming from Stein herself, such judgements might seem a bit rich. The book is full of hyperbolic claims, often outrageous, though delivered with deft ironic spin. *The Making of Americans* is a 'great book', 'a history of all human beings, all who ever were or are or could be living'; Stein is a 'genius'; someone who has single-handedly revolutionized modern writing, inventing 'those long sentences which were to change the literary ideas of a great many people.'[53] To some readers this will seem intolerably vain; and compounded by the way she could be accused of hiding behind Toklas; getting her to say the things she wants said about herself.

But there is often something disconcerting about the way Toklas says them— as in that remark about Stein realizing that 'she is the only one': the only one what? Writer? Modernist? Mentor? Or take Stein's purported response: 'She says yes of course.' What is she supposed to be assenting to: that she is proud? That her pride is inordinate? This doesn't sound right, since if she thinks 'she is the only one', surely the pride she's being accused of would be appropriate. Or is she accepting that the young make such accusations, especially after they have learned from her? The response, that is, is a slight non-sequitur, or slightly oblique in relation to the preceding sentence. And the slight awkwardness opens up a range of perspectives on what Stein has done, what other writers think of it, and what her own attitude is to her work. In a sense the style is a kind of anti-*style indirect libre*, since Toklas echoes Stein's alleged words, but the effect is to make us feel that Stein's actual thoughts, feelings, mind, constantly elude us. From Stein's point of view, the exercise at this point is close to Joyce's, since the consciousness she makes more alive the less Toklas seems able to create it is her own. It isn't just that she finds a brilliant way of dealing with the problem of egotism in autobiography—as Lejeune says, it is 'a cunning form of self-hagiography' which 'neutralizes or forestalls criticism'; it is also a new mode of autobiographic self-objectification.[54]

The mode through which she is able to bring off such feats is through an equally subtle play with ideas of naivety. As with the question of egotism, this too is very up-front—literally, as only three pages into the text, Toklas describes her first meeting with Stein:

I was impressed by the coral brooch she wore and by her voice. I may say that only three times in my life have I met a genius and each time a bell within me rang and I was not mistaken, and I may say in each case it was before there was any general recognition of the quality of genius in them. The three geniuses of whom I wish to speak are Gertrude Stein, Pablo Picasso and Alfred Whitehead. I have met many important people, I have met several great people but I have only known three first class geniuses and in each case on sight within me something rang. In no one of the three cases have I been mistaken. In this way my new full life began.[55]

---

[53] Ibid., pp. 60–1.   [54] Lejeune, 'Autobiography in the Third Person', p. 43.
[55] *The Autobiography of Alice B. Toklas*, p. 3.

Now this would have seemed even more extraordinary in 1933, since the *Autobiography* was the book that made Stein a celebrity, and which got everybody parodying what became known as 'Steinese'. Before publication of *The Autobiography of Alice B. Toklas* not many people had heard of her outside of a small modernist literary and artistic coterie. So the claim of her being not only just any old genius, but a 'first class genius' would have rung a bell, certainly, but probably an alarm bell.

Indeed, the more you look at this passage the harder it gets to imagine how it could have been made more brazen. Stein is not only a first class genius, but this is instantly recognizable on first meeting, even though she's written little and published nothing. She's better than the merely great or important people. And meeting her has the power to change Alice's life, to make it 'full'. You could say that this may well have been what Alice Toklas really thought, both when she first met Stein, and later, after Stein really had transformed her life, placing her at the centre of the modernist movement. Toklas certainly comes across as naive. For example, those repetitions about meeting geniuses, bells ringing, not being mistaken, give her a slightly plodding, even autistic quality. There's a bathos in the move between the coral brooch and the world-class geniuses in philosophy and painting.

But of course the naivety is assumed. Even if Toklas was actually that naive, Stein certainly was not. So it could be read as an example of the *faux-naïf,* or false naivety; like *Bridget Jones's Diary,* say. But there's another level to the game in Stein's case, whereby you keep seeing her peep around the mask of Alice Toklas and wink at her reader. The *Atlantic Monthly* version did this from the start, presenting the paradox of vicarious autobiography, so readers of that knew all along it wasn't really Toklas writing, so that all the praise of Stein is ironized. I've suggested that the centrality of Stein to the story undermines its claim to be Toklas's story. And I've discussed particular passages—especially those discussing writing—which can also be read as coded signatures. But the book's playful doubleness is predominantly a matter of tone, whereby Stein lets us hear the irony in the writing itself, as in those awkward repetitions and unpunctuations. What they let us see is that Toklas's naivety, which would be false naivety if Stein simply tried to make her seem naive, is in fact false-false-naivety, which is much more complex: a performance of false-naivety that is revealed as a performance. Which seems to have been a style of living for the two, as well as a style of writing.

If Stein really did think of herself as a genius, she was also aware of how genius had to be a kind of performance, like the *Autobiography,* and especially for a woman genius—of which of course in that trio she is the only one. Here it is both naivety and the idea of 'genius' which are being created through being at once accepted and denied. Part of her performance of these things is to mock the conventions of their performance. If Toklas's heroine-worship of Stein makes us uneasy when she elaborates Stein's 'genius', it is supposed to: it satirizes the fetishizing of predominantly male geniuses, to undermine the hero-worship, perhaps, but not to undermine the idea of women's gifts. This kind of performance and concealment are functions of all autobiography, but were perhaps necessary to a woman autobiographer—and especially to a lesbian autobiographer writing about love at first meeting.[56] Stein deploys false naivety in a way that makes another more general point about autobiography, by ironizing its reliance on false naivety. To show how wise they are now, and how wisely they understand themselves now, autobiographers are tempted to exaggerate the naivety (or innocence) of their past selves. This leads to a sense of the comedy of autobiography:

And identity is funny being yourself is funny as you are never yourself to yourself except as you remember yourself and then of course you do not believe yourself. That is really the trouble with an autobiography you do not of course you do not really believe yourself why should you, you know so well so very well that it is not yourself, it could not be yourself because you cannot remember right and if you do remember right it does not sound right and of course it does not sound right because it is not right. You are of course never yourself.[57]

Autobiography is supposed to let writers make sense of themselves. But as it turns into autobiografiction it can let them see how far the sense they make is, precisely, something they have *made*; or made up; or (in Henry James's phrase) made over.[58] That is, part of the radical effect of such anti-realist autobiography, or modernist anti-autobiography, is that it doesn't just reveal how autobiographical subjectivity is performative. It reveals how subjectivity itself has to be brought into being through being performed.[59]

What Stein's and Joyce's texts help us to see is that all the composite portraits and photographs trying to represent 'genius', all the imaginary portraits of the artist, emerge when the ideas of genius and the artist came under a new form of scepticism, just as notions of 'personality' and 'self' in which they were supposed to reside themselves became subject to doubt; no longer appeared the unitary, coherent, organic, natural things they had seemed. Marx said famously that history repeated itself, the first time as tragedy and the second time as farce. Where *fin de siècle* authors reacted to these identity-uncertainties with anxiety and awe, modernists like Stein, and her postmodernist successors, find that 'Identity is funny'. In terms of narrative structure Stein's trick is a simpler one than Joyce's, and her book is a comic version of fictionalized autobiography.

[56] See Sidonie Smith, 'Performativity, Autobiographical Practice, Resistance', in *Women, Autobiography, Theory: A Reader*, ed. Sidonie Smith and Julia Watson (Madison: University of Wisconsin Press, 1998), pp. 108–15.

[57] Stein, *Everybody's Autobiography*, p. 68.

[58] James, *Autobiography*, p. 227. See p. 279.

[59] Ideas of performativity are developed in the Conclusion.

CUBIST SELF-PORTRAITURE

Where most *Künstlerroman* autobiografiction fictionalizes autobiography with pseudonyms or heteronyms, Stein creates a different effect; one of Cubist juxtaposition or superimposition; superimposing over her and Toklas's real lives the veil of fictionalized telling that turns the narrative into much more than confession or transcription. A particularly self-referential example comes when Toklas talks about names:

> Everybody called Gertrude Stein Gertrude, or at most Mademoiselle Gertrude, everybody called Picasso Pablo and Fernande Fernande and everybody called Guillaume Apollinaire Guillaume and Max Jacob Max but everybody called Marie Laurencin Marie Laurencin.[60]

What a shame she doesn't tell us what everyone called Ford Madox Ford or William Carlos Williams! The joke here is that, as in that clause 'Everybody called Gertrude Stein Gertrude', what Toklas does throughout is call Stein 'Gertrude Stein', and never abbreviate her to just 'Gertrude'—which then ironizes that repeated 'Everybody'. What she's doing here is purporting to imitate a naive attempt to be literal, but, through that, what interests Stein is abstract verbal patterning. The *Autobiography* connects this move towards abstraction with what Picasso was doing in painting; and significantly, Stein says it was while Picasso was struggling to paint his celebrated portrait of her, that he made this landmark transformation.

> It had been a fruitful winter. In the long struggle with the portrait of Gertrude Stein, Picasso passed from the Harlequin, the charming early italian period to the intensive struggle which was to end in cubism. Gertrude Stein had written the story of Melanctha the negress, the second story of Three Lives which was the first definite step away from the nineteenth century and into the twentieth century in literature.[61]

Here we have Gertrude Stein not only writing the story that modernizes literature, but being the subject of the painting that modernizes painting. And there's some truth in it, thought art historians now see Picasso's 1907 painting *Les Demoiselles D'Avignon* as the landmark picture that led to Cubism, and Picasso had done most of his studies for that picture, drawing on African and Iberian sculpture before he finished Gertrude Stein's portrait—which he finished by painting out the head and replacing it with a mask-like African-inflected head. But it's in that paradoxical phrase 'fruitful winter' that you can hear Stein beginning to laugh behind her fictional mask; and continuing as she traces the parallel between Picasso's attempt to represent her, and her own attempt to represent herself in the *Autobiography*.

---

[60] *The Autobiography of Alice B. Toklas*, p. 65. [61] Ibid., p. 58.

The idea of a mask is crucial here. It connects what the one genius, Picasso, is doing in painting, with what another, Stein, is doing in prose. In another intriguing passage on Picasso she both makes and complicates the connexions between African art, abstraction, and naivety:

In these early days when he created cubism the effect of the african art was purely upon his vision and his forms, his imagination remained purely spanish. The spanish quality of ritual and abstraction had been indeed stimulated by his painting the portrait of Gertrude Stein. She had a definite impulse then and always toward elemental abstraction. She was not at any time interested in african sculpture. She always says that she liked it well enough but that it has nothing to do with europeans, that it lacks naïveté [. . .]⁶²

Stein's engagements with egotism and naivety are therefore more than purely ethical concerns: they are also formal experiments; part of her experiment with the forms of auto/biography and auto/biografiction, and parallel with what she has Picasso describe as the period of primitivism in Modern Art. If the *Autobiography* is another version of aesthetic autobiography, its aesthetics are those of Cubism and modernism rather than Impressionism. Just as in Cubism the painter breaks up the picture plane and traditional ideas of perspective, and shows a subject from several different angles at the same time, so Stein's might be what Cubist autobiography—or Cubist auto/biografiction—looks like.⁶³ It is a self-portrait viewing the subject from different perspectives: Toklas's, her own, their friends, younger writers, and so on. The parallels with Picasso's innovations are not just the casual name-dropping they might sound like, trying to make herself sound important by association. She is genuinely trying something new in literature. Just as in an analytical-cubist portrait by Picasso or Braque, you can't identify the subject as an individual, but just as someone with attributes (of a musician, say, or an *habitué* of cafés), so Stein too is giving us her imaginary Portrait of the Artist in general, blurring together the individualities of writer, painter, philosopher, friend, and lover—or a composite portrait of artistic genius, superimposing Stein, Picasso, Matisse, Whitehead, and various writers. Picasso signals what makes Stein's composite portrait different from Victorian or *fin de siècle* forerunners: it'll be Cubist, abstracting space, time, personality, so that you become more aware of the composition than the subject—which is especially pertinent given that Stein is a writer: someone who *composes*: who sees (as she put it) 'Composition as Explanation.'⁶⁴ For when you write a portrait of

---

⁶² Ibid., p. 68.

⁶³ See Wendy Steiner, *Exact Resemblance to Exact Resemblance: The Literary Portraiture of Gertrude Stein* (New Haven, CT: Yale University Press, 1978), for a discussion of Stein and cubism. The first chapter, pp. 1–26, also gives a valuable account of 'The Literary Portrait: History and Theory'.

⁶⁴ Carolyn A Barros, 'Getting Modern: *The Autobiography of Alice B. Toklas*', *Biography: An Interdisciplinary Quarterly*, 22:2 (1999), 177–208, gives a good account of the multiple ways in which portraits and portraiture figure in the text. She argues that Stein effects a 'major shift to modernist autobiography by eschewing the romantic conception of the autobiographical subject—a

the artist, the writing *is* the subject. Making people hear and feel and see her language was always Stein's aim in her writing experiments. The major achievement of the *Autobiography* is that by turning the form of auto/biography inside out she found a way to do that which is also intensely engaging.

The *Autobiography of Alice B. Toklas* is nowhere more brilliant than in its ending, which shares the aesthetic circularity of Proust's and Joyce's imaginary self-portraits, but ends in a crescendo of aesthetic self-consciousness that highlights the formal games it has been playing with naivety, egotism, auto/biography and fiction, as, for the first time, she explicitly flips the author-attribution back from Toklas to herself:

> About six weeks ago Gertrude Stein said, it does not look to me as if you were ever going to write that autobiography. You know what I am going to do. I am going to write it for you. I am going to write it as simply as Defoe did the autobiography of Robinson Crusoe. And she has and this is it.[65]

Yet even here something bizarre happens. At the moment Stein has Toklas acknowledge that Toklas's autobiography has in fact been written by Stein, she maintains the pretence: 'And she [Stein] has'. Here, presumably, for the first time (explicitly, at least) is Stein talking as Toklas talking about Stein. Which has of course been the game all along. Yet other complications impinge on this bravura passage. It implies Toklas had really had the idea/intention of writing an autobiography, so in conception at least it really is hers; it is as if Stein is just being *her* secretary. Then there's the strange intrusion of Defoe, who of course did not write the *autobiography* of Robinson Crusoe, or at least, not 'simply', since Robinson Crusoe was not a real person. He was based on a real person, Alexander Selkirk, who had already written his autobiography. What Defoe wrote was a novel posing as an autobiography; a fictionally authored autobiography; simple because appearing to be written in the simple words Crusoe would have used, but aesthetically complex since this simplicity is a fiction. That back-flip makes for metafiction, and looks forward to the idea of auto/biographic metafiction discussed in Chapter 12.

I argued that the notion of fictional creativity was a particular challenge; and that Pessoa certainly attempted it with his heteronyms, and that Joyce certainly attempted it with the presentation of Stephen's poem- and journal-writing, and perhaps attempted it in the *Portrait* as a whole. But what of the other two main examples in this and the previous chapters, by Svevo and Stein? Are the narratives fictionally authored by Zeno and by Toklas works of art? The answer is probably no, though for different reasons. In Zeno's case, he appears not to have intended to publish his memoirs; to have thought of them as psychoanalytic notes rather

self of feeling and internal motives—to construct herself as a modernist work of art comprised of multiple voices and portraits, which destroy what Stein herself called "associational emotion"; p. 177.

[65]   *The Autobiography of Alice B. Toklas*, p. [268].

than as a book. Svevo's novel is certainly metafictional—writing about writing—but the writing we see Zeno doing is different from the writing a novelist does (though the words are the same). Thus, according to Linda Hutcheon's definitions of metafiction (discussed in Chapter 12), though the process of writing is thematized in the novel, it is thematized not as literary writing—it isn't a novel about writing a novel—but as psychoanalytically oriented autobiography. As a new variety of autobiografiction, it is fiction that allegorizes its own processes as psychoanalytic life-writing. It is thus a kind of halfway house between fictionally authored non-art and fictionally authored art. The persona of Toklas in Stein's book does think of herself as writing a book. When we start reading it, its title announces it as an autobiography, and we assume that (like all classic autobiography) the autobiographer has given it that name. But when we learn that Stein has actually written the book, and given it its title, the generic label becomes ironized. Toklas may think of it as a serious, book-like, factual project, worthy of the name 'autobiography'. But her characteristic naivety in the book means that what she thinks of as 'autobiography' may not qualify as a work of art, and perhaps not even as formal autobiography: it reads, anyway, more like a memoir of her life with Stein, rather than trying to make sense of her life in the way classic autobiography is supposed to do. Whether she thinks 'autobiography' is 'art' is the sort of question Stein might well ask; and whether Stein thinks it is also a moot point. The device of assumed naivety can mean that Stein thinks Toklas does think the book 'art', but insofar as the narrative is Toklas's, Stein thinks it isn't, whereas insofar as it's Stein's, it is; in which case it would modulate from plodding documentation to art as it modulated from Toklas's genuine naivety to Stein's false naivety. But that is another way of saying that if the ending provides a frame, the framing makes a work of art out of naive life-writing.

The same could be said for a very different work of *faux-naïveté*, Anita Loos's smash hit of 1925, *Gentlemen Prefer Blondes*, in which it's clear from the start that Lorelei's diary is a comic fake (of the kind discussed in Chapter 5)—a mock-diary:

March 16th
A gentleman friend and I were dining at the Ritz last evening and he said that if I took a pencil and a paper and put down all of my thoughts it would make a book. This almost made me smile as what it would really make would be a whole row of encyclopediacs. I mean I seem to be thinking practically all of the time.[66]

Lorelei has things to say about art, if only to repeat what her better-informed friend Dorothy says about it (in Munich 'Dorothy looked around and Dorothy said, if this is "kunst", the art center of the world is Union Hill New Jersey').[67] Lorelei has things to say about psychoanalysis, too. In Vienna she is analysed by

---

[66] Anita Loos, *Gentlemen Prefer Blondes* (London: Picador, 1974), p. 19.
[67] Ibid., p. 111.

'Dr Froyd', who advises her 'to cultivate a few inhibitions and get some sleep.'[68] Loos's book manages deftly to mock both American naivety and European pretension, making one admire Lorelei's directness and success even as she exposes her ignorance. But what pretensions she might have to be thought of as a 'writer' are also being mocked. She is clearly not an artist. Her gentlemen prefer their blondes dumb, and when Lorelei's 'thinking' does amount to more than a stream of mindless consciousness, it's despite herself. *Gentlemen Prefer Blondes* might seem an improbable pre-text for *The Autobiography of Alice B. Toklas,* but the escapades of the two women, Lorelei and Dorothy, among the gentlemen in Europe, may have lent something of the content, form, and tone to Stein's account of two women among the artists in Europe during the same period.

Thus Zeno's autobiography is ultimately the portrait of a patient, not an artist. Similarly, the naivety of Toklas's narrative precludes it from being her art work. Her autobiography is the portrait of an artist's companion. But it is a portrait of the artist in another sense, in that it is the portrait of another who is an artist: Gertrude Stein. In the case of *The Notebook of Malte Laurids Brigge,* Rilke presents the mind of an artist in crisis, undergoing a form of breakdown and treatment. So while he too is representing the aesthetic life, a portrait of the artist, and doing so in terms of the character's fictional writing, the fact that Brigge's notebook is a journal establishes a gap between its form and that of the novel Rilke is writing using it. That gap offers a kind of frame; a frame so thin it's almost implied. Only the most minimal annotations indicate the presence of the framer. But nonetheless even such virtually imaginary framing allows us to distinguish Brigge's journal, which he presumably does not intend as his novel, from the art-work Rilke has made by creating it. In which case, there are few rivals to Joyce's innovation in *Portrait,* even if we doubt the fictional-author theory about the whole book. So he may have been justified in thinking (if he did) that he had indeed altered the laws of art . . .

---

[68] Loos, *Gentlemen Prefer Blondes,* p. 119.

9

Auto/biographese and Auto/biografiction in Verse: Ezra Pound and *Hugh Selwyn Mauberley*

'The artist, like the God of creation, remains within or behind or beyond or above his handiwork, invisible, refined out of existence, indifferent, paring his fingernails.'[1]

VOICE AND FORM

Stephen Dedalus's Flaubertian image of artistic impersonality is often quoted as Joyce's credo, usually without the irony being noted of its being uttered by a fictionalized persona, in a novel so intensely autobiographical that the artist is visible everywhere. I have proposed a particular way of conceiving *A Portrait of the Artist* as an instance of modernist im/personality. That reading accepts earlier interpretations which have stressed the autobiographical content (such as Ellmann's), or which read the novel as 'aesthetic autobiography' (such as Nalbantian's). I enclose these readings within another, arguing that Joyce may have found a technical device that enabled him to turn himself inside out, and achieve a greater impersonality than has previously been recognized, by presenting not his own autobiographical novel, but the one that Stephen might have written: even critics reluctant to entertain that possibility will recognize that it *is* an experiment in autobiografiction.

Of all the modernists, it is Eliot and Pound who seem most intractable to such claims. Few might have predicted that the scourge of 'personality' and liberal individualism, Wyndham Lewis, would write autobiography, but he did. Some, like Virginia Woolf, who didn't write formal autobiography nonetheless wrote autobiographical novels, diaries, even autobiographical sketches and biography. Eliot, whose essay 'Tradition and the Individual Talent' was the most influential single contribution to establishing the doctrine of modernist impersonality,

---

[1] Joyce, *A Portrait of the Artist as a Young Man*, ed. Jeri Johnson (Oxford: Oxford University Press, 2000), p. 181.

consistently defended his position, and sustained a principled refusal of biographical readings of his own work. Eliot's immense influence on Anglo-American literature for at least half a century both guaranteed the dominance of his critical position, and provoked discussions of ways in which his work appears more autobiographical than his precepts allow.[2] Pound's case is both less familiar and more complex, at least from the point of view of im/personality, and it is with his work that this chapter is concerned.

'AS usual, pubrs/ continue to want naughtyboyography', Pound wrote to Ford Madox Ford in 1933: 'IF I expressed my opinion of 20% of the shits I have encountered the bk/ wd. Be too libelous to print. And what intelligence I have encountered, I have already mentioned in my articles on this thet an tother.'[3] 'Naughtyboyography' is an inspired Pound coinage, suggesting both what he thought his own would be like (or at least what he thought his publishers wanted it to be like), and what he thought was wrong with the form: a smug and staid retrospect on a misspent youth, titillating its readers with escapades for which it purports to express contrition. Yet it is typical of Pound's genius that such imaginative energies are inseparable from the energy of vituperation, which can only imagine his life story as a narrative of encounters with one damned shit after another. If he was wise to resist the advances of publishers then, how much wiser not to attempt autobiography after his disastrous involvement with Italian Fascism.

This chapter is concerned with an earlier phase of Pound's life and work, before he moved to Italy in 1925, three years after Mussolini had come to power. My argument is that while Pound appears to distance himself from auto/biography, his work represents a significant modernist engagement with it. There is a trace of it even as he distances himself from 'naughtyboyography', when he adds: 'what intelligence I have encountered, I have already mentioned in my articles [...]'; as if to concede (following Wilde and Nietzsche) that his autobiography—at least his intellectual autobiography—can be found in his criticism: that in other words all his writing has an autobiographical dimension, though not of the salacious kind to interest the publishers. As suggested in the Preface, the Wilde–Nietzsche argument can be read as an extension of Romantic expressive theory: insofar as works of art are the best expression of an author's personality, they are equally his or her best autobiography. Pound does here exactly what Philippe Lejeune notes about the trope of writers calling their fiction their true autobiography: denigrating the notion of formal autobiography, while nonetheless using the autobiographic as the criterion for judgement (i.e. the critical essays

---

[2] See for example William Empson's biographical reading of 'The Waste Land': 'My God, man, there's bears on it', in his *Using Biography* (London: Chatto & Windus and The Hogarth Press, 1984), pp. 189–200.

[3] *Pound/Ford: The Story of a Literary Friendship*, ed. Brita Lindberg-Seyersted (London: Faber and Faber, 1982), p. 126.

8 Vortograph of Ezra Pound by Alvin Langdon Coburn, 1917, gelatin silver print.

constitute a more significant autobiography than a 'naughtyboyography' would).[4] I shall argue that Pound's engagement with auto/biography goes much deeper than this, however, and manifests itself in ingenious formal ways which necessitate a rereading of his early poetry in the light of the issues of imaginary portraiture and imaginary writing that have emerged from our earlier discussions. Pound's comparable experimentation in these areas has been eclipsed by the scandal of his politics, which, together with his close association with Eliot, the chief spokesman for modernist impersonality, has skewed readings of Pound's most important early work, *Hugh Selwyn Mauberley*.

Hugh Selwyn Mauberley was first published by John Rodker's Ovid Press in London in 1920. It consists of a pair of sequences of short poems. Part I, which has no overall title, contains twelve poems, five of which are titled, the other seven headed just by roman numerals. Then there is an 'Envoi: 1919', marked off as a separate section on the title page, but usually taken by critics as the end of Part I, in parallel to the final poem of Part II. Part II is headed by the date '1920', with '(Mauberley)' below it.[5] It consists of just five poems. These all have roman numerals (on the title page, though the first loses its numeral above the poem itself). Two also have titles: 'The Age Demanded', which phrase is a quotation from the first line of poem II in Part I; and the final poem, 'Medallion'.

The whole work is notoriously difficult, of comparable difficulty to Eliot's 'The Waste Land'. It is richly allusive; profoundly elliptical, ironic, and ambiguous. Unlike 'The Waste Land', it is mostly stanzaic, predominantly in partially rhymed quatrains, of fairly short (mainly trimeter) lines. But while each individual poem thus looks complete on the page, the effect of the whole work is of a gathering of disparate fragments. In his famously surgical editing of 'The Waste Land', Pound made Eliot's poem more like his own, opening up the gaps between the sections to problematize the coherence of the whole.

Much of the critical commentary on *Hugh Selwyn Mauberley* has been concerned with just that: its coherence or unity; and specifically, with how to understand the relations between the various parts. And, as with 'The Waste Land', the issue of coherence is bound up with the issue of voice: of who is speaking, and how we can know. Eliot's poem is a mélange of voices (a working title was 'He do the Police in Different Voices', quoted from a voice in Dickens's *Our Mutual Friend*). We saw how Eliot's notes describe Tiresias as not a

---

[4] Philippe Lejeune, 'The Autobiographical Contract', in *French Literary Theory Today*, ed. Tzvetan Todorov (Cambridge: Cambridge University Press, 1982), pp. 192–222.

[5] Some of these presentational details were changed in subsequent editions. The division into parts disappears; and the title of the second sequence varies, appearing as 'MAUBERLEY / 1920' in *Personae* (1926), as 'MAUBERLEY (1920)' in the 1949 *Selected Poems*, and as 'MAUBERLEY / (1920)' in *Diptych: Rome—London* (1958)—hence the need to refer to it here as the 'second sequence'. The changes perhaps indicate a hesitation on Pound's part as to how much the focus is on the man and how much on his postwar milieu. The edition used for quotations here is the *Selected Poems*, ed. T. S. Eliot (London: Faber, 1973).

'character' but a 'personage'. But what is the difference? Tiresias is said to unite the other people in the poem (and what of them? Are they characters, or also only personages? Eliot doesn't say) because as a seer he participates in events at all times, and according to the myth he has lived as both man and woman. But perhaps this very inclusiveness is what prevents him from having an individual 'character' at all. In this respect, 'The Waste Land' is anti-biography; an expression of someone who cannot be said to have an individual life story. 'What Tiresias *sees*,' the note continues, 'in fact, is the substance of the poem.' But without Eliot's note, we couldn't guess that the focalizer of the other voices was Tiresias. The notes also suggest that the other personages combine to form an imaginary portrait of Tiresias: 'Just as the one-eyed merchant seller of currants, melts into the Phoenician Sailor, and the latter is now wholly distinct from Ferdinand Prince of Naples, so all the women are one woman, and the two sexes meet in Tiresias.' *Hugh Selwyn Mauberley* finds its own ways of problematizing person-hood and subjectivity; in establishing where one person or voice ends, and the next begins.

Pound's poem makes us ask why it has been separated into two sequences; why the second alludes to the first; and why the second is headed with the eponym's surname (as if to suggest that the second sequence is somehow more 'Mauberley' than the first). As Peter Brooker explains, 'the essential critical debate' about the whole poem is 'the relation of Pound to the fictitious Mauberley.'[6] He quotes the letter to Felix Schelling in which Pound says: '(Of course, I'm no more Mauberley than Eliot is Prufrock. Mais passons.) Mauberley is a mere surface. Again a study in form, an attempt to condense the James novel.'[7] Brooker's *A Student's Guide to the Selected Poems of Ezra Pound* is an indispensable resource for the understanding of *Hugh Selwyn Mauberley*, and I am more grateful for his scrupulous scholarship than might appear from my occasional dissent from his interpretations. Brooker cites this passage as evidence that 'Pound himself maintained that Mauberley was unequivocally a distinct persona'. Certainly he distinguished Mauberley from himself; but is it so clear that Mauberley is a 'persona'? Or, more to the point, if he is, is he more of a 'personage' than a 'character'? These questions would matter were the form that of a dramatic monologue, in which the separation between poet and speaker is required for the monologue to *be* dramatic. If we were to feel that a Browning monologue were just the poet in yet another fancy-dress outfit, the poem would have failed, since the raison d'être of dramatic monologue is to present a character, torn out of the context of their life, but speaking so as to convince us of the reality of their character and predicament. There's no doubt who the speaker is in a poem like

---

[6] Peter Brooker, *A Student's Guide to the Selected Poems of Ezra Pound* (London: Faber, 1979), p. 183. Brooker builds on the work of earlier scholarship on the sequence, especially by Herbert Schneidau, J. J. Espey, and K. K. Ruthven.

[7] Pound to Felix Schelling, 8–9 July 1922; *Selected Letters of Ezra Pound* (New York: New Directions, 1971), pp. 178–82 (p. 180).

'My Last Duchess', or in 'The Love Song of J. Alfred Prufrock'. The problem in Pound's 'study in form' is that it is impossible to be certain who is speaking which poem. Furthermore (as argued in Chapter 7), in a Victorian dramatic monologue, part of the convention is usually that the speaker is just talking, and not aware that s/he is uttering verse. The versification signals the distance between speaker and poet. Thus the poet can truly be said to be 'behind or beyond or above his handiwork'; 'invisible' in the sense that the only words we have are the speaker's; but visible in the sense that the poetry is the poet's, not the speaker's. But in Pound's poem, Mauberley is a poet; and the first poem mentions another poet, one 'E. P.', in its title: 'E. P.: ODE POUR L'ÉLECTION DE SON SÉPULCHRE'. The commentators tell us that this is an allusion to Ronsard's 'De l'Élection de son sépulchre' (On the Choice of his Grave), combined with a pun on the classical term 'Epode': 'a lyric metre, or after-song of sombre character.'[8] But such explications are further complications. The poem alludes to another poem in which the poet imagines his own premature death: Villon's 'Le Testament':

> Unaffected by 'the march of events',
> He passed from men's memory in *l'an trentuniesme*
> *De son eage*, the case presents
> No adjunct to the Muses' diadem.

Both the Ronsard and the Villon allusions align the poem as the poet's utterance: 'E. P.' imagining his own death; writing his own obituary. Yet Pound appeared to have something else in mind, at least in his subsequent comment on his critics: 'The worst muddle they make is in failing to see that Mauberley buries E. P. in the first poem; gets rid of all his troublesome energies.'[9] If Mauberley buries E. P., then Mauberley is speaking, or writing, the first poem. The debate about the relation between Pound and Mauberley has thus also been a debate about which of the two voices to attribute to each poem. And, as here, it is disingenuous of Pound to claim that the muddle is of the critics' making, since he has left the poems so open to such debates.

To say that Mauberley buries E. P. in the first poem, and that Pound is 'no more Mauberley than Eliot is Prufrock', is to suggest that Mauberley is to be conceived as the speaker of the entire work. However, there are two problems with this position. First, whereas the poems in the first sequence are either impersonal comments on the age, or sketches of other literary figures, the emphasis in the second sequence appears to be on Mauberley himself. Yet the first sequence includes first-person singular utterances in three poems: 'Siena mi

---

[8] Brooker, *A Student's Guide*, p. 188.
[9] T. Connolly, 'Further Notes on Mauberley', *Accent* (1956), 59; quoted Brooker, *A Student's Guide*, p. 188.

Fe'; 'Mr. Nixon'; and poem XII; four if the 'Envoi' is included. Whereas the second sequence is all in the third person, and is lethally critical of its object:

> Incapable of the least utterance or composition,
> Emendation, conservation of the 'better tradition',
> Refinement of medium, elimination of superfluities,
> August attraction or concentration.
> Nothing, in brief, but maudlin confession [...][10]

It is not inconceivable that a writer could be so damning of himself. Perhaps Pound's point is that such a writer is paralysed by his self-consciousness. Perhaps it's an example of a kind of English false modesty that he might have found exasperating. Yet it concurs with Pound's judgement of the kind of aesthete that Mauberley is. He wrote (to Schelling again) that 'the aesthetes since 1880' weren't 'a very sturdy lot.'[11] To call the writer presented in the poem 'The Age Demanded' not very sturdy would be an understatement. His 'desire for survival' is 'Faint' even 'in the most strenuous moods', and he seems to dwindle into obscurity. Thus the attitude towards Mauberley expressed in the second sequence exerts a pressure on us to read that sequence as the comment of someone else—E. P., posterity—on Mauberley, rather than his self-analysis. (Though again, it's arguable that the form somehow combines the two, inverting the combination I proposed for the first poem: Mauberley impersonating the kind of verdict he knows posterity will accord him.) Such a reading might point to a division whereby Mauberley is the speaker in the first sequence, commenting on E. P., other literary figures, and his times; and the subject of the second sequence is an assessment of him by others.

To illustrate how the critical 'muddle' survived Pound's attempt to clear it up, witness Peter Brooker's comment on Pound's admiration for what he called the 'hardness' of French poetry such as Gautier's:

But this would hardly seem to distinguish Pound from Mauberley since it is in fact Mauberley himself who in his own defence invokes Gautier in the phrase 'the "sculpture" of rhyme'. And if the attribution here is uncertain, since the speaker at this point in the poem is uncertain, then what of 'Medallion', the last poem in the sequence and one generally agreed to be Mauberley's own? (But cf. notes on this poem.)[12]

In what sense are the words about the sculpture of rhyme 'in fact' Mauberley's, if the speaker is uncertain? The final parenthesis concedes that agreement about the speaker of 'Medallion' isn't general at all. The notes cite Jo Brantley Berryman's argument that both the 'Envoi' and 'Medallion' refer to the same person, the singer Raymonde Collignon, whom Pound had heard, admired, and reviewed.[13] Brooker doesn't mention that Donald Davie, perhaps the most influential British

---

[10] 'The Age Demanded', from the second sequence.
[11] Pound to Schelling, 8–9 July 1922: *Selected Letters*, p. 180.
[12] Brooker, *A Student's Guide*, p. 186.
[13] Ibid., p. 223. Berryman, '"Medallion": Pound's Poem', *Paideuma*, 2:3 (1973), 391–8.

Poundian, had in 1975 very deliberately recanted his view that 'Medallion' was offered as an example of Mauberley's work, in a rather Poundian attempt to respond to the uncertainty by finding new grounds for denying it:

Hugh Selwyn Mauberley is a mask that continually slips [. . .] What is the mask for if, as often as not, the poet throws it off and speaks vulnerably as from himself? More distractingly still, since we are advised of the mask in the very title, how are we to know in which poems Pound speaks through the mask, in which he doesn't? An end came to much special pleading on this score when Mrs Berryman showed that 'Medallion' must be taken as spoken with pride *in propria persona*, though most earlier commentaries (including my own) had supposed it must be uttered in the assumed character of Mauberley.[14]

'[M]ust be taken'? Berryman's evidence 'showed' that 'Medallion' echoes Pound's reviews of Collignon. But it can't prove what attitude he took, or expects us to take, towards the two poems recalling her singing. Berryman argues that Pound means to contrast two poetic modes of responding to the same event: the lyric mode of 'Envoi', or the more visual, sculptural mode of 'Medallion'. Yet he could equally be imagining how a good poet and a bad poet would both represent the same event. Just as I have suggested Joyce needed to purge himself of aestheticism through representing Stephen's aestheticism, might not Pound be impersonating the kind of poet he feared he had been, or feared he might have become, had he not met and read modernists such as Ford, Lewis, Eliot, and Joyce?[15] In other words, he might be recalling Collignon's concert in order to show how perilously close he had come to turning into Mauberley. (That is to suggest that Mauberley is not only an imaginary portrait, but also an imaginary self-portrait: more of that anon.) Davie saw *Hugh Selwyn Mauberley* as overrated, in comparison to *The Cantos*. Even if one disagrees with his valuation (as I do), his criticism of its slipping mask is a cogent statement of the uncertainty about utterance throughout the poem. The attempt to find at least one site of certainty comes comically unstuck when, having noted that Pound's admiration of 'robust self-exposure' in poets such as Villon was 'precisely what the doctrines of "persona" and "mask" were designed to obviate' in Eliot and Yeats, he writes of Pound speaking '*in propria persona*'. This raises precisely the possibility that his argument is trying to obviate: that Pound's self might, at least in a poem such as this, be another 'persona', an impersonation of an attitude rather than a robust expression of a conviction.

---

[14] Davie, *Pound* (London: Fontana, 1975), p. 55.

[15] See Paul Skinner, '"Speak Up, Fordie!": How Some People Want to Go to Carcassonne', *Ford Madox Ford and the City*, ed. Sara Haslam (New York and Amsterdam: Rodopi, 2005), pp. 197–210 (p. 205): 'In *Hugh Selwyn Mauberley*, Ezra Pound describes the minor poet that he might have been or remained—without Imagism, Vorticism, Fenollosa and others, including Ford Madox Ford—and both completes and demonstrates his escape from that role through and by the writing of *Mauberley*.'

A. David Moody is equally impatient with the debate about the poem's voices. In his study *Ezra Pound: Poet* he comments wearily apropos 'Medallion': 'Again the question is raised, whose poem is this?' And as when it was raised apropos the 'Envoi', he answers: 'again, the answer must be that it is E. P.'s treatment of Mauberley's art.'[16] But this forecloses all the questions the poem opens up. What is the relation between E. P. and Ezra Pound? What kind of 'treatment' is at stake? Is it a fictionalized or semi-fictionalized narrator, 'E. P.', giving his verdict on Mauberley's art? That is, is E. P. commenting on Mauberley? Or is it an impersonation of Mauberley? And if so, by whom? Is it a fully fictionally authored poem: an example of a poem written by Mauberley? Or is it possible (if improbable) that Pound might have toyed with the idea of writing a fictionally authored parody by 'E. P.' of the fictional-authored poems by Mauberley in the first sequence? William H. Pritchard described Moody's book as including: 'a heroic attempt to sort out the complicated interplay between Pound the writer, and his persona, Mauberley (also a poet), by way of ascertaining just who is speaking at this or that moment and in what tone.'[17] Pritchard acknowledges *Mauberley* to be 'dense with ambiguity'. But Moody's 'careful and strenuous attempt to sort it out' doesn't convince him that, 'in places, ambiguity is not confusion and incoherence'. The extraordinary allusive density of Pound's work is the source of much of the ambiguity, and many of the anxieties of coherence. But one possible allusion that has largely gone unnoticed points to a different axis of coherence. The image of a medallion for a piece of writing—and a piece of writing about a writer—probably alludes to Mallarmé's *Quelques Médaillons et portraits en pied* ('Some Medallions and full-length portraits'). These sketches of different lengths, (of Villiers de L'Isle-Adam, Poe, Verlaine, Rimbaud, and others, were collected in a volume called *Divagations* (1897), which Pound surely knew (and presumably had in mind when he titled his own later collection of prose pieces *Pavannes and Divagations*; 1958).[18] The possibility that Pound's poem 'Medallion' alludes to Mallarmé doesn't disambiguate the question of voice. But it does add to the weight of evidence placing the poem, and the sequences, in a tradition of poets writing epitaphs on fellow-poets. And, more germanely to our study, it emphasizes the idea of the poem as condensed life-writing: biographical or autobiographical studies presented as 'medallions'. *Hugh Selwyn Mauberley*, that is, can be read as an experiment in the presentation of the literary life. It isn't

<hr />

[16] Moody, *Ezra Pound: Poet*, vol. 1 (Oxford: Oxford University Press, 2007), p. 385.

[17] Pritchard, 'Poet of the Public Stage', *Washington Times* (20 January 2008).

[18] Patrick McGuinness, 'From Mallarmé to Pound: The "Franco-Anglo-American" Axis', in *Symbolism, Decadence and the Fin de Siècle: French and European Perspectives*, ed. McGuinness (Exeter: University of Exeter Press, 2000), pp. 264–79, says that Pound 'remained distressingly blind to Mallarmé' (p. 273). That he doesn't note Pound's allusions to Mallarmean terms like 'divagation' or 'medallion' doesn't vitiate his argument: Pound may have remained dubious of Mallarmé's virtues even while alluding to him; and indeed, may have been alluding to him as an example of practice to avoid. In other words, the 'Medallion' in *Mauberley* may be meant as parodic of Mallarmé, or a critique of Mauberley as a pasticheur of Mallarmé.

only that it can be read in this way regardless of whose voice is imagined speaking each poem; but that the haze of ambiguity about individual voices is what allows its outlines as auto/biography to emerge all the more clearly.

The debate about who is speaking has obscured a second kind of ambiguity—that E. P. and Mauberley are both poets; so whichever of them might be 'speaking' any particular poem, we cannot be sure whether the writing is offered as an example of their speech (or thought, in Flaubertian free indirect style) or whether it's being offered as an example of their writing, their *poetry*. Davie's verbs—'spoken *in propria persona*'; 'uttered in the assumed character'—curiously insist on the speech act in discussing words that are in verse, and possibly intended as song. It is perhaps the habit of a poet used to reciting his own verse. But for most readers, the possibility that what we have, at least in some of *Hugh Selwyn Mauberley*, and possibly in a lot of it, is Pound's impersonation not of Mauberley's speaking, but of his poetry-*writing*, adds a further degree of uncertainty. I think this is what accounts for much of the critical perplexity, though the reason has not been identified, namely, that as in Joyce's *Portrait*, what Pound is doing is presenting fictional creativity: imaginary authorship: heteronymity. Given Stephen's aestheticism, and that of his villanelle, it may well have been *Portrait* that gave Pound the idea. Fictional creativity complicates our response because whereas a poet publishing a poem as his or her own must be assumed to think it good enough, a poet publishing a poem as if written by a fictional poet may think differently, and we have to try to second-guess the real poet's opinion of the fictional one. Peter Brooker quotes Gautier's account of his own *Émaux et Camées* ('Chaque pièce devait être un médaillon. . . .'), saying of 'Medallion': 'Whether the poem is then to be regarded as Pound's own or Mauberley's is a question of its success in these terms.'[19] Meaning that if it fails, it's Mauberley's, whereas if it succeeds, it's Pound's. But what if Pound had intended it as an example of Mauberley's one success? What if he sees it as a successful example of a mode he disliked? What if he intends it as an example of 'E. P.' trying to write the wrong kind of poem—and doing it either well or badly?

The conceit that 'E. P.' has died could be said to have a curious effect on Pound's *propria persona*. It makes the 'E. P.' commented on by Mauberley into precisely, a persona of Pound's: 'E. P.' rather than 'Ezra Pound'. And this gives any words uttered by that persona a curious doubleness, since they also become examples of fictional creativity: poems that the 'E. P.' who died might have written, rather than the Ezra Pound writing *Hugh Selwyn Mauberley*. But then, in its first edition, *Hugh Selwyn Mauberley* wasn't published as being by Ezra Pound. The only identification on the title-page and cover was that the volume was by—'E. P.' The 'E. P.' device thus also manages to turn 'Ezra Pound' himself

---

[19] Brooker, *A Student's Guide*, p. 222.

into an imaginary portrait too, who signs himself with the semi-anonymizing initials familiar from *fin de siècle* autobiografiction.

During the First World War, some six years before he completed *Hugh Selwyn Mauberley*, Pound had elaborated his interest in the ideas of mask and persona in an essay on Vorticism, which he reprinted in his book of 1916—itself an important example of innovative Modernist memoir—on the sculptor Henri Gaudier-Brzeska:

> In the 'search for oneself', in the search for 'sincere self-expression', one gropes, one finds some seeming verity. One says 'I am' this, that, or the other, and with the words scarcely uttered one ceases to be that thing.
>
> I began this search for the real in a book called *Personae*, casting off, as it were, complete masks of the self in each poem. I continued in the long series of translations, which were but more elaborate masks.[20]

This is enough to make one wonder whether it really was 'robust self-expression' that Pound admired in other poets, or whether it wasn't instead the kind of impersonation of subjectivity countenanced here. Presumably Davie, himself a master of what he (autobiographically?) calls 'robust self-expression', would have rejected the idea that with such self-expression the self ceases to be what has been expressed. Pound wasn't writing here about *Hugh Selwyn Mauberley*. But the translation of the author's name from Ezra Pound into just his initials may indicate that he intended 'E. P.' as just such a complete mask of the self, or that he intended both Mauberley and E. P.—and perhaps the other figures in the sequence too—as an elaborate confrontation of such masks.

POUND'S IMAGINARY PORTRAITURE

Pound had been experimenting energetically with the persona for a decade at least: in his 1909 poems *Personae*; in his adaptations from the Chinese in *Cathay*; and the Latin in *Homage to Sextus Propertius*; and in a series of 'Imaginary Letters' from the fictional persona of 'Walter Villerant' (which have been discussed in relation to the persona of Mauberley, but not to imaginary portraiture).[21] The mask or persona is a development of the Aesthetic idea of the imaginary portrait. It is more stylized, more modernist, certainly. But it extends aestheticism's exploration of imaginary, or fictional subjectivities. And it is with Pound's appropriation of these ideas, in a work unmistakably about aestheticism, that this chapter is concerned. I have suggested that (as in Joyce) the imagining of

---

[20] Pound, *Gaudier-Brzeska* (New York: New Directions, 1974), p. 85.
[21] 'Imaginary Letters', *Pavannes and Divagations* (New York: New Directions, 1974), pp. 55–76. See for example Davie, *Ezra Pound: Poet as Sculptor* (London: Routledge and Kegan Paul, 1965), chapter 5; Davie, *Ezra Pound*, p. 55; and Brooker, *A Student's Guide*, pp. 184–6.

fictional creativity is often bound up with the production of an imaginary portrait. Whereas Susanne Nalbantian argues that her key works proceed as autobiography combined with commentary on their own aesthetics, I submit that many key works of modernist autobiografiction incorporate or consist of examples of heteronymous creativity: that they are often imaginary auto/biography, in which rather than telling the story of how the author became an author, the emergence of a creative persona is projected onto a fictional character— Stephen Dedalus or Hugh Selwyn Mauberley. I shall return to Pound's use of fictional creativity later, but first need to consider exactly how *Hugh Selwyn Mauberley* engages with the idea of auto/biography.

John J. Espey notes that in Pound's 1949 *Selected Poems*, the subtitle of the whole work, '(Life and Contacts)', was removed, together with the epigraph from Nemesianus, and a note added for the 1926 collection *Personae* saying: 'The sequence is so distinctly a farewell to London that the reader who chooses to regard this as an exclusively American edition may as well omit it and turn at once to page 205.' Espey says 'These deletions seem to be indications of the relative unimportance of the original epigraph and subtitle.'[22] My contention is that he couldn't be more wrong. He wasn't to know in 1955 that in 1958 both epigraph and subtitle were to be reintroduced, but with the subtitle revised into 'Contacts and Life.'[23] Their reintroduction casts doubt over whether Pound had in fact sanctioned their omission in 1949, when, confined to St Elizabeths Hospital for the Criminally Insane, and arguably still traumatized by his captivity, and the arguments over whether he should be tried (and perhaps executed) for treason, he had other things on his mind. The only piece Pound published called 'Autobiography' was a single page prefatory sketch in telegraphese for the 1949 *Selected Poems*:

> E.P.
> Born, Hailey, Idaho, 30 Oct. 1885.
> Educ. U. of Penn and Hamilton. PhD. '05. M.A. '06
>
> Published. 1908. Venice; A Lume Spento.
>
> 1909, Mathews, London. Personae, Exultations.
> Thereafter some 40 volumes, in London till 1910.[24]

---

[22] John J. Espey, *Ezra Pound's 'Mauberley': A Study in Composition* (London: Faber, 1955) p. 23.
[23] Brooker, *A Student's Guide*, p. 187. The volume *Diptych: Rome—London* (London: Faber, 1958), combines *Propertius* and *Mauberley*, and includes the subtitle 'Contacts and Life' for the latter on the title-page and slipcase label. While this clearly suggests that the subtitle covers the whole of *Hugh Selwyn Mauberley*, the contents page adds another level of confusion, however, putting 'Contacts and Life' and 'Mauberley' as if they were the sub-titles for the first and second sequences respectively: in other words, as if 'Contacts and Life' only covered the first sequence. This structure is supported by the separate sub-title pages given to each in the text itself.
[24] Pound, *Selected Poems* (New York: New Directions, 1949), p. viii. As Donald Gallup notes in his *Ezra Pound: A Bibliography* (Charlottesville: University Press of Virginia, 1983), p. 82, the later (New York, 1957) edition changes 'Autobiography' to 'Biography'. I am grateful to Paul Skinner for this information. '1910' is presumably an error for '1920'.

Some staccato paragraphs follow retailing his study of economic theory, carefully described here as 'investigation of causes of war, to oppose same', and leading to his 'first visit to U.S. since 1910 in endeavour to stave off war' in 1939, and the claim that his notorious Rome radio broadcasts were 'for personal propaganda in support of U. S. Constitution, continuing after America's official entry into the war only on condition that he should never be asked to say anything contrary to his conscience or contrary to his duties as an American Citizen.'[25] That emergence of the third-person pronoun out of the impersonal curriculum vitae is not the most interesting thing about this understandably defensive document. But it does suggest that the notion of impersonal or third person highly stylized auto/biography, like his initializing and objectifying himself as 'E.P.', was still of interest to him.

Pound told his New Directions publisher, James Laughlin, that the rearranged subtitle of *Mauberley*—'Contacts and Life'—followed 'the actual order of the subject matter.'[26] In the rest of this chapter I propose a new reading of *Hugh Selwyn Mauberley* that takes its subtitle or subtitles seriously; that draws on K. K. Ruthven's suggestion that 'The original subtitle parodies the phrase "life and letters" and is an ironic comment on the modern formula for literary success';[27] and that reads the work in the light of Pound's claim that 'Contacts and Life' represents 'the actual order of the subject matter'. It was certainly his view of *Mauberley*'s order when, soon after writing it, he included a sketch of its plan in a letter to a potential French translator:

Et puis il y a 'Hugh Selwyn Mauberley, life and contacts' mon dernier petit livre, qui est le sujet modern avec le decor modern. Je crois que je vous ai explique [*sic*] l'architecture de cet libre [*sic*].

> Le jeun[e] homme
> Les gens qu'il rencontre a Londres.
> Lui meme [*sic*]
> Son roman,
> Fin.[28]

Pound's change of mind over the order of the subtitle (here as later) both confirms the importance of auto/biography to the work, and explains what is probably the reason for its neglect: namely that there is a tension between the

---

[25] Pound's wording here was closely based on the statement he drafted, and which was used to introduce his broadcasts, when he resumed them after a break of over seven weeks after Pearl Harbor. See Leonard W. Doob, ed., *'Ezra Pound Speaking': Radio Speeches of World War II* (Westport, CT and London: Greenwood Press, 1978), p. xiii.

[26] K. K. Ruthven, *A Guide to Ezra Pound's Personae (1926)* (Berkeley: University of California Press, 1969), p. 127. Pound made the comment when returning the proofs of *Diptych Rome—London* (1957).

[27] Ibid.

[28] Pound to Georges Herbiet, (undated but probably mid-1920), quoted by Ronald Bush, '"It Draws One to Consider Time Wasted": Hugh Selwyn Mauberley', *American Literary History*, 2:1 (1990), 56–78 (pp. 59–60). 'Son roman' primarily refers to Mauberley's adventures with the Lady Valentine. Though the term can also mean a 'novel', there's no indication in the poems that Mauberley writes anything but poems.

cliché or near-cliché phrase, 'Life and Contacts', signalling how Pound is parodying or pastiching the etiolated literary memoir of a minor aesthete, and the order in which the sequences actually operate, giving us the 'Contacts' before the 'Life'. That is, there is a flaw in the composition which has obscured Pound's design. He needed the phrase 'Life and Contacts', the order of which chimes with other familiar biographical forms—'Life and Times', 'Life and Letters', 'Life and Work'. 'Contacts and Life' sounds awkwardly inverted, and wouldn't alert us to the formal games he is playing with the conventions of literary memoir-writing. But 'Life and Contacts' didn't alert his readers to it either, because the order of the poem didn't match it. Any attempt to equate the first sequence with Mauberley's 'Life' (it is about a series of other literary figures; his 'contacts') and the second sequence with his 'Contacts' (it is headed with Mauberley's name, and is about the life of an otherwise unnamed aesthete, presumably a single person, and thus presumably Mauberley) is doomed to failure. It is easy to see how critics would be discouraged from attending to the subtitle.

But what if we do read the whole work as Pound tells us to: as a poem whose subject matter is Mauberley's 'Contacts and Life'? What difference might this make to the received critical debate over the attribution of each component poem to Mauberley or Pound (or 'E. P.')?

The first thing to say (to focus on what has already been implied) is that this is to read the whole work as a gallery of imaginary portraits. Mauberley himself is undeniably the central figure: not only the subject of at least the first four poems of the second sequence, possibly the author of the last poem, 'Medallion', and also the person whose name the whole work bears as its title. 'E. P.' is perhaps the next most important figure, though as we have seen, Pound said Mauberley buried him in the first poem: the only one in which he is mentioned. But there are various others, several named, others indicated. In the first sequence there is the woman of 'Yeux Glauques'; 'Monsieur Verog' of 'Siena Mi fe', disfecemi Maremma'; 'Brennbaum'; 'Mr. Nixon'; there is 'the Lady Valentine' of poem XII. There are also the two unnamed figures: 'the stylist' of poem X; and the '"Conservatrix of Milésien" / Habits of mind and feeling' of poem XI.

With the second sequence there is more uncertainty. The subject of each component poem is not named. My reading presumes they are all aspects of Mauberley (hence 'lui même'); that they represent his 'Life', and that is why his name appears in the overall title for this sequence. The pattern established by the first sequence, in which most of the component poems sketch a different portrait, may set up an expectation that these are distinct figures. If they are all spoken by Mauberley, they might be imaginary portraits of aesthetes which together compose an imaginary self-portrait. I shall return to this sequence later, but first let us consider Part I, and its less phantasmal portraits.

E. P. in the first poem has already been discussed. What needs adding here is the way he is introduced: as a writer striving 'to resuscitate the dead art / Of poetry', but somehow 'out of key with his time', because 'Unaffected by "the march of events"'. The narrator only buries him to the extent of saying 'He passed from men's memory' in his thirtieth (or in one variant, thirty first) year; not that he actually died. Pound was thirty in 1915; the year he read 'Prufrock', in which Eliot imagined a speaker much older than himself, who may (the epigraph implies) already be dead. In August 1911 he had visited Ford Madox Ford (then Hueffer) in Germany for three weeks, and acted as his secretary. With his usual generosity to younger writers, Ford read Pound's later poems, and enacted the most unforgettable criticism Pound received. Nearly thirty years later, in Ford's obituary, he wrote how Ford 'felt the errors' of the writing:

to the point of rolling (physically, and if you look at it as mere superficial snob, ridiculously) on the floor [...] when my third volume displayed me trapped, fly-papered, gummed and strapped down in a jejune provincial effort to learn, *mehercule*, the stilted language that then passed for 'good English' in the arthritic milieu that held control of the respected British critical circles [...]

And that roll saved me at least two years, perhaps more. It sent me back to my own proper effort, namely, toward using the living tongue (with younger men after me), though none of us has found a more natural language than Ford did.[29]

Pound remained grateful for what he recognized was a turning point in his literary career; the realization he needed to be able to turn himself from a pasticheur of the aesthetes into a truly modern, or as we would say now, modernist, poet. The E. P. in the first poem of *Hugh Selwyn Mauberley* may thus be Pound's mask of the poet he was until around 1915; the thing Ford had helped him cease to be.

The next four poems in Part I explore the time that E. P. was out of key with. Though no specific characters are presented, they form an important set of contexts for the presentation not only of E. P., but also of the imaginary portraits which follow. Each is a complex performance, bristling with savage irony, wordplay, allusion and provocation. At the risk of gross oversimplification (not least because the poems' concerns overlap) their primary concerns are respectively: modern art; modern culture; the First World War; and its effect on civilization.

Poem II appears to contrast the Imagist movement with popular art and entertainment. 'The age demanded an image', but not the 'image' of the Imagists; rather, an image 'of its accelerated grimace'. Here Pound appears to be saying a farewell to the London-based Imagism of which he was prime mover,

---

[29] Pound, 'Ford Madox (Hueffer) Ford: Obit', *Nineteenth Century and After*, 126 (1939), 178–81; reprinted in *Selected Prose*, ed. William Cookson (London: Faber, 1978), pp. 431–3 (pp. 431–2). The book was probably *Canzoni*, published in July, but actually Pound's fifth volume of verse. For further discussion of this episode see Saunders, *Ford Madox Ford: A Dual Life*, vol. 1 (Oxford: Oxford University Press, 1996), pp. 342–5. For the relationship between Ford and Pound see Lindberg-Seyersted, ed., *Pound/Ford*; Robert Hampson, '"Experiments in Modernity": Ford and Pound', in Andrew Gibson, ed., *Pound in Multiple Perspective: A Collection of Critical Essays* (Basingstoke and London: Macmillan, 1993), pp. 93–125; and Max Saunders, 'Ford/Pound', *Agenda*, 27:4/28:1 (1989/1990), 93–102.

as part of his farewell to London; and also to what he calls 'the "sculpture" of rhyme', alluding to his admiration not only for Gautier's sculptural images for poetry, but for his near-namesake the Vorticist sculptor Gaudier.

The third poem presents a broader picture of cultural change, encompassing fashion, lyric, religion, aesthetics, and politics. No explicit judgement is made, but the laconic bitter tone suggests degeneration in all aspects: a time which it would be no disgrace to be out of key with.

The fourth poem stands out from all the others. It is the only poem in the whole of *Hugh Selwyn Mauberley* without regular stanzas, though it has stanza breaks. It has some half rhymes in lines 5–10, and some line-end repetitions, but is otherwise unrhymed. Pound said: 'The metre in *Mauberley* is Gautier and Bion's "Adonis"; or at least those are the two grafts I was trying to flavour it with. Syncopation from the Greek; and a general distaste for the slushiness and swishiness of the post-Swinburnian British line.'[30] Where the metrics of the other poems are those of Gautier or Laforgue, it is this one that has been seen as most closely modelled on Bion. That Pound uses the model of Bion's *Lament for Adonis* for a poem about the war is a poignant irony: the language itself is deeply unsentimental:

> These fought in any case,
> and some believing,
>   pro domo, in any case . . .
>
> Some quick to arm,
> some for adventure,
> some from fear of weakness,
> some from fear of censure,
> some for love of slaughter, in imagination,
> learning later . . .
> some in fear, learning love of slaughter;

But the rhythmic allusion allows the poem to stand as a lament for the war's waste of youth and beauty, while avoiding the sentimental idealizations of the Swinburnian aesthetes or their Georgian successors. It also stands out as the most rhetorical and impassioned poem in the work. It doesn't seem possible that it could have been produced by the Mauberley anatomized in the second sequence; nor does it seem to have any connection with Pound's critique of Mauberley's aestheticism (except by avoiding it). It does however express Pound's outrage at the war's slaughter, and especially at the loss of artists such as his friend Gaudier-Brzeska. It sounds out of key with the rest of the volume. But that is perhaps Pound's point: the war was the central event of the time with which 'E. P.' was 'out of key'. Yet Pound himself refuses to attune himself to what the age demands: especially when it demands topically militaristic clichés such as 'the march of events'. Those

---

[30] Pound to Schelling, 9 July 1922: *Selected Letters*, p. 181.

Poundian inverted commas enact a refusal to be in key with the times, to adopt uncritically the phrases of the day.

The other function of this magnificent poem—one of the best war poems written by a non-combatant—is to emphasize the war as a context for the whole work. 'Vocat æstus in umbram'. Whatever else Pound may have intended by the epigraph, the idea that 'the heat calls us into the shade', stated in 1920, must surely have suggested the heat of battle and the shades of the dead, or the shade of Hades.[31] The first of Pound's *Cantos*, early versions of which had been published during the war, and in 1919, includes a rite in which Odysseus and his companions offer a blood sacrifice to summon the ghosts of the dead, especially that of the seer Tiresias.[32] The Trojan War was the inevitable parallel to the Great War for classically minded modernists such as Joyce, Richard Aldington, or Pound. To be alive in London in 1920 must have been to be aware of the ghosts of the war-dead. 'I had not thought death had undone so many', as Eliot has Tiresias see or say in 'The Waste Land'. The guilt of being alive when so many of your contemporaries and friends had died was intolerable, which is perhaps why Pound imagines his own death in the first poem.

The fifth poem, one of the shortest in the volume, considers the notion that the war-dead sacrificed themselves to save civilization:

> There died a myriad,
> And of the best, among them,
> For an old bitch gone in the teeth,
> For a botched civilization [. . . .]
> For two gross of broken statues,
> For a few thousand battered books.

These are the last words before the transition to 'Yeux Glauques', and the first of the poems anatomizing precisely that pre-war civilization and its representatives.

The first five poems thus present the contemporary predicament for the artist: especially the demands of modernity, and the after-effects of the war. Seen in this way, the bitterness in the tone towards the aesthetes becomes clearer. Pound is setting the prevailing poetics before Modernism (what he calls the 'post-Swinburnian British line') in balance with the magnitude of the war, to ask whether it is adequate to the occasion: to ask how aestheticism looks now; what visions of beauty can survive the horror of the Western Front. But he is also, to some extent, holding pre-war culture responsible for the war. Pound was of course not alone in feeling the need to find someone to blame for the war; not alone, later, in trying to pin the blame on Jews, Liberals, or elders. What is surprising here is the

---

[31] See Brooker, *A Student's Guide*, pp. 187–8.

[32] In the 'Three Cantos' published in *Poetry* (June–August 1917), the passage in question appears in Canto III, as it does in the slightly revised text published in *Quia Pauper Amavi* (London: The Ovid Press, 1919). See Ronald Bush, *The Genesis of Ezra Pound's 'Cantos'* (Princeton: Princeton University Press, 1976), pp. xiii, 71.

suggestion that Pre-Raphaelite artists or aesthetes were somehow culpable. Equally surprising, perhaps, is the fact the he was not alone here either.[33] It may sound an absurd position, but it indicates that Pound's attack on the aesthetes didn't mean that he didn't take aesthetics seriously. On the contrary: his point is that a failure of clarity in language ('slushiness and swishiness') conduces to a culpable hypocrisy, solipsism, muddle, and impotence; and in political as well as personal terms. Which is the basis of his critique of an aesthete such as Mauberley; and of the literary establishment's cult of memorializing such minor figures. Pound's verdict on the 'botched' pre-war civilization—'two gross of broken statues', 'a few thousand battered books'—may echo Ford's verdict on the Pre-Raphaelite Brotherhood: 'As a producing agency it gave to the world ten or a dozen pictures, five or six poems, a few statues and it has caused an inordinate heap of Memoirs.'[34]

'Yeux Glauques', the next poem, is the first of the other 'imaginary portraits' in the volume, and it is of a figure from just this Pre-Raphaelite milieu. The subject is a woman. She is not named directly, but has been identified as Lizzie Siddal, the model used by Millais and Holman Hunt, and particularly by Rossetti, whom she eventually married.[35] The third stanza refers to Burne-Jones's 'Cophetua' (i.e. *King Cophetua and the Beggar-Maid*) at the Tate Gallery. The disconnected quotation 'Ah, poor Jenny's case' also perhaps points to Siddal, via Rossetti's poem 'Jenny', which had been attacked by the critic Robert Buchanan ('Foetid Buchanan', to Pound) in a notorious article called 'The Fleshly School of Poetry' in the *Contemporary Review* of 1871. Peter Brooker writes, with impressive concision:

This and the following six poems present a gallery of symptomatic writers, representing the character of literary culture in the latter half of the nineteenth and the early twentieth centuries. Their inherent limitations and the philistinism of the age are precedents for Mauberley's own 'case.'[36]

Certainly writers are mentioned in 'Yeux Glauques' (Ruskin, Rossetti) as is Fitzgerald's 'English Rubaiyat'. The central figure isn't a writer, but a model; two artists who painted Siddal's imaginary portrait as mythical or symbolic figures also figure: Rossetti again (who used her as the model for such paintings as *Beata Beatrix*), and Burne-Jones. It is right that this portrait is part of a 'gallery'; but if 'symptomatic', of what? The poem moves from a statement of how the Pre-Raphaelites were 'abused', which appears to defend them, to a criticism of the 'vacant gaze' of the archetypal Pre-Raphaelite woman, as if their presentation of

---

[33] See Joseph Wiesenfarth, 'Ford Madox Ford and the Pre-Raphaelites or how Dante Gabriel Rossetti Started the First World War', *REAL: Yearbook of Research in English and American Literature*, ed. Herbert Grabes, Winfried Fluck, and Jürgen Schlaeger, vol. 9 (Tübingen: Gunter Narr Verlag, 1993) pp. 109–48.
[34] Ford Madox Hueffer, *The Pre-Raphaelite Brotherhood* (London: Duckworth, 1907), pp. 2–3.
[35] Brooker, *A Student's Guide*, p. 203.
[36] Ibid., p. 201.

passion were itself hopelessly vacuous. There are two issues here. First, Pound takes aestheticism's celebration of the blending of the arts seriously, addressing the function of the visual in poetry not just metaphorically, but through a consideration of real visual artists. Second, though his tone may imply a diagnostic relation to a morbid culture (in which writers may be 'symptomatic'), his form develops the aesthetic experiment with imaginary portraiture.

One reason for thinking this is that the woman may not be a portrait of Siddal, or not only of her. Violet Hunt, Ford's lover when Pound met him in London, had also modelled for Burne-Jones. One of her recent biographers argues that 'Although other women claimed to have sat for the virgin in Burne-Jones's *King Cophetua and the Beggar Maid*, Violet's features are evident.'[37] Pound knew Hunt well, and is bound to have heard about the Pre-Raphaelites from her, or from her mother Margaret Raine Hunt, when he visited them and Ford in Kensington. Whoever was actually the sitter, what they sat for was an imaginary portrait; a lending of their features for a portrait of an imaginary couple. (King Cophetua is described in Brewer's *Dictionary of Phrase and Fable* as an 'imaginary King of Africa', referred to by Shakespeare.) If the portrait of the beggar-maid is a composite portrait of two sitters, it is doubly imaginary. Such concerns matter because they militate against the objection that Pound is writing satires of individual writers, and that satire belongs to a different genre from the imaginary portrait. It is true that the Aesthetic imaginary portraits lack satire. They might be better for it. And it is true that Pound is satirizing the aesthetic milieu. But part of his innovation in *Hugh Selwyn Mauberley* is to achieve just that combination of satiric tone with imaginary portraiture: to engage with the Aesthetic version of auto/biography, but transform it into something more 'robust' and energetic. Where Joyce's *Portrait* satirizes a youthful stage of aesthetic pretension, Pound not only satirizes the whole milieu of aestheticism, but also the way it writes about itself.

The obscurity of *Hugh Selwyn Mauberley*, partly a product of its allusiveness, and partly due to its attack on a milieu long-forgotten, has had the understandable effect of making critics want to decode it: to identify both the allusions and the figures in the milieu. Readers need expert guides such as Peter Brooker's, which helpfully annotates all the names mentioned. The effect of such annotation, though, is to read the poems as actual portraits, not imaginary ones. In the case of the next poem, 'Siena Mi fe', disfecemi Maremma', the case for a specific identification is much stronger:

> Among the pickled fœtuses and bottled bones,
> Engaged in perfecting the catalogue,

---

[37] Barbara Belford, *Violet* (New York: Simon and Schuster, 1990), caption for plate 12, between pp. 160–1. Ford's *Collected Poems* (London: Max Goschen, 1914), which Pound reviewed, included a 'Song Drama' on 'King Cophetua's Wooing'.

I found the last scion of the
Senatorial families of Strasbourg, Monsieur Verog.

Verog talks to the speaker 'For two hours' of Lionel Johnson, Ernest Dowson, and other members of the 'Rhymers' Club'. 'So spoke the author of "The Dorian Mood"', says the speaker. Brooker glosses Verog as 'Victor Gustav Plarr (1863–1929)'. Plarr had indeed been born in Strasburg; had indeed published a volume of poems called *In the Dorian Mood* (1896); had indeed become Librarian for the Royal College of Surgeons; and Pound had indeed heard his talk, referring to it twice in the *Cantos*.[38]

It wasn't only in *Hugh Selwyn Mauberley* that Pound wanted to produce what he called 'a portrait of contemporary England, or at least Eng. As she wuz when I left her.'[39] In the so-called 'Hell Cantos', XIV and XV, written between 1923 and 1925, his subject was 'specifically LONDON, the state of English mind in 1919 and 1920'—the year of writing and publishing *Hugh Selwyn Mauberley*.[40] Indeed, the fact that Pound puts the year 1920 together with Mauberley's name as the title to the second sequence suggests that *Mauberley* portrays a representative of 'the state of [the] English mind' at exactly that time. As Peter Brooker notes in connection with the 'Hell Cantos':

Pound had attempted such a portrait earlier in Mœurs Contemporaines' (1918), but wrote to James Joyce already in that year of the 'need of bottling London, some more ample modus than permitted in free-verse scherzos, and thumb-nail sketches of Marie Corelli, H. James etc. (in Mœurs Contemporaines).'[41]

In many ways 'Mœurs Contemporaines' is a closer precursor of *Hugh Selwyn Mauberley*, though one Brooker misses. It is a suite of eight such brief sketches of London types mostly concerned with art and aesthetics, with the exception of the first, 'Mr. Hecatomb Styrax', whose sexual 'ineptitudes' have driven his wife 'from one religious excess to another', yet 'even now Mr. Styrax / Does not believe in aesthetics.'[42] It might have been possible to guess that one of the 'old men with beautiful manners' in the penultimate poem was Henry James, but only because Pound uses there the same phrase from Dante that he associates with James in Canto VII: 'Con gli occhi onesti e tardi' (with honest and slow eyes). Otherwise, only those who knew the subjects personally would have had much chance of guessing who they are, or even that they are based on real figures, had Pound not told Joyce he was 'bottling' London. This is either because they are based on personal details that the subjects would have kept as private as

---

[38] See *The Cantos* (London: Faber, 1975); XVI (p. 70) and LXXIV (p. 433).

[39] Pound to Wyndham Lewis, 3 December 1924: *Selected Letters*, p. 191.

[40] Bush, *The Genesis of Ezra Pound's 'Cantos'*, p. 183. Pound to John Drummond, 18 February 1932, *Selected Letters*, p. 239.

[41] Brooker, *A Student's Guide*, pp. 259–60; quoting *Pound/Joyce*, p. 149.

[42] 'Mœurs Contemporaines', *Selected Poems*, ed. T. S. Eliot (London: Faber, 1973), pp. 165–9 (p. 165).

possible, such as the sex life of Styrax. Or because both the poems and their observations are so slight as to give the literary detective little clue, as with the subject of the fourth poem, whose parents still open his mail, even though he is twenty-seven, 'an officer, / and a gentleman, / and an architect'.

The 'thumb-nail sketches' of 'Mœurs Contemporaines' do not work like Max Beerbohm's caricature drawings of writers, say, in which a personality is clearly identified by a caption as well as the familiar features which the artist exaggerates. They are 'scherzos' in the musical sense as much as in the literal sense of 'jokes', since few beyond Pound's inner circle would have got their jokes. What Pound sought to do in 'Mœurs Contemporaines' is clear from the title, out of Remy de Gourmont, speaking of Flaubert, who had subtitled *Madame Bovary* 'Mœurs de Province' (provincial manners, morality, habits).[43] It was the social 'tone' of London he wanted to catch: people's ways of behaving and feeling; what they cared about or didn't; how they spoke, thought, and interacted. This was what he particularly admired in James, on whom he had written a long essay in 1918.[44] The letter to Felix Schelling about Mauberley also discusses humour. Pound is perhaps thinking ahead to the Hell Cantos he was about to write. But his remarks also touch on the tone of 'Mœurs Contemporaines' and *Hugh Selwyn Mauberley*, which makes some readers wince when it seems to aim at satiric wit but merely steamrollers over butterflies:

Next point: This being buoyed by wit. No. Punch and the rest of them have too long gone on treating the foetor of England as if it were something to be joked about. There is an evil without dignity and without tragedy, and it is dishonest art to treat it as if it were funny. It is perhaps difficult to treat it at all; the Brit. Empire is rotting because no one in England tries to treat it. Juvenal isn't witty. Joyce's isn't harsh enough. One hasn't any theology to fall back on.[45]

'[F]oetor'; 'Foetid Buchanan'; 'pickled fœtuses and bottled bones'. Pound presents the Aesthetic movement as at once still-born and stinking. The savage energy of condemnation here is disturbing, and looks forward to Pound's fascism. It is not absent from *Hugh Selwyn Mauberley*, though the poems' saving grace is that they lack this brutal judgementality. It is as if the tight Laforguean forms hold in check Pound's tendency to denounce. The best satire knows that energy of denunciation without discrimination can tend to hysteria. The letter also pulls itself back from this position a few lines later, as it catches itself having slipped from talking of 'treating the foetor' in the sense of literary treatment, to the sense of treating it medically or hygienically, as you'd treat something 'rotting': 'Art can't offer a patent medicine. A failure to dissociate that from a

---

[43] Humphrey Carpenter, *A Serious Character* (London: Faber, 1988), p. 324.
[44] Pound 'Henry James', *Literary Essays of Ezra Pound*, ed. T. S. Eliot (London: Faber, 1974), pp. 295–338.
[45] Pound to Felix Schelling, 9 July [1922]: *Selected Letters*, p. 180.

profounder didacticism has led to the errors of "aesthete's" critique.' I take this to mean that in trying to free art from religious and bourgeois morality, the Aesthetes detached it altogether from the world, and painted themselves into a corner, solipsist and impotent. Whereas Pound's poetry aims at 'a profounder didacticism'. *Hugh Selwyn Mauberley* is a critique of 'the errors of "aesthete's" critique'.

This analysis of the methods and aims of the poetry may appear to digress from the topic of imaginary portraiture. But what it shows is that what Pound wanted to portray was not individuals, treated satirically or comically, so much as the general milieu: 'Mœurs Contemporaines'; 'the foetor of England'; 'the errors of "aesthete's" critique'; 'atmospheres, nuances, impressions of personal tone and quality';[46] 'LONDON, the state of English mind in 1919 and 1920'. What he was offering was 'a portrait of contemporary England'; an attempt at 'bottling London', presumably in the medical sense of bottling specimens to exemplify a type, rather than for their individual sakes. That, I take it, is the significance of Monsieur Verog's surroundings of 'pickled fœtuses and bottled bones'. And that is why it is less important that he is based on Victor Plarr, than that he is the type of the European émigré writing in London, himself a walking catalogue of the Aesthetic movement, and like them, though a talented writer, too inward-looking to connect either with his own generation or the next: 'Neglected by the young, / Because of these reveries'. After all, why did Pound need to disguise the name? Of all the portraits in the volume, this is the least satirical of its subject; more an act of homage to a writer whose work he genuinely valued. True, Plarr was still alive in 1920. But then so were 'Headlam' (Revd Stewart D.), and 'Image' (wait for it: Selwyn), who are named in the fourth stanza. It seems, rather, that Pound wanted to create an uncertainty about whether the subjects were real literary figures, like Plarr, or fictional ones, like Mauberley; to infiltrate imaginary portraits, especially that of Mauberley, amongst real and almost real ones: to create the impression that Mauberley really moved among these histori-cal figures; or, conversely, in Paul Skinner's evocative words, to create the impression that the real figures about whom Pound enjoyed hearing Yeats and Ford reminisce were 'already flickering and becoming insubstantial'; that, after the 'vast, single obliterating force' of the war, 'who was left and remembered must have been an abruptly pertinent question.'[47] Such a method has the virtue of criticizing the aesthete's critique by presenting one through the aesthete's own technique of imaginary portraiture.

The vitriol in Pound's remarks on literary London was not only the product of his encounters with aestheticism, of course. Established writers and critics hostile to modernism had more to do with it, as we shall see in the next two portraits. But before we move on to those, consider his comments on another writer's

---

[46] Pound 'Henry James', *Literary Essays of Ezra Pound*, p. 324.
[47] Paul Skinner, email to Max Saunders, 15 March 2008.

satirical treatment of the pre-war English literary scene. He wrote that it was 'difficult for those not in eng. at least from 1908–20' to appreciate Ford Madox Ford, and said that Ford's satires *The Simple Life Limited* and *Mr. Fleight* were:

both in surface technique, presumably brilliant, and but for levity, wd. be recognized as hist. docs. are so recog. by those who know how close their apparent fantasia was to the utter imbecilities of milieu they portray. Unbelieved because the sober foreigner has no mean of knowing how far they corresponded to an external reality.[48]

Pound's farewell to London, then, is an attempt to show how fantastical the literary milieu seemed to a 'sober foreigner' who was there: to present not 'the series / Of curious heads in medallion', like Mauberley, but a series of heads pickled like medical curiosities, to recapture the surreal 'imbecilities' of the time and place.

BEERBOHM

The next two poems in the first sequence stand out as the only ones with names for titles: 'Brennbaum' and 'Mr. Nixon'. These portraits too seem readily identifiable. Indeed, Pound is on record as saying Mr. Nixon was 'a fictitious name for a real person', generally taken to be Arnold Bennett.[49] Like Nixon, Bennett had made enough money from his writing to buy yachts. Not only does Brennbaum's name echo Beerbohm's, but the caricature of his 'circular infant's face' sounds like both Beerbohm and one of his self-caricatures. Furthermore, the last line calls him 'Brennbaum "The Impeccable"', echoing the phrase used of Beerbohm, 'The Incomparable Max', as well as Pound's mention, in an essay published the same year, of 'the impeccable Beerbohm.'[50] Clearly, these portraits are less imaginary than the rest, though I shall argue that even they engage with the idea of the imaginary portrait obliquely. First, though, we need to ask why the names needed changing. In the case of 'Brennbaum', the reason appears to be a gratuitous anti-semitism. Gratuitous because in fact Beerbohm was not Jewish, though he said he would have been pleased to have been.[51] However, Pound's portrait attributes to him the racial 'memories' of the Hebraic exodus—'of Horeb, Sinai and the forty years'; and the name ('burnt tree' in German) adds to these, suggesting the burning bush. This short poem effectively reduces him to

[48] Pound, '[The Inquest]' [1924?], in Lindberg-Seyersted, ed., *Pound/Ford*, p. 70.
[49] Kimon Friar and John Malcolm Brinnin, eds, *Modern Poetry: American and British* (New York: Appleton-Century-Crofts, 1951), p. 529.
[50] Brooker, *A Student's Guide*, p. 208. *Literary Essays*, p. 340.
[51] Brooker, *A Student's Guide*, p. 208. David Cecil, *Max: A Biography* (London: Constable, 1964), p. 4, quotes Beerbohm saying 'I would be delighted to know that the Beerbohms had that very agreeable and encouraging thing, Jewish blood'; but he gives no source, so it's not clear whether Pound could have read it before 1920. Even if he hadn't, he could still have thought of Brennbaum as an imaginary portrait of Beerbohm as a Jew.

a racial type;[52] and the change of name has the effect of a reproach or an unmasking, as if to say that Jewish émigrés who changed their names to assimilate should not be allowed to conceal their Jewishness. This has the further, and equally unpleasant effect, of making the phrase 'The Impeccable' sound sarcastic, as if there might be something peccable in being Jewish. Insofar as this is a portrait of Beerbohm, the only imaginary element is the Jewish one. That could only stand as evidence that this was a truly imaginary portrait if one thought Pound intended it as imaginary, which is doubtful.

However, Beerbohm (*in propria persona*) is an important figure in relation to *Hugh Selwyn Mauberley* in another way. And it may be for this reason that Pound wants him more easily identifiable. Beerbohm had published in 1919 a book treating comically the same milieu Pound was presenting. It was called *Seven Men*, and is one of the supreme examples of aesthetic imaginary portraits. Beerbohm's is the comic version of the imaginary portrait, and as such avoids the cloyingness of Pater's. Not all Beerbohm's men are writers. 'James Pethell' is a gambler. Beerbohm writes about how he was first intrigued, and later shocked, by Pethell's motivation. When he is introduced to Pethell he is told he is 'a great character': the terms already introduce a frisson of fictionality.[53] Pethell turns out to be a thrill-seeker; someone who only feels alive when the risks are high, and he is even prepared to risk not only his own life, but the lives of his family and friends, in his addiction to excitement. With 'A. V. Laider', Beerbohm moves closer to an exploration of fiction. Laider is the only other character who isn't a writer. But he turns out to be a consummate storyteller. Beerbohm returns to a seaside hotel to recuperate from influenza, and finds that a letter he wrote to Laider when they met there the previous year is still there, on the 'letter board' for mail addressed to absent guests. The pathos of unreceived letters allows Beerbohm to launch into a characteristic piece of hilarious fantasy: an imaginary dialogue between 'A Very Young Envelope' and 'A Very Old Envelope'. ('One only has to look at you to see there's nothing in you but a note scribbled to him by a cousin. Look at *me!* There are three sheets, closely written, in me. The lady to whom I am addressed —' / 'Yes, sir, yes; you told me all about her yesterday' etc.)[54] At first this may seem merely a piece of whimsy, but it exemplifies an idea that runs through the entire volume, of literature not being where it should be; not being what it should be, or what people want it to be, or what they expect it to be. Beerbohm had written to Laider out of sympathy. He explains how they had got into conversation, and a discussion of palmistry had led to Laider's chilling story of how he felt responsible for murder. He was on a railway journey, and when his fellow travellers discover his interest in palmistry, they insist he

---

[52] Compare Pound's contemporary remark to William Carlos Williams, 11 September 1920: 'I don't care a fried —— about nationality. But race is probably real. It is real', *Selected Letters*, p. 158.
[53] Beerbohm, *Seven Men: and Two Others* (Oxford: Oxford University Press, 1980), p. 100.
[54] Ibid., pp. 126–7.

reads their fates. He is appalled to find that all their fate-lines indicate an imminent violent death, whereas his does not. Laider feels he should have pulled the communication cord to stop the train; but that he was too weak-willed, and didn't. The train crashed, leaving him the only survivor of the group. The story made a great impression on Beerbohm. Laider returns to the hotel and reads the letter, and they talk again. Now Laider expresses a different guilt. He explains that it is true that weakness of will is his problem. But that the form it takes is in being unable to control his 'very strong imagination.'[55] Now he confesses that the mere mention of the topic of palmistry provoked him to invent the whole tale, which was 'a sheer improvisation.'[56] He is a fantasist, but one who talks like an artist about his fantasies, feeling guilty not only for taking in his listeners, but also for 'not doing justice to my idea.'[57]

Laider thus may not write down his stories, but he is certainly a creator of fiction; and Beerbohm has given us a fictional story by a fictional narrator. In the other chapters of *Seven Men*, the characters are all published authors. 'Hilary Maltby and Stephen Braxton' are both successful novelists writing before the First World War. They are rivals, and much of the story is about their rivalry for acceptance by London's High Society—very much as in Pound's twelfth poem, about 'the Lady Valentine' and 'the Lady Jane'. Like several of Beerbohm's stories here, there is a gothic twist. Maltby successfully outmanoeuvres Braxton, making sure that he is invited to an aristocratic country house weekend but Braxton is not. Yet while he is there, he is tormented by the apparition of Braxton, which haunts him like a ghost—a 'simulacrum of himself'; and which makes him commit a series of ever more humiliating *faux pas*.[58] Maltby thinks that Braxton has managed to 'project' himself through the force of his 'envy, hatred, and malice.'[59] But of course (and like the apparition of Banquo's ghost in *Macbeth*, to which Beerbohm is perhaps alluding) the story leaves the possibility open that the projection is from Maltby's conscience-stricken head. Either way, there is a sense in which the writer's 'strong imagination' is subversive of the good manners prized so highly by the upper class milieu which is as important a part of Beerbohm's subject; that just as it disrupts the social order to the extent of getting writers invited to parties above their social station, it can also disturb the moral order and the order of the real too. It is, after all, an essential part of the realist or impressionist artist's effort to make simulacra appear to live.

One of the most entertaining stories in the volume is '"Savonarola" Brown'. Primarily a satire on an aspiring but hopelessly inept dramatist, this is also a story in which words and names don't stay in their proper time or place. 'I like to remember that I was the first to call him so', Beerbohm begins, suggesting that others have also applied the nickname to Brown; and that therefore he is a real person, available for discussion before Beerbohm had written his story.[60] This

---

[55] Ibid., p. 150. [56] Ibid. [57] Ibid.
[58] Ibid., p. 77. [59] Ibid. [60] Ibid., p. 198.

slippage between the fictional and the real, or the attempt to insert fictional characters into the literary and social worlds is one of the collection's central devices. Brown had been unfortunately christened 'Ladbroke', because his parents lived at Ladbroke Crescent at the time. Beerbohm knew him at school, where he was teased for his name; and meets him later at the theatre. Brown explains that he intends to write a play about Savonarola:

> He made me understand, however, that it was rather the name than the man that had first attracted him. He said that the name was in itself a great incentive to blank verse. He uttered it to me slowly, in a voice so much deeper than his usual voice that I nearly laughed.[61]

This rings alarm bells. Some names are a dangerously sonorous incentive to blank verse: 'O Huncamunca, Huncamunca, O'. Will Savonarola Brown prove the Tom Thumb amongst dramatists? The anxious near-schoolboy near-laughter over voice-pitch suggests that Brown's attraction to the sound of the name may be equally jejune. There's also a sense that Brown's unease with his own name is what draws him to write about others. The two men continue to meet, the alarm continuing to sound, if muffled, in Beerbohm's scathingly tactful comment that he found Brown's 'company restful rather than inspiring'. Brown begins writing the play, and gives regular progress reports:

> 'I've hit on an initial idea', he said, 'and that's enough to start with. I gave up my notion of inventing a plot in advance. I thought it would be a mistake. I don't want puppets on wires. I want Savonarola to work out his destiny in his own way. Now that I have the initial idea, what I've got to do is to make Savonarola *live*. I hope I shall be able to do this. Once he's alive, I shan't interfere with him. I shall just watch him.[62]

The eschewing of falsifying plots is almost plausible as an impressionist aspiration, if absurd apropos of a subject whose destiny is given by history. But Beerbohm takes issue with it, arguing that 'the end of the hero *must* be logical and rational.'[63] Brown disagrees, saying 'In actual life it isn't so. What is there to prevent a motor-omnibus from knocking me over and killing me at this moment?':

> At that moment, by what has always seemed to me the strangest of coincidences, and just the sort of thing that playwrights ought to avoid, a motor-omnibus knocked Brown over and killed him.[64]

It's hard to tell which cheek Beerbohm's tongue is in here, but the cruelly funny joke barely allows us to entertain the possibility of suicidal intent. Brown has made Beerbohm his executor. Beerbohm prints the four completed acts, sketching how the play might have been completed. In part what is being parodied,

[61] Beerbohm, *Seven Men: and Two Others*, p. 200.
[62] Ibid., p. 201.   [63] Ibid., p. 203.   [64] Ibid., p. 204.

then, is the form of the 'literary remains' of an author. Beerbohm's prefatory remarks are deeply ironic, feigning admiration while making the fragment's faults all too evident:

Remembering the visionary look in his eyes, remembering that he was as displeased as I by the work of all living playwrights, and as dissatisfied with the great efforts of the Elizabethans, I wonder that he was not more immune from influences.[65]

'I am not blind to the great merits of the play as it stands', says Beerbohm, knowing full well that its great merits are its echoes of those great Elizabethans. 'Savonarola' is a hilarious pastiche of Renaissance revenge drama, complete with gaoler, Shakespearean singing Fool, disguise, secret passion, and murder. Much of the hilarity comes from its immunity to history. Not only does Brown have Lucrezia Borgia falling in love with Savonarola, and her brother Cesare murdering him. But he also conflates times to give other legendary Italians walk-on parts. The first scene is set in 1490. Leonardo da Vinci, who was alive then, is joined by St Francis of Assisi, who died in 1226, and Dante, who died in 1321. Of course Shakespeare was notoriously inventive with his history. But even a supreme parodist such as Beerbohm needs to be wary in attempting to parody Shakespeare. So the double-articulation of the story—inventing Brown and then writing his play—enables him to parody Shakespeare at one remove, introducing an uncertainty as to when he is parodying Renaissance drama, and when he is parodying authors unable to escape its influences. What is clear is that Brown wasn't intending to parody. His play is an unintentional pastiche. It is equally clear that Beerbohm is mocking Brown. Yet Brown's pastiche does also have considerable parodic force, which though unintended by him, is presumably part of Beerbohm's intention. Though it should be said that whatever the juvenile high spirits at trying to knock the unmockable off his pedestal, the aim is as much to make fun of the conventions of Elizabethan drama, especially once they are wrenched out of their original contexts, and expected to carry the weight of a later, and absurd, play. Nothing Ezra Pound had written looked like pastiche Shakespeare; though his redactions of poetry by Provençal Troubadours and Medieval and Renaissance Italians may have made him feel that Beerbohm was looking in his direction.

It will have been evident that what Beerbohm also provides in '"Savonarola" Brown' is a sustained example of an imaginary work of literature, by an imaginary author. Despite his ironic claims for its merits, it is not offered as genuinely creative, though it has an inadvertent insane energy. The point for our purposes is that Beerbohm, like George Eliot, Symons, and others, including Joyce and Pound, is adhering to the form of the portrait-collection that includes imaginary artists and includes examples of their work. This notion of imaginary authorship is a feature of the two other stories in *Seven Men.* One of them, 'Felix Argallo and

---

[65] Ibid., p. 205.

Walter Ledgett', was in fact written later, in 1927, and added when the book was republished in 1950 as *Seven Men: and Two Others*. It is not therefore strictly relevant to our discussion of Pound's use of imaginary portraiture; though it does demonstrate Beerbohm's continuing interest into the 1920s in imaginary authorship. He begins with another knowing play with fictionality: 'It may be that in these days, among the young, Argallo's name is the main thing about him. His books are but little read, I daresay, save by us elders.'[66] How flattering, Mr. B! If we haven't read him, then, we are the young. If we haven't even heard of him, more cool us. Argallo is a major writer; Ledgett a successful minor one. Beerbohm is fond of Ledgett, and increasingly dismayed by the disparaging references which occur to him in the published correspondence of other authors. This notion allows Beerbohm to fake letters from Robert Louis Stevenson, Coventry Patmore, Henry Irving, George Meredith—each an opportunity to parody the author's style: 'Yesterday an eager homunculus named L— struck foot across this threshold, sputtering encomiastic cackle', and so on.[67] Beerbohm takes an altruistic decision to do something to counter these denigrations. He decides to use his friendship with Argallo, persuading Argallo to write out and sign letters addressed to Beerbohm (that Beerbohm has actually composed, and dictates to him) praising Ledgett and his work. Argallo has never actually met Ledgett, but Beerbohm rightly assumes that his melancholic disposition will make him sympathize with Ledgett's case. The idea is to insert these letters into Literary History; so that when Argallo's correspondence is eventually published, there will be strong praise from at least one great writer to counterbalance the slights from the others. The working through of this strategy is handled with all Beerbohm's ingenuity, and is extremely funny, not only for the way Argallo starts wanting to improve the letters, but also for the way Beerbohm slyly works in some praise of his own work too. The letters from Argallo have a different status from the ones by Stevenson, Patmore, or Meredith. Where in those cases Beerbohm invents imaginary letters by real authors, here he invents letters from an imaginary author. But there is no pretence that Argallo composed them. Yet they are not quite fakes. They are genuinely in Argallo's hand, and with his signature. He wrote them out, even if he didn't write them. Though the dramatic situation in which Beerbohm places them is fictitious, they have a real existence, published in their entirety. Their effect is to disturb one's assumptions about the reality of Literary History. If such a trick could be perpetrated, then how many other published letters might not equally be faked? This could be read as a satirical look at how that is exactly what sometimes happens: as when an author writes a letter of praise to a writer friend, with the intention that it be shown to a prospective publisher. It also reads as a satire of the public's appetite for literary memorabilia. But once again the effect is to disturb the order of the real. The fantasy of being

---

[66] Beerbohm, *Seven Men: and Two Others*, p. 157.
[67] Ibid., p. 167.

able to insert fictional letters into the public domain turns real letters into potentially imaginary works of literature.

It is the remaining story from *Seven Men*, the first in the volume, 'Enoch Soames', which bears most upon *Hugh Selwyn Mauberley*. It satirizes London literary life in the 1890s. Enoch Soames is in many ways a comparable figure to Mauberley. He is a study of ineffectualness. Beerbohm plays with the imaginariness of his portraiture, saying that Soames's chief quality was of being 'dim', of appearing not to exist. The comical plot has Soames, resigned to failure during his lifetime, making a pact with the devil in order to discover what posterity will make of him. He returns from his futuristic trip to the British Museum in 1997 demoralized by the realization that not only is his work totally forgotten, but he is only known through Beerbohm's imaginary portrait, and is thus believed to be a fictional character. It is a hilarious and ingenious story, the kind Borges would have loved, anticipating postmodern concerns with simulacra—here not only of people, but also of books and paintings. The story starts with Holbrook Jackson's *The Eighteen Nineties*,[68] which may also have brought the period into focus for Pound, and ends with an imaginary literary history (written in a kind of phonetic state-socialist Newspeak) which Soames has brought back from the future. Take away the plot of Soames's 'Catholic Diabolism', supernaturalism and time-travel, and what remains is a caricature of the aesthete convinced of his own superiority, but unable to make his mark on the world. Beerbohm, again the supreme parodist, includes examples of his verse too, from an imaginary volume called *Fungoids*. Though the title is clearly parodic, arguably the poems are more than parody, since they touch Soames's fate: the first lyric turns on the question of the existence or non-existence of the love-object (anticipating Soames's own dematerialization out of fictional history); the second is a spirited account of an encounter with the Devil, replayed as tragedy in Soames's own subsequent life and damnation. The point is that both are plausible as emanations from Soames's mind, rather than being merely Beerbohm's mockery of him:

> For this it is
> That is thy counterpart
> Of age-long mockeries
> *Thou hast not been nor art!*[69]

They are genuine examples of fictional creativity. And the caricature of the 'Nineties poet, complete with examples of his work, may well have contributed to Pound's invention of Mauberley.

Numerate readers will have noticed that only six men from the 1919 edition have been mentioned. As Lord David Cecil explained, 'The Seventh Man is Max

---

[68] Holbrook Jackson, *The Eighteen Nineties: A Review of Art and Ideas at the Close of the Nineteenth Century* (London: Grant Richards, 1913).

[69] *Seven Men: and Two Others*, p. 15.

himself who both narrates the tale and takes part in the action.'[70] Thus, as in Pater's portraits, though in a different way, Beerbohm's are also self-portraits: 'Altogether *Seven Men* is the most autobiographical of Max's works.' Or is it an imaginary self-portrait? Cecil continues: 'Not very autobiographical, however! Even when it is not too fantastic, it is too amusing.'

Vincent Sherry has made a subtle case for the presence of *Seven Men* behind *Hugh Selwyn Mauberley*, which also grants Mauberley an 'autobiographical depth' not generally recognized.[71] He shows that *Mauberley* was written during a hiatus in Pound's writing of the early *Cantos*. Sherry reads the sequence as expressing Pound's anxiety that the 'ideogrammic method' he had hoped would be his breakthrough, was beginning to issue in obscurity and incoherence, and that this would result in the kind of judgements about his inefficacy that the sequence makes on Mauberley. Sherry sees Beerbohm's 'Hilary Maltby and Stephen Braxton' as helping to shape the conception of *Mauberley* as a work about literary failure: a view that postulates 'the ironic continuity between E. P. and Mauberley as the rueful design of the sequence', such that 'E. P.' passes into Mauberley, who (as in the Beerbohm story) then expires a year after his alter ego.

Readers of Pound's volume would have recognized 'Brennbaum' as the author of *Seven Men*, which had been published the previous year. It is thus possible that Pound intended them to connect the form of *Hugh Selwyn Mauberley* with that of Beerbohm's imaginary portraits, in which he inserts himself, as Pound does (as 'E. P.') into Mauberley's world. It is also possible, though perhaps less probable, that he intended his readers to recognize the changing of Beerbohm's name to 'Brennbaum' as a gesture of homage, acknowledging the formal debt by turning Beerbohm into an imaginary portrait himself, amongst the seven portraits beginning with 'Yeux Glauques'.

ORIGINALS

The tenth poem is the clearest example of how the Poundian annotation industry can violate what Pound was trying to do. The subject is only identified as 'The stylist', who has withdrawn to rural poverty with 'a placid and uneducated mistress'. Most commentaries say the stylist is Ford, who had indeed left London for a leaking Sussex cottage in 1919, though his mistress was the Australian artist (who had studied at the Westminster School of Art, under Sickert), Stella Bowen. Brooker also suggests that Pound might have had Joyce in mind, whom he had called 'the stylist', and said that Joyce had 'lived for ten years in obscurity and

---

[70] Introduction by Lord David Cecil, *Seven Men and Two Others*, p. x.
[71] Sherry, 'From the Twenties to the Nineties: Pound, Beerbohm, and the Making of Mauberley', *PN Review* 20:5 (97) (1994), 40–2.

poverty, that he might perfect his writing and be uninfluenced by commercial demands and standards.'[72] This is very valuable, not least in suggesting how this poem follows on from the portrait of Mr. Nixon's commercialism. But the rest of Brooker's annotations all concern Ford. I don't doubt that Pound had Ford in mind here (or that he may have also had Joyce in mind, whose wife Nora had left school aged twelve, though she was not placid).[73] They were very close friends. Pound visited Ford and Stella at their cottage, and teased Ford about his playing the role of gentleman-farmer, writing to him as (amongst other things) 'Dear Hesiod.'[74] The point is that the fact Pound may have had either man in mind doesn't mean that he wanted us to have him in mind when reading the poem. Few could have had Ford in mind in 1920. A prolific author before and after the war, he had enlisted in 1915, been badly shell-shocked, but had stayed in the army until 1919. He published only one book between 1915 and 1921, a volume of poems. He had left London largely to escape from a fraught relationship with Violet Hunt (already mentioned in connection with 'Yeux Glauques'), and needed to remain obscure at least while recuperating from the war.

Ah, the annotator might annotate, Pound, who also knew Violet Hunt well, was covering up for his friend: keeping him anonymous so as not to give anything away about his post-war whereabouts; or lest Hunt should try to prise further information out of him. This is possible. Two months after the publication of *Hugh Selwyn Mauberley* in June, Hunt had discovered Ford's whereabouts, and Ford told Pound she 'has planted herself in the neighbourhood & runs about interrupting my workmen and generally making things lively. I fancy she had you followed by a detective when you came down & so got the address.'[75] Such readings, however enjoyable for biographers, insist on reading the poems as literal-minded: Pound was thinking of Ford (or Joyce), so the 'stylist' *is* Ford (or Joyce). What such readings cannot account for is the centre of the poem: Mauberley himself, who has not been traced to a single individual (though of course he draws on Pound's own experience). If all the minor portraits are read as unimaginary ones, why should the major portrait be thought imaginary? I believe that while Pound is drawing on his knowledge of real stylists like Joyce and Ford, his aim is to create an imaginary portrait of someone who is neither Joyce nor Ford, nor even a composite of both, but who is a generic artist: the type of 'the stylist', someone who, like Flaubert, like Pound himself, is prepared to ignore the forces represented by Mr. Nixon, and dedicate himself to his art whatever the cost.

---

[72] *Pound/Joyce*, pp. 115, 39: quoted by Brooker, *A Student's Guide*, pp. 209–10.

[73] Brenda Maddox, *Nora* (Boston: Houghton Mifflin, 1988), p. 13, rejects the view of Nora Barnacle as 'illiterate', saying that she had the maximum education available for girls at that time without fees.

[74] Lindberg-Seyersted, ed., *Pound/Ford*, p. 65.

[75] Ford to Pound, 30 August 1920: *Letters of Ford Madox Ford*, ed. Richard M. Ludwig (Princeton: Princeton University Press, 1965), p. 122.

The last three poems of this first sequence are all about women. In poem XI and the 'Envoi' they are not named; in poem XII they are only half-named, as 'the Lady Valentine' and 'the Lady Jane'. As before it is possible to speculate on who the 'originals' were that Pound might have had in mind. Yet these three poems have been the most resistant to such biographical decoding, and there is a hint of desperation in the annotations that have tried to attach them to particular originals. True, as we have seen, in the case of 'Envoi' we now have good reason to think Pound had a particular singer in mind, though it took half a century for a real name (Raymonde Collignon) to be connected with the poem. But we have to set that against Pound's response when asked in 1959 'Who sang you once that song of Lawes?': 'Your question is the kind of damn fool enquiry into what is nobody's damn business.'[76] Taking that tone with his naughtyboyographer shows a classic modernist antipathy to conventional literary biography. Note that he doesn't deny that there was a specific occasion; merely that it is irrelevant to an understanding of the poem. A resourceful biographical sleuth may trace a poem back to a particular time and a place. But the point is that these three poems (like poem X about 'the stylist') give little away that can serve as a clue. Pound, that is, seems again to be delineating types, and presenting them in such a way as to give them the concreteness of an individual, but simultaneously to frustrate any attempt to scratch the biographical itch.

Poem XI is perhaps the clearest instance:

> 'Conservatrix of Milésien'
> Habits of mind and feeling,
> Possibly. But in Ealing
> With the most bank-clerkly of Englishmen?

The quotation, as Peter Brooker notes, is adapted from Remy de Gourmont. Pound quotes it in one of his essays on de Gourmont, and glosses it in the postscript he wrote to his translation of de Gourmont's *The Natural Philosophy of Love* as 'Woman, the conservator, the inheritor of past gestures.'[77] The essay was published in 1919; the translation in 1922; so de Gourmont was on his mind while writing *Hugh Selwyn Mauberley*.[78] But what does the phrase mean? The problem, again expertly unravelled by Brooker, is that it means two rather different things. The 'Milesian Tales' were 'erotic romances of the first century

---

[76] Charles Norman, *Ezra Pound* (New York: Macmillan, 1969), p. 224.

[77] Pound, *Pavannes and Divagations*, p. 213. Brooker, *A Student's Guide*, p. 210. *The Natural Philosophy of Love* (New York: Boni and Liveright, 1922).

[78] Pound, 'De Gourmont: A Distinction (Followed by Notes)', *Little Review*, 5:10–11 (1919), 1–19. Republished (as 'Remy de Gourmont, a Distinction, Followed by Notes') in *Instigations* (New York: Boni and Liveright, 1920); and in *Literary Essays*, pp. 339–58 (p. 345). He had also written two essays on de Gourmont during the war: 'Remy de Gourmont', *Fortnightly Review*, 98:588 (New Series) (1 December 1915), 1159–66; and 'Remy de Gourmont', *Poetry*, 7:4 (1916), 197–202; reprinted as 'Remy de Gourmont' in *Pavannes and Divisions* (New York: Knopf, 1918); and in *Selected Prose*, pp. 383–93.

B.C., none of which are extant'. (So much for conservatrixes?) But 'Milesian' can also signify 'Irish', 'after King Milesius whose sons are reputed to have conquered ancient Ireland.'[79] The stanza swivels on its 'But', but what is the basis of the opposition? Is it a contrast of pagan eroticism with modern suburban lower-middle class uptightness? Or of Irish with English? Or does it somehow combine the two, juxtaposing Irish eroticism with English suburbanism? Brooker quotes a letter in which Pound reports to the American John Quinn just after the armistice about Maud Gonne's release from arrest:

The other point M.G. omits from her case is that she went to Ireland without permit and in disguise, in the first place, during war time.

'Conservatrice des traditions Milesienne,' as de Gourmont calls them. There are people who have no sense of the value of 'civilization' or public order.[80]

The letter goes on to ask: 'Have *all* the Irish a monomania?', and to characterize Gonne as a temperament that wants 'revolution *with* violence; no special aim or objective, but just pure and platonic love of a row'. It may then be that what Pound intends here, whether de Gourmont meant it or not, is a humorously precious phrase to describe a brawling tendency associated with the Irish. As who should say: Irish conservation: a contradiction in terms. The prejudices in and around this poem are evidently legion. Poundian advocates might argue that what he seeks is a 'constatation' of attitudes: that is, to juxtapose a Celtic exuberance with English prudery and to enjoy the spectacle of their mutual disapproval. But the evidence of the letter is that Pound was not that aloof from such prejudices: '*all* the Irish'; 'as de Gourmont calls *them* [my emphasis]'. Calls who? Women? The Irish? Revolutionists? In a case like this the poetry would be better if it were biographically more specific. Imaginary portraiture, that is, like any other form of portraiture, is as likely to reflect the qualities of its artist as well as its subjects, and is not necessarily always admirable. A satiric sketch of a particular person such as Maud Gonne might have several kinds of interest. But the letter about Gonne doesn't seem to me to legitimize such a reading of the poem (which I should acknowledge that Brooker is too tactful an annotator to force: he merely juxtaposes).[81] Rather, it indicates a prejudicial reflex whereby Pound's response to Gonne's political activities is to compound three prejudices: against woman, the mad, and the Irish. The phrase 'as de Gourmont calls them' could apply to any or all of the three. What it also suggests, though, is precisely that for Pound the phrase applies to a 'them' rather than to a 'her'. Whether he had Gonne in mind or not (and there is no other reason for thinking he did—she

---

[79] Brooker, *A Student's Guide*, p. 210.
[80] Pound to John Quinn, 15 November [1918]: *Selected Letters*, p. 140.
[81] I am grateful to Warwick Gould for confirming that there is no known connexion between Gonne and Ealing: Gould to Saunders, 20 October 2004.

had no connection with Ealing or bank-clerkly Englishmen) what he is doing in the poem is to present what seems to him a particular type of woman:

> No, 'Milesian' is an exaggeration.
> No instinct has survived in her
> Older than those her grandmother
> Told her would fit her station.

The self-qualification at the start of the second (and final) stanza suggests that something else is happening here. If it's true that this woman's instincts have been suppressed into a social conformity (such as presumably comports with Ealing bank-clerkliness) then it's less clear what the poem is about. She might be one of these people; no, that's an exaggeration. Hello? As one moves from one stanza to the next the woman becomes baffling; and the effect is (as in Impressionist art) to pull the focus onto the bafflement of the perceiver. That is, the poem becomes an exploration of the aesthete's (presumably Mauberley's) consciousness, trying to find words to express the baffling relation between the erotic and the repressed in pre-war London.

   Though poem XII is longer, its relation to the biographical is similar, so the discussion can be briefer. Like XI, it begins with a quotation, this time from Gautier, about Daphne being turned into a laurel. The irony is that whereas Apollo the god of Poetry pursued Daphne, the poet is here being commanded by 'the Lady Valentine'. Brooker cites the occasion when 'Pound, Eliot and Yeats were collected together on 2 April 1916 for the first performance of Yeats's "At the Hawk's Well" in the drawing room of Lady Cunard.'[82] The poem mentions the Lady Valentine's 'vocation: / Poetry'; and lists amongst her 'means of blending / With other strata' 'A modulation towards the theatre'. That's not quite the same as saying she put on a performance of a play in her drawing-room. The annotation-method is curiously laconic and oblique here, since the next stanza is said to be like Eliot's 'Prufrock', so Eliot's introduction to Lady Ottoline Morrell's circle is adduced as relevant, though, as Humphrey Carpenter says, Pound had 'no contact' with her.[83] Why not any aristocratic art-patrons, then? A letter from H. G. Wells to Ford, written around the time Ford was taking Pound around London introducing him as his latest discovery of a 'genius', indicates the milieu just as well: 'I enclose two letters, one from Lady Elcho, and one from Lady Desborough . . . I do not fail to pursue these ladies with subscription forms. Tell me shall I write to Lady Tennant?'[84] I'm not proposing that 'the Lady Valentine' is one of these either. Rather, that the comment of Pound's that

---

[82] Brooker, *A Student's Guide*, p. 211.

[83] Carpenter, *A Serious Character*, p. 412.

[84] Wells to Ford, 26 November 1908: quoted by Arthur Mizener, *The Saddest Story* (London: The Bodley Head, 1972), p. 155. Also see Lawrence Rainey's *Institutions of Modernism: Literary Elites and Public Culture* (New Haven: Yale University Press, 1998), ch. 1, on Pamela Wyndham Tennant, Lady Glenconner.

Brooker quotes to annotate the fourth stanza is the crucial one: 'It has been well said of the "lady in society" that art criticism is one of her functions. She babbles of it as of "the play", or of hockey, or of '"town topics".'[85] That is the lady 'the lady Valentine' portrays: the generic 'lady in society': a stereotype, the misogyny of which is palpable. This is the danger of the Poundian method of imaginary portrait by stereotype. Whereas in Pater, say, the imaginariness of the portrait was precisely bound up with the difficulty of defining and visualizing the subject, where Pound's portraits are animated by energies of condemnation, they settle for brutally facile generalizations.

Nonetheless, all but four of the thirteen poems of this first sequence can thus be seen as forming a gallery of imaginary portraits, delineating various 'types' constituting the early twentieth-century London literati. These are Mauberley's 'Contacts'. What of his 'Life'—assuming the poem is to be read according to Pound's reversal of the subtitle? How does the second sequence engage with auto/biography?

THE SECOND SEQUENCE: ALLOBIOGRAPHY, AUTOBIOGRAPHY, METABIOGRAPHY

To recapitulate—at the risk of obviousness, but for the sake of clarity: apart from the final poem, 'Medallion', which may or may not be *by* Mauberley, all the other poems in this second sequence appear to be *about* him: to compose his imaginary portrait. This sequence is thus an attempt to condense the form of a literary memoir (by analogy with Pound's description of the whole work as an 'attempt to condense the James novel'). It is an example of biografiction: imaginary biography, though at one remove; not written in the manner of conventional biography, but as a parodic reduction of it—to absurdity, perhaps.

In one of the best discussions of *Hugh Selwyn Mauberley*, Ronald Bush quotes the first poem of this sequence alongside a passage from *A Portrait of the Artist as a Young Man*, arguing that 'The point of view as given by the shading of phrases is Mauberley's own, but Pound's use of the third person is as impersonal as Joyce's own.'[86] That is, Pound is using a versified kind of free indirect style, fusing an external narrator with the language of Mauberley's consciousness. That consciousness is focalized as if seen from outside, but the focalizer is Mauberley himself. Bush seeks to quash the received debate about personae by claiming that 'There can be no question of a narrative persona here.' Yet, as we have seen, there has been precisely that question, and it won't do merely to deny it. To be fair, he argues that the second sequence is unproblematically objective, whereas the problems all arise from the

---

[85] Pound, *Patria Mia* (London: Peter Owen, 1962), p. 43; quoted Brooker, *A Student's Guide*, p. 211.
[86] Bush, *The Genesis of Ezra Pound's 'Cantos'*, p. 258.

first. Yet, as we have seen, it is the juxtaposition of poems within the sequences, and of the two sequences, that generates the debate about voices and personae.

The argument that follows is not intended as a rebuttal of Bush's reading, since it seems to me that fundamentally he, and others who take the second sequence as about Mauberley, are right. My argument is intended to incorporate this position into a broader reading of the volume in terms of imaginary portraiture, auto-biography and auto/biografiction, that finds three further kinds of nuance in the poems (just as my account of Joyce's *Portrait* thinks there is more to be said about that work than that it is Joyce's objective presentation of Stephen's subjectivity; that what he is also objectifying is autobiography). These are essentially the allobiographical, the autobiographical, and the metabiographical.

By 'allobiographical' I mean that the 'objective' presentation of Mauberley draws upon, or can be connected with, biographies of other people—real biographies rather than the imaginary one of Mauberley.[87] It is not merely a matter of lives, but of the aesthetic activities and standpoints of other people as well. Now the second sequence is as allusive and elliptical as the first, and gestures towards many figures. To be exhaustive would exhaust readers unnecessarily. Brooker's *Student's Guide* is recommended to the tireless for its marvellous detail here too. I shall concentrate on one important 'Contact' of Pound's as a representative illustration: Ford once again. I make no apology for reintroducing him here, having already discussed him in relation to Poem X of the first sequence, because it is precisely the fact that he does figure in, or at least can be read into, both sequences, that problematizes our reading of the volume.

Whereas Poem X concentrated on the stylist's style of life, poem II of the second sequence concentrates on the poet's poetics:

> —Given that is his 'fundamental passion',
> This urge to convey the relation
> Of eyelid and cheek-bone
> By verbal manifestations;

According to Bush's reading, this 'fundamental passion' would be Mauberley's, and would have to be ironized by Pound. The inverted commas suggest exactly that: that Mauberley has made a fetish of trying to capture visual forms in words, and that it is a debilitating sublimation of his sexuality. However, that deliberate phrase, 'verbal manifestations', gets repeated in one of Pound's most important aesthetic essays, 'How to Read', in the celebrated manifesto distinguishing between three modes of poetry:

MELOPOEIA, wherein the words are charged, over and above their plain meaning, with some musical property, which directs the bearing or trend of that meaning.

---

[87] As in Kingsley Amis's distinction between 'allo- rather than autobiography': *Memoirs* (London: Hutchinson, 1991), p. xvi.

PHANOPOEIA, which is the casting of images upon the visual imagination.

LOGOPOEIA, 'the dance of the intellect among words,' that is to say, it employs words not only for their direct meaning, but it takes count in a special way of habits of usage, of the context we *expect* to find with the word, its usual concomitants, of its known acceptances, and of ironical play. It holds the aesthetic content which is peculiarly the domain of verbal manifestations, and cannot possibly be contained in plastic or in music. It is the latest come, and perhaps most tricky and undependable mode.[88]

Yet there is an apparent contradiction between the two passages. Mauberley's passion is to convey the relation of eye-lid and cheek-bone—an essentially spatial, visual image—by 'verbal manifestation', the ironic play that 'cannot possibly be contained in plastic or in music'. Mauberley, according to these later definitions, is confusing Phanopoeia and Logopoeia. It might seem an accidental echo. But I think the phrase appealed to Pound for its suggestion of something supernatural, manifesting itself in the language as a god makes itself manifest in a metamorphosis. When he echoes the passage from *Hugh Selwyn Mauberley* in Canto LXXIV, he relates it to one of the most famous images of exactly that manifestation of the divine, Botticelli's *The Birth of Venus*:

> . . . cheek-bone, by verbal manifestation,
> her eyes as in 'La Nascita'[89]

What has this to do with Ford? Pound may have been echoing Ford's use of the same phrase in an important pair of articles on the Imagists and Futurists, the first of which discussed and quoted Pound. In the second piece on the volume *Des Imagistes*, Ford wrote:

on the one hand, whilst all the literary, all the verbal manifestations of Futurism are representational, and representational, and again representational, all the plastic-aesthetic products of the new movement are becoming more and more geometric, mystic, non-material, or what you will. The Futurist painters were doing very much what novelists of the type of Flaubert or short-story writers of the type of Maupassant aimed at. They gave you not so much the reconstitution of a crystallised scene in which all the figures were arrested—not so much that, as fragments of impressions gathered during a period of time, during a period of emotion, or during a period of travel.[90]

A 'crystallised scene'; 'Luini in porcelain! . . . The face-oval beneath the glaze . . .'. It would be surprising if Pound hadn't known these essays. He always took Ford's critical views seriously. In 1914 he ranked Ford as 'the best critic in England, one might say the only critic of any importance.'[91] Pound was helping

---

[88] Pound, 'How to Read', *Literary Essays*, p. 25. The articles were originally published in the *New York Herald Tribune Books* from 13 to 27 January 1929.

[89] *The Cantos*, p. 446. See Brooker, *A Student's Guide*, p. 217.

[90] 'Literary Portraits—XXXVI. Les Jeunes and "Des Imagistes" (Second Notice)', *Outlook*, 33 (16 May 1914), 682–3.

[91] Lindberg-Seyersted, ed., *Pound/Ford*, p. 16.

Lewis with the Rebel Art Centre and *Blast*, and was closely involved with the questions Ford was discussing: Futurism, poetics, the relation of the verbal to the visual and the musical. The musical? One of the contrasts that has been observed in *Hugh Selwyn Mauberley* is between the lyrical investment of the first sequence, and the visual imagination of the second; as if Melopoeia were being set off against Phanopoeia; poetry as song against poetry as impression.

Ford is relevant here too, I suggest, because Pound could never quite settle where Ford stood in relation to these different emphases. He admired Ford's insistence that poetry should be a living language, 'the speech of to-day', the poetry of the voice. 'It is he who has insisted, in the face of a still Victorian press, upon the importance of good writing as opposed to the opalescent word, the rhetorical tradition.'[92] As we saw apropos of 'the stylist', Pound admired Ford's (and Joyce's) Flaubertian quest for *le mot juste*, for 'style'. In addition, 'Mr. Hueffer has also the gift for making lyrics that will sing', he said, adding: 'we would not be far wrong in calling Mr. Hueffer the best lyrist in England.'[93] In a word, Melopoeia. Yet at the same time he criticized Ford's avowed 'impressionism' as hyper-ocular: 'Impressionism belongs in paint', he wrote. And he later said of Ford's criticism: 'I think Hueffer goes wrong because he bases his criticism on the eye, and almost solely on the eye.'[94] In another word, Phanopoeia. And one way in which he makes a point against the haziness of Fordian impressionism is by giving as an example of what not to write a phrase from a poem of Ford's: 'Don't use such an expression as "dim lands of peace". It dulls the image.'[95] So we should not be surprised to find him echoing Ford's words elsewhere.

Pound's portrait of Mauberley glazed in ineffectual rapture over his visions of beauty touches the heart of his criticism of impressionism, which he said (writing of music) had 'reduced us to such a dough-like state of receptivity that we have ceased to like concentration.'[96] It also touches his criticism of Ford:

> In a country in love with amateurs, in a country where the incompetent have such beautiful manners [...] it is well that one man should have a vision of perfection and that he should be sick to the death and disconsolate because he cannot attain it.
>
> That Ford was almost an *halluciné* few of his intimates can doubt. He felt until it paralysed his efficient action, he saw quite distinctly the Venus immortal crossing the tram tracks.[97]

---

[92] Pound, 'Mr. Hueffer and the Prose Tradition in Verse', *Poetry*, 4 (1914), 111–20; Lindberg-Seyersted, ed., *Pound/Ford*, p. 16.

[93] Lindberg-Seyersted, ed., *Pound/Ford*, p. 10.

[94] Ibid., pp. 10, 68.

[95] 'A Retrospect', *Literary Essays*, p. 5. The phrase is from Ford's poem of 1904 'On a Marsh Road': see Ford, *Selected Poems* (Manchester: Carcanet, 1997), p. 35.

[96] Pound, 'Arnold Dolmetsch', *Literary Essays*, p. 433.

[97] 'Mr. Hueffer and the Prose Tradition in Verse', in *Pound/Ford*, p. 16. Pound, 'Ford Madox (Hueffer) Ford: Obit', *Selected Prose*, pp. 431–3; and Lindberg-Seyersted, ed., *Pound/Ford*, pp. 171–4 (p. 172).

The first quotation is pre-Mauberley, from an appreciation of Ford's *Collected Poems*. Most of the review is about the importance of Ford as a critic, but Pound nonetheless praises his poems as 'gracious impressions'. By the second quotation, post-Mauberley, from Pound's obituary for Ford in 1939, his views have hardened, and the earlier praise for Ford's effectiveness as both critic and poetic example has been overshadowed by his admiration for the 'factive personalities' he lumped together indiscriminately, as in his book *Jefferson and/or Mussolini*: people who forced their will on events.[98] This illustrates the danger of the annotation-method that ransacks Pound's entire oeuvre for pertinent parallels. With regard to impressionism, as to much else in the volume of his *Literary Essays*, Pound's views were undergoing transformation during the war and while he was writing *Hugh Selwyn Mauberley*.

To demonstrate parallels between Mauberley and Ford is not to make the facile claim that Hugh Selwyn Mauberley *is* Ford Madox Hueffer. Poundian scholarship has shown how many more prototypes are involved.[99] And anyway, my argument concerning the first sequence was that to allege traces of an original in the genealogy of a poem is not the same thing as saying that poem is about that original. Rather than saying Mauberley is partly Ford, just as 'the stylist' is partly Ford, I'm saying that both draw on Ford's aesthetics, but neither is a portrait of him. It might then be countered that I'm just using the same method: entertaining claims of likenesses only to discount them. This is true. But the fact that the same method can be used, and that the same 'originals' come up in both sequences strengthens my argument. As 'the stylist' is one of Mauberley's 'Contacts', it's hard to see how he and Mauberley could *both* have been meant as portraits of Ford.

Mauberley too, like his contacts, is, rather, a vortex drawing in a range of Decadents, Edwardians, and Georgians, and also their antitheses (like Arnold Bennett) and critics (like Pound and Ford themselves): an ideogram of the pre-war literary scene. Or, to recall a different image, he is an example of the 'composite portraiture' pioneered by Francis Galton.[100] Thus the first sequence would produce a composite portrait of 'the world of letters', and the second, of 'the aesthete'; the Paterian epicure or hedonist.

According to this view, the sequence is still imaginary biography, but of a composite figure, combining characteristics of unsturdy aestheticism with Fordian impressionism. Yet insofar as its composite portraiture is of Pound's own contacts, it is also imaginary autobiography: fictionalizing Pound's own experience as the

---

[98] Pound's contrast between an active Imagism and passive impressionism has remained influential. See for example Peter Nicholls, *Modernisms: A Literary Guide* (Basingstoke: Macmillan, 1995). It has had unfortunate consequences for Ford's critical reputation though, since Pound has nothing to say about Ford's impressionist masterpiece *The Good Soldier*, in which the passivity of the narrator is not to be confused with the formal energy of the author. See Saunders, 'Ford/Pound', *Agenda*, 27:4/28:1 (1989/1990), 93–102.

[99] Brooker's annotations to the second sequence cite de Gourmont, James or his character Lambert Strether, Huntley Carter, John Gould Fletcher, and Dante Gabriel Rossetti.

[100] Galton's Composite Portraiture is discussed in Chapter 5.

experience of a fictional persona. One of the main differences between *Hugh Selwyn Mauberley* and Joyce's *Portrait* is that Pound's criticism of Mauberley has seemed much less equivocal than Joyce's criticism of Stephen. That might seem to imply a greater distance between author and portrait in Pound's case. As Brooker argues about Pound's personae, in both cases one's judgement about the real author's attitude to the imaginary author is a function of how successful you think the imaginary author's work is. Pound's judgement on Mauberley's aesthetic as leading to his degeneration into a kind of autism, is much harsher than anything in the Joyce. Joyce's impersonality renders Stephen's febrile enthusiasm in his own words with a finesse that occasionally lets us glimpse an author that has moved beyond the young aesthete's precious verbosity. Pound tells us that Mauberley's hedonistic impressionism renders him incapable of anything other than failure.

But. That need not preclude the possibility that Mauberley is to some extent autobiographical: an imaginary *self*-portrait as well. Indeed, the epitaph Pound has Mauberley write for himself (to contrast, perhaps, with the obituary for 'E. P.' that starts the first sequence) picks up the idea (from poem II of the second sequence) of Maubeley's drifting:

> 'I was
> And I no more exist;
> Here drifted
> An hedonist.'

If Mauberley's drifting out of existence recalls Beerbohm's play with Enoch Soames's failure to exist, his fantasy of himself as a sort of castaway (he imagines the epitaph on an oar) recalls the poem Pound published in *Blast* No. 2:

> I cling to the spar,
> Washed with the cold salt ice
> I cling to the spar—
> Insidious modern waves, civilization, civilized hidden snares.
> Cowardly editors threaten: 'If I dare'
> Say this or that, or speak my open mind
> [. . .]
> Then they will have my guts;[101]

Mauberley is not how Pound saw himself in 1920, certainly. Pound is critical of the way Mauberley's aesthetic, in the aftermath of his one, failed, 'amorous adventure' (in poem II of the second sequence), 'paralysed his efficient action'; just as he would have criticized his anachronistic poeticisms: the inversion of 'I no more exist' does little to convince us of his substance when he claims he did

---

[101] 'Et Faim Sallir Le Loup des Boys', *Blast*, 2 (1915), 22. I am grateful to Rebecca Beasley for drawing my attention to this poem.

exist.[102] Yet with a passage such as the following, isn't there a sense that Pound has some sympathies with Mauberley's attitude?

> Non-esteem of self-styled 'his betters'
> Leading, as he well knew,
> To his final
> Exclusion from the world of letters.

Mauberley's acquiescence in his literary oblivion is the antithesis of Pound's ferocious activity in promoting his aesthetics and his friends' work. To that extent Pound is criticizing the limp pride that will not make the effort to continue creating and get its art acknowledged. Yet Pound shares Mauberley's sense that members of that 'world of letters' who style themselves 'his betters' are not worth the candle. Writers like Mr. Nixon, whose advice Pound wasn't prepared to take any more than Mauberley. Exclusion from *that* world of letters is a mark of integrity rather than failure. This is tantamount to saying that insofar as Mauberley is a self-portrait of Pound he is an imaginary one: not a portrait of Pound as he was in 1920; not even one of Pound as he had been; but one of Pound as he felt he might have become, had he not decided to leave London (as Stephen Dedalus in *Ulysses* might be Joyce's portrait of the self he might have become had he not left Dublin); had he not become 'modernized'. (Eliot, he said with envious admiration, had 'modernized himself *on his own*'; whereas Pound had needed efficient actions like Ford's roll to steer him away from an aesthetic cul de sac.)[103] Perhaps the animus in the poem comes from just this: that Mauberley is a portrait of what Pound most mistrusted in himself.[104]

Milan Kundera finds an ingenious metaphor to account for the way in which fictional characters both are and are not autobiographical:

The characters in my novels are my own unrealized possibilities. That is why I am equally fond of them all and equally horrified by them. Each one has crossed a border that I myself have circumvented. It is that crossed border (the border beyond which my own 'I' ends) which attracts me most. For beyond that border begins the secret the novel asks about. The novel is not the author's confession; it is an investigation of human life in the trap the world has become.[105]

It is the other way around with Mauberley or Dedalus: Mauberley has failed to cross, and Dedalus has not yet crossed, the borders their authors have crossed. Where Pound spoke of 'casting off, as it were, complete masks of the self in each

---

[102] With thanks to Paul Skinner for this shrewd observation: email to Max Saunders, 15 March 2008.

[103] Pound to Harriet Monroe, 30 September 1914: *Selected Letters*, p. 40.

[104] Carpenter, *A Serious Character*, p. 241, makes a comparable case about 'Mœurs Contemporaines', arguing: 'There could be a buried reference to his own condition' in 'Mr Styrax', who was still a virgin when he married aged twenty-eight.

[105] Milan Kundera, *The Unbearable Lightness of Being*, trans. Michael Henry Heim (London: Faber and Faber, 1985), p. 221.

poem', another way to put it would be that each poem is a mask of a self he has cast off. The danger of the method is of complacency about the new, improved self; and a limiting of the imagination to negativity about what is already familiar. Kundera's image is of an exploration of unknown possibilities, which can attract and horrify; whereas the compass of *Hugh Selwyn Mauberley* is constricted to an ironic jadedness.

The argument so far has claimed that the volume is autobiographical in multiple ways: through the discussion of 'E. P.' in the first poem of the first sequence; in the use of autobiographical material in the other portraits in that sequence (Pound's meetings with Plarr, Bennett, Beerbohm, Ford, and others); and now in the ways in which Mauberley himself draws upon elements of Pound. But 'autobiography' here is also 'auto/biography': because 'E. P.''s career is sketched in the third person, as if by Mauberley; and because when Pound describes Mauberley, he fuses him with elements of other real figures such as Ford. This fusing of biography and autobiography, subjective and objective, is what we might expect, given his comment about the processes of composition of a poem such as the magnificent haiku 'In a Station of the Metro': 'In a poem of this sort one is trying to record the precise instant when a thing outward and objective transforms itself, or darts into a thing inward and subjective.'[106] At first this seems counter-intuitive coming from a modernist advocate of concreteness, hardness, objectivity. It is consciously opposed to the Romantic aesthetic whereby the poem takes a subjective feeling and expresses it, transforms it into something outward. Yet (as according to the Wilde–Nietzsche paradox) the flip-side of modernist objectivity is that the outward things turn into autobiography.

I now want to consider the third kind of nuance in the volume that makes it an even more complex and slippery work than has been acknowledged: what I called the metabiographical. This is the core of my reading, which is not concerned merely to annotate the auto/biographical elements *in* the poetry, but to consider the ways in which Pound simultaneously *comments upon* auto/biography and uses its forms as a creative resource. *Hugh Selwyn Mauberley* does not just recycle autobiographical material. Its form and style is also a critique of the literary memoir. It is this dimension that is missed by an interpretation such as Bush's, which effectively reads the volume as one large imaginary portrait of Mauberley, comparable to his reading of Joyce's *Portrait* as rendering Stephen's 'tones of mind', but in an objective, third-person way. As with Flaubert and Joyce, the refining out of existence of the artist from his work is achieved not by a disappearance into pure objectivity, but behind a smokescreen of parody. Of course it has been well-established that Pound is parodying people—whether particular individuals (Plarr, Beerbohm, Ford, etc.) or types (the aesthete, the

---

[106] Pound, *Gaudier-Brzeska*, p. 89.

classicist, the society lady, etc.). What has been missed is how he is also parodying forms and styles, as suggested at the start of this chapter. The 'Life and Contacts' subtitle indicates that the volume's form is a dig at the literary memoir, especially the memoir of a minor figure, which pads out an insubstantial life with the testimony of acquaintances, and tries to use the celebrity of these to validate the life in question. Such volumes are easier to find when on major figures:

W. Hall Griffin and Harry C. Minchin, *The Life of Robert Browning With Notices of His Writings His Family, & His Friends* (London: Methuen, 1911)

Sidney Colvin, *John Keats: His Life and Poetry, His Friends, Critics, and After-Fame* (New York: The Macmillan Company, 1917)

S. M. Ellis, *George Meredith: His Life and Friends* (London: Grant Richards, 1920)

By way of examples commemorating the lesser known, consider the group portrait of the literary world constituted by this random collage:

J. Howlett-Ross, *A Memoir of the Life of Adam Lindsay Gordon. The 'Laureate of the Centaurs' with new poems, prose sketches, political speeches and reminiscences, and an 'In Memoriam' by Kendall* (London: S. J. Mullen, 1888)

Francis Espinasse, *Literary Recollections and Sketches. Including the Carlyles and a segment of their Circle* (New York: Dodd, Mead and Co., 1893)

Life, Letters and Literary Remains of J. H. Shorthouse, edited by S. Shorthouse, 2 volumes (London: Macmillan, 1905)

W. Scott Palmer and A. M. Haggard, *Michael Fairless: Her Life and Writings* (London: Duckworth, 1917)

There is no reason to believe Pound knew of any of these. But one he is much more likely to have come across in London from 1908 is Henry Treffry Dunn, *Recollections of Dante Gabriel Rossetti & His Circle: or, Cheyne Walk Life* (London: Elkin Mathews, 1904), so perhaps that could stand as a representative of the kind of aesthetic bio-babble he sets his teeth against in *Hugh Selwyn Mauberley.*

It isn't only the title and structure of such literary memoirs that Pound parodies, but also their language and style. (After all, as we saw in Chapter 1, what modernists like Eliot and Pound said they objected to about Decadence was different from what everyone else was objecting to in the wake of the Wilde trial: they offered a critique of Decadent language as itself, well, decadent.) This isn't a matter of sustained parody. No one is likely to mistake the volume for a real memoir; not only because it is in verse, but because the parodic effect is intermittent: struck by a phrase or a clause, which sounds as if it is in imaginary inverted commas. 'For three years, out of key with his time'; 'seeing he had been born / In a half savage country'; 'His true Penelope was Flaubert'; 'the march of events'; 'The age demanded'; 'To Fleet St. where / Dr. Johnson flourished'; 'Not the full smile, / His art, but an art / In profile'; 'Leading, as he well knew, / To his final / Exclusion from the world of letters'. This is Pound mimicking the mandarin tone of the literary establishment: precious, pleased with its own conceit, superior. The trouble is, of course, that some of these phrases either already are in real inverted commas, or are quoted or alluded to later. Thus there appear to be two levels of self-consciousness: one of a free indirect style that speaks through the clichés of the literati; and within that, one which signals its self-consciousness of those clichés. This may be Pound indicating that Mauberley has a critical awareness of what's wrong with the literary scene, but is too trapped within it to be able to transform himself or change it. Rather as Pound had been, perhaps, for that excruciating moment when Ford was rolling on the floor at his language. Perhaps, then, Pound's *anger* at aesthetic impotence is autobiographical too: an investigation of human life in the trap the literary world had become.

What difference does this 'metabiographical' dimension make to a reading of *Hugh Selwyn Mauberley*? As we have seen, the main critical debate has been about the function of two voices, Mauberley's and Pound's. (Or three voices, if 'E. P.' is distinguished from Pound.) My reading introduces a third (or fourth) enunciator: the voice of the belletrist, the tone of the literary memoirist. This seems to make Pound's satire much more effective, turning it from being a rant about personality failings to a critique of a mode of writing. The ingenuity of Pound's form—and this is the most significant sense in which the volume is 'a study in form'—is that it performs its critique simultaneously as a parody of aesthetic poetry, and of aesthetic literary memoir. This adds a further layer of difficulty to the task of critics determined to attach poems to biographical originals or fictional personae, since not only do they have to worry about whether Pound (or E. P.) or Mauberley is speaking, but (if I am right) they would also have to worry about whether it is these voices speaking, or the voice of the belletrist speaking about them.

Thus I still see the volume as centrally concerned with 'voice', but suggest that Pound's approach to the literary milieu through its own ways of talking about itself makes the collage of voices even more complex. Why then was Pound so unconcerned about critics' concerns over who speaks which poems? Though his remark about the 'muddle' critics make in not seeing that Mauberley buries E. P. in the first poem suggests he did have a clear sense of who was speaking, and that it was Mauberley, I have argued that the volume is more concerned with portraits of imaginary figures, types rather than historical individuals. I want now to take this argument further, and propose that rather than focus on traditional notions of 'character-types', what Pound is satirizing is literary styles. It is here that he is perhaps most modern, foregrounding the language of what he saw as cultural malaise so as to disembody it, let it float free of particular human characters and psychologies. This may be what he meant when he said Mauberley was 'a mere surface'; and it is certainly what he meant by 'logopoeia'; and it is with this concept, and how it is enriched by the issues of imaginary portraiture and fictional creativity, that I want to conclude. For part of the difference this reading makes is to contribute another aspect of imaginary portraiture (of what I have called the belletristic); and another aspect of fictional creativity: an imaginary work, albeit one only cited or alluded to rather than impersonated in entirety: the fictional literary memoir.

'LOGOPOEIA, "the dance of the intellect among words."' Is that a quotation, or an example of the logopoeic method, prising words out of their context for critical investigation? Pound was always committed to all three modes, the musical, the visual, and the verbal. But logopoeia comes to the fore in his writing after his realization in Giessen that something was wrong with his language. He had imitated the musicality of the Provençal troubadours; he had moved on to a more visual emphasis in Imagism. ('The apparition of these faces in the crowd; / Petals on a wet, black, bough' works not only by contrasting two visual experiences, but also by explicitly discussing the visual: 'The *apparition*'.) In his subsequent work, and especially in *Homage to Sextus Propertius* and *Hugh Selwyn Mauberley*, the art is predominantly verbal: concerned, if you like, with 'verbal manifestations' rather than visual apparitions or musical effects.

This is most evident in *Hugh Selwyn Mauberley*, where, as we have seen, critics have posited a contrast between the final poems of both sequences: a reaching back to the world of Elizabethan lyric, of poetry as song, in 'Envoi'; and the Gautier-influenced ideal of poetry as like the visual arts (engraving, carving, cameos etc.) in 'Medallion'. In his work on Chinese poetry Pound had come to advocate what he called the 'ideogrammic method.'[107] In an earlier essay I argued that *Hugh Selwyn Mauberley* combines together the three modes of poetry; juxtaposing, with ideogramic suppression of logical or narrative connexion, the two sequences, the one more melopoeic, the second more phanopoeic, in order to energize 'the dance of the intellect among words' as the mind darts back and forth between them.[108] True, either sequence alone demonstrates enough ironic verbal play to qualify for logopoeic status; but one sense in which the volume is 'a study in form' is the way it uses this form of montage as a structure to heighten our sense of verbal nuance.

TRANSLATORESE

To show what difference the metabiographical reading makes, consider a related argument. This is Donald Davie's brilliant perception about Pound's longest work before *Hugh Selwyn Mauberley*, the *Homage to Sextus Propertius*, that much of the language in it is what Davie calls 'translatorese', or '*babu* English'; 'examples of how not to do it', 'it' being translation from the Latin.[109] Much of the earlier critical debate on that sequence concentrated on whether or not Pound had made

[107] Pound, *ABC of Reading* (London: Faber, 1951), pp. 17–27.
[108] Saunders, 'Verbal and Other Manifestations: Further thoughts on Ford/Pound/Ford', in *Redefining the Modern: Essays on Literature and Society in Honor of Joseph Wiesenfarth*, ed. William Baker and Ira B. Nadel (Madison, WI and London: Fairleigh Dickinson University Press, 2004), pp. 165–80. Also see Stephen J. Adams, 'Irony and Common Sense: The Genre of *Mauberley*', *Paideuma*, 18, 1 & 2 (1989), 147–60.
[109] Davie, *Ezra Pound*, pp. 58–9. Also see his *Ezra Pound: Poet as Sculptor*, p. 87.

'howlers' in his Englishing of Propertius. Pound's champions pointed to the conscious anachronisms (words like 'Wordsworthian' or 'frigidaire') as evidence that the sequence was clearly doing something other than merely translating Propertius' words. More classicist-minded critics, outraged by the liberties Pound took in cutting and pasting individual lyrics as well as his liberties of phrasing, countered that that didn't mean he hadn't also made mistakes.

Take, for example, the line that Brooker (whose annotations to *Propertius* are also invaluable) says is 'Perhaps the most controversial line in the poem': '"Gaudeat in solito tacta puella sonso" ("Let my girl be touched by the sound of a familiar music and rejoice in it").'[110] Pound translates 'tacta puella' as 'devirginated young ladies'. This was attacked as 'particularly unpleasant' with no basis in the original, and indicative of Pound's 'ignorance and bad taste'. Pound however claimed that the near proximity of 'in' and 'tacta' summoned up the notion of 'puella intacta', a virgin, and that this made 'tacta' ambiguous: someone touched by music, but also someone sexually experienced. As Brooker says, clearly Pound 'saw in Propertius' line an example of "logopoeia"', and he cites Hugh Kenner's defence of Pound's 'scepticism directed at Latin professors'.

Most of Pound's work, like much of high modernism, is manically intertextual. Translatorese, which is amongst other things a way of drawing attention to intertextuality, is also a site where 'logopoeia' coexists with questions of fictional creativity. *Propertius* is a dramatization of someone translating, awkwardly, ineptly, but in a way which allows us to glimpse a better work within or behind or beyond or above the one in front of us. If a translation like 'devirginated' is a mistake, then we just have Pound as translator obstructing our view of Propertius' text. If—as the comic awkwardness of the term surely suggests—it is a joke, then it interposes a parody of a translation between us and the original. That is, it is an example of imaginary authorship: the work of an imaginary translator of an inept kind, which Pound uses in a cunningly triple-jointed fashion to mock the literary ineptness of bad translators, and the tone-deafness of classicists unattuned to Propertius' wit, while also drawing our attention to precisely that quality of wit. In short, it is an application of Pound's 'logopoeia' to bring out Propertius'—a dramatization of someone translating freely, which anticipates the objections classicists will make where it departs from literal translation, but triumphs over them with its inspired jokes and moments of surrealism. Admittedly the persona of the inept translator is a mask which—as in *Hugh Selwyn Mauberley*—often slips. But it is one crucial to the *Cantos* too, in which he often dramatizes someone poring over earlier writings, translating or interpreting or rereading.

Pound's invention of translatorese, then, is purposeful mistranslation which simultaneously reveals something about the original. It is the fictional creation of a text—the bad translation—which implies an imaginary persona—the bad

---

[110] Brooker, *A Student's Guide*, pp. 161–2.

translator. Much of Pound's translation works like this, not modernizing its original so the translator disappears into the contemporary vernacular, but by using a language that draws attention to itself: either as the best language that the history of English has produced to render a particular style (as when he translates Cavalcanti into Elizabethan English) or as an example of a translator fixated upon archaism as he had been himself. Or both, as when, in Canto I, he manages both to parody Pre-Raphaelite medievalism as a response to the Greek of Homer, while also drawing on the energies of the earliest poetry known to Anglo-Saxon ears—the alliterative verse of poems like 'The Seafarer'—as a way of conveying his sense of older layers within the *Odyssey*.[111]

In his translation, or poems conducted via translation, such as *Cathay* or *Propertius*, Pound starts with the real words of others, and makes out of them his own poems, which may use the persona of the original poet (like Propertius), or create the imaginary persona of the obtuse or unreliable translator (in parallel with modernist fiction's exploration of the obtuse or unreliable narrator); or they may be uttered *in propria persona*. In *Hugh Selwyn Mauberley*, though, he reverses the process. He starts with his own poetic development, out of aestheticism and imagism, and works from that to the imaginary words of imaginary authors— whether Mauberley or his contacts, critics, and biographers. The language of these imaginary authors is treated in the same way as 'translatorese' in poems like *Propertius*: as both inadequate but also critically revealing both of its object and subject speaking.

The experiments with 'translatorese' in *Propertius* alerted Pound to the possibilities not just of the persona (through which much of his early verse is articulated) but of the slippage between personae; to the use, that is, of uncertainty about personae to generate the energies of logopoeia. What he achieves in *Propertius* through translatorese, he develops in *Hugh Selwyn Mauberley*—and this is what my reading adds to the debate—through the play with imaginary portraits, the fictional creation of poems, and the partial or refracted fictional creation of an imaginary memoir. It is, in short, a crucial example of how modernism's engagement with life-writing is more than a mere rejection of auto/biography, or even naughtyboyography. Pound's mimicking of the clichés of memoir-writing—'life and contacts', 'the age demanded', 'out of key with his time', etc.—might best be termed 'auto/biographese' by analogy.

Hugh Selwyn Mauberley is a structure of mirrors, ingeniously angled to keep us guessing at each moment whether we are reading Pound's imaginary portrait of Mauberley, Mauberley's fictional creativity, or both simultaneously, or a literary mandarin's judgement on Mauberley (and/or Pound). I'd like to be able to argue

---

[111] See for example the version of 'Donna mi priegha' in *The Translations of Ezra Pound*, introduced by Hugh Kenner (London: Faber, 1970), p. 133. Pound wrote to W. H. D. Rouse, 23 May 1935: 'The Nekuia shouts aloud that it is *older* than the rest, all that island, Cretan, etc., hinter-time, that is *not* Praxiteles, not Athens of Pericles, but Odysseus': *Selected Letters*, p. 274.

that it was consciously intended like this, and had a writer as calculating as Joyce, Nabokov, or Borges written it, I might be able to persuade myself. But Pound's remarks about the whole work suggest he thought of it as more fixed than that—though nonetheless as a sustained example of fictional creativity. According to Basil Bunting, Pound had been thinking of *Mauberley* from its inception in terms of heteronymy and parody. As James Laughlin retold the story:

Speaking of *Mauberley*, the story of its genesis as a hoax is perhaps relevant. One convivial evening in London, Pound and Eliot decided that it would be amusing to invent an impossible poet who would write parodies of poets they didn't like and lampooning reviews of such poets' books. Hugh Selwyn Mauberley was the name they dreamed up.[112]

How, then, are the uncertainties about attribution to be construed? Are they mistakes: slips of the mask, as Davie has it, when Pound loses interest in the dramatic monologue he has set up, to deliver something else?—like poem IV of the first sequence, which seems too impassioned and astringent and un-aesthetic and robustly moving to issue from Mauberley? Or is it something other than a masquerade: a wearing of the semi-transparent mask of an imaginary portrait (which, insofar as it is transparent, is an imaginary self-portrait)? Or, again, is it that Pound's didacticism conceived the work as a dramatic monologue—a straightforward exposé of aesthetic unsturdiness—but that his verbal brilliance occasionally got the better of him, and out of him, by imagining other possibilities in the form? According to this view, he was responding to two things: the formal possibilities of auto/biography as reinvented by the Aesthetic movement; and the formal possibilities of fictional authorship, and their possibilities for parody, as reinvented by Joyce and Beerbohm responding to the Aesthetic movement. Pound's responses to these things was perhaps subliminal, escaping any didactic purpose he had framed for the poem, but nonetheless lending it more troublesome energies than he could recognize.

Ultimately, then, what the volume is an imaginary portrait *of*, is literary consciousness. And it is in this sense that it represents a condensation of Henry James, for whom writing (in Terry Eagleton's words) 'represents an adventure into individual consciousness of unique worth.'[113] This is approximately what F. R. Leavis said about *Hugh Selwyn Mauberley*, arguing that it embodied a particular 'sensibility.'[114] Leavis appreciated Pound's expression of a cultivated sensibility, and for all his investment in the anti-biographical method of Practical Criticism, could recognize that *Mauberley* was engaging with life-writing. He read it as 'the summing-up of an individual life', and added that 'One might, at the risk

[112] James Laughlin, *Pound as Wuz* (London: Peter Owen, 1989), p. 173.

[113] Terry Eagleton, 'Living as Little as Possible', *London Review of Books* (23 September 2004), 23–4.

[114] 'The verse is extraordinarily subtle, and its subtlety is the subtlety of the sensibility it expresses': Leavis, *New Bearings in English Poetry* (1932) (Harmondsworth: Penguin, 1972), pp. 104–5.

of impertinence, call it quintessential autobiography, taking care, however, to add that it has the impersonality of great poetry.'[115] It is Pound's dealings with auto/ biography and metabiography, I would add, that allows him to achieve at once sensibility and impersonality. Pound's aim in surgically detaching consciousness from individual minds, the individuals having been etherized upon the writing table, and anatomizing it, is profoundly ambivalent. Rather like Eagleton, who sees 'consciousness' as a reified term, 'the transcendent truth of the modern liberal age', he sees the cult of consciousness as revealing a crisis in liberalism: an alienation of the atomized individual, whose hyper-awareness makes him unable to act (though the political remedies they envisage are diametrically opposed). Arguably, then, Mauberley is a kind of composite imaginary self portrait in negative; a portrait of the aesthete as a middle-aged man.

Soon after Pound had finished his 'farewell to London', he left for Paris around the end of April 1920, and then went on to Venice.[116] The work he began there shows the extent to which autobiography, and the ironizing of auto/ biographical form, was still preoccupying him. This was the prose work 'Indis-cretions', first published in the *New Age* in twelve instalments from 27 May to 12 August 1920. Donald Gallup describes it as 'a thinly disguised autobiographical fragment concerned chiefly with Pound's father.'[117] If it isn't Pound's 'naughty-boyography', exactly, and scarcely delivers the kind of 'indiscretions' which that label suggests, and with which its title titillates its readers, it does shed further light on his concern with autobiography—with 'how to display anything remotely resembling our subjectivity';[118] and with the related issue of family memoir: 'It is one thing to feel that one could write the whole social history of the United States from one's family annals, and vastly another to embark upon any such Balzacian and voluminous endeavour', writes Pound.[119] This is the nub of his unease with auto/biography. His project was always to condense the voluminous into the luminous; 'one's family annals' were required to be not only selective, but represen-tative. The subtitle of 'Indiscretions' is 'or, Une Revue De Deux Mondes'; and its Jamesian aim is to juxtapose the American experience and the European point of view. What its fifty or so pages give us has been described as 'slightly-fictionalized autobiography'; and as 'Recording his semi-mythical family history with Henry Jamesian mock solemnity.'[120] 'Indiscretions' too, that is, fictionalizes and mocks the forms and tones of life-writing.

[115] Ibid., p. 105.
[116] Carpenter, *A Serious Character*, p. 372.
[117] Gallup, *Ezra Pound: A Bibliography*, p. 35.
[118] Pound, 'Indiscretions', in *Pavannes and Divagations* (New York: New Directions, 1974), p. 3.
[119] Ibid., p. 6.
[120] See the *Modernist Journals Project* website. Carpenter, *A Serious Character*, p. 3.

10

Satirical Auto/biografiction: Wyndham Lewis and Richard Aldington

'I never knew a man who seemed more to be living from a character not his own, than you.'[1]

The danger of the kind of argument I have advanced about Pound is that it could in theory be used indiscriminately to disarm works that were intended as satires of specific people. It is open to the objection that an imaginary portrait is different from a satire, and that rather than exploring the impressionistic concept of personality (in the manner of Pater), Pound intends to satirize precisely any such aesthetic leanings.

There are two main counter-arguments. First, as has been shown, the auto-biographical dimension of *Hugh Selwyn Mauberley* reveals it as more than satiric character assassination. Second, and this is the argument of the present chapter, that satire, far from being antithetical to auto/biography, is one of the modes in which modernism engages with the auto/biographic. Indeed, it follows from the Wilde–Nietzsche argument that it could not do otherwise, since satire, like any other aesthetic mode, can be read *as* autobiography.

But how does satiric differ from parodic auto/biography? And how does modernist parody differ from pastiche? Pastiche is generally defined as imitation, which may have parodic purposes or may not. It is a term that can be used to criticize a failure of originality, or unconscious imitation, as when Stephen's thought processes during composing his villanelle are deemed pastiches of aesthetic prose. According to this view, Stephen is pastiching, but Joyce is parodying. The fictional-author reading adds another possibility of a similar kind: that Joyce is parodying Stephen's writing rather than, or as well as, his thinking. Even if we agree with Joyce that he hasn't let his 'young man' off very lightly, we're unlikely to feel that he is satirizing him. Stephen is too close to him for satire's vitriol. Whatever his excesses of self-indulgence or narcissism, they are stages on the way to the art of Joyce's maturity.

---

[1] D. H. Lawrence to Aldington, 24 May 1927: quoted in Charles Doyle, *Richard Aldington: A Biography* (Basingstoke: Macmillan, 1989), p. 112.

With Beerbohm's 'Enoch Soames' there is perhaps a glint of satire. But its central trope—that Soames doesn't have a definite enough existence—effectively precludes him from being a satirical object. Pound's *Hugh Selwyn Mauberley* has a more definite satiric dimension. Though (as argued in the previous chapter) its portraits are not always directly identifiable with individual specific real figures, and though Mauberley himself partakes of some of Pound's own qualities, the tone is undeniably a satiric one, edged with animosity, contempt, anger. For the most part, Pound's aim isn't so much *ad hominem* satire, as the diagnosis of a culture's *malaise*. However, to see the clearest examples of modernist combinations of satire and life-writing we need to consider two of its other exponents, Wyndham Lewis and Richard Aldington.

WYNDHAM LEWIS

Lewis's novels are where literary critics might begin when considering his satire. But it is also an inextricable component of his criticism, as well as his painting. It is in his immense book of critical and philosophical polemic, *Time and Western Man*, that he most explicitly considers auto/biography.[2] His objection to the auto/biographic is that it is a manifestation of the world-view the whole book opposes, in which reality is organized according to categories of temporality: what he calls the 'Time-mind', which is exemplified by the philosophies of Bergson and Einstein, but which Lewis sees as much more pervasive.[3]

He has been arguing that 'to the popular mind "a history" is always a true account of something as it *really* happened', whereas we should be aware that 'the historian is a politician; attempting, by the colour he gives to his version of the Past [. . .] to influence his contemporaries to imitate that particular version of the Past.'[4] So far, so familiar, anticipating postmodern scepticism that narrativization is fictionalization: that representations are simulacra. Lewis's whole book is a vast assault on what he calls 'the philosophy of "time"', which he sees as the prevalent but erroneous mode of modern understanding. He has the historian in his sights because 'the science or art which is *par excellence* that of the time-philosophy, is history.'[5] This leads to an attack on a range of other arts or sciences—disciplines we now call human sciences or humanities: 'How much ethnology, biology, archaeology, sociology and so forth to-day is really history, is not sufficiently realized.'[6] He picks out Darwin and Freud as examples of what he terms the 'veiled historian'.

---

[2] Wyndham Lewis, *Time and Western Man* (London: Chatto & Windus, 1927).
[3] Ibid., p. 3.
[4] Ibid., pp. 263, 264.
[5] Ibid., pp. 265, 264.
[6] Ibid., p. 264.

Unsurprising, then, that auto/biography comes in for particular animus, since it is for him the pre-eminent literary expression of the 'Time-mind'; nor that Proust emerges as art's pre-eminent time-villain:

With the history of a person written by himself, or any form of autobiography or self-portrait, the same impulses are at work. They are often propagandist—propaganda for all that the 'time'-hero has favoured. In Proust, for instance—one of the ideal examples of a projection on the grand scale, in narrative form, of the philosophy of 'time'—we have in a sense a new type of historical practitioner. Proust embalmed himself alive. He died as a sensational creature in order that he should live as an historian of his dead sensational self, which expired about the time that lyrical poets are supposed to snuff out. Or rather, he did in a sense really die; when those complicated and peculiar meeds of admiration exacted by his slight, ailing, feminine body, with deep expansions of bottomless vanity, were in the nature of things no longer forthcoming, and life's (for him) paradoxical repetitive trance was terminated, he bleakly awoke: in his wakeful industrious nights he began stealthily revisiting the glimpses of the sun of the past time-scene. That was his way of making himself into an historical personage, by embalming himself in a mechanical medium of 'time.'[7]

Let us recall (pausing only parenthetically to wonder what scorn Lewis might have invented for our own form of time-mentality, New Historicism) that *Time and Western Man* appeared in 1927. It is a classic exposition of high modernist philosophy, advocating against all forms of '"time"-notions' what he calls the '"spatializing" process of a mind *not* a Time-mind'. He knew Hulme, Ford, Pound, Eliot, and Joyce well, and was writing with knowledge of their experiments with what Joseph Frank later called 'spatial form.'[8] His criticism of Proust is typical of Lewis's ability to get hold of the wrong end of the right stick.[9] He calls Proust 'in a sense a new type of historical practitioner', because he sees him as pushing the chronological obsession to an extreme: a kind of *augmentio ad absurdam*. But if we turn it around, we can see that Proust's project, which to Lewis seems like the elaboration of the Time-mind on a grand scale, can be seen as the opposite: a pushing of the time-philosophy to the point where it collapses. As Jesse Matz argues, the force of Proustian involuntary memory is directed *against* time and death, producing impressions that are outside time. At least, insofar as there is a 'time-philosophy' in Proust it is very different from the historicizing imagination of Hegel, Sainte-Beuve, or Taine.

Correspondingly, the project also represents an unease about auto/biography. It's not exactly wrong to call *A la recherche* 'the history of a person written by himself' or a 'form of autobiography or self-portrait'. But it's not exactly right

---

[7] Wyndham Lewis, *Time and Western Man*, p. 265.
[8] See Joseph Frank, 'Spatial Form in Modern Literature', *Sewanee Review*, 53 (1945), 221–40, 433–56, 643–53.
[9] As Hugh Kenner argues, for example, about Lewis's spotting of Joyce's use of cliché in *Portrait*, but failing to appreciate it as a sign of Joyce's use of free indirect style: *Joyce's Voices* (London: Faber, 1978), pp. 16–17.

either, and Proust's careful erasure of any unequivocal identification of the work's 'Marcel' with the 'Marcel Proust' on its title pages is just one sign of unease with the genre. It is here that Proust is truly 'a new type of historical practitioner'. The flood of involuntary memory released by the taste of the madeleine at the beginning of *Du côté de chez Swann* signals that his interest in time is to liberate it from the historicism of the nineteenth century; to experience time as an escape from temporality. What this tells us is that far from being the age of the Time-mind, the early twentieth century is the age when the Time-mind, *homo auto/biographicus*, is called into question.

When Lewis read Joyce's *Portrait* he found it 'a rather cold and priggish book', 'well done', 'and that was all, that I could discover.'[10] This was perhaps because he read *Portrait* too as a 'form of autobiography or self-portrait'. He glosses Stephen as 'the author, of whom that is a self-portrait as a young man' (though perhaps the awkwardness of that phrasing, which seems alive to the art-historical connotations of the title, also registers an uncertainty about who exactly is the author here: Joyce or Stephen . . .).[11]

The ground of Lewis's attack on the historical is, in his analysis of Proust, curiously *historical*, biographical. He traces Proust's development, alleging a transition from experience to embalming. The energies of his portrait of Proust are characteristically satiric, combining a moral critique of 'bottomless vanity' with a hint of homophobia in the description of 'his slight, ailing, feminine body'. Much of *Time and Western Man* (like much of Lewis's work) operates by this kind of *ad hominem* satiric sketch. Writers and philosophers are treated with comparable ruthlessness, whether Lewis admires their work or not. His discussion of Pound is representative, and also indicative of the biographical element in Lewis's method. He describes Pound as a kind of 'great intellectual parasite'; 'a kind of intellectual eunuch'; 'that curious thing, a person without a trace of originality of any sort':

When he writes about living people of his acquaintance, as sometimes he has done, he shows himself possessed of a sort of conventional malice, perhaps, that says about them things that other people would say about them; but he never seems to have *seen* the individual at all. He sees people and things as other people would see them [. . .][12]

No one would accuse Lewis here, who is himself writing about a living person of his acquaintance, of saying the things other people would say about Pound, who is generally taken for one of the prime modernist innovators. Though Lewis claims to disabuse any readers who might take him to mean 'that Ezra Pound is a nobody', it's hard to imagine Pound as having taken any solace from Lewis's account of him. Lewis effectively damns him with praise of his fainter works

---

[10] *Time and Western Man*, p. 91.
[11] Ibid., p. 94.
[12] Ibid., pp. 86, 87, 85.

('His best translations [*the Seafarer*, for instance] are classics'), and admires his ability to 'get into the skin of somebody else, of power and renown, a Propertius or an Arnaut Daniel' and become 'a lion or a lynx on the spot.'[13] As he explains, though, despite his 'respect' for Pound, he felt the need to dissociate himself from his 'old friend' when he felt that Pound had reneged on his opposition (which opposition Lewis claims was based on Lewis's own) to 'the histrionics of the prefascist milanese', Marinetti.[14] According to Lewis, the form Pound's parasitism takes is in requiring the disturbance produced by more active figures. This enables Lewis to say: 'Pound is, I believe, only pretending to be alive for form's sake.'[15]

In some ways this is shrewd about Pound: about his genius for imaginary portraits of other writers through the mode of translation; and about the attraction for what he called 'factive' personalities, such as Sigismundo Malatesta.[16] When Lewis objects that Pound seems never to have *seen* the acquaintances he writes about, he is implicitly contrasting his own method, which is presumably intended to present a portrait of Pound as vivid as one of his aggressively distorted Cubist-influenced paintings. The images he uses to describe him—'big bug', Sphinx—have a vividness which is meant to persuade us that Lewis has *seen* him, and in a truly original way. Lewis's images are spatializing ones.[17] Yet here too there is a temporal story underlying the spatializing analysis. It is Pound's evolution that has disturbed Lewis, and makes him feel that 'I am sorry to say that I believe Ezra's effective life-work is over.'[18] There is a grim humour in Lewis's insistence that Pound 'should not be taken seriously as a living being at all', not only because he derives his energy from the creators he consumes, but because 'his field is purely that of *the dead*.'[19] But just as the ground of his objection to Marinetti is a form of vitalism (because Futurism is 'that intellectualist *commis* of Big Business—especially the armament line'; in the thrall of 'the great god, Industry'), so his criticism of Pound seems grounded on a sense that Pound lacks his own vitality (though he seems unaware of how his metaphors get mixed, as the 'parasite' is deemed 'unfit [...] to deal with living material at all.'[20] And this vitalism is inseparable from a historical sense of a life; a *bios*; biography. Rarely can life-writing have been so lethal.

In a sense, this contradiction is written into the heart of *Time and Western Man*. In accounting for the 'undisputed ascendancy' of the Time-mind, the historicizing mentality, Lewis needs to give something of the history of its

13 *Time and Western Man*, pp. 87, 86.
14 Ibid., pp. 87, 56, 57–8.
15 Ibid., pp. 56–7.
16 See Pound, *Guide to Kulchur* (London: Faber, 1938), p. 194.
17 *Time and Western Man*, pp. 86, 85.
18 Ibid., p. 85.
19 Ibid., p. 87.
20 Ibid., pp. 57–8, 87.

ascent.[21] When he poses the 'main characteristic' of such a mind as 'from the outset' (note the time-marker) a 'hostility to what it calls the "spatializing" process of a mind *not* a Time-mind' he is projecting his own hostility to the temporalizing mind. The notion of 'a mind *not* a Time-mind' is less impersonal than it is made to sound here. It is evidently Lewis's own mind that is *not* (or wants not to be) a Time-mind, and which seeks to contradict the prevalent temporalizing tendency of the era. Lewis is candid about his own 'political' (or as we might say, polemical) intent: 'The position from which this essay is written is outwardly a "narrow" one': 'But certainly I am issuing a "challenge" to the community in which I live. I am "criticizing all its institutions and modes of action and of thought".' And he continues:

I will next try to give some compendious idea of the manner in which I regard the claims of *individuality*. First then, although it is true that a pig would be a strange pig who dreamt himself a cat, or a cat that allowed the psychology of the horse to overpower it, and so forgot it was a cat, for this life, at least, a man still is the most detached and eclectic of creatures. But if his life is centred upon some deep-seated instinct or some faculty, he will find a natural exclusiveness necessary to proper functioning. For our only terra firma in a boiling and shifting world is, after all, our 'self'. That must cohere for us to be capable at all of behaving in any way but as mirror-images of alien realities, or as the most helpless and lowest organisms, as worms or as sponges.

I have said to myself that I will fix my attention upon those things that have most meaning for me.[22]

This move of opposing the fixed self to an unstable world is the opposite of Paterian impressionism, and evidently intended as a refutation of it or rebuke to it. Having defined his 'formally fixed "self"' in terms of his partisan character, he goes on to echo Nietzsche's remark about the philosophy being unconscious autobiography. He attributes his 'philosophic position' to his choice of art as an occupation:

So as the occupation is an art [. . .] it could perhaps more exactly be described as the expression of the instincts of a particular kind of man, rather than as an artist among men of other occupations. What philosophy is not that?—you could say, however, with truth. But the definiteness of those instincts, those of a plastic or graphic artist, make his responses to the philosophic tendencies around him more pointed than if he were a scholar mainly, or if he approached them from a political position, or as a professional of philosophical thought.[23]

Few readers who have read *Time and Western Man* right the way through are likely to remember it as autobiographical. But it is something of the kind, despite the third-personality and the self-presentation as a visual rather than verbal artist.

---

[21] Ibid., p. 3.
[22] Ibid., pp. 4–6.
[23] Ibid., p. 7.

That is to say, the book responds to the ascendancy of the Time-mind by trying to counter with a self-portrait of the artist as a Space-mind. It is certainly not a self-portrait in the manner in which it reads Joyce and Proust as self-portraitists. But even when it is most implacably opposed to the autobiographical in its time-dominated form, its opposition is offered in the form of a different version of the autobiographical. Certainly, though the book is not a historical narrative of Lewis's development, it is an intensely personal work, and leaves one with a clear sense of his personality and opinions. So it may seem less surprising than it might initially appear that Lewis was to go on to write two volumes of (albeit unconventional) autobiography: *Blasting and Bombardiering* (1937), dealing with the period of the First World War, and *Rude Assignment: An Intellectual Autobiography* (1950). Yet *Time and Western Man* should not be claimed as 'autobiography' despite its hostility to the Time-mind. Rather, it enables us to distinguish more clearly between autobiography and self-portrait, along the lines suggested by Philippe Lejeune, when he observes that Montaigne has 'no connection with, as we define it, autobiography; there is no continuous narrative nor any systematic history of the personality. Self-portrait rather than autobiography.'[24] Michel Beaujour, in his study *Poetics of the Literary Self-Portrait*, develops this definition of the self-portrait as organized not by continuous narrative but by analogy, metaphor, poetic superimposition. For him, literary self-portraits are arranged logically or dialectically instead of chronologically. 'The operational formula for the self-portrait', he says, is ' "I won't tell you what I've done, but I shall tell you *who I am*". '[25] That is Lewis's position exactly. He gives a self-portrait of himself as 'Western Man' not in terms of 'Time', but as a 'self' that can be abstracted out of time; self-portrait as anti-autobiography.

RICHARD ALDINGTON

Two crucial points have emerged from this discussion of Lewis. First, that even high modernist works associated with impersonality and spatiality can proceed by engaging with auto/biography. Modernist objections to auto/biography tend to be objections to specific received *forms* of auto/biography, rather than to the auto/biographic project itself. Second, that one form modernist engagements with auto/biography take is satire. We have already encountered moments of satire, or of the possibility of satire, in Pound and Lewis. We now turn to another modernist, Richard Aldington: a highly versatile and prolific writer, in whose

---

[24] Lejeune, *L'Autobiographie en France* ('U2' Series, Paris: Armand Collin, 1971), p. 57; trans. Beaujour, p. 2.

[25] Michel Beaujour, *Poetics of the Literary Self-Portrait*, trans. Yara Milos (New York: New York University Press, 1991), pp. 2–3.

work satire plays an even more prominent part.[26] Aldington was one of the three founders of Imagism in 1912, together with Pound, and Pound's ex-lover 'H. D.', Hilda Doolittle, whom he married in 1913. He was befriended by Ford, working as his secretary for a time just before the First World War.

He had met T. S. Eliot during the war, when Eliot took over Aldington's editorial duties on the *Egoist*. After the war Aldington began to work for the *Times Literary Supplement* as a regular reviewer of French books, and it was through his intercession that Eliot began to appear there from 1919. Aldington was expected to become editor of the *Times Literary Supplement* but after a visit from D. H. Lawrence—whom he had known since 1914, and who was the modern novelist he most admired—he decided he needed to write more personally, and to make a decisive break with England, and with Eliot's influence. His rejection of Eliot was in part a reaction to his war experiences. He came to see Eliot as death-obsessed, and he had had enough of death on the Western Front. His later work increasingly celebrates vitality, as is evident from his admiration for Lawrence, or his later autobiography, written during the next world war, and significantly entitled *Life for Life's Sake* (1941).

His distancing himself from Eliot and Pound dates from the late 1920s. Though Aldington continued to write poetry, he was entering a decade in which his major achievements were the satirical novels such as *Death of a Hero* (1929), *The Colonel's Daughter* (1931), *All Men are Enemies* (1933), and *Women must Work* (1934). This, followed by a last phase of auto/biographical production, may suggest that Aldington was moving away from modernism, capitulating to a more conservative version of the 'man of letters'. Yet that would be an over-simplification. His auto/biographical writing was rarely conventional, as we shall see from his use of satire. It was, rather, a case of realigning himself with a different version of modernism: that of Lawrence and Ford, rather than Eliot, Pound, and Joyce. Besides, my overall argument resists the implication that engagement with auto/biography is antithetical to modernism. Rather than being seen as a reneging on modernism's hostility to auto/biography, the emergence of the satiric should be seen as a phase in the sequence of sceptical engagements with it: through pastiche, parody, irony, and satire.

Death of a Hero includes satiric sketches of modernists in its depiction of prewar bohemian life. Waldo Tubbe, later Lord Tubbe, is unmistakably meant for Eliot. Mr or Herr Shobbe, 'a sort of literary Falstaff', is Ford Madox (Hueffer) Ford. Comrade Bobbe has Lawrence's working-class background as well as his illness. The painter Upjohn appears to combine traits of Pound and Lewis.[27] The novel's satire is much broader, and its pervasive anger is an attempt to expiate the war's blood-guilt, and to recover from his own traumatic experiences. The war is largely blamed on his parents' generation, and what Aldington sees as its

---

[26] See Saunders, entry on Richard Aldington, *Oxford Dictionary of National Biography*.
[27] See Doyle, *Richard Aldington*, p. 132. *Death of a Hero* (London: Chatto & Windus, 1929), p. 143.

Victorian cant; though pre-war and wartime bohemian gender politics come under attack as well. *Death of a Hero* is thus a complex, disturbed and necessarily sprawling satire. Its satirical sketches of the culturati place it in the genre of the modernist *roman à clef,* with books such as Ford's *The Simple Life Limited* (1911, satirizing Conrad, Edward Garnett, and Frank Harris), Huxley's *Point Counter-Point* (1928, with fictionalizations of D. H. Lawrence and Middleton Murry), and Lewis's *The Roaring Queen* (suppressed in 1936 by its wouldn't-be publisher for its satires of Arnold Bennett, Woolf, Walter Sickert, and Nancy Cunard amongst others).

Aldington followed *Death of a Hero* with a series of much more focused satiric sketches, collected together in *Soft Answers* (1932). The book consists of five imaginary portraits in the British first edition.[28] The form is similar to Beerbohm's *Seven Men:* a suite of fictional or fictionalized sketches, predominantly concerned with the aesthetic life. Two of Aldington's portraits develop the satire of English middle-class complacency begun in *The Colonel's Daughter.* 'A Gentleman of England: A Speculation' resumes Aldington's attack on cant, and especially on the 'religion of Money' and the moral smugness it engenders.[29] Harold Formby-Pett thinks he's perfect, but is in fact incompetent; a walking exposé of the inadequacy of the business ethic. He tries using his wife's sexuality to attract clients, but she ends up falling for one, then betraying and leaving him. '"Yes, Aunt": A Warning', charts the fate of a prissy dilettante who's conned into a literary life and a bad marriage out of financial dependence on his aunts. It's hard not to suspect at least an element of self-satire:

He would join the London Library and write a book on Elizabethan drama. He had planned a series of witty and satirical portrait-biographies in the manner of Mr. Strachey. He also intended a long novel, somewhat in the manner of Monsieur Proust, depicting the social and intellectual life of London. And he would 'criticise for the newspapers.'[30]

This is also a *mise en abyme* imaging *Soft Answers'* own witty and satirical portrait biographies depicting the social and intellectual life of artistic London. The other three stories are also concerned with art. 'Now Lies She There' is said to be based on Nancy Cunard. It's a disturbingly vicious account of a *femme fatale* who ends

---

[28] Aldington, *Soft Answers* (London: Chatto & Windus, 1932). Unless otherwise stated, references are to this edition. The American first edition (New York: Doubleday Doran, also 1932) added a sixth chapter, 'Last Straws' which had been published the previous year by Nancy Cunard's Hours Press at Réanville. See Harry T. Moore, 'Preface' to Aldington, *Soft Answers* (Carbondale and Edwardsville: Southern Illinois University Press, 1967), p. vi. Presumably it wasn't included in the Chatto & Windus edition because it was already available in Europe, and/or already in copyright. Moore's edition includes 'Last Straws', which tells of three cynical ex-soldiers, commenting on, but affected by, the destructiveness of the war. Its tone and melodrama are those of Aldington's *Death of a Hero,* suggesting that it may be partly autobiographical. It is otherwise an imaginary portrait of members of the lost generation.

[29] *Soft Answers,* p. 196.

[30] Ibid., pp. 14–15.

up with a feeble lion tamer—though the narrative structure is effective, as the narrator obsessively and baffledly pieces together her story, as she so humiliates his ex- that she attacks her, disfiguring Constance, who loses an eye. 'Nobody's Baby' is about a charlatan American composer, Mr Charlemagne Cox. If his music makes him sound like George Antheil, his megalomania and genius for self-publicizing are clearly those of Ezra Pound—who, if not a composer, did none-theless compose strange operas about Villon and Cavalcanti, and was also a prolific music critic.[31] But it is with the last satire in the book, 'Stepping Heavenward', on which this chapter will focus: Aldington's most savage attack on Eliot.

Aldington had thought highly enough of 'Stepping Heavenward' to publish it twice: first as a separate volume in 1931 and then the following year in *Soft Answers*. Peter Ackroyd, in his biography of Eliot, says of it: 'The novel itself is clearly animated by spite and jealousy, but although it presents only a caricature of Eliot it was accurate enough to be immediately recognizable to his friends.'[32] It's less clear that he has actually read it, since the work he twice calls a novel is only sixty-three and sixty pages in the respective editions. Jason Harding—who certainly *has* read it—calls it 'mean-spirited.'[33] But any meanness of spirit may be attributable as much to its target (Eliot) as its author, and as much the subject of the piece as its vice. It is, after all, a satire—not a mode known for generosity and forgiveness.

'Stepping Heavenward' is a satirical hagiography of Jeremy Cibber, like Eliot an American who comes to Europe and marries a neurasthenic wife. He is a historian rather than a poet, and is eventually beatified. But (as Ackroyd says) there is no doubt whom Aldington has in his sights:

With these valued allies, Cibber exactly at the right moment produced his epoch-making Notes on the Provincial Itinerary of the Emperor Antoninus. At first sight it seems impossible that so abstruse a work should have epoch-making consequences; but then, as we all know, it is the method and not the substance of a work which makes its value. And Cibber had method. The Itinerary itself was relegated to footnotes, while the notes, cast in the form of a commentary, became the text. In the opening pages Cibber politely but decisively annihilated every living historian of eminence except Cholmp. Then, in passages of unparalleled eloquence, now known to every schoolboy outside the great Public Schools, he lamented the decay and disappearance of so many once great and prosperous cities. In prose which moved with the stately tread of conscious superiority, he lamented the degradation of Kingship and the fetid growth of democracy, and pointed out that the ruinous European War had been the combined work of the Socialist Free-thinkers and the Jews. But the War, he insisted, was but a trifle, a mere symptom...[34]

[31] See *Ezra Pound and Music: The Complete Criticism*, ed. R. Murray Schafer (London: Faber, 1978).

[32] Peter Ackroyd, *T. S. Eliot* (London: Abacus, 1985), p. 186.

[33] Jason Harding, *The Critesion: Cultural Politics and Periodical Networks in Inter-war Britain* (Oxford: Oxford University Press, 2002), p. 20.

[34] *Soft Answers*, p. 284.

There's more happening here than a spirited travesty of 'The Waste Land'. There are four main strands to Aldington's critique of Eliot. First, the politics, which are a concise catalogue of exactly the views that get Eliot discussed alongside fascism. Aldington is sometimes discussed as a fellow-traveller of the Right.[35] Certainly, his friendships with right-inclined writers predominated—Eliot, Pound, Wyndham Lewis, and later Roy Campbell. But he was equally scathing about all political or religious systems. He was really an epicurean individualist, who resented any threat to individual fulfilment, whether from communism, capitalism, bureaucracy, or Christianity. The whole tract is evidently a satire on Eliot's religiosity; his 'conscious superiority' which is at once social and spiritual. In *Life for Life's Sake* (his memoirs, which incidentally show how little malice he bore Eliot in 1941),[36] he is as shrewd about Eliot's attractions to Toryism as to Royalism and Anglo-Catholicism:

Eliot was quietly laying the foundations of his future influence by cultivating the right people. . . . Another valuable ally, but a pernicious influence on Eliot, was Charles Whibley. Eliot was already too much influenced by Irving Babbit's pedantic and carping analysis of Rousseau—indeed to some extent he founded his prose style on Babbit—and in Whibley he found a British counterpart to his old Harvard professor. Whibley was a Fellow of Jesus College, Cambridge, a good scholar, but a hopeless crank about politics. He was the very embodiment of the English Tory don, completely out of touch with the realities of his time.[37]

Second, and related to this: Aldington targets what he sees in Eliot as a mania for control; for doing things at 'exactly at the right moment':

Cibber was always remarkable for prudence and decency. Everything he said and did bore the mark of careful premeditation. He left nothing to chance, never abandoned himself to any of those spontaneous impulses which, once yielded to, leave a lifetime of regret.[38]

Part of the satire here involves the narrator meticulously dissociating himself from demeaning attacks reducing continence to anality: 'But nothing but envy and a kind of secular bigotry would claim that the WHOLE of Cibber's career can be explained in terms of constipation.'[39] This in turn relates to the fetishization of 'method', which Aldington saw Eliot's growing critical authority as enforcing on everyone in a coercive fashion: 'as we all know, it is the method and not the substance of a work which makes its value'.

Finally, the argument that there is something inherently negative about this method: 'This, in fact, was the famous "oblique" method which Cibber made so

---

[35] See David Ayers, 'Richard Aldington's *Death of a Hero*: A Proto-Fascist Novel', *English*, 47 (1998), 89–98.
[36] Aldington, Life for Life's Sake (New York: Viking, 1941). See for example pp. 198–9.
[37] Ibid., p. 201.
[38] *Soft Answers*, p. 241.
[39] Ibid., p. 236.

formidable, i.e. always to create by destruction, to seek truth for oneself by exposing the errors of others.'[40] Critically, this reflects Aldington's view that Eliot's position involved an arrogant rubbishing of too many great writers, especially of the nineteenth century. Eliot wrote to Pound that Aldington had reproved him for 'expressing contempt . . . for eminent writers.'[41] This is another reason why Aldington's position at the *Criterion* eventually became untenable.

Biographically, his critique of Eliot's 'oblique method' sets him up as a Hollow Man, all hypocritical surface and no heart. When, in the 1950s, he turned his attention to a demythologizing biography of T. E. Lawrence, he told Alan Bird: 'after TEL I consider Eliot the biggest fraud and cleverest literary strategist and self-advertiser of this century. It is interesting to note how the English intellectuals have allowed themselves to be cowed by a series of American dictators, from Russell Lowell to Berenson and Eliot.'[42] But it also constitutes a criticism that Aldington was increasingly to make against the aesthetics of high modernism as nihilistic and death-obsessed. He had begun to intimate as much in 1920, telling Eliot that for all his poetic intelligence his poetry lacked something:

I know it is exceedingly brilliant and thoughtful; I see it as miles above most contemporary stuff; I recognize an irony which is 'vraiment supérieur'. But, I do feel sometimes, that you, like Ezra, have sacrificed something to this exquisite surface . . .[43]

Later this became the view that it is 'the intellectual concentration which so effectively conceals Eliot's emotional sterility.'[44]

I don't inventory these criticisms to endorse them from a position of moral superiority. They say nothing that Eliot wasn't already agonizingly aware of, and making agonized poetic use of. But they seem intelligently to summarize an aesthetic choice of modernisms: between, schematically, Eliot and D. H. Lawrence. D. H. Lawrence had a more decisive effect on Aldington's work than any writer, in a sense converting him from a classicizing Imagist poet to a satirical novelist. The conversion was gradual, and happened in the late 1920s. Indeed, *Stepping Heavenward* is one of its first published fruits, and it was soon joined by the other satirical sketches that make up *Soft Answers*. Satire and biography were to continue to become the essence of much of his work—whether satirical biographies like *Lawrence of Arabia*—or satirical biografiction like *Soft Answers*.

What was remarkable, I reflected, was Lawrence's immense capacity for experience and almost uncanny power of re-living it in words afterwards. Of all human beings I have known he was by far the most continuously and vividly alive and receptive. . . . I thought

---

[40] Ibid., p. 254.
[41] Eliot to Pound, 19 July 1922: *The Letters of T. S. Eliot*, vol. 1, ed. Valerie Eliot (London: Faber, 1988), p. 549.
[42] 15 March 1953: *A Passionate Prodigality: Letters to Alan Bird from Richard Aldington*, ed. Miriam J. Benkovitz (New York: New York Public Library and Readex Books, 1975), p. 87.
[43] Aldington to Eliot, 11 June 1920: Doyle, p. 91.
[44] *Life for Life's Sake*, p. 203.

of him a good deal. His talk and personality, the many glimpses of his life, gave point and concentration to the vague rebellious tendencies I have described in myself. It seemed to me that I was being rather cowardly and foolish in allowing so much of life to slip by in mere labour and by allowing my energies to be diverted from writing about what I myself felt and thought to other subjects.[45]

'The upshot of this', he continues, was to write a pamphlet about Lawrence 'in which I abandoned the hocus-pocus of "objective criticism" and the desiccated style it imposes'—in other words, the method of Eliot. When it was published as *D. H. Lawrence: An Indiscretion*, in 1927, Lawrence wrote one of his extraordinary, surgically perceptive letters:

No need to be in any trepidation on my account—you hand me out plenty of bouquets, as you say.... But *caro*, you are so funny. Why do you write on the one hand as if you were my grandmother—about sixty years older than me, and forced rather to apologize for the *enfant terrible* in the family?.... And on the other hand, why do you write as if you were on hot bricks? Is the game worth the candle, or isn't it? Make up your mind. I mean the whole game of life and literature—not merely my worthy self. You don't believe it's worth it, anyhow. Well then, don't worry any more, be good and commercial. But don't, don't feel yourself one of the pillars of society. My dear chap, *where* did you get all this conscience of yours? You haven't got it really.... I never knew a man who seemed more to be living from a character not his own, than you. What *is* it that you are afraid of?—ultimately?—is it death? Or pain? Or just fear of the negative infinite of all things? What ails thee, lad?[46]

And perhaps that was it—that sense of 'the negative infinite of all things', which glowers at the heart of Eliot's writing—that caused him to reject Eliot. Aldington certainly objected to what he saw as Eliot's 'death-worshipping'. He gives a parody of 'The Hollow Men' in one article:

A greatly admired poem by the most admired poet of the day may be summarized in the following excerpted words:

Hollow-dried-meaningless-dry-broken-dry-paralysed-death's-hollow-I-dare-not-death's-broken-fading-death's-final-twilight-dead-cactus-stone-dead-fading-death's-broken-dying-broken-last-sightless-death.

The poet's genius is not in question, but I hate this exhibitionism of a perpetual suicide mania which never, never, comes to the point. ... It is the War despair which involved so many of us and from which the healthy-minded have been struggling to escape, not yearning to wallow in.[47]

This might sound like the moral superiority of the veteran, who has a more real experience of death, over the non-combatant. Yet Eliot's comment to Herbert Read that 'there are plenty of people suffering from much more real torments

---

[45] *Life for Life's Sake*, pp. 278–9.
[46] Lawrence to Aldington, 24 May 1927: quoted in Doyle, *Richard Aldington*, p. 112.
[47] *Sunday Referee*, 15 Dec. 1929: quoted Doyle, *Richard Aldington*, pp. 148–9.

than his own' suggests a lack of sympathy for Aldington's very real traumatic stress; and that Aldington wasn't far wrong in having Cibber insist that the war was 'but a trifle, a mere symptom.'[48] And his reaction to Lawrence shows how genuinely Aldington meant his criticism. It didn't matter that Lawrence hadn't fought. What mattered was that he had struggled against the 'War despair'. It was part of Eliot's genius to articulate that despair in 'The Waste Land', and find a strange and compelling new music in negativity. Aldington felt that, but felt it as something he needed to struggle to escape.

Aldington's biographer Charles Doyle wonders what caused Lawrence to 'flourish the stiletto' in response to Aldington's tribute, and says it must have been hard to bear, especially coming when he was at loggerheads with Eliot. But I don't believe Aldington took it as a stab in the back. Rather, it came at just the right moment, and helped cut free Aldington's most creative work in his novel-writing decade, starting with the book that confronted the terror of the negative infinite, *Death of a Hero*—the watershed in his career, and the book that made him famous. George Orwell thought it 'much the best of the English war books.'[49] It was the first real intimation of his satirical power: an angry denunci-ation of Victorian hypocrisy, social stupidity crushing individual happiness. These were to be his main fictional themes. It is also a rawly autobiographical work, expressing his anger towards his parents (especially his mother), the war, and the literary establishment.

Yet his dealings with Lawrence show how un-touchy Aldington could be in a friendship he trusted as genuine. Indeed, Aldington devoted much of his time to celebrating, and editing Lawrence.[50] Lawrence, he said, 'was literally "satirical", really like a wild half-trapped creature, a satyr, desperately fighting to get free.'[51] And he particularly admired satirical energy of his talk: 'Curious that Lawrence, who was such a good satirist in conversation, was a comparatively poor one in writing. The reason is, I think, that in talk his satire was mostly laughter, whereas in print he scolded.'[52] Lawrence's analysis of him also unleashed Aldington's own satirical energy. For the pressing need to unmask other false selves, which caused his career so much trouble, appears to date from Lawrence saying that he was 'living from a character not his own'.

---

[48] He also told Read that Aldington was 'full of false pride'. Quoted in Doyle, *Richard Aldington*, p. 103.
[49] Doyle, *Richard Aldington*, p. 128.
[50] Aldington had edited Lawrence's *Selected Poems* (1932), and was now influential in getting Lawrence's prose republished, writing fourteen introductions for Heinemann and Penguin, and writing *D. H. Lawrence: An Appreciation* (Harmondsworth: Penguin, 1950) (in which he argues that '*Women in Love* contains a good deal of satire'; p. 19). He also produced the important early biography, *D. H. Lawrence: Portrait of a Genius, But ...* (London: Heinemann, 1950).
[51] *Life for Life's Sake*, p. 212.
[52] Ibid., p. 277.

What he resented wasn't Eliot's genius, but what he saw as his undue influence. Even at the heart of 'Stepping Heavenward' there is a recognition, however ambivalent, of the power and eloquence of Eliot even at his most abstruse; a generosity notably lacking from Eliot's attack on Lawrence three years after his death, in the disgraceful book *After Strange Gods: A Primer for Modern Heresy* (1934). (One could say 'Stepping Heavenward' is eerily prophetic of that book, except that presumably Aldington had been hearing similar views from Eliot during the 1920s.) There's more laughter in Aldington's satire of Eliot than has been recognized, and also more intelligence than spite or jealousy.

We have seen different modes in which satire can engage with the biographic, such as Pound's poem-portraits; or Lewis's spatializing seeing of character. In Aldington's case not only does he draw upon the biographies of real figures, but (like Pound) he also satirizes biographical practice. In *Death of a Hero* there is a gesture in this direction when, having introduced Shobbe, Bobbe, and Tubbe, we are assured about each in turn that he is 'a very great man.'[53] The satire is directed largely at the characters' self-importance, as well as that of their bohemian milieu; but it also has it in for the kind of hagiographical canting biographic tradition that needs to elevate its artists to superhuman status. (It was in response to this tendency that Aldington subtitled his biography of D. H. Lawrence *Portrait of a Genius, But...*; 1950.) In *Soft Answers*, the satire of biographical forms is double-edged. The opening of 'Stepping Heavenward', for example, resumes the attack on biographical cant:

Naturally the careers of great men are differently interpreted, and estimates of their characters vary surprisingly. Various, indeed, have been the portraits recently offered by a fecund tribe of biographers, professing to give adequate accounts and explanations of the life of the late Jeremy Pratt Sybba, afterwards Father Cibber, O. S. B., recently beatified by the Roman Curia.[54]

The ironies are scarcely subtle here: the undermining of the claim that Cibber is one of the very great men, as well as of the true fruitfulness of the 'fecund tribe of biographers'. Yet it is significant that they are cast in the form of a parody of biographical decorum and piety. To this extent Aldington might be said to be following Strachey, and producing a volume of 'Eminent Moderns'. Yet, as is implied by the comment already quoted which mentions him, Aldington is also satirizing Strachey: not only adopting Strachey's compass, the brief essay-length life, and his tone, the mandarin irony, but also satirizing that form and tone. After all, one of the effects of applying familiar biographical modes to imaginary subjects is to hold the mirror up to biography itself (as Woolf was to do superlatively in *Orlando*, discussed in the next chapter).

---

[53] *Death of a Hero*, pp. 118–19.
[54] *Soft Answers*, p. 235.

Some readers who are persuaded by my accounts of the conjunction of the auto/biographical and the satirical in modernism may nonetheless feel that it is illicit to conflate these arguments with one about Imaginary Portraits: that to the extent to which a piece of writing is a satire of a real historical figure, it is not imaginary. According to this view, when a satire which has a real target in its sights changes any details—such as the real name, occupation, achievements, and so on of the target—it only does so by convention: to evade possible charges of libel and thus to be safely publishable. Cibber is *really* Eliot, and the reasons he is not named Eliot are merely contingent; signifying only satiric convention and not otherwise meriting attention. Of course, Aldington may have chosen the name to suggest that Eliot has something in common with the eighteenth-century actor-manager and earlier autobiographer Colley Cibber, by way of stressing his manipulation of his career. But the piece is seen, from this point of view, as inescapably *about* Eliot.

However, it is not clear that satire works in quite this way. Certainly, part of its pleasure comes from the recognition of its targets. Yet, as with cartoons and caricatures, that pleasure derives from the combination of familiarity and otherness; from the paradox of recognition *despite*, or *in*, otherness. Similarly, what it is that is being recognized is paradoxical too. We recognized Eliot in Cibber. But the satire also enables us to see qualities in Cibber that we had perhaps not recognized in Eliot—such as pedantry, sanctimoniousness, negativity, and so forth. Swift's famous observation that 'Satyr is a sort of Glass, wherein Beholders do generally discover every body's Face but their Own; which is the chief Reason for that kind of Reception it meets in the World, and that so very few are offended with it' is alive to the way satire's otherness can blind us to the way it might implicate us.[55] While ostensibly a claim that readers read satire biographically, and not autobiographically, Swift's point is that they see the satire as applying to everyone else precisely because they cannot, or will not, or cannot bear to, see that it applies to themselves; whereas a fully sane and perceptive reading would recognize their autobiography in the satire.

But satire is also necessarily general; attacking generalized human vices, perhaps as they are manifested in individuals; but not merely for the sake of castigating those individuals, but as a 'warning' to others. Part of its pleasure comes from the energy with which it distorts the individual to make it represent the general quality. Satire always involves imaginative extrapolation. To this extent, the portraits Aldington presents in *Soft Answers are* imaginary ones. Though writers like Pound, Cunard, and Eliot can be glimpsed in them, the distortions are so exaggerated as to create wonderfully grotesque figures different from any putative originals. Such satires work by suggesting that the subjects satirized are themselves grotesquely distorted impressions of their original selves;

---

[55] Jonathan Swift, 'The Preface of the Author', *The Battle of the Books*, in *A Tale of a Tub and Other Satires*, ed. Kathleen Williams, revised edition (London: J. M. Dent, 1975), [p. 140].

that, as Lawrence suggested of Aldington himself, they are living from characters 'not their own'. To this extent satiric biografiction works by opposite principles to the Reynoldsian autobiografiction which seeks to express the true psychic life by fictional means. Instead, it insinuates that it's the psychic life of its targets (their spiritual experiences) that are themselves fictional.

Like most biografiction, Aldington's portraits start from characteristics of real people, but combine and transform them to create imaginary, other people. The satire then exists not to mock specific individuals, but as a formal property. It was a method that, to some extent, one might even say that Aldington had learned from Eliot himself. After all, as suggested in Chapter 1, many of Eliot's early poems are not only sharp imaginary portraits but also sometimes sharper imaginary self-portraits. The aim is perhaps to emulate the effect of much classical satire on modern readers, when the specific original context hasn't survived, so we no longer know whether a proper name is the subject's real name, or an easily identifiable pseudonym, or whether it merely designates an easily recognizable type. This kind of effect was one Pound sought too in his classicizing epigrams:

> Leucis, who intended a Grand Passion,
> Ends with a willingness-to-oblige.[56]

Similarly, a visual caricature might be a criticism of an identifiable original (as in a political cartoon); or it might simply be an idiom for expressing identifiable human behaviour or experiences with greater sharpness than by more realistic treatment (as in the drawings of Daumier, say, or George Grosz). In such cases the satiric form is better suited to more negative content: the expression of human suffering, folly, malignity.

Aldington's pre-war gifts were predominantly lyrical; it was the war that gave him his fury. And though Lewis's satirical, oppositional stance—his mission to 'Blast' the sacred cows of bourgeois culture—was manifest before the war, the books by both men discussed here are post-war works, and their anger at anyone they felt had misled them (whether about philosophy, history, time, culture, or human relationships) must in part be attributed to the aftermath of that catastrophe. The preceding chapter argued that Pound's satire of the aesthetes and Georgians also derived its fire from the war: both from his anger that from a post-war perspective the cultural ideas of the 1890s seemed so ineffectual; and his anger at the destruction of many of the talents who had seemed best able to create a modern alternative, such as the philosopher T. E. Hulme or the sculptor Gaudier-Brzeska.

The First World War, that is to say, produced for these modernists the next stage of the crisis we have been tracing in life-writing. A particularly clear expression of the crisis erupted in France in 1923. A vignette of Ford's gives the gist:

---

[56] Ezra Pound, 'Epitaph', *Selected Poems*, ed. T. S. Eliot (London: Faber, 1973), p. 104.

I was sitting in the Closerie des Lilas and some French novelist or other was discanting [*sic*] on the disappearance of the Great Figure from the Earth. He was a violent anti-Plutarchian and declared that the war just ended had made all the leaders of men appear such feckless fools that never again would Society consent to be led by Great Men.[57]

'[A]nti-Plutarchian' might sound like a bit of public-school showing off. But it refers to a specific French controversy sparked off by the publication (the year after Joyce had reimagined the great military and political figure of Ulysses as a cuckolded Jewish advertising salesman) of a book by Jean de Pierrefeu called *Plutarque a menti—Plutarch Lied*. As the *New York Times* was to put it three years later, reviewing his follow-up, *L'Anti Plutarque*:

> Although M. Pierrefeu's earlier book which opened the Plutarch controversy, 'Plutarque a Menti,' was promptly put under the ban by the 'grande presse' of Paris when it appeared in May, 1923 (considerably later translated under the title 'Plutarch Lied'), it appears from the notice in 'l'Anti-Plutarque' that it has gone through 198 editions.[58]

While the ban indicates the politically subversive nature of the controversy, the refracting of the question of leadership through the figure of Plutarch indicates that this is also a question of how historical figures are represented: in short, a question of biography. (Surprisingly, it's one of the few instances missed by Ann Jefferson in *Biography and the Question of Literature in France*.) It's well-known how the torrent of war memoirs published in the late 1920s and early 1930s transformed the writing of autobiography. The anti-Plutarchian controversy reveals how this shift was being prepared by a post-war crisis in biography through the 1920s—or even earlier; since for English readers it was the publication in 1918 of Lytton Strachey's *Eminent Victorians* that signalled the end of the biographical tradition venerating elders and worshipping ancestors, and a turn towards a more ironic or even satirical approach. As we shall see in the next chapter, discussing his fellow Bloomsbury writers Virginia Woolf and Harold Nicolson, after the war, life-writing, and its relation to literature, was being reinvented yet again.

[57] Ford, *Portraits from Life*, p. 120. Ford's point is that while this may be true of military or political leaders, there are still writers who are 'Great Figures': he cites H. G. Wells as his incontestable example.

[58] Jean de Pierrefeu, *l'Anti-Plutarque* (Paris: Les Editions de France, 1926); rev. *New York Times* (14 February 1926) Book Review Section, p. 6.

11

Woolf, Bloomsbury, the 'New Biography', and the New Auto/biografiction

> 'Invented, this escapade with the girl; made up, as one makes up the better part of life, he thought—making oneself up; making her up; creating an exquisite amusement, and something more. But odd it was, and quite true; all this one could never share—it smashed to atoms.'[1]

Of all modernist engagements with life-writing, Virginia Woolf's is the most visible, and her work represents the most sustained and diverse exploration of the relation between fiction and auto/biography—at least in English, since the example of Proust was her major precursor. This chapter will show how many of the concerns that Woolf shares with other modernists, such as time, consciousness, memory, memorialization, obscurity, identity, sexuality and gender, aesthetics, form, technique, and so on, are expressed through her experiments with life-writing. She was, as Linda Anderson says, 'critically engaged all her life in the problem of writing lives and, in particular, the problem of writing women's lives.'[2]

It is not only a matter of using her own life as an artist as material for (autobiographical) fiction, though she certainly did that as much as everybody. Since almost every aspect of Bloomsbury has been saturated with biographical curiosity and scholarship for almost a century, the ways in which she reinvented her own life-facts in a prolific oeuvre have been minutely examined. To take only the most obvious instances, novels such as *Mrs Dalloway* and *To the Lighthouse* have been read as profoundly autobiographical; as respectively about her anxieties about insanity and suicidal impulses; and about her parents, and her struggle to become an artist.

Her family and friendships connected her in a unique way with the defining and redefining of biography from the late nineteenth to the early twentieth centuries. Her father, Sir Leslie Stephen, was not only a major intellectual historian and biographer, but also the founding editor of the *Dictionary of National Biography* (from 1882 to 1891). Woolf's own life-writing and writing about life-writing is a complex reaction against the kind of Victorian 'official'

---

[1] Peter Walsh's interior monologue, in *Mrs Dalloway* (Oxford: Oxford University Press, 1992), p. 70.
[2] Linda Anderson, *Autobiography* (London and New York: Routledge, 2001), p. 92.

biographic tradition that the *DNB* represented: conventional, patriarchal, impersonal, censorious, and censored. She was at the heart of the modernist reinvention of life-writing; and gave it a name: 'The New Biography.'[3] Its other key exponent was Lytton Strachey, her fellow Bloomsbury group member and close friend. The Bloomsbury group was largely responsible for the introduction of Freudian ideas into British intellectual life. They also established a 'Memoir Club', to which members would read autobiographical papers of a psychosexual frankness unthinkable to their parents' generation.[4]

'I was thinking the other night that there's never been a womans [*sic*] autobiography', Woolf wrote to her friend the composer Ethel Smyth: 'Nothing to compare with Rousseau'. She went on to ask why Smyth shouldn't be 'not only the first woman to write an opera, but equally the first to tell the truths about herself.'[5] As Anna Snaith observes, 'Woolf, for many reasons, is unable to write this autobiography herself', though she did write in an explicitly autobiographical mode in the experimental 'A Sketch of the Past', and the other memoirs and reminiscences collected posthumously as *Moments of Being*.[6] But, as Snaith notes, 'her stylistic and imaginative vision took her to places other than the unequivocally stable "I" of a conventional autobiography.'[7] While, as we have been witnessing, the 'I' of *literary* autobiographical texts is scarcely unequivocal or stable, Snaith is right to see Woolf's modernism as questioning 'the linear, fact-based style of Victorian auto/biography'. Though, as she says, Woolf 'was never to write a conventional biography of a woman', her fictional works like *Orlando*, *Flush*, and *To the Lighthouse*, as well as autobiografictionalizing essays such *A Room of One's Own*, regularly 'contain representations of real women's lives.'[8] She did try to write what Snaith describes as her 'one conventional biography', but of a man—another Bloomsbury friend, the art critic and painter Roger Fry—but it 'caused her much turmoil because she was obliged to stick to facts', and she proposed turning it into something 'more fictitious' at the point she entered the narrative in 1909.[9] Woolf also wrote numerous biographical essays. Many of her reviews and essays are on particular biographies, autobiographies, and memoirs. Just as some of her essays have become canonical

[3] Woolf, 'The New Biography' (1927), in *The Essays of Virginia Woolf*, vol. 4, ed. Andrew McNeillie (London: The Hogarth Press, 1994), 473–80.

[4] See S. P. Rosenbaum, ed., *The Bloomsbury Group: A Collection of Memoirs and Commentary* (Toronto: University of Toronto Press, 1995).

[5] Woolf to Smyth, 24 December 1940: *Leave the Letters till We're Dead: The Letters of Virginia Woolf*, vol. 6 (London: The Hogarth Press, 1980), p. 453.

[6] Woolf, *Moments of Being*, ed. Jeanne Schulkind (London: Chatto & Windus and Sussex University Press, 1986). See also Virginia Woolf, *The Platform of Time: Memoirs of Family and Friends*, expanded edition, ed. S. P. Rosenbaum (London: Hesperus, 2008).

[7] Anna Snaith, 'My Poor Private Voice: Virginia Woolf and Auto/biography', in *Representing Lives: Women and Auto/biography*, ed. Alison Donnell and Pauline Polkey (Houndmills: Macmillan, 2000), pp. 96–104 (p. 96).

[8] Snaith, 'My Poor Private Voice', pp. 97, 96.

[9] Ibid., p. 97. *Roger Fry: A Biography* (London: The Hogarth Press, 1940).

modernist statements on the novel—'Modern Fiction', say, or 'Mr Bennett and Mrs Brown'—so her essays on auto/biography are key theoretical documents of 'The New Biography'. Indeed, as in that essay, she was not only a major theorist of life-writing as well as fiction, but also of their possible combinations: of what we are terming auto/biografiction.

Above all, though, it is as a practitioner of such composite forms that she is most significant for our purposes.[10] It would be unthinkable not to include her groundbreaking works parodying, mocking, and fantasizing upon biography: *Jacob's Room* (1922); *Orlando* (1928), and *Flush* (1933). *Jacob's Room* is unmistakably a novel, though, as Michael Whitworth argues:

> If the novel is a parody of a *bildungsroman*, in which the hero fails to reach maturity, it is also a parody of a biography, in which the biographer-narrator fails to capture his subject, fails to accommodate him within the conventional framework of biography, but cannot concede the impossibility of the task he has set himself.[11]

In *Jacob's Room* the central character is set the essay title 'Does history consist in the biographies of great men?' Jacob is not presented as a 'great man' in the Carlylean sense, though his classical beauty makes an impression on many of his contacts. And the relationship of Woolf's novel to biography is an antithetical one. 'It is no use trying to sum people up', she writes, countering the entire *DNB* ethos of doing exactly that in a few pages: 'One must follow hints, not exactly what is said, nor yet entirely what is done.'[12] A *DNB* life necessarily prioritizes the subject's public acts: what was said and done. Whereas Woolf follows the antithetical strategy of following hints instead. She gives what she calls a 'scrap of conversation' instead of a fully transcribed discussion. Characteristically, *Jacob's Room* forms a collage of such scraps, conveying tones and moods as Jacob and his friends spend time together, without giving any traditional sense of their 'intellectual development', say, or the history of their ideas:

> 'I rather think,' said Jacob, taking his pipe from his mouth, 'it's in Virgil,' and pushing back his chair, he went to the window.[13]

This is a whole paragraph at the start of chapter 5. Woolf doesn't tell us what the 'it' is which Jacob thinks is in Virgil; nor whether he's right, knows where in Virgil, nor why whatever it is might be important to Jacob or to anyone else. These are unthinkable omissions for a realist novelist such as George Eliot, for

---

[10] As Anna Snaith notes, the playing of such games with life-writing forms appears at the start of Woolf's writing life, in such early works as 'Journal of Mistress Joan Martyn'; and the 'Mysterious Case of Miss V'. Snaith to Saunders, 25 April 2008. See *The Complete Shorter Fiction of Virginia Woolf*, ed. Susan Dick (London: Hogarth Press, 1985).

[11] Michael Whitworth, *Einstein's Wake* (Oxford: Oxford University Press, 2001), p. 155. Also see Judy Little, '*Jacob's Room* as Comedy: Woolf's Parodic *bildungsroman*', in Jane Marcus, ed., *New Feminist Essays on Virginia Woolf* (London: Macmillan, 1981), 105–24.

[12] Woolf, *Jacob's Room*, ed. Kate Flint (Oxford: Oxford University Press, 1992), p. 214.

[13] Ibid., p. 84.

whom a full view of Jacob would necessitate such information, and judgements about the nature and quality of his mind. It is for these reasons that *Jacob's Room* is often read as what Rachel Bowlby calls the 'debunking of the ideals of Victorian biography.'[14] She calls such debunking 'implicit', although, as in the argument against 'summing up' characters, it is fairly explicit. Nor is Woolf content merely to denigrate Victorian biography: she opposes her method of impressionistic collage. Much of the registrations a realist might desire could be said to be implicit in Woolf's method. Jacob's vagueness comes across in the phrase 'I rather think', and in the sense in which such a remark seems to close a discussion; even, perhaps, in the way he says half the sentence with the pipe still in his mouth, suggesting perhaps that for him talk is as much a physical instinct or activity as smoking, or walking over to a window; or as much a matter of making the right social gestures.

Her terms and techniques are the same, whether applied to life-writing or to fiction. The same opposition, and the same preference, is the basis for her best-known aesthetic manifesto, the essay 'Modern Fiction'. The privileging of internal, private, and evanescent impressions over the external, public and regulated markers is her cardinal principle for writing lives, or for writing 'life'. It is a method that suggests both how much can be observed, but also how opaque the self can remain to even the most observant eye:

The proximity of the omnibuses gave the outside passengers an opportunity to stare into each other's faces. Yet few took advantage of it. Each had his own business to think of. Each had his past shut in him like the leaves of a book known to him by heart; and his friends could only read the title, James Spalding, or Charles Budgeon. . . .[15]

The past of each passenger is scarcely going to resemble the kind of Victorian biography that puts its subject's name on the cover; or to be written in the impersonal, judgemental style of the *DNB*:

It seems that a profound, impartial, and absolutely just opinion of our fellow-creatures is utterly unknown. Either we are men, or we are women. Either we are cold, or we are sentimental. Either we are young, or growing old.[16]

Biographical or interpretative objectivity is impossible, given that it issues from the subjective viewpoint of a biographer or interpreter. Yet Woolf's antitheses are not all commensurable. Gendering is either/or in a way that aging is not. The distinction between coldness and sentimentality, poised between these two kinds of antithesis, is equivocal. Some may be more inclined towards coldness, some towards sentimentality. But may we not be cold and then sentimental, and vice

---

[14] Bowlby, 'Introduction', Woolf, *Orlando*, World's Classics (Oxford: Oxford University Press, 1992), p. xxii.
[15] *Jacob's Room*, p. 85.
[16] Ibid., p. 96.

versa, by turns? And, if that antithesis is permeable, might not that of gender be so too? After all, sexologists such as Edward Carpenter were arguing for a spectrum of gender composites: the more or less masculine man, the less or more feminine man, the more or less masculine woman, the less or more feminine woman. And Freudian psychoanalysis was arguing that, within an individual, sexuality is dynamic and polymorphous. Even the antithesis between men and women was proving negotiable. So perhaps in this book of 1922 Woolf was already anticipating her 1928 experiment in *Orlando*, in which one imaginary fellow-creature is neither only man nor only woman, but a composite of the two, who remains young for centuries.

The novella *Flush*, though ultimately a *jeu d'esprit*, is similarly subversive. The antithesis it worries away at is that between animal and human. One way it is unmistakably a parody of biography is in its mock-ponderous application of the conventions of human biography to a dog. *Flush* isn't any old dog, however, but a literary one: Elizabeth Barrett Browning's spaniel. Thus Woolf takes as her subject area one of the great Victorian biographical stories—the love story of Robert Browning and Elizabeth Barrett—as written about as anything in Bloomsbury, by the lovers themselves in their letters and poems, as well as by their biographers. Woolf had written earlier of how the result had been the relative neglect of Barrett Browning's work.[17] Telling the story from the dog's point of view certainly returns attention to the mistress. But it also wrenches the point of view away from the human participants. This too has its serious motives. As with many animal narratives it serves to make human judgements seem strange, and to un-found hierarchies of class and gender. Its empathy with the non-human is fascinating and often poignant, as in the vivid description of Flush's sensitivity to scents:

The greatest poets in the world have smelt nothing but roses on the one hand, and dung on the other. The infinite gradations that lie between are unrecorded. Yet it was in the world of smell that Flush mostly lived. Love was chiefly smell; form and colour were smell; music and architecture, law, politics and science were smell. To him religion itself was smell [. . .][18]

Using Flush as a focalizer shows the limitations of the human point of view in these ways. It also makes Woolf's point that (as Lily Briscoe reflects in *To the Lighthouse*), 'One wanted fifty pairs of eyes to see with'; 'Fifty pairs of eyes were not enough to get round that one woman with.'[19] *Flush* makes us aware of other pairs of eyes watching the Brownings—their servants, family, the criminals who kidnap Flush. But it also wants to make us aware that one of the limitations of

---

[17] Woolf, 'Poets' Letters', *The Essays of Virginia Woolf*, ed. Andrew McNeillie, vol. 1 (London: Hogarth, 1986), pp. 101–5.

[18] Woolf, *Flush* (Harmondsworth: Penguin, 1977), pp. 83–4.

[19] Woolf, *To the Lighthouse*, ed. Margaret Drabble (Oxford: Oxford University Press, 1992), p. 266.

the human point of view is to assume that the only eyes that matter are his and hers. There is something profoundly paradoxical about the way in which the hyper-sensitivity to impressions of the spaniel takes us inside the minutiae of a consciousness, but that it is a non-human consciousness. In a sense, it is an attempt at impersonality, in its escape from human personality; though part of the comedy comes from the way human foibles creep back in, via Flush's snobbery, xenophobia, pride in property, and possessiveness.[20] As in the experimental central section of *To the Lighthouse*, Woolf imagines whether stories might be told from outside human consciousness, and if so, how. But where in that novel the story is of the empty house, here it includes the human participants, but turns biography inside out, so the humans only populate the margins, and the elements that biographers leave on the margins or leave out altogether become the centre.

Orlando, written between *Jacob's Room* and *Flush*, embodies aspects of both. Like *Jacob's Room* it is a full-length novel focused on the life of a single human subject. Like *Flush*, it uses the form of 'fake biography', even to the extent of bearing the subtitle 'A Biography'. As Hermione Lee tells us in her superb biography of Woolf, because of this subtitle the novel 'was being placed on the biography shelves of bookshops, so advance sales were poor.'[21] It is almost as hard to imagine readers mistaking *Orlando* for a genuine biography as it is salutary to be reminded that there was a time when biography didn't top the bestseller lists.

Perhaps the booksellers didn't read further than the subtitle. They'd only have to have read as far as the Preface (which fulsomely acknowledges such eminent but dead influences as Walter Pater) to realize that something was awry. Or if they had started at the other end, the Index might have told the same story. It begins with 'A., Lord', and includes 'Anne, Queen'; 'C., Marquis of'; 'Canute, the elk-hound'; 'Field, Mrs.'; 'Nell' followed immediately by 'Nelson'; and 'R., Lady' followed immediately by 'Railway, the'; and so on. In between is the notoriously fantastical construct of Orlando, exceeding the fundamental biographical categories of lifespan (by living for at least 400 years) and gender (by changing spontaneously from a man to a woman). The notion of the book being a 'biography' is clearly as fictional as anything else in it.

Orlando's first reviewers immediately recognized that it was a sustained parody of biography, and tended to appreciate the joke. 'The preface is a parody of prefaces and the whole book is written in tearing high spirits', wrote Raymond Mortimer.[22] It is by now a well-established view that the book plays with 'the conventions of biographical and historical writing.'[23] But it is a view that raises two questions.

---

[20] See Anna Snaith, 'Of Fanciers, Footnotes, and Fascism: Virginia Woolf's *Flush*', *Modern Fiction Studies*, 48:3 (2002), 614–36.

[21] Hermione Lee, *Virginia Woolf* (London: Vintage, 1997), pp. 512, 516.

[22] Quoted Bowlby, 'Introduction', p. xv.

[23] Bowlby, 'Introduction', p. xii.

Which biographical conventions does Woolf have in mind? And what relation to them does her book have?—is it parody, satire, fake, or just high-spirited game-playing? Since *Orlando* actually alludes to the *DNB*, that is as good a place as any to start investigating what kind of biography Woolf wants to make fun of:

And indeed, it cannot be denied that the most successful practitioners of the art of life, often unknown people by the way, somehow contrive to synchronize the sixty or seventy different times which beat simultaneously in every normal human system so that when eleven strikes, all the rest chime in unison, and the present is neither a violent disruption nor completely forgotten in the past. Of them we can justly say that they live precisely the sixty-eight or seventy-two years allotted them on the tombstone. Of the rest some we know to be dead though they walk among us; some are not yet born though they go through the forms of life; others are hundreds of years old though they call themselves thirty-six. The true length of a person's life, whatever the *Dictionary of National Biography* may say, is always a matter of dispute.[24]

There is a serious criticism of biographical practice beneath the cliché that what matters is life's intensity rather than its duration: an argument that the shaping of a life according to conventional time-markers (such as birth, education, marriage, career, children, honours, death) falsifies the *experience* of life; that our *experience* of time eludes the nets of clock and calendar time. As Woolf put it in her essay 'The Art of Biography':

Many of the old chapter headings—life at college, marriage, career—are shown to be very arbitrary and artificial distinctions. The real current of the hero's existence took, very likely, a different course.[25]

The problem is that 'the old chapter headings' are not confined to stuffy biographies, but have organized the way we think about our experience. So Woolf's problem, in her fiction as well as her thinking about auto/biography, is to imagine alternative forms for that experience. As in the passage about the *DNB*, this needs to be done *against* the prevailing modes of representation. After all, if the *DNB* is likely to be wrong even about 'The true length of a person's life'—the span between the markers that might seem the least negotiable: of birth and death—then how can the biographer be trusted to represent what happens during that life? *Orlando* combines the telling of a biographical story with a recurrent unease with biographical conventions. For example, the narrator tells of Orlando's habit of lying under his favourite oak tree. He describes the changes in the landscape, but then continues:

but probably the reader can imagine the passage which should follow and how every tree and plant in the neighbourhood is described first green, then golden; how moons rise and

---

[24] *Orlando*, p. 291.
[25] Woolf, 'The Art of Biography' (1939), *The Death of the Moth and Other Essays* (London: The Hogarth Press, 1942), pp. 119–26 (p. 124).

suns set; how spring follows winter and autumn summer [. . .] a conclusion which, one cannot help feeling, might have been reached more quickly by the simple statement that 'Time passed' (here the exact amount could be indicated in brackets) and nothing whatever happened.[26]

Rachel Bowlby's note to this passage in her valuable Oxford World's Classics edition calls this a self-parody of the 'Time Passes' section of *To the Lighthouse*, written immediately before *Orlando*. It's a shrewd connection. But self-parody; or self-reference? Part of the point of 'Time Passes' is to show that even down those passages of time in which biographers or novelists might say 'nothing whatever happened', something always is happening. Time passes. What both passages show is that you cannot merely write 'Time passed', because that's not how we experience experience. As Bowlby's note adds, 'In the manuscript, it is followed by a passage on the impossibility of biographical comprehensiveness.'[27]

Orlando is full of such metabiographical fantasias on how to write life-time. Conventional notions of chronology are presented as absurdly inadequate in various passages, some of which explicitly discuss the 'method of writing biography', in one case by merely counting off the months of a year.[28] Instead of this calendar method, and instead of attempting biographical comprehensiveness, she offers a classic modernist account of *duration* (drawing upon Bergson's and Proust's exploration of the subjective experience of time): 'It would be no exaggeration to say that he would go out after breakfast a man of thirty and come home to dinner a man of fifty-five at least.'[29] She combines it with other classic modernist tropes: of the multiplicity of subjectivity (perhaps drawing on the psychoanalytic model of the self as a composite personality); on the co-existence of different times within the mind (drawing again perhaps on psycho-analysis—the unconscious is no respecter of the calendar either—or perhaps on the narrative experiments in the 'time-shift' of Conrad or Ford). But out of these possible influences she makes something new: the idea of 'the sixty or seventy different times which beat simultaneously in every normal human system'. And she uses this idea of temporal multiplicity to 'dispute' the authority of an establishment publication such as the *DNB*, and along with it the authority of the patriarchy and her own familial patriarch. It certainly seems reasonable to read this as mockery of the established tradition of official, pious, 'authorized' biography. But (unless you find the notion of 'sixty or seventy different times which beat simultaneously in every normal human system' ridiculous) it doesn't seem to be 'parody', or to be making fun of the biographer-narrator. Or at least, if there is an element of mockery of his style and pomposity—'it cannot be denied that the most successful practitioners of the art of life, often unknown people by the way'—the *ideas* he is advocating seem close to the ideas Woolf

---

[26] *Orlando*, p. 94.   [27] Ibid., p. 324.
[28] Ibid., p. 254.   [29] Ibid., pp. 95–6.

herself expresses elsewhere. That one is the rationale for recovering what she called 'The Lives of the Obscure' (of which, more anon). Or take the remark that 'This extraordinary discrepancy between time on the clock and time in the mind is less known than it should be and deserves fuller investigation.'[30] There is perhaps a parody of a tone there—the tone of patriarchal rationalism, confident it will be able to make known what in fact it has done its best to repress. But again, the idea being expressed is fundamental to Woolf's aesthetic.

If we juxtapose these with some of the many passages that are clearly mocking biographical conventions the problem is more evident. Take for example a passage expressing frustration that Orlando has to be portrayed as thinking. Part of the problem is, as the narrator puts it, in rather Sterne fashion, that 'Orlando is a woman, but won't slip off her petticoat and —.'[31] By thinking, Orlando is transgressing gender stereotypes. But she also poses a problem common to literary biographies of how to represent thinking or writing, in a life where these activities predominate over passions and action: 'If, then, the subject of one's biography will neither love nor kill, but will only think and imagine, we may conclude that he or she is no better than a corpse and so leave her.'[32] '[W]e may conclude' is clearly ironic: Woolf wants us to avoid such gender stereotyping that closes our minds. '[N]o better than a corpse' is more disturbing, however, in the way it appears in excess of conventional disparagement of the creative or contemplative life. Historians may traditionally have valued men of action or women of passion, but not have gone so far as to leave artists for dead. There is perhaps a playful suggestion that the biographer is fetishizing the dynamism of his subject. Or is it a note of irony or self-parody? And if so, is it on the part of the fictional biographer, or Woolf? While accepting that such distinctions may be of the kind that *Orlando* is expressly designed to outflank—not least because of the difficulty of deciding whether Woolf is granting the narrator self-awareness, or merely letting the mask slip—the questions bring out two subtleties that don't tend to get noticed. First, that rather than (or even in addition to) parodying a stupid biographer, she might be impersonating a self-aware, ironic one. I shall say more soon about why she might want to attempt this, but first, let's consider the second subtlety, which becomes more evident if we go further back towards Orlando's earlier years:

the wild and the weeds even had always a fascination for him.

Here, indeed, we lay bare rudely, as a biography may, a curious trait in him, to be accounted for, perhaps, by the fact that a certain grandmother of his had worn a smock and carried milkpails [. . .] Certain it is that he had always a liking for low company [. . .][33]

---

[30] *Orlando*, p. 95.   [31] Ibid., p. 257.
[32] Ibid.   [33] Ibid., p. 27.

As in most of the sentences of this agile book, there is much going on. Vita Sackville-West's pride in her bohemian ancestry is gently mocked: she was compounded of opposites: part noble respectable family, part gypsy ancestry. Yet, as Rachel Bowlby explains, Vita's grandmother was an 'internationally famous Spanish dancer called Pepita', who became involved with her grandfather, Lionel, the second Baron Sackville. (This history is given a parodic glance when one of the charges brought against Orlando when she returns to England is 'that she was an English Duke who had married one Rosina Pepita, a dancer'.)[34] When Lionel became Ambassador to the United States, Victoria, their illegitimate daughter, who had been brought up in the south of France, was taken to America to act as society hostess for her father.[35] Victoria later married her cousin, another Lionel, and the heir to the stately home Knole in Sevenoaks, Kent. If her life involved milkpails and smocks, it must have been in the sense that Marie Antoinette's involved tending sheep.

The teasing goes further, both suggesting that Orlando likes a bit of rough ('low company'), and parodying the patronizing or snobbish reaction of readers supposed to be shocked (in a titillated sort of way) by the revelation. This could be taken as parody of biographic salaciousness posing as circumspection. But the language points elsewhere. '[T]he wild and the weeds even' has an archaic ring, as does the adverb 'rudely', and the phrase 'Certain it is'. So, perhaps, does the trope of the smock and milkpails. The point here is that, as in much of *Orlando*, the vocabulary and phrases and cadences seem to mimic those of the period Woolf is narrating—the period of John Aubrey's *Brief Lives*, say. As Kathryn Miles argues, 'As we follow Orlando from the Elizabethan age to the height of modernism, it becomes clear that we are also following the evolution of biography through these ages as well.'[36] In particular, Woolf gets this effect by mimicking the *biographical* style— 'biographese'—of different periods; or by showing how the biographese of a period is inflected by that period's other mannerisms and preoccupations. Thus, for example, Orlando the Renaissance man is narrated in a Renaissance manner:

For though these are not matters on which a biographer can profitably enlarge it is plain enough to those who have done a reader's part in making up from bare hints dropped here and there the whole boundary and circumference of a living person [...] that Orlando was strangely compounded of many humours—of melancholy, of indolence, of passion, of love of solitude [...][37]

---

[34] Ibid., p. 161.

[35] Bowlby, 'Introduction', pp. xx–xxi.

[36] Kathryn Miles, '"That perpetual marriage of granite and rainbow": Searching for "The New Biography" in Virginia Woolf's Orlando', *Virginia Woolf and Communities*, ed. Jeanette McVicker and Laura Davis (New York: Pace University Press, 1999), pp. 212–18 (p. 213).

[37] *Orlando*, pp. 70–1.

Among the voices strangely and parodically compounded here are those of writers such as Thomas Browne and Robert Burton. If it is a reader's part to make up a living person from verbal 'bare hints', it is a writer's part to have made up the hints. 'Have I made you up?' Woolf was to ask Sackville-West when she had finished the book.[38] The pun on 'making up' is crucial, not just for its hint of applying make-up for a performance, or gender masquerade, but for the hesitation between composing and fabricating or fantasizing. Orlando 'was a nobleman afflicted with a love of literature'; 'It was the fatal nature of this disease to substitute a phantom for reality',[39] which is a way of saying that his reading turns into a desire to write. But he pauses just as he's about to start writing: 'As this pause was of extreme significance in his history, more so, indeed, than many acts which bring men to their knees and make rivers run with blood, it behoves us to ask why he paused.'[40] The answer is another of the narrator's 'marvellously contorted cogitations' in the manner of Sir Thomas Browne.[41] A four-page rumination on memory: how it shows Orlando first a vision of his lost princess, then of the succession of his heroic military ancestors; all of which determines him to achieve immortality by writing. To transcend the whole boundary and circumference of a living person.

One of the most intriguing examples comes when Orlando reaches the Victorian age. In a bizarre paraphrase of Ruskin's 'The Storm-Cloud of the Nineteenth Century' (1884), Woolf elaborates the fantasy of a historical period being represented in terms of climate-change: 'The great cloud which hung, not only over London, but over the whole of the British Isles on the first day of the nineteenth century stayed, or rather, did not stay [...] A change seemed to have come over the climate of England.'[42]

But whereas Ruskin's is clearly a metaphor for industrialization and the social tensions it has produced, Woolf's is metaphysical: a change in the mental and moral climate. Woolf uses the image of dampness to characterize the Victorian age; a dampness which is transcendental, moral, and linguistic:

The damp struck within. Men felt the chill in their hearts; the damp in their minds. In a desperate effort to snuggle their feelings into some sort of warmth one subterfuge was tried after another. Love, birth, and death were all swaddled in a variety of fine phrases [...] Thus the British Empire came into existence; and thus—for there is no stopping damp; it gets into the inkpot as it gets into the woodwork—sentences swelled, adjectives multiplied, lyrics became epics, and little

---

[38] Woolf to Vita Sackville-West [20? March 1928]: *A Change of Perspective: The Letters of Virginia Woolf*, vol. 3, ed. Nigel Nicolson and Joanne Trautmann (London: Hogarth Press, 1977), p. 474.
[39] *Orlando*, p. 71.   [40] Ibid., p. 75.
[41] Ibid., p. 70.   [42] Ibid., p. 217.

trifles that had been essays a column long were now encyclopaedias in ten or twenty volumes.[43]

Or multi-volume reference works like the *Dictionary of National Biography*, perhaps? As Bowlby argues, Woolf is here mocking the modes in which ages are represented, and in particular 'the theory of climatic determination'[44]—the Tainean notion of how literature is shaped by 'milieu'. What is being parodied here is thus not only the nineteenth century's view of itself (or at least Ruskin's influential view of it), but its way of conceptualizing and articulating that view. As before, there is a serious critique: of imperialism as a form of moral deterioration, complicit in the subjection of women; and a serious critique of how such moral aporia seep into the language, fostering euphemism and prolixity. In comparable ways *Orlando* parodies not just a *single* mode of biographical or historical writing, but just about every mode from the Renaissance to the twentieth century. Jacob Flanders has a shock of awareness aged twenty, of 'the obstinate irrepressible conviction which makes youth so intolerably disagreeable—"I am what I am, and intend to be it", for which there will be no form in the world unless Jacob makes one for himself.'[45] This suggests that what Woolf really wants to dislodge is biography's arrogant assumption that it can find the form in someone else's life; a form that only the subject can make for herself or himself. That feeling, combined with a resistance to the idea of how she might herself be portrayed as a biographical subject, came to the fore in September 1927, as she was about to begin *Orlando*, and was looking back to her depression of the previous year: 'No biographer could possibly guess this important fact about my life in the late summer of 1926; yet biographers pretend they know people.'[46] *Flush*, too, was prompted by Woolf's anxieties about what biography might do to her own literary reputation, as first E. M. Forster then Harold Nicolson were approached to write a book about her.[47] Both her biographical fantasy fictions thus originate in auto/biografiction, seeking to pre-empt her own crystallization as a biographical subject.

Whatever else Orlando's last cry—'The wild goose!'—at the end may represent, it implies biography is always a wild goose chase. In some ways this is how *Orlando* works: in each period the style morphs into the cadences of that period. Another way of expressing the implications of this device is to say that the figure of the biographer himself becomes subject to the same kind of temporal and personal complications as Orlando. It isn't only Orlando, but the narrator, who

---

[43] Ibid., p. 219.

[44] Bowlby, 'Introduction', p. xxxii.

[45] *Jacob's Room*, p. 44.

[46] Entry for 4 September 1927, *The Diary of Virginia Woolf*, vol. 3, ed. Anne Olivier Bell, assisted by Andrew McNeillie (London: The Hogarth Press, 1980), p. 153. See Lyndall Gordon, *Virginia Woolf: A Writer's Life* (Oxford: Oxford University Press, 1986), p. 203.

[47] See Snaith, 'Of Fanciers, Footnotes, and Fascism: Virginia Woolf's *Flush*', pp. 616–17.

becomes a composite portrait, in this case of biographers from the Renaissance to the twentieth century. Woolf does for biography what Joyce in *Ulysses* had done for prose fiction, parodying its development through epic, romance, and the novel. According to this view, the narrator too has Orlando's extraordinary longevity and multiplicity of personae. (To the extent that he is also a persona for Woolf, he is another version of gender-bending, too.)

In an important letter to Clive Bell, she makes a vertiginous transition from meeting Noel Coward at lunch, to reading Michelet. It prompts a question:

Does it strike you that history is one of the most fantastic concoctions of the human brain? That it bears the remotest likeness to the truth seems to me unthinkable. Consider the character of Louis 14th. Incredible. And those wars—unthinkable. Ought it not all to be re-written instantly? Yet he fascinates me.[48]

In *Orlando* she takes on the historical sweep of Michelet's massive nineteen-volume *Histoire de France* (1867), using the fantastic concoction of Orlando to bring out the fantastic concoctions of historiography and biography.

In this respect what Woolf is doing is continuous with the transformations of auto/biography discussed in earlier chapters. She is developing the turn-of-the-century awareness that the conventions of biography (like history) are beginning to seem absurd: that as soon as they begin to become visible *as* conventions, they can no longer do their work of transparently creating the impression of authority and objectivity. That argument was perhaps in danger of posing 'biography' as a monolithic, timeless entity. Whereas of course biography has a history. It responds to other literary developments. This is one of the stories *Orlando* tells. It had also been told, in the previous year, by Vita's husband Harold Nicolson, in his book *The Development of English Biography* (1927). It seemed particularly important to grasp the changing nature of biography at this time, because it was a time when biography (like autobiography) was itself changing dramatically.

'THE NEW BIOGRAPHY', BLOOMSBURY, AND FREUD[49]

Woolf, Nicolson, and the Bloomsbury group were at the centre of the 'New Biography'—so much so that the concept has a tinge of Bloomsbury mutual admiration. Woolf's complex involvement in it—as critic, biographer, novelist, diarist, letter-writer—is in part, as I have suggested, a reaction against her father, the historian of ideas, editor and biographer Leslie Stephen (1832–1904). Stephen had himself written literary biographies of Samuel Johnson (1878),

---

[48] Woolf to Clive Bell, 31 January 1928: *A Change of Perspective: The Letters of Virginia Woolf*, vol. 3, p. 454.

[49] Some paragraphs from this section have been revised from my chapter on 'Biography and Autobiography', *Cambridge History of Twentieth-Century English Literature*, ed. Laura Marcus and Peter Nicholls (Cambridge: Cambridge University Press, 2004), pp. 286–303.

Pope (1880), Swift (1882), Hobbes (1904) and—surprisingly, given that it appears in the same series of 'English Men of Letters'—George Eliot (1902). The *DNB* was not only a Victorian institution, but (despite Stephen's agnosticism) might be considered the biographical wing of the Establishment: an enterprise dedicated to defining nationality and national history in terms of the 'lives of great men'. Yet Sidney Lee, to whom the editorship of the *DNB* passed in 1891, himself noted how Edwardian biography had evolved from its Victorian predecessors. In his book *Principles of Biography* (1911) he wrote: 'The aim of biography is not the moral edification which may flow from the survey of either vice or virtue; it is the truthful transmission of personality.' Woolf quoted this comment at the beginning of her essay 'The New Biography' (1927).[50] And she had read the book when it came out in 1911.[51] So her playfully absurd claim that 'on or about December 1910 human character changed', besides being understood in terms of the end of the Edwardian era, or the mounting of the first Post-Impressionist exhibition in London, should perhaps also be read as reflecting a new concept of the character of biography as well as fiction.[52]

Like the 'New Woman' in the period, 'The New Biography' kept getting newer. If biography had *already* changed by 1910–11, it was to change further thanks largely to the work of the Bloomsbury Group. The first Post-Impressionist show had included portraits by Cézanne, Gaugin, Manet, Picasso, Matisse, and Van Gogh. It was organized by Roger Fry, and his own portraits, which together with those of his fellow Bloomsbury artists Vanessa Bell and Duncan Grant were heavily derivative of the continental work, have been described as 'Essays in Biography'; part of the modernist renegotiation of how to represent the subject.[53]

When Woolf wrote of 'The New Biography', however, it was Bloomsbury writing she had in mind. The essay was a review of another book by Harold Nicolson—of whom more soon—the author of many biographies and diaries. Vita Sackville-West herself wrote biography as well as novels. Her book about her family and its stately home, *Knole and the Sackvilles*, appeared in 1922, and was followed by two books of saints' lives: *Saint Joan of Arc* (1936) and *The Eagle and the Dove: St. Teresa of Avila, St. Thérèse of Lisieux* (1943). Bloomsbury's other major novelist besides Woolf, E. M. Forster, wrote a life of the Cambridge political

---

[50] Cited in *The Essays of Virginia Woolf*, vol. 4, pp. 473, 479 n. 2.

[51] Woolf, Letter to Sidney Lee, 29 July 1911: *The Flight of the Mind: The Letters of Virginia Woolf*: Vol. 1: *1888–1912*, ed. Nigel Nicolson (London: Chatto & Windus, 1975), p. 473.

[52] Woolf, 'Character in Fiction' (1924; an expanded version of 'Mr Bennett and Mrs Brown'), *The Essays of Virginia Woolf*, vol. 3, ed. Andrew McNeillie (London: The Hogarth Press, 1988), pp. 420–38 (p. 421). Edward VII had died on 6 May. The exhibition was open from 8 November 1910 to 15 January 1911. Samuel Hynes, *The Edwardian Turn of Mind* (Princeton: Princeton University Press, 1975), pp. 325–6.

[53] Richard Shone, *The Art of Bloomsbury: Roger Fry, Vanessa Bell and Duncan Grant* (London: Tate Gallery Publishing, 1999), p. 93.

scientist Goldsworthy Lowes Dickinson (1934); one of his great-aunt, *Marianne Thornton: A Domestic Biography* (1956); as well as various biographical essays.[54]

But it was Lytton Strachey who was the chief Bloomsbury practitioner of 'The New Biography'. His landmark volume *Eminent Victorians* had appeared in May 1918, during the last year of the war, and, as Laura Marcus says, was perceived as 'the first book of post-war England.'[55] John Sutherland has placed it 'among that small corpus of books which have changed the genre to which they belong.'[56] It is also itself the most eminent portrait collection of twentieth-century prose. Its four studies, of varying lengths, of Cardinal Manning, Florence Nightingale, Dr Arnold, and General Gordon, form a panoply of what we might now call, with an irony made possible largely thanks to Strachey, as the great and the good; representatives of key Victorian professions: the Church; medicine; education; the Army. Nineteenth-century official biographies of such figures frequently ran into multiple volumes to provide 'moral edification'. As Strachey laments in his 'Preface':

Those two fat volumes, with which it is our custom to commemorate the dead—who does not know them, with their ill-digested masses of material, their slipshod style, their tone of tedious panegyric, their lamentable lack of selection, of detachment, of design? They are as familiar as the *cortège* of the undertaker, and wear the same air of slow, funereal barbarism.[57]

'The art of biography seems to have fallen on evil times in England', he argues. In part the New Biography was an attempt to foster the kind of 'great biographical tradition' that he saw in French literature. 'We have had, it is true, a few master-pieces'; but 'we have had no Fontenelles and Condorcets, with their incomparable *éloges*, compressing into a few shining pages the manifold existences of men.'[58] Strachey's lives were certainly brief: Thomas Arnold gets a mere twenty-five pages in *Eminent Victorians*; and Strachey went on to produce three volumes of what he called 'Characters', or *Portraits in Miniature*. As he explains, he is abandoning 'the direct method of a scrupulous narration' in favour of 'a subtler strategy', which privileges 'a becoming brevity—a brevity which excludes everything that is redundant and nothing that is significant' (his critics have complained that he abandoned other scruples as well, including that of accurate narration).[59] Biography, that is,

---

[54] See *Abinger Harvest* (London: Edward Arnold and Co., 1936) and *Two Cheers for Democracy* (London: Edward Arnold and Co., 1951). Saunders, 'Forster's Life and Life-writing', *The Cambridge Companion to E. M. Forster*, ed. David Bradshaw (Cambridge: Cambridge University Press, 2007), pp. 8–31.

[55] Marcus, *Auto/biographical Discourses* (Manchester University Press, 1994), p. 115.

[56] *Eminent Victorians*, ed. Sutherland, World's Classics (Oxford: Oxford University Press, 2003), p. vii.

[57] *Eminent Victorians* (Harmondsworth: Penguin, 1986), p. 10.

[58] Ibid., p. 10.

[59] Ibid., pp. 9, 10. For the criticisms, see, for example, the annotations to the Oxford World's Classics text, ed. John Sutherland.

was to be reconfigured according to modernist aesthetics. In transforming it from tedious barbarism to an art, he would adopt the methods of modern fiction—selection; obliqueness; indirection—in the name of that 'significant form' that Clive Bell had argued, in his equally iconoclastic 1914 treatise *Art*, was 'the quality shared by all objects that provoke our aesthetic emotions.'[60]

Strachey's strategy was not directed only against biographers, however, but against his subjects. He wrote from what he called 'a slightly cynical point of view.'[61] But as he continues his military metaphors in the 'Preface', readers might wonder whether the cynicism didn't go deeper:

> He will attack his subject in unexpected places; he will fall upon the flank, or the rear; he will shoot a sudden, revealing searchlight into obscure recesses, hitherto undivined. He will row over that great ocean of material, and lower down into it, here and there, a little bucket, which will bring up to the light of day some characteristic specimen, from those far depths, to be examined with a careful curiosity.[62]

Strachey was one of the pioneers Nicolson had in mind when he argued that 'the main element in twentieth-century biography' was a 'peculiar brand of sceptical detachment.'[63] The point of the biographer's detachment—like the impersonality of the modernist artist—is to ironize the subject, while expressing (as here) the artist's personality. (Like other Bloomsbury biographers, Strachey only intermittently wrote on artists.) He pulls his pillars of the community down to the depths, where they seem as bizarre as the life-forms studied by marine biologists. The main effect, as is often said of Strachey, is to 'debunk'. In 1916 Henry Ford had famously said, more or less, that History was bunk (what he actually said was that 'History is more or less bunk')—abbreviated from 'bunkum', or nonsense. Strachey was to imply that biography was more or less bunk too, at least in its Victorian hero-worship mode. The first instance of the word 'debunk' given in the *Oxford English Dictionary* is from 1923, which suggests not only a post-war slang but a post-war attitude.

Eminent Victorians certainly cuts its subjects down to size. Manning emerges as an ambitious Machiavellian. Strachey puts aside the 'popular conception' of Nightingale as 'the Lady of the Lamp', and presents instead someone driven by a 'Demon', a manipulative neurotic. Arnold, the earnest advocate of religion and athletics in education, is mocked for having perverted the educational system into 'the worship of athletics and the worship of good form.'[64] The essay on 'The End of General Gordon' again takes apart the popular conception of the heroic imperialist to reveal him as 'a little off his head, perhaps'; a man obsessed with his

---

[60] Clive Bell, *Art*, ed. J. B. Bullen (Oxford: Oxford University Press, 1987), p. 8.
[61] Letter to Ottoline Morrell, 17 October 1912: quoted in Michael Holroyd, Introduction to *Eminent Victorians* (Harmondsworth: Penguin, 1986), p. viii.
[62] *Eminent Victorians* (Harmondsworth: Penguin, 1986), p. 9.
[63] *The Development of English Biography* (London: The Hogarth Press, 1927), pp. 134–5.
[64] *Eminent Victorians* (Harmondsworth: Penguin, 1986), p. 187.

own fame, and instrumental in the bloodthirstiness of 'a glorious slaughter of 20,000 Arabs.'[65] All four subjects are represented mischievously as being fanatical, ambitious, and misguided. As Cyril Connolly saw, *Eminent Victorians* is 'a revolutionary textbook on bourgeois society written in the language through which the bourgeois ear could be lulled and beguiled, the Mandarin style'; and he called it 'the work of a great anarch.'[66] Strachey followed it with a biography of the most eminent Victorian of all, *Queen Victoria* (1921), in which he played with nineteenth-century conventions of romantic fiction and melodrama. His last book, *Elizabeth and Essex* (1928), is another experimental work, combining the structure of an Elizabethan drama with Freudian ideas.

Psychoanalysis was of course a major influence on human character's changing representations. Again Bloomsbury is central to the story of the impact of Freudian ideas on British culture, and to their impact upon biographical and autobiographical writing. The Hogarth Press, which had been founded in 1917 by Leonard and Virginia Woolf, published the papers of the International Psycho-Analytical Institute from 1924, thereby becoming the authorized British publisher for Sigmund Freud (mainly in translations by Strachey's brother and sister-in-law, James and Alix), and making psychoanalytic theory available to English readers.[67] Freud's concepts of the unconscious, the repression of sexual wishes, neurosis, dream, fantasy, delusion, and the Oedipus complex, were all rapidly taken up, with varying degrees of scepticism, by novelists and poets such as D. H. Lawrence, May Sinclair, and W. H. Auden. Freud's own narrative forms offered possible models, too, especially to life-writers. His 'Case Histories' are more clinical and theoretical than Strachey's, but they are biographical studies proceeding by the criteria Strachey was to borrow: exploring the 'unexpected places' and 'obscure recesses, hitherto undivined'. *The Interpretation of Dreams* is, besides a masterpiece of theory, an oblique autobiography, or perhaps an inverted autobiography. Whereas autobiographers traditionally take the material of a life and seek a form or pattern with which to interpret it, Freud begins with the concept of interpretation, and seeks the material from his life that will substantiate it.

Strachey's method owed something to the work of the pioneering British sexologist Havelock Ellis; since, according to Ellis's editor J. S. Collis, 'It may well be owing to [him] that it is at last recognized that weakness is the very hall-mark of genius, for it provides the point of least resistance in human nature through which the force of Nature may enter the human world.' Collis argues that after the example of Ellis's psychological biographical studies of figures such as Nietzsche and Casanova in his 1898 collection *Affirmations*, 'Biographers now realize that while exposing the weaknesses of great men they are not therefore called upon to despise

---

[65] *Eminent Victorians* (Harmondsworth: Penguin, 1986), p. 266.
[66] Quoted in ibid., p. xi.
[67] See *Bloomsbury/Freud: The Letters of James and Alix Strachey 1924–25*, ed. Perry Meisel and Walter Kendrick (New York: Basic Books, 1985).

them.'[68] Edmund Gosse agreed, arguing (in 1911; the same year Sidney Lee's *Principles of Biography* came out) that where modern biography sought to understand 'genius' (which he thought was the only legitimate survival of an earlier tradition of narrating lives as moral examples), the biographer should be careful not to 'glose over frailties or obscure irregularities.'[69] Strachey's thrust is that his Victorians aren't great figures; merely 'eminent' ones, and he reserves the right to deprecate if not to despise them. Ellis's method is certainly Strachey's too: to posit personal 'demons' of a morally dubious and unsavoury nature that drive figures to attain heights of public heroism and moral exemplariness. In a sense, the tension in Ellis's writing between showing up the hidden abnormalities, then being tolerant towards them, is the source of Strachey's irony. In his case, though, it is a kind of revenge for society's intolerance of homosexuality—showing that the official moral heroes have more disturbing skeletons in their closets.

It wasn't until after the Second World War that biographers began to adopt the Freudian vision of the centrality of sexuality to the 'personality' of their subjects. But if the New Biography didn't quite constitute the tradition Strachey desired, it did produce a new enthusiasm for the form. As Laura Marcus argues, 'The rise in popularity of biographies was linked to the perception that biography had been reinvented for the twentieth century, requiring a new level of critical self-awareness'; and she quotes Hesketh Pearson, saying in 1930: 'It is the day of the biographer'; and Lord David Cecil, arguing in 1936 that biography was 'the only new form' of modern literature.[70] These comments may look not just self-aggrandizing, coming from two biographers, but silly now, coming from the era witnessing the profound innovations of Lawrence, Joyce, Eliot, Woolf, Pound, Auden, Orwell, Greene, and Brecht. But it wasn't only biographers who noticed the phenomenon. Ford Madox Ford wrote, in a book on *The English Novel*, written in the same year *Orlando* was published: 'That the republic—the body politic—has need of these human-filtered insights into lives is amply proved by the present vogue of what I will call novelized biography.'[71] He was certainly right about the vogue. The success of Emil Ludwig's *biographies romancées* or André Maurois's *vies romancées* is indicative; as is Ernest Boyd's identification four years later of what he called '"modern" biographies, "novelized" lives.'[72]

---

[68] J. S. Collis, 'Introduction' to Havelock Ellis, *Selected Essays* (London: Dent, 1936), pp. viii–ix.

[69] Edmund Gosse, 'Biography', *Encyclopedia Britannica*, 11th edn (Cambridge: Cambridge University Press, 1911) Volume 3, p. 954.

[70] Marcus, 'The Newness of the "New Biography"', in *Mapping Lives: The Uses of Biography*, ed. Peter France (Oxford: Oxford University Press, 2002), pp. 193–218 (pp. 193–4).

[71] Ford, *The English Novel* (Philadelphia: J. B. Lippincott, 1929), p. 20.

[72] Ernest Boyd, from 'Sex in Biography', *Harper's Magazine*, November 1932, 753–6; quoted in James L. Clifford, ed., *Biography as an Art: Selected Criticism, 1560–1960* (London: Oxford University Press, 1962), p. 141. See David Gervais, 'Stories of Real Life', *Cambridge Quarterly*, 9:1 (1979), 56–64 (p. 62), objecting to Maurois' 'false imaginativeness'. Sartre's biography of Flaubert, which he described as a 'roman vrai' (a true novel) might be seen as developing this line: Sartre, 'Sur *L'Idiot de la famille*', *Situations*, X (Paris: Gallimard, 1976), p. 94.

As the New Biography responded to modernist experiments, so the modernists were reacting against biography in turn (and against Bloomsbury, some of them); and not just its Victorian forms, but the New Biography too. This sense of a renaissance of the literature of personality was one factor leading Eliot to write (in the year following *Eminent Victorians*): 'Poetry is . . . not the expression of personality, but an escape from personality.'[73] The New Biography thus catalysed a new and substantial challenge to the idea of biography, which had a profound effect on creative writers, critics, and teachers. Where a Victorian or Edwardian person of letters would be expected to produce biographies as part of an oeuvre, authors like Joyce, Eliot, or Wyndham Lewis did not. Nor did the New Critics. Biography seemed irrelevant to literary studies; a survival from a belletristic age. This meant both that modernist writers were (as we might now say) 'in denial' of the biographic; and also that their critics were in denial that the modernists had enough investment in the biographic to be in denial of it. Yet, as we have seen, life-writing is central to modernism, in ways that have only recently begun to be appreciated. This is particularly true of the autobiographic. But we should note here that several writers allied with modernism wrote biographically too: not only Woolf and Forster, but also Ford (*Ford Madox Brown*; *Joseph Conrad*; *Portraits from Life*), Ezra Pound (*Gaudier-Brzeska*), May Sinclair (*The Three Brontës*), and Richard Aldington (in biographies of both T. E. and D. H. Lawrence; of Norman Douglas and his friends; and of the Duke of Wellington).

Woolf was explicit about the impact of *Eminent Victorians*. In her essay on 'The Art of Biography', she wrote in 1939 that when Strachey had 'made his first attempt, biography, with its new liberties, was a form that offered great attractions.'[74] These were attractions for a novelist as well as a biographer. Much of her subsequent work would engage with Strachey's novelization of biography; his experiments with the portrait collection; and his ironic, whimsical tone—whether she was to apply them to her own family in *To the Lighthouse*; or to invert them in her musings on the non-eminent, in 'Lives of the Obscure'; or to mock them in *Orlando*.

I suggested earlier that the narrator of *Orlando* might not be as obtuse as he is often assumed to be, but that some of the text's irony might be hers. (After all, this narrative which begins by asserting of young Orlando that 'there could be no doubt of his sex, though the fashion of the time did something to disguise it', is narrated by someone whose sex is never asserted, though s/he assumes the garb of patriarchal authority.)[75] This possibility of the narrator's being ironic arose again apropos the passage about nineteenth-century dampness, since there (as in the idea of damp getting into the inkpot as well as the woodwork) the language

[73] Eliot, 'Tradition and the Individual Talent' (1919), *Selected Essays*, 3rd enlarged edn (London: Faber and Faber, 1951), pp. 13–22 (p. 21).
[74] Woolf, 'The Art of Biography', *The Death of the Moth and Other Essays*, p. 121.
[75] See Bowlby, 'Introduction', p. xii.

becomes too metaphorical for us to be sure the narrator isn't making fun of the period.

The biographer of the early twentieth century best known for irony was of course Strachey. When *Orlando*'s narrator sounds ironic or parodic, then, it is possible that besides mocking Victorian notions of biography Woolf is also hinting at a pastiche, or even a gentle parody, of Strachey's celebrated 'debunking' of the same notions. Woolf said of *Flush* as she was working on it: 'I meant it for a joke with Lytton, and a skit on him.'[76] Could not her other great mock-biography of only four years earlier have equally been a joke with, and a skit on, Strachey—who like Orlando could move effortlessly between the time of *Elizabeth and Essex* (1928) and *Queen Victoria* (1921) whose sexuality was no less transgressive? Or perhaps it's also a pastiche of Strachey's mockery of Victorian notions; pushing his *jeux d'esprit* and caprices a little further, to the point where biography turns into something else: rhetoric, fantasy, imagination.

Woolf appears not to have read *Elizabeth and Essex* until November 1928, a month after *Orlando* was published. She found it 'a poor book' and associated her response with a change in her feelings towards Strachey: 'I kept thinking: well, if he can palm that off on us after years of effort—that lively superficial meretricious book.'[77] Although *Orlando* cannot be a response to *Elizabeth and Essex*, she certainly knew he was working on it while she was finishing *Orlando*. She told Clive Bell: 'I have every reason to suppose that his Elizabeth [and Essex] is a masterpiece.' But she gives us every reason to suspect at least irony, not only by adding: 'I have every reason to suppose that my own judgement is vitiated. I have been writing to Max Beerbohm [. . .]', but also because of the way she asks Bell about 'Lytton's articles', saying: 'I can't get into the skip of them. But they enchant the fashionables.'[78] These were the essays on the four historians, Macaulay, Hume, Gibbon, and Carlyle, later collected in *Portraits in Miniature and Other Essays* (1932). Yet she admired the volume as a whole—another portrait-collection:

Lytton's book: very good. That's his line. The compressed yet glowing account which requires logic, reason, learning, taste, wit order & infinite skill—this suits him far better, I think than the larger scale, needing boldness, originality, sweep.[79]

Most of the essays of *Portraits in Miniature* are compressed into ten or so pages apiece. She probably meant this scale suited him better than the full-length study

---

[76] Woolf to John Lehmann, 31 July 1932, *The Sickle Side of the Moon: The Letters of Virginia Woolf*, vol. 5, ed. Nigel Nicolson (London: Chatto & Windus, 1982), p. 83.

[77] *The Diary of Virginia Woolf*, vol. 3, p. 208.

[78] Woolf to Clive Bell, 31 January 1928: *A Change of Perspective: The Letters of Virginia Woolf*, vol. 3, p. 454.

[79] Entry for Tuesday 19 May (1931), *The Diary of Virginia Woolf*, vol. 4, ed. Anne Olivier Bell and Andrew McNeillie (London: The Hogarth Press, 1982), p. 26.

of *Elizabeth and Essex*. But she may also have been thinking of the boldness, originality, and sweep of the larger scale of *Orlando*.

In her own volume of essays, *The Common Reader*, which Woolf had dedicated to Strachey in 1925, she included two essays under the heading 'The Lives of the Obscure'. As Julia Briggs argued, 'One of the chief problems that Woolf confronted as a biographer was how to write the lives that the *Dictionary* had ignored, those lives of the obscure that remained unrecorded, that were lived out, unconsidered and unvalued, in the shadows.'[80] In a sense the 'Lives of the Obscure' are also a counter to Strachey: an attending to those not eminent enough to deserve his mockery. You couldn't get much less obscure than Vita Sackville-West, whether in terms of high society or literary celebrity; and *Orlando* is not a life of the obscure to that extent. There is a sense in which Orlando's life was previously unrecorded because s/he is fictional. But there is a more important way in which 'The Lives of the Obscure' anticipate *Orlando*:

It is one of the attractions of the unknown, their multitude, their vastness; for, instead of keeping their identity separate, as remarkable people do, they seem to merge into one another, their very boards and title-pages and frontispieces dissolving, and their innumerable pages melting into continuous years so that we can lie back and look up into the fine mist-like substance of countless lives, and pass unhindered from century to century, from life to life.[81]

Orlando is a remarkable person for not keeping his identity separate from hers, and for merging into different selves for different historical moments: for, precisely, passing 'unhindered from century to century, from life to life'. That is as much a part of *Orlando*'s boldness and originality and sweep. That idea of great historical sweep was something that was increasingly to preoccupy Woolf, culminating in the historical pageant of *Between the Acts*.

'THE NEW BIOGRAPHY' ESSAY AND *SOME PEOPLE*

The work that prompted her to analyse 'The New Biography' in 1927, just before she wrote *Orlando*, was not a biography; though its author, Harold Nicolson, was best known as a biographer.[82] Indeed, he has been seen as a pioneer in the stretching of biographical conventions. Richard Holmes explains how Nicolson 'demystified the lordly Poet Laureate in *Tennyson*, and wrote one of the pioneering studies of the

---

[80] Briggs, chapter on 'The Proper Writing of Lives', *Reading Virginia Woolf* (Edinburgh: Edinburgh University Press, 2006), p. 27.

[81] Woolf, 'The Lives of the Obscure', *The Common Reader* (London: The Hogarth Press, 1925), p. 149.

[82] For a recent biography, see Norman Rose, *Harold Nicolson* (London: Cape, 2005). Frank Kermode's review offers a critical account of both Nicolson's personality and his writing: 'A Very Smart Bedint', *London Review of Books*, 27:6 (17 March 2005), 15–16.

whole form in *The Development of English Biography*, in which Boswell is praised as a cinematographer.'[83] But the book Woolf was reviewing in 1927, *Some People*, is structured as a series of character sketches. These are all characters the narrator has known, and his story emerges as they are told in sequence. That is, the book fuses biography with autobiography. It also reads like fiction. As Holmes says, Nicolson 'described his early intimates [. . .] in the manner of Chekhovian short stories'. His aim, he said, was 'to put real people in imaginary situations, and imaginary people in real situations.'[84] Woolf picked out exactly this quality. Though she admired 'his method of writing about people and about himself as though they were at once real and imaginary', she was clearly unsettled by it. She told him 'how absolutely delightful' she thought it; and that it made her feel 'jealous' 'that all these things should have happened' to him instead of to her. She doesn't quite say she envied his literary talent; but she did write to him: 'I can't make out how you combine the advantages of fact and fiction as you do.'[85] Though this was presumably supposed to flatter him into thinking his skills were inscrutable even to such a sharp literary eye, in the review she wonders whether he had combined fact and fiction; or whether they weren't perhaps simply impossible to combine. In *Orlando*, she found ways of combining 'the advantages of fact' (rather than actual facts) with fiction that satisfied her. It was her unsettling reading of *Some People* that prompted her next experimental engagement with life-writing. The way she described that act of reading is a strikingly autobiographical account of how autobiography or auto-biografiction can provoke the kind of autobiographical questioning that produces further writing (equally autobiographical or autobiografictional) in its turn:

And also, for some reason I feel profoundly and mysteriously shy. What this arises from I have not yet discovered: some horror of the past no doubt: but I think it is a great tribute to a book when it makes one fumble in ones own inside.[86]

Some People consists of nine chapters. The first five concern Nicolson's education. 'Miss Plimsoll', about his and his brothers' governess, and 'J. D. Marstock', about a promising schoolfellow, cover his childhood. 'Lambert Orme' and 'The Marquis de Chaumont' are both writer-friends met at university. The central chapter, 'Jeanne de Hénaut', describes the Paris landlady who lodges young Englishmen studying for their examination for the Diplomatic Service.[87] This chapter is thus also the first of the sequence which completes the volume, detailing Nicolson's life as a diplomat. 'Titty' describes his senior, the memorably inept Nevile Titmarsh. 'Professor

---

[83] Richard Holmes, <http://sunsite.wits.ac.za/holistic/boswell.htm>.
Also see Harold Nicolson, 'The Practice of Biography', *American Scholar*, 23 (1954), 153–61.
[84] Nicolson, *Some People*, 'Introduction' by Nigel Nicolson (London: Constable, 1982), p. vii.
[85] Woolf to Nicolson, [15 June 1927]: *A Change of Perspective: The Letters of Virginia Woolf*, vol. 3, p. 392.
[86] Ibid.
[87] The Woolfs' Hogarth Press printed fifty-five copies of 'Jeanne de Henaut' as a separate pamphlet in 1924.

Malone' is an arrogant independent expert; 'Arketall' the alcoholic valet to Lord Curzon; and 'Miriam Codd' an American psychologist Nicolson meets en route to Tehran.

As Harold Nicolson's son Nigel explains in his introduction, all these characters had some basis in real people, though 'All of them are now forgotten except Ronald Firbank, the model for Lambert Orme, and Henry Wickham Steed who with Dr. D. J. Dillon posed for the composite portrait of Professor Malone.'[88] Harold Nicolson gave a complexly self-contradictory account to his parents of what he called his 'silly book', as he wondered whether it would cause offence:

The idea of the book is original. I take nine people and describe them in the manner I described Jeanne de Hénaut. You see, it is really an autobiography—only each person is made the centre of the picture and I only appear in the background. Most of the people are wholly imaginary, only real people and real incidents mix in with them. Everybody will be terribly puzzled as to who everybody else is, and there will be a great deal of identification going on. But as a matter of fact, they are all composite portraits except Jeanne who is of course drawn straight from life.[89]

These descriptions already suggest several versions of 'composite portrait': a portrait composed of more than one original; a composite of a real original with fictionalization; the juxtaposition of a real character with a fictionalized one. *Some People* is a composite portrait in another sense too—one common to this genre of portrait-galleries, as we have already seen. It is also a composite self-portrait, in that it outlines Nicolson's autobiography through his encounters with these others. Nigel Nicolson thought that:

He had discovered, as if by accident, an original way of stating a novel point of view. He had put into the book more of his philosophy than he realized when writing it. His allusive, self-mocking, pictorial style might, after all, be something more than a parody of Lytton Strachey and Max Beerbohm. It was a tone of voice which the recipient of any of his letters, and later his vast radio audience, would immediately recognize as his own.[90]

The claim for the originality of method is excessive here. What Nicolson is doing goes back to the late nineteenth-century experiments with life-writing discussed in Part I. In particular, Walter Pater's *Imaginary Portraits*, which appeared from 1878, seem to lie behind Nicolson's mixing of imaginary and real portraits and self portraits; his mixing of autobiography and biography, and of both with fiction.[91] It is also curious to think of *Some People* as a parody of Beerbohm, given Beerbohm's construction of *Seven Men* by parody. The New Biography, in other

---

[88] p. x. See James Lees-Milne, *Harold Nicolson: A Biography*, 2 vols (London: Chatto & Windus, 1980–3), for identifications of others.

[89] Nicolson, letter to his parents, 14 January 1927: *Diaries and Letters: 1907–1964*, ed. Nigel Nicolson (London: Weidenfeld and Nicolson, 2004), p. 50.

[90] *Some People*, pp. viii–ix.

[91] See *Some People*, pp. 34, 46, and 62 for references to Pater.

words, wasn't as new as all that. Indeed, in the context of our study, it begins to look less new in formal terms, and to be more a matter of a new mode of autobiografiction, with an ironic tone. Certainly Nicolson's patrician, somewhat supercilious tone does bear comparison with Strachey's. *Some People* can be read as an account of the achievement of that tone: the getting of wisdom that warrants the narrator's aloof superiority—which is perhaps why readers haven't shared Nicolson's view that he keeps himself in the background. The *Times Literary Supplement* reviewer characterized the book as 'part fiction, part biography, but most of all, autobiography.'[92] Nor did all its contemporary readers share in Bloomsbury's congratulation of itself. Nicolson's boss, Sir Percy Loraine, called *Some People* 'A cad's book.'[93] Yet Vladimir Nabokov proved an admirer, telling Nicolson that 'all his life he had been fighting against the influence of *Some People*, like a drug.'[94]

Nigel Nicolson also describes the book as primarily autobiographical. Its account of the education of an observer is more than a matter of the school-university-early-career outline given above:

In fact the book is a record of how the precocious Harold gradually grew up, how he rejected in turn Empire-worship (Miss Plimsoll), the public-school spirit (Marstock), self-conscious aestheticism (Orme), snobbishness (de Chaumont) bland affability (Titty), and arrogance (Malone) [. . .][95]

Few readers now are likely to be convinced that Nicolson managed entirely to reject any of these things. But otherwise, this gives a convincing account of the book's structure as a set of developmental phases; though, as Nigel Nicolson also shrewdly observes, his father omits sexual life from the book, and marriage to Sackville-West.

Much of the wit of *Some People* turns on the paradox of a realistic representation of unreal characters:

Of course I behaved caddishly towards Malone. It may be thought even that in publishing this story I am adding to my fault. But here you are wrong. Malone is not an individual but a type: the incidents recorded in this story are true incidents, but they didn't happen to Malone: had he been present, he would have behaved as I have made him behave. But he was not present. The incidents occurred without him, since Malone, except potentially, does not exist.[96]

This is more than an elegant insurance policy against possible libel actions, or accusations that he was violating the Foreign Office's 'Obligation of Secrecy.'[97] If the incidents were true, they must have happened to someone individual: or

---

[92] *Times Literary Supplement* (7 July 1927), 468. The *Times Literary Supplement* Centenary Archive identifies the anonymous reviewer as Marjorie Grant Cook.

[93] Gordon Waterfield, *Professional Diplomat: Sir Percy Loraine of Kirkharle Bt.* (London: John Murray, 1973), p. 116.

[94] See Lees-Milne, *Harold Nicolson: A Biography*, vol. 1, p. 310.

[95] *Some People*, p. xiii.

[96] Ibid., p. 120.

[97] Ibid., p. 123.

perhaps something comparable happened to more than one individual (if this part of 'Malone''s story is indebted to both Wickham Steed and Dillon). In that case, all that is being disclaimed is the name. It didn't happen to 'Malone', but nonetheless it did happen to someone real. And yet the language also equivocates between history and fiction. Is Nicolson merely recording and publishing, or is he making his characters behave the way they do?

The discourse of individuals and types is crucial to imaginary portraiture. Whereas representational art generally begins from real individuals and idealizes and generalizes from them, to produce a portrait more universally communicable, the imaginary portraitist begins with a type or idealization, and particularizes it by casting it in biographical form. (Indeed, one criticism that can be leveled against Pater's Imaginary Portraits is that they fail to get away from idealization and generality; are not adequately or convincingly individualized, except as spectres of their author.) This discourse forms an important strand in *Some People*, and is I take it one way in which the book could be said to offer a reflection on its world. Thus Nicolson begins 'J. D. Marstock' with a discussion of 'British education', saying that he is not one 'of those who thoroughly disbelieve' in it: 'It is true, of course, that it standardizes character and suppresses originality: that it somewhat ruthlessly subordinates the musical to the gymnastic. I am not convinced, however, that this is a bad thing.'[98] As the book progresses, though, it becomes less clear how unconvinced he is. Marstock is a study of someone taken by the schoolboy Nicolson as an admirable individual, following a path of outstanding success in school terms: 'head of the house, then captain of the XV, then school prefect and then head of the school.'[99] But Nicolson says it took him six years 'to realise that Marstock, although stuffed with opinions, had never had a thought at all.'[100] It is the idea of a head according to the school ethos: full of received opinion, but as far as originality or individuality is concerned, empty. When Nicolson meets him later there is a sense of pathos as he finds Marstock's early promise has proved illusory: he has turned into an indecisive bachelor whose only occupation is to be a Lloyds underwriter.

With the case of 'Titty', however, Nicolson gives these ideas a different twist. After describing Titmarsh's naivety and timidity, he contemplates his fate:

I am aware that at this stage, should I so desire, I could give to Titty an important or dramatic ending. After all, the European War came along, and Titty might well have been at Brussels or in the *Lusitania*. I considered this, walking up and down with Gladwyn Jebb under the plane-trees at Gulahek. But the whole point of Titty was that he existed, and that the circumstances above described were actual circumstances. My story might be a dull one, but Titty must be allowed, as God allowed him, to peter out.[101]

---

[98] *Some People*, p. 21.   [99] Ibid., pp. 27–8.
[100] Ibid., p. 24.   [101] Ibid., p. 105.

As with Malone, the suggestion of the narrator operating the strings of his character is entertained, only to be countered by the claim that the circumstances were factual. But where Nicolson says Malone's events happened, but not to him, here he claims that Titty's non-events did happen to him. As with Malone, there is a note of regret for behaving badly towards his subject. But whereas some of the characters inspire animosity and vengefulness (Miss Plimsoll, the Marquis de Chaumont, Miriam Codd), others draw out an affection in Nicolson almost in spite of himself, or at least in spite of his class-prejudices. Of Titmarsh he continues:

I must tell the truth. It is not interesting, and Titty would not have liked it. I was fond of Titty, in an unrealised way: he was one of those who taught me to break with the conventions. He was the first, I think, to show me that our inherited standards were unintelligent. He violated those standards. And yet there was something about him, there was something personal about him. I wish I knew.[102]

The chapter ends with Nicolson discussing Titty, who has since died of influenza, with his former boss, Lord Bognor, at Bognor's club. True to the lesson he has learned from Titty, Nicolson breaks with the conventions indeed, losing his temper when Bognor refers to Titty as a 'poor little blighter', and insinuates that 'really, you know, between you and me and the doorpost he wasn't quite....'[103] Nicolson says by this time he had 'increased in self-confidence', and he attacks Bognor in a 'loud and angry voice', hoping their influential neighbours will overhear. 'It is people like you', he says:

[...] who make diplomacy ridiculous: you simply aren't real at all: you have got no reality: you're merely bland: that's what you are, and you're smug [...] compared to you, Titty was a real person [....] surely you feel somewhere that Titty was more of a personality than yourself?[104]

Thus Titty's individuality, however absurd it had seemed from the point of view of the aspiring career-diplomat, assumes a positive value in retrospect: a sign of personality which the system seeks to repress, but the creative writer appreciates. (Here the title suggests that what might have looked like a random album of sketches—oh, here are just some people—has delivered real human beings rather than social ciphers: some *people*.)

The self Nicolson presents in the forefront is that of the professional diplomat: keeping his head in the Balkans when those like Titty are losing theirs as the war begins; valued junior adviser to the British delegation at the Paris peace conference after the war; indispensable private secretary to Lord Curzon at the Lausanne conference of 1922–3. Yet he was also a prolific writer, and especially

---

[102] Ibid., p. 105.   [103] Ibid., p. 109.   [104] Ibid., p. 110.

biographer, managing in his spare time to publish lives of Verlaine (1921), Tennyson (1923) and Swinburne (1926), as well as later biographies of Constant (1945), King George V (1952), and Sainte-Beuve (1957). As we have seen, *Some People* occasionally refers to Nicolson as its author. It also includes two portraits of writers—not only marking Nicolson's passage through a phase of aestheticism, but conforming to the pattern of imaginary portraiture being drawn towards portraits of artists. They are also where he takes his play with the reality and fictionality of his characters a stage further.

Nicolson juxtaposes the portraits of his two writers, 'Lambert Orme' and 'The Marquis de Chaumont', saying that together they represent his 'interest in the freaks of literary temperament'. They are complementary:

Lambert began so foolishly and ended on such a note of seriousness: de Chaumont possessed such possibilities but became in the end idiotic beyond the realm of comprehension. His story, fortunately, will not be believed: but I give it none the less.[105]

Nicolson meets de Chaumont at Oxford. He is an intellectual, but oppressed by his sense of his own aristocracy. 'His ancestry, his parents, his collaterals loomed in front of him in vast and menacing proportions.'[106] His disconcertingly cockney accent when speaking English is explained by his having been taught the language by his nurse. Yet his speech continually serves to undermine his desire to comport himself aristocratically.

The chapter ends with a brilliant (if Beerbohmesque) metafictional flourish. Nicolson meets Proust at a reception for members of the Peace Conference, and finds that Proust also knows de Chaumont. Proust disagrees that de Chaumont has his priorities wrong, saying that many young men can write better than de Chaumont, who is wise to concentrate on what he does best. He then offers to speak to Nicolson 'on the subject of elegance', but they are interrupted, and Nicolson says 'fate cheated me of that discourse.'[107] In the closing section, de Chaumont visits Nicolson, bearing a letter from Proust, who has been working on *Pastiches et Mélanges*. Proust says he had 'written a short sketch in the manner of St. Simon and would Jacques mind if he figured in it by name?' De Chaumont is 'in obvious tribulation'. He doesn't want to offend Proust, 'yet on the other hand, well, really . . .'. He claims that 'moy mother would not loike it'. Nicolson points out that he has met the mother, and thinks it unlikely she would mind, at which point de Chaumont mentions 'moy aunt, de Maubize. She 'ates Jews.' Nicolson argues that he would be missing a chance of 'a free gift of immortality' from the hand of 'the greatest living writer.'[108] But de Chaumont turns the letter over in his hands, then impulsively tears it up and throws it away.

---

[105] *Some People*, p. 57.   [106] Ibid., p. 61.
[107] Ibid., p. 73.   [108] Ibid., p. 74.

Thus Nicolson (as writer) skillfully disposes of the evidence of Proust's letter, which fictionally inserts de Chaumont into real literary history but only by virtue of missing his chance to figure by name in a real text. 'The book appeared some months later and it contained no mention of Jacques de Chaumont.'[109] The absence of his name from Proust's text seems paradoxically to confirm Nicolson's story. Yet the chapter leaves us with the implication that de Chaumont is somehow nonetheless *in* Proust's text, as an 'original', even though he is not named; a suggestion which again paradoxically adds to the sense of the reality of this unbelievable character.

The best of the chapters, 'Lambert Orme', is a contrasting case-history of 'literary temperament'. Whereas de Chaumont let his concerns for 'society' block his literary aspirations, Orme lives the aesthetic creed fully, valuing art above social life. He too is a study in the implausible, beginning: 'It would be impossible, I feel, to actually be as decadent as Lambert looked.'[110] It is the funniest of the sketches, not only for its mockery of Orme, but for a self-mockery more genuine than appears in the other chapters, perhaps attributable to Nicolson's sense of attraction to, and kinship with, Orme at the time of their acquaintance:

It interests me to recapture my own frame of mind at the time of this my first meeting with Lambert Orme. It amuses me to look back upon the block of intervening years in which I also aped æstheticism, toyed with the theory that I also could become an intellectual.[111]

The climax of the chapter follows from an anti-climactic episode when Orme visits Constantinople, and Nicolson invites him on a sailing trip on the Bosphorus. Orme stands him up, merely sending a note: '"To-day is too wonderful", he wrote, "it is the most wonderful day that ever happened: it would be too much for me: let us keep to-day as something marvellous that did not occur."' Nicolson is furious, and says 'I thereafter and for many years dismissed Lambert from my mind': as a person he didn't seem 'worth the bother', and 'as an intellect he was absurdly childish—he represented the rotted rose-leaves of the *Yellow Book*.'[112] The war comes. Orme rather unexpectedly fights in France then dies in Mesopotamia. The chapter ends with a post-war Bloomsbury gathering (there are sly digs at Keynes—'An untidy man'—and Ottoline Morrell—'The lady whom, from a distance, I had so much admired') at which Nicolson discovers Orme had written a poem about the boat trip they didn't take:

> Thera, if it indeed be you,
> That are Santorin,
> You will fully understand

---

[109] Ibid., p. 75.   [110] Ibid., p. 39.
[111] Ibid., p. 41.   [112] Ibid., p. 49.

This my cleansing—
At which he leant forward and pulled a rope toward him,
And the yacht sidled cross-ways,
At an angle
'That,' he said (he was a man of obtuse sensibilities),
'Is Bebek.'[113]

The untidy man reads out the poem, describing it as about a day spent with a 'local bore', and arguing that Orme was 'a real pioneer in his way', and that had he lived, he 'would have been important.'[114] Nicolson is irritated again, telling himself that he wouldn't have been so obtuse as to be an unwelcome tour guide had the trip actually happened, and trying to let himself off the hook by reminding himself that it didn't. Yet the discussion of Orme's significance indicates that his sensibilities were obtuse in another way, for not taking Orme's poetry seriously. And that thought enables us to reconsider Orme's note. What seemed precious egotism at first sight now might be something else, since it turned out that there was something genuinely wonderful in the day: if their trip was 'something marvelous that did not occur', it was marvellous because it inspired one of his best poems—a poem which exists on the same frontier as Nicolson's own sketches, marvellous episodes which do not (quite) occur.

If Lambert Orme is recognizable as Firbank (who did not die in the war, but in 1926), he is also recognizable as another kind of figure we have already encountered: the parody of the aesthete, to be set alongside Beerbohm's Enoch Soames and Pound's Hugh Selwyn Mauberley. He is a little more modern, a Georgian rather than Victorian, and following his volume of *Lay Figures* with one of *War Poems*. As with Joyce, Beerbohm, and Pound, Nicolson writes some of the poet's poetry. Not a complete poem, but two of the 'several stanzas' of 'Thera'. As with the earlier examples (but unlike Pessoa's heteronyms), the limitations of the imaginary poet relieve his creator from having to produce verse of the highest quality: it needs merely to indicate potential, which it does, if a little awkwardly, in its evocation of Imagism and deployment of free verse. If, like Beerbohm's sample of Soames's verse, it has a parodic edge, it doesn't have the full parodic force of Savonarola Brown's playlet—presumably because Nicolson's affinity with Orme extends to his versifying mind-set. The important point for our purposes is that it is entirely plausible as a piece of writing by a Georgian aesthete who was beginning to mature into something more experimental and significant; and that, in addition to imaginary letters from and conversations with a real figure such as Proust, Nicolson's imaginary portrait of Orme includes some of his imaginary writing: fictional creativity.

---

[113] *Some People*, pp. 54, 56, 55.   [114] Ibid., p. 56.

It is easy to see how the imaginative fertility of Nicolson's experiments with auto/biografiction might have attracted Woolf, and fed into her fictional biography of his wife as Orlando, struggling over several centuries with his/her epic poem 'The Oak Tree'. Yet Woolf's review discussing *Some People* expressed doubts about the formal composite of fiction and auto/biography which might seem surprising. While his 'lack of pose, humbug, solemnity' embody the achievements of the New Biography, Woolf notes that 'the truth of real life' and 'the truth of fiction' are explosively antagonistic. 'Let it be fact, one feels, or let it be fiction; the imagination will not serve under two masters simultaneously.'[115] Yet the twentieth century's literary imagination increasingly did. We have seen the volatility of the combination, from Pater and Hale White to figures like Hesketh Pearson and Ford. Woolf was one of its twentieth-century pioneers, and nowhere more emphatically than in *Orlando*. So we could read the essay as the stirrings of a new engagement with auto/biografiction. Indeed, Woolf's essays—'Mr. Bennett and Mrs. Brown', say, or *A Room of One's Own*—are characterized by shifting into and between auto/biography and fiction, just as her fiction is characterized by shifting into and between auto/biography and essay (thus continuing to bear out Stephen Reynolds's definition of autobiografiction). And yet in Woolf's other essay devoted to biography—'The Art of Biography'—written a decade after *Orlando*, she was still asserting an irreconcilability, a destructive antagonism, between fact and fiction: 'If he invents facts as an artist invents them—facts that no one else can verify—and tries to combine them with facts of the other sort, they destroy each other.'[116] In this case perhaps she was expressing an anxiety that her attempts to combine the two kinds of 'fact' in *Orlando* and *Flush* had been misconceived. Otherwise it seems strange that these essays written either side of those two biografictions are so opposed to the method they use so triumphantly. Stranger still, given how much of her best work is deeply auto/biografictional. How we are to understand these objections to combining fact and fiction, coming from the British writer herself pre-eminent in fusing auto/biography and fiction? In 'The Art of Biography' her stricture against combining invented and other facts is apropos Strachey. So perhaps her point is that such combinations are inadmissible in *biography*, but not in fiction. Biography is valuable when it gives us 'the creative fact; the fertile fact; the fact that suggests and engenders', she argues.[117] But entirely invented facts undermine trust in anything offered as fact; which in turn undermines the text's claim to be a biography at all. But as few reading *Orlando* would confuse it with factual biography or history, fiction's effect on fact is liberating rather than disabling. In other words, writers shouldn't combine fact and fiction under the sign of biography; but if they do it under the sign of fiction it will be a different story; especially if they fictionalize the biographic process as

---

[115] 'The New Biography', pp. 475–8.
[116] Woolf, 'The Art of Biography', p. 123.
[117] Ibid., p. 126.

well. Strachey and Nicolson had, in their different ways, written auto/biography as novelists. Woolf would write a novel as a biographer. As *Orlando* has it:

> To give a truthful account of London society at that or indeed at any other time, is beyond the powers of the biographer or the historian. Only those who have little need of the truth, and no respect for it—the poets and the novelists—can be trusted to do it, for this is one of the cases where the truth does not exist. Nothing exists.[118]

This points to another component of parody in *Orlando*. Its fantasy elements suggest how real lives are even more fantastical than in most biographers' meretricious fantasies—such as, for example, Strachey's Freudian construction of the story of Elizabeth and Essex. Woolf had written in a review of a biography of Sterne: 'a real life is wonderfully prolific; it passes through such strange places and draws along with it a train of adventures that no novelist can better them [...].'[119] This in turn suggests that what is being parodied in *Orlando* is the biographer's straying from fact as much as plodding alongside it. In other words, that its fantastical elements might be another aspect of its parody of 'New Biographers' like Strachey or Nicolson.

It was Strachey, then, who elicited Woolf's energies of parody in *Orlando*— parody of him, and also of the subjects and epochs he ironized. Nicolson's *Some People* helped provoke *Orlando*'s experiment in autobiografiction. But his next book, which the Woolfs published at the Hogarth Press, *The Development of English Biography*, also contributed to her thinking about these questions of life-writing. Nicolson finished the book in October 1927, and it was published before the end of the year, as the fourth in the 'Hogarth Lectures on Literature Series.'[120] Woolf had been planning *Orlando* since September, and was working on it until March 1928. Even if she hadn't known any of Nicolson's book before she began *Orlando*, she is very likely to have heard about it; and she is very likely to have read it while working on the novel. Indeed, it is possible she read it, and likely that she had a good idea of what was in it, by the time she wrote 'The New Biography', which was published at the end of October 1927 in America. Her concern there for the difficulties of combining fact and fiction provides the main axis for Nicolson's study. He begins with different terms, contrasting the pursuit of 'historical truth' and 'complete and accurate portraiture', which he calls 'pure' biography, which must unite 'truth, individuality, and art', with its 'impure' counterpart: works whose truthfulness is unadulterated by three motives: celebrating the dead; wanting to turn them into moral examples; or the intrusion of the biographer's subjectivity.[121] These terms, common-sensical

---

[118] *Orlando*, p. 184.
[119] Woolf, 'Sterne' (1909), in *The Essays of Virginia Woolf*, vol. 4, pp. 280–8 (p. 281). See Julia Briggs, 'Virginia Woolf and "The Proper Writing of Lives"', in *The Art of Literary Biography*, ed. John Batchelor (Oxford: Clarendon Press, 1995), pp. 245–65.
[120] See Lees-Milne, *Harold Nicolson: A Biography*, pp. 310, 318–20.
[121] Nicolson, *The Development of English Biography* (London: The Hogarth Press, 1927), pp. 157, 9–11.

though they are, draw on Edmund Gosse's entry on 'Biography' for the 1911 *Encyclopedia Britannica*.[122] Nicolson also poses a conflict between the 'scientific' and 'literary' interest of biography—the scientific using psychological theory and a scholarly exhaustiveness of historical detail, and the literary foregrounding the personality and intelligence of the biographer. His antitheses appear to suggest distinct kinds of biographical text, which are better kept apart, rather as Woolf suggests that fact and fiction are better kept apart. But his examples are hybrids; necessarily so, since the fully 'scientific' biography would be as unreadable as unwriteable; and the notion of 'purity' admits impurity, given the difficulty of drawing the line between the biographer achieving a personal view and voice, and intruding a personality and manner. Indeed, Nicolson concludes by arguing that the tendency towards scientific biography has 'put an end to "pure" biography as a branch of literature.'[123] Thus his argument has moved towards accepting hybridity. To see how closely this anticipates the development of Woolf's English biografiction, consider Nicolson's concluding pages:

But in general literary biography will, I suppose, wander off into the imaginative, leaving the strident streets of science for the open fields of fiction. The biographical form will be given to fiction, the fictional form will be given to biography.[124]

That apparently tentative clause, 'I suppose', is as disingenuous as the prophetic strain, since Strachey had already gone a long way towards giving fictional form to biography; and Nicolson himself, like the writers of autobiografiction discussed in Part I, had already given biographical form to fiction. Perhaps he didn't want to appear to be congratulating himself on the techniques he had just been using; or perhaps he was acknowledging the limits of what he had been able to achieve with those techniques, as when he writes: 'We shall have franker and fuller autobiographies than we have yet been accorded.'[125] If there is also a note of Bloomsbury mutual back-scratching in the way these comments appear to announce *Orlando* (which Nicolson had probably heard about before he finished the book) it is nonetheless striking how closely his terms anticipate Woolf's; and also how well his speculation anticipates the project she was engaged upon.

---

[122] Gosse argues that before the seventeenth century, 'The personage described was [...] treated either from the philosophical or from the historical point of view. In the former case, *rhetoric* inevitably clouded the definiteness of the picture; the object was to produce a grandiose *moral effect*, to clothe the subject with all the virtues or with all the vices; to make his career a splendid example or else a solemn warning [...] In considering what biography, in its *pure* sense, ought to be, we must insist on what it is not. It is not a philosophical treatise nor a polemical pamphlet [...] It was very difficult to persuade the literary world that, whatever biography is, it is not an opportunity for *panegyric* or invective, and the lack of this perception destroys our faith in most of the records of personal life in ancient and medieval times' (my emphases). Edmund Gosse, 'Biography', *Encyclopedia Britannica*, 11th edn (Cambridge: Cambridge University Press, 1911) vol. 3, p. 954.

[123] *The Development of English Biography*, pp. 157–8.

[124] Ibid., pp. 155–6.

[125] Ibid., [p. 158].

Literature, he wrote, 'by devoting itself to "impure" or applied biography, may well discover a new scope, an unexplored method of conveying human experience.'[126]

COMPOSITE PORTRAITURE

Orlando, then, is Woolf's most sustained imaginative engagement with life-writing, drawing on her evolving ideas about the received forms of biography, but also exploring the possibilities offered by the New Biography represented by Strachey, the new auto/biography represented by Nicolson, and the new sense of the history of biography explored by both men. But it is central to my argument that, like these other experiments, it also draws on the previous half-century's tradition of experiments in auto/biografiction. The remainder of this chapter will consider the ways in which *Orlando* both reflects and develops several of the concepts and techniques that have threaded their way through that tradition, such as the composite portrait, the imaginary portrait, the notion of the fake or mock biography, imaginary authorship, and fictional creativity.

Orlando does composite portraiture in a way that is itself a composite, of multiple times and periods, multiple people, multiple selves, multiple genders, multiple literary forms; and these will be discussed first. *Orlando* is a striking chronological composite portrait of different ages from the Renaissance to the time of publication.[127] It is also a domestic version of this temporal composite: a composite of family history, using Vita's *Knole and the Sackvilles* (1922)—an example of the topographical portrait gallery—for background material.[128] But rather than telling of the Sackvilles from the Elizabethan to Victorian periods, say, Woolf presents one figure who combines them all. The 'Oak Tree' of Orlando's poem is thus a metonymy for the idea of a family tree; and for Orlando him/herself as the embodiment of that family tree: a walking composite biography and history. In the illustrations, Vita poses for several of the periods. Orlando is thus a composite of multiple Vitas. But also a composite of her and the other Sackvilles whose portraits are reproduced opposite.[129] Woolf's book thus itself becomes a gallery of portraits, some of which are real and some of which are imaginary. Woolf chooses paintings for the illustrations with long Van Dyck faces that reflect Vita's; as if to suggest that Orlando works his/her way through the generations in much the same way as family traits work through family portraits. From one point of view it might seem a conservative strategy,

---

[126] *The Development of English Biography*, [p. 158].
[127] Suzanne Nalbantian describes it as 'a historical composite', in *Aesthetic Autobiography*, p. 167.
[128] Bowlby, 'Introduction', p. xx.
[129] The Frontispiece to the 1928 Hogarth Press edition (reproduced in Bowlby's edition, facing p. 146), and titled: 'Orlando as a Boy' is cropped (so as to remove the second boy) from the illustration facing p. 106 in Sackville-West's book.

9 Two illustrations from Virginia Woolf's *Orlando*, 'Orlando as Ambassador' and 'Orlando Back in England'.

emphasizing the stability of identity through family history (as traced through works like the *DNB*, in which family identity is constructed as a constituent of national identity). But Orlando's transmigrations through times and genders is more radical even than Woolf's anti-patriarchal handling of family in *To the Lighthouse*, say, suggesting instead a more modernist notion of a trans-personal or impersonal identity.

When she had begun to map out *Orlando* in her diary, Woolf wrote:

One of these days, though, I shall sketch here, like a grand historical picture, the outlines of all my friends.... It might be a way of writing the memoirs of one's own times during peoples [*sic*] lifetimes. It might be a most amusing book. The question is how to do it. Vita should be Orlando, a young nobleman. There should be Lytton [Strachey], & it should be truthful; but fantastic. Roger [Fry]. Duncan [Grant]. Clive [Bell]. Adrian [Stephen].[130]

---

[130] *Diary of Virginia Woolf*, vol. 3, pp. 156–7: entry for Tuesday 20 September 1927.

This would have made it more like the composite portraiture of *Some People*. As Bowlby observes, while this directly announces the transformation of Vita into Orlando, it adds several of Woolf's other friends who don't feature in *Orlando*.[131] Whereas the project outlining all her friends anticipates *The Waves*, which collects together characters usually identified as portraits of other Bloomsbury figures such as Strachey, J. M. Keynes, Vanessa Bell, T. S. Eliot, and Leonard Woolf.

Biography is always necessarily composite portraiture to the extent that the subject's life is inextricable from other people's lives. But the fantasy biography of Orlando gives us a subject who is him/herself a composite of many lives and many times. *Orlando* doesn't constitute a portrait collection in the way *Some People* or *Portraits in Miniature* do, devoting separate chapters to separate individuals. I have tried not to use the term metaphorically, merely to describe novels including a number of striking characters. But though it is a single continuous narrative, *Orlando* does offer itself as a work which extends the

---

[131] Bowlby, 'Introduction', p. xvii.

form in two ways. First, it includes a portrait gallery of illustrations, alternating between photographs of actual paintings and photographs of Vita posing, as if a painting, such as 'Orlando about the year 1840'. Second, the fact that most of the portraits in this gallery are (or at least are said to be) of a single character stands as an emblem of the whole book, which could be described as a series of portraits of Orlandos from different periods: the Renaissance Orlando, Augustan Orlando, early-Victorian Orlando, or 'Orlando at the Present Time' (as the last photograph is captioned).

Insofar as it runs these different avatars into a single figure, it is better described as a composite portrait. Galtonian composite portraiture in the visual arts implies a timeless universality. But *Orlando* is a composite of snapshots taken through history; a composite in which the differences between times does matter. This produces a paradoxical result. While Orlando has an identifiable character throughout the narrative, the contrasts between different periods militates against both the sense of his individuality and of her universality.

Thus the effect of the composite portrait in *Orlando* is not to fuse many individuals into a single image, but to take a single character and explore its multiplicity. This is not only Woolf's radical development of the technique of literary portraiture, but also a deconstruction of the Victorian notion of 'character', smuggled in under the guise of fantasy:

For if there are (at a venture) seventy-six different times all ticking in the mind at once, how many different people are there not—Heaven help us—all having lodgement at one time or another in the human spirit? Some say two thousand and fifty-two [. . .][132]

In the late essay on 'The Art of Biography' Woolf connects this idea of multiple subjectivity with the modern culture of publicity and celebrity. As suggested in Chapter 1, notions of portraiture were changing in response to photography and the media's insatiable demands for author-interviews:

since we live in an age when a thousand cameras are pointed, by newspapers, letters, and diaries, at every character from every angle, he must be prepared to admit contradictory versions of the same face. Biography will enlarge its scope by hanging up looking glasses at odd corners. And yet from all this diversity it will bring out, not a riot of confusion, but a richer unity. And again, since so much is known that used to be unknown, the question now inevitably asks itself, whether the lives of great men only should be recorded. Is not anyone who has lived a life, and left a record of that life, worthy of biography[?][133]

Had this passage appeared in *Orlando*, it might have been tempting to read it as part of the book's parody of Strachey (whom the essay has in mind: its catching the famous out with covert mirrors is comparable to his image of lowering his bucket to the hidden depths); or at least to read it ironically, as the narrator's

---

[132] *Orlando*, pp. 293–4.
[133] Woolf, 'The Art of Biography', pp. 124–5.

echoing of what the spirit of the age kept saying about photography and publicity, rather than as Woolf's own view. But even though it appears to be her own view, that is not to say that authors cannot express their views through irony and parody, even in essays.

Certainly, *Orlando* is explicit about the challenge posed to biography by the idea of multiple personality:

> she had a great variety of selves to call upon, far more than we have been able to find room for, since a biography is considered complete if it merely accounts for six or seven selves, whereas a person may well have as many thousand.[134]

Hermione Lee notes that Woolf wanted to move narrative away from what she called 'the damned egotistical self.'[135] One way to do this is to recognize that the ego is not itself, but is legion: 'of what odds and ends are we compounded [...] What a phantasmagoria the mind is and meeting-place of dissemblables!'[136] The text of *Orlando* is itself a 'phantasmagoria' (an exhibition of optical illusions, originally associated with magic lantern effects), in that it uses the optical illusion of projecting Sackville-West back through time to show how we are all compounded of (amongst other things) the odds and ends of history, family history, literary history. Its fantasmatic aspect expresses the presence of fantasy in everyday mental life—an idea Woolf would have known well from Freud (as for example in his essay on 'Creative Writers and Daydreaming').[137] As Lee comments: 'Orlando's biographer, preoccupied with questions of how lives can be written (in a way quite alien to Vita's more conventional preferences in fiction and poetry) ends up dissolving all concepts of a stable "self".'[138]

We have seen how *Orlando*, like many of our modernist examples, proceeds by parody. Style thus becomes as unstable as the self through time. One reason for this is Woolf's sense that to write is to confront a dissolution of the self when faced with the demands of great writers from the past: 'They made one feel, she continued, that one must always, always write like somebody else.'[139] *Orlando*'s parody turns sounding like someone else into high creativity and individuality. But it also enables Woolf to produce something greater than a self-satisfied mockery of Victorianism. Which is one reason why Woolf is so much better a writer than Strachey. As she says, his irony is too backward looking.

The most surprising way in which Orlando's personality or character is multiple is of course in changing gender, which produces one of the fictional biographer's purplest passages:

[134] *Orlando*, pp. 294–5.
[135] Lee, *Virginia Woolf*, p. 523.
[136] *Orlando*, p. 169.
[137] Freud, 'Creative Writers and Day-Dreaming' (1908), in *The Standard Edition of the Complete Psychological Works of Sigmund Freud*, vol. 9 (London: The Hogarth Press and the Institute of Psycho-Analysis, 1959), pp. 141–53.
[138] Lee, *Virginia Woolf*, p. 523.
[139] *Orlando*, p. 272.

And now again obscurity descends, and would indeed that it were deeper! Would, we almost have it in our hearts to exclaim, that it were so deep that we could see nothing whatever through its opacity! Would that we might here take the pen and write *Finis* to our work! Would that we might spare the reader what is to come and say to him in so many words, Orlando died and was buried. But here, alas, Truth, Candour, and Honesty, the austere Gods who keep watch and ward by the inkpot of the biographer, cry No! Putting their silver trumpets to their lips they demand in one blast, Truth![140]

This note of hysteria is continued for a further three pages, until the narrator can put off the revelation no longer: 'we have no choice left but confess—he was a woman.'[141] The hysteria is very much to the point, of course, suggesting that the characteristics men attribute to women are projections of what they mistrust in themselves; but also that the very point of high Victorianism when the argument that the two spheres of male and female should be kept separate occurs as (and perhaps because) the differences have come to seem less absolute, more negotiable. Orlando momentarily shares Tiresias' trans-gendered identity: 'indeed, for the time being, she seemed to vacillate; she was man; she was woman; she knew the secrets, shared the weaknesses of each. It was a most bewildering and whirligig state of mind to be in.'[142]

   This extraordinary fantasy-transformation is susceptible of multiple readings. Culturally, it is an allegory of authorship, occurring at the point when women writers no longer needed to adopt male pseudonyms, especially if they wanted to write frankly about sexual relationships. As Woolf put it in 'The Art of Biography', 'The accent on sex has changed within living memory.'[143] That was because the accent *of* sex had also changed: it could now speak with a woman's voice.

   Like multiple times and selves, multiple gender offers a challenge to essentialist notions of character and personality and nature. Woolf's method here is to parody the very sexologists who were themselves undermining essentialist assumptions about sex and gender:

In every human being a vacillation from one sex to the other takes place, and often it is only the clothes that keep the male or female likeness, while underneath the sex is the very opposite of what it is above. Of the complications and confusions which thus result everyone has had experience.[144]

The authoritative generalization gives the game away, which is to sound like Havelock Ellis. Yet when the Freudian question of 'What Women Want' is being broached, and the risqué question arises of what happens 'when women get together', Woolf plays more Sterne games with narrative interruption (and presumably shares an in-joke with Vita). The revelation 'All they desire is—' is interrupted as a man comes up the stairs: 'the gentleman took the very words out of our mouths. Women have no desires, says this gentleman, coming into Nell's

---

[140] Ibid., pp. 128–9.
[141] Ibid., p. 132.
[142] Ibid., p. 152.
[143] Woolf, 'The Art of Biography', p. 124.
[144] *Orlando*, p. 181.

parlour.'[145] In the year of the trial of *The Well of Loneliness* the topic of homosexual female desire required gentle treatment, and Woolf's impersonation of a male biographer (at least at this point) provides the perfect mock-gentility:

what can we suppose that women do when they seek out each other's society?

As that is not a question that can engage the attention of a sensible man, let us, who enjoy the immunity of all biographers and historians from any sex whatever, pass it over [...][146]

The gender-swapping raises such issues because Orlando, who was a man who had had affairs with women, is now a woman who had had affairs with women. But it also raises the question of human nature again, in the form of asking how gendered it is: can one have the same nature as a man and as a woman?

Yet through all these changes she had remained, she reflected, fundamentally the same. She had the same brooding meditative temper, the same love of animals and nature, the same passion for the country and the seasons.[147]

Rachel Bowlby persuasively relates the sexual 'indeterminacy' of Orlando to the ideal of androgyny in the essay of the following year, *A Room of One's Own*. 'It is fatal for anyone who writes to think of their sex', Woolf wrote there.[148] Orlando's composite gender is one way in which the book is autobiographical, then: Orlando is a writer who composes both sexes into one, thus enacting the ideal of androgyny that Woolf was advancing in the contemporary essay. The notion of literary androgyny has been criticized by Roger Poole as something that can only be wish-fulfilment, and that it can only be found in *Orlando* because Orlando is a 'fantasy.'[149] His certainty is based on a certainty that male and female minds have to be different because of different embodiment. Bowlby, by contrast, places the emphasis on the relation between gender and language: 'There is no using language, or being represented in it, without initially being "he or she".'[150] The fantasy in *Orlando* of embodiment as he *and* she enables Woolf to imagine using language as he *and* she, not as any novelist does, from different subject positions, but from the position of a single subject. Thus Bowlby compares Woolf and Freud, as both expressing the subject moving through different gender roles and positions. The legacy of such experiments, especially in Judith Butler's theory of gender as performative, is to see the fantasmatic as inseparable from any gender-identifications. Yes, Orlando's trans-gendering is a fantasy (one wonders what Woolf would have made of subsequent medical advances which have realized it as a surgical possibility). But part of its cunning is to suggest how gender is itself a fantasy; and how fantasies of gender form just a part of our fantasy performances of the lives of others and of ourselves.

---

[145] *Orlando*, p. 210.
[146] Ibid., See Lee, p. 524.
[147] *Orlando*, p. 226.
[148] Bowlby, 'Introduction', p. xlii. *A Room of One's Own: Three Guineas*, ed. Morag Shiach (Oxford: Oxford University Press, 1992), p. 136.
[149] Poole, *The Unknown Virginia Woolf* (Cambridge: Cambridge University Press, 1978), p. 263.
[150] Bowlby, 'Introduction', p. xxxix.

IMAGINARY PORTRAITURE AND
FICTIONAL CREATIVITY

Like many of the works under discussion, *Orlando* presents imaginary portraiture through imaginary authorship. The biographer-narrator is more than an obtuse first-person narrator. He or she is *writing* the book we read, and presumably giving it its generic subtitle, adding its photographs, and compiling its index. It is undoubtedly an example of ventriloquial authorship. If we read it (as it has often been read) as merely a parody of patriarchal Victorian biography, then that authorship is being mocked, and the fictional biographer's writing is imaginary but not imaginative. If, however, it is seen (as I have been proposing it should) as a response to the New Biography as well, and to Lytton Strachey in particular, the argument becomes more complex. Woolf might be using the form to mock Strachey too—in a more affectionate way, to be sure, but nonetheless showing the limitations of his rather pre-modernist assumption of novelistic omniscience. Or it might be an act of homage to the liberating potential of the New Biography, intended as an example of a work which, though fictionally authored, is genuinely creative—since, after all, the fictional biographer's book *is* an extraordinarily original narrative. If one reads this biographer as an individual fictional character, rather than a cento of biographical voices from different ages, then the form generates an uncertainty as to how far we are to see the achievement as the biographer's, and how far as Woolf's.

Orlando further complicates the argument by doubling the number of fictional authors: not only the biographer, but also Orlando. Where Joyce included his own villanelle in *Portrait of the Artist as a Young Man* as one of Stephen's compositions, Woolf includes some poetry, supposedly written by Orlando, which has sometimes been taken for Woolf's own: Bowlby suggests that 'the "quotations" appear to have been invented by Woolf for the occasion.'[151] But in fact they are from two poems by Letitia Elizabeth Landon (1802–38): 'Lines of Life' and 'Fragment'. In the first case, Woolf reproduces two stanzas from a poem about poetry. When Orlando reads it, it proves 'the most insipid verse she had ever read in her life'; but then something else takes over: 'she became conscious, as she stood at the window, of an extraordinary tingling and vibration all over her, as if she were made of a thousand wires upon which some breeze or errant fingers were playing scales.'[152] It is the Romantic trope of the poet as Aeolian harp, played upon by inspiration as the harp is played upon by the wind. As with many of our texts of aesthetic autobiography or autobiografiction this turns into

---

[151] *Orlando*, pp. 227–8, 334. See 'Introductory Essay to the Work of Letitia Elizabeth Landon' by Dr. Glenn Dibert-Himes, at <http://www.people.iup.edu/ghimes/gdhessay.htm> (accessed 18 December 2007).

[152] *Orlando*, pp. 227, 228.

the story of the source of the artist's art. Like Joyce, Woolf includes a poem as evidence of the artist-character's first inspiration. But there is also an ironic edge. It's an example of a Romantic poet feeling inspired, described in the terms in which Romantic poets described their inspiration—a notion which is itself a product of Romanticism. The 'spirit' of the age, according to the Romantic trope that equates breath, wind, spirit, and inspiration (via the Latin 'spiritus') is playing across her. But Woolf reverses the trope, since the spirit of the age is not the inspiration of 'genius' or semi-divine creativity, but the style of the time. This second poem may be less insipid, and describes a woman's metamorphosis ('She was so changed'); but it is still conventional. The change Orlando writes about seems to express the change beginning to manifest itself in her, since four pages later she makes another, momentous, but also conventional change. She is 'forced at length to consider the most desperate of remedies, which was to yield completely and submissively to the spirit of the age, and take a husband.'[153]

Woolf uses a fragment of existing verse of the period, where Joyce had used an earlier piece of his own. But he was basing Stephen on his own youth, whereas Orlando is not based on Woolf's own life (though of course s/he draws on it). Though she didn't attempt to write the verse herself (as our postmodern biografiction writers Nabokov and A. S. Byatt do in the next chapter), the verse she chose has another kind of appropriateness. It tells the story of an imaginary girl, 'whose loveliness yet lives / In village legends', abandoned by her lover and dying of despair. In short, it is an imaginary portrait, rendered with a painterly and sculptural detail that adds it to *Orlando*'s portrait-gallery.

Woolf's attribution of an existing work of literature to a fictional character makes her point that the literary canon makes everyone write like someone else. But it is also a *mise en abyme* of the book's central technique of superimposing a fictional identity over a real one: Orlando over Vita. It might be countered that Orlando isn't a fully fictional character, so it is only the attribution of Landon's poem to her that is fictional. This is fair enough; but it merely concedes the technique of superimposition as a feature of Orlando her/himself. And it is that superimposition that represents the real novelty of the book. The technique of inserting imaginary portraits *alongside* real people was already well tried. It's the staple of the Shakespearean History play, the Historical Novel, Nicolson's version of the New Biography, and the postmodern historiographical metafiction discussed in the next chapter. Woolf had done it herself, putting the fictional Mrs Brown in the same essay as the realist Arnold Bennett, and would do it again in *A Room of One's Own*, giving Judith Shakespeare a literary history of her own. But in *Orlando* she lays the imaginary portrait over the real one. Orlando is both real (Vita) and imaginary (a pastiche of historical types). As Rachel Bowlby brings out so well, the movement between real and fictional works in both directions.

[153] *Orlando*, p. 232.

'*Orlando* is not exactly a fake biography, of a purely fictitious subject', she writes; 'but nor is it much like a biographical *roman-à-clef*, in which the subject would secretly stand for some real-life personage.'[154] As Bowlby says:

There is Vita herself, in the photographs, on the dedication page, for all the world to see and read: the fiction links it to a real person. Yet at the same time, the photographs show the 'real' Vita posing, taking on parts from her own life and her ancestors', so that real life itself is shown to be made up of imaginary identifications.[155]

'She was so changed.' 'Vita kept reappearing; but she kept being written over, too', says Lee: '*Orlando* both was and was not her portrait.'[156] That composite of verbal and visual is an essential aspect of the book. Woolf saw how photography, and the play between the paintings and photographs, could lend itself to her purposes. We saw in the chapter on Pater's Imaginary Portraits how he drew on the idea that painters could imagine the likeness of people they'd never seen (though they might imagine them as like the model they had seen, but which viewers of the painting generally hadn't). But a photograph isn't a likeness of someone; it is the image of that person. To caption a photograph of Vita 'Orlando on her return to England' might be seen as an in-joke—those who knew Sackville-West or had seen other photos of her would have recognized her; for others, it could be a photograph of anybody, being co-opted as an image of Orlando. But it is also to insist on the reality of Orlando—here she is; the camera never lies! The photographs pull the text's fantasy into the real; the text pulls the photographs' reality into fantasy.

AUTO/BIOGRAFICTION

Orlando is often described as 'mock-biography'. Though that description would accord with the taxonomy of Chapter 5 (which distinguished pseudo- from mock-auto/biography according to whether the form was being impersonated or parodied), my reading has suggested *Orlando*'s biografiction does more than this: that it is better understood as imaginary portraiture, however ironic, of both Orlando (who includes Vita Sackville-West) and the biographer-narrator (who includes Lytton Strachey). To conclude, I want to turn to the last but not least way in which *Orlando* engages with life-writing: the autobiographical. While the family history and the photographs are of Sackville-West, Orlando's chief characteristics are Woolf's too: especially bisexuality and writing. And if Woolf has made Sackville-West up, the result tells us as much about herself. It is also imaginary *self*-portraiture: *auto*biografiction. To wonder if you have turned someone into fiction is to acknowledge the

---

[154] Bowlby, 'Introduction', p. xix.
[155] Ibid.
[156] Lee, *Virginia Woolf*, p. 522.

fantasmatic at the heart of your everyday relations. Psychoanalysis had been finding different terms—'identification', 'love object', 'transference'—for the way in which the mind can swarm with shadow selves of our loved ones.

Of course such a metabiographical work as *Orlando* includes this very idea of reading literature as autobiographical. As the narrator says, apropos Alexander Pope's character being legible in his verse:

In short, every secret of a writer's soul, every experience of his life, every quality of his mind is written large in his works, yet we require critics to explain the one and biographers to expound the other. That time hangs heavy on people's hands is the only explanation of the monstrous growth.[157]

Expounding biographers and explaining critics evidently need to beware in the face of such mockery. What is less clear is Woolf's attitude to the idea used to legitimize such monstrous growth of discourse. That idea is another version of the Nietzsche–Wilde argument—that all expression is autobiographical, whether it expresses the writer's 'soul' or psyche, biography, or personality. It turns up here just on cue at the *fin de siècle* in Orlando's gallop through cultural history. The narrator, as a literary biographer, presumably believes it. But does Woolf endorse it too, or is she mocking the age's theory of biography as well as its practice?

And what happens when we consider this argument alongside the view we have also encountered in the period, of reading as an autobiographical act—as in Wilde's claim that what immorality readers found in *Dorian Gray* was in themselves; or Proust's image of a book as 'a kind of optical instrument' for readers to see into themselves.[158] If we read a book by a writer who doesn't know us, but makes us feel the book sees into us, then such a book has an autobiografictional relation to us: it threads our spiritual experiences on a narrative about someone other. In practice, as post-Wildeans and post-Freudians, perhaps we mostly read a book in both ways, as autobiografiction about the writer and also about ourselves.

Biography, too, according to the Wilde–Nietzsche argument, must also be auto-biography. When the biographical subject—herself a biographer—is likely to be one of the book's readers, the dynamics get more convoluted. The autobiographical function is triangulated: the book reveals Sackville-West, Woolf, and the reader. When Woolf offered Sackville-West the optical instrument of *Orlando*, what did she see in it: herself, as portrayed in Woolf's biography; Woolf, as expressed autobiographically in her biography of another; or the self she (Sackville-West) read into Woolf's text? Such multiplicity of readings is invoked by the cross-addressings of *Orlando*'s play with writers and readers. And it is one way in which Woolf can bring into being within the text the multiplicity of selves she wants us to recognize.

[157] *Orlando*, p. 200.
[158] See Wilde, *The Picture of Dorian Gray*, ed. Michael Patrick Gillespie (New York: W. W. Norton, 2006), p. 3; discussed in the Introduction; and Proust, *Time Regained*, trans. Andreas Mayor (London: Chatto & Windus, 1970), p. 283; discussed in Chapter 2.

In his earlier meditation on what he called 'mental optics' Proust had given a different emphasis to the idea of reading as autobiographical, arguing that authors give us not answers, but desires, because 'we can receive the truth from nobody, and that we must create it for ourselves.'[159] This argues for a more creative sense of what 'the autobiographical' means. It doesn't work like a translation or decryption machine, on which we set the dials and reading translates *Orlando* into Woolf's autobiography on one setting, or the reader's, on another. Instead of being the autobiography, reading prompts the creation of autobiography. If texts energize our imaginations in this way, as they surely do, then the boundaries between self and other, fact and fiction, writer and reader, become even harder to maintain. This view was shared by another of Woolf's Bloomsbury friends, E. M. Forster, who, writing about anonymity, gave a characteristically mystical account of how art challenges the superficial, social sense of self:

Just as words have two functions—information and creation—so each human mind has two personalities, one on the surface, one deeper down. The upper personality has a name. It is called S. T. Coleridge, or William Shakespeare, or Mrs. Humphry Ward. It is conscious and alert, it does things like dining out, answering letters, etc., and it differs vividly and amusingly from other personalities. The lower personality is a very queer affair. In many ways it is a perfect fool, but without it there is no literature [. . .] It has something in common with all other deeper personalities, and the mystic will assert that the common quality is God, and that here, in the obscure recesses of our being, we near the gates of the Divine [. . .] What is so wonderful about great literature is that it transforms the man who reads it towards the condition of the man who wrote, and brings to birth in us also the creative impulse.[160]

Woolf gives a more psychological account of the encounter between self and other as we read; as for example in this review of a biography of Shelley, in which she ponders, just as she begins sketching out *Orlando*, why we read the optical instruments which are biographies of the 'Eminent':

There are some stories which have to be retold by each generation, not that we have anything new to add to them, but because of some queer quality in them which makes them not only Shelley's story but our own. Eminent and durable they stand on the skyline, a mark past which we sail, which moves as we move and yet remains the same.
[. . .]
And now comes our turn to make up our minds what manner of man Shelley was; so that we read Professor Peck's volumes, not to find out new facts, but to get Shelley more sharply outlined against the shifting image of ourselves.[161]

[159] Marcel Proust, *On Reading Ruskin: Prefaces to 'La Bible d'Amiens' and 'Sésame et les lys'*, with *Selections from the Notes to the Translated Texts*, trans. and ed. Jean Autret, William Burford, and Phillip J. Wolfe; introduction by Richard Macksey (New Haven: Yale University Press, 1987), pp. 114–15. See Chapter 2, p. 93.

[160] Forster, 'Anonymity: An Inquiry', in his *Two Cheers for Democracy* (London: Edward Arnold and Co., 1951), p. 93.

[161] Virginia Woolf, 'Not One of Us', A review of *Shelley; His Life and Work*, by Walter Edwin Peck, October 1927. *The Death of the Moth, and Other Essays* (London: The Hogarth Press, 1942),

If a book enables us to see into the shifting image of ourselves, but we start imagining as soon as we stop reading, then the selves we see into are imaginative constructs: fictionalized selves. Thus Proust writes the fictionalized autobiography of an imaginary alter ego, who happens to share his first name, because as soon as he starts looking into himself he begins to rewrite himself. Woolf writes an imaginary portrait of a real friend, only to worry that she has made her up. Insofar as her fantasy about Vita as Orlando expresses her own self too, is that self not equally susceptible to being made up, or over? If *Orlando* can be read autobiographically—as about Woolf's love, and those aspects of Vita with which she could identify—then it must also be read as a turning of autobiography into fiction: as auto/biografiction indeed.[162]

Orlando's multiple hybridities have resulted in its uncertain critical status. Some scholars dismiss it as a snobbish diversion from Woolf's real work.[163] Others see it as a watershed text: as, in Susan Squier's words, her 'literary emancipation', in which 'she confronted the influence of both literal and literary fathers to reshape the novel, and so create a place for herself in the English novelist tradition which was their legacy to her.'[164] Karyn Sproles also sees it as subverting the patriarchal authority of biography.[165] Hermione Lee shows Woolf as less confident of the book's efficacy, suggesting that 'Virginia may have felt that she had evaded the issues':[166]

And I cannot think what to 'write next'. I mean the situation is, this Orlando is of course a very quick brilliant book. Yes, but I did not try to explore [. . .] Orlando taught me how to write a direct sentence; taught me continuity & narrative, & how to keep the realities at bay. But I purposely avoided of course any other difficulty. I never got down to my depths & made shapes square up, as I did in To the Lighthouse.

Well but Orlando was the outcome of a perfectly definite, indeed overmastering impulse. I want fun. I want fantasy. I want (& this was serious) to give things their caricature value.[167]

In some ways *Orlando* is an exercise in evasion. It evades censorious attitudes towards women, towards women writers, towards lesbian desire. But rather, its

pp. 78–83 (p. 78). Lee, *Virginia Woolf*, p. 511. I am grateful to Laura Marcus for drawing my attention to this passage.

[162] See Suzanne Raitt's excellent study, *Vita and Virginia: The Work and Friendship of V. Sackville-West and Virginia Woolf* (Oxford: Clarendon Press, 1993).

[163] See for example Susan Dick, *Virginia Woolf* (London: Edward Arnold, 1989), pp. 59–60; and Gordon, *Virginia Woolf: A Writer's Life*, pp. 187–8.

[164] Susan Squier, 'Tradition and Revision in Woolf's *Orlando*: Defoe and "The Jessamy Brides"', *Women's Studies*, 12:2 (1986), 166–77 (p. 167).

[165] Karyn Sproles, *Desiring Women: The Partnership of Virginia Woolf and Vita Sackville-West* (Toronto: University of Toronto Press, 2006), p. 88.

[166] Lee, *Virginia Woolf*, p. 527.

[167] *The Diary of Virginia Woolf*, vol. 3, pp. 202–3.

achievement is the precarious balancing act of managing to express just those things it appears to avoid.

And, perhaps, conversely, also to escape those things it appears to express. The inward turn of the century had made biography and autobiography seem tyrannical, all-consuming. From one point of view this foregrounding of personal experience and feeling could be liberating; especially for writers who felt stifled. But the extended reach of auto/biographical readings could also seem intrusive. The parody of *Orlando*'s biographer doesn't just reveal his lack of finesse for the task, but the way his task strips the subject, especially when the subject is a writer, of any privacy. Woolf knew that her best writing was profoundly personal: involved getting down to what she called her 'depths'. But for her, as for other modernists, this descent into personality was done not for the sake of expressing that personality, or not only for that, but for something impersonal: making 'shapes square up'. The expression is telling: a craftswoman might square things up to make sure the pieces all fit together; but one generally 'squares up' *to* something else: an ethical challenge; a situation; the demands of the other. There is thus a double sense of making shapes which harmonize with each other and themselves—rather as a Cubist painter might want to make shapes square up; but which also answer to something beyond themselves. If the thing they answer to is the self that made them square up, while they might be said to express that self, they don't represent it as itself, but substitute something abstract. Thus although I have pursued the trail of the autobiografictional in *Orlando*, it ultimately also contains this antidote to autobiography. Like so much modernist impersonality—in Eliot, in Joyce, in Pound—*Orlando*'s is arrived at not by evading or escaping the personal, but by descending into it, and turning it inside out. Woolf's art of autobiografiction squares up to the institution of biography—in particular of literary biography—and confronts it head-on. Instead of trying to avoid the possibly prurient attentions of biographers trying to expose her lesbian affair with Sackville-West, or trying to psychoanalyse her depression, Woolf turns these things, including their biographical pursuit, into the subjects of her book. But she does so, not in order to pre-empt their exposure of her personality, but to turn that exposure into something other: abstract patterning; a work of art. She was to argue the following year, in *A Room of One's Own*, that the novel by a woman writer had changed in the early twentieth century: 'The impulse towards autobiography may be spent. She may be beginning to use writing as an art, not as a method of self-expression.'[168] Once again, the assumption that impersonal art and self-expression could be so easily separated out is surprising, given Woolf's own genius for the auto/biografiction, which combines them.

---

[168] Woolf, *A Room of One's Own*, p. 103.

12

After-Lives: Postmodern Experiments in Meta-Auto/biografiction: Sartre, Nabokov, Lessing, Byatt

'it still strikes me myself as strange that the case histories I write should read like short stories.'[1]

There is life-writing after modernism, of course, and postmodernism becomes ever more playful in its fictionalizing games with it. The body of my story must expire around the early 1930s; when the New Biography had been identified, and had shown itself to be at the same time auto/biography, biografiction, and auto/biografiction. The story of what this multiple personality did next would be another book. That would need to chart how modern literature's escape out of 'personality', and into auto/biografiction, was interrupted by two world wars, which forced people back on their selves, their memories, their illusions, and their hopes and projects for humanity. The prevalence of this form of personal testimony has contributed to a new understanding of autobiography. However, the purpose of this book is not to write the history of autobiography, but to explore forms in which auto/biography and fiction have interacted. That inter-action has become the dominant mode of postmodernism. This brief chapter—really a coda—will begin by merely indicating a small selection of examples of key postmodern texts that significantly develop the central ideas we have been tracing, of unease with auto/biography, aesthetic autobiography, auto/biografiction, imaginary portraits, and concepts of faking and imaginary writing.

The books treated in the first section of this chapter—Jean-Paul Sartre's *Les Mots* and Vladimir Nabokov's *Speak, Memory*—do not play the same auto/biografictional games explored in the rest of Part II. They are both works of formal autobiography. Yet they are playfully experimental in other ways, offering new models of imaginary portraiture and aesthetic autobiography, as they respond to major intellectual currents of the period such as aestheticism, sociology, psychology, and psychoanalysis. In doing so they continue to explore the

---

[1] 'Fräulein Elizabeth von R.', in Sigmund Freud and Joseph Breuer, *Studies on Hysteria* (1895), *The Standard Edition of the Complete Psychological Works of Sigmund Freud*, vol. 2 (London: The Hogarth Press and the Institute of Psycho-Analysis, 1955), pp. 135–81 (p. 160).

limits of autobiography, providing new versions of 'anti-autobiography'. Just as modernism can be seen struggling ambivalently with auto/biography, so postmodernism struggles ambivalently with psychoanalysis.

PSYCHOANALYSIS

Psychoanalysis, which as Freud freely acknowledged, drew on the insights of earlier literature, has in turn had an incalculable impact on subsequent writing. As psychoanalytic views of the mind acquired increasing prestige in the 1920s it became impossible for writers not to respond, even if negatively. Many of those discussed here, and especially Joyce, Svevo, Ford, and Woolf were familiar with psychoanalytic theories and practices. The psychoanalytic portrait of the mind, and especially the concept of the unconscious, presents a particular set of challenges to creative writers. It wasn't just that Freud found a new name for an insight that had been emerging throughout the nineteenth century,[2] he also elaborated a system for apprehending it, which placed the concepts of sexuality and repression at its core. This presents one kind of challenge to fiction writers (as it did to biographers), since it implied that the keys to human character were precisely those ideas and experiences that literature conventionally excluded. The idea of the unconscious presents autobiography with a different kind of problem. If a crucial component of your psyche is obscure to your conscious mind, what is the value of whatever degree of self-knowledge you can attain? And if you don't know the sources of your self, how can you represent yourself? In *The Interpretation of Dreams* (first translated into English in 1913) Freud indicates how radically psychoanalysis transformed the understanding of 'character':

It is the [*Perceptual*] system, which is without the capacity to retain modification and is thus without memory, that provides our consciousness with the whole multiplicity of sensory qualities. On the other hand, our memories—not excepting those which are most deeply stamped on our minds—are themselves unconscious. They can be made conscious; but there can be no doubt that they can produce all their effects while in an unconscious condition. What we describe as our 'character' is based on the memory-traces of our impressions; and, moreover, the impressions which have had the greatest effect on us—those of our earliest youth—are precisely the ones which scarcely ever become conscious.[3]

Once the self begins to be perceived as non-self-present, then its representations become problematic, dynamic, impressionist. Such a view revolutionizes not only

---

[2] See Meg Harris Williams and Margot Waddell, *The Chamber of Maiden Thought: Literary Origins of the Psychoanalytic Model of the Mind* (London: Tavistock and Routledge, 1991).
[3] Sigmund Freud, *The Interpretation of Dreams*, trans. James Strachey, *The Standard Edition of the Complete Psychological Works of Sigmund Freud*, vol. 5 (London: The Hogarth Press and the Institute of Psycho-Analysis, 1953), pp. 539–40.

the reading of autobiography but the writing of it. There have been great psycho-analytically inflected autobiographies, certainly, of which the first is arguably *The Interpretation of Dreams* itself.[4] It was Freud's self-analysis that gave him the breakthrough in his ideas, allowing him to shift from the early theory that all hysterias came from actual child abuse by parents, to the theory that children fantasized about such intimacies. This enabled him to address fantasies, dreams, unconscious wishes, screen memories. It also allowed for the idea of the Oedipus complex as universal (and not confined to abused children).[5] *The Interpretation of Dreams* is a surprisingly and deeply autobiographical text; one that stems—like many of our earlier examples—from an autobiographical crisis: Freud's mourning for his father; feeling hysterical as a result; feeling his work was stalled; feeling all kinds of (possibly psychosomatic) pains. It also constitutes a new kind of autobio-graphical quest: pursuing earliest memories and fantasies and dreams and associa-tions for what they could tell him about himself, his feelings about his father and his father's death. But if our most powerful influences 'hardly ever become conscious', then autobiography would appear to be either irrelevant, or only worth conducting as psychoanalytic case history—which, as Freud observed, was likely to read like fiction. From a psychoanalytic perspective, the unconscious is the autobiographer, retaining the memories that make up our character. Autobiogra-phy becomes unconscious—unconscious impressionism. But the unconscious also intervenes to displace autobiography into unconscious autobiografiction.

It's scarcely surprising, then, that autobiographers are often so wary of psy-choanalysis. In Gertrude Stein's phrase (about how a genius should approach time), post-Freudian autobiographers who approach the unconscious tend to 'accept it and deny it by creating it'. In the following two examples of postmod-ern life-writing, the location of a self in the text proves deeply problematic as they engage in new ways with fiction in autobiography, developing modernism's experiments with the displacements and transformations of subjectivity.

LES MOTS

Les Mots (1964) is essentially a memoir of childhood, with a particular focus on just a few years of that childhood.[6] But it isn't a nostalgia trip back to an idyllic fragment of the past. Far from it. Sartre says: 'I loathe my childhood and all that

---

[4] Which gives a much more intimate history than *An Autobiographical Study*, translation by James Strachey (London: Hogarth Press, 1935), in which Freud is much more concerned with the stages of his development of psychoanalysis.

[5] See J. Laplanche and J.-B. Pontalis, *The Language of Psycho-Analysis* (London: The Hogarth Press and the Institute of Psycho-Analysis, 1983), pp. 404–7.

[6] See Michael Scriven, *Sartre's Existentialist Biographies* (London and Basingstoke: Macmillan, 1984).

remains of it.'[7] In a work that is both a profound piece of self-analysis, and formally highly inventive, he projects this childhood both backwards and forwards, making it emblematic of his whole life. He loathes it because it created a false self—the construct of adults' fantasies and desires: what Sartre had elsewhere called 'being for others.'[8] The story of the book is the switch from reading to writing; moving from receiving the descriptions of others, to being free to describe oneself; moving from acceptance, through denial, to creation.

I was born from writing: before that, there was only a reflection in a mirror. From my first novel, I knew that a child had entered the palace of mirrors. By writing, I existed, I escaped from the grown-ups; but I existed only to write and if I said: me—that meant the me who wrote.[9]

Sartre describes a book he had as a child, called *L'Enfance des hommes illustres*, the childhood of famous men. The author doesn't mention their surnames, they're just Johann Sebastian or Jean-Jacques. But he 'deployed his skill in planting allusions everywhere to their future greatness, recalling casually, by some detail, their most famous works or actions, and arranging his narrative so that you could not grasp the most trivial incident without relating it to subsequent events'. Young 'Rafaello' is taken to see the Pope, and asked about him afterwards: 'What Holy father?', he replies; 'All I saw was colours!' Miguel, reading a romance of chivalry, sees a ruined country gentleman bouncing along on an old horse, and waving his lance at a windmill. Miguel tells everyone about the encounter at dinner, and has his family in stitches, but later tears up his romance in tears.[10]

For a lesser autobiographer such a reminiscence could lead to fatal egotistical complacency: 'And though my parents couldn't have known how significant it would prove, this innocent gift sowed the seeds of my future conviction that I, too, should write/paint/compose.' Indeed, by making his own first name sound like those of Rousseau or Bach in the following passage, he appears to be parodying that kind of teleological self-congratulation. Yet he does so in order to present an extraordinary moment, in which Sartre reads himself, and reads himself reading himself.

These children lived in error: they thought they were acting and speaking fortuitously whereas the true goal of their most trivial remarks was to proclaim their Destiny. The author and I exchanged smiles above their heads; I read the lives of these false mediocrities as God had envisaged them: beginning at the end. At first, I triumphed: they were my brothers and their glory would be mine. And then everything rocked: I found myself on

---

[7] Jean-Paul Sartre, *Les Mots* (1964) trans. as *Words* by Irene Clephane (Harmondsworth: Penguin, 1967), p. 104.
[8] See Sartre, *Being and Nothingness*, trans. Hazel E. Barnes (London: Methuen, 1986), Part Three.
[9] *Words*, p. 97.
[10] Ibid., pp. 127–8.

the other side of the page, *in the book*. Jean-Paul's childhood was like those of Jean-Jacques and Johann Sebastian, and nothing happened to him that was not for the most part a foreshadowing.[11]

'Foreshadowing' is normally a property of a text rather than a life: the advancing of a narrative under the shadow of the knowledge of what is to come.[12] Both writers and readers tend to approach autobiography from this teleological viewpoint. In telling the stories of their lives up to the point of writing, authors certainly know the endings to which their narratives lead. Generally, if readers have been interested enough in them to buy their autobiographies, then probably they do too. Even if the title didn't give away the plot, you wouldn't read Nelson Mandela's *Long Walk to Freedom* (2000) wondering what became of the man. As Sartre puts it with characteristic lucid paradox: 'in a completed life, the end is taken as the truth of the beginning'; and he cites an appropriately macabre example of such an end: 'a young lawyer is carrying his head under his arm because he is the late Robespierre.'[13]

When Sartre finds himself on the other side of the page, it panics him, because it makes him feel he cannot understand the meanings of his experiences. They'll only be clear after his death, to people who come after him. He tries to get back across the page to the reader's side—that is, to try to read his life in the present as if it were in the past. But he's caught in the trap, because even that attempt, that moment of panic, becomes a sign to be interpreted after his death. 'I chose for a future the past of a famous dead man, and I tried to live backwards. Between the ages of nine and ten, I became entirely posthumous', he says: 'I am my own obituary notice.'[14] Of course, in autobiography he is both reader and writer. He is the child, wondering how his childhood will be read later, and the reader reading it later. He is the child determining his life, creating it so that it can be read; and he is the writer that child became, writing his own childhood posthumously. This is also a problem of freedom: the great topic of Sartre's Existentialism. The famous children think their actions are fortuitous, but from another point of view they are part of a destiny.

The book Sartre describes is a collection of imaginary portraits (in the sense of fictionalized recreations of the early lives of real people). Rather than writing imaginary portraits, Sartre dramatizes himself reading them. The placing of this book within his own book is an example of the *mise en abyme*, comparable to earlier examples of imaginary portraits within a collection that appear emblematic of the whole. But Sartre's version of this trope offers something startlingly new, however. It's a *mise en abyme* in a more specific sense, in that the whole book

---

[11] *Words*, p. 128.

[12] See Gary Saul Morson, *Narrative and Freedom: The Shadows of Time* (New Haven: Yale University Press, 1994). I am grateful to Nicola King for this reference.

[13] *Words*, p. 126.

[14] Ibid., pp. 125, 129.

is after all precisely a childhood of someone who was later to become famous; and who was very famous by the time he wrote the book. Sartre thus takes the familiar form of the childhood memoir, but makes it peculiarly self-reflexive, focusing on a fairly short period of childhood, but reading his whole life out of it. In other words, *Les Mots* is a knowing example of that genre of the childhood of famous men, presenting young Jean-Paul carrying his philosophical head under his arm. In formal terms, he incorporates imaginary portraits (of others, as in this childhood book, but also of himself) into formal autobiography. *L'Enfance des hommes illustres* is biografiction. But Sartre uses it in an ingenious way. He watches his young self turning into something from the book. So it's auto/biografiction to that extent, and turns into an imaginary self-portrait: a portrait of the young author as a character in a book. This episode produces another kind of *mise en abyme*, in that the children in the book are fated to live each moment as if it encapsulates the whole of their future lives. That is, each moment becomes a representation of a whole life (rather like Nietzsche's thought experiment of Eternal Recurrence). As he feels trapped inside the book, young Jean-Paul feels obliged to live his life under this pressure of foreshadowing.

SPEAK, MEMORY

The first major postmodern autobiography was arguably Vladimir Nabokov's *Conclusive Evidence* (1947); expanded, and revised self-reflexively, into *Speak, Memory: An Autobiography Revisited* (1967). It, too, introduced a new degree of formal detachment and inventiveness to autobiography.

Nabokov's *Speak, Memory* is also largely concerned with childhood. Five-sixths of it deal with his life before he went to university in Cambridge. But his attitudes towards his childhood couldn't be more different from Sartre's. Nabokov's attitude towards time is also very different. Though both make childhood a set of mirrors or magnifying glasses with which to examine the rest of their lives, where Sartre's story is of trying to escape from alienation and a false self, Nabokov's is a more Wordsworthian project, to explore the loss of a childhood sense of plenitude and reality. And where Sartre uses style to attack bourgeois literariness, Nabokov uses style like a hallucinogen, to try to escape from exile and reconnect with his past. Yet both men proceed with irony, realizing the traps on their way, and always suggesting ways in which they escape their own representations of themselves.

Speak, Memory represents a new stage in 'aesthetic autobiography'. Where earlier examples take an aesthetic attitude towards life—try to understand it, or live it, as a work of art—for Nabokov the aesthetic becomes dominant: more important than life; more interesting than autobiography. To take a representative example, when Nabokov is a young child, he is brought down to meet a friend of the family, General Kuropatkin. The General plays a game with young

Vladimir involving matches. Suddenly he is called away to be appointed supreme commander of Russian army in the Russo-Japanese war. Fifteen years later, Nabokov's father is escaping from St Petersburg during the Russian Revolution, to avoid being captured by the Bolsheviks:

he was accosted while crossing a bridge, by an old man who looked like a gray-bearded peasant in his sheepskin coat. He asked my father for a light. The next moment each recognized the other. I hope old Kuropatkin, in his rustic disguise, managed to evade Soviet imprisonment, but that is not the point. What pleases me is the evolution of the match theme: those magic ones he had shown me had been trifled with and mislaid, and his armies had also vanished [. . .] The following of such thematic designs through one's life should be, I think, the true purpose of autobiography.[15]

You might think the political background to Nabokov's life is the important thing. His grandfather had been Minister of Justice, and his father was an important statesman, involved in Kerensky's liberal government just before the Revolution. That's why top generals came to visit. You might think historical events like wars and revolutions were the important thing; especially for a writer like Nabokov, an émigré after the Russian Revolution, who studied at Cambridge, settled in Berlin after the First World War—where his father was assassinated at a political meeting—and then had to emigrate again, this time to America, to escape the Nazis in the Second World War. Another autobiographer might find that the extraordinary coincidence of this meeting amidst revolutionary turmoil was what gave its memory significance. But no! For Nabokov, 'the point', the true purpose of autobiography, is aesthetic: the evolution of themes. It isn't even the matches themselves, since they've vanished long ago like the armies and the wars and the General and Nabokov's father. It's the match *theme* that matters to Nabokov—the way he appreciates a pattern in his life. The national crises, and crises of others, provide the background to his perceptions and memories.

We now think of Nabokov as postmodern, for his lexical ingenuity; his fascination with simulacra, puzzles, the endless play of representations. *Speak, Memory* displays all these traits, and nowhere more so than when he gives a new twist to the imaginary self-portrait, splitting into various identities, concealed under lexical and formal playfulnesses. When he is discussing the émigré Russian authors he met in Paris, he says:

But the author that interested me most was naturally Sirin. He belonged to my generation. Among the young writers produced in exile he was the loneliest and most arrogant one. Beginning with the appearance of his first novel in 1925 and throughout the next fifteen years, until he vanished as strangely as he had come, his work kept provoking an acute and rather morbid interest on the part of critics [. . .] Conversely, Sirin's admirers made much, perhaps too much, of his unusual style, brilliant precision, functional

---

[15] Nabokov, *Speak, Memory: An Autobiography Revisited* (London: Penguin, 2000), p. 23.

imagery and that sort of thing. Russian readers who had been raised on the sturdy straightforwardness of Russian realism and had called the bluff of decadent cheats, were impressed by the mirror-like angles of his clear but weirdly misleading sentences and by the fact that the real life of his books flowed in his figures of speech, which one critic has compared to 'windows giving upon a contiguous world [. . .]'[16]

Those critics and admirers would have recognized the game Nabokov is playing with life-writing here, since he had published his early books in Russian as Vladimir Sirin, and then his first English translations as Vladimir Nabokoff-Sirin. The portrait of Sirin has thus been written from a mirror-like angle, so that if we look into it we see Nabokov. It is an imaginary portrait insofar as Sirin is a pseudonym (hence his mysterious arrival without a history, and disappearance without a death). And it is an imaginary self-portrait, in which Nabokov—'naturally' interested in him above all other writers—can comment on his own work. To that extent it is also another *mise en abyme*: an autobiographical sketch within an autobiography. What he says about Sirin's prose offers further clues, both to the puzzle of Sirin's identity, and to the nature of Nabokovian autobiography. For this passage is itself composed of 'clear but weirdly misleading sentences': weirdly misleading us to think Sirin is another person; clear because what they say is true, but true of Nabokov. It is also composed of allusions to Nabokov's works: *The Real Life of Sebastian Knight* in the phrase 'the real life of his books'; or *Pale Fire*, whose eponymous poem begins with a waxwing killed 'by the false azure in the windowpane', as it mistakes the glass for a 'contiguous world'.

The Real Life of Sebastian Knight is a fictional biography of an author by his half-brother, and thus the phrase 'real life' plays there between lived experience and life-writing. But when Nabokov revisits it in his autobiography something else happens to it. To say 'the real life of his books flowed in his figures of speech' is profoundly ambiguous. It could be taken as a modernist/formalist rejection of biography: the energy of his language is what matters in a writer, not his life outside the books. Or it could be taken as a version of the Wilde–Nietzsche argument that even such apparently impersonal, formalist writing is autobiography; or even of Lejeune's trope that it is in such works of art that the truest autobiography—the *real* life—is to be located. Or, as Nabokov put it: 'The best part of a writer's biography is not the record of his adventures but the story of his style.'[17] Part of the story of Nabokov's own style is that it plays these games with imaginary self-portraits: with biography, autobiography, and their inter-reflections. Indeed, as Herbert Grabes has shown, Nabokov's novels 'are all fictitious biographies or fictitious autobiographies.'[18] In his fictitious review of *Conclusive Evidence*, Nabokov argued that among the features setting it 'completely apart

---

[16] *Speak, Memory*, p. 220–1.
[17] *Strong Opinions* (London: Weidenfeld and Nicolson, 1974), pp. 154–5.
[18] Herbert Grabes, *Fictitious Biographies: Vladimir Nabokov's English Novels* (The Hague: Mouton & Co., 1977), p. ix.

from extant autobiographies, true, more or less true, or deliberately fictitious', was its 'being the meeting point of an impersonal art form and a very personal life story.'[19] This perfectly articulates postmodernism's turn of the trope of im/personality, and of the new games it finds to play with life-writing.

By the time Nabokov published *Conclusive Evidence* he had been living in America for seven years. By the time *Speak, Memory* appeared, he had taught literature at Wellesley and Cornell. Literary criticism, like psychoanalysis, had acquired a much stronger institutional presence after the Second World War, and Nabokov had experienced it first hand. To encrypt your meanings and your life in this way is to anticipate critics and psychoanalysts going over your work; it is also to attempt to confuse or mislead them. Where Sartre takes up the terms of both and incorporates them into his own more complex system, Nabokov creates complex puzzles to frustrate them, meanwhile denouncing their methods. When an interviewer questioned him about his mockery of 'Freud, the Viennese witchdoctor', Nabokov was quick to spot the potential psychoanalytic trap of letting resistance be read as agreement, but nonetheless wouldn't restrain his contempt: 'I detest not one but four doctors: Dr. Freud, Dr. Zhivago, Dr. Schweitzer, and Dr. Castro.'[20] This at once turns him into a parody paranoid, while simultaneously ruling out a set of conflicting perspectives: not just psychoanalytical, but religious; not just Marxist revolutionary, but moral-idealistic. As with the imaginary self-portrait of Sirin, the game-playing prevents us from locating the autobiographer.

Where *fin de siècle* autobiografiction was tentative and anxious, and modernist engagements with life-writing were formally more experimental, Postmodernist autobiographies like these are more ludic and performative in their explorations of the aesthetic life. Yet their debt to our earlier experiments with life-writing and fiction are evident. It isn't only postmodern autobiography, but also a major strand of postmodernist fiction, that draws on these modernist precursors and their *fin de siècle* precursors. For many key postmodern novels can be described as works of autobiografiction, or auto/biografiction. Chapter 7 contemplated reading a classic modernist text by Joyce with postmodernist eyes. Historically speaking, it is because postmodernists like Nabokov and Sartre were so saturated in modernist aesthetics that such retrospective reinterpretation is possible.

This discussion of Sartre and Nabokov, is intended to show how some of the themes traced earlier in the book—imaginary portraiture, portrait-collections, aesthetic autobiography—continued to be taken up and developed from the 1930s. Certain of our other central themes also have an important postmodernist legacy. In particular, auto/biografiction, and imaginary authorship, have become

[19] 'Appendix: "Chapter Sixteen" or "On *Conclusive Evidence*', *Speak, Memory*, pp. 238–51 (pp. 238–9).
[20] Nabokov, interviewed by Nicholas Garnham, *Listener*, 10 October 1968: *Strong Opinions*, pp. 115–19 (p. 115).

essential components of the postmodern mode that Linda Hutcheon has identified as 'historiographic metafiction'—which she characterizes in *A Poetics of Postmodernism* as 'those well-known and popular novels which are both intensely self-reflexive and yet paradoxically also lay claim to historical events and personages';[21] and analyses them in *The Politics of Postmodernism* in these terms:

Facts are events to which we have given meaning [...] Postmodern fiction often thematizes this process of turning events into facts through the filtering and interpreting of archival documents [...] in historiographic metafiction the very process of turning events into facts through the interpretation of archival evidence is shown to be a process of turning the traces of the past (our only access to those events today) into historical representation.[22]

Such fiction, she argues, brings out the way, in Dominick LaCapra's words, 'the past is not an "it" in the sense of an objectified entity that may either be neutrally represented in and for itself or projectively reprocessed in terms of our own narrowly "presentist" interests.'[23] Hutcheon continues:

While these are the words of a historian writing about historical representation, they also describe well the postmodern lessons about fictionalized representation [...] we only have representations of the past from which to construct our narratives or explanations. In a very real sense, postmodernism reveals a desire to understand present culture as the product of previous representations. The representation of history becomes the history of representation. What this means is that postmodern art acknowledges and accepts the challenge of tradition: the history of representation cannot be escaped but it can be both exploited and commented on critically through irony and parody [...][24]

Those historical traces so important for Hutcheon's argument—archival documents, testimony of witnesses—come down to us, in part, through forms of life-writing: letters, diaries, journals, memoirs, interviews, autobiographies. The works examined in earlier chapters comprise a tradition of the ironizing and parodying of these forms of life-writing. 'Auto/biografiction', in other words, can be understood as a strand of historiographic metafiction. Where classic works of historiographic metafiction focus on the representations of historical crises or trauma—Indian Independence and Partition in Rushdie's *Midnight's Children*; the Somme in Pat Baker's *Ghost Road Trilogy*; the Holocaust in Sebald's *Austerlitz*—auto/biografiction focuses on the representations of individual life-stories.

While 'metafiction' may feel like an anachronistic term to describe turn-of-the-century auto/biografiction by writers like 'Rutherford', Gosse, or Benson, by

[21] Linda Hutcheon, *A Poetics of Postmodernism* (New York and London: Routledge, 1988), p. 5.
[22] Linda Hutcheon *The Politics of Postmodernism* (London: Routledge, 1989), p. 57.
[23] Dominick LaCapra, *History, Politics, and the Novel* (Ithaca, NY: Cornell University Press, 1987), p. 10.
[24] Hutcheon, *The Politics of Postmodernism*, pp. 57–8.

the time we reach the modernism of Woolf and Stein there is no question that works like *Orlando* or *The Autobiography of Alice B. Toklas* are thematizing their own processes of representation. Such works, together with those by Pessoa and Joyce discussed in Chapter 7, represent the beginnings of what we might call, by way of another neologism (alas, this chapter must introduce three more such terms), *auto/biographic metafiction*. Where historiographic metafiction represents a post-modernizing of the historical novel, auto/biographic metafiction represents a post-modernizing of auto/biography.

POSTMODERN AUTO/BIOGRAPHIC METAFICTION

The notions of framing and hierarchy have proved crucial to the presentation of autobiografiction, as we have seen through the use of fictional editors, prefaces, and *mises en abyme*. Putting a work of art within a fictional frame, can let the frame govern it. The frame seems to have more authority than what it contains. The creation within the creation seems like secondary creation. Critics often seem uneasy with it, as it shows the frames up as themselves fictionalized, thus disturbing any certainties we may have thought we had about the boundary between originality and impersonation. But such difficulties indicate that creation within creation is more difficult to bring off. Rather than a second-order achievement, it should be recognized as a sign of a double talent.

To illustrate these ideas, let us briefly consider three virtuoso postmodernist works that all turn on these questions of autobiografiction, imaginary writing, and the use of frames:

- Doris Lessing's *The Golden Notebook* (1962) as autobiographic metafiction.
- Vladimir Nabokov's *Pale Fire* (1962) as auto/biographic metafiction.
- A. S. Byatt's *Possession* (1990), as biographic metafiction.

The Golden Notebook

The work Lessing describes in her Preface as 'a conventional, short novel', entitled 'Free Women', she calls 'a skeleton, or frame.'[25] It is broken up into five sections, each separated by 'stages of the four Notebooks, Black, Red, Yellow and Blue'. But 'Free Women' is only a conventional novel in an unconventional sense: it is another example of the convention (or trope) of fictional fictions, since it is the novel written by Anna Wulf, one of *The Golden Notebook*'s central characters. We wouldn't know this if we didn't have the Notebooks as well. Structurally, then, yes, the novel 'Free Women' is the frame containing the

---

[25] Lessing, *The Golden Notebook* (London: Flamingo, 1993), p. 7.

Notebooks. But, logically, the Notebooks frame 'Free Women', show its genesis. In a way, this would be the more conventional approach, seeing the Notebooks as 'source' material, raw, or at least less cooked, biographical data, which then gets 'transmuted', by some creative magic or mystery, into art, a 'novel'. And the work as a whole could be read as telling a story that has now become 'conventional' to a post-psychoanalytic audience: the story of the process an artist needs to go through to produce authentic, challenging work: a process of disintegration, splitting, and breakdown, before a new form can be constructed out of the fragments.

But to put it like this is to begin to see it in another way. For, if the book shows the fictional author, Anna, moving from emotional problems to literary solutions (from the notebooks to the novel 'Free Women'), it shows the author Doris Lessing moving in the other direction, from conventional novel to the breakdown of convention; from the Forsterian novel of personal relations to the psychodrama of Anna's and Saul's intense, often unreal, virtually psychic, relationship; from balanced, coherent narrative, to the multiple, overlapping, split notations in the various notebooks. Rather than reading as auto/biographical source material, the notebooks feel at least as fictionalized (by Anna, as well as by Lessing) as anything in 'Free Women'. Lessing is using this paradox of frame and picture not just to play perceptual games: it relates seriously to her ethical and philosophical concerns; concerns with how the personal relates to the public (do we determine our society, or does it determine us?); and her existential concern with freedom. In this book she has used imaginary writing, fictional creativity, to find a new form to express that idea: since neither the novel 'Free Women', nor the Notebooks, really contains or determines the other, but each is both related to yet also free from the other, as her friends, relations, and lovers strive to be. By calling the whole novel the title of one of the notebooks (not just a part, but a part of a part), she undoes the distinction between whole and part, between source and work.

Pale Fire

Something comparable occurs in another book of Nabokov's, the novel *Pale Fire* (1962), already touched on in terms of fake auto/biography, but offered here as an example of 'auto/biographic metafiction'. Framing and imaginary authorship are crucial here too, as is the focus on life-writing. Nabokov multiplies imaginary authors. At the heart of the novel is John Shade's poem 'Pale Fire', which Nabokov reproduces in full. He combines it in a life-and-death struggle with a fictional work of scholarship: Charles Kinbote's bizarre notes to the poem, which threaten to engulf it.

Again, there's a paradox about which is the source, which is the text. Kinbote thinks he suggested the idea of the poem, and that his story is its source. He wants to read into it, or write into it where he cannot, his own story. On the surface, Shade's poem about a suburban academic family grieving for a dead child, seems to have no connection with Kinbote's alleged autobiography, of being a deposed king of a country called 'Zembla', in exile in America and in fear of espionage and assassination. Nabokov achieves an exquisite balance, whereby on the one hand, the correspondences Kinbote claims with the text are so detailed and systematic they begin to seem possible, but on the other, his story could equally be read as paranoid fantasy in both its persecutory extremity and its relentlessly systematic quality. Yet commenting on Shade's poem lets Kinbote articulate his autobiography; so in that sense the poem is the source of the story he tells us.

Nabokov's novel thus not only combines two acts of literary ventriloquism, impersonating the authorship of Shade's poem and Kinbote's commentary. It also explores two contrary ways of understanding the relation between them in terms of ventriloquial influence. Kinbote, who has a higher opinion of Shade's gifts than the poem quite warrants, is convinced that his conversations with Shade about his Zemblan past have inspired the poem. His determination to read every detail as somehow alluding to him is tantamount to claiming his words have ventriloquially produced Shade's. But, in a novel preoccupied with mirrors and mirror-images from the first lines of the poem, this is the reflection of Kinbote's belief that Shade's words somehow ventriloquially produce his, Kinbote's, biography. Competent though the poem is, it is rather pedestrian, and deeply imitative of its models (especially Alexander Pope). There's a paradox that what Kinbote makes of it is something more imaginative; something which has the true madness of imagination, if not the true imagination of madness which Nabokov's novel's frame provides.

Pale Fire is a detective story, not only about murder, but about theft.

> The suns a thief, and with his great attraction
> Robs the vast sea. The moon's an arrant thief,
> And her pale fire she snatches from the sun.[26]

If Kinbote is mad to think Shade's poem alludes to him, then he has not only stolen the text of the poem, but its meaning too. Or, he has murdered Shade's poem, and made his own version of it assume its identity (rather as he may himself madly have assumed the identity of the Zemblan king Charles). Or is his belief justified that his own experiences (even though they don't figure explicitly in the poem) are both its inspiration and veiled subject?

Both Shade and Kinbote write autobiographically. Both autobiographies might be autobiografictional; Shade's for its wishful thematizing of the afterlife of his daughter; Kinbote's if his story is fantasy. Nabokov's novel can itself be

---

[26] *Timon of Athens*, IV. iii. 438–40.

seen as allegorizing autobiografiction in the way it tracks how the pedestrian everyday life can be transmuted into something fantastical.

The Golden Notebook and *Pale Fire* are thus works of postmodern auto/ biografiction. One of the legacies of postmodernism (even in its Nietzschean or Wildean avatars) is a sharper sense of how the biographic is inextricable from the autobiographic. Yet *Pale Fire* might be considered something of a transitional text, in the way it recapitulates a shift from the modern engagements with autobiography discussed throughout this study to the engagements with biography perhaps equally characteristic of postmodernism. Fiction about biography, and about biographers, has become an increasingly important strand of 'historiographic metafiction' since, say, 1941—the year of Nabokov's *The Real Life of Sebastian Knight*.[27]

Possession

The prime example, though, is A. S. Byatt's *Possession* (1990), offered here as our example of 'biographic metafiction'. *Possession* is a masterpiece of fictional creativity; like the act of a good impersonator. Byatt not only writes poems by her characters, the two very different Victorian poets R. H. Ash and Christabel LaMotte; she also writes some of their letters; of the journals of his wife and her cousin; then parts of an academic biography of Ash, entitled *The Great Ventriloquist*; and pieces of criticism of both (and so on). *Possession* thus not only exemplifies literary ventriloquism, but thematizes it and offers beautiful ventriloquized discussion of it, both placing it as taboo for the nineteenth century, while offering a twentieth-century solution. Ash writes to LaMotte:

I have no right to extend my unfortunate curiosity to your work, your writing. You will accuse me of trying to write your Melusina, but it is not so—it is only my unfortunate propensity to try to make concrete in my brain how you would do it—and the truly exciting possibilities open up before me [. . .] And yet I know your work is nothing if not truly original—my speculations are an impertinence.[28]

Ash turns out to be implicated in LaMotte's poem 'The Fairy Melusine'. There's even a moment when Roland, the Ash scholar, says '*Melusina* sounds often as though he wrote it.'[29] So it may be some kind of instance of possession or ventriloquism; though Byatt leaves this marvellously open. More importantly, Ash's letter to LaMotte about the poem raises another accusation: that *Byatt* is writing other people's works for them. 'And yet I know your work is nothing if not truly original.' Fictional creativity is by definition not truly original. Must it

---

[27] See the discussion of 'biografiction' in Chapter 5, and especially of postmodern works about biographers and biography on p. 218.
[28] A. S. Byatt, *Possession* (London: Vintage, 1991), p. 177.
[29] Ibid., p. 265.

therefore be 'nothing'? Must it always be dismissed as impertinence, as pastiche, as fake? Byatt's novel proves the reverse: that the truest poetry is the most faking; that it isn't impossible to write convincing poems or stories by other people; it's just harder.

Pastiche can be uncomfortably close to a form of theft. *Possession* starts with a theft—a purloined letter, in fact—Roland's stealing of Ash's draft letter he comes across in a volume in the library—and ends with another kind of detective denouement, which combines theft and death: the digging up of the box containing a letter buried with the poet.

In *Possession*, too, the frame could be said to take over the pastiches, in two senses at least. First, because the detective story becomes the story of how Roland and Maud (the LaMotte scholar) find out who they are, and what they want. She turns out to be a descendant of Ash (which she didn't know) as well as of LaMotte (which she did know). Roland finds out he wants to be a poet, not a scholar. They find out they want each other, which they have been spending most of the novel trying to ignore. Their literary work thus turns out to matter to them as biography rather than as literature.

The second sense in which the frame might seem to take over the fictional writings within it is that Roland's and Maud's detective work shows them that the literary works they are studying turn out to have mattered to their writers more as biography than as literature. They discover that the poems and stories and journals they thought they knew as scholars actually concealed a different meaning, which is to do with the life stories of the writers (their meeting, their affair, their illegitimate child, their separation), rather than with their ostensible subjects of fantasy, mythology, and history.

Thought of in this way, Byatt's pastiches might seem a side-show, which exists for the sake of the more important stories of human relationships in the present and in the past. And yet; it is the literary works that have 'possessed' the scholars, and made them care about the biographies. These literary works are then found to 'contain' the stories that contain them. No instance of the word 'ash' can then be thought 'innocent' in LaMotte's writings. So not only does the Ash/LaMotte story interpret Roland and Maud for us, as they interpret it. But also their *writings* interpret them, and their readers. The picture won't stay in its frame. Roland even takes a postmodern pleasure in recognizing that he's living out someone else's plot.

These examples of 'auto/biographic metafiction' also incorporate versions of imaginary portraiture, though in each case in a different metafictional way. *Possession* not only creates portraits of its two imaginary Victorian authors, but reads their imaginary writings as imaginary self-portraits of their authors, while showing their biographer-readers discerning these portraits, and thus furnishing their own imaginary self-portraits in the process. The *Golden Notebook* is a portrait of the artist as a woman, in which Anna Wulf is an imaginary self-portrait of Lessing, and Anna's imaginary fiction, *Free Women* is the imaginary self-portrait of a fictional character. John Shade's auto/biographical poem in *Pale Fire* is a self-portrait in imaginary writing. It's jarringly different from the imaginary portrait of Shade that Kinbote's notes become (because the poem seems oblivious to Kinbote, which doesn't stop Kinbote reading it as about himself). The autobiographical account Kinbote gives of himself in the notes may be an imaginary self-portrait in the sense of a delusory identity. Whether it is or not, his reading of Shade's poem turns it into an imaginary portrait of Kinbote (thus his reading is an imaginary self-portrait, even if Shade didn't intend the poem as an imaginary portrait of him).

These three novels offer a representative sample of how fiction about biographers and autobiographers has formed so important a part of the postmodern literary landscape, and of how constitutive of the projects of modernity and postmodernity an engagement with life-writing has been. They show how the crescendo of auto/biografiction and imaginary writing in modernism is important not only for its own sake, but for its legacy to postmodernism, too.

Conclusion

'A man who invents himself needs someone to believe in him, to prove he's managed it.'[1]

'I suppose that a novelist who produces an autobiography has the right to expect that most of its readers will also be readers of his fiction. As a good deal of real life has got into my fiction, I forbear to unscramble it all into what has been fabled by the daughters of memory, though I have unscrambled some.'[2]

MEDIATIONS OF SUBJECTIVITY

The story followed in this book is necessarily complex and has many strands. It is as recalcitrant to generalization as is the story of the novel, not least because it often *is* the story of the novel, or parallels and intersects with that story. Nevertheless, a central strand has traced how auto/biography and auto/biographical writing from the 1870s to the 1930s becomes shadowed by an increasing scepticism. Distinct phases can be identified in the works we have examined. While they do not constitute an ineluctable chronological sequence—they sometimes overlap or return—they do manifest a logical sequence of increasing scepticism about subjectivity and its representations, which takes various forms, according to where the scepticism is directed:[3] scepticism about the formal conventions of representation issues in ironic or pseudo- or mock-auto/biography; scepticism about the intelligibility or reality of the self fosters impressionism, autobiografiction, and formalism; scepticism about the capturability of the self in writing issues in anti-autobiography; scepticism about the notion of the self as essential produces an awareness of performativity.

Certainly, not all auto/biographic production has been affected. The majority of biographies and autobiographies that flood the market are still predominantly

---

[1] Salman Rushdie, *The Satanic Verses* (London: Vintage, 1998), p. 49.

[2] Anthony Burgess, *Little Wilson and Big God* (London: Heinemann, 1987), p. viii.

[3] For example Harold Nicolson's identification of 'sceptical detachment' as 'the main element in twentieth-century biography': *The Development of English Biography* (London: Hogarth Press, 1927), pp. 134–5; discussed in Chapter 11.

realist, bourgeois, and formally or technically null. But the conceptually and technically more sophisticated versions, such as are studied here, increasingly come to question and transform the form.

Post-structuralist critics have argued that autobiography is subject to 'displacement' and 'excess'; baffled in its attempt to deliver the promised self, and thus performing an excess of substitute figures serving to obscure such displacements.[4] However, the auto/biographical works discussed in this book effect their displacements, performative excesses, and opacities in different ways from those posited by deconstruction. They do so by specific structural or formal means, rather than as a result of a general condition of language or textuality. According to the deconstructive readings, what I have designated formal autobiography (in which a first-person narrator who is also the author whose name appears on the title-page claims to tell his or her own story) will never quite deliver what it promises. Yet the late nineteenth- and early twentieth-century works discussed here dismantle precisely this structure of formal autobiography. Their opacities and unpredictabilities are produced by their strategies of narrating autobiography not in the first person; or by using a narrator or focalizer whose name is not that of the author; or by publishing autobiography pseudonymously or anonymously; or by displacing their own story into those of others; giving a fictional character the author's life-story; or producing entirely fictional auto/biography that mimics the forms of conventional life-writing: or writing fake journals, diaries, letters, poems, novels. Such transformations of life-writing can be accounted for in multiple ways, all with their own plausibility: as a return to eighteenth-century carnivalesque experiments with life-narratives; as the aftermath of the problematics of Romantic autobiography; as a response to changing ideas about the relation between language, the self, society, and the universe in the nineteenth century;[5] or to changing technologies of subjectivity, including bourgeois ideology, the increasing deployment of publicity to market authors, and developments in autobiographical fiction, sociology and psychoanalysis; or as indicative of an increasing scepticism not only about religious authority but also literary authority.

Late nineteenth-century autobiographies such as those by Mill, Ruskin, and Nietzsche move away from a sense of the self as essential, given, and intelligible, and towards narratives of multiplicity, uncertainty, breakdown, and loss. This is the starting point for *fin de siècle* and impressionist experiments in life-writing. The self there appears elusive, liquid, intermittent, and unreliable. The scepticism about its knowability generates an uncertainty about whose self is being narrated, so (as in Pater's Imaginary Portraits) the lines between autobiography, biography, and fiction become harder to draw. The outpouring of forms of

[4] See Linda Anderson, *Autobiography* (London and New York: Routledge, 2001), p. 53.
[5] See for example Linda Dowling, *Language and Decadence in the Victorian Fin de Siècle* (Princeton: Princeton University Press, 1986).

'displaced' or 'disturbed' pseudonymous autobiography begins to appear increasingly fictionalized, or to be read as such, at the point where Stephen Reynolds was able to identify a puzzling hybridity; a deluge of 'autobiografiction'.

To some extent this increasing awareness of fictionality inhering in the auto/biographic project can be accounted for by the machineries of displacement. That is, the plethora of pseudonyms, prefaces, fictional editors and annotators, the presentation of putative diaries, journals, autobiographies, letters framed and interrupted by other textual matter produces an awareness of the auto/biographic as inescapably *textual*, mediated by such textual traces; and of the self as legible only in such partial and displaced textualized forms. That is, the view of the self as given and self-present (as in the Cartesian *cogito*: 'I think therefore I am'), gives way to a view of the self as constructed in the process of expression. If Pater sounds melancholy that the self unweaves itself and vanishes away as you try to analyse it, and his contemporaries like Hale White and Benson write as if they were frantically constructing fictional selves in order to compensate for the self that felt lost, our later writers have celebrated the unweaving and vanishing as precisely where and how one achieves a sense of selfhood (rather as you only attain a sense of having been dreaming as the dream dissolves).

Chapter 4 argued that the major shift represented by the flourishing of auto/biografiction in this period was towards a sense of character as something that needs to be constructed. If selfhood is only knowable through its representations, then there is a sense in which those representations produce the subject as an object of knowledge. Whether or not one believes there is a pre-existent, essential self—even if its process of construction is really a process of re-construction—it only becomes a self for us as it is represented, mediated, constructed. The aspects of construction and of process are both crucial. But they have been understood in different ways, variously emphasizing self-creation, multiplicity and possibility; narrativity; fictionality; or performativity. All these ideas have threaded their way through our discussion. They will be briefly recapitulated here, before concluding with an account of auto/biografiction as not so much a historically specific instance of a hybrid form, but as a discursive system which operates through a problematic opposition between autobiography and fiction.

When Gosse ended *Father and Son* with the claim that he 'took a human being's privilege to fashion his inner life for himself', I suggested that he was punning between two senses: he had chosen to live a life different from the one his father had lived, or the one his father wanted for him; he had chosen his own way of writing his life. Indeed, his choice of a literary life was one of the ways in which he had departed from the life-script his father had prescribed. The form of life-writing he employs—autobiografiction—is itself a departure from his father's fundamentalism. Critics nowadays are so familiar with the notion of 'self-fashioning' as a hallmark of New Historicist terminology that they might miss how self-consciousness about fashioning the self is announced here as already integral to the project of modern life-writing. That is, Gosse's crucial ambiguity raises a question that had been becoming increasingly pressing for life-writing: how far is the self presented equivalent to an actual or pre-existent self, and how far is it something created or transformed by the process of its fashioning. This would be one way of understanding Heidegger's magisterial paradox from 'The Origin of the Work of Art': 'The artist is the origin of the work. The work is the origin of the artist.'[6]

In Paul Valéry's words (which are not Paul Valéry): 'I am aware that, once my pen intervenes, I can make whatever I like out of what I was.'[7] Or, as Sartre put it: 'I never stopped creating myself.'[8] It is possible to see such self-creation as anticipated by the lyric poet's increasing sense of dramatization throughout the nineteenth century. When Emily Dickinson wrote that 'When I state myself [. . .] it does not mean—me—but a supposed person', she means (primarily) that the first person in literature need not refer to the actual author, but may be a fictional first person, 'a supposed person.'[9] But what about when she states 'me'? Is that the hesitation the characteristic dashes indicate? In other words, the recognition that the 'I' can be fictionalized, heteronymous, cuts both ways. If it means that readers cannot assume that the first person is autobiographical because the author may mean it to be an alter ego, by the same token, even when the writer means it to refer to herself it's possible it might refer to another; that, in Rimbaud's mind-bending and grammar-bending phrase, 'Je est un autre' ('I is another').[10] One reason 'I is another', for Rimbaud at least, is that (as he has just explained in the same letter) 'C'est faux de dire: Je pense: on devrait dire: On me pense' ('It's wrong to say "I think"; one ought to say "I am being thought"'). That could be read as saying that the 'I' isn't experienced as subject of thought, only as the object of thought: and thus that the self that we are aware of when we try to think of ourselves is estranged from the subject doing the thinking, and always appears as 'other' to it. I think therefore I am another.

In formal autobiography, this effect is heightened by the time-gap between the narrating and the narrated selves. Edith Wharton's autobiography, *A Backward Glance*, begins with a paradoxical slippage between first and third persons:

It was on a bright day of midwinter, in New York. The little girl who eventually became me, but as yet was neither me nor anybody else in particular, but merely a soft anonymous morsel of humanity—this little girl, who bore my name, was going for a walk with her

[6] Heidegger, 'The Origin of the Work of Art', in *Poetry, Language, Thought*, trans. Albert Hofstadter (New York: Harper Colophon, 1975), p. 17.
[7] Valéry, 'Remarks about Myself', in *Moi*, trans. Marthiel and Jackson Mathews, Bollingen Series XLV; 15 (Princeton: Princeton University Press, 1975), pp. 301–2.
[8] Sartre, *Les Mots*, citation from *Words*, trans. Irene Clephane (Harmondsworth: Penguin, 1967), p. 23.
[9] Emily Dickinson to T. W. Higginson, July 1862: *Emily Dickinson: selected Letters*, ed. Thomas H. Johnson (Cambridge, MA: Belknap Press, 1971), p. 176.
[10] Rimbaud, letter to George Izambard, 13 May 1871, in *Oeuvres Completes*, ed. Rolland de Renéville and Jules Mouquet (Paris: Gallimard, 1963), p. 268.

father. The episode is literally the first thing I can remember about her, and therefore I date the birth of her identity from that day.[11]

In her 'Foreword' to *Testament of Youth*, Vera Brittain quotes from the early twentieth-century novelist Charles Morgan's book *The Fountain*:

In each instant of their lives men die to that instant. It is not time that passes away from them, but they who recede from the constancy, the immutability of time, so that when afterwards they look back upon themselves it is not themselves they see, not even—as it is customary to say—themselves as they formerly were, but strange ghosts made in their image, with whom they have no communication.[12]

Because Brittain is so haunted by the ghosts of loved ones she lost through the war, she feels like her own ghost. But as Morgan's passage indicates, such self-estrangement can beset any autobiographical act of retrospect. Insofar as a self is constructed or performed in the autobiographical act, it is a self that did not previously exist. It cannot but feel 'other'.

This perception of the autobiographic self as 'other' can lead in several directions. One response is to feel that auto/biography is an impossibility. Deconstruction in particular has argued that auto/biography uses words in quest of subjectivity, but what it gives us is not subjectivity, consciousness, the self, but words. As Linda Anderson explains, paraphrasing Derrida: 'Autobiography as a demand for unmediated selfhood is, it seems, doomed to reiterate itself endlessly as text.'[13] The question is, what kind of doom does this represent? At one level, for all the critical sophistication of such a position, the insight it leaves us with is banal. A text is not a person. In Barthes's formulation, 'the *I* which writes the text [...] is never more than a paper-*I*.'[14] The best autobiographers have always known this; and it is an awareness that comes to the fore at the turn of the century. If writers are understandably less inclined to accept that the auto/biographic project can generate only records of failure, they are no more naive in confusing their narratives with themselves. But even when they are hopeful about the ability of words to metamorphose into selves, they are often struck by the otherness of the selves so created.

This predicament prompts three broad categories of response. First, to explore that otherness imaginatively, extrapolating it into fictional other selves in the forms described here as auto/biografiction. According to Reynolds's formula, autobiografiction involves autobiographical content (what he calls 'spiritual experience') displaced onto a fictionalized narrative form. But in the modernist versions of autobiografiction discussed in Part II, we have traced the emergence

---

[11] Edith Wharton, *A Backward Glance* (New York: D. Appleton-Century, 1934), p. 1.
[12] Vera Brittain, *Testament of* Youth (London: Virago, 1983), p. 13.
[13] Anderson, *Autobiography*, p. 79.
[14] Barthes, 'From Work to Text', in R. Rylance, ed., *Debating Texts* (Toronto: University of Toronto Press, 1987), p. 120.

of a different formula, which postulates the autobiographical as residing not in the content, but in the form. This is the second kind of distancing of the created self. In the words of Paul Valéry (apropos of his poem 'La jeune Parque'): 'Qui saura me lire lira une autobiographie, dans la forme' ('He who will know how to read me will read an autobiography, in the form').[15] Valéry's phrasing implies that autobiography is to be found in the form instead of the content—a more formalist position than we have found in our modernist examples, which could all be described as combining autobiography of content with autobiography of form—though in different ratios. Joyce doesn't just give Stephen his own formative experiences, but shows him learning how to represent them, in a portrait of artistry. Pound obscures his own life to a much greater extent (so that it requires painstaking annotation to restore it); but it is in the verse's control, irony, and bite that his presence is felt; in the way of saying, rather than the thing said. What autobiography there is in *Orlando* is comparably encoded; much of it only decodable to those in the know about Woolf's love for Sackville-West. Woolf, too, felt that it was in terms of form that her work was most significantly autobiographical; when she 'got down to my depths & made shapes square up'.

The third kind of response to the sense of the represented self as estranged is to explore it critically. What Terry Eagleton terms 'anti-autobiography' is not so much a negation of the possibility of writing autobiographically as a commitment to a form of autobiography enacted with scepticism; a turning of the form against itself, which nonetheless does write the self, however ironically (in the case of Eagleton's own memoir, *The Gatekeeper*) or poetically (in the case of André Malraux's *Anti-memoires*).[16] Anti-autobiography is an important form too, and constantly intertwines with autobiografiction (Proust's *Contre Sainte-Beuve* is an example, which anti-autobiography he turned into the autobiografiction of *A la recherche*). But it is also surprisingly well populated, and deserves separate treatment.

Sometimes the incommensurability of self and text has been taken to lead in another direction, focusing its scepticism not on the autobiographic text but on the nature of the selfhood it purports (but fails) to deliver. That is, it can lead to a corrosive scepticism not only about narratives of selfhood, but also about the existence of the very selfhood which they narrate. As Conrad suggested, the understanding of the self as a process of construction can lead to a despair of its ever being anything:

When once the truth is grasped that one's own personality is only a ridiculous and aimless masquerade of something hopelessly unknown the attainment of serenity is not very far

[15] Valéry, *Oeuvres*, ed. Jean Hytier (Paris: Gallimard, 1957), vol. 1, pp. 1631–2.
[16] Eagleton, *The Gatekeeper: A Memoir* (London: Allen Lane and the Penguin Press, 2001), p. 57. Malraux, *Antimémoires* (1967), trans. Terence Kilmartin as *Antimemoirs* (London: Hamish Hamilton, 1968).

off [. . .] If we are 'ever becoming—never being' then I would be a fool if I tried to become this thing rather than that; for I know well that I never will be anything.[17]

That remark is from 1896, very much the heart of the period under consideration here. We have seen how that sense of a crisis of self and personality was integral to autobiography and autobiographic writing from the mid-nineteenth century; how it is integral both to the emergence of autobiografiction and to the emergence of modernist impersonality. The emotional response to such scepticism about selfhood varies. One response—the anxious or agonistic version typified by 'Mark Rutherford' or A. C. Benson, say—is disturbed by the loss of (or the loss of the idea of) self-presence, self-knowledge. Another response takes comic forms, either entertaining itself with the absurdities produced as others' attempts to render themselves only demonstrate the fictionality of their subjectivity; or alternatively, meeting the challenge by turning the fictionality of their own subjectivity into a comic resource, and performing it for all it's worth. In a sense Existentialism fuses these two responses, understanding that anxiety and absurdity are two faces of the same coin—as Conrad's tortuous tone there indicates.

When modernist anxious scepticism about selfhood modulates into the post-structuralist negation of individualism, the notorious 'Death of the Author' can be a prelude not to lament but celebration. Barthes is positively cheery about the process by which authors are encoded as textual effects:

The pleasure of the Text also includes the amicable return of the author. Of course, the author who returns is not the one identified by our institutions (history and courses in literature, philosophy, church discourse); he is not even the biographical hero. The author who leaves his text and comes into our life has no unity; he is a mere plural of 'charms,' the site of a few tenuous details, yet the source of vivid novelistic glimmerings, a discontinuous chant of amiabilities, in which we nevertheless read death more certainly than in the epic of a fate; he is not a (civil, moral) person, he is a body. [. . .] What I get from Fourier's life is his liking for *mirlitons* (little Parisian spice cakes), his belated sympathy for lesbians, his death among the flowerpots [. . .][18]

As Barthes put it in his own stylish anti-autobiography, *Roland Barthes by Roland Barthes*: 'He wants to side with any writing whose principle is that *the subject is merely an effect of language.*'[19] This pushes the idea that the self is only known *through* language to the conclusion that it *is* only language, or at least it is only a side-effect *produced by* language: a kind of verbal mirage. In a classic moment of

---

[17] Conrad to Edward Garnett, 23/24 March 1896: *The Collected Letters of Joseph Conrad*, ed. Frederick R. Karl and Laurence Davies, vol. 1 (Cambridge: Cambridge University Press, 1983), pp. 267–8.
[18] Roland Barthes, *Sade, Fourier, Loyola*, trans. Richard Miller (New York: Hill and Wang, 1976), p. 8.
[19] *Roland Barthes by Roland Barthes*, trans. Richard Howard (New York: Hill and Wang, 1977), p. 79.

postmodern auto/biografiction, he even imagines himself transformed into such effects:

were I a writer, and dead, how I would love it if my life, through the pains of some friendly and detached biographer, were to reduce itself to a few details, a few preferences, a few inflections—let us say 'biographemes' [...][20]

'Biographemes' would be the units of biographical signification; elements of meaning in the 'grammar' of biography. In *Roland Barthes by Roland Barthes* he does just that to himself: reduces himself to a list of preferences, interests, ideas; what we might call 'autobiographemes'. The terms are suggestive of the ways in which auto/biography has its own code or conventions of signification. (Though the danger with structuralist applications of linguistic theory to literature is that the best writers are as often concerned to change the rules as obey them. 'For a long time I used to go to bed early' is an autobiographeme, but arguably one the 'grammar' of autobiography would not have deemed a possible opening before Proust.)

A more common response to the constructedness or otherness of the autobiographical self in the modernist period was to see it as suggesting the *multiplicity* of subjectivity. The Freudian picture of the personality as a system of conflicting agencies is decisive here. The psychoanalytic notion of fantasy was also contributory, showing how we produce fantasmatic versions of ourself in order not to have to recognize other versions of our past. Insofar as the fantasmatic dimension is structured by unconscious desire, the fantasy self can be seen as a symptom; something which traps the subject, preventing him from being himself. But there is another, more celebratory approach to fantasy selves, exemplified here especially by Pessoa and Woolf. In Pessoa's heteronyms, in *Orlando*, or even in *Flush*, the ability to inhabit fantasy selves is liberating. Thus the problematizing of the link between self and text can also be a site of possibility and freedom (as it is, in the end, for Sartre too).

NARRATIVITY, FICTIONALITY, AND THE AESTHETIC

Such awareness of the artifice of subjectivity—of the self *as* an impression—coincides with what we have called aesthetic autobiography. After all, to perceive or consider lives as like works of art is to entertain the idea of lives, and the persons and selves living them, as both creative and created; self-transforming, and thus artificial, and generally subject to the same aesthetic principles as works of art, including works of literature. For writers like Ruskin, or James, for example, it is the process of narrative that creates a sense of self-presence by

[20] Barthes, *Sade, Fourier, Loyola*, p. 9.

passing over, or making over, past selves. Some moral philosophers, notably Alasdair MacIntyre and Charles Taylor, have seen selfhood as essentially a narrative concept. In *After Virtue* MacIntyre argues: 'I am what I may justifiably be taken by others to be in the course of living out a story that runs from my birth to my death; I am the *subject* of a history that is my own and no one else's, that has its own peculiar meaning.'[21] Rather than locating personal identity in putative psychological traits, say, this view posits that the unity and coherence of an individual life is provided by the unity and coherence of its narrative. Yet just as criticism is sceptical that a single narrative can be reduced to a single meaning, so it knows how a single experience is representable by more than a single narrative. The narrative conception of self thus ushers in the very scepticism, relativism, and multiplicity it sought to fend off.

We might also note that, if subjectivity can only be understood discursively or narratively, and no direct or unmediated access is possible, there is no way of being sure the self exists in and for itself, rather than being a by-product of our narratives and discourses. This point of view can lead back towards scepticism about the existence of selfhood; or it can introduce a radical uncertainty about the epistemological status of subjectivity. Either way, subjectivity begins to look increasingly fictional. Similarly, if the sense of self is achieved through the telling of the self as a story, story always has a tendency to grow taller than history.

For literary scholars, especially, the line between narrativity and fictionality is hard to draw. This position was elaborated most influentially by Hayden White, in his book *Metahistory: The Historical Imagination in Nineteenth-Century Europe* (1973), which argued that the literary tropes in historiography shaped the meanings of history. MacIntyre and Taylor do not equate narrativity with fictionality. To do so would undermine their project of taking the narrative self as a basis for ethical and political understanding. But autobiography is clearly at least as tropic as history.

Thus the sense of the constructedness and mediatedness of autobiography conduces rapidly to a sense of its fictionality. Paul Ricoeur, commenting on MacIntyre's 'notion of the narrative unity of a life', argues in terms suggestive of why autobiography should metamorphose into autobiografiction:

it must be seen as an unstable mixture of fabulation and actual experience. It is precisely because of the elusive character of real life that we need the help of fiction to organize life retrospectively, after the fact, prepared to take as provisions and open to revision any figure of emplotment borrowed from fiction or from history.[22]

---

[21] Alasdair MacIntyre, *After Virtue: A Study in Moral Theory*, 2nd edn (London: Duckworth, 1993), p. 217. Charles Taylor, *Sources of the Self: The Making of the Modern Identity* (Cambridge: Cambridge University Press, 1989), especially pp. 47–52.
[22] Paul Ricoeur, *Oneself as Another*, trans. Kathleen Blamey (Chicago: The University of Chicago Press, 1992), p. 162.

Poststructuralist criticism, by contrast, has tended to see autobiography's tendency to fictionalize less as expressing a need, and more as a kind of deception or self-deception. As Shari Benstock writes:

Autobiography reveals gaps, and not only gaps in time and space or between the individual or the social, but also a widening divergence between the manner and matter of its discourse. That is, autobiography reveals the impossibility of its own dream: what begins on the presumption of self-knowledge ends in the creation of a fiction that covers over the premises of its construction.[23]

It is a short step from saying (as here, in Lacanian style) that autobiography is a fiction which conceals a lack—the absence of the self it purports to narrate—to saying that because the narrated self is a fiction, any conception of selfhood is fiction, and the fiction is the self. But if the self which autobiography narrates can only be grasped through its narration, it follows that subjectivity itself is likely to be perceived as inherently fictionalized.

Recent autobiography theory has been unequivocal in assuming that to write the self is to write fiction. Linda Anderson expresses an even more extreme form of this position, according to which autobiography is not merely doomed to fictionalize, but cannot even be understood to refer to anything non-fictional that precedes it: 'The autobiographical self is a fictional construct within the text, which can neither have its origins anterior to the text, nor indeed coalesce with its creator.'[24] To say an autobiographical *text* is a fictional construct is one thing. To say an autobiographical *self* is a fictional construct is almost something else. At least, Anderson's phrasing might imply that an 'autobiographical self'—a self written in an autobiography—is a fictional construct, as opposed to the self doing the writing or the self doing the reading. But taken together with the philosophical position that the self can only be understood narratively, it appears to imply something much more sweeping: namely, that the self is altogether a fictional construct.

That is, if we believe, with MacIntyre, that the unity of a life is given by narrative; and with Taylor, we understand ourselves only in the form of narrative; then once these narratives are perceived as autobiografiction rather than autobiography, the nature of that self-understanding inevitably shifts. Contemporary critical theorists like to imply that such ideas began with contemporary critical theory. But it is central to my exposition that the fictionalization of autobiography was something writers became aware of a century before Deconstruction.

We began with the Wilde–Nietzsche argument that everything is autobiography. But where it has led us (as Wilde and Nietzsche had always already known)

---

[23] Shari Benstock, 'Authoring the Autobiographical', in her *The Private Self: Theory and Practice of Women's Autobiographical Writings* (Chapel Hill: University of North Carolina Press, 1988), 10–33, 11.
[24] Linda Anderson, 'At the Threshold of the Self: Women and Autobiography', in *Women's Writing: A Challenge to Theory*, ed. Moira Monteith (Brighton: Harvester, 1986), p. 59.

is to the realization that autobiography is something else—someone else, even. The something else that autobiography increasingly is during the period, is, increasingly, fiction; or autobiografiction: a form which is caught in the act of turning from confession into a making up of a self, or selves. Rather than 'writing the self', most of the writers discussed here are creating selves, which may or may not be their own; or rather, which are and are not their own, especially when the autobiography is constructed by a novelist.

This is one response to the insight that autobiography partakes of fictionality: to claim that fiction can therefore provide the best autobiography. But again, this idea of auto/biography as fabulous artifice can produce very different responses. The one which dominated in the period immediately after that from the 1870s to the 1930s favoured forms of documentary writing that attempted to turn life-writing into testimony not of the self alone but of society. If this tendency emerged from the war memoirs of the late 1920s, bearing witness to the sufferings and deaths of other selves as well as to the disturbances of the self witnessing them, it was strengthened by the socialism of the 1930s; and again later by the catastrophe of the Holocaust. Orwell, for example, could be said to be turning himself inside out, but the result is the opposite of Henry James's elaborate self-concentration: instead of opening out the workings of the man of imagination, Orwell wants to make himself transparent (as he wanted to make language transparent) so we can see society, and social injustice. He has to be the man of compassion and common decency, but what this shows is what unites him to the common man, not what separates him. Such new forms of auto/biography appear to have little to do with the kinds of playful engagements with life-writing forms which we have been discussing, even if Orwell, like most autobiographers, uses artistic licence to reinvent facts and chronologies in the name of honesty.

PERFORMATIVITY THEORY AND LIFE-WRITING

Another response, related to the idea of the constructedness of subjectivity, is the view that has gained currency over the last two decades of the self as performance. Where earlier cultures have understood selfhood as fate or character, we prefer the more ironic view: selfhood as a part we play; a view that, if it expresses our alienation from a dream of unmediated subjectivity, also promises to empower us to rewrite our selves at will.

Insofar as we are considering autobiographic *texts*, ideas of mediation and construction are useful in capturing the artifice at the heart of the representation of self. But the concentration on written texts can bring with it severe limitations. After all, the self being written about is not only the self that writes, but the living, speaking, interacting self. In our everyday life, that self doesn't only express itself in writing, but in speech, sound, gesture, movement, facial expression, with costumes and props and settings—all the paraphernalia of what Erving Goffman called *The Presentation of Self in Everyday Life*, in his analysis of the way selfhood has to be performed socially. Goffman cast the net of performance ironically wide, writing that 'All the world is not, of course, a stage, but the crucial ways in which it isn't are not easy to specify.'[25]

After Derrida, we know that such things, insofar as we can talk about them, are themselves textual; and we are wary of claims that creatures of language can exist beyond textuality. But if deconstruction argues that performance is textual, the more recent theorizing of performativity has sought to regain the initiative in a different way, arguing the converse: that text is itself inherently performative. Performativity has increasingly become *the* influential paradigm for thinking about literature. This is of course largely thanks to the work of Judith Butler, which brings together speech-act theory, post-structuralism, queer theory, and ideas of performance. Butler's theory of the performative builds on the concept of the illocutionary and perlocutionary force of performative utterances in the speech-act theory of philosophers like Austin and Searle. As she explains: 'Within speech act theory, a performative is that discursive practice that enacts or produces that which it names.'[26] But whereas for speech-act philosophers performative utterances are seen as socially consensual and useful forms, enabling marriages and other contracts, and are known by the participants to be doing what they are doing, the argument that subjectivity is produced performatively is rather different, since it starts with something we thought had another form of (prior) existence, and tells us that it doesn't; that it only comes into being as we perform it. As life-writing studies have proliferated recently, there has been a turn from approaches based on identity politics or figuration towards performativity. Such theories of performativity are further arguments against essentialism. Autobiography does not transcribe a self that already exists. The act of narrating brings that self into being. From one point of view this plays to a Sartrean Existentialist view of the possibility of self-creation. We need no longer be constrained by received versions—especially theologically driven ones—of our role in the world. Instead, we can write our own script; invent ourselves; create our own destiny.

But there is a philosophical problem here—one of agency. Writing one's own script for atheism, politics, society, sexuality, is one thing. But writing one's own script for one's self is another; since, if the self doesn't exist until it is brought into being by the script, who or what is going to do the writing that brings it into being?

Sartre solves this problem in *Les Mots* by showing his self-creating, writerly self emerging from the falsity of his childhood theatrical self, being solely for others;

---

[25] Goffman, *The Presentation of Self in Everyday Life* (Garden City, NY: Doubleday Anchor, 1959), p. 72.

[26] Judith Butler, *Bodies that Matter: On the Discursive Limits of 'Sex'* (New York: Routledge, 1993), p. 13.

existing for the performances of his own prodigiousness. Performativity theorists of life-writing like Sidonie Smith put it differently. In her seminal essay of 1995, 'Performativity, Autobiographical Practice, Resistance', Smith distinguishes different versions of the self: the 'I before the text'; 'the I of the narrator'; and 'the I of the narrated subject'. Performativity theory refuses the identity of these three subjects:

> There is no essential, original, coherent autobiographical self before the moment of self-narrating. Nor is the autobiographical self expressive in the sense that it is the manifestation of an interiority that is somehow ontologically whole, seamless, and 'true' [. . . .] the interiority or self that is said to be prior to the autobiographical expression or reflection is an *effect* of autobiographical storytelling.[27]

This version doesn't quite deny the pre-existence of a self that produces the writing (though that last remark makes it sound like it wants to). It simply argues that that self is different from the one we read. As one commentator puts it, 'The "authentic" self that is sought in autobiography by both writer and reader is not a pre-existent, pre-formed self, but is written into existence [. . .] The very self of self-narratives is conjured up, not found.'[28] That is, the 'self of self-narratives' is just a different self; the one which is 'sought in autobiography by both writer and reader' but is not identical with the self of the person writing it. Those reading the self as performance thus arrive at the same place as those reading the self as narrative—unsurprisingly, since narrative itself can be read as performance.

This splitting of selves is itself well established in autobiography theory, and we have seen a special case of it in autobiografiction. It is seen as inherent in the structure of autobiographical narrative, if only because of the different phases of the self involved. Because of the retrospective nature of the form, the 'I' that is narrating is other than the 'I' that is narrated (as in the examples from Wharton and Brittain). The gap may close as the story gets nearer to the time of writing. But however hard the author may want to prove that (in Wordsworth's paradox) 'The Child is father of the Man', it is the man who is writing who can see that, in a way that the child could not.

What then does performativity theory add to this notion of the multiple personality of autobiography? One answer comes out of a profound scepticism about the agency and epistemology of the self; about our freedom to be how we want; or even, to know who we are. Paul De Man, for example, placed the autobiographic at the heart of his sceptical assault on humanism. In his analysis of Rousseau's *Confessions* in *Allegories of Reading* (1979), he argued that the quest

---

[27] Sidonie Smith, 'Performativity, Autobiographical Practice, Resistance', in *Women, Autobiography, Theory: A Reader*, ed. Sidonie Smith and Julia Watson (Madison: University of Wisconsin Press, 1998), pp. 108–15 (pp. 108–9).

[28] Christine Overall, review of *Women, Autobiography, Theory: A Reader*, in *APA Newsletters*, 00:1 (2000), <http://www.apaonline.org/publications/newsletters/v00n1_Feminism_20.aspx> (accessed 23 April 2009).

for knowledge of the self is displaced by stagings of guilt, shame, and confession.[29] In 'Autobiography as De-Facement' (1979) De Man argues again for this slippage from the cognitive to the performative. In such readings, the performative is seen as a failure of self-knowledge; a symptom of the impossibility of the enlightenment project.

This deconstructionist refusal of the concept of self-expression takes us back from the Sartrean idea of self-creation to the Butlerian version of performativity as bringing into being the very subject it purports to express. For Butler, there is no originary heterosexuality or homosexuality; each imply the other, and need parodically to imitate each other precisely because neither are fixed essences which simply exist. They must be produced, and it is conduct, performance, action, that produces them. It is because the role is impossible that we have to keep up the performance, repeatedly. Which might account for the feature noted in several modern autobiographers (James, Proust, Ford, Nabokov) of what we might term 'revision compulsion'. This is an argument about interpellation; performance as something we're compelled to do by a system.

But such social-construction theories risk falling into determinism, if they deny the possibility of radical action by denying any agency that could change the system. Butler's alternative is to recognize the performativity of everyday life and to break with the gender script through performing gender roles in new (and often parodic, and often humorous) ways—in the terms of performance art, to engage in a subversion of the script, to disavow the repetitious control of the theatrical text and director, allowing for 'self-determining' performance art rather than prefigured roles.[30] This is different from Sartre's position. The self is less stable, less in control of its own production.[31] It's rattling the chains that have constructed its identity.

There is thus an identifiable split in performative theories of autobiography. One reason for the success of such theories is that they draw upon already widely accepted, or at least familiar, deconstructive theories of language and meaning; and thus appear to constitute a negation of humanist ideas of subjectivity. Yet on the other hand they seem to leave the door open to the possibility of self-creation, thus of agency and self-transformation, radicalism; and thus offer an escape from post-structuralism's deconstruction of selfhood.[32] The best account of this ambiguity at the heart of performative theory was given by Laura Marcus, in

---

[29] See De Man, *Allegories of Reading: Figural Language in Rousseau, Nietzsche, Rilke and Proust* (New Haven and London: Yale University Press, 1979), pp. 283–6. I am indebted to Linda Anderson's account of De Man's argument in her *Autobiography*, pp. 49–51.

[30] Mal Ahern, 'performative' (2003), University of Chicago: Theories of Media: Keywords Glossary, <http://csmt.uchicago.edu/glossary2004/performance.htm> (accessed 23 April 2009).

[31] Ibid.

[32] H. Porter Abbott, *The Cambridge Introduction to Narrative* (Cambridge: Cambridge University Press, 2002), 'Life Writing as Performative', pp. 134–7, takes a broader view of the performative, closer to what other critics call autobiography's 'pragmatic' dimension: what it does in the world or to the world or for its author.

her book *Auto/biographical Discourses*, and is the more impressive for having been written so soon after emergence of Butler's work:

First, it exists in Butler's account as a form of ideological mystification in which 'doing' serves to confirm or compel gender as 'being'—identity is performatively constituted [...] Secondly, the 'performative' and 'the performance' seem to become synonymous, or at least closely related, terms, and are discussed as radical ways of revealing the multiple constructions of gender identity and of opening up to the 'parodic proliferation and subversive play of gendered meanings.'[33]

Marcus goes on to argue for 'the concept of the performative' as 'One major link between the disparate forms' of auto/biographical discourse discussed in her book. Yet she also acknowledges that 'the performative is defined in a variety of ways: as experience/action as opposed to theory; as de-authorising play and performance; as authenticating identity and positionality; as deceit, duplicity and self-referentiality; as an ethical discourse of commitment; as testimony.'[34] The ambiguity is already there in the verb 'to perform': to perform a task or a function; or to perform a role. The version of performativity given to us by Speech-Act Theory is the former. If we vow to marry someone, we do; if we agree to a contract, it exists. But performing a role is different. Acting Othello did not make Laurence Olivier a Moor.

Performativity in autobiografiction predates Sartrean Existentialism, and had been becoming gradually more prominent in the previous half-century. It is arguably inherent in our earlier texts: in pseudonymity; in imaginary self-portraiture; in Henry James's arch self-involutions. It is most evident in Wilde's theatricalization of the self; turning his life into a sell-out public performance. But it is less apparent in the other turn-of-the-century anxieties about self-representation analysed in Part I; whereas it is in the increasing fictionalizations of subjectivity that we have charted through modernism in Part II that performativity becomes foregrounded, as melancholic bafflement is gradually replaced by ludic virtuosity of impersonation: in the syntactic virtuosity of Proust; the stylistic virtuosity of Joyce as he metamorphoses into Stephen Dedalus, or the prolific heteronyms of Pessoa; the virtuoso comedy of Woolf's and Stein's games with auto/biographic representation and gender-representation; or the parodic and satiric energies of Pound, Lewis, and Aldington; when giving the self's impressions gives way to giving impressions of the self. Writing is a kind of public performance. When writers are public figures—and it is a corollary of the convention that autobiographies are desired when someone is already established as a public figure that our writers of literary autobiographies are just that—then their writing does have an inescapably performative dimension: a sense of playing

---

[33] Laura Marcus, *Auto/biographical Discourses* (Manchester: Manchester University Press, 1994), p. 284.
[34] Ibid., p. 287.

to an audience, having a confidence that they will be read. We have noted a marked thematization of the acts of reading as well as writing in autobiographic writing from Ruskin and Pater onwards; and similarly, of the writing of autobiography *as* an unfolding performance; as an interpretative process rather than delivery of known quantity, or instantaneous epiphany.

An approach to the autobiographic via recent performativity theory can help us make sense not only of these aspects, but also of others. Conrad's description of 'one's own personality' as 'only a ridiculous and aimless masquerade of something hopelessly unknown' doesn't just indicate a sense of self-estrangement (partly caught in the awkward formality of the impersonal pronoun being applied to the quintessentially personal); and a sense of 'personality' as suddenly and vertiginously appearing as absurd and unintelligible—very much the precursor to the modernist turn from personality as exemplified by T. S. Eliot. It also, in that word 'masquerade', gives an impression of the self as a *performance* of otherness and disguise or impersonation. 'Masquerade' has acquired a particular valency in Butlerian performativity theory in terms of the performance of gender. That is not irrelevant to Conradian masculinity. But it is striking how many of the writers studied here are exemplary not only for their autobiographic writing, but for their radical engagements with gender. Wilde, Pater, James, Proust, Woolf, and Stein, are all landmark figures in the history of transgressive gender representations, as well as those for whom the auto/biographic figures most markedly as performance.

The other aspect of our subject that performativity theory might shed most light upon is the practice of heteronymous or imaginary writing: the point at which a portrait of the artist turns into a masquerade of the artist; an impersonation of writing, as well as the writing of impersonation; the performance of the aesthetic life.

Such, then, are the ways in which modern auto/biografiction might be read as performative. I haven't offered a 'Butlerian' reading of auto/biografiction in the course of this book; though the account of performativity here, is intended to suggest ways in which it might be done. The reason for holding back such concepts until now was to avoid reading the auto/biografictional texts anachronistically; but rather, to suggest not just that performativity theory can help us understand auto/biografiction, but also that auto/biografiction can help us understand the origins of performativity theory.

One consequence of considering life-writing as performance is that if you view the self as performative rather than transcendental, the life-writing shifts from the quest to record an essence to an attempt to transcribe a performance. But that act of transcription is another, second-level performance, a fact that has further consequences for auto/biography. Autobiography is a particularly revealing case, since from this perspective a form that poses as a kind of stepping out of one's primary public role (as politician, author, or even actor), removing the mask and revealing the self, appears doubly artificial: a performance of a performance. In artists' autobiographies these two performances are inextricably linked. After all, how better to show the story of an artist's life than by giving an example of his art? This technical self-consciousness isn't just a matter of saying that an artist's autobiography must attend primarily to that subject's aesthetic sensibilities. It is also to say that the writing of the autobiography is itself an aesthetic act: in short, a performance of being an artist; of being that artist, who had that life story. This location of the artificial at the heart of authenticity, while it may look like an extreme case, may in fact simply reveal the performativity of all life-writing; which may in turn shed light on why it is that historically the emergence of life-writing is inextricable from the experimentation in fictionality that gave birth to the modern novel. The agency that is felt by the reader is felt not in the self being produced, but in the process of the writing. This is partly why autobiography tends towards intertextuality.

AFTERWORDS—SUPPLEMENTARITY

The form of intertextuality constitutive of literary autobiography is the relation between the autobiography and the autobiographer's other texts. So I shall conclude by reconsidering the function of autobiography within an author's oeuvre.[35]

There are exceptions, but the autobiography is usually thought of as a kind of afterword to a writer's career; a coda. In Serge Doubrowsky's ironic terms, it is 'un privilège réservé aux importants de ce monde, au soir de leur vie, et dans un beau style' ('a privilege reserved for the important of this world, in the evening of their lives, and in a fine style').[36] Mill, Nietzsche, James, H. G. Wells, Sartre, Simone De Beauvoir, Doris Lessing, Chinua Achebe, to name but a few, all turn to autobiography after they have written their most important work. This structure is naturalized as the aged dwelling increasingly amid memories; the storyteller entering the phase of anecdotage. The desire to pre-empt a posthumous biographer, and get your say in first, while you still can, underlines the point. Autobiography is often conceived as written from a position of near death. The writing is thus given a quasi-transcendental status, akin to that of 'last words'; as offering a kind of wisdom that only those who have contemplated, and perhaps reconciled themselves to, death, could achieve. Autobiography is almost by definition, 'late work'—not necessarily because it comes late in life, but because it comes later than a corpus of work: 'later work', perhaps.[37] Even when

---

[35] See Chapter 5.

[36] Doubrowsky, cover blurb to *Fils* (Paris: Éditions Galilée, 1977).

[37] See Edward Said, *On Late Style* (London: Bloomsbury, 2006); and Gordon McMullan, *Shakespeare and the Idea of Late Writing: Authorship in the Proximity of Death* (Cambridge: Cambridge University Press, 2007).

literary autobiographers have been precocious—William Gerhardie; Siegfried Sassoon; Martin Amis—their memoirs have come after a substantial body of writing. That fact is important too. Writers' autobiographies differ from others' autobiographies because their subject is at least in part their authors' *texts*—the story of their stories, not just of their lives, inner lives, selves, or personalities. And the relationship of autobiography to oeuvre tends to assume a standard shape in a novelist's career. Life-writing often forms a tailpiece to an oeuvre as well as to a life. B. S. Johnson caught this convention in his wonderful title for his collection of short pieces: *Aren't You Rather Young to be Writing Your Memoirs?* Autobiography, that is, asserts a peculiar kind of intertextuality. It stands outside a prior oeuvre, to comment upon it. It seeks to incorporate or contain that oeuvre. It takes its place within the oeuvre it supplements.

Once this pattern is grasped as a cultural practice, it is thus possible to see that autobiography is a perfect example of a discourse that works according to what Derrida called the logic of the supplement.[38] Something is a supplement if it is not essential to the thing it supplements. But it is a paradoxical notion, since what needs supplementing is incomplete; in which case the supplement is essential to its completion. For Derrida the logic of the supplement describes our general textual condition. Writing poses as supplementary to speech or experience; text as supplementary to *hors-texte* (whereas, famously for Derrida, there *is* only supplement, because there is nothing beyond text). Such ideas have been applied to autobiography, notably by Derrida himself writing about Rousseau, and Geoffrey Hartman writing about Wordsworth.[39] There, too, the emphasis is on the way autobiography both exemplifies and frustrates the Enlightenment ideal of transparent self-knowledge. But there is another sense in which autobiography can be understood in terms of the supplement; and this is to see it as writing which supplements a life's work; and in the case of literary autobiography, which supplements a body of texts: the author's oeuvre.

A public figure may feel that their actions have been misunderstood, or need some explanation to appear in their true light. Political memoirs, like many other types, are conducting debates by other means: justifying decisions; claiming 'legacies'; answering critics. But when a literary autobiography touches on the author's fictional works, the situation is different. A work of art is supposed to be complete in itself; to carry its explanation within itself. Thus for a writer to explain what he meant to do in a novel, or even to describe what she thought she was doing—to explain a book's origins or context—is to suggest that the work of art requires a supplement. Or, to put it slightly differently, we could say that such autobiographical explanation is a supplement that produces or re-produces the

---

[38] See for example Derrida, *Of Grammatology*, trans. Gayatri Chakravorty Spivak (Baltimore and London: Johns Hopkins University Press, 1978), pp. 144–5.

[39] See Linda Anderson, *Autobiography*, pp. 52–3.

thing it means to supplement—by analogy with the way autobiography (according to the performative theory) produces the self it claims to describe.

Besides supplementing individual works, literary autobiography can also supplement the whole oeuvre. Conrad, for example, explained to his agent how he wanted *A Personal Record* to account for the differences between his books: 'I wished to explain (in a sense) how I came to write such a novel as *Under Western Eyes* (I shall say that much in the preface) so utterly unlike in subject and treatment from anything I had done before.'[40] What he actually wrote, in 'A Familiar Preface' to the published volume, places the emphasis differently, on the integration that underlies any disparateness:

The hope that from the reading of these pages there may emerge at last the vision of a personality; the man behind the books so fundamentally dissimilar as, for instance, *Almayer's Folly* and *The Secret Agent*, and yet a coherent, justifiable personality both in its origin and in its action.[41]

This is a clear instance of what De Man means by *prosopopeia* in autobiography.[42] The autobiography is thus presented as the supplement which will make the oeuvre cohere, by producing a 'vision of a personality' which will 'explain' how such diverse books issued from something unified: a 'coherent, justifiable personality'. What's odd is how this vision of 'the man behind the books' requires another book to make us see it. By another paradox, the personality thus conjured up is supposed to explain the novelist. But it is actually the novelist—the storyteller, the masterly author—who explains the personality.

The implication is that the autobiography, which will allow 'the man behind the books' to appear, is different in kind from the books (the novels) the man was behind. Their dissimilarities obscured the personality behind them. The autobiography will make its coherence manifest, justify it. Yet like those novels, it is another narrative text; it can supplement them by adding more stories; more of the same. Once again, it is the performance of the novelistic which produces the self that is supposed to have produced the novels.

Conrad's phrase 'the man behind the books' (itself something of a biographical cliché) implies the personality preceded the novels and is separable from them; whereas the Philippe Lejeune trope, arguing that writers' novels are the best expression of their personalities, suggests a different model, according to which, the personality is inseparable from its performances. Ford's phrase for this notion of what one might call instead 'the man within the books' was, as we have seen, 'literary personality.'[43] As he wrote to Galsworthy: 'When one reads a book

---

[40] Conrad to J. B. Pinker, 13 September 1911: *Collected Letters*, vol. 4, ed. Frederick R. Karl and Laurence Davies (Cambridge: Cambridge University Press, 1990), p. 477.

[41] Conrad, 'A Familiar Preface', *The Mirror of the Sea* [and] *A Personal Record* (London: Dent, 1975), p. xxi.

[42] See pp. 4–5.

[43] For a full discussion of this concept, see Saunders, *Ford Madox Ford: A Dual Life*, vol. 2 (Oxford: Oxford University Press, 1996), ch. 23.

one is always wondering what kind of man the writer is—as writer be it said.'[44] That is, one is reading a novel as autobiographical, but the autobiography it gives you is not so much the private life, as the creative life of the artist's mind. Conrad 'was an unrivalled autobiographer', says Ford, 'not only in his records and reminiscences but in all his writings for publication.'[45] But, as with the trope discussed by Lejeune, the idea of 'literary personality' takes things further. Rather than implying there is a prior self that can be read out of the imaginative works, this suggests that those works express an autobiographical dimension that you cannot read anywhere else. Thus in a sense, then, according to this view too, the personality that gets expressed doesn't pre-exist the novels, but is performed by them, as an epiphenomenon of their primary, fictional, processes. In Ford's words again, 'Conrad was Conrad because he was his books.'[46] To redescribe this paradox in terms of performativity: fiction displaces the autobiographic performance onto other performances, which, though fictional, express the writer's autobiography, or aspects of it. But such fictional performance brings a different subjectivity into being. The existence of many fictions seems to imply (by the logic of the analogy) a multiple personality expressed by an oeuvre. Or rather, it is the oeuvre that best expresses the multiplicity of subjectivity.[47] This is how Proust came to think of his nineteenth-century precursors. The separate books of writers like Balzac, Michelet, and Hugo 'fail to sustain the powerful schemes they invented later (and expressed in prefaces) to create one massive work encompassing the individual volumes.'[48] It was another figure who, as we have seen, shaped Proust's sense of the relation between reading and autobiography, John Ruskin, who became a turn-of-the-century emblem of how a writer's entire oeuvre could be read as autobiography. For this is exactly what was argued by his editors E. T. Cook and Alexander Wedderburn, in their 1903 Preface to their definitive thirty-nine-volume Library Edition of *The Works of John Ruskin*:

Ruskin was the most personal of writers. It is one of the secrets of his charm. Behind every book he ever wrote one catches the personality of the man [. . .] Increasingly, as he went on writing, he aimed at speaking to his readers face to face. His personality was very marked; he was a man of many moods. It is impossible to understand aright the works of this author without following also the moods of the man. But again, Ruskin's life is contained in his writings [. . .] Thus, as one reads him through, one gets his biography— the facts of his life, the history of the development of his mind. We have his pen-work

---

[44] Ford to Galsworthy, [October 1900]: *Letters*, ed. Richard M. Ludwig (Princeton: Princeton University Press, 1965), p. 10.
[45] Ford, 'The Other House', *New York Herald Tribune Books* (2 October 1927), 2.
[46] Ford, *Joseph Conrad*, p. 25.
[47] See the last section of Chapter 5.
[48] See Roger Shattuck, *Proust* (London: Fontana/Collins, 1975), p. 150.

from the age of seven or eight to the age of seventy. In him, more perhaps than in any other writer, the style is the man, the Works are the Life.[49]

It is perhaps the classic *fin de siècle* application of the Wilde–Nietzsche argument: 'the Works are the Life' not just because Ruskin's was a life devoted to the work of writing, but because his books constitute his autobiography, and this gigantic edition of them (which includes volumes of his letters as well) is his auto/ biography.

Thought of in terms of supplementarity, then, literary autobiography in general has just that kind of liminal status that fascinated Derrida writing about Nietzsche's *Ecce Homo*, and what he calls the 'exergue' of that book, which is both part of the text but precedes the text, sandwiched between the preface and the text itself.[50] This is because of its implicit claim to stand outside the writer's other (fictional, creative, poetic, literary) work; to produce the effect, as suggested, of an actor stepping out of character. Especially if a writer hasn't written autobiographically before, a late autobiography may purport to remove the mask and reveal the self that has been responsible for the performances we have known previously. Yet the autobiography is at the same time another work in that same oeuvre; and hence, another example of the art that transforms its subject matter. And the self that it presents must operate by the same standards of persuasiveness, credibility, verisimilitude perhaps, and literary competence, that his other work is judged by. Every moment has to provide a credible construction of the self. So the author has not quite stepped out of the role of *author*.

SYSTEM

To recapitulate: the notion of the performative reintroduces the ideas of fictionality and creativity to the heart of the autobiographic project; and to that extent could be said to inscribe even in formal autobiography some of the key concepts we have been tracing in more hybrid works, of 'autobiografiction' and imaginary writing. According to performativity theory, that is, even formal autobiography is a version of autobiografiction: it purports to write the self autobiographically,

---

[49] *Library Edition* of *The Works of John Ruskin*, ed. E. T. Cook and Alexander Wedderburn, vol. 1 (London: George Allen, 1903). 'Preface to this Edition', pp. v–xi (p. ix). I am grateful to Jerome Maunsell for drawing this passage to my attention.

[50] Derrida, 'Otobiographies: The Teaching of Nietzsche and the Politics of the Proper Name', in *The Ear of the Other*, ed. Christie McDonald (Lincoln: University of Nebraska Press, 1988), p. 11. Ann Jefferson, *Biography and the Question of Literature in France* (Oxford: Oxford University Press, 2007), p. 20, argues that: 'Biography is traditionally a liminal genre: it is, in the broadest sense, a textual coda to a lived existence [. . .] the "life" frequently takes the form of a preface to the collected works of an author; or else it serves as a supplement to suggest the reading and interpretation of a literary text.'

but actually performs a fictional narrative to put in its place. To that extent, performativity theory concurs with the deconstructive critique of autobiography.

The notion of literary autobiography as a supplement to fiction produces a similar effect. Its status as commentary upon a body of work, as a deferred accompaniment, poses the autobiographical supplement as different in kind from the fictional work being supplemented—as non-fiction. On the other hand, this other literary work being added to the author's existing works, which is able to complete or clarify the earlier fictions, is not only itself a contribution to an oeuvre, but identifies itself as stylistically the product of the same imagination; an identification which then raises the question as to whether the autobiography isn't itself fictionalized, or at least autobiografictionalized. A work that re-mediates novels as explanations of novels is not simply writing a novel, of course; but it is rewriting novels, in a discourse which is itself susceptible of fictionalization.

What both kinds of argument—for the performativity and supplementarity of autobiography—bring out is how autobiography and fiction, while posed as mutually exclusive, are in fact profoundly and paradoxically interdependent. Novelists turning to auto/biography must find their sense of fiction being altered. Similarly, philosophers turning to autobiography must become aware how once they start writing the self, the pursuit of truth becomes mediated by narrativity and fictionality. Contemporary autobiography theory has become accustomed to moving amid such paradoxes. Paul John Eakin, for example, argued in 1985 that 'the self that is the centre of all autobiographical narrative is necessarily a fictive structure [. . .]'; and in 1992 that while 'autobiography is nothing if not a referential art; it is also and always a kind of fiction'; and that 'the constraint of fact is not necessarily a limitation of artistic freedom, and conversely, the invention of fiction in autobiography may be undertaken in the pursuit of biographical truth.'[51] Yet stylish assertions of a paradoxical equivalence between autobiography and fiction do not illuminate how their relationship functions. Whereas the literary history we have been tracing not only enables us to ground such claims in specific historical developments of literary forms, but also demonstrates an emerging awareness of autobiografiction as a symptom of a systematic relationship between the two terms; and it is with this idea that this study will close.

The interdependence of auto/biography and fiction is claimed by the two tropes threading their way through this study, which I have associated with Nietzsche and Wilde, and with Philippe Lejeune. What Lejeune argues about the trope he analyses (that fiction is truer autobiography), could be applied to both: that they appear to compare the two modes but use one of the terms—autobiography—as the ground of the comparison. In other words, what matters

---

[51] Paul John Eakin, *Fictions in Autobiography: Studies in the Art of Self-Invention* (Princeton: Princeton University Press, 1985), p. 3; *Touching the World* (Princeton: Princeton University Press, 1992), p. 31.

ultimately is how autobiographical something is, whatever the form in which it appears. This is ingenious, but reversible. To say that the true autobiography is really the fiction, is to re-ground autobiography on fiction. Or to put it another way, when we seek to map fiction back on to life, we always risk subverting its purity as autobiography: to the extent that the writer's life can be mapped in terms of her fiction, then her life story might share its quality of fictionality. That is the situation so elegantly described by Barthes:

[The text] can be read without the guarantee of its father, the restitution of the inter-text paradoxically abolishing any legacy. It is not that the Author may not 'come back' in the Text, in his text, but he then does so as a 'guest'. If he is a novelist, he is inscribed in the novel like one of his characters, figured in the carpet; no longer privileged, paternal, aletheological, his inscription is ludic. He becomes, as it were, a paper-author: his life is no longer the origin of his fictions but a fiction contributing to his work; there is a reversion of the work on to the life (and no longer the contrary); it is the work of Proust, of Genet which allows their lives to be read as text. The word 'bio-graphy' re-acquires a strong, etymological sense [...][52]

This paradoxical relation between autobiography and fiction seems to be a late nineteenth-century product. Most readers of eighteenth-century fiction would probably not have thought of it as autobiographical, not just because the term hadn't been invented, but because fiction's links were stronger with other modes: satire, the picaresque, the sentimental, the criminal, the journalistic, the epistolary, forgery, and so on; whereas by the late nineteenth century it was widely assumed that fiction was displaced autobiography; and that it was therefore appropriate for literary autobiography to recover its material from the writer's fictional works.

This double-jointedness, whereby autobiography and fiction can be flipped over (or turned inside out) into each other, is implicit in the terminology. After all, as argued at the outset, the 'autobiograph*ical*' is a profoundly paradoxical, even schizophrenic, term. It can describe something which is autobiography. This is how it is glossed in the *Oxford English Dictionary*: 'Belonging to, connected with, autobiography'; or as equivalent to 'autobiographic', which is glossed as 'of the nature of autobiography'. Almost all the *Dictionary*'s historical examples refer to works of autobiography or memoir. But the term is just as likely—possibly now even more likely—to describe something within a predominantly *non*-autobiographical work; as when we speak of an 'autobiographical novel'. The *OED*'s examples are all nineteenth-century ones, and the latest one, from Leslie Stephen in 1880, is moving in this direction: 'Pope takes advantage of the suggestions in Horace to be thoroughly autobiographical.' Stephen doesn't mean that Pope is writing a formal autobiography, but that he incorporates autobiographical material into his Horatian Epistles: 'He manages to run his own

[52] Barthes, 'From Work to Text', in R. Rylance, ed., *Debating Texts*, p. 120.

experience and feelings into the moulds provided for him by his predecessor.'[53] One other example is telling: James Russell Lowell, writing in the 1870s of the writings of Dante that:

they are all (with the possible exception of the treatise *De Vulgari Eloquio*) autobiographic, and that all of them, including that, are parts of a mutually related system, of which the central point is the individuality and experience of the poet.[54]

Even the allegorical and theological vision of the *Divine Comedy* contributes to this vision of the 'autobiographic'. Lowell is clearly using the term against the grain, to cover works it would not normally cover: works which are not autobiographies. This is the sense we use when we call a fiction 'autobiographical'. That the first instance recorded in the *Dictionary* is from 1870 indicates that it is a later sense, which only begins to be used towards the end of the century. I suggested in Chapter 3 that the meaning of the term 'autobiography' had shifted from the public record of social interaction to the narrative of interiority. The implication of a splitting within auto/biography, whereby the story of the inner life may no longer correspond to the external, visible, public life, here finds its counterpart in modes of reading. For when we read stories about fictional characters as autobiography, the 'autobiographical' has become covert, encoded. The *Dictionary* not only supports the argument that writers and readers felt the meanings of 'autobiography' and its cognates were changing from about the 1870s; and that (as claimed in the Preface) the argument that autobiography could be read into any discourse became prominent at the *fin de siècle*. It also shows us how De Man's argument that autobiography is a figure of reading needs to be historicized: that rather than standing as a timeless truth, it is a view of the nature of autobiography that only begins to be articulated around 1870—about seventy years after the emergence of the term 'autobiography' itself.

Literary autobiography thus establishes a structure in which a boundary is drawn between fiction and autobiography; but at the same time, the form undoes the boundary, suggesting both the autobiographic within the fictional works that appear to lie outside the autobiography; and also, conversely, the fictional within the autobiography itself. Thus autobiografiction can be seen not so much as a separate genre or hybrid of two genres, as an expression of the structuration of genres: a relationship between the fictional and the autobiographic that defines them as different from each other by means of a moving between them.

Autobiografiction in this sense, then, as well as being a name for *works* which hybridize autobiography and fiction, might also provide a name for the *system* which locks autobiography and fiction together, in order to claim to keep them apart. This is partly as a result of defining them as in opposition to each other, and

---

[53] Leslie Stephen, *Pope* (London: Macmillan, 1880), pp. 185–6.

[54] James Russell Lowell, 'Dante', *Among my Books*, second series (London: Sampson Low, Marston, Searle & Rivington, 1876), p. 26.

thus by reference to each other: fiction is a departure from autobiographical truth; autobiographical truth is purged of fiction. Yet one story traced here is of how the progressive interiorization of autobiography makes 'truth' an increasingly private quality. It is precisely the anxiety that the truthfulness of inner-life-writing could not be evaluated by others that fostered the development of autobiografiction, and the concomitant self-consciousness about life-writing form that this book has charted. Autobiografiction understood as a system is not a matter of combining statements of fact with statements of fabulation, since in many cases, and most cases concerning interiority, readers would be unlikely to be able to tell the difference. It is, instead, more a matter of combining *forms*; fusing, blurring, or moving between the forms of autobiography, story, diary, preface, and so on.

It is this system which, ultimately, enables many of the discourses traced through this book to signify: discourses of imaginary portraiture, fictionalized autobiography, works of autobiografiction, fictional autobiography, fake life-writings, aesthetic autobiography, impressionist autobiography, *Künstlerroman*, heteronymity, imaginary writing, and auto/biographic metafiction.

Thinking of autobiography-and-fiction as a system or set of discursive and formal practices in this way sheds lights on the fraught question of whether autobiography can be said to constitute a genre; or (as De Man argues) it is merely a mode of reading. Instead, it can be seen as a term within the system, which gains its significance according to its relation to the term 'fiction' (whether opposed or combined). The story told in this study could be described as an increasing awareness of this system—the gravitational pull between auto/biography and fiction. It falls into four phases. First, autobiography is increasingly felt through the nineteenth century to be required—as a test of sincerity and authenticity—and also to be problematic, elusive, even impossible. At the turn of the century, such anxiety results in a proliferation of fictionalizations of the auto/biographical. The next phases include the reciprocal responses of modernism and postmodernism. Modernists appear to reject the auto/biographical, but experiment with it as they claim to be disengaging themselves from it. Postmodernists, conversely, embrace life-writing, not in the Rousseauistic spirit of transparency or an Enlightenment quest for objectivity; but as a metafictional mode of self-performance. They take an ironic stance, meaning that even as they write the auto/biographical, they disengage from it.

The deep and extensive interconnectedness of the categories of autobiography and fiction in the period demonstrated in this book correlates with the interdependence between history and fiction elaborated by Paul Ricoeur and Hayden White.[55] Such interconnectedness is commonly described (as it has sometimes

---

[55] Paul Ricoeur, *Time and Narrative*, vol. 2, trans. Kathleen McLaughlin and David Pellauer (Chicago: University of Chicago Press, 1985), pp. 155–8, argues that provided one brackets off the question of truth, historical and fictional narratives are configured similarly. Hayden White, *The Content of the Form: Narrative Discourse and Historical Representation* (Baltimore: Johns Hopkins

been described in the preceding chapters) as a blurring of boundaries, or a process of hybridization. But such terminology tells us little about why such fusions should occur. Whereas the arguments about performativity and supplementarity lead to a view of autobiography and fiction together constituting throughout the last two centuries a single system for representing subjectivity. In proposing that it is this system which we should call 'autobiografiction', I recognize that that is not how an Edwardian writer like Reynolds would have thought of it when he gave the name to particular hybrid works. But it does offer an explanation of the curious multi-valency of the term 'autobiographical' in the period (according to whether it's applied to autobiography or fiction); of what makes auto/biografic-tional works possible; and also of why so many writers were drawn to experiment with them. The focus of this book has been how the concept of autobiografiction emerged and played across modernism and into postmodernism. But it would be wrong to suggest that the only modern writing affected by it were modernist or postmodernist. In fact, many other novelists turned autobiographers, and auto-biographical novelists, explicitly discuss the paradoxical intimacy between the forms, indicating that the explanatory power of the idea of autobiografiction as a discursive system is by no means confined to specific movements or periods.

Freud wrote to Arnold Zweig in 1936:

To be a biographer you must tie yourself up in lies, concealments, hypocrisies, false colourings, and even in hiding a lack of understanding, for biographical truth is not to be had, and if it were to be had, we could not use it.[56]

Autobiographers had been finding (over the previous half-century or more) that autobiographical truth was equally elusive, because it tended to sound like, and to turn into, fiction. But, paradoxically, and equally elusively, they found that that showed them how they could use it, precisely by giving rein to its fictional-ity, by writing autobiografiction. Conversely, writers setting out to write fiction were increasingly attending to the ways in which their work expressed, or could be read as expressing, autobiographical truths about themselves. The emerging discourse of interiority was learning to read the 'inner life' of the 'psyche' and its unconscious through the traces of its disturbances: the repressions,

University Press, 1992), pp. 179–80: 'Historical stories and fictional stories resemble one another because whatever the differences between their immediate contents (real events and imaginary events, respectively), their ultimate content is the same: the structures of human time. Their shared form, narrative, is a function of this shared content. There is nothing more real for human beings than the experience of temporality [. . .]'. See Tonya Blowers, 'Distinguishing Autobiography from the Novel', in *Representing Lives: Women and Auto/biography*, ed. Alison Donnell and Pauline Polkey (Basingstoke: Macmillan, 2000), pp. 105–16.

[56] Freud, letter to Arnold Zweig, 31 May 1936. *The Letters of Sigmund Freud and Arnold Zweig*, ed. Ernst L. Freud, trans. W. D. Robson-Scott and Mrs Robson-Scott (London: The Hogarth Press and the Institute of Psycho-Analysis, 1970), p. 127; translation amended by Richard Ellmann, 'Freud and Literary Biography', in Peregrine Hordern, ed., *Freud and the Humanities* (London: Duckworth, 1985), pp. 58–75 (p. 63).

displacements, condensations, slips, hesitations, on which psychoanalysis was to base its methods. Autobiography recognizes itself as having a fictional dimension. Fiction recognizes itself as having an autobiographical dimension. Autobiografiction is not only where these two recognitions coincide, but is also the recognition that they are inseparable; and that they have been since the beginning.

However, to speak of structures, systems, or hybrids, is to attempt to render static what is in fact a dynamic process. It isn't so much that autobiography and fiction stay where they are, and that the boundary between them dissolves. Rather, it is the passage of works across the border that calls the force of the border into question. Or perhaps that metaphor too is grounded in notions which are excessively static, of autobiography or fiction inhabiting defined spatial positions. Perhaps instead we should speak of the *autobiographic effect*, or the *fictional effect*, and recognize that particular works can produce first one then the other. That may be where Reynold's account of autobiografiction might be most vulnerable: he wants to define it as a delicate stasis, an interstitial state hovering between autobiography, fiction, and essay. But when we read the works he has in mind, or indeed any of the works in this book, don't we instead move between moments of perceiving the narrative as autobiographical, and moments of perceiving it as fictional? Isn't autobiografiction precisely that sense of movement, rather than a border country at which we arrive? A particularly suggestive way of theorizing such relationships is offered by Slavoj Žižek in *The Parallax View*. Parallax normally describes an optical effect: 'the apparent displacement of an object (the shift of its position against a background), caused by a change in observational position that provides a new line of sight.'[57] Žižek uses the term 'parallax gap' metaphorically to describe the relationship between 'two closely linked perspectives between which no neutral common ground is possible.'[58] As Nick Hubble explains, Žižek means more than a mere shift of perspective:

the added philosophical twist is that the observed difference is not simply 'subjective' but that the '"epistemological" shift in the subject's point of view always reflects an "ontological" shift in the object itself' [. . .] That is to say that what is revealed to us is the object's non-coincidence with itself, its parallax gap. Žižek's main point, which he constantly reiterates and elaborates, is that it is the parallax gap or shift—the difference seen in the object as a result of the shift of perspective—which constitutes the Real, rather than either a presence or an absence.[59]

However, while the Real is revealed as the shifting product of a multitude of symbolic formulations, this is often further concealed by the tendency of the two

---

[57] Slavoj Žižek, *The Parallax View* (Cambridge, MA and London: The MIT Press, 2006), p. 17.
[58] Ibid., p. 4.
[59] Nick Hubble, 'The Origins of Intermodernism in Ford Madox Ford's Parallax View', in *Ford Madox Ford: Literary Networks and Cultural Transformations*, ed. Andrzej Gasiorek and Daniel Moore, International Ford Madox Ford Studies, vol. 7 (Amsterdam and New York: Rodopi, 2008), pp. 167–88 (pp. 169–70). The quotation is from Žižek, *The Parallax View*, p. 17.

levels involved in the parallax shift to be radically asymmetric: 'One of the two levels appears to be able to stand on its own, while the other stands for the shift as such, for the gap between the two. In other words, Two are not simply One and One, since Two stands for the very move/shift from One to Two.'[60]

Hubble deftly shows how this account of parallax shift can be applied to literary 'movements': 'it can now be seen that what is concealed by the privileging of Modernism over social realism', he argues, 'is that "Modernism" is not an authentic presence, but the shift itself, and therefore that it necessarily incorporates interconnections with social realism within itself.'[61] The displacements described in this book from auto/biography to auto/biografiction could be described in similar terms. That is, auto/biografiction is not the thing auto/biography moves towards, or becomes, but it is the move itself. Its name certainly makes explicit the way it incorporates interconnexions with the auto/biography it has departed from. Indeed, the term 'auto/biography' itself is structured around a parallax gap. Whether writers start by writing the lives of others, and find themselves shifting into autobiography; or whether they start by writing autobiography, and find the self they are writing shifting into another's, auto/biography is the movement between the two, which shows how one term incorporates interconnections with the other term it thought it had departed from. Similarly, my discussion of modernist 'impersonality' understood it in a similar way: as partaking in a discourse of 'im/personality', in which 'impersonality' is not just itself, but the move away from 'personality' to 'impersonality'.

The notion of 'autobiografiction' was identified as writers became increasingly preoccupied with the autobiographical aspect of fiction, or of other forms of writing (as we saw from Wilde and Nietzsche onwards). In such readings, the autobiographical is experienced not as a separable, self-contained form, but as a shift from other forms (fiction, philosophy, drama) into autobiography. Autobiography is thus seen to incorporate interconnections with these other forms. Which in effect means that the shift occurs in the other direction too, since autobiography cannot just be itself, but shifts back into the fiction or philosophy or drama from which it has been constituted. Finally, then, though of course it is the opposite of finality, auto/biografiction is the effect of this two-way traffic: a parallax shift from auto/biography to fiction, and back again. Though the writers of the modernist period didn't express it in these Postmodern terms, the emergence of auto/biografiction seems to have given them a similar sense of shifting or circulation back and forth between the terms. Robert Littell, for example, wrote a dialogue between writers of fiction and biography in 1925, in which the biographer says: 'The people you believe you have invented get their start from people you have known in real life, or have read about. And the

---

[60] Žižek, *The Parallax View*, p. 42.
[61] Ibid.

statesmen or adventurers whose lives I choose to retell are in great part my own creations.'[62] That the traffic goes two ways is fundamental.

The idea that Žižek's 'parallax gap' reveals 'the object's non-coincidence with itself' has particular force and relevance when applied to autobiography (though Žižek does not particularly have autobiography in mind, except in the psychoanalytic sense of the unconscious inscribing itself across all our utterance). This is because autobiography is a specific version of that non-coincidence, namely of the self's non coincidence with itself, since the written self can never coincide exactly with the lived sense of self. As with deconstructive theories of autobiography, Žižek's account of this radical non-coincidence is articulated as loss, gap, absence, trauma. The 'Real' that is seen in the shift in the object, in its difference from itself, is the Lacanian Real: not what we normally take to be reality, but a threat to its stability and solidity.

Auto/biografiction, like any literature, can certainly express that sense of the unweaving of the fabric of the real; and it can express our anxieties about its unweaving. But it can also minister to those anxieties; perhaps even counter them. Pater doesn't just write of the unweaving of the self, but of its weaving as well. Our experience of reading auto/biography, autobiografiction, or fiction, isn't just of negativity and fragmentation; but also, when they are as well written as most of the books described here, of the values of style, beauty, humour, memory, imagination, feeling, experience, knowledge, care. If these things were inadequate consolation to some of our authors for the unweaving of god, the soul, and the self, that they could be recreated as values in the face of such absences is the measure of the work auto/biografiction could do.

If its performances of subjectivity express anxiety about the self's essence and coherence, they nevertheless produce subjectivities that achieve remarkable coherence. Writers increasingly fictionalized their autobiographies not only out of anxiety or despair of selfhood, or of the possibility of expressing selfhood; but also because the shift towards fiction helped them to express it better, and thus to counter anxiety and despair. When auto/biography has been theorized in terms of performativity, it is usually formal autobiography that is shown to be performative. Here too, auto/biografiction offers better evidence of the self as created through role-playing, since its writers are consciously and deliberately shifting into the shapes of other subjectivities, and thus revealing the performance involved in the achievement of any subjectivity. But this, too, is something other than a story of failure. If subjectivity wasn't what you thought it was, or even where you thought it was, the performance that is auto/biografiction manages to make it appear, as someone other, somewhere else. And that is a remarkable, distinctive, achievement.

---

[62] Robert Littell, Dialogue in *The New Republic* (1925), in James L. Clifford, ed., *Biography as an Art: Selected Criticism, 1560–1960* (London: Oxford University Press, 1962), pp. 123–5 (p. 123).

Bibliography

Abbott, H. Porter, *The Cambridge Introduction to Narrative* (Cambridge: Cambridge University Press, 2002).

Ackroyd, Peter, *T. S. Eliot* (London: Abacus, 1985).

Adams, Henry, *The Education of Henry Adams*, ed. Ernest Samuels (Boston: Houghton Mifflin, 1974).

Adams, Stephen J., 'Irony and Common Sense: The Genre of *Mauberley*', *Paideuma*, 18: 1 and 2 (1989), 147–60.

Ahern, Mal, 'Performative' (2003), University of Chicago: Theories of Media: Keywords Glossary, <http://csmt.uchicago.edu/glossary2004/performance.htm> (accessed 23 April 2009).

Aldington, Richard, *Death of a Hero* (London: Chatto & Windus, 1929).

——, *Soft Answers* (London: Chatto & Windus; New York: Doubleday Doran, 1932).

——, *Life for Life's Sake* (New York: Viking, 1941).

——, *D. H. Lawrence: An Appreciation* (Harmondsworth: Penguin, 1950).

——, *D. H. Lawrence: Portrait of a Genius, But . . .* (London: Heinemann, 1950).

——, ed. *The Religion of Beauty: Selections from the Æsthetes* (London: Heinemann, 1950).

——, *Soft Answers*, ed. Harry T. Moore (Carbondale and Edwardsville: Southern Illinois University Press, 1967).

——, *A Passionate Prodigality: Letters to Alan Bird from Richard Aldington*, ed. Miriam J. Benkovitz (New York: New York Public Library and Readex Books, 1975).

Amigoni, David, *Colonies, Cults and Evolution: Literature, Science and Culture in Nineteenth-Century Writing* (Cambridge: Cambridge University Press, 2007).

Amis, Kingsley, *Memoirs* (London: Hutchinson, 1991).

Anderson, Linda, 'At the Threshold of the Self: Women and Autobiography', in *Women's Writing: A Challenge to Theory*, ed. Moira Monteith (Brighton: Harvester, 1986), pp. 54–71.

——, *Autobiography* (London and New York: Routledge, 2001).

Angeles, Peter A., *A Dictionary of Philosophy* (London: Harper and Row, 1981).

Anon., 'Art. IV.': review of I. D'Israeli, *Miscellanies; or, Literary Recreations*, *Monthly Review*, 2nd series, 24 (December 1797), 374–9.

Armstrong, Paul B., 'The Hermeneutics of Literary Impressionism', *Centennial Review*, 27:4 (1983), 244–69.

——, *The Challenge of Bewilderment: Understanding and Representation in James, Conrad, and Ford* (Ithaca and London: Cornell University Press, 1987).

——, 'The Epistemology of Ford's Impressionism', in Richard A. Cassell, ed., *Critical Essays on Ford Madox Ford* (Boston: G. K. Hall, 1987), pp. 135–42.

Arnold, Matthew, 'The Function of Criticism at the Present Time' (1864; published in *Essays in Criticism*, 1865), *Selected Criticism of Matthew Arnold*, ed. Christopher Ricks (New York: New American Library, 1972), pp. 92–117.

——, 'Preface to First Edition of *Poems*, 1853', *Selected Criticism of Matthew Arnold*, ed. Christopher Ricks (New York: Signet, 1972), pp. 27–40.

Arnold, Matthew, *The Poems of Matthew Arnold*, 2nd edn, ed. Kenneth Allott and Miriam Allott (London: Longman, 1979).

Arnold, W. D., *Oakfield: or, Fellowship in the East*. Pseud. Punjabee, 2 vols (London: Longman, 1853).

Ascari, Maurizio, 'The Mask without the Face: Walter Pater's *Imaginary Portraits*', *Textus*, 12:1 (1999), 97–112.

——, 'Mapping the Private Life and the Literary Canon: Ford Madox Ford's *Mightier Than the Sword*', in *Ford Madox Ford and 'The Republic of Letters'*, ed. Vita Fortunati and Elena Lamberti (Bologna: CLUEB, 2002), pp. 73–9.

Attridge, Derek, reviewing Robert Spoo's *James Joyce and the Language of History: Dedalus' Nightmare* (Oxford: Oxford University Press, 1994), in *Modern Fiction Studies*, 42:4 (1996), 888–90.

——, 'How to Read Joyce', <http://www.fathom.com/course/10701034/session3.html> (accessed 19 April 2009).

Ayers, David, 'Richard Aldington's Death of a Hero: A Proto-Fascist Novel', *English*, 47 (1998), 89–98.

Bailey, Peter J., '"Why Not Tell the Truth?": The Autobiographies of Three Fiction Writers', *Critique*, 32 (1991), 1–23.

'Barbellion, W. N. P.' [pseud. of Bruce Cummings], *The Journal of a Disappointed Man* (London: Chatto & Windus, 1919).

Barber, D. F., ed., *Concerning Thomas Hardy: A Composite Portrait from Memory* (London: Charles Skilton, 1968).

Barbour, John D., *Versions of Deconversion: Autobiography and the Loss of Faith* (Charlottesville: University Press of Virginia, 1994).

Barham, Peter, *Forgotten Lunatics of the Great War* (New Haven: Yale University Press, 2004).

Baring, Maurice, *Lost Diaries* [1913] (London: Duckworth, 1929).

——, *Unreliable History* (London: Heinemann, 1934).

——, *The Puppet Show of Memory* (London: Cassell, 1987).

Barrie, J. M., 'Pro Bono Publico', *Fortnightly Review*, 48, new series (1 July to 1 December 1890) (vol. 54 old series), 398–407.

Barros, Carolyn A., 'Getting Modern: *The Autobiography of Alice B. Toklas*', *Biography: An Interdisciplinary Quarterly*, 22:2 (1999), 177–208.

Barthes, Roland, *Sade, Fourier, Loyola*, trans. Richard Miller (New York: Hill and Wang, 1976).

——, 'The Death of the Author', in *Image, Music, Text*, trans. Stephen Heath (London: Fontana, 1977), pp. 142–8.

——, *Roland Barthes by Roland Barthes*, trans. Richard Howard (New York: Hill and Wang, 1977).

——, 'From Work to Text', in R. Rylance, ed., *Debating Texts* (Toronto: University of Toronto Press, 1987), pp. 117–22.

Bartocci, Clara, 'John Barth's *Once Upon a Time*: Fiction or Autobiography?', Associazione Italiana di Studi Nord-Americani (Italian Association for North American Studies), <http://www.aisna.net/rsajournal6/bartocci.html> (accessed 20 April 2006).

[Bashford, Henry], *Augustus Carp, Esq. By Himself* (Harmondsworth: Penguin, 1987).

Bassett, Troy J., 'T. Fisher Unwin's Pseudonym Library: Literary Marketing and Authorial Identity', *English Literature in Transition 1880–1920*, 47:2 (2004), 143–60.

Batchelor, John, *H. G. Wells* (Cambridge: Cambridge University Press, 1985).

Bates, William, and Daniel Maclise, *The Maclise Portrait Gallery of Illustrious Literary Characters. With Memoirs Biographical, Critical, Bibliographical, and Anecdotal Illustrative of the Literature of the Former Half of the Present Century* (London: Chatto & Windus, 1883).

Baudelaire, Charles, *The Painter of Modern Life and Other Essays*, ed. Jonathan Mayne (London: Phaidon, 1995).

Bayley, John, 'Other Selves', *London Review of Books* (27 October 1987), 19–20.

Beaujour, Michel, *Poetics of the Literary Self-Portrait*, trans. Yara Milos (New York: New York University Press, 1991).

Beckson, Karl, 'Symons' "A Prelude to Life", Joyce's *A Portrait*, and the Religion of Art', *James Joyce Quarterly*, 15 (1978), 222–8.

——, *Arthur Symons: A Life* (Oxford: Clarendon Press, 1987).

Beerbohm, Max, *And Even Now* (London: Heinemann, 1950).

——, *Seven Men: and Two Others* (Oxford: Oxford University Press, 1980).

Beja, Morris, ed., *James Joyce: 'Dubliners' and 'A Portrait of the Artist as a Young Man': A Casebook* (London and Basingstoke: Macmillan, 1979).

Belford, Barbara, *Violet* (New York: Simon and Schuster, 1990).

Bell, Clive, *Art*, ed. J. B. Bullen (Oxford: Oxford University Press, 1987).

Bell, Millicent, 'Henry James and the Fiction of Autobiography', *Southern Review*, 18:3 (1982), 463–79.

Bender, Todd K., *Literary Impressionism in Jean Rhys, Ford Madox Ford, Joseph Conrad, and Charlotte Brontë* (New York and London: Garland, 1997).

Bennett, Andrew, ed., *Readers and Reading* (London and New York: Longman, 1995).

Benson, A. C., *The Diary of Arthur Christopher Benson*, edited by Percy Lubbock (London: Hutchinson, [1926]).

——, *Escape and Other Essays* (London: Smith, Elder & Co., 1915).

[Benson, A. C.], *The Gate of Death: A Diary* (London: Smith, Elder, 1906).

——, *The House of Quiet: An Autobiography*, ed. 'J. T.' (London: John Murray, 1904).

Benson, A. C., *Hugh: Memoirs of a Brother* (London: Smith, Elder, 1915).

——, *The Life of Edward White Benson by his son Arthur Christopher Benson*, 2 vols (London: Macmillan, 1899).

[Benson, A. C.], *The Thread of Gold* (John Murray: London, 1905).

——, *The Upton Letters* (London: Smith, Elder & Co., 1905).

Benson, A. C., *Walter Pater* (London: Macmillan, 1906).

——, and R. H., *The Temple of Death & Other Stories*, ed. David Stuart Davies (Ware, Hertfordshire: Wordsworth, 2007).

Benson E. F., *As We Were: A Victorian Peep Show* (London: Longmans Green, 1930).

——, *As We Are: A Modern Revue* (London: Longmans, 1932).

Benson, R. H., *The Holy Blissful Martyr Saint Thomas of Canterbury* (London: Macdonald & Evans, 1908).

——, *Confessions of a Convert* (London: Longmans, 1913).

——, and Frederick Rolfe, *Saint Thomas*, ed. Donald Weeks (Edinburgh: Tragara Press, 1979).

Benstock, Shari, 'Authoring the Autobiographical', in *The Private Self: Theory and Practice of Women's Autobiographical Writings* (Chapel Hill: University of North Carolina Press, 1988), 10–33.

Berryman, Jo Brantley, '"Medallion": Pound's Poem', *Paideuma*, 2:3 (1973), 391–8.

Birch, Dinah, 'Fathers and Sons: Ruskin, John James Ruskin, and Turner', *Nineteenth-Century Contexts*, 18 (1994), 147–62.

Birrell, T. A., 'Notes on the new *Cambridge Bibliography of English Literature* vol. 4 (1900–1950)', *Neophilologus*, 59:2 (1975), 306–15.

Bleikasten, André, 'Of Sailboats and Kites: The "Dying Fall" in Faulkner's *Sanctuary* and Beckett's *Murphy*', in *Intertextuality in Faulkner*, ed. Michel Gresset and Noel Polk (Jackson: University Press of Mississippi, 1985), pp. 57–72.

Block, Ed. Jr, 'Walter Pater, Arthur Symons, W. B. Yeats, and the Fortunes of the Literary Portrait', *Studies in English Literature, 1500–1900*, 26:4 (1986), 759–76.

Bloom, Harold, ed., *Selected Writings of Walter Pater* (New York: Columbia University Press, 1974).

Bloom, Lynn Z., 'Gertrude Is Alice Is Everybody: Innovation and Point of View in Gertrude Stein's Autobiographies', *Twentieth Century Literature*, 24:1 (1978), 81–93.

Blowers, Tonya, 'Distinguishing Autobiography from the Novel', in *Representing Lives: Women and Auto/biography*, ed. Alison Donnell and Pauline Polkey (Basingstoke: Macmillan, 2000), pp. 105–16.

Boldrini, Lucia, and Peter Davies, eds, *Autobiografictions: Comparatist Essays*, *Comparative Critical Studies*, 1:3 (2004).

Boldrini, Lucia, *Biografie Fittizie* (Pisa: ETS, 1998).

Booth, Wayne C., *The Rhetoric of Fiction* (Chicago: University of Chicago Press, 1961).

Bowen, Zack, and James F. Carens, eds, *A Companion to Joyce Studies* (Westport, CT: Greenwood, 1984).

Bowlby, Rachel, 'Introduction', Woolf, *Orlando*, World's Classics (Oxford: Oxford University Press, 1992), pp. xii–xlvii.

Boyd, Ernest, 'Sex in Biography', *Harper's Magazine*, 165 (November 1932), 753–6.

Brake, Laurel, *Walter Pater* (Plymouth: Northcote House, 1994).

——, *s.v.* Walter Pater, *Oxford DNB*.

Brake, Lesley Higgins, and Carolyn Williams, eds, *Walter Pater: Transparencies of Desire* (Greensboro, NC: ELT Press, 2002).

Breslin, James, 'Gertrude Stein and the Problems of Autobiography', in Jelinek, Estelle C., *Women's Autobiography: Essays in Criticism* (Bloomington, IN: Indiana University Press, 1980), pp. 149–62.

Bretell, Richard, *Modern Art: 1851–1929: Capitalism and Representation* (Oxford: Oxford University Press, 1999).

Bridgman, Richard, *Gertrude Stein in Pieces* (New York: Oxford University Press, 1970).

Briggs, Julia, 'Virginia Woolf and "The Proper Writing of Lives"', in *The Art of Literary Biography*, ed. John Batchelor (Oxford: Clarendon Press, 1995), pp. 245–65.

——, *Reading Virginia Woolf* (Edinburgh: Edinburgh University Press, 2006).

Brinnin, John Malcolm *The Third Rose: Gertrude Stein and her World* (London: Weidenfeld and Nicolson, 1960).

Brittain, Vera, *Testament of Youth* (London: Virago, 1983).

Brontë, Charlotte, *Jane Eyre* (London: Smith, Elder, 1847).

Brooker, Peter, *A Student's Guide to the Selected Poems of Ezra Pound* (London: Faber, 1979).

Brooks, Peter, *Henry James Goes to Paris* (Princeton: Princeton University Press, 2007).

Brunetière, Ferdinand, 'L'impressionisme dans le roman', *Revue des deux mondes*, 49:3 (1879), 450.

Butler, Judith, *Bodies that Matter: On the Discursive Limits of 'Sex'* (New York: Routledge, 1993).

Byatt, A. S., *Possession* (London: Vintage, 1991).

Buckler, William E., *Walter Pater: Three Major Texts* (New York and London: New York University Press, 1986).

Budgen, Frank, *James Joyce and the Making of 'Ulysses' and Other Writings* (London: Grayson and Grayson, 1934).

Buitenhuis, Peter 'The Golden Moment', *New York Times* (20 December 1970).

Bush, Ronald, *The Genesis of Ezra Pound's 'Cantos'* (Princeton: Princeton University Press, 1976).

——, '"It Draws One to Consider Time Wasted": Hugh Selwyn Mauberley', *American Literary History*, 2:1 (1990), 56–78.

——, 'Rereading the exodus: *Frankenstein, Ulysses, The Satanic Verses*, and other Post-colonial Texts', in *Transcultural Joyce*, ed. Karen R. Lawrence (Cambridge: Cambridge University Press, 1998), pp. 129–50.

Butler, Samuel, *The Way of All Flesh* (Harmondsworth: Penguin, 1986).

Byatt, A. S., 'Scenes from a Provincial Life: Part two', *Guardian* (Saturday 27 July 2002), <http://www.guardian.co.uk/books/2002/jul/27/classics.highereducation> (accessed 18 April 2008).

Calvin, Thomas, 'Stephen in Process/Stephen on Trial: The Anxiety of Production in Joyce's *Portrait*', *Novel*, 23:3 (1990), 282–302.

Camus, Albert, *The Myth of Sisyphus*, trans. Justin O'Brien (Harmondsworth: Penguin, 1975).

Caramello, Charles, *Henry James, Gertrude Stein, and the Biographical Act* (Chapel Hill and London: University of North Carolina Press, 1996).

Carlyle, Thomas, Lecture on The Hero as Divinity. *Heroes, Hero-Worship and the Heroic in History* (New York: The Macmillan Company, 1897).

——, 'Biography', in *English and Other Critical Essays* (London: Dent, 1915), pp. 65–79.

——, *Sartor Resartus*, ed. Kerry McSweeney and Peter Sabor (Oxford: Oxford University Press, 1987).

Carpenter, Humphrey, *A Serious Character: The Life of Ezra Pound* (London: Faber, 1988).

Carswell, Catherine, 'Proust's Women', in *Marcel Proust: An English Tribute*, ed. C. K. Scott Moncrieff (New York: Thomas Seltzer, 1923), pp. 66–77.

Castle, Terry, *Masquerade and Civilisation* (Stanford: Stanford University Press, 1986).

Caws, Mary Ann, *Reading Frames in Modern Fiction* (Princeton: Princeton University Press, c.1985).

——, 'Ruskin's Madness and Ours', in *Victorian Literature and Culture*, ed. John Maynard and Adrienne Munich (New York: AMS Press, 1991).

Cecil, David, *Max: A Biography* (London: Constable, 1964).

Cianci, Giovanni, and Peter Nicholls, eds, *Ruskin and Modernism* (Basingstoke: Palgrave, 2001).

Clark, Kenneth, 'Introduction', *Præterita* (London: Rupert Hart-Davis, 1949), pp. vii–xxii.

Clifford, James L., ed., *Biography as an Art: Selected Criticism, 1560–1960* (London: Oxford University Press, 1962).

Coleridge, S. T., *Biographia Literaria: Or: Biographical Sketches of My Literary Life and Opinions*, ed. James Engell and W. Jackson Bate, 2 vols (London: Routledge and Kegan Paul, 1983).

Cone, Helen Gray, and Jeannette L. Gilder, *Pen-Portraits of Literary Women* (New York: Cassell & Co., 1887).

Connolly, Cyril, *Enemies of Promise* (London: George Routledge & Sons, 1938).

Conrad, Joseph, *The Mirror of the Sea* [and] *A Personal Record* (London: Dent, 1975).

——, *The Collected Letters of Joseph Conrad*, vol. 1, ed. Frederick Karl and Laurence Davies (Cambridge: Cambridge University Press, 1983).

——, *The Collected Letters of Joseph Conrad*, vol. 2, ed. Frederick Karl and Laurence Davies (Cambridge: Cambridge University Press, 1986).

——, *The Collected Letters of Joseph Conrad*, vol. 3, ed. Frederick Karl and Laurence Davies (Cambridge: Cambridge University Press, 1988).

——, *The Collected Letters of Joseph Conrad*, vol. 4, ed. Frederick Karl and Laurence Davies (Cambridge: Cambridge University Press, 1990).

——, *Heart of Darkness*, ed. Robert Hampson (London: Penguin, 1995).

Conway, Jill Ker, *When Memory Speaks* (New York: Knopf, 1998).

Cook, E. T., and Alexander Wedderburn, eds, 'Preface to this Edition', Library Edition, vol. 1, *The Works of John Ruskin* (London: George Allen, 1903), pp. v–xi.

Cunningham, Valentine, *s.v.* William Hale White ['Mark Rutherford'], *Oxford DNB*.

Cupitt, Don, 'Introduction', William Hale White, *The Autobiography of Mark Rutherford and Mark Rutherford's Deliverance, edited by his friend Reuben Shapcott* (London: Libris, 1988).

Dällenbach, Lucien, *Le Récit spéculaire* (Paris: Seuil, 1977); trans. Jeremy Whiteley and Emma Hughes as *The Mirror in the Text* (Cambridge and Oxford: Polity Press, 1989).

Dällenbach, 'Reflexivity and Reading', *New Literary History*, 11 (1980), 435–49.

Davenport-Hines, Richard, 'Tinned Nellie', *Times Literary Supplement* (14 December 2007), 26.

Davie, Donald, *Ezra Pound: Poet as Sculptor* (London: Routledge and Kegan Paul, 1965).

——, *Pound* (London: Fontana, 1975).

Davies, Dido, *William Gerhardie: A Biography* (Oxford: Oxford University Press, 1990).

Davis, Philip, *The Victorians*, Oxford English Literary History, vol. 8 (Oxford: Oxford University Press, 2002).

Day, Robert Adams, 'The Villanelle Perplex: Reading Joyce', *James Joyce Quarterly*, 25 (1986), 69–85.

Deane, Seamus, *A Short History of Irish Literature* (Indiana: University of Notre Dame Press, 1986).

——, 'Introduction', Joyce, *A Portrait of the Artist as a Young Man* (London: Penguin, 1992).

de Gourmont, Remy, *The Natural Philosophy of Love*, trans. Ezra Pound (New York: Boni and Liveright, 1922).

Dellamora, Richard, *Masculine Desire: The Sexual Politics of Victorian Aestheticism* (Chapel Hill: University of North Carolina Press, 1990).

De Man, Paul, 'Autobiography as De-Facement', *Modern Language Notes*, 94:5 (1979), 919–30.

——, *Allegories of Reading: Figural Language in Rousseau, Nietzsche, Rilke and Proust* (New Haven and London: Yale University Press, 1979).

Derrida, *Of Grammatology*, trans. Gayatri Chakravorty Spivak (Baltimore and London: Johns Hopkins University Press, 1978).

——, 'The Law of Genre', *Critical Inquiry*, 7:1 (1980), 55–81.

——, *The Ear of the Other*, ed. Christie McDonald (Lincoln: University of Nebraska Press, 1988).

Devlin, Kimberly J., *James Joyce's "Fraudstuff"* (Gainesville: University Press of Florida, 2002).

Dibert-Himes, Glenn, 'Introductory Essay to the Work of Letitia Elizabeth Landon' at <http://www.people.iup.edu/ghimes/gdhessay.htm> (accessed 18 December 2007).

Dick, Susan, *Virginia Woolf* (London: Edward Arnold, 1989).

Dickens, Charles, *David Copperfield* (Harmondsworth: Penguin, 1976).

Dickinson, Emily, *Emily Dickinson: Selected Letters*, ed. Thomas H. Johnson (Cambridge, MA: Belknap Press, 1971).

Donoghue, Denis, *Walter Pater: Lover of Strange Souls* (New York: Knopf, 1995).

Doob, Leonard W., ed., *'Ezra Pound Speaking': Radio Speeches of World War II* (Westport, CT and London: Greenwood Press, 1978).

Doubrouwsky, Serge, *Fils* (Paris: Éditions Galilée, 1977).

Dowling, Linda, *Language and Decadence in the Victorian Fin de Siècle* (Princeton: Princeton University Press, 1986).

Doyle, Charles, *Richard Aldington: A Biography* (Basingstoke: Macmillan, 1989).

Drabble, Margaret, ed., *Oxford Companion to English Literature* (Oxford: Oxford University Press, 2000).

Dvorak, Marta, 'Autobiografiction: Strategies of (Self) Representation', *Commonwealth Essays and Studies* 24:1 (2001), 91–101.

Eagleton, Terry, *Literary Theory: An Introduction* (Oxford: Blackwell, 1994).

——, *The Gatekeeper: A Memoir* (London: Allen Lane, the Penguin Press, 2001).

——, 'Living as Little as Possible', *London Review of Books* (23 September 2004), 23–4.

Eakin, Paul John, *Fictions in Autobiography: Studies in the Art of Self-Invention* (Princeton: Princeton University Press, 1985).

——, *Touching the World* (Princeton: Princeton University Press, 1992).

Easley, Alexis, *First Person Anonymous: Women Writers and Victorian Print Media, 1830–70* (Aldershot: Ashgate, 2004).

Edel, Leon, *Henry James: A Life* (New York: Harper & Row, 1985).

——, and Gordon Ray, eds, *Henry James and H. G. Wells* (London: Rupert Hart-Davis, 1959).

Elbaz, *The Changing Nature of the Self: A Critical Study of the Autobiographic Discourse* (London: Croom Helm, 1988).

Eliot, George, *The Impressions of Theophrastus Such* (London: J. M. Dent, 1995).

Eliot, T. S., *After Strange Gods: A Primer of Modern Heresy* (London: Faber, 1934).

——, *Selected Essays*, third enlarged edition (London: Faber and Faber Limited, 1951).

——, *The Sacred Wood* (London: Methuen, 1980).

——, *The Letters of T. S. Eliot*, vol. 1, ed. Valerie Eliot (London: Faber, 1988).

——, *The Varieties of Metaphysical Poetry*, ed. Ronald Schuchard (London: Faber, 1993).

Ellis, Havelock, *Selected Essays*, ed. J. S. Collis (London: Dent, 1943).

——, *Studies in the Psychology of Sex.* Vol. 1: *Sexual Inversion* (London: Wilson and Macmillan, 1897).

Ellmann, Richard, *James Joyce*, revised edition (Oxford: Oxford University Press, 1983).

——, 'Freud and Literary Biography', in *Freud and the Humanities*, ed. Peregrine Hordern (London: Duckworth, 1985), pp. 58–75.

——, *Oscar Wilde* (London: Hamish Hamilton, 1988).

Empson, William, *Using Biography* (London: Chatto & Windus and The Hogarth Press, 1984).

——, 'Virginia Woolf' (1931), in *Argufying* (London: Chatto & Windus, 1987), 443–9.

Espey, John J., *Ezra Pound's 'Mauberley': A Study in Composition* (London: Faber, 1955).

Evans, Lawrence, ed., *Letters of Walter Pater* (Oxford: Clarendon Press, 1970).

Fellows, Jay, *Ruskin's Maze: Mastery and Madness in His Art* (Princeton, NJ: Princeton University Press, 1981).

Fisch, Menachem, and Simon Schaffer, eds, *William Whewell: A Composite Portrait* (Oxford: Clarendon, 1991).

Fish, Stanley, *Doing What Comes Naturally* (Durham, NC: Duke University Press, 1989).

Ford [Hueffer], Ford Madox, *The Pre-Raphaelite Brotherhood* (London: Duckworth, 1907).

——, *The Spirit of the People* (London: Alston Rivers, 1907).

——, *Ancient Lights* (London: Chapman and Hall, 1911).

——, *The Critical Attitude* (London: Duckworth, 1911).

——, *Henry James* (London: Martin Secker, 1913).

——, 'Impresssionism—Some Speculations', *Poetry*, 2 (August and September 1913), 177–87, 215–25.

——, *Collected Poems* (London: Max Goschen, 1914).

——, 'Literary Portraits—XXVIII. Mr. Morley Roberts and *Time and Thomas Waring*', *Outlook*, 33 (21 March 1914), 390–1.

——, 'Literary Portraits—XXXVI. Les Jeunes and "Des Imagistes" (Second Notice)', *Outlook*, 33 (16 May 1914), 682–3.

——, 'On Impressionism', *Poetry and Drama*, 2 (June and December 1914), 166–75, 323–34.

——, *The Good Soldier* (London: John Lane; the Bodley Head, 1915).

——, *Between St. Dennis and St. George* (London: Hodder and Stoughton, 1915).

——, *Thus to Revisit* (London: Chapman and Hall, 1921).

——, [under the pseudonym 'Daniel Chaucer'], 'Stocktaking: Towards a Revaluation of English Literature', *transatlantic review* (Jan.–Dec. 1924), passim.

——, *Joseph Conrad: A Personal Remembrance* (London: Duckworth, 1924).

——, and Joseph Conrad, *The Nature of a Crime* (London: Duckworth, 1924).

——, *A Mirror to France* (New York: Boni, 1926).

——, 'The Other House', *New York Herald Tribune Books* (2 October 1927), 2.

——, *The English Novel* (Philadelphia: J. B. Lippincott, 1929).

——, *Return to Yesterday* (London: Gollancz, 1931).

——, *It Was the Nightingale* (London: Heinemann, 1934).

——, 'Techniques', *Southern Review*, 1 (1935), 20–35.

——, 'Men and Books', *Time and Tide*, 17:21 (23 May 1936), 761.

——, *Portraits from Life* (Boston: Houghton Mifflin, 1937); published in Britain as *Mightier Than the Sword* (London: Allen & Unwin, 1938).

——, *The March of Literature* (New York: Dial Press, 1938; London: Allen & Unwin, 1939).

——, *Letters of Ford Madox Ford*, ed. Richard M. Ludwig (Princeton: Princeton University Press, 1965).

——, *A History of Our Own Times*, ed. Solon Beinfeld and Sondra Stang (Bloomington and Indianapolis: Indiana University Press, 1988).

——, *Critical Essays*, ed. Max Saunders and Richard Stang (Manchester: Carcanet, 2002).

Forster, E. M., *Abinger Harvest* (London: Edward Arnold and Co., 1936).

——, *Two Cheers for Democracy* (London: Edward Arnold and Co., 1951).

——, *Selected Letters of E. M. Forster*, ed. Mary Lago and P. N. Furbank, vol. 1 (London: Collins, 1983).

Foucault, Michel, 'What is an Author' (1969), in *Language, Counter-Memory, Practice*, ed. Donald F. Bouchard (Ithaca: Cornell University Press, 1980), pp. 113–38.

Frank, Joseph, 'Spatial Form in Modern Literature', *Sewanee Review*, 53 (1945), 221–40, 433–56, 643–53.

Friar, Kimon, and John Malcolm Brinnin, eds, *Modern Poetry: American and British* (New York: Appleton-Century-Crofts, 1951).

Freud, Sigmund, *An Autobiographical Study*, translation by James Strachey (London: Hogarth Press, 1935).

——, *The Interpretation of Dreams*, trans. James Strachey, *The Standard Edition of the Complete Psychological Works of Sigmund Freud*, 24 vols, vol. 5 (London: The Hogarth Press and the Institute of Psycho-Analysis, 1953).

——, 'Creative Writers and Day-Dreaming' [1908], in *Standard Edition*, vol. 9 (London: The Hogarth Press and the Institute of Psycho-Analysis, 1959), pp. 141–53.

——, 'Childhood Memories and Screen Memories', in *The Psychopathology of Everyday Life, Standard Edition*, vol. 6 (London: The Hogarth Press and the Institute of Psycho-Analysis, 1960), pp. 43–52.

——, 'Introductory Lectures on Psycho-Analysis', *Standard Edition*, trans. James Strachey, vol. 15 (London: The Hogarth Press and the Institute of Psycho-Analysis, 1963).

——, *The Letters of Sigmund Freud and Arnold Zweig*, ed. Ernst L. Freud, trans. W. D. Robson-Scott and Mrs Robson-Scott (London: The Hogarth Press and the Institute of Psycho-Analysis, 1970).

——, and Joseph Breuer, *Studies on Hysteria* (1895), *Standard Edition*, vol. 2 (London: The Hogarth Press and the Institute of Psycho-Analysis, 1955).

Gallup, Donald, *Ezra Pound: A Bibliography* (Charlottesville: University Press of Virginia, 1983).

Galsworthy, John, 'A Portrait', *A Motley* (London: Heinemann, 1910), pp. 1–29.

——, *Caravan: The Assembled Tales of John Galsworthy* (New York: Charles Scribner's Sons, 1925).

Galton, Francis, 'Composite Portraits', *Nature*, 18 (23 May 1878), 97–100.

——, *Memories of My Life* (London: Methuen, 1908).

Gerhardi, William, and Brian Lunn, *The Memoirs of Satan* (London: Cassell, 1932).

Gervais, David, 'Stories of Real Life', *Cambridge Quarterly*, 9:1 (1979), 56–64.

Gide, André, *The Notebooks of André Walter*, trans. Wade Baskin (London: Peter Owen, 1968).

——, *The Counterfeiters*, trans. Dorothy Bussy (Harmondsworth: Penguin, 1985).

Gilcher, Edwin, *s.v.* George Augustus Moore, *Oxford DNB*.

Gilfillan, George *Gilfillan's Literary Portraits*, ed. with an introduction by W. Robertson Nicoll (London: Dent, 1909).

Gillhof, Gerd, 'Introduction', *Diary of a Seducer* (London: Elek, 1969).

Gissing, George, *The Private Papers of Henry Ryecroft* (London: Constable, 1928).

Goffman, Erving, *The Presentation of Self in Everyday Life* (Garden City, NY: Doubleday Anchor, 1959).

Gombrich, E. H., 'Standards of Truth: The Arrested Image and the Moving Eye', *Critical Inquiry* 7:2 (1980), 237–73.

Gordon, Jan B., 'The Dialogue of Life and Art in Arthur Symons' Spiritual Adventures', *English Literature in Transition*, 12:3 (1969), 105–17.

Gordon, Lyndall, *Virginia Woolf: A Writer's Life* (Oxford: Oxford University Press, 1986).

Gosse, Edmund 'Biography', *Encyclopedia Britannica*, 11th edn (Cambridge: Cambridge University Press, 1911), vol. 3, p. 954.

——, 'The Ethics of Biography' [1903], excerpted in James L. Clifford, ed., *Biography as an Art: Selected Criticism, 1560–1960* (London: Oxford University Press, 1962), 113–19.

——, *Father and Son*, ed. Peter Abbs (London: Penguin, 1989).

——, *Father and Son: A Study of Two Temperaments*, ed. Michael Newton (Oxford: Oxford University Press, 2004).

Grabes, Herbert, *Fictitious Biographies: Vladimir Nabokov's English Novels* (The Hague: Mouton & Co, 1977).

Graves, Robert, *Goodbye to All That* (Harmondsworth: Penguin, 1960).

Griffiths, Eric, *The Printed Voice of Victorian Poetry* (Oxford: The Clarendon Press, 1989).

Groom, Nick, *The Forger's Shadow* (London: Picador, 2002).

Gross, John, *James Joyce* (New York: The Viking Press, 1972).

Grossmith, George and Weedon, *The Diary of a Nobody* (Bristol: J. W. Arrowsmith, 1892).

Guerard, Albert J., *Conrad the Novelist* (Cambridge, MA: Harvard University Press, 1979).

Hale White, William, *see* 'Rutherford, Mark'.

Hampson, Robert, ' "Experiments in Modernity": Ford and Pound', in Andrew Gibson, ed., *Pound in Multiple Perspective: A Collection of Critical Essays* (Basingstoke and London: Macmillan, 1993), pp. 93–125.

Harding, Jason, *The Criterion: Cultural Politics and Periodical Networks in Inter-war Britian* (Oxford: Oxford University Press, 2002).

Harris, Frank, *Contemporary Portraits* (New York: Mitchell Kennerley, 1915).

Hay, Eloise Knapp, 'Impressionism Limited', *Joseph Conrad: A Commemoration* (London: Macmillan, 1976).

Heath, Stephen, *Gustave Flaubert: Madame Bovary* (Cambridge: Cambridge University Press, 1992).

Heidegger, Martin, *Poetry, Language, Thought*, trans. Albert Hofstadter (New York: Harper Colophon, 1975).

Heilman, Robert B., review of F. O. Matthiessen, in *Henry James: The Major Phase New England Quarterly*, 18:2 (1945), 268–71.

Hennegan, Alison, 'Personalities and Principles: Aspects of Literature and Life in *Fin-de-Siècle* England', in *Fin de Siècle and its Legacy*, ed. Mikuláš Teich and Roy Porter (Cambridge: Cambridge University Press, 1990).

Hill, Geoffrey, 'Gurney's Hobby', *Essays in Criticism*, 34:2 (1984), 97–128.

Holmes, Richard, 'Boswell's Bicentenary', at <http://web.wits.ac.za/Academic/Humanities/SLLS/Holistic/Boswell.htm> (accessed 24 April 2009).

Hoople, Robin, *In Darkest James: Reviewing Impressionism, 1900–1905* (Lewisburg, PA: Bucknell University Press, 2000).

Horne, Philip, *Henry James and Revision* (Oxford: Clarendon, 1990).

——, ed., *Henry James: A Life in Letters* (London: Allen Lane, 1999).

Howells, W. D., 'The Editor's Study': 'Two Remarkable Examples of Sincerity in Fiction', *Harper's*, 72 (1886) 485–6.

——, 'The Editor's Easy Chair', *Harper's*, 108 (1904), 478–82.

Hubble, Nick, 'The Origins of Intermodernism in Ford Madox Ford's Parallax View', *Ford Madox Ford: Literary Networks and Cultural Transformations*, ed. Andrzej Gasiorek and Daniel Moore, International Ford Madox Ford Studies, vol. 7 (Amsterdam and New York: Rodopi, 2008), pp. 167–88.

Hume, David, *A Treatise of Human Nature*, ed. L. A. Selby-Bigge, 2nd edn (Oxford: Oxford University Press, 1983).

Hutcheon, Linda, *A Poetics of Postmodernism* (New York and London: Routledge, 1988).

——, *The Politics of Postmodernism* (London: Routledge, 1989).

Hutton, R. H., 'Mr. Browning', *Literary Essays* (London: Macmillan, 1896), pp. 188–243.

Huxley, Aldous, *Point Counter Point* (1928; Harmondsworth: Penguin, 1961).

Huysmans, J.-K., *Against Nature*, trans. Robert Baldick (Harmondsworth: Penguin, 1959).

Hynes, Samuel, *The Edwardian Turn of Mind* (Princeton: Princeton University Press, 1975).

——, *A War Imagined: The First World War and English Culture* (London: The Bodley Head, 1990).

Iser, Wolfgang, *Walter Pater: The Aesthetic Moment*, trans. David Henry Wilson (Cambridge: Cambridge University Press, 1987).

Jackson, Holbrook, *The Eighteen Nineties: A Review of Art and Ideas at the Close of the Nineteenth Century* (London: Grant Richards, 1913).

Jackson, Kevin, *Invisible Forms: A Guide to Literary Curiosities* (London: Picador, 1999).

James, Henry, 'John S. Sargent', *Harper's*, 75 (October 1887), 683–91.

——, *The Notebooks of Henry James*, ed. F. O. Mathiessen and Kenneth B. Murdock (New York: Oxford University Press, 1947).

——, 'The Figure in the Carpet', in *The Lesson of the Master; and Other Stories* (London: John Lehmann, 1948), pp. 149–84.

——, 'The Impressionists' (1876), in *The Painter's Eye*, ed. John L. Sweeney (London: Rupert Hart-Davis, 1956), pp. 114–15.

——, *The Princess Casamassima* (Harmondsworth: Penguin, 1977).

——, *Letters*, vol. 3, ed. Leon Edel (London: Macmillan, 1981).

——, *Selected Literary Criticism*, ed. Morris Shapira (Cambridge: Cambridge University Press, 1981).

——, *Autobiography*, ed. Frederick W. Dupee (Princeton: Princeton University Press, 1983).

——, 'The Art of Fiction' (1884), in *Literary Criticism: Essays on Literature: American Writers: English Writers* (New York: Library of America, 1984).

James, P. D., *Time to be in Earnest: A Fragment of Autobiography* (NY and Toronto: Knopf, 2000).

Janowsky, Oscar, ed., *The American Jew. A Composite Portrait* (New York: Harper & Bros, 1942).

Jefferson, Ann, *Biography and the Question of Literature in France* (Oxford: Oxford University Press, 2007).

Jolas, Eugene, *Testimony against Gertrude Stein* (supplement of *transition*) (Servire Press: The Hague, 1935).

Jolly, Margareta, ed., *Encyclopedia of Life Writing: Autobiographical and Biographical Forms*, 2 vols (London and Chicago: Fitzroy Dearborn, 2002).

Jones, Thomas, 'Short Cuts', *London Review of Books* (16 November 2000), 18.

Joyce, James, *Finnegans Wake* (London: Faber, 1971).

——, *Selected Letters of James Joyce*, ed. Richard Ellmann (London: Faber, 1975).

——, *James Joyce: Poems and Shorter Writings*, ed. Richard Ellmann, A. Walton Litz, and John Whittier-Ferguson (London: Faber, 1991).

——, *Ulysses*, ed. Jeri Johnson (Oxford: Oxford University Press, 1993).

——, *A Portrait of the Artist as a Young Man*, ed. Jeri Johnson (Oxford: Oxford University Press, 2000).

Joyce, Stanislaus, *Complete Dublin Diary*, ed. George H. Healey (Ithaca: Cornell University Press, 1971).

——, *My Brother's Keeper* (London: Faber, 1982).

Kappeler, Susanne, *Writing and Reading in Henry James* (London and Basingstoke: Macmillan, 1980).

Karl, Frederick R., *Joseph Conrad: The Three Lives* (London: Faber and Faber, 1979).

Katz, Tamar, *Impressionist Subjects: Gender, Interiority, and Modernist Fiction in England* (Urbana and Chicago: University of Illinois Press, 2000).

Keating, Peter, *The Haunted Study: A Social History of the English Novel 1875–1914* (London: Fontana, 1991).

Kemp, Sandra, Charlotte Mitchell, and David Trotter, *Edwardian Fiction: An Oxford Companion* (Oxford: Oxford University Press, 1997).

Kenner, 'Joyce's Anti-Selves', *Shenandoah*, 4:1 (1953), 24–41.

Kenner, Hugh, *Dublin's Joyce* (Boston: Beacon Press, 1962).

——, '*The Portrait* in Perspective', in Thomas Connolly, *Joyce's Portrait: Criticism and Critiques* (London: Peter Owen, 1964), pp. 25–60.

——, 'The Cubist Portrait', in *Approaches to Joyce's Portrait*, ed. Thomas F. Staley and Bernard Benstock (Pittsburgh: University of Pittsburgh Press, 1976), pp. 171–84.

Kenner, Hugh, *Joyce's Voices* (London: Faber, 1978).

Kermode, Frank, 'A Very Smart Bedint', *London Review of Books* (17 March 2005), 15–16.

Kierkegaard, Søren, *Concluding Unscientific Postscript*, trans. David F. Swenson, ed. Walter Lowrie (London: Humphrey Milford and Oxford University Press, 1941).

King, John, 'Trapping the Fox You Are with a Riddle: The Autobiographical Crisis of Stephen Dedalus in *Ulysses*', *Twentieth-Century Literature*, 45 (1999), 299–316.

Kingsley, Charles [as 'C. K.'], review of Froude's History of England, vols 7 and 8, in *Macmillan's Magazine* (January 1864), 216–17.

Kirby, David K., 'Henry James: Art and Autobiography', *Dalhousie Review*, 52:4 (1972–3), 637–44.

Kirschke, James J., 'Impressionist Painting and the Reflexive Novel of the Early Twentieth Century', *Proceedings of the 8th Congress of the International Comparative Literature Association: Three Epoch-Making Literary Changes: Renaissance, Enlightenment, Early Twentieth Century*, ed. Bela Kopeczi and Gyorgy M. Vajda (Stuttgart: Bieber, 1980), pp. 567–73.

——, *Henry James and Impressionism* (Troy, NY: Whitson, 1981).

Kittredge, Daniel Wright, *The Memoirs of a Failure* (Toronto: Albert Britnell; and James: Cincinatti: University Press, 1908).

Kittredge, *A Mind Adrift* (Seattle, WA: S. F. Shorey, 1920).

Knowles, Owen, *A Conrad Chronology* (Basingstoke: Macmillan, 1989).

Korg, Jacob, *George Gissing: A Critical Biography* (Brighton: Harvester, 1980).

Kundera, Milan, *The Unbearable Lightness of Being*, trans. Michael Henry Heim (London: Faber and Faber, 1985).

LaCapra, Dominick, *History, Politics, and the Novel* (Ithaca, NY: Cornell University Press, 1987).

Lambert-Charbonnier, Martine, *Walter Pater et Les Portraits Imaginaires* (Paris, L'Harmattan, 2004).

Landow, George, *Ruskin* (Oxford: Oxford University Press, 1985).

——, ed., *Approaches to Victorian Autobiography* (Athens: Ohio University Press, 1979).

Landy, Joshua, *Philosophy As Fiction: Self, Deception, and Knowledge in Proust* (Oxford: Oxford University Press, 2004).

Lane, Barbara M., *Architecture and Politics in Germany 1918–1945* (Cambridge, MA: Harvard University Press, 1968).

Laplanche, J., and J.-B. Pontalis, *The Language of Psycho-Analysis* (London: The Hogarth Press and the Institute of Psycho-Analysis, 1983).

Laughlin, James, *Pound as Wuz* (London: Peter Owen, 1989).

Lawrence, D. H., *Phoenix*, ed. Edward. D. McDonald (London: Heineman, 1936).

——, *The Letters of D. H. Lawrence*, vol. 2., ed. George J. Zytaruk and James T. Boulton (Cambridge: Cambridge University Press, 1981).

——, *The Complete Poems*, ed. and intro. Vivian De Sola Pinto and Warren Roberts (New York: Penguin, 1982).

Lear, Jonathan, 'Author of authors', *Times Literary Supplement* (28 January 2005), 3–4.

Leavis, F. R., *New Bearings in English Poetry* (1932) (Harmondsworth: Penguin, 1972).

Lee, Hermione, *Virginia Woolf* (London: Vintage, 1997).

——, *Body Parts* (London: Chatto & Windus, 2005).

'Lee, Vernon' [Pseud. of Violet Paget], *Laurus Nobilis: Chapters on Art and Life* (London: John Lane, The Bodley Head, 1909).

——, *Proteus: or the Future of Intelligence* (New York: Dutton, 1925).

Leighton, Angela, *On Form: Poetry, Aestheticism, and the Legacy of a Word* (Oxford: Oxford University Press, 2007).

Lees-Milne, James, *Harold Nicolson: A Biography*, 2 vols (London: Chatto & Windus, 1980–3).

Lejeune, Philippe, *L'Autobiographie en France* ('U2' Series, Paris: Armand Collin, 1971).

——, *Le pacte autobiographique* (Paris: Editions du Seuil, 1975).

——, 'Autobiography in the Third Person', *New Literary History*, 9:1 (1977), 27–50.

——, 'The Autobiographical Contract', in *French Literary Theory Today*, ed. Tzvetan Todorov (Cambridge: Cambridge University Press, 1982), pp. 192–222.

Lejeune, Philippe, *On Autobiography*, ed. Paul John Eakin, trans. Katherine Leary (Minneapolis: University of Minnesota Press, 1989).

Lessing, Doris, *The Golden Notebook* (London: Flamingo, 1993).

Levenson, Michael, 'Stephen's Diary in *Portrait*: The Shape of Life', *ELH*, 52 (1985), 1017–35.

Levin, Harry, *James Joyce: A Critical Introduction* (London: Faber, 1971).

Lewis, Percy Wyndham, *Men Without Art* (London: Cassell, 1934).

Lewis, Wyndham, *Time and Western Man* (London: Chatto & Windus, 1927).

Lindberg-Seyersted, Brita, ed., *Pound/Ford: The Story of a Literary Friendship* (London: Faber and Faber [1983]).

Linzie, Anna, *The True Story of Alice B. Toklas: A Study of Three Autobiographies* (Iowa City: University of Iowa Press, 2006).

Little, Judy, '*Jacob's Room* as Comedy: Woolf's Parodic *bildungsroman*', in Jane Marcus, ed., *New Feminist Essays on Virginia Woolf* (London: Macmillan, 1981), 105–24.

Lock, Charles, 'On Biographical Proportions: A Review-Essay', *The Powys Journal*, 13 (2003), 240–7.

Loos, Anita, *Gentlemen Prefer Blondes* (London: Picador, 1974).

Lowell, James Russell, 'Dante', *Among My Books*, second series (London: Sampson Low, Marston, Searle & Rivington, 1876).

Lucas, E. V., Preface to *The Best of Lamb* (London: Methuen, 1914).

'L[ucas], E. V., and G. M[orrow]', *What a Life!* (London: Collins, 1987).

Ludwig, Emil, *Genius and Character* (1925), English translation (London: Jonathan Cape, 1927).

McBride, Margaret, *'Ulysses' and the Metamorphosis of Stephen Dedalus* (London: Associated University Presses, 2001).

McGuinness, Patrick, ed., *Symbolism, Decadence and the Fin de Siècle: French and European Perspectives* (Exeter: University of Exeter Press, 2000).

MacIntyre, Alasdair, *After Virtue: A Study in Moral Theory*, 2nd edn (London: Duckworth, 1993).

Maclean, C. Macdonald, *Mark Rutherford: A Biography of William Hale White* (London: Macdonald, 1955).

McMullan, Gordon, *Shakespeare and the Idea of Late Writing: Authorship in the Proximity of Death* (Cambridge: Cambridge University Press, 2007).

Maddox, Brenda, *Nora* (Boston: Houghton Mifflin, 1988).

Mahaffey, Vicki, *Reauthorizing Joyce* (Cambridge: Cambridge University Press, 1988).

Mallarmé, Stéphane, *The Poems*, trans. Keith Bosley (Harmondsworth: Penguin Books, 1977).

Mann, Thomas, *The Story of a Novel: The Genesis of Doctor Faustus*, trans. R. and C. Winston (New York: Knopf, 1961).

Mansfield, Katherine, *Selected Letters*, ed. Vincent O'Sullivan (Oxford: Clarendon Press, 1989).

Marcus, Laura, *Auto/biographical Discourses* (Manchester: Manchester University Press, 1994).

——, 'The Newness of the "New Biography"', in *Mapping Lives: The Uses of Biography*, ed. Peter France (Oxford: Oxford University Press, 2002), pp. 193–218.

Martin, Linda Wagner, 'Stein, Woolf, and Parody', in *Telling Women's Lives: The New Biography* (New Jersey: Rutgers University Press, 1994), pp. 72–7.

Marx, Emanuel, ed., *A Composite Portrait of Israel* (London: Academic Press, 1980).

Matz, Jesse, *Literary Impressionism and Modernist Aesthetics* (Cambridge: Cambridge University Press, 2001).

Meisel, Perry, *The Absent Father: Virginia Woolf and Walter Pater* (New Haven and London: Yale University Press, 1980).

——, and Walter Kendrick, eds, *Bloomsbury/Freud: The Letters of James and Alix Strachey 1924–25* (New York: Basic Books, 1985).

Middeke, Martin, Introduction to Huber, Werner, and Martin Middeke, eds, *Biofictions: The Rewriting of Romantic Lives in Contemporary Fiction and Drama* (Woodbridge, Suffolk: Boydell and Brewer (Camden House), 1999).

Miles, Kathryn, '"That Perpetual Marriage of Granite and Rainbow": Searching for "The New Biography" in Virginia Woolf's Orlando', *Virginia Woolf and Communities*, ed. Jeanette McVicker and Laura Davis (New York: Pace University Press, 1999), pp. 212–18.

Mizener, Arthur, *The Saddest Story: A Biography of Ford Madox Ford* (London: The Bodley Head, 1972).

Monsman, Gerald, 'Gaston de Latour and Pater's Art of Autobiography', *Nineteenth-Century Fiction*, 33:4 (1979), 411–33.

——, *Walter Pater's Art of Autobiography* (New Haven and London: Yale University Press, 1980).

Moody, A. David, *Ezra Pound: Poet*, vol. 1 (Oxford: Oxford University Press, 2007).

Moore, George, *Hail and Farewell*, ed. Richard Cave (Gerrrards Cross, Bucks: Colin Smythe, 1985).

Morson, Gary Saul, *Narrative and Freedom: The Shadows of Time* (New Haven: Yale University Press, 1994).

Moser, Thomas C., *The Life in the Fiction of Ford Madox Ford* (Princeton: Princeton University Press, 1980).

Muir, Edwin, *An Autobiography* (1954) (St Paul, MN: Graywolf Press, 1990).

Mullan, John, *Anonymity: A Secret History of English Literature* (London: Faber and Faber, 2008).

Muller, Marcel, *Les Voix narratives dans la recherche du temps perdu* (Geneva: Droz, 1965).

Nabokov, Vladimir, *Pale Fire* (New York: G. P. Putnam's Sons, 1962).

——, *Speak, Memory: An Autobiography Revisited* (London: Penguin, 2000).

——, *Strong Opinions* (London: Weidenfeld and Nicolson, 1974).

Nagel, James, *Stephen Crane and Literary Impressionism* (Pennsylvania: Pennsylvania State University Press, 1980).

Najder, Zdzisław, *Conrad in Perspective: Essays on Art and Fidelity* (Cambridge: Cambridge University Press, 1997).

Nalbantian, Suzanne, *Aesthetic Autobiography: From Life to Art in Marcel Proust, James Joyce, Virginia Woolf and Anaïs Nin* (New York: St Martin's Press, 1997).

Nehls, E., ed., *D. H. Lawrence: A Composite Biography*, 3 vols (Madison: University of Wisconsin Press, 1957–9).

Newman, John Henry, *Apologia*, ed. Philip Hughes (Garden City, NY: Image Books, 1956).

Newsome, David, *On the Edge of Paradise: A. C. Benson, the Diarist* (London: John Murray, 1980).

Newsome, David, *Edwardian Excursions* (London: Murray, 1981).

Nicholls, Peter, *Modernisms: A Literary Guide* (Basingstoke: Macmillan, 1995).

Nicoll, W. Robertson, *A Bookman's Letters* (London: Hodder and Stoughton, 1913).

Nicolson, Harold, *The Development of English Biography* (London: The Hogarth Press, 1927).

——, 'The Practice of Biography', *American Scholar*, 23 (1954), 153–61.

——, *Diaries and Letters: 1907–1964*, ed. Nigel Nicolson (London: Weidenfeld and Nicolson, 2004).

——, *Some People*, 'Introduction' by Nigel Nicolson (London: Constable, 1982).

Nietzsche, Friedrich, *Beyond Good and Evil*, tr. Helen Zimmern (London and Edinburgh: T. N. Foulis, 1914).

——, *Will to Power*, trans. Anthony M. Ludovici, vol. 15 of *Complete Works*, ed. Oscar Levy (Edinburgh: T. N. Foulis, 1910).

Nochlin, Linda, ed. *Impressionism and Post-Impressionism 1874–1904: Sources and Documents* (Englewood Cliffs, NJ: Prentice-Hall, 1966).

Norman, Charles, *Ezra Pound* (New York: Macmillan, 1969).

Norris, Margot, review of Anna Linzie, *The True Story of Alice B. Toklas: A Study of Three Autobiographies* (Iowa City: University of Iowa Press, 2006), in *Biography*, 30:1 (2007) 108–11.

O'Brien, Justin, 'Gide's Fictional Technique', *Yale French Studies*, 7 (1951), 81–90.

Overall, Christine, review of *Women, Autobiography, Theory: A Reader*, in *APA Newsletters*, 00:1 (2000), <http://www.apaonline.org/publications/newsletters/v00n1_Feminism_20.aspx> (accessed 23 April 2009).

Ovid, *Metamorphoses*, trans. Frank J. Miller, 2 vols, vol. 1, Loeb Classical Library (Cambridge, MA: Harvard University Press; London: Heinemann, 1971).

Pater, Walter, 'Poems by William Morris', *Westminster Review*, 90 (October 1868), 300–12.

——, *The Renaissance* (London: Macmillan, 1893).

——, *Miscellaneous Studies*, ed. Charles Shadwell (London: Macmillan, 1895).

——, *Emerald Uthwart: An Imaginary Portrait* (Portland, ME: Thomas B. Mosher, 1899).

——, *Appreciations: With an Essay on Style* (London: Macmillan, 1907).

——, *Imaginary Portraits* (London: Macmillan, 1922 [repr. of the 1910 Library Edition]).

——, *Marius the Epicurean* (London: Dent, 1934).

——, *Imaginary Portraits by Walter Pater: A New Collection*, ed. Eugene J. Brzenk (New York, Evanston, and London: Harper and Row, 1964).

——, 'A Novel by Mr Oscar Wilde', *Bookman* [November 1891]: repr. in Pater, *Essays on Literature and Art*, ed. Jennifer Uglow (London: Dent, 1971), pp. 142–5.

——, *The Renaissance: Studies in Art and Poetry: the 1893 Text*, ed. Donald L. Hill (Berkeley: University of California Press, 1980).

Pearson, Hesketh, *Extraordinary People* (London: Heinemann, 1965).

[Pearson, Hesketh], *The Whispering Gallery*, ed. Michael Holroyd (London: Phoenix, 2000).

Pessoa, Fernando, *A Centenary Pessoa*, ed. Eugénio Lisboa with L. C. Taylor (Manchester: Carcanet, 1995).

——, *The Book of Disquietude: by Bernardo Soares, Assistant Bookkeeper in the City of Lisbon*, trans. Richard Zenith (Manchester: Carcanet, 1996).

Peters, John G., *Conrad and Impressionism* (Cambridge: Cambridge University Press, 2001).

Phillips, Adam, *On Flirtation* (London: Faber, 1994).

——, Introduction to Pater, *The Renaissance*, Oxford World's Classics (Oxford: Oxford University Press, 1998).

——, 'Newfangled Inner Worlds', *London Review of Books* (3 March 2005), 21–2.

Pierrefeu, Jean de, *l'Anti-Plutarque* (Paris: Editions de France, 1926).

'Plain Woman, A', *My Trivial Life and Misfortune*, 3 vols (Edinburgh: Blackwood, 1883).

Poe, Edgar Allan, *Selected Tales*, ed. Julian Symons (Oxford: Oxford University Press, 1980).

Pontalis, J.-B., *Love of Beginnings*, trans. James Greene with Marie-Christine Réguis (London: Free Association Books, 1993).

Poole, Adrian, *Gissing in Context* (Basingstoke: Macmillan, 1975).

Poole, Roger, *The Unknown Virginia Woolf* (Cambridge: Cambridge University Press, 1978).

Poulet, Georges, 'Phenomenology of Reading', *New Literary History*, 1:1 (October 1969), 53–68.

Pound, Ezra, 'VORTEX. POUND', *Blast*, 1 (June 1914), 153–4.

——, 'Et Faim Sallir Le Loup des Boys', *Blast*, 2 (July 1915), 22.

——, *Pavannes and Divisions* (New York: Knopf, 1918).

——, *Instigations* (New York: Boni and Liveright, 1920).

——, *Hugh Selwyn Mauberley* (London: Ovid Press, 1920).

——, *Personae* (Norfolk, CT: New Directions, 1926).

——, *Guide to Kulchur* (London: Faber, 1938).

——, *Selected Poems* (New York: New Directions, 1949).

——, *ABC of Reading* (London: Faber, 1951).

——, *Literary Essays*, ed. T. S. Eliot (London: Faber, 1954).

——, *Diptych: Rome—London* (London: Faber, 1958).

——, *Patria Mia* (London: Peter Owen, 1962).

——, *The Translations of Ezra Pound*, introduced by Hugh Kenner (London: Faber, 1970).

——, *Selected Letters of Ezra Pound*, ed. D. D. Paige (New York: New Directions, 1971).

——, *Selected Poems* (London: Faber, 1973).

——, *Pavannes and Divagations* (New York: New Directions, 1974).

——, *The Cantos* (London: Faber, 1975).

——, *Gaudier-Brzeska* (New York: New Directions, 1974).

——, 'Ford Madox (Hueffer) Ford: Obit', *Selected Prose*, ed. William Cookson (London: Faber, 1978), pp. 431–3.

Pritchard, William H., 'Poet of the public stage', *Washington Times* (20 January 2008).

Proust, Marcel, *A la recherche du temps perdu*, vol. 12: *Time Regained*, trans. Andreas Mayor (London: Chatto & Windus, 1970).

——, *A la recherche du temps perdu*, vol. I: *Swann's Way*, trans. C. K. Scott Moncrieff (London: Chatto & Windus, 1971).

——, *On Reading*, trans. and ed. Jean Autret and William Burford (London: Souvenir Press, 1972).

Proust, Marcel, *On Reading Ruskin: Prefaces to 'La Bible d'Amiens' and 'Sésame et les lys'*, *with Selections from the Notes to the Translated Texts*, trans. and ed. Jean Autret, William Burford, and Phillip J. Wolfe; introduction by Richard Macksey (New Haven: Yale University Press, 1987).

——, *Contre Sainte-Beuve*, in *Marcel Proust on Art and Literature: 1896–1919*, trans. Sylvia Townsend Warner; introduced by Terence Kilmartin (New York: Carroll & Graf, 1997).

Queneau, Raymond, 'What a Life!', *Bâtons, chiffres et letters* (Paris: Gallimard, 1950), pp. 197–207.

Rainey, Lawrence, *Institutions of Modernism: Literary Elites and Public Culture* (New Haven: Yale University Press, 1998).

Raitt, Suzanne, *Vita and Virginia: The Work and Friendship of V. Sackville-West and Virginia Woolf* (Oxford: Clarendon Press, 1993).

——, *May Sinclair: A Modern Victorian* (Oxford: Clarendon Press, 2000).

Raymond, Ernest, ed., *The Autobiography of David* —— (London: Gollancz, 1946).

Rajan, Tillotama, 'Autonarration and Genotext in Mary Hays' *Memoirs of Emma Court-ney*', *Studies in Romanticism*, 32:2 (1993), 149–76.

Read, Forrest, ed., *Pound/Joyce* (London: Faber, 1968).

Reynolds, Stephen, 'Autobiografiction', *Speaker*, new series, 15:366 (1906), 28, 30.

——, 'Preface to the New Edition' (1911), *A Poor Man's House* (Oxford: Oxford University Press, 1982).

Ricks, Christopher, *The Force of Poetry* (Oxford: Clarendon Press, 1984).

——, ed., *The New Oxford Book of Victorian Verse* (Oxford: Oxford University Press, 1987).

Ricoeur, Paul, *Time and Narrative*, vol. 2, trans. Kathleen McLaughlin and David Pellauer (Chicago: University of Chicago Press, 1985).

——, *Oneself as Another*, trans. Kathleen Blamey (Chicago: The University of Chicago Press, 1992).

Rimbaud, *Oeuvres Completes*, ed. Rolland de Renéville and Jules Mouquet (Paris: Galli-mard, 1963).

Rimmon-Kenan, Shlomith, *Narrative Fiction: Contemporary Poetics* (London: Methuen, 1983).

Riquelme, John Paul, *Teller and Tale in Joyce's Fiction* (Baltimore: Johns Hopkins University Press, 1983).

——, '*Stephen Hero, Dubliners*, and *A Portrait of the Artist as a Young Man*: styles of realism and fantasy', *Cambridge Companion to James Joyce*, ed. Derek Attridge (Cam-bridge: Cambridge University Press, 1990), pp. 103–30.

Roberts, Morley, *The Private Life of Henry Maitland* (London: Eveleigh Nash, 1912).

Rose, Norman, *Harold Nicolson* (London: Cape, 2005).

Rosenbaum, S. P., ed., *The Bloomsbury Group: A Collection of Memoirs and Commentary* (Toronto: University of Toronto Press, 1995).

Rossetti, Christina, *The Poetical Works of Christina Georgina Rossetti*, with Memoir and Notes &C by William Michael Rossetti (London: Macmillan, 1904).

Rousseau, Jean-Jacques, *The Confessions*, trans. J. M. Cohen (Harmondsworth: Penguin, 1975).

Ruskin, John, *Modern Painters*, Library Edition, vol. 3, *The Works of John Ruskin*, ed. E. T. Cook and Alexander Wedderburn (London, George Allen, 1903).

——, *La Bible d'Amiens*, trans. Marcel Proust (Paris: Mercure de France, 1904).

——, *Sesame and Lilies*, Library Edition, vol. 18, *The Works of John Ruskin*, ed. E. T. Cook and Alexander Wedderburn (London: George Allen, 1905).

——, *Sésame et les lys*, trans. Marcel Proust (Paris: Mercure de France, 1906).

——, *Fors Clavigera: Letters 37–72*, Library Edition, vol. 28, *The Works of John Ruskin*, ed. E. T. Cook and Alexander Wedderburn (London: George Allen, 1907).

——, *Præterita and Dilecta*, Library Edition, vol. 35, *The Works of John Ruskin*, ed. E. T. Cook and Alexander Wedderburn (London: George Allen, 1908).

——, *The Letters of John Ruskin: 1827–1869*, Library Edition, vol. 36, *The Works of John Ruskin*, ed. Cook and Wedderburn (London: George Allen, 1909).

Russett, Margaret, *Fictions and Fakes: Forging Romantic Authenticity, 1760–1845* (Cambridge University Press, 2006).

'Rutherford, Mark' [pseud. of William Hale White], *The Autobiography of Mark Rutherford, Dissenting Minister* (London: Trübner & Co., 1881).

——, *Mark Rutherford's Deliverance* (London: Trübner & Co., 1885).

——, *The Autobiography of Mark Rutherford and Mark Rutherford's Deliverance* (London: Trübner & Co., 1889).

——, *Pages from a Journal, with Other Papers* (London: T. Fisher Unwin, 1900).

——, *More Pages from a Journal: with Other Papers* (London: Oxford University Press, 1910), p. 178.

——, *Last Pages from a Journal: with Other Papers: by Mark Rutherford: Edited by his Wife* (London: Oxford University Press, 1915).

——, *Mark Rutherford's Deliverance* (London: Trübner & Co., 1885).

Ruthven, K. K., *A Guide to Ezra Pound's Personae (1926)* (Berkeley: University of California Press, 1969).

——, *Faking Literature* (Cambridge: Cambridge University Press, 2001).

Said, Edward, *Beginnings* (New York: Basic, 1975).

——, *On Late Style* (London: Bloomsbury, 2006).

Sanders, Valerie, 'Victorian Life Writing', *Literature Compass*, 1:1 (2004), 1–17.

——, '"House of Disquiet": The Benson Family Auto/biographies', in *Life Writing and Victorian Culture*, ed. David Amigoni (Aldershot: Ashgate, 2006), pp. 292–315.

Sartre, Jean-Paul, *Les Mots* (1964) trans. as *Words* by Irene Clephane (Harmondsworth: Penguin, 1967).

——, 'Sur L'Idiot de la famille', *Situations*, X (Paris: Gallimard, 1976).

——, *Being and Nothingness*, trans. Hazel E. Barnes (London Methuen, 1986).

Sassoon, Siegfried, *Memoirs of a Fox-Hunting Man* (London: Faber, 1928).

——, *Memoirs of an Infantry Officer* (London: Faber, 1930).

Saunders, Max, 'A Life in Writing: Ford Madox Ford's Dispersed Autobiographies', *Antæus*, 56 (1986), 47–69.

——, 'Ford/Pound', *Agenda*, 27:4/28:1 (1989/1990), 93–102.

——, *Ford Madox Ford: A Dual Life*, 2 vols (Oxford: Oxford University Press, 1996).

——, 'Ford, Eliot, Joyce, and the Problems of Literary Biography', in *Writing the Lives of Writers*, ed. Warwick Gould and Thomas F. Staley (London and New York: Macmillan and St Martin's Press, 1998), pp. 150–72.

Saunders, Max, 'Reflections on Impressionist Autobiography: James, Conrad and Ford', *Inter-relations: Conrad, James, Ford, and Others* in the series 'Joseph Conrad: Eastern and Western Perspectives', gen. ed. Wieslaw Krajka (Lublin/Columbia University Press, 2003), 7–41.

——, 'Verbal and Other Manifestations: Further Thoughts on Ford/Pound/Ford', in *Redefining the Modern: Essays on Literature and Society in Honor of Joseph Wiesenfarth*, ed. William Baker and Ira B. Nadel (Madison, WI and London: Fairleigh Dickinson University Press, 2004), pp. 165–80.

——, 'Biography and Autobiography', *Cambridge History of Twentieth-Century English Literature*, ed. Laura Marcus and Peter Nicholls (Cambridge: Cambridge University Press, 2004), pp. 286–303.

——, 'Literary Impressionism', in *A Companion to Modernist Literature and Culture*, ed. David Bradshaw and Kevin Dettmar (Oxford: Blackwell, 2005), pp. 204–11.

——, 'Forster's Life and Life-writing', *The Cambridge Companion to E. M. Forster*, ed. David Bradshaw (Cambridge: Cambridge University Press, 2007), pp. 8–31.

——, 'From Pre-Raphaelism to Impressionism', *Ford Madox Ford and Visual Culture*, ed. Laura Colombino (Amsterdam and New York: Rodopi, 2009), pp. 51–70.

——, *s.v.* May Sinclair, *Oxford DNB*.

——, *s.v.* Richard Aldington, *Oxford DNB*.

——, *s.v.* 'Literary Impressionists', *Oxford DNB* Reference Group article (2008).

Sawyer, Roger, *The Island from Within: A Composite Portrait of the Isle of Wight* (Isle of Wight: Robook, 1990).

Schafer, R. Murray, ed., *Ezra Pound and Music: The Complete Criticism* (London: Faber, 1978).

Schlicke, Paul, ed., *Oxford Reader's Companion to Dickens* (Oxford: Oxford University Press, 1999).

Scholes, Robert, 'Stephen Dedalus, poet or esthete?', *PMLA*, 89 (1964), 484–9.

——, *In Search of James Joyce* (Urbana and Chicago: University of Illinois Press, 1992).

Rossman, Charles, 'Stephen Dedalus' Villanelle', *James Joyce Quarterly*, 12 (1975), 281–93.

Schreiber, Georges, collected and illustrated, *Portraits and Self-Portraits* (Boston: Houghton Mifflin Company, 1936).

Schwob, Marcel, *Vies imaginaires* (Paris: Bibliothèque Charpentier, 1896).

Schwob, Marcel, 'Selections: Marcel Schwob', trans. Iain White, *Comparative Criticism*, vol. 2, ed. Elinor Shaffer (Cambridge: Cambridge University Press, 1980), pp. 265–90.

Scoble, Christopher, *Fisherman's Friend: A Life of Stephen Reynolds: 1881–1919* (Tiverton, Devon: Halsgrove, 2000).

——, *s.v.* Stephen Reynolds in the *Oxford DNB*.

Scriven, Michael, *Sartre's Existentialist Biographies* (London and Basingstoke: Macmillan, 1984).

Seidel, Michael, *James Joyce: A Short Introduction* (Oxford: Blackwell, 2002).

Senn, Fritz, 'The Challenge', in *James Joyce's 'A Portrait of the Artist as a Young Man': A Casebook*, ed. Mark Wollaeger (New York: Oxford University Press, 2003), pp. 129–42.

Severijnen, Olav, 'The Renaissance of a Genre: Autobiography and Modernism', *New Comparison*, 9 (1990), 41–59.

Shaw, George Bernard, *Pen Portraits and Reviews* (London: Constable, 1932).

Shakespeare, William, *The Complete Works*, general eds Stanley Wells and Gray Taylor (Oxford: Clarendon Press, 1986).

Shattuck, Roger, *Proust* (London: Fontana and Collins, 1975).

Sheringham, Michael, *French Autobiography: Devices and Desires* (Oxford: Clarendon Press, 1993).

Sherry, Vincent, 'From the Twenties to the Nineties: Pound, Beerbohm, and the Making of Mauberley', *PN Review* 20:5 (97) (1994), 40–2.

Shone, Richard, *The Art of Bloomsbury: Roger Fry, Vanessa Bell and Duncan Grant* (London: Tate Gallery Publishing, 1999).

Shorthouse, J. H., *John Inglesant* (Birmingham: Cornish Brothers, 1880).

Simon, Linda, ed., *Gertrude Stein: A Composite Portrait* (New York: Avon and Discus Books, 1974).

Skinner, Paul ' "Speak Up, Fordie!": How Some People Want to Go to Carcassonne', *Ford Madox Ford and the City*, ed. Sara Haslam (New York and Amsterdam: Rodopi, 2005), pp. 197–210.

Small, Ian, *Conditions for Criticism* (Oxford: Clarendon, 1991).

Smith, David C., *H. G. Wells: Desperately Mortal* (New Haven: Yale University Press, 1986).

Smith, Sidonie, 'Performativity, Autobiographical Practice, Resistance', in *Women, Autobiography, Theory: A Reader*, ed. Sidonie Smith and Julia Watson (Madison: University of Wisconsin Press, 1998), pp. 108–15.

Snaith, Anna, 'My Poor Private Voice: Virginia Woolf and Auto/biography', in *Representing Lives: Women and Auto/biography*, ed. Alison Donnell and Pauline Polkey (Houndmills: Macmillan, 2000), pp. 96–104.

——, 'Of Fanciers, Footnotes, and Fascism: Virginia Woolf's *Flush*', *Modern Fiction Studies*, 48:3 (2002), 614–36.

Spengemann, William C., *Forms of Autobiography: Episodes in the History of a Literary Genre* (New Haven: Yale University Press, 1980).

Sproles, Karyn, *Desiring Women: The Partnership of Virginia Woolf and Vita Sackville-West* (Toronto: University of Toronto Press, 2006).

Squier, Susan, 'Tradition and Revision in Woolf's *Orlando*: Defoe and "The Jessamy Brides"', *Women's Studies*, 12:2 (1986), 166–77.

Stannard, Martin, ed., selection of sources on 'Literary Impressionism', in Ford Madox Ford, *The Good Soldier* (New York and London: W. W. Norton, 1995), pp. 239–300.

Stein, Gertrude, *The Autobiography of Alice B. Toklas* (London: John Lane, 1933).

——, *Everybody's Autobiography* (New York: Random House, 1937).

Steiner, Wendy, *Exact Resemblance to Exact Resemblance: The Literary Portraiture of Gertrude Stein* (New Haven, CT: Yale University Press, 1978).

Stephen, Leslie, *Pope* (London: Macmillan, 1880).

——, 'Biography', *National Review*, 22 (1893), 171–83.

——, *Studies of a Biographer*, 4 vols (London: Duckworth 1898–1902).

Stevenson, Robert Louis, *Memories and Portraits* (London: Chatto & Windus, 1887).

——, *Vailima Letters: Being Correspondence addressed by Robert Louis Stevenson to Sidney Colvin* (London: Methuen, 1895).

Stouck, David, 'Willa Cather and the Impressionist Novel', in *Critical Essays on Willa Cather*, ed. John J. Murphy (Boston: G. K. Hall, 1984), 48–66.

Stowell, H. Peter, *Literary Impressionism, James and Chekhov* (Athens: University of Georgia Press, c.1980).

Strachey, Lytton, *Eminent Victorians*, ed. Michael Holroyd (Harmondsworth: Penguin, 1986), p. 10.

Strachey, Lytton, *Eminent Victorians*, ed. John Sutherland, World's Classics (Oxford: Oxford University Press, 2003).

Strawson, Galen, 'A fallacy of our age: Not every life is a narrative', *Times Literary Supplement* (15 October 2004), 13–15.

Svevo, Italo, *La Coscienza di Zeno*, trans. Beryl de Zoete (1930) (Harmondsworth: Penguin, 1964).

Swann, Charles, '"Autobiografiction": Problems with Autobiographical Fictions and Fictional Autobiographies. Mark Rutherford's *Autobiography* and *Deliverance*, and Others', *Modern Language Review*, 96:1 (2001), 21–37.

Jonathan Swift, *The Battle of the Books*, in *A Tale of a Tub and Other Satires*, ed. Kathleen Williams, revised edition (London: J. M. Dent, 1975).

Swinnerton, Frank, *George Gissing: A Critical Study* (London: Martin Secker, 1912).

Symonds, John Addington, *The Memoirs of John Addington Symonds*, ed. Phyllis Grosskurth (New York: Random House/London: Hutchinson, 1984).

Symons, Arthur, *Spiritual Adventures* (London: Archibald Constable, 1905).

——, *The Collected Work of Arthur Symons* (London: Martin Secker, 1924).

——, *Confessions: A Study in Pathology* (New York: The Fountain Press, 1930).

——, *Poetry and Prose* (Cheadle Hulme: Carcanet, 1974).

——, *The Memoirs of Arthur Symons: Life and Art in the 1890s*, ed. Karl Beckson (University Park, PA: Pennsylvania State University Press, 1977).

Taylor, Charles, *Sources of the Self: The Making of the Modern Identity* (Cambridge: Cambridge University Press, 1989).

Theobald, Catherine J. Lewis, 'Layers of Portraiture in *Manon Lescaut*: Changing Modes of Representation in a Changing Society', *French Forum*, 28 (2003), 1–19.

Thwaite, Ann, *Edmund Gosse* (London: Secker & Warburg, 1984).

——, 'Rereadings', *Guardian* Review (2 November 2002), 37.

Timpanaro, Sebastiano, *The Freudian Slip: Psychoanalysis and Textual Criticism* (London: Verso, 1985).

Tindall, William York, *A Reader's Guide to James Joyce* (New York: The Noonday Press, Inc., 1959).

Tintner, Adeline R., 'Autobiography as Fiction: "The Usurping Consciousness" as Hero of James's Memoirs', *Twentieth Century Literature*, 23:2 (1977), 239–60.

Tönnies, Merle, 'Radicalising Postmodern Biofictions: British Fictional Autobiogaphy of the Twenty-First Century', in *Fiction and Autobiography: Modes and Models of Interaction*, Salzburg Studies in English Literature and Culture, vol. 3, ed. Sabine Coelsch-Foisner and Wolfgang Görtschacher (Frankfurt: Peter Lang, 2006), pp. 305–14.

Trollope, Anthony, *An Autobiography*, ed. Michael Sadleir and Frederick Page, World's Classics (Oxford: Oxford University Press, 1980).

Turgenev, Ivan, *A Sportsman's Sketches*, trans. Constance Garnett, vols 8 and 9 of *The Novels of Ivan Turgenev* (London: William Heinemann, 1895).

Twain, Mark, *Chapters from My Autobiography* (New York: Oxford University Press, 1996).

Valéry, Paul, *Oeuvres*, ed. Jean Hytier (Paris: Gallimard, 1957), vol. 1.

——, *Moi*, trans. Marthiel and Jackson Mathews, Bollingen Series 45; 15 (Princeton: Princeton University Press, 1975).

van Gunsteren, Julia, *Katherine Mansfield and Literary Impressionism* (Amsterdam and Atlanta: Rodopi, 1990).

Wahrman, Dror, *The Making of the Modern Self* (New Haven: Yale University Press, 2004).

Waterfield, Gordon, *Professional Diplomat: Sir Percy Loraine of Kirkharle Bt.* (London: John Murray, 1973).

Watts, Cedric, *Joseph Conrad: A Literary Life* (London: Macmillan, Basingstoke, 1989).

Welch, Robert, and Bruce Stewart, *The Oxford Companion to Irish Literature* (Oxford: Oxford University Press, 1996).

Wells, H. G., *Boon, The Mind of the Race, The Wild Asses of the Devil* and *The Last Trump* (London: T. Fisher Unwin, 1915).

——, *The World of William Clissold*, vol. 1 (Ernest Benn, London, 1926).

——, *Experiment in Autobiography: Discoveries and Conclusions of a Very Ordinary Brain (since 1866)* (London: Victor Gollancz and The Cresset Press, 1934).

——, 'World Brain: The Idea of a Permanent World Encyclopaedia', written in 1937 for the new *Encyclopédie Française*, and reprinted in his book *World Brain* (London: Methuen, 1938).

West, Anthony, *H. G. Wells: Aspects of a Life* (Harmondsworth: Penguin, 1985).

Wharton, Edith, *A Backward Glance* (New York: D. Appleton-Century, 1934).

White, Hayden, *The Content of the Form: Narrative Discourse and Historical Representation* (Baltimore: Johns Hopkins University Press, 1992).

Whitworth, Michael, *Einstein's Wake* (Oxford: Oxford University Press, 2001).

Wiesenfarth, Joseph, 'Ford's *Joseph Conrad: A Personal Remembrance* as Metafiction: Or, How Conrad Became an Elizabethan Poet', *Renascence*, 53:1 (2000), 43–60.

——, 'Ford Madox Ford and the Pre-Raphaelites or how Dante Gabriel Rossetti Started the First World War', *REAL: Yearbook of Research in English and American Literature*, ed. Herbert Grabes, Winfried Fluck, and Jürgen Schlaeger, vol. 9 (Tübingen: Gunter Narr Verlag, 1993), pp. 109–48.

Wilde, Oscar, 'Mr. Pater's Imaginary Portraits', *Pall Mall Gazette* (June 11, 1887), 2–3.

——, *Complete Writings of Oscar Wilde* (New York: The Nottingham Society, 1909).

——, *The Letters of Oscar Wilde*, ed. R. Hart-Davis (London: Hart-Davis, 1962).

——, *The Picture of Dorian Gray*, ed. Michael Patrick Gillespie (New York: W. W. Norton, 2006).

Willcocks, M. P., *Between the Old World and the New: Being Studies in Literary Personality from Goethe and Balzac to Anatole France and Thomas Hardy* (London: George Allen & Unwin Ltd, 1925).

Willey, Basil, *More Nineteenth-Century Studies* (Cambridge: Cambridge University Press, 1980).

Williams, Carolyn D., *Transfigured World: Walter Pater's Aesthetic Historicism* (Ithaca: Cornell University Press, 1989).

Williams, Meg Harris, and Margot Waddell, *The Chamber of Maiden Thought: Literary Origins of the Psychoanalytic Model of the Mind* (London: Tavistock and Routledge, 1991).

Wilson, Edmund, *Axel's Castle* (New York: Charles Scribner's Sons, 1931).

Wilson, Jean Moorcroft, *Siegfried Sassoon: The Journey from the Trenches* (London: Duckworth, 2003).

Winslow, Donald J., *Life-writing: A Glossary of Terms in Biography, Autobiography, and Related Forms* (Hawaii: University of Hawaii Press, 1995).

Winterson, Jeanette, *Art Objects* (London: Jonathan Cape, 1995).

Woolf, Virginia, 'The Art of Biography' [1939], *The Death of the Moth and Other Essays* (London: The Hogarth Press, 1942), pp. 119–26.

——, 'Not One of Us', *The Death of the Moth, and Other Essays* (London: The Hogarth Press, 1942), pp. 78–83.

——, 'The Lives of the Obscure', *The Common Reader: First Series* [1925] (London: The Hogarth Press, 1968), pp. 146–67.

——, 'Modern Fiction', *The Common Reader* (London: Hogarth Press, 1968).

——, *The Flight of the Mind: The Letters of Virginia Woolf*, vol. 1, ed. Nigel Nicolson and Joanne Trautmann (London: Chatto & Windus, 1975).

——, *A Change of Perspective: The Letters of Virginia Woolf*, vol. 3, ed. Nicolson and Trautmann (London: Hogarth Press, 1977).

——, *The Diary of Virginia Woolf*, vol. 3, ed. Anne Olivier Bell, assisted by Andrew McNeillie (London: The Hogarth Press, 1980).

——, *Leave the Letters till We're Dead: The Letters of Virginia Woolf*, vol. 6, ed. Nicolson and Trautmann (London: The Hogarth Press, 1980).

——, *The Diary of Virginia Woolf*, vol. 4, ed. Anne Olivier Bell and Andrew McNeillie (London: The Hogarth Press, 1982).

——, *The Sickle Side of the Moon: The Letters of Virginia Woolf*, vol. 5, ed. Nicolson and Trautmann (London: Chatto & Windus, 1982).

——, *The Complete Shorter Fiction of Virginia Woolf*, ed. Susan Dick (London: Hogarth Press, 1985).

——, 'Poets' Letters', *The Essays of Virginia Woolf*, vol. 1, ed. Andrew McNeillie, (London: Hogarth, 1986), pp. 101–5.

——, 'Sterne' (1909), in *The Essays of Virginia Woolf*, vol. 4, ed. Andrew McNeillie (London: The Hogarth Press, 1986), pp. 280–8.

——, *Moments of Being*, ed. Jeanne Schulkind (London: Chatto & Windus and Sussex University Press, 1986).

——, *The Essays of Virginia Woolf*, vol. 3, ed. Andrew McNeillie (London: The Hogarth Press, 1988).

——, *Jacob's Room*, ed. Kate Flint (Oxford: Oxford University Press, 1992).

——, *Mrs Dalloway* (Oxford: Oxford University Press, 1992).

——, *Orlando*, World's Classics (Oxford: Oxford University Press, 1992).

——, *A Room of One's Own: Three Guineas*, ed. Morag Shiach (Oxford: Oxford University Press, 1992).

——, *To the Lighthouse*, ed. Margaret Drabble (Oxford: Oxford University Press, 1992).

——, 'The New Biography' (1927), in *The Essays of Virginia Woolf*, vol. 4, ed. Andrew McNeillie (London: The Hogarth Press, 1994), 473–80.

——, *The Essays of Virginia Woolf*, vol. 4, ed. Andrew McNeillie (London: The Hogarth Press, 1994).

——, *The Platform of Time: Memoirs of Family and Friends*, expanded edn, ed. S. P. Rosenbaum (London: Hesperus, 2008).

Wright, Samuel, *A Bibliography of the Writings of Walter H. Pater* (New York: Garland, 1975).

'Y', *The Autobiography of an Englishman* (London: Paul Elek, 1975).

Yeats, W. B., *Autobiographies* (London: Macmillan, 1980).

——, From 'The Philosophy of Shelley's Poetry', in *The Major Works: Including Poems, Plays, and Critical Prose*, ed. Edward Larrissy, Oxford World's Classics (Oxford: Oxford University Press, 2001), 350–1.

Ziegler, Robert, 'Fictions of the Forgotten in Marcel Schwob', *Forum for Modern Language Studies*, 28:3 (1991), 227–37.

Žižek, Slavoj, *The Parallax View* (Cambridge, MA and London: The MIT Press, 2006).

Zweig, Stefan, *Der Kampf mit dem Dämon* (Leipzig: Insel-Verlag, 1925).

——, *Drei Dichter ihres Lebens* (1928), trans. as *Adepts in Self-Portraiture* (New York: Viking, 1928).

——, *Drei Meister* (1920); trans. as *Three Masters* (New York: Viking Press, 1930).

——, *Die Heilung durch den Geist* (1931), trans. as *Mental Healers* (New York: Viking, 1932).

Index

Note: the following terms occur too frequently in this book to warrant indexing: autobiografiction, autobiography, biography, fiction, life-writing.

Index

Index

Index